ISBN 978-1-334-45661-9
PIBN 10642381

This book is a reproduction of an important historical work. Forgotten Books uses
state-of-the-art technology to digitally reconstruct the work, preserving the original format
whilst repairing imperfections present in the aged copy. In rare cases, an imperfection in
the original, such as a blemish or missing page, may be replicated in our edition. We do,
however, repair the vast majority of imperfections successfully; any imperfections that
remain are intentionally left to preserve the state of such historical works.

1 MONTH OF
FREE
READING

at

www.ForgottenBooks.com

By purchasing this book you are eligible for one month membership to ForgottenBooks.com, giving you unlimited access to our entire collection of over 700,000 titles via our web site and mobile apps.

To claim your free month visit:

www.forgottenbooks.com/free642381

Commonwealth and

THE EMPIRE

REVIEW

AND MAGAZINE

EDITED BY

SIR CLEMENT KINLOCH-COOKE

VOLUME XX

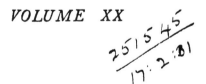

LONDON

CONTENTS

Contents

THE EMPIRE REVIEW

"Far as the breeze can bear, the billows foam,
Survey our empire, and behold our home."—*Byron.*

| VOL. XX. | AUGUST, 1910. | No. 115 |

AUSTRALIAN IMMIGRATION

By F. A. W. GISBORNE

[*Of Tasmania*]

THE most urgent problem that demands the attention of the new Federal Government is unquestionably that of immigration. On its successful and early solution depends, not merely the economic welfare, but the very existence of the Australian Commonwealth as a national entity. Without a largely augmented population there can neither be an effective army of defence, nor a sufficient number of taxpayers to provide the necessary armaments and equipments.

Warnings innumerable have already been given on this point, the latest, and perhaps, most authoritative, being that uttered by Lord Kitchener. His words have created more than a transient impression on the minds of thoughtful Australians. Yet the continued reiteration of truth of fundamental importance is necessary to make the citizens of the Commonwealth as a whole, who, thanks to the protection so long gratuitously afforded by their kinsmen in a far country, have never yet been brought face to face with grave and imminent danger, realise their importance. *Repetitio est mater studiorum* in the democracy as in the school. Until the present population of the Australian Commonwealth shall have been increased at least fourfold the cry for more people must be raised.

The new Labour Ministry, while, in a general sense, no doubt, anxious to promote Australian immigration, will unfortunately find the subject rather a thorny one to deal with. Its more enlightened supporters strongly advocate the adoption of a liberal policy in this direction. But a strong section is either openly or secretly hostile to the importation of people from outside. "Australia for the Australians" expresses the rather crude and narrow patriotism of the average trade unionist. The British working man immigrant he views with jealousy as a possible poacher on his own preserves. To the oligarchy of labour preference for unionists means monopoly of employment for the chosen people of Australian industry. Even the imported plough-man is looked upon with distrust as a possible strike-breaker. Consequently, Mr. Fisher and his colleagues will have the rather difficult task of educating their masters to accomplish before they can take any effective action. And, in common with all their predecessors in office, they are confronted with the land difficulty. Excepting only the area of less than a thousand square miles, embracing the site and surroundings of the future Australian Washington, the Commonwealth is absolutely landless. Each State possesses sole control over its own territories. It is imperiatve, therefore, that a working agreement shall be arranged between the Commonwealth and the various State Governments before the former can carry out a comprehensive scheme of immigration.

Just now nearly all the States are bestirring themselves vigorously with a view to the filling of their waste spaces. West Australia and Queensland are showing particular zeal in this direction. But as the Editor of this Review pointed out at the recent emigration conference held in London under the auspices of the Royal Colonial Institute, there is a lack of co-ordination of effort, of unity of plan; each State works only for itself, and treats its neighbour as a rival and almost hostile suitor for the horny hand of the sturdy British rustic. What seems to be wanting is a Central Immigration Board, under non-political management, and representative of all the States alike. Such a body should be supplied with adequate funds specially allocated out of the Commonwealth revenues, and each State should place at its disposal certain areas of Crown lands to be distributed at the Board's discretion among the immigrants introduced. Thus the Commonwealth would provide the funds, the States the land, and the two combined the machinery required to import and distribute the people. Such seems to be a fair basis of partnership.

The codification of the various land laws that now exist would be a necessary preliminary step, and a single body of regulations substituted for the present multitude of confusing and conflict-ing enactments. In New South Wales especially the com-plexity of the laws relating to the disposal of the Crown lands is notorious, and even experts have been known to become lost in the labyrinth ingeniously contrived by generations of legislators. To expect a newly-arrived settler, first to engage in a long and painful study of the local land laws, or to pay high fees to their legal interpreters, and then to set out on an equally protracted exploring tour in search of suitable land is unreasonable. The land laws now in force throughout Australia might well be submitted to a joint committee of practical administrators and skilled jurists with a view to rendering them simple and comprehensible, and as uniform as local conditions would permit; and the areas open to settlement should be classified, subdivided, and rendered accessible. In certain States, notably Queensland and West Australia, admirable work has been done in this direction of late years; but there is still a grievous lack of uniformity throughout the continent, and no general scheme for the promotion of immigration yet exists. When it is borne in mind that during the period intervening between the commencement of the years 1896 and the close of 1905, the whole Commonwealth gained less than a beggarly 5,200 people through immigration, the extent of the arrears to be made good can be estimated. All the resources of statesmanship will be required to atone for the apathy of the past.

But only half the difficulty will have been overcome when the land question has been successfully dealt with. There still remain the formidable questions of the selection and the transportation of emigrants. At first sight the former seems simple enough. Great Britain and other European countries overflow with inhabitants. Australia is nearly empty. The old countries possess many people but scanty land; the new have illimitable territories and few people to occupy them. It would seem, then, that the deficiency in the one case would be easily satisfied out of the superabundance of the other. In last October's number of this Review figures were quoted to show how enormous was then the amount of territory in Australia available to appease the land hunger of the compressed multitudes at home. In round numbers, some 1,100,000,000 acres in the Commonwealth are either wholly unoccupied, or are but inadequately utilised. Of this quantity, making the amplest allowances for sterility and climatic disabilities, at least one-third may be described as habitable. While the United Kingdom possesses, according to the Statesman's Year Book for 1908, over 363 persons to the square mile, and the whole of Europe about 112, Australia has only one civilised human being and a half to the same area. The aborigines, in numbers at least, are a negligible quantity. That Great Britain and Australia can mutually supply each other's wants is a fact that requires no further demonstration. A satisfactory working agreement, then, is all that is necessary to safeguard the one against the internal dangers of congestion, and the other against the external dangers of conquest.

Unfortunately, at the outset, a distinct though not irreconcilable conflict of interests arises. The empty country desires people of a class the overcrowded land is reluctant to part with. While young communities require young settlers, it by no means follows that old countries will be content to remain but asylums for the aged. Both alike covet the fit. Australia particularly needs robust agriculturists, men of the very class that England wishes to retain to preserve an industry already languishing under the blight of Free Trade. It is hard on a country to rear and train its citizens and then see them lured away to another land when their services have become valuable. The value of each efficient agricultural labourer imported into Australia has been rather sordidly estimated at £300. The flower of Britain's manhood undoubtedly represents the chief source of the national wealth, and Great Britain cannot be expected to view its exportation, even to kindred shores, with approval. The hardship seems emphasised when we reflect that the British oversea dominions owed their existence, and still in the main owe their security, to the expenditure of British blood and treasure.

More than a century ago, Adam Smith, in the chapter of his classic dealing with colonies, complained that a then recent colonial war had cost the mother-country £90,000,000; and apart from the gigantic sum now paid annually by British taxpayers for the support of the fleet required to protect a world-wide empire, a very large proportion of the yearly interest on the National Debt represents payment by instalments for the vast Imperial estates whose use is now peacefully and gratuitously enjoyed by the descendants of British pioneers abroad. The latter would act with signal ingratitude were they to pursue a vampire policy in regard to the mother-country, and endeavour to drain her of her very life-blood in order to increase their own vitality. Such a policy would be doubly injurious. It would tend to weaken Great Britain to such a degree as to render her incapable of supporting the armaments necessary as much to the safety of her colonies as to her own. It would also create feelings of resentment that would grievously impair the sentiment of Imperial solidarity, and forbid the consummation of a lasting union.

Yet, while Great Britain naturally desires to keep at home the pick of her brains and sinews, there is an undesirable element in her population which she is more than willing to spare. Every old country possesses a human residuum it is only too glad to get rid of. But the degenerate, the incompetents and the loafers of European city slums are not wanted in Australia. To undeserved misfortune she offers a kindly helping hand, but for vice and incorrigible indolence she has no welcome. Each country may deal with its social waste products as it thinks best; it is not at liberty to dump its slag and tailings on its neighbour's ground.

Perhaps private benevolence at home has in the past ignored these considerations, and has attributed both to Canada and Australia powers of moral purification to which neither country can lay claim. It should be remembered that moral disease is at least as infectious as physical; and those philanthropists who hold that the best way to cure a criminal or profligate is to throw him into association with people who are honest and respectable, might as reasonably contend that to cure a person suffering from small-pox or leprosy one need but give him complete liberty to mix with healthy persons. Neither the physically nor the morally unfit is a suitable immigrant. To both the policy of the closed door must be rigorously applied.

Great Britain does not want to part with her sound workers; Australia does not wish to receive either the inefficient or the depraved. Where then is the solution of the problem of emigration to be found? The suggestion made a few years ago by the Editor of this Review and anticipated in practice to a certain degree by Dr. Barnardo seems to open the required *via media*. The transfer of young and healthy children selected from among the redundant urban population of the United Kingdom, and approved by colonial representatives at home, from their hopeless native environment to colonial training farms or other establishments, with Government assistance and under Government supervision, would be an undoubted blessing both to the mother country and to Australia, and would be the redemption of countless young lives. For the successful carrying out of any scheme of the kind suggested State aid would be required, and the principle should be recognised that the control both of emigration and immigration comes within the legitimate functions of Government. Admirable as has been the work of many private associations in this direction, such bodies necessarily lack both the money and the legal authority requisite to the achievement of a great Imperial task. To perform it effectively receiving establishments on a large scale, and under official management, would have to be formed both in Great Britain and in the emigrant-receiving colonies. Steamers would have to be subsidised to convey the partially trained children from the old country to the new, where their education would be completed, and where they would be thoroughly habituated to novel conditions of life before being thrown on their own resources.

There is no reason to doubt that under scientific and sympathetic management the slum boy, who, if neglected, would develop into the hooligan or gaol-bird, might be transformed into an industrious and profitable citizen of his adopted country. He would carry with him there no painful memories. Any sense of the private wrong that tends to impair civic efficiency would be obliterated by feelings of gratitude to those who had freely bestowed on him full opportunities for self-improvement. Thus the ties between Great Britain and her daughter Dominions would be continually strengthened, the homogeneity of the Empire promoted, and the path prepared to an ultimate political union. The mutual, economic and material benefits that would arise from such an interchange of population are obvious. The Briton abroad would provide food and raw material for his kinsman at home, and, at the same time, by his consumption of British manufactures, increase their opportunities of employment.

Land hunger would be satisfied on the one side; population hunger on the other. Great Britain by the periodic withdrawal of her surplus juvenile inhabitants might eventually be spared the social convulsions arising from glut of population; while the overflow would enhance the prosperity, and ensure the safety of her dependencies abroad. These great blessings for coming generations are worthy of some effort and sacrifice on the part of Britons to-day. What cynics speak scornfully of as human refuse is, after all, but animate matter in the wrong place. Both philanthropy and policy alike demand that it should be transferred to the right place. The necessarily fitful and disconnected efforts of private charity cannot achieve a task of such magnitude. The resources of the State, now too often squandered in alleviating quite avoidable distress, must be applied to its prevention.

The proposal that a central emigration board should be formed composed of representatives of Great Britain and of each emigrant-receiving colony affiliated to local committees in the provinces seems to be a very feasible one. A similar bureau, or board, in each colony or Dominion would undertake the necessary arrangements in regard to the receiving of immigrants, their distribution where required, and their settlement on land; and, in the case of juveniles, control their preparatory training. The ancient Greek Republics, we know, systematically arranged for the periodic transportation of their surplus inhabitants and their settlement in new territories, though, with singular fatuity, they neglected to devise political bonds to unite the colonies with the mother cities. That the plough should follow the sword was a fundamental maxim of Roman policy, and by its consistent observance the Romans not only conquered, but retained. Modern statecraft should be able to combine the freedom of the one system with the permanence and political stability of the other.

Another, and very potent, agency by which population might be attracted to Australia would be the construction of railways on the land-grant system. The inveterate prejudice that at present exists in the Commonwealth against a method of developing unoccupied territories which is universally practised in America, and which in Western Canada particularly has worked miracles in extending settlement and civilisation, is deeply to be deplored. No country in the world seems to require development by the means indicated more imperatively, and none could derive greater benefit by their adoption. Permanent settlement in Australia to-day is still almost confined to the coast and the regions immediately adjacent to it. Much of the interior is an uninhabited waste, and the rest but sparsely occupied by pastoralists holding their lands on lease. Railways are required to open up the interior, and, in particular to bridge the huge gaps that now separate Adelaide from Albany, and Oodnadatta, the present northern terminus of the trans-continental railway from Pine Creek, the southern terminus of the line from Port Darwin.

In 1902 the South Australian Parliament did, indeed, pass an Act by which the Government was empowered to invite offers from capitalists to construct a line between the two places last mentioned on certain specified conditions. In return for fulfilling those conditions the syndicate whose offer was accepted was to receive in alternate blocks along the line areas of land not exceeding 75,000 acres each for every mile of railway constructed. Tempted by the liberal inducements offered a syndicate was formed some time afterwards, and the sum of £10,000 was deposited to the credit of the South Australian Government as required by the Act. Unfortunately, however, before the contract was finally signed, a general election took place with the result that a Labour ministry under the premiership of the late Mr. Price came into office, and negotiations with the syndicate were at once broken off. But for this unlucky occurrence a line connecting the Northern Territory with the settled regions of the continent would be now nearly completed, as the syndicate was prepared to undertake to build the railway within eight years. From the fact that the expenditure in wages alone during that period was computed at £300,000 per annum, the magnitude of the work may be estimated; and the benefit derived by the people of Australia in general from the circulation of such large amounts of imported capital would have been very substantial. But the narrow prejudice against visionary "monopolies" prevailed, and defeated an enterprise of a most beneficent description. Two similar attempts to construct land-grant railways on a large scale previously made in Queensland and Tasmania respectively proved equally unsuccessful.

Rational objections to the land-grant system applied to railway construction in unoccupied regions are hard to discover, provided of course, each contract stipulates for efficiency of construction and service, and reasonable expedition in completing the work ; and imposes a maximum rate of charges for goods and passengers.   As a safeguard, too, the right of re-purchase by the State at a fair valuation should be reserved, such right to be exercised, if thought expedient, at the end of a fixed term.   In return for a certain quantity of land, at the time absolutely useless to it, the State would then receive the two direct advantages of the expenditure of a large sum of money in building the line, and the use of the line itself.   The lands retained along the route would also be largely increased in value and rendered fit for settlement.   While private individuals would bear the whole risk, their interests and those of the country served by the railway would be absolutely identical.   Its prosperity would be essential to their prosperity.   Land and railway alike are useless, indeed burdensome, to their owners without people to occupy the one and provide traffic for the other.   Consequently, among other signal benefits conferred by a land-grant railway company on the country which is the scene of its operations, is that of providing the State with a most effective and entirely gratuitous, immigration agency.

Settlers being needed to cultivate the Company's lands the people introduced are of the best type—in the main, skilled agriculturists and adventurous pioneers.   In reality, too, the Company deprives the country it thus benefits of nothing in the form of wealth.   It receives no cash, and it certainly cannot carry its broad acres away and deposit them elsewhere.   On the other hand, it bestows on the State men, money and large increasing revenues, apart, possibly, from strategic advantages of inestimable value.   The fear entertained by certain suspicious, and not very enlarged, minds that a certain number of capitalists, or shareholders, on whom had been bestowed large areas of land would deliberately lock these up against settlement, paying taxes on them meanwhile, and running trains through them at a heavy loss, patiently awaiting an " unearned " and very shadowy increment of the remote future, excites risibility.   Business men are not as a rule prepared to lay out large sums of money solely for the benefit of their great-grandchildren.   The natural craving for the dividend would effectually operate in the way of " bursting up " their huge landed estates.   A survey of the history and the present operations of the Canadian Pacific Railway Company is alone sufficient to dispel many of the small prejudices which with so many men pass for opinions on the great questions of communications and agrarian settlement.   The Australian working man, ignoring the admonitions of not wholly disinterested political mentors, might dispassionately consider the emphatic opinions adverse to the State ownership of railways that have been expressed among others by such eminent authorities as Sir Wilfrid Laurier and ex-President Roosevelt.

But Australia offers a warm welcome and a plenteous share of the good things of life to others besides those who, perhaps reluctantly, seek her shores, driven from their own homes by pressure of want. Her numerous and diverse industries, and others yet to be born, present the most inviting prospects to the enterprising capitalist, small as well as great. Her yet untrodden plains and forests await the advent of the adventurous pioneer with his flocks and herds, or the equally hardy treasure-seeker. To the man of mature years, with a limited income and possibly an unlimited family, she offers both comfort and opportunity. The irksome conventions that compel the retired officer or civilian at home who enjoys a fixed income to maintain a certain style of living under penalty of social ostracism are happily unknown in Australia. The man there counts for more than the purse. And, unlike Canada and South Africa, Australia is essentially British in blood, tastes, habits and sympathies.

"No Englishman need apply" is a form of welcome that never appears in an Australian advertisement. All new arrivals from the United Kingdom are at once adopted as members of the Australian family, and are made to feel, in the full sense, at home. All tastes as to situation, climate and general surroundings can be gratified. The entrancing loveliness of tropical Queensland invites those who love warm sunshine and the glory of flower and foliage. Hardier constitutions may revel among the snows of the Australian Alps, or enjoy the bracing atmosphere and noble landscapes of the Tasmanian tableland. For salubrity and equability of temperature the elevated regions that separate the coast ranges of Queensland and New South Wales from the burning plains of the interior are unrivalled, and certain portions of the south-west of West Australia suggest the climatic charms of the Mediterranean Riviera.

It is pitiable to read of British emigrants of means seeking in large numbers each year the shores of the United States and Argentina, while Australia thirsts for the waters of life. The invitation she extends is also the animating call of patriotism. For the sake, not only of individual happiness and collective prosperity, but of the very existence of the kindred civilisation now menaced by the growing powers and ambitions of the Oriental nations, let us hope that reinforcements of strenuous British workers will soon flow in an unceasing and increasing stream to the great outpost of the white race in the southern seas.

F. A. W. GISBORNE.

TASMANIA, *June* 19.

FOREIGN AFFAIRS

By EDWARD DICEY, C.B.

THE RUSSO-JAPANESE AGREEMENT

THE conclusion of a new agreement between Russia and Japan is by far the most important event in foreign affairs that has occurred during the month just closing. If we are to accept the view put forward officially on behalf of both the contracting Powers, the new treaty forms a supplement to the Russo-Japanese Agreement of 1907, and is to be regarded as a further surety for the maintenance of the *status quo* and of peace in the Far East. And so far as one can judge from the summarised text of the arrangement telegraphed by the *Times* correspondent at St. Petersburg it would appear that both these statements are correct. I take leave to append the summary, dated July 7th, three days after the signatures were attached.

> Sincèrement attachées aux principes de la convention du 17 Juillet 1907, et désireuses de développer ses effets en vue de la consolidation de la paix en Extrême Orient, les hautes parties contractantes sont convenues de compléter ledit arrangement par les dispositions suivantes.
>
> Dans le but de faciliter les communications et de développer le commerce entre les nations elles s'engagent mutuellement à la coopération amicale en vue de l'amélioration de leurs lignes de chemin de fer respectives en Mandchourie et du perfectionnement du service de raccordement des voies ferrées, et de s'abstenir de toute concurrence nuisible.
>
> Elles s'engagent de maintenir et de respecter le *statu quo* conformément à tous les traités conclus jusqu'à ce jour, soit entre la Russie et le Japon, soit entre ces deux puissances et la Chine.
>
> Dans le cas où les évènements viendraient à menacer le *statu quo* les deux parties contractantes s'entendront sur les mesures pour son maintien.

From this summary it will be seen that although the open door is not directly mentioned it is covered by the wording of the treaty, which pledges the signatories to maintain all previous agreements. The matter, however, did not escape the attention of the representative of the German Foreign Office when the text of the treaty was conveyed to the German Government, and in thanking the Ambassadors of Russia and Japan for their communication, Baron von Shoen expressed the expectation that the principle of the open door, so important to Germany in the prosecution of her economic efforts in the Far East, would be maintained, and received an assurance to that effect. In view of the action taken by Germany to secure the open door in Morocco and other places, one can appreciate her anxiety to make certain that what has always been regarded as a cardinal point in German foreign policy was not being avoided. And I sincerely hope that the assurance given will be kept in the spirit as well as in the letter. Certainly looking back on the past dealings of Japan in commercial matters ample ground exists for Germany's anxiety, and one might almost say for anxiety on the part of Great Britain.

The new treaty will doubtless be a disappointment to Mr. Knox, whose recent drastic proposals for removing the Manchurian railways out of the sphere of politics so greatly astonished both Russia and Japan. These proposals were of such a nature that one could hardly expect them to be received with acclamation, but although the non-assent of Russia and Japan was extremely polite, it did not quite convey the meaning that some other plan was in contemplation which, if carried out, must inevitably postpone Mr. Knox's proposals till the Greek Kalends. Contrary to expectation, however, the American press has been singularly reticent about the treaty, and even if in some circles a suspicion prevails that all is not well, it is difficult to find chapter and verse for any statement to that effect. Perhaps the nearest is the warning note in the *Tribune*. That journal supports the agreement so long as the relations established " are not hostile in their intent to the United States or to any other nation," but follows up its rather chilly reception by suggesting that " the agreement might mean the perpetuation of the present exclusive control of those Chinese provinces by two alien Powers. It might mean the continued monopoly of travel and transportation in all directions by the existing Russo-Japanese railroads and the prohibition of the construction of any new lines." These suggestive remarks seem to find an echo in the *Evening Post*, which goes out of its way to assure the American public that the two nations, Russia and Japan, mean to discriminate against American enterprise in Manchuria, but this has yet to be proved.

Reading between the lines it can hardly be said that the reception of the arrangement by America is altogether genial, and one can hardly expect Americans to receive with open arms the view expressed very freely in the Japanese press that the idea of the treaty was conceived long before Mr. Knox brought forward his proposals. The story put forward in Japan, presumably with official cognizance, is that the treaty was delayed owing to the untimely death of Prince Ito. Both Russia and Japan had learned by experience, we are told, that competition was mutually injurious and therefore it was resolved to settle the railway question as the chief source of possible friction. Concerning the question of possible friction there can be no doubt, and if proof were wanted it is supplied by the fact that the same possibility was present to the mind of Mr. Knox; accordingly he can scarcely complain if that cause of friction has been removed, even though he himself has not been allowed to have a hand in the removal and the method of removal does not exactly coincide with the scheme he put forward. Any suggestion that a secret understanding has all along existed between Russia and Japan is indignantly denied by Japan, nor does there appear to be ground for any suggestion of the kind.

China finds no fault; in fact it may be said that the verdict in Peking is favourable to the new treaty. In the formal reply sent by the Chinese Government satisfaction is expressed at the decision of Russia and Japan to adhere to the Portsmouth Treaty and the *status quo* in Manchuria. Further, China declares her intention in future to act in accordance with the provisions of the Portsmouth and China-Japanese treaties, and intimates that she will continue as before to use every effort, when exercising her sovereign rights, to maintain equal opportunity for the development of commerce and industry in Manchuria with the object of furthering the best wishes of all countries.* With China friendly and America apparently willing to await results, Japan and Russia have secured two bull points. France gives a warm welcome to the Treaty as becomes an ally of Russia, while Great Britain extends a most cordial welcome to an understanding which marks another stage in the course taken by her ally Japan to maintain peace in the Far East. So long as any cause existed that might tend to create difficulties between Russia and Japan the danger of hostilities was ever present. Happily the new agreement sets our minds at rest on that score, and the fact that China is content offers an additional guarantee of peace and progress.

Germany has no economic interests in Manchuria, and the *Kölnische Zeitung* correctly voices German opinion when it says the new treaty is welcomed in Germany as a guarantee of peace in the Far East, a view that receives confirmation from the *North German Gazette*, which also sees in the Russo-Japanese

* See *Times* telegram from Peking, July 22.

agreement "a security for the maintenance of peace in the Far East." On the other hand the same semi-official journal does not hesitate to mention that German satisfaction would have been "more unadulterated and more emphatically expressed if Russian and French newspapers had not—and that even before the publication of the Agreement—suggested that Russian policy, now that the Agreement with Japan had been secured, would take in the Near East a turn against Germany and Austria-Hungary. It must be stated with special emphasis that this perversion of the tendency of the Russo-Japanese Agreement is not of German origin." One cannot help regretting that the press of Russia and France should have given any cause for this not unnatural complaint, but it may, I trust, be assumed that the organs to which reference is made in no way represent the official view either of France or Russia. Possibly the true inwardness of the new treaty is correctly diagnosed by the statement that the Agreement emanated from the desire of Russia to pursue her policy in Asia undisturbed, and from the wish of Japan to build up in peace what she acquired in war. In any case it is eminently satisfactory to know that the treaty meets with approbation in Germany.

Austria-Hungary seems to fear the freeing of Russia in the Far East will mean greater strength for that power in Europe, a strength which in view of recent events in the Balkans one can understand Austria-Hungary failing to appreciate. On the whole, however, the treaty has been very favourably received all round, and certainly we in this country have every reason to be satisfied, while the fact that the arrangement has met with no direct opposition from any quarter is a sure indication that what has been done is well done, As far as one can see the treaty not only reflects credit upon the signatory Powers but must tend to secure the peace of the world.

GERMANY AND GREAT BRITAIN

As one who for many years has advocated an *entente* with Germany, I welcome the better feeling that exists between the two countries. Nothing shows this advance more than the recent debate on the Navy Estimates. I do not mean to say that all criticism of the German naval programme disappeared from the discussion; that, of course, was not possible, especially in view of the statements made by the First Lord of the Admiralty last year, but on this occasion there was an entire absence of animosity. Even the most bitter critics of Germany's naval policy did not express any ill-feeling towards our friends across the channel, and Lord Charles Beresford was most careful to point out that we had no quarrel with Germany, who had a right, an inherent right, to build what ships she liked and when she liked. This sentiment marked the debate throughout except for one disagreeable incident which was well treated by Mr. Asquith and Mr. Balfour.

The Prime Minister endeavoured in every way to show the friendly feelings of this country towards Germany. " It is a matter for deep regret that the increase in our naval expenditure should have been associated with the notion that we are, in any sense, hostile to, or entertain hostile designs against the friendly nation of Germany. Nothing is further from the truth," were the words used by Mr. Asquith quite early in the debate. And in the course of the same speech he said :—

> I can say, with the most perfect sincerity, that our relations with Germany have been, and at this moment are, of the most cordial character. I look for increasing warmth and fervour and intimacy in those relations year by year. I welcome— every man on both sides with any sense of patriotism must welcome—the various agencies and movements by which the two peoples are getting more and more to under- stand each other. I do not believe the German Government would in the least subscribe to the view that our naval preparations are directed against them any more than I subscribe to the view that the German naval preparations are directed against us. Germany has her own policy to pursue, her own interests to safeguard. She is a great world-Power. She has outlying dependencies. She is constantly sending her sons and daughters to the uttermost parts of the earth. Her trade is increasing everywhere. The German statesmen and people honestly and legitimately believe—and it is not with us a question whether the manner in which they express and carry out their belief is politic or wise ; that is a matter for them—they believe they cannot maintain their position as a great world-Power, with the numerous and constantly increasing interests they are bound to defend in every quarter of the globe, unless they increase their navy. That is, so far as I know, the German position.

That is the exact position of Germany and with that position it is no business of ours to find fault. We may not like Germany's go-ahead policy either in commerce or in naval matters, but after all that is her affair and not ours. What we have to do is to set our own house in order and to keep it in order, and that is what the little navy party in the House of Commons and in this country are trying their best to prevent. Let Germany work out her own policy and let this country work out her own policy, but do not let us quarrel over the inherent right of every nation to do what seemeth best for its own advancement and its own safety. That is opposed to common sense, and any attempt to fall foul of common sense must inevitably end in the discomfiture of the party foolish enough to try the experiment.

Strong Unionist as I am, I congratulate Mr. Asquith on his statesmanlike utterance, which cannot fail to be appreciated by all who have the peace of the world at heart. That so forcible and so timely a statement in the House of Commons by the Prime Minister should meet with a cordial reception in the Fatherland is only what one might expect, and the feeling of the German nation is well represented by the comments that appeared in the *North German Gazette*, from which I take the following extract :—

> Spoken in the House of Commons by the statesman who is responsible for the policy of the Government as a whole, these utterances have a weight that can hardly be exaggerated. In this pronouncement Germany sees absolute evidence of a happy change in the method of judging Anglo-German relations on the other side of the North Sea. In recent years it has repeatedly been pointed out on the British no less than on the German side that there was no true and reasonable ground for serious dispute between Germany and England. The natural inference, however—that there was, therefore, no obstacle to a thoroughly friendly development of mutual relations—was always wrecked upon the English "but" concerning German naval expansion. Now, in complete harmony with the views expressed in all authoritative German quarters upon every opportunity, Mr. Asquith has laid down that it is a complete mistake to ascribe to the construction of the German Navy an anti-English tendency, just as it is erroneous to attribute anti-German intentions to British naval armaments. . . .
>
> The German building programme is based not upon hostility to any other country, for that is absolutely foreign to German policy, but upon practical consideration of the means of defence which are necessary and sufficient in all the circumstances which have to be considered. It marks a welcome advance in the public treatment of Anglo-German relations when recognition of the real motives which have led Germany to expand her means of naval defence finds such clear expression in England as it has just found in the speech of the British Prime Minister. No sensible German politician will desire to deny Great Britain the right to set what bounds she thinks fit to her naval power, the strength of which, as Mr. Asquith insisted, must be regulated according to the shipbuilding programme of the world. So far from denying that, we have a thorough appreciation of the importance which, in view of its world-wide interests, the British nation attributes to its navy.
>
> It can only be hoped that the question of naval armaments will henceforth be judged on both sides with the calm and the objectivity which the question deserves. By these means the relations of the two peoples would be freed from a factor

which at times has lamentably counteracted welcome and praiseworthy attempts to give to the relations between the German and the British peoples a cordiality which corresponds with the interest of the two Powers. The utterances of Mr. Asquith open up the prospect of a public treatment of questions that affect the two Powers, which will be less heavily loaded with misunderstandings, and therefore more profitable. Such a turn of events would not only serve Germany and Great Britain in equal degree, but would confirm afresh and in a most valuable way the general confidence in peace.

Contrast the debate on the March Estimates this year with that of last year, and contrast the reception given to the utterances of the spokesmen on the Government front bench with that given this year in the German press, and the most casual observer must admit that, while the same determination exists in both countries to pursue a programme which each thinks necessary to provide for the proper and efficient defence of their respective shores and political interests, there is a considerable advance in that give and take which is so essential to preserve friendly relations between one nation and another. Another step forward has been taken towards a better state of feeling between this country and Germany. Let us trust it is but the forerunner of other steps, and that before long we may see a similar *entente* to that now existing between this country and France and this country and Russia.

EDWARD DICEY.

GENERAL BOTHA'S TACTICS

By A SOUTH AFRICAN

THE appointment of General Botha to be the first Premier of United South Africa was, on the whole, welcomed by Afrikanders holding diverging political views. This general satisfaction has, however, not been maintained, and Mr. Duncan Baxter, late member for Cape Town, speaking at a Unionist meeting held in the legislative capital of the Union, on June 17, accurately expressed the present views of a very large section of moderate South Africans, when he called attention to the fact that " the South African party had combined with the forces of Het Volk and the Unie, and 'had determined to fight a strict party fight." He pointed out the duty of Unionists to meet the tactics of their opponents, adding that " the Government had been in power for a fortnight, and if ever there were shown to be a necessity for vigilance on the part of a vigorous Opposition to watch the Government, it had been demonstrated by the happenings of that fortnight."

At the outset confidence was shaken by the inclusion of Mr. Fischer and General Hertzog in the cabinet, and it has certainly not been restored by General Botha's declarations, or by Mr. Fischer's repudiation of racialism as being evidenced in General Hertzog's past educational policy. The " Nationalist " manifesto declared at Pretoria reads delightfully to those eager to proclaim it a triumphant vindication of the success of " Liberal policy," and ignorant of the reactionary forces at work within the provinces of the Union. To South Africans who have learned by heart the lessons of the past, and to whom actions speak louder than words, it tells another story. The press comments in leading South African papers severely criticise the consolidation of the three " Bond " parties under the name of " the South African Nationalist Party," while General Botha at the same time strenuously endeavours to obtain election support by urging the necessity of a clean slate, and by " hoping " that through the publication of his political programme the old parties will cease to exist on the old lines, but will fall into line with the Nationalists.

The Union's administration has been constructed on the most rigid and uncompromising party lines, and, as the *Cape Times* justly comments :

It is preposterous, therefore, to come forward now and declaim eloquently about the wisdom of ignoring all party distinctions and bringing every South African elector into one and the same political fold. Either the grounds on which the necessity for a party administration is urged are mere pretexts, or the grounds of the appeals for non-party support are pretences, and pretences only. Party until we get the portfolios, no party afterwards. If any set of politicians could persuade a country to accept a formula of this kind, naturally they would have every reason to congratulate themselves. They would have a fair chance of retaining office for the terms of their natural lives. But we can scarcely imagine the electorate being hoodwinked in this fashion.

The varying forms " noble phrases " may assume in legislative and administrative practice are instanced by a notable illustration when the *Cape Times* remarks : " We know that one member of General Botha's Ministry, General Hertzog, imagined he was dealing tolerantly and equitably, and in accordance with the Act of Union, in enforcing an educational policy in the Free State which English-speaking South Africans regard as tyrannously coercive."

No one having the true interests of South Africa at heart and desiring to carry out the Act of Union in a fair and liberal spirit, could fail to deplore the reactionary educational policy laid down by General Hertzog in the Orange Free State, a policy which he and his adherents are anxious to impose on the whole of South Africa, and the argument advanced, that elementary education comes within the administration of the Provincial Councils, by no means minimises the gravity of a crisis which led to the formation of the Central Council of Education at Bloemfontein to deal with the question of Separatist Schools.

In expressing his admiration of the courageous action of the small minority in the Orange Free State when they found that the only remedy was the creation of separate schools, Dr. Jameson pointed out that it was " after stretching every point, after trying everything possible to come to a compromise, after fighting the Act to the last ditch, they took the only course open to them. They did not do anything to make a party question out of this controversy. It was far too serious a question. It was a matter of handicap to the future generations of the Orange Free State." To enter into all the provisions of the Orange Free State Education Act would be impossible in so limited a space, but the full reports of the lengthy Parliamentary debates which took place in Bloemfontein deal with various aspects of the question, and explain why such solemn protests have been made " against an Act which denies to every English child the right possessed elsewhere in South Africa and throughout the Empire," and which further militates unjustly against unilingual teachers. An article by Mr. Dewdney Drew, of the late Legislative Council, Bloemfontein, exhaustively explains the position of English teachers and pupils in the Orange Free State, and it has been widely endorsed in South Africa by all who have studied the Hertzog Act with care and attention.

The *Cape Times* fairly summed up the educational crisis and the responsibility of General Hertzog and his colleagues as follows :

Until they came into office, the educational machine in the Orange Free State was working as smoothly as it is in the Cape Colony, we might almost say as smoothly as it is in Scotland. Since General Hertzog set to work to remodel the education system in accordance with his views, friction has developed into dissension, and dissension into conflict, until now the English-speaking parents are faced with the alternative either of accepting a system of racial tyranny which their brethren in the Cape Colony would never dream of tolerating, or of setting up schools of their own. General Hertzog's conception of education in a United South Africa is not the development of the powers of the mind and the provision of the earliest mode of access to vital knowledge, to paraphrase Matthew Arnold, but the insistence on a rigid system of bilingualism, the most conspicuous result of which must be to turn out half-educated racialists.

And yet it is to General Hertzog that the portfolio of " Minister of Justice " has been allotted in the Union Ministry led by the preacher of fairplay and conciliation. Small wonder that those who are true to British ideals and traditions, and who desire a real Union, and allegiance to Imperialism, are gravely apprehensive of what the future may hold.

A SOUTH AFRICAN.

PRACTICAL SCHOOL OF FRUIT FARMING ON THE DRY BELT OF BRITISH COLUMBIA

NUMBERS of young men are educated at our public schools for whom no prospect exists in the old country beyond the office desk without expectations—young men with a marked preference for open-air life—and perhaps unfitted by nature for a University career and the learned professions. For these, fruit farming on the Dry Belt of British Columbia probably offers a better and more attractive opening than any other calling, provided that their parents can start them with, say, £1,000 capital.

To ensure success, however, a proper training is absolutely necessary, and this training cannot be obtained in England, because the climate and physical conditions of this country do not lend themselves to the teaching of fruit culture as practised on the Dry Belt of British Columbia. Such training must therefore be obtained on the spot. People are apt to talk about fruit farming in British Columbia as if the industry was the same all over the Province, whereas fruit farming on the Dry Belt under irrigation conditions is altogether different from fruit culture on the Wet Belt, where irrigation is not required. Unfortunately it does not appear to be the business of anyone to explain to the intending settler the difference between the two methods of fruit culture and the widely different results that are obtained, with the not unnatural result that the uninformed Englishman almost invariably starts fruit farming on the Wet Belt of British Columbia, because the conditions resemble those he has been accustomed to see at home. And not until he has made a failure of his experiment does he begin to understand how different might have been his fate had he only turned his attention to fruit culture under irrigation on the Dry Belt. An excellent guide for the young emigrant fruit farmer, telling him what to do and what to avoid, is Mr. Redmayne's little book * on the subject.

* To be obtained from the *Times* Book Club or from the British Columbia Development Association, Limited, 115, High Holborn, W.C. For further particulars see advt. p. 4 of Cover.

The typical Dry Belt fruit farm in British Columbia is as a rule generally about ten acres in extent, which is much smaller than the Wet Belt fruit farm. The system of culture is intensive, and the results far exceed those of the Wet Belt farm. The ten acre Dry Belt fruit farm leads to close settlement, i.e., in any Dry Belt district the farmers live in closer proximity, and the orchard land being expensive the farmers are more likely to be of the same class as the English public school boy.

Hitherto the chief difficulty has been how to obtain the necessary training, for there is no college in British Columbia where this training can be fully obtained, and it can only be given on the Dry Belt itself. Accordingly it has been necessary to advise young Englishmen intending to take up this kind of fruit culture to take a course at the Washington State College, Pullman, U.S.A. But while the Pullman College authorities are most considerate and attentive to the requirements of the English students, there is always the natural dislike to put oneself under an obligation to another country for the training of British students—who ought to be trained under "the Flag." Besides there is the inconvenience and expense of journeys to and from Pullman to be considered.

As the result of long experience, as well as of parental pressure, the British Columbia Development Association are now organising a Practical School of Dry Belt Horticulture under irrigation conditions at Walhachin, near Ashcroft. This school will necessarily be conducted on self-supporting lines and every precaution taken to see that the students mean business, and join with the intention of being made thoroughly practical Dry Belt fruit farmers. In England one hardly realises how important it is to all fruit land development companies on the Dry Belt of British Columbia that their lands should only be sold to persons who know how to handle the land properly. An indifferent fruit farmer is as it were a plague spot in a Dry Belt fruit farming district: he pulls down the average of excellence in the district. And how important this high average is to a district is best understood when one realises that the marketing of fruit farm produce on the Dry Belt is for the most part done on co-operative principles. In fact the efficiency of the Dry Belt fruit farmer is as important to his district as it is to himself.

The familiar English method of getting one's training by going as a private premium pupil to some individual farmer does not exist in Canada—or if it does it is unpopular. The pupil is regarded as being a bit of a fool and the farmer that takes him as something worse. The successful fruit farmer has no time or inclination to teach a raw hand, and will at most only put him to cut logs or drive a team—anything to keep him away from the fruit trees. And no wonder, seeing that a raw hand has been known to do some hundreds of pounds' worth of damage in an hour by the wrong use of the spraying machine. An unsuccessful fruit farmer on Wet Belt may occasionally advertise in British (not Canadian) newspapers for a premium pupil—but this only means that the farmer wants to make a living out of the pupil's premium.

In the Walhachin School all the practical work of the pupils will be done under adequate supervision of experts specially retained for the purpose, and their instructions will be supplemented by lectures and lessons on theory during the winter months when outdoor work on the ground is suspended. The actual work done by the pupils on the estate will be paid for at its market value in the form of wages to be applied in the first instance to the reduction of the student's fees, any balance being placed to the student's credit and handed to him on the completion of his training. The fees are arranged to cover the cost of board and tuition, and are fixed at the lowest possible figure, having regard to the fact that there is at present no government grant or endowment fund in connection with the school.

A useful adjunct of the school will be the horticultural experiment station and nursery, in which it is expected many of the problems affecting the culture of fruit under irrigation conditions will be solved, and a professional library of literature bearing on fruit culture is to be attached to the school. Experimental work in connection with tobacco culture and curing and in the handling of the by-products of fruit culture will also be undertaken, and instruction given in the grading, packing, and marketing of fruit.

At first the accommodation will be necessarily limited and a careful selection of intending students will be necessary. In the case of public school-boys, the headmaster's certificate will be required to gain admission to the school. It is hoped that a system may be established of having a correspondent at each of the leading schools in the homeland—possibly one of the junior masters who may be specially interesting himself in finding openings in the overseas dominions for boys about to leave school. At present all communications should be addressed either to Mr. W. A. Evans, Secretary of the Public Schools Emigration League, or to Mr. J. S. Redmayne, British Columbia Development Association, 17, Waterloo Place, Pall Mall, S.W. It is intended to open the school next spring with a minimum of ten students, and as arrangements have to be made considerably in advance, early application will be necessary; names should, if possible, be sent in before Christmas in order to secure admission during the coming year.

It is not improbable that an affiliated separate branch for lady fruit farmers may come into existence later, for Dry Belt fruit farming is an industry well adapted for ladies. But the Association, in the first instance, will concentrate its energies in making provision for training young men. As one of the most successful fruit farmers on the Dry Belt has said—the fame and future of his particular fruit farming district has been built up by the efforts of young fruit farmers from the English public schools.

The following ladies and gentlemen have already agreed to serve on the consultative committee which has been formed here in England. To this committee any points arising in connection with the working of the scheme will be referred. It will be seen that the headmasters of the leading public schools are well represented—as well as scientific and horticultural experts.

G. McL. Brown, European Manager of the Canadian Pacific Railway Company; the Hon. Mrs. Evelyn Cecil; Sir Clement Kinloch-Cooke, M.P., Editor of the *Empire Review* and Chairman of the Central Emigration Board; Catherine Lady Decies; the Rev. A. A. David, Headmaster of Rugby; Henry Devine, Director of the Future Career Association; Professor Wyndham Dunstan, F.R.S., Director of the Imperial Institute; Mr. W. A. Evans, Hon. Secretary of the Public Schools Emigration League and of the Headmasters Conference; the Rev. Lionel Ford, Headmaster of Harrow; Miss L. Francis; Sir Gilbert Greenall, Bart., President of the Royal Agricultural Society; Mr. A. St. G. Hammersley, M.P.; the Rev. W. A. Heard, Headmaster of Fettes College; the Rev. S. R. James, Headmaster of Malvern College; Sir John Jardine, K.C.I.E., M.P.; the Rt. Rev. the Bishop of Lichfield; the Hon. and Rev. Edward Lyttelton, LL.D., Headmaster of Eton College; the Rev. H. W. McKenzie, M.A., Headmaster of Uppingham School; Mr. J. O'Regan, of Marlborough College; the Rev. Jocelyn Perkins, Organising Secretary of New Westminster Mission Association, B.C.; Mr. Spencer Pickering, F.R.S., Director of the Woburn Experimental Fruit Farm; Professor Adam Sedgwick, F.R.S., London University; Sir Henry Seton-Karr, C.M.G.; Mr. Nowell Smith, Headmaster of Sherborne School; the Hon. J. H. Turner, Agent-General for British Columbia; Miss J. S. Turner, F.R.H.S., Principal of the Ladies' Colonial Training School, Hitchin; Mr. F. Wade, B.C.; and the Rev. St. J. B. Wynne Willson, Headmaster of Haileybury College.*

* Further invitations have been issued, but replies have not yet been received.

In connection with the horticultural and agricultural estates of the British Columbia Development Association, Limited, a Technical School is being formed to undertake the practical training of a limited number of young men in fruit growing, intensive and general farming and other subjects necessary to the equipment of a successful settler. The conditions will be as follows :—

A fee of £35 per term (the year being divided into three terms) *covering the cost of board and tuition*, the first year's fees being paid in advance.

The students to be employed in a variety of work : planting, ploughing, carpentering, mechanical work, etc., including everything required in a new country, on the estates under the management of the resident local director and his staff, the value of the work so performed being paid for in the form of wages to the School Account, so reducing the scholar's fees the following term.

The work will be so arranged that each student shall gain practical experience of all branches, from the breaking up and ploughing of the rough ground, irrigation. construction, etc., including the necessary elements of surveying and engineering, followed by planting, pruning, care of orchards, cultivation of various side crops, fruit packing, grading and marketing, etc., supplemented by theoretical instruction and lectures by the estate horticulturist and expert (who is a graduate of the famous Pullman College, Washington State, U.S.A.), during the winter, when little outdoor work can be done.

With the resident director and his staff will be associated an English Public School man, who is in charge of special industrial operations that are being conducted in relation to these estates. In securing the services of this gentleman, the Association has had due regard to the fact that the majority of pupils attending the School would probably be English Public School boys.

In order to give the students a special and personal interest in their work, they or their parents or guardians will be allowed to secure, on specially favourable terms, a five-acre plot of fruit land on the estate where they are actually working, the land to be paid for in four equal annual instalments, and it will be so arranged that part of the practical instruction shall be given to each student on and in respect of the actual plot, or similar plots, to those which he will afterwards own. [This land has been withdrawn from sale expressly for the above purpose.]

The pupils, or in the case of minors, the parents or guardians on their behalf, will be required to sign an undertaking to obey the rules and regulations of the School, and to subject themselves generally to the control of its officers, and in default of such obedience they will be liable to removal and the forfeiture of fees already paid.

Should the pupil remove himself, or should the parent or guardian remove the pupil, or should the chief officers of the School determine that the pupil at the end of the first year was unsuitable and unlikely to make a successful settler (in which case the authorities would report to the parent or guardian accordingly), the student will be required to leave the School.

The normal course will be three years.

In all cases where the pupil is not retained a second or third year, the five-acre plot assigned to such individual student or his parent or guardian, in relation to which purchase instalments have been paid by the student, or parent or guardian, acting on his behalf, shall pass back into the hands of the estate development company and cease to be the property of the student, his parent or guardian, while the company on its part shall refund any instalment payments that may have been made on account of the purchase of such plot, less expenses in connection therewith. The intention being that if a student does not justify by his industry his ability to earn for himself at least £50 per annum after the first year, he cannot make a successful and desirable settler, and therefore cannot do credit to his instructors. An efficient student should earn as much as £75 to £125 the second year, and £125 the third year.

The Headmaster's certificate as to character will be required in the case of all students coming from the English Public Schools, and no student will be admitted to the School who is under the age of eighteen years unless specially recommended by his master at an earlier age for good and sufficient reason.

In special cases the length of the course may be reduced to a period of two instead of the full period of three years.

The authorities of the School undertake to furnish an annual report to the parent or guardian of the pupil as to his progress in the School.

On the completion of the course a certificate of proficiency will be given.

A Horticultural Experiment Station and Nursery will form part of the Practical School Scheme and deal specially with problems affecting horticulture under irrigation conditions.

The main object in view is to teach young Englishmen to become efficient, self-supporting settlers, and the whole aim of the School will be to secure this end. It is not the intention of the promoters to furnish a domicile for young men who go out to

British Columbia just " to see how they like it." Every possible precaution will also be taken to exclude this class of pioneer, the lazy youth and the waster, for the Association is fully alive to the fact that the presence of even one or two young men of that kind would be most detrimental to the general welfare of the School. Hence the need for stringent regulations.

AGRICULTURAL EDUCATION IN CANADA

Dr. Robertson, late Principal of the Macdonald College, Montreal, and previously Commissioner of Agriculture and Dairying for the Dominion of Canada, in the course of an interesting address at the Guildhall, laid stress on the educational methods adopted in the Dominion for the improvement of moral conditions in Canada. He regarded the welfare of the children as most important — the better chance, the better child. Education had no such helper as agriculture, using both words in their wide and true sense. England had forgotten that agriculture was the greatest educational experience her people had ever had for teaching citizenship, self-reliance, and all kinds of adventurous courage. In Canada the proper culture of the land was looked on as a matter of national interest. It was a great social force for the humanizing of the people and the cultivating of a proper spirit of pride of race. Substantial aid was given by the Federal Government, not directly to primary education, but to experimental and illustration farms for the education of grown-up people. Real education was founded on nature study, manual training, and household science, with as much reading, writing, and arithmetic as time could be found for. That might be heresy; but such education fitted boys and girls for their surroundings. Some of the Canadian school gardens had been most successful, appealing as they did to the imagination and pride of the whole neighbourhood. The agricultural population should be educated to the highest that was in man, and they would respond to the appeal. They maintained in Canada agricultural colleges in three centres, besides illustration farms. The Governments granted aids to the extent of £470,000 for other than elementary education, and it paid immensely. In ten years the crops had increased from £42,000,000 to nearly £110,000,000. Their educative method was to work at both ends of the problem—both children and grown-ups—and that was why they had been so successful.

IMPERIALISM AND TARIFF REFORM

By SAMUEL SKELHORN

PROFESSOR SEELEY once said that the British Empire was founded in a fit of absence of mind, which, if true, must surely be reckoned among the miracles of the ages. Imperial Rome was the product of a disciplined and determined race bent with iron will upon the conquest of the world; but the British Empire— Rome's only rival—came into being during the reverie of a race of dreamers. The Oxford historian may be right. The birth of Britain may have been an accident; but its endurance and final destiny depends upon the resolute and designing intelligence of the democracy.

Certain it is that the *status quo* cannot possibly endure. At the present time we have not so much an Empire as the colossal material of one, the possibility of one. Britain, like a Spartan mother, sits cold and isolated among her daughter States who yearn for sympathy and love. This policy of aloofness and drift, which may be said to include the whole theory and practice of Cobdenism, is doomed. It is wearing away like a castle of sand before the incoming tide. It is oblivious to the facts of the past, the actualities of the present, and the hopes of the future. It is one branch on the sapless and decadent tree of radicalism of which a recent critic, Mr. J. A. Hobson, has said: " It has shown defects of vision and of purpose which sowed doubt and distraction among its followers. .... For over a quarter of a century it has wandered in this valley of indecision—halting, weak, vacillating, divided and concessive. Not gaining ground it yielded it." It is sometimes claimed as the legitimate child of Adam Smith, but to base the case for Cobdenism upon Adam Smith is like basing the case for passive resistance upon Macchiavelli's " Prince." " You can," said Schwarzenberg, " do anything with bayonets except sit on them." You can make anything of 'The Wealth of Nations' except a case for Cobdenism. Adam Smith was neither individualist nor cosmopolitan. He was intensely Nationalist and sturdily Imperialist. His Imperialism was not indeed flamboyant,

D 2

but it was none the less real, and as fervent as a Scotch philosopher's phlegm would permit.

The following quotation shows how very far removed was Adam Smith from the "Little Englandism" of his professed disciples, and how egregiously they have misread their master:

The rulers of Great Britain have for more than a century past amused the people that they possessed a great empire on the west side of the Atlantic. This empire has hitherto existed in imagination only. It has hitherto been not an empire but the project of an empire; not a gold mine but the project of a gold mine; a project which has cost, which continues to cost, and which, if pursued in the same way as it has been hitherto, is likely to cost immense expense without being likely to bring any profit. It is surely now time that our rulers should either realise this golden dream in which they have been indulging themselves, perhaps, as well as the people, or that they should awake from it themselves and endeavour to awaken the people. If the project cannot be completed it ought to be given up. If any of the provinces of the British Empire cannot be made to contribute towards the support of the whole Empire, it is surely time that Great Britain should free herself from the expense of defending those provinces in time of war, and of supporting any part of their civil or military establishments in time of peace, and endeavour to accommodate her future views and designs to the real mediocrity of her circumstances.*

Cobdenism again misreads the present. To say or suggest, as have some of its representatives, that the Fiscal Reform propaganda was merely a piece of political patchwork to distract an irate people from the blunders of South African diplomacy, is quite childish, even inane, in its simplicity. The Tariff Reform movement, especially in its Imperial or Preferential aspects, was the creature of conditions as much as the Reformation or the Renaissance. Mr. Joseph Chamberlain did not make it. It made Mr. Chamberlain. Before it arose there was no Mr. Chamberlain as we have known him since. There was the clever politician and debater, but the great Imperial statesman was not born. In other words, the movement produced the man not the man the movement. It was Mr. Chamberlain's merit that he saw it afar off, that he stamped his strong personality upon it, and so voiced its meaning as to make it live and throb in the mind of the nation. That is why Mr. Chamberlain's policy holds the field without a rival. Not because he made the memorable speech at Birmingham, but because the facts and conditions which were behind the speech and determined its character were such that no other policy is possible. Behind the Birmingham speech was the "Zeitgeist"—the spirit of the age, manifesting itself in "Nationalist" movements, laying the foundation of massive States and building up hostile tariffs—uncontrollable forces that made the speech imperative. Hence the movement with which Mr. Chamberlain's name is indissolubly associated was essentially part of a larger movement,

* Book V., Chap. III.

a movement which may be described as an instinctive apprehension of danger, a feeling after security, and the consequent need for Imperial Union and Defence. This brings us to the pivot upon which the whole problem and policy of Imperialism turns. The irresponsible levity with which the typical Cobdenite trifles with this master-problem of modern politics is appalling. He imagines that all is well because Mr. Haldane has created his phantom army of office boys, and because in naval armaments we are still ahead of Germany. He does not realise that on existing terms we are playing a game which we are fated to lose; that our very existence is at stake, because we can no more maintain the *status quo* than a top can maintain its equilibrium after it has stopped spinning.

The fact is orthodox Cobdenism is played out, if, indeed, it can ever be said to have been more than a pious aspiration. Its best defenders, like Mr. Asquith with his " eternal economic law," remind us of that school of Spanish fencers who fenced according to rules derived from " the mathematics," of whom it is recorded that they could only fight duels among themselves, because antagonists with less science always ran them through in the first bout. The best intellect of the day has repudiated Cobdenism and its works for ever, and is more and more drawn in the direction of a constructive Imperialism.

One happy omen is the publication of Professor J. Shield Nicholson's recent book, 'A Project of Empire.' The issue of this brilliant book marks an era in the discussion of Imperial problems. Dr. Nicholson holds a distinguished position among British economists, and his 'Political Economy' has been pronounced by a very competent critic, Dr. W. Cunningham, " the best complete treatise on the subject in the English language." Seven years ago he signed the famous manifesto against Mr. Chamberlain, yet now we find him moving, not indeed with haste, but with measured steps, in the direction of Mr. Chamberlain's Imperial ideals. A more striking instance of a first-class mind shifting its moorings and gravitating towards the inevitable could scarcely be given.

Professor Nicholson says:

The question of imperial defence has suddenly become of pressing importance, and has directed public attention to other aspects of imperial union. The object of the present book is to reconsider the economic problems involved in their due order and proportions. And first of defence; so long as this country could maintain the undisputed command of the sea we could afford to wait in case of need for the aid of the overseas dominions. But recent events have shown that this country ought no longer to attempt to provide from its own resources for the naval defence of the whole Empire; and in a great naval war there would be no time to call up the ultimate or potential reserves of men and money from the ends of the earth. The self-governing colonies have grown into self-conscious colonies, have grown into self-governing nations, and the recent Conference has shown that they recognise that the primary duty of every nation is to provide for its own defence against foreign attack. . . . It is obvious that a real imperial union of this kind would involve the institution of some form of federal government, in which the constituent States were represented. It is beyond the range of the present inquiry to consider the political difficulties involved. It is clear, however, that a real federal government of this kind, although established in the first place for defence, would naturally be used for the furtherance of other objects. Of these secondary objects of political union the most closely connected with defence is the growth of wealth, population, and organisation. And for this economic development a common defensive policy would naturally be supplemented by a common policy, both as regards trade within the Empire, and also as regards commercial relations with foreign States; and in both cases the ruling idea would be the economic development of the Empire as a whole. For this further development Free Trade within the Empire seems to be one of the fundamental requirements, especially if the appeal is made to recent experience in Empire-making. Internal Free Trade (*i.e.*, between the constituent parts of the Empire) is consistent either with external protection of the most extreme kind or with the complete absence of differential duties or with any *via media.*

As regards industrial defence, history shows that our only security lies in the economic union of the Empire. This has been the experience of nearly all the great modern States. It was Alexander Hamilton's insistence upon mutual trade that made America; it was the Zollverein that made Germany; it was the Canadian Tariff that established economic interchange between Eastern and Western Canada. No theorem of Euclid can be clearer than that, so far as the present position is concerned, the Empire depends upon our commerce, and our commerce depends upon the Empire, and our place as a progressive world-power upon both. The argument of the "Free-Trader" that Germany and the United States represent great "Free Trade" areas is fatuous to a degree. Germany and America do undoubtedly believe in Free Trade—for themselves. They are Free-Traders as between each other, but they are sternly Protectionist against the foreigner, in the solid conviction that by Protection they are benefiting their own countrymen at the expense of the foreigner. Absolute Free Trade within the Empire may be a dream beyond reach of realisation, although on this point Professor Nicholson, while acknowledging the practical difficulties, is by no means so convinced as to its impracticability as were the Premiers at the Imperial Conference of 1907, and he pertinently remarks:—

So long as statesmen are content to repeat, one after the other, that a thing is impossible, it is, *ipso facto*, impossible. It will cease to be impossible as soon as it seizes the imagination of a great Colonial leader of the order that believes a thing because it is impossible. Every great success in war and in peace has been impossible until it has been accomplished. In the background there are the prejudices of the people; but though the race continues the individuals change, and the prejudices change with them.

But if we cannot achieve the whole, must we sacrifice the vital contributory parts? Must we do nothing because we cannot do everything? If we have not enough string to make a perfect parcel, must we leave the contents loose and exposed? Difficulties will undoubtedly arise, and perhaps formidable difficulties, for it is not possible to horoscope the future. In matters of practical organisation it is rarely possible to see further than the next step. But does this justify a condition of inertia, a display of apathetic indifference, and an attitude of official obstruction or cynical scepticism? Surely not. The issues are too vast, the dangers too serious. Never did British statesmanship show to less advantage than when the door was "banged, bolted, and barred" in the face of our kinsmen from across the seas at the last Imperial Conference. The air of superior knowledge, the display of casuistry, the lack of constructive imagination, the cheap cynicism and sneering exhibited at that gathering was pitiful and unpardonable. It could only be paralleled by the pedantry of the old Spanish etiquette which forbade unauthorised persons to throw water upon the king even when he was burning. To sneer at a vision greater and grander than any that has filled the eyes of statesmen since the days of Chatham; that has stirred the souls and fired the hearts of a body of patriots like Joseph Howe, John Macdonald, Cecil Rhodes, Sir Wilfrid Laurier and Mr. Joseph Chamberlain, shows a poor appreciation of what is best and noblest in British politics. To speak of the "sordid" ideals of such men must surely be the last resource of partisan politicians, as destitute of fine feeling as they are lacking in gratitude. To speak of their common aim as a leap in the dark is no less ridiculous. We are groping in darkness now, and we are groping on sinking sand. The policy of constructive Imperialism means a removal to solid rock, to a place of permanent safety. Timorous souls may prate about sacrifice and risk, but the question is, Is the reward worth the risk, and are we worthy of it? Do we want an Empire in reality as we have an Empire in name? If we do, then we must be determined to engineer all our resources to mould this "congeries of Empire" lying shapeless on the seven seas into a consolidated and self-contained Empire, unapproachable in splendour and unrivalled in strength.

Such is the immediate task before us to-day, not indeed more vital now than yesterday, but infinitely more urgent. Every consideration, from calculating prudence to purest patriotism, urges it upon us, and suggests the awful alternative. How long shall we halt between two opinions? Are we without vision, judgment, and practical business sagacity, that we hesitate? Do we prefer the shibboleths and catch-cries of the ignorant to the penetrating insight and foresight of seers? Shall we continue to dally with the unimaginative mandarins of Cobdenism and be deterred from our destined goal by their protests about "Dear Food"? Shall we lose a sure and inestimable gain because of a problematic and trifling loss? To refuse the policy of Imperial Preference because it may involve some slight sacrifice, is like refusing to pick up a diamond because a clot of earth may adhere to it. Shall we turn our faces from the sun because of its spots? "Enough of this foolery." Great empires are not made, nor are they maintained by men who think only of their bellies.

But these, after all, are idle fears. Imperialism and Tariff Reform appeals with equal strength to self-interest and patriotism. We live in democratic days, and democracy has resolved upon a programme of social reform. Like distant thunder we hear the tread of its advance, advancing to demand its rights. Soon it will be knocking clamorously at our doors. But the first condition of social policy is Imperial policy. Any forced antithesis between the two is both false and vicious. The relation is one of friendship. Without reform, Imperialism means revolution; without Imperialism, social reform means stultification. Even socialism must be barren unless based on racial instinct. In politics, as in biological science, the species rests upon the genus.

More and more social problems resolve into financial problems, and financial problems can only be solved by Imperial policy. Democracy must be taught to understand this. Like a storm-tossed ship she ploughs her way through troubled seas, seeking a desired haven. Only by a policy of sane and enlightened Imperialism can the crew realise their hopes; otherwise they may founder in darkness. If the well-being of democracy is our greatest concern, we can only find a secure basis for greater well-being in a united Empire.

SAMUEL SKELHORN.

THE CANADIAN INDIAN TO-DAY

By ELIZABETH WALMSLEY

It is a remarkable thing how completely the North American Indian seems to have vanished, not only from romance, but from sight. Not so many years ago the Fenimore Cooper type of tale still held its readers breathless, and Buffalo Bill thrilled the audiences at Earl's Court with scenes in which he had originally acted in grim earnest as pony express rider, stage coach driver, or military leader.

To-day Sir Gilbert Parker's 'Translation of a Savage' must take the place of some blood-curdling story of Indian warfare, or the handsome Sioux who come to Atlantic City in the season, hawking the barbaric articles they make in exchange for Yankee dollars, incidentally afford the Indians' last display. In Canada, too, it is only on some such occasion as that of a local sports day or agricultural show that the Indians issue in festive native dress from the nearest Reserve to add a touch of something wild and pristine to the day's attractions. Otherwise they are not only out of sight, but out of the mind of all save the Minister for Indian Affairs, and of those responsible under him for the compilation of the annual Blue-Book on the subject.

All that the immigrant, for instance, is likely to see of the red man nowadays is his half-breed representative hanging about with a knot of white settlers on the platforms of the little stations dotting the track of the great trans-continental railways. The Treaty Indians, i.e., those remnants of the once wandering tribes who have entered into relationship with the Canadian Government, keep very generally to their Reserves, to the lands set apart under the supervision of a local agent, for their exclusive use and occupation. Here they experiment in agriculture, avail themselves more or less of such advantages as come to them in the shape of missions, schools, and hospitals, sigh for the strictly forbidden "fire-water" of the pale faces, and lead inoffensive lives as much in keeping with their primitive traditions as the totally altered conditions of things will allow. This system of Indian Reservations also obtains in the United States, but in

Canada, in the Yukon, and North-West Territories there are still
numbers of Indians who have not come into the Treaty, and
who maintain their old nomadic habits, and subsist entirely by
hunting, trapping and fishing.

The line of the great Canadian Pacific Railway strikes the
northern shore of Lake Superior (the "Gitchee Gumee," the
shining "Big-Sea-Water" of Hiawatha) at a point called Heron
Bay, and runs along it to that city of elevators, Fort William,
nearly two hundred miles further west. Thus it traverses the
"pleasant land of the Ojibways," and no one who has not
known what it is to speed onwards day after day through the
sun-smitten wilderness of rocks and pine trees, lakes and rushing
rivers that stretches all the way from Montreal to Winnipeg,
can fully understand how exquisitely apt are the metre and the
simplicity of Longfellow's immortal poem to the very spirit of
Canadian landscape, to the soul of Canadian nature. For one
who has felt the enchantment of its immensity, its loneliness,
its titanic virginity, Longfellow's use of simple adjectives, of
quaint repetition, above all of poetic Indian names, "Mahng the
loon, the wild-goose Wa-wa," has an almost magical power to
recall "the Muskoday, the meadow, the prairie full of blossoms,"
with longing so great it would be homesickness if felt for
another land. Hiawatha himself, however, has little in common
with the "neche" of to-day. Nor have the legends of that Song
of his, into which the poet has woven many a reminiscence of
classic mythology and even of Christian sacrament, much resemblance to the fables of the modern remnants of Indian heathenism.
Hiawatha belongs to American literature, but not to the Red
Indian.

It is said that three dates alone serve to mark Indian history,
from the time when the land which originally united North
America to Asia fell through, and oceans rolled between those
fragments of it left in Baffin's Land, Greenland, Iceland and
Scandinavia. Those tribes of prehistoric men which had already
migrated thus far west, were then cut off from the parent stocks
of the East and isolated. The two great Americas, North and
South, formed an island, and their inhabitants were left—till
the coming of the white man late in historic time—to their own
development. From Hudson's Bay to Tierra del Fuego the
native Americans are one great race. Those in the South have
remained barbaric to the present day; civilisations have arisen
and died away in the central parts of the continent; and for the
North it is approximately true to say that two dates only, or
three, have marked Indian time. They are very recent dates,
too. The first is that of the introduction of the horse about
the eighteenth century; the second is that of the extermination

of the bison during the winter of 1886–87; and the third, surely, is that of the first treaty made with the invading white man. We need assign no specific day or year for it, as of course the States made their own, and Canada made her own, and even at the present time the treaty is continually being made afresh whenever non-treaty Indians desire to enter into it.

The day has long gone by in the States and in Canada when the white man had anything to fear from the red. With the Riel rebellions of 1870 and 1885 an end came to that long series of wars by which the pale face established his right to inhabit and develop the forests of North America. Pitiless and savage as the Indian showed himself to be, Colonel Butler wrote in his book of rovings, "I have no hesitation in saying that five-sixths of our African wars, and a still larger proportion of the Indian wars in America, have had their beginning in wrongs done in the first instance by white men upon natives." *

However this may be—and it can serve no purpose to examine the indictment now—the Government of our great Dominion overseas treats the Indians of the present day with more than scrupulous justice, with extraordinary solicitude. The remnants of all those fine tribes whose very names are fast being forgotten, the Crees, Chippewayans, Ojibways, Delawares, Blackfeet, Abenakis, Mohawks, Iroquois, Dakotas, Assiniboines, etc., are carefully located in Reserves, taught the arts and decencies of settled life, nursed in sickness, assisted in their efforts to make the land productive or to find work elsewhere, paid for their concessions to the white man, and encouraged to transform themselves into enfranchised Canadians.

Much of all this is due to Mr. David Laird, now Chief Adviser in the Department of Indian Affairs at Ottawa, the first Governor of the North-West Territories.

"Never had a public man so large an opportunity in directing the destiny of an almost unknown land, for in 1873 there was practically no Winnipeg, no Edmonton, nor Calgary. Not a mile of railway had been laid on the floor of the prairie, and the wheat-growing possibilities of the West had not even been discovered. Rancher and cow-boy were unknown. British Columbia was isolated by a mountain barrier as if it belonged to another continent. It was at this time that Mr. Laird entered upon a new career of usefulness as a public man. One of the most pressing problems facing the Minister of the Interior was the Indian. The majority of the hundred thousand Canadian red men live west of Lake Superior, and some system of Government control of the Indian was necessary if settlement was to be encouraged and law and order preserved. It was indeed fortunate that it fell to the

* 'Far-out: Rovings Retold.' Introduction, p. xi.

lot of a man of such high character to negotiate some of the principal treaties with the Western tribes. No more fitting encomium could be paid to Mr. Laird than the red men themselves, who, with their unerring insight into human nature, gave him the flattering name of 'The-man-whose-tongue-is-not-forked!' In the year 1876 the North-West Territories were organised, with Mr. Laird as their first resident Lieutenant-Governor. Battleford became the capital of the country now the provinces of Saskatchewan and Alberta, and from the executive mansion of this then isolated centre the government of Canada exercised a more direct sway over both white and red men and half-breeds than had before been possible.

"During the succeeding years Mr. Laird, in his positions of Lieutenant-Governor and Superintendent of Indian Affairs, was in constant contact with the Indians. Deputations of the dusky sons of the plains were frequently encamped on the Battleford outskirts, and there and at other points in the territories he met with the great Indian leaders, such as Crowfoot, the famous chief of the Blackfoot nation, a man of remarkable native genius for government. On numerous occasions the tall chief, for Mr. Laird exceeds a six-foot stature, smoked the pipe of peace with his bronze brothers. It was in 1877 that Treaty No. 7 was concluded with the Assiniboines and Blackfeet—the most powerful of all the prairie tribes. Under it and previous treaties the whole of the country from Lake Winnipeg to the Rocky Mountains and north to the Athabasca, was ceded to the Government, leaving the red men of the farther north to be dealt with at a later period, a much more difficult task owing to their inaccessibility and long freedom from control. In 1899 Mr. Laird concluded the great treaty, known as Treaty 8, with the Crees, Beavers and Chippewayans of the Peace River and contiguous country. It was another remarkable agreement in which the red men signed away for ever their blood rights in a territory five hundred miles in length from the Athabasca River to Great Slave Lake, a treaty that, in the picturesque language of the document, is to last 'as long as the sun shines and the water runs.' The journey of the Treaty Commission with Mr. Laird at its head, was a notable one. It was notable as a matter of contrast. Whereas in the 'Seventies' he had to cover the distance between Winnipeg and Battleford by cart or on horseback, across great stretches of unoccupied and untilled lands, on this journey the railway had reached Strathcona with all the changes and developments involved in its building. From Edmonton northward, however, the primitive overland trail had to be taken to Athabasca Landing, and thereafter covering rivers, lakes and land, as they form the two thousand mile route by the Peace River north, and return by the Athabasca. Reaching Lesser Slave Lake, a memorable gathering took place, when hundreds of tribesmen with their chiefs formed a great tented city surrounding the whiter tents of the Treaty Commissioners. It was a significant day, too, for the red men, for they were asked to part with their rights in an area as large as an empire.

" ' Possessing a nature in which firmness and fairness met,' as Mr. Laird has been happily characterised, he and his fellow Commissioners conducted the negotiations so tactfully and successfully as to secure the consent of the Indians to the proposition and the symbolic signatures of their chiefs to the important document. Addressing the assembled throng as his ' Red Brothers,' Mr. Laird explained the terms by which everyone would get \$12 in that year, and for every year afterwards \$5, for each person for ever, chiefs receiving \$25, a silver medal and a flag, and counsellors \$15, with suits of clothes for both dignitaries. One hundred and twenty-eight acres of land also were offered to each Indian in reserves, the Government promising to further help them with farm implements and grains or cattle if they preferred stock-raising. Schools were also promised. To-day over three hundred schools in the West accommodate ten thousand Indian children. Thus at the most critical period of its history Mr. Laird has rendered high service not only in formulating a beneficent and humane policy regarding the Indian, but in the general development of the great lone land. The trackless prairie of the ' Seventies ' has become the Mecca of the world's surplus peoples ; the unknown West has become the gold West ; the parish of a single administrator has been made into two great provinces, and all this transformation has taken place since Mr. Laird himself went West thirty-three years ago." *

No more interesting comment on his work and on the condition of the Indians under the system he established is to be found than in the Report for the year ending March 31st, 1909, of the Deputy Superintendent-General for Indian Affairs.

First and foremost we find the idea that the Indians are dying out rapidly, qualified (for 1909 at least) by the statement that the births among them outnumbered the deaths by 838. The census return totalled their numbers at 111,043,† and British Columbia with 24,871 has the largest Indian population of Canada. Of all the tribes, the Sioux or the Salteaux are considered perhaps the finest, and the Thlinkets of Alaska and the Klondyke route the poorest specimens. It is not, however, likely that the pure blood Indian will survive very much longer. He must either be absorbed by the big class of half-breeds, the formation of which is the

* The *Edmonton Daily Bulletin.*
† About equal to the population of Brighton.

natural result of an invading white population, or succumb to the fell disease which has gained such a terrible and widespread hold on the red man, viz., tuberculosis. For the Canadian Indian is no longer an Indian, though he persists in behaving as though he were, to the destruction of his health and the depletion of his race. The "brave" no longer lives in a wigwam or "tepee" as his forefathers did, more or less exposed to the inclemencies of all weathers and consequently hardened to them, but in a "shack" much like an immigrant settler's. But he cannot also accustom himself to the white man's mode of life. He combines the disadvantages to health of bad ventilation indoors and exposure outside. For the nature of the Indian is still Indian, and until he can be taught how to adapt himself to the higher standards of comfort which contact with civilisation has brought him, the result must inevitably be extinction. Lung disease is the great menace of the race; if indeed consumption could be effectually prevented or stamped out among the Indians, there is no reason why they should not increase as normally as the white populations around them.

"First contact with civilisation," says Mr. Pedley, "rarely proves an unmixed blessing to aboriginal races," and in the case of those Indians to be found in the more newly-opened provinces of Western Canada, the diversified character of the stream of immigration makes it difficult to decide whether the upshot for them is good or bad. "Down East," where the Indians have long been in contact with the "superior race," they have not failed to recognise the benefits likely to accrue to them from the adoption of its methods. It is interesting to note that in 1909 the Indians made nearly three times as much money from agriculture as from their natural resources of hunting, fishing and trapping, and that they made more from wages than from agriculture. In religion the greater number of Indians are Catholics, but nine thousand six hundred odd still adhere to those queer pagan beliefs which make it so difficult for the various agents to report justly as to what may or not be considered the "morality" of the bands under their charge. The validity of pagan Indian marriage rites is recognised by the Canadian courts in so far as these rites contemplate monogamy and the permanency of the marriage tie. Fortunately the Indians seldom now have recourse to the barbaric services of their "medicine men," but Dr. Bryce reports that it is often owing to the extraordinary "native customs" that still prevail at child-birth that certain classes of diseases are found among the women.

The question as to how the Indians avail themselves of the educational advantages provided for them in the shape of excellent schools, which the children are bound to attend—often managed by qualified teachers from the Indian bands themselves—raises the interesting ethnological point as to the relative "highness" or "lowness" of nations in the evolutionary scale. Are the American aborigines, for instance, capable of assimilating education, and, if so, to what extent? It seems that the welfare of the red man in Canada depends entirely upon his own power of coming into line, so to speak, with the white, for of prejudice against him there is none. The Government is always ready to extend the franchise to the Indian and to encourage him to take an administrative interest in the affairs of his "Band" the moment he has attained the few necessary qualifications. Here we have the argument in a nutshell against the contention that the "natural" races of mankind (as distinguished from the "savage" or the "cultured") are necessarily any lower in intellectual capacity than those which have attained civilisation in more or less higher degrees. Some ethnologists hold that the natural races are absolutely in line intrinsically with the civilised races, that there is, perhaps, less of the animal about a Somali or a Cree than about a "degenerate" in Paris or London. An uncivilised being is "all man," equal in mental and spiritual capacity with the cultivated one. But the difference between a civilised and a natural race is that the former has embraced, and the latter has missed, opportunities of racial advancement. The reasons for this, of course, are to be sought in climate, environment, contact with others, etc. Thus the races of mankind are to be viewed rather as a squadron on the level in rough echelon formation than by a perpendicular standard with rungs. The civilised nations of the world "toe the line," and the uncivilised straggle away behind them in various degrees short of it.

Now, indeed, advantages such as he has never won for himself have been brought to the Redskin, and if he could only live as a race long enough to profit by them it would remain to be seen whether or no he could vindicate a claim to equality with the white man.

' From reading the hundred and fifty odd pages of school reports in the Indian Blue Book it is difficult to arrive at a wholesale estimate of the progress of education among the children. Here it is eminently satisfactory: "An unusual interest is taken in education by these Indians," writes one agent of a band in Alberta, "and it is the exception, not the rule, for their children to be away from a school." There it is disheartening: "The subject of education is one our Indians do not seem to appreciate," writes Mr. MacPherson of a Nova Scotian band of Micmacs; "attendance is meagre and progress slow." In one place school buildings are urgently required, in another such as exist are being closed. Perhaps the only unqualified remark to be passed on the subject is one of admiration for the care the Government and the local school authorities expend on the children and the justice of the principle applied, that the denomination of the teacher should be decided by the religious majority in the school. In Quebec and Ontario, of course, the schools are largely in the hands of Catholics. "I may say confidently," writes Father Conture S.J., of the Wikwenikong Industrial School, Ontario, "that the school is contributing largely to the elevation of the moral tone and development of habits of thrift and industry, the enlightenment of the mind generally and the improvement of physique among our Indians. Our present pupils appreciate more their training, and rise to a higher level than our former ones. . . . A few of our Iroquois boys have gone to college in Quebec. . . ." Mr. Matherson, principal of the Battleford Industrial School, says: "Some of our pupils are engaged in various places as teachers or helpers in connection with the Indian schools; two have taken a course at St. John's College, Winnipeg, and have been ordained to the sacred ministry of the Church. One is married to an English lady, and is in charge of one of our boarding schools and missions. The other took his degree of Bachelor of Arts in the university of Manitoba, and is also now in charge of one of our missions. Nearly all the girls that have been discharged are married, most of them on the Reserves, to ex-pupils and others, but several of them are married to white settlers, and are keeping their homes in creditable condition." An Indian from the big reserve belonging to the famous Six Nations in Ontario is studying medicine at Toledo, Ohio. Some of the Indians have taken, too, to literature, and a paper appeared in the *Forum* for July, 1898, written by a Pottawatomi chief, dealing with Indian legends.

The tone of the reports of the various Indian agents is always patient, tolerant and even affectionate; sometimes the Blue Book rises to psychological analysis and insight.

"Progress on the Reserves is apparently very slow," we read in one place. "To uplift an Indian his whole character has to be reformed, and how this is to be accomplished on an Indian Reserve with its usual surroundings I fail to see; but if an Indian with his family goes off the Reserve to work for a good class of farmers for a year or two his development in character is quite apparent to anyone; and if this is carried on it will in time produce the survival of the fittest, and the next generation will develop on the character of their parents."

And again: "The characteristics of the Sioux are very apparent to those working with him. He is wary, subtle and suspicious of a lurking enemy somewhere in hiding. He is proud of himself and his capabilities. He has also a fertile imagination, which is easily capable of expansion. These are some of his positive qualities. Negatively he has no idea of economy, and thriftiness is altogether foreign to his nature. Combine these characteristics with a love of the marvellous and magic, and of the power of the spirits over him, and we have a make-up different from most other Indian tribes. He is likewise very industrious and has a lively imagination, and these help him in a variety of ways to secure his ends. It leads him to live on futures, which are always large; he spends freely, and if possible faster than he makes, so he does not get ahead very fast."

The Indians are generally quick linguists and soon acquire French and English. Some have a care for their own tongue, and in one Abenaki school the native language is carefully preserved. It is said that the stock languages of the American natives are extremely numerous, perhaps more so than all the stock languages of all the other orders of speech in the world. Indeed every band and tribe of Indians seems to have a speech of its own not understood by the rest. The Indian languages are very poetical and their metaphors are derived from the clouds, the birds, beasts, seasons and heavenly bodies. While many bands still have a system of picture writing, like that Hiawatha is supposed to have taught them, it has remained for the modern missionary to devise an alphabet which represents the sounds of the Indian tongues and serves for clerkly purposes. In print it looks much like shorthand.

Civilised man has undoubtedly forfeited many of those extraordinary instincts which in the Indian still amount to sixth and seventh senses. Last summer when the difficulty occurred of tracking down some escaped convicts near Strathcona, it was suggested that half-a-dozen Stoney Indians should be procured from the Stoney Reserve and placed on the trail. They would follow it, said one who was fully conversant with Indian guides and trappers, almost as accurately as a bloodhound. "I have seen them pick up horse tracks where a white man could see absolutely no trace." Another Stoney Indian shammed paralysis, in order to escape a charge of horse-stealing, so marvellously that for days two medical men were completely baffled as to whether it was simulation or real illness that had reduced the man to the condition of a log ever since he was brought to the mounted police barracks.

"The extent to which Indian interests are confined to the Reserves" makes for the absence of serious crime, but on the other hand, Mr. Pedley says, "the deprivation of various forms of legitimate excitement and amusement encourages the inclination among them to seek refuge from the monotony of existence by means of the coveted 'scuteo apwe,' the fire-water of the whites." An Indian will kill himself by whisky drinking in three days if he gets the chance. The element of danger involved in contraband trade involves profits unfortunately, such as ensure its active prosecution by lawless and unscrupulous vendors. "The Department by no means flatters itself that its efforts are successful to prevent intoxicants from reaching . . . communities bent upon obtaining them . . . " but in some places "the orgies of which so much was heard a few years ago among Indians in from their hunt have quite ceased to occur."

Romance, in fact, of every description has deserted the Canadian Indian. He is no longer thrilling in any way. Never more will fierce battles between a handful of white adventurers and the savage tribes of the forest rage round the stockades of isolated trading forts, nor will swift hordes of yelling Indians swoop down on the labouring train of "prairie schooners" and scalp every man of the luckless convoy. The wild children of the plains, of the wilderness of lake-lands, are carefully herded in Government "parks" and artificially preserved, like the few remaining bison. They are now tame and spiritless.

If ever a tale of the Indians is forthcoming touched with something of primitive danger and wildness, 'tis sure to hail from the States !

ELIZABETH WALMSLEY.

THE EASTERN ARCHIPELAGO AND ITS FUTURE

II.*

By L. V. HELMS

WHEN Great Britain, in 1819, formed the settlement of Singapore, the Chinese were mainly settled in Java, where, according to Raffles' estimate, they numbered about a hundred thousand. The other Malay countries being then in a state of decay, offered little inducement to the adventurous and industrious Chinese, but the opportunity and protection which the British flag in Singapore gave soon attracted them, and they began to arrive in ever-increasing numbers. At the present time, taking the Straits Settlements and the Federated Malay States together, the Chinese outnumber the Malays by nearly two to one, and supply the workers for almost every industry.

The Chinese are the middlemen who stimulate the natives all over the Archipelago to produce and gather the products of their various regions. In every branch of commerce, whether as shipowners, merchants, or shopkeepers, the Chinese press close upon the white man and in many cases oust him from enterprises once all his own. The Malay had long been accustomed to lead an idle, but where circumstances permitted, not unhappy life in a country where with little labour the soil yielded him his food, where the clothing of his body, and the shelter of his home, need but be of the slightest, and where he was free from those anxieties which a higher civilisation often brings in its train. But for good or evil, this idyllic existence of the race is now threatened from north and west. Between the Chinaman's ideal of toil and the white man's restless craving for wealth—the brown race which inhabits these beautiful Islands is awaiting its destiny, not to be decided by any action of their own, but by those greater world movements to which the Russo-Japanese War gave the impetus. For the further development of the momentous issues to which that war gave birth, the world is now watching with interest not unmixed with doubt, for it is felt that a new chapter in the world's history has begun.

* For I. see April No., 1910.

The two great Asiatic Powers, which, half a century ago, were by diplomatists considered *une quantité negligeable*, have become important factors in international politics. What will be the policy of greater Japan? Will the fruits of the Chinese and Russian wars content her, or will the glamour of past glories lure her on to new ventures? Japan astonished the world by the rapidity with which she transformed herself from the most exclusive despotism of even Asiatic Powers, to a constitutional *régime* on the most approved European pattern. And this transformation, which extended to most branches of the national life, was often carried out with a recklessness which sometimes led to strange incidents. Let me relate one of which I was an eyewitness. In June, 1872, I was standing with some friends outside the Hiago Hotel. The sun was just setting when a large Japanese steamer came into the harbour. It was evident that the engineer could not stop the engine, but instead of turning and standing out to sea, to our amazement the captain ran the ship full speed on shore and then bolted with the officers. It was recklessness of this kind and disregard of consequences which effected the fall of Port Arthur, and which, combined with those other great qualities that the Japanese possess, individually and as a nation, enabled them, in half a century, to convert their country from the condition of mediæval times to that which she now holds as an equal to first class European Powers.

In 1872 the country, in spite of the bizarre scenes which the sudden change from old to new world conditions had produced, was still old Japan. It was but a year since a party of gentlemen with one lady rode out of Yokohama, when they met a Daimio with a party of armed retainers; the Europeans were too much in the prince's way, he gave a signal to clear the road, and in a moment Mr. Richardson was cut down and others wounded. In 1860 I was fellow-passenger in the East with Mr. Lawrence Oliphant who, with his arm in a sling, was still suffering from the wound received in the night attack upon the British Embassy in Jeddo. But travellers who entered Japan in 1872 found it hard to realise that such acts could so recently have been perpetrated. Hitherto but few tourists had visited the country, and nothing could exceed the friendliness of the people, the charm of their manners, or the joyous and happy appearance of the masses.

In my diary for that period I read: "From the balcony of Jota's Hotel (Osaka) which overhangs the canal, I look down upon the constantly passing pleasure-boats, containing merry parties, singing, playing the guitar, drinking tea, and greatly enjoying themselves, everybody seems happy." Another entry runs thus:—"Our boat was carried down by the rapid current of the canal, and multitudes witnessed our descent, for the people were crowding by thousands to witness the expected arrival of the Mikado who had as yet rarely been seen by the populace; even the bridges under which we drifted were thickly covered with heads. I was greatly impressed by the enormous crowds which lined the banks, it was something like what might be seen in London on a Lord Mayor's day. Now as our boat was the only one moving down (a special pass had been granted to us, as all traffic had been suspended either by jinrikshas or boats—an extraordinary favour under the circum-stances, and no doubt intended to emphasise the altered feeling towards the white man), and the canal not being very broad, my friend and I felt ourselves exalted by having thus, as it were, become the heralds of H.M. the Mikado: but when the first surprise was over, and our bashfulness had given way to con-fidence, we did justice to our position, and exchanged salutations by answering 'Ohaio' to the crowd's repeated calls of 'Sajanara' —which, if I remember rightly, meant 'Good morning' and 'Good day'—and this continued for some miles. A more orderly or pleasant crowd I never saw." Another extract shows a very pretty scene. "Over paths from which mountain peaks, lovely valleys, village groves, and paddy-fields were seen, a ride brought us to the village of Arima, lying in a valley, a very paradise of pastoral restful beauty in gardens, fields, and bamboo groves. Men, women, and even children were at work, some in agricultural pursuits, others busy with the beautiful basket-work for which Arima is famous, and all exhibited that gay cheerful-ness which seemed to pervade the very atmosphere of Japan."

The question arises, was it a happy day for Japan when she opened her gates to the outer world? Will her sacrifices in blood and treasure, her new responsibilities as a world power, the transfer of men and women and even children from pastoral pursuits and home industries to grimy factories and wearing toils compensate her for that simpler, but maybe happier, state which I witnessed?

Having adopted western methods, Japan is exhibiting great qualities in war and peace, in tactical skill, in bravery. and disregard of death, in administrative ability, and fervent patriotism. But underlying these admirable qualities, there exists a psychological difference between the races—a difference which has led to different modes of civilisation, and kept that of the yellow man within bounds—bounds which he was unable to pass till the patterns of Western science and invention came to his knowledge. But this psychological difference has an even deeper foundation, for under the suave and charming manner of the Japanese is hidden that indifference to human suffering, that cynicism in their dealings with the rights and wrongs in human affairs which, on the testimony of Lord Stanhope, they have shown in the administration of Formosa and Korea. Torture, it is stated, was there applied without the slightest regard to guilt or innocence of the victim.

But if Japan shows such symptoms of a lower sense of humanity, if her administration tolerates methods which it is unthinkable that white administrators should apply, how much more must this insensibility to human suffering be charged to China. In Japan, Lord Stanhope writes, the minor officials deal cruelly only with those whom they consider of an inferior race. In China, English gentlemen, under circumstances which should have rendered their persons sacred, were subjected to torturous treatment. Yet four thousand years ago China had an organised government; and later, her world-renowned conquerors moved with vast armies and magnificent courts across the world, destroying nations in their progress, but also executing public works which for their magnitude are the wonder of this modern world; her sages wrote those classics the knowledge of which has been the only road to office and official distinction in the Empire. Her silks adorned the great and wealthy in the Roman Empire, but the civilisation of which all this was a type was stationary, and the China of ages past remained in all essentials, and is in the main, still the China of to-day.

From this digression in the north I must again return to the Archipelago, and especially to the Malay peninsula, now so much in the public eye; if the name of "Golden Chersonesus," which ancient nations bestowed upon it, was not then fully justified, it has in these later days received its justification, for from the Stock Exchanges of Britain's busy cities has descended upon lucky speculators that golden rain of wealth which has its source in the plantations of the dim, untrodden forests of Malaya.

In my former article I asked the question: "Will the white maintain that dominating superiority in the Archipelago which a few centuries of successful dominion has accustomed some of them to consider a law of nature?" The question would seem primarily to rest with the Malays, especially in the Dutch sphere of the Archipelago—if the aspiration of Asia for the Asiatics spreads there, and especially in Java, the position of the Dutch, if left alone to deal with it, might become untenable—that the Malays would rise in the British zone is more unlikely.

But this is probably not the danger that would threaten white rule in the Archipelago. The cause which has produced unrest in India is mainly the uprooting of the ancestral faith and traditions in thousands of young men who, during college and university studies, have become imbued with the latest Western thoughts and speculative subtleties. Filled with aspirations which can have no fulfilment, and finding themselves without any prospect of obtaining those Government appointments, for the attainment of which they have made great sacrifices, they become discontented, and a danger to the State. In the Archipelago, with the exception of some of the sons of Malay rulers, or boys who in the higher local schools have distinguished themselves, and perhaps obtained scholarships—young natives have not been encouraged to obliterate the traditions of their country by studies and residence in Europe, and the discontented element, so strong in India, does not exist in the Archipelago. Nor do I think that the Malays are insensible to the benefits which white rule has conferred upon them, or that they would prefer Chinese or Japanese dominion to that of the white man.

The question of rulers in the Archipelago is perhaps of greater importance to the white race than to the Malays themselves. So long as a great gulf separates the white and yellow races in all the moral and physical relations of life, it must be the object of the one to prevent the other from exercising an overwhelming influence over so large a branch of the human family as that which occupies the island world of the Archipelago, and indeed the greater part of the Pacific Ocean. This would be dangerous to the white race, not only in a political and material sense, but to Western civilisation itself.

The shadow of China fell through centuries as an incubus over Asia, and in the South, Annam, Siam and Burmah were the intermediaries through whom the minor States were reached—in the Malay Archipelago it was Siam which held the Sultans and rulers of minor States under subjection. Nowhere perhaps has Great Britain's work as a civiliser in barbarous countries yielded more blessed results than here. Let me take the reader back a few years.

In 1849, Phra Harirak was king of Cambodia. Harried by his neighbours the Annamites and Siamese, he desired to seek protection from Great Britain, and sent an emisary to Singapore to represent his position, and to make the resources of his country known, with a view to commercial relations. An enterprising firm undertook to meet the king's wishes, and I was invited to take charge of an experimental expedition which, besides Cambodia, would include the States on the east coast of the Malay peninsula, viz., Tringanu, Kalantan and Sangona. It was well known that the Sultans and Rajas, who at that time ruled in the peninsula, were themselves more or less interested in piratical enterprises, and of this I found clear evidence. In Tringanu lay three Chinese junks, partly burnt, and in one of them I learnt that twenty-three men had been killed: the Sultan's story was that they were pirates whom he had captured, but other informants reversed his tale. When nearing Kalantan, we saw five junks anchored off the river, and their appearance left no doubt as to their character. Our vessel was well armed, but our mission was not for fighting —it was a case where discretion was better than valour, and ours took the form of masquerading as a man-of-war. We had anchored well within view of the Chinese; we had ten guns, not of a very formidable calibre, yet well calculated to serve our purpose; we hoisted a pennant and, having made all possible preparations to meet eventualities, we awaited the result. It was near sundown, there was a great movement of boats between the junks and the river, but for what purpose we could not guess, and night soon concealed them from our view. It was a night for keen watchfulness, but nothing happened, and early dawn revealed the welcome news that the junks had disappeared. Our strategy had been successful—we had doubtless disturbed the Raja of Kalantan's very good friends, but politeness required, when I called upon him, that no such delicate matters should be mentioned. Sangona, the last place of call, was in Siamese territory, and it was with some difficulty that I obtained admittance to its ruler, but the reason he informed me was that he had but recently been released from captivity by Chinese pirates on the payment of a large sum of money. But the main object of the expedition was Cambodia, and thither we now laid our course.

The gorgeous East is a phrase which still has a meaning in India, but scarcely has the significance which pertained to the scenes which Marco Polo and the early missionaries witnessed in the camps and cities of the great Khans of those days, in Samarkand or in Peking. But the tradition of these barbaric splendours belong to history, and the mementos and drawings of the ruins of Nineveh and Babylon are familiar objects in collections and museums—but with the vast and magnificent relics from an unknown past, which the jungle in further East holds concealed in all their architectual details, the world was to within recent years unacquainted; yet the Cambodian ruins, which were only made known to the world in 1859, rank for magnitude and grandeur with the greatest from antiquity. They are found, says a writer in "Encyclopædia Britannica," in forty or more localities, embracing walled cities of large extent, palaces and temples stupendous in scale and rich in design, often most elaborately decorated, with long galleries and storied bas-reliefs, artificial lakes enclosed in walls of cut stones, stone bridges of extraordinary design and excellent execution, elaborate embanked highways across the alluvial flats. The walls of the ancient capital Angkor form a quadrangle of 8½ miles in circuit and 30 feet in height; 5 miles south of the city is the great temple, one

of the most extraordinary architectual relics in the world—its
corridors, sculptures and towers rise upwards of 180 feet.

Of the builders of these wondrous structures, now concealed
in densest jungle—of the people and rulers of an empire which
must have ranked with the greatest of the ancient world, no
historic record remains. Cambodia's written annals commence
in 1346 A.D. when its civilisation had already passed its climax
—but Cambodia became tributary to China in 125 B.C., and
in 1295–1297, an envoy, sent from Peking shortly after Kublai
Khan's death, describes the Court and capital as very splendid,
but its power was declining, and the country has ever since
been wearing away.

This then was the country towards which we were steering
our course after leaving the Malay Coast, and with a favouring
wind crossed the Gulf of Siam, but even the Admiralty charts
were unreliable there, and the discovery of Komput, Cambodia's
only seaport, was found to be no easy matter, and when found,
it proved to be a miserable collection of thatched bamboo huts,
surrounded by filth and mud, with a population consisting
mainly of Chinese, of a depraved and emaciated opium smoking
class. The Governor who came to see me was a greedy savage,
and only by the assistance of the King's envoy was I enabled
to obtain means of conveyance to Udong, the king's capital,
situated about 135 miles north-west of Komput. The conveyances
consisted of a number of bullock-carts, of very wretched construction, and very poor oxen to draw them. Our road lay over
marshy plains and through magnificent forests abounding with
wild animals. Water was scarce, confined to green slimy pools,
the margins of which were trampled by animals of every description, elephant, rhinoceros, wild buffalo, tiger, leopard, bear and
deer. There was little underwood, and under the leafy canopy
great flocks of wild cattle and deer could be seen grazing, while
overhead were the peacock, paraquet, eagle, pigeon, etc. The
dry sandy soil made travelling heavy and slow, the carts constantly broke down and had to be repaired with such means
(mainly rattans) as could be found in the forest. Human habita-
tions were rare, nature was left in pristine silence, only the
animal world lorded it in undisturbed security.

On the evening of the tenth day we reached Udong; the
elephants which the King had sent for my conveyance had missed
us, and the journey had been wearisome. Udong, like Komput,
proved a poor looking place, composed of thatched bamboo houses,
but was stated to contain about ten thousand inhabitants. In the
centre was a large square surrounded by walls, of no great strength,
and within was the King's Palace built of wood; which like the
town gave the impression of a temporary and insecure existence.

The King, whose full style and titles were Phra Harirak Maka Issara Tibodi, was not only a tributary to Annam (Cochin China) but also a vassal of Siam ; he was enthroned in 1846 under the joint investiture of both countries. A residence had been prepared for me, and here I soon received a message to attend the King. He received me with a rather poor attempt at regal state, but with much cordiality. Our first meeting was at a public audience, when he was very reserved, knowing that spies surrounded him, but later in private he spoke sadly of his position ; of the great past and present humiliation of his country.

I brought back his request for British protection, but the rehabilitation of his country fell to France. His eldest son, Rachabodi, was at that time a hostage in Siam, where later I made his acquaintance, and I assume it is he whom the French, in 1864, crowned King of Cambodia.

The history of Cambodia is the history of all the ancient Asiatic States ; the indifference to human life, and insensibility to human suffering which marked the devastating incursions of the Mongols and Tartars, in former days, is still inherent in the race, as was shown during the Taiping rebellion, when entire provinces were laid waste, and the people exterminated.

A feeling akin to patriotism involving hatred of the foreigner is now revealing itself in China. As in Egypt and India, so here, the closer and more intimate contact with the West bears its obvious fruit, and as there, so here, it is the young men, who have visited and perhaps studied in Western Countries and Japan, who are most keenly affected ; they return to their own country with their own conceptions of social and political conditions disturbed, and with aspirations for changes for which their countrymen are as yet unfit.

But the conditions in China differ from those of Egypt or India, and involve graver and more imminent problems. The Chinese of the south have never been content with Manchu rule, they are now conscious of its weakness, they have seen parts of China ceded to foreign Powers, and an uneasy feeling pervades the masses, which has just been evidenced by serious riots in Changsha, the capital of Hunan, the cry being that the " Foreign Devils " want to divide their country, a cry which may have been instigated, but will certainly be utilised, by the Cantonese and " Young China " party. But it is not merely political but also commercial and financial questions which are agitating China. She owes to European countries and mainly to Great Britain those large loans which have enabled the Peking Government to overcome grave financial crises ; she also owes to the white nations those railways which are, and, if extended, will become still more, a blessing to the country. But not content with these benefits, the "Forward ' or "Young China" party would now themselves build the railways, run them, and keep them in their own hands. And meanwhile the Peking Government is attempting to acquire the supreme control of the Maritime Customs, which is the security for the millions lent to China—in both cases ignoring or over-riding binding contracts and engagements.

If the Chinese Government was well organised, if her officials were well .paid and incorruptible, and if her financial condition was sound, friends of China would sympathise with these aspirations, and would admit that the dealings of European nations with China have not always been blameless in the past; but at present, the condition of China is the reverse of that above postulated, and in her own interest these claims should be strongly resisted. But obviously these are grave matters and will require careful handling; they might lead to the actualisation of that "Yellow Peril," which seems looming in the future, and which should unite the white race for defence against, or possible prevention of, a common danger.

L. V. HELMS.

CHRISTMAS ISLAND

IN his last report on the Straits Settlements Sir John Anderson tells us that the population of Christmas Island on December 31, 1908, was 1,101, and comprised 28 Europeans and Eurasians, 990 Chinese, 10 Japanese, 35 Sikhs, and 38 Malays and other nationalities, The death-rate was 14·93 per mille per annum as compared with 12·27 in 1907 and 28·5 in 1906. The public health was good and beri-beri continues to decrease, there having been only 101 new cases and 7 deaths. Comparison of these figures with those for 1901, when no less than 229 deaths occurred from beri-beri alone, shows what good progress has been made in a few years by means of scientific attention to matters of housing, sanitation, food, and water supply. The only other disease which shows a tendency to appear in epidemic form is conjunctivitis, of which there were in 1908 61 cases (132 in 1907). There are no anopheles mosquitos on the island, and malaria is unknown. The revenue collected locally was $735.91 against $861.53 in 1907, these figures being exclusive of postage stamps, of which the District Officer buys a stock from the Postmaster-General for re-sale. Payments made locally amounted to $8,883,30. Very remarkable is the amount paid in royalties on phosphates to His Majesty's Government in 1909 in respect of phosphate exported in 1908. The total reached £10,482 12s. against £8,411 16s. 2d. for 1907, and £7,153 8s. 10d. for 1906.

SIDELIGHTS ON COLONIAL LIFE

The Editor will be glad to receive voluntary contributions to these pages
from oversea readers.

Canada and British Artizans.

We have received, says the *Montreal Medical Journal*, a communication from the Superintendent of Immigration informing us that much unfavourable comment has appeared in English papers upon the present rules which apply to immigrants entering Canada. The comment, we are informed, applies chiefly to two regulations; the first, requiring immigrants coming to employment other than farm work, or in the case of females, to domestic service, to have in their possession at time of landing the sum of twenty-five dollars, in addition to railway transportation to ultimate destination; the second, providing that the consent to emigrate to Canada, required by law to be granted by the Assistant Superintendent of Emigration for Canada in London, to such charity-aided emigrants as he considers suited to this country, shall be given only to such as are suited for, willing to accept, and have assured employment at farm work. We are asked to offer an opinion upon these regulations, so that it may be placed before the reading public of the British Islands, or "Isles," as the dominions of England, Scotland, and Ireland are described. We fail to see the necessity for this additional light, as we are told somewhat gratuitously, that "practically every Canadian paper irrespective of political connection, which has so far dealt with the subject, has upheld the regulations, and insisted upon Canada being the sole judge as to who shall or shall not be allowed to enter this country." We shall set aside at once the truculent suggestion, that any serious person has denied that Canada is "the sole judge as to who shall or shall not be allowed to enter this country;" and we shall content ourselves by making the equally obvious statement, that the Immigration authorities and the Labour Unions do not constitute the people of Canada by any large majority.

Canadian Criticism.

The movement to keep British artisans out of Canada is instigated by those who desire to see labour scarce, wages high, and the product of craftsmanship dear, and we fail to see why farmers are not equally entitled to demand the exclusion of farm labour so that food will cost even more than it actually does at the present moment. If the regulations were designed to keep out of this country only the diseased, the vicious, and those who are likely to become a charge upon the community, it would be difficult to controvert them with any chance of being understood ; though it could be urged with perfect truthfulness that not all of us are utterly callous to the situation of our more miserable brethren in the Old Country who have done so much for us in laying the foundations of Canada and in protecting us all these years, whilst we have been growing big, and sleek, and fat. We cannot refrain from adding that, if this regulation compelling immigrants to be in possession of £5 had always been in force, many of those now in Canada would not be here or anywhere else. In this attempt to manufacture expression which it is proposed to place before the reading public of England as " the consensus of Canadian opinion," we hope the Immigration authorities will not omit to include this opinion which is expressed by the *Montreal Medical Journal*, even if they are disappointed in our response to their lead, or do not like this dance to their piping. If they do forget, we shall take the proper steps to remedy the omission.

New Zealand Immigration.

Sir Joseph Ward, Prime Minister of New Zealand, in a recent address to his constituents, made the following interesting statement on Immigration :—

The arrangement with the several shipping companies trading to New Zealand from the United Kingdom, allowing persons who are approved or selected by the High Commissioner in London to be provided with passages at reduced rates, is still in existence. This arrangement enables the High Commissioner to provide farmers and farm labourers who are possessed of some capital, and who will make satisfactory colonists, with passages at low rates, so as to induce some of them to come to New Zealand instead of going elsewhere. Any farmer or agriculturist can, through this system, obtain a passage to the Dominion for the sum of £10. In order that agriculturists may have a chance of at once obtaining employment, passages are being granted so that they shall only arrive during the early summer months. The first vessel to arrive during the coming season will be the

Tongariro, which is expected to leave London on the 4th of August, and is due in New Zealand on the 20th of September. As there is a constant demand for domestic servants, the Government has continued to grant passages at reduced rates to suitable workers ; and no restriction has been placed upon the dates when they may arrive. Every vessel brings as many as can be induced to come to New Zealand. The Government continues also to accept nominations from householders in the Dominion for domestic servants.

An Important Proposal.

Husbands who come out to New Zealand to see if they can adapt themselves to our mode of living, and wish to have their families with them, are also allowed to nominate their wives and families for reduced rate passages. The number of Government assisted passengers who arrived in the Dominion during the year 1909–1910 was 2,797 souls. The number of persons who were nominated and accepted in New Zealand during the year for reduced rate passages was 1,341 souls ; and the cash payments made by the nominators amounted to £11,339 5s 5d. I think, however, in addition to what we are doing a system might well be established under which any one or more people in New Zealand requiring labour, which the Labour Department admits cannot be obtained here in the numbers required, might ask the Government to arrange for the importation of such labour from Great Britain, provided that those desiring this labour undertake to employ the persons so introduced in the work mentioned for a period of at least six months after their arrival in the Dominion and at a wage uniform with the wages paid for that class of work now. This will obviate, first the objection to a large number of people landing in New Zealand and having no immediate employment in view, and secondly will remove any complaint that may be made by the workers that the ranks of any particular industry are being unduly swelled by imported labour.

Fishing in St. Helena.

In the course of an interesting report on St. Helena some particulars are given by Mr. Mosely concerning the Island's fisheries. All fish are caught with hook and line, a somewhat tedious process when large quantities are required. Nets are practically unknown. In fact, it has been proved that the St. Helena mackerel will not look at a net. I refer to nets of ordinary colour—black or brown. Possibly a light-coloured net (as near the colour of the water as possible) might prove efficacious. There is a remarkable variety of fish in St. Helena waters, the chief being: mackerel, albacore, bull's eyes, old wives, silver fish, stoney brass, soldiers, barracoota, bonito, cavally, yellow tail, bill fish, and cole fish. Of the above the cole fish is by far the most palatable, but very few are caught. Albacore and mackerel are the cheapest fish and form the chief diet of the poorer classes. Mackerel range from 1s. to 2d. per dozen. They are not nearly as good eating as the English mackerel. During the last nine months of the year under review 3,579 albacore and 6,130 dozen mackerel were landed at Jamestown. These fish were caught by nine boats. The fishermen, however, only catch what they think they can sell; that number being reached, they cease their labours. The quantity of the different fish varies with the season of the year. In the summer months enough fish could be caught in a week to provide for local consumption for probably a whole year. At other times there is a scarcity of the article, and prices go up. With more boats, and more honest labour, I am convinced the Islanders could obtain considerably more benefit from their fisheries than they have in the past. There are three kinds of fishing: ground fishing, deep-water fishing, and float fishing. The first extends from the shore outwards until a depth of 40 fathoms is reached. The second extends from 40 to 100 fathoms; whilst "float fishing" refers to surface-feeding fish, such as mackerel. All fishing is done in small open boats. Consequently, except in calm weather, fishing is chiefly confined to the lee side of the Island. Hitherto only sufficient fish for local consumption has been caught. It is not, therefore, possible at this stage to calculate the extent of the supply of fish in St. Helena waters. If the Islanders, however, wish to get full value out of their fisheries, they must adopt a more energetic and industrious attitude than has been apparent in the past.

Among the Shangaans.

Living in the Shangaan country, writes Mr. Hall in the *Rhodesian Journal*, are to be found, in small and very scattered kraals, a most interesting people known as the Va-Duma, to whom my porters were often referring, though we did not meet any of them. Along the south bank of the Rundi, east of Mount Vumbi, there are only a very few Shangaan kraals, and they are small and have thick beam stockades. These people do not appear to be nearly so devoted to agriculture as the Karanga on the north side of the river, and their plantations are very small. But they are most industrious and are exceedingly clever in making wicker-work articles and cord cloth and matting, in which correct patterns are woven. The method of dressing the hair into long cords is striking. The whole of the mass of wool is plaited into long cords, all hanging down to the same level round the head and also over their foreheads. This style gives them, especially the women, an Egyptian appearance, and one is reminded forcibly of the Sphinx's head. This resemblance is considerably heightened by a general Egyptian cast of countenance, especially in the shape of the lips, the full round contented eyes, their far-off gaze, the chubby cheeks, and rounded chin. These features reminded us of the Egyptian paintings in the British Museum, in which the cords of hair, as well as the colour of the skin are shown in red. Strange to say, here one finds some natives with the cords coloured a brick-red with clay, and their faces and whole bodies being also so coloured. The Portuguese records (1505-1760) give several instances of the general practice of south-east African tribes reddening their hair, faces, bodies, and limbs with clay. Covering their entire bodies with red clay is a common feature with certain Ama-prefix tribes, but so far this has not been discovered among the Karanga variety tribes, though these, at certain great dances, which some might think obscene, cover the naked bodies of the young men with white clay. The love of beads for ornament is an intense passion with the Shangaan women, white and red being their invariable vogue in colours. Most of the women appear to have skull caps made entirely of these coloured beads, the designs being very regularly worked out. Broad bands of bead-work for armlets, bangles and anklets occupy the place of the heavy brass ornaments of the Karanga.

Direction of Ashanti Trade.

The Revenue of Gambia for 1909 is the largest yet recorded in the colony, amounting to £72,675 11s. 10d., while the expenditure dropped nearly £5,000 compared with the preceding year. Both the particulars and the direction of the export trade deserve attention. The total value of all exports during the year was £477,964, being an increase of £103,826 over 1908, the principal articles exported being ground-nuts, hides, kola-nuts, palm kernels, beeswax, and rubber. A record crop of ground-nuts was gathered, and the total amount exported, 53,644 tons, shows an increase of 21,680 tons beyond the preceding year and an increase of 8,170 tons over 1903, the record year prior to 1909. This trade, which commenced in the year 1835 in consequence of the demand for nuts in America and England, has now almost entirely passed over to France. It is understood that an attempt is to be made by a firm in England to manufacture oil from the nuts supplied from the Gambia, and it is hoped that this may result in a greater proportion of the trade going to the mother country. Hides show a further increase, the number, 33,411, being 1,731 in excess of those exported in 1908, with an increased value of £1,887. The trade in kola-nuts consists of re-exported kolas sent from this colony to the adjacent French possessions. The falling-off in the quantity of rubber exported in 1909 was not so large as in the preceding year, but the trade continues on the downward grade, showing a decrease of 3,020 lbs. from 1908. This is probably due to the large amount of cultivated rubber obtained from other countries and the improved method of extraction used. There are no rubber plantations in this country; the rubber exported is taken direct from forest trees. Of the total exports, exclusive of specie, 82 per cent. goes to France and its colonies, 7 per cent. to Great Britain and its colonies, and 4 per cent. to Germany.

Bad Year at the Gold Coast (Northern Territories).

Things in the Northern Territories of the Gold Coast, to judge from the Governor's report for 1909, do not appear to be in a very happy condition: the total revenue collected for the year amounted only to £16,989, with a decrease of over £9,000 on the previous year, whereas the expenditure has gone up from £50,261 to £52,056. The health statistics too are scarcely encouraging. The health of Europeans, we are told, was far from good, three deaths occurring amongst the officials and one amongst the non-officials, while three officials were invalided. The deaths of the officials were due to malaria, and that of the non-official to heart failure. In 1908 two officials were invalided, but no deaths occurred amongst either officials or non-officials. The death-rate for officials was 5·17 per cent., that for non-officials was 6·25 per cent., and the invaliding rate for officials was 5·17 per cent. The health of native officials was not so good as in previous years; two deaths occurred and a larger number than usual were placed on the sick list; but the health of the company of the Gold Coast Regiment stationed at Gambaga and of the Northern Territories Constabulary at all stations is reported good. With regard to epidemics a decided improvement has taken place, compared with the year before, no cases of cerebro-spinal meningitis being reported, whereas, during the two previous years, the disease was very prevalent in the North-Western Province. There was an epidemic of small-pox in many parts of the Protectorate, but the percentage of mortality was small, as many as a hundred cases being noted without a single death.

About Fiji.

Fiji, Sir Charles Lucas tells us, is a Crown colony whose dealings are principally with self-governing dominions. The Crown colony system is here, so to speak, constantly put on its trial, and tested by contrast. From what I saw, and from what

I have heard and read, I should gather that the system has been to the full as successful in Fiji as it has been elsewhere in His Majesty's tropical dominions. My stay was made specially pleasant by the obvious indications of confidence in the present Governor on the part of both the white and the coloured community, and the equally obvious indications of prosperity. For this sugar cultivated by East Indian labour is largely responsible. But there is much development still to come ; and even at headquarters the fine natural harbour of Suva is in equipment sadly behind the American port of Honolulu. The representatives of the mercantile community urged strongly, and with sound reason, the necessity for a loan for public works, and their request, supported by the Governor, has been granted by the Secretary of State. One very great want of Suva is that of a good hotel. There is, however, a prospect that one will be built at an early date, and it should prove a great attraction to tourist traffic.

The Bouvette Islands.

Captain Ryan, a Canadian mariner, discussing the recent cruise of the schooner *Latooka*, 118 tons register, engaged in the sealing trade, gives some interesting particulars of Southern islands rediscovered. The ship sailed from Canada some months ago, and after calling at Rio and Bahia, set a course for the Bouvette Islands, or Sandwich Land, which according to the Admiralty books are situated 54·15 degrees S. latitude, and 6·11 degrees E. longitude, that is, roughly, 1,200 miles S.S.W. of the Cape of Good Hope. The same Admiralty books supply the information that the islands were first discovered by a French navigator, Captain Bouvette, in 1808, and in 1822 were visited by an English navigator, Captain Morell. Since the latter date, until the *Latooka* rediscovered them, no person has visited the islands. For eighty-eight years the Bouvette Islands have merely been a speck on the chart, with a note that the position designated may be a degree or so out. " I went to look for the islands," says Captain Ryan, " at the position marked on the chart, and cruised about for twenty-seven days before finding them. After making the most careful observations, I ascertained the actual position of the islands to be 210 miles from the latitude and longitude given on the charts.

Icebergs and Penguins.

We stayed there for about five weeks, and all the time, day and night, had sunlight. Without continual light it would be impossible for any craft to survive those awful seas and icebergs. It is a terrible place, with fierce ocean currents and tides tearing along at from 8 to 10 knots an hour, shoal waters, and waterfalls the same as may be seen when the waters of a mountain stream tumble over rocks. The icebergs are terrific. Several were from 4,000 to 5,000 feet high, and from 5 to 10 miles long. A peculiar feature about the icebergs of those seas is that they are all flat-topped. In the South Shetlands the bergs are broken, and run to a peak. We could not tell the islands from icebergs, except for the penguins, the fact that the bergs are always drifting; and the islands, of course, are stationary. The islands are ice-clad right down to the water's edge. Reefs run out from the islands for miles into the sea over which currents of water rush in cataracts.

Whales.

" We only worked them for seven or eight days, and in that time managed to make a good catch of seals. But I never want to go there again, except in steam. It is an awful spot. We don't mind the everlasting gales, because we can weather them with comfort; but we do care for the myriad icebergs and reefs, which we must always be dodging. If a vessel came to grief in the vicinity of the Bouvettes, nothing much would ever be heard of anyone aboard. I never saw so many whales in my life," said Captain Ryan; " and most of them were the 'right' whale. There were 'tons' of them about us on every side. All the islands of the group are volcanic. We saw no signs whatever of any life, either recent or ancient. They are perpetually covered with ice. In fact they lie within the Antarctic Circle." The lowest latitude reached by the *Latooka* was 58·3 degrees S. She cruised down to that position, and about 10 degrees either side of the meridian of Greenwich. "In all my life I never experienced such terrible weather. During the five weeks we were down south, I never slept for two consecutive hours."

Game in East Africa Protectorate.

In his excellent report upon the East Africa Protectorate Sir Percy Girouard informs us that although there has been a considerable falling off in the number of sportsmen who have visited the Protectorate during the year, yet owing to the country being better known the bags of game have been larger and more varied. Three hundred lions were killed during the year, a considerable increase on the numbers in previous years, and it would appear that they are still numerous, though the increase is possibly due in some measure to the larger areas of country now open to sportsmen. There has been a notable reduction in the number of bull elephants, though the number of cows and calves seem to have been maintained. Giraffe, buffalo, and eland are all increasing, and it is satisfactory to note a distinct increase also in the number of greater kudu, which for some years had remained stationary. Hyænas, hunting dogs, and jackal do not appear to have recovered from the outbreak of distemper reported last year, and there was a fresh outbreak on the Uasin Gishu plateau during the year. On the Athi Plains game continues to be numerous, but, owing to the drought, somewhat local. Comparatively little shooting has been done in this district on account of the enormous quantities of ticks. On the Tana river and east of Mt. Kenya game is very plentiful, but is little shot, being in a fly-infested and feverish district. Owing to the amount of settlement which has taken place in the Rift Valley, this is not now such a popular resort for sportsmen as formerly, though many fine trophies are obtainable, especially in the Baringo District.

Southern Rhodesia: Agricultural Progress.

The Director of Agriculture, in his latest Bulletin, states that British settlers of an exceptionally good class are now entering the country in steadily increasing numbers. Crop prospects throughout the country, and particularly as regards maize, are highly satisfactory. Pastures are looking well and cattle are in excellent condition, whilst the prices of live stock are firm and show a strong upward tendency. Large importations of cattle and sheep for breeding purposes are taking place. At the Chamber of Mines meeting, early in the month, the president observed that the new developments were accentuating the inadequacy of the labour supply. Gold discoveries were being made throughout Rhodesia, and numerous mines were nearing the milling stage, while others were preparing to increase their plants, and dividends were being paid. All these things indicate that the country is on a solid foundation.

INDIAN AND COLONIAL INVESTMENTS*

Lack of business has again been the principal characteristic of the Stock Exchange during the past month. The holiday atmosphere has, of course, something to do with the slackness of the markets, and the investing and speculating public is still suffering from the lassitude that naturally follows such a boom as was enjoyed earlier in the year. Monetary conditions, however, are all to the good, and it would require but a slight change in the attitude of the public to effect a rapid rise in prices.

A currency loan amounting to Rs. 1,50,00,000 in 3½ per cents. has been successfully placed by the Indian Government. The tenders amounted in all to Rs. 6,94,45,600, and the minimum rate accepted was 95¾ per cent., the average being £96 1*s.* 4*d.* per cent.

Canadian railway securities have been overshadowed by the labour troubles, and the influence of the excellent traffic returns has thus been counteracted. The Canadian Pacific's financial year ended on June 30, and the aggregate receipts for the period amounted to $94,585,000, an increase of no less than $18,272,000 above the receipts for the preceding year, whereas the increase

INDIAN GOVERNMENT SECURITIES.

Title.	Present Amount.	When Redeemable.	Price.	Yield.	Interest Payable.
India.	£				
3½% Stock (t . . .	85,304,848	1931	95¾	3⅝	Quarterly.
3% ,, (t) . . .	66,724,530	1948	82¾	3⅝	,,
2½% ,, Inscribed (t)	11,892,207	1926	69	3⅝	,,
3½% Rupee Paper 1854–5	..	(a)	95¼	3⅝	30 June—31 Dec.
3% ,, ,, 1896–7	..	1916	79½	3¾	30 June—30 Dec.

(t) Eligible for Trustee investments.
(a) Redeemable at a Quarter's notice.

* The tabular matter in this article will appear month by month, the figures being corrected to date. Stocks eligible for Trustee investments are so designated.—Ed.

INDIAN RAILWAYS AND BANKS.

Title.	Subscribed.	Last year's dividend.	Share or Stock.	Price.	Yield.
RAILWAYS.	£				
Assam—Bengal, L., guaranteed 3% .	1,500,000	3	100	79	$3\frac{3}{4}$
Bengal and North-Western (Limited)	3,000,000	$7\frac{1}{2}$	100	$142\frac{1}{4}$	$5\frac{1}{4}$
Bengal Dooars, L.	400,000	4	100	$86\frac{1}{4}$	$4\frac{5}{8}$
Bengal Nagpur (L), gtd. 4%+¼th profits	3,000,000	5	100	101	$4\frac{4}{5}$
Burma Guar. 2½% and propn. of profits	3,000,000	$5\frac{1}{4}$	100	110	$4\frac{3}{4}$
Delhi Umballa Kalka, L., guar. 3¼% + net earnings . . . . }	800,000	7	100	$144\frac{1}{2}$	$4\frac{13}{16}$
East Indian Def. ann. cap. g. 4% + ⅛ sur. profits (t) . . . . . . }	1,912,804	$5\frac{1}{2}$	100	98	$5\frac{9}{16}$
Do. do, class " D," repayable 1953 (t) .	4,637,196	$4\frac{7}{8}$	100	$115\frac{1}{4}$	$4\frac{3}{16}$
Do. 4½% perpet. deb. stock (t) . . .	1,435,650	$4\frac{1}{2}$	100	118	$3\frac{13}{16}$
Do. new 3% deb. red. (t)	8,000,000	3	100	80x	$3\frac{3}{4}$
Great Indian Peninsula 4% deb. Stock (t)	2,701,450	4	100	$105\frac{1}{2}$	$3\frac{3}{4}$
Do. 3% Gua. and 20 surp. profits 1925 (t)	2,575,000	3	100	96	$3\frac{1}{8}$
Indian Mid. L. gua. 4% & ¼ surp. profits (t)	2,250,000	4	100	$98\frac{1}{4}$	$4\frac{1}{16}$
Madras and South Mahratta . . .	5,000,000	4	100	102	$3\frac{7}{8}$
Nizam's State Rail. Gtd. 5% Stock .	2,000,000	5	100	$110\frac{1}{4}$	$4\frac{1}{2}$
Do. 3½% red. mort. debs.	1,074,700	$3\frac{1}{2}$	100	$84\frac{1}{2}$	$4\frac{1}{8}$
Rohilkund and Kumaon, Limited . .	400,000	7	100	$130\frac{1}{2}$	$5\frac{5}{16}$
South Behar, Limited	379,580	5	100	101x	$4\frac{4}{5}$
South Indian 4½% per. deb. stock, gtd.	425,000	$4\frac{1}{2}$	100	117	$3\frac{13}{16}$
Do. capital stock	1,000,000	$7\frac{1}{5}$	100	$101\frac{1}{4}$	$7\frac{3}{4}$
Southern Punjab, Limited	1,000,000	$7\frac{1}{2}$	100	134	$5\frac{9}{16}$
Do. 3½% deb. stock red.	500,000	$3\frac{1}{2}$	100	87	4
West of India Portuguese Guar. L. . .	800,000	5	100	$95\frac{1}{2}x$	$5\frac{3}{16}$
Do. 5% debenture stock	550,000	5	100	$101\frac{1}{2}x$	$4\frac{4}{5}$
BANKS.	Number of Shares.				
Chartered Bank of India, Australia, and China . . . . }	60,000	14	20	59	$4\frac{11}{16}$
National Bank of India	64,000	12	$12\frac{1}{2}$	42	$3\frac{9}{16}$

(t) Eligible for Trustee investments.
(x) Ex dividend.

in the mileage worked was quite trifling. The net revenue statements so far published cover only the first eleven months of the year. This period showed an increase of $16,418,000 in gross receipts, of which as much as $10,055,000 was retained as an increase in net earnings. Thus there is ample margin for an increase in dividend if the directors should think it advisable to raise the rate.

In the case of the Grand Trunk Railway the accounts are made up to December 31st, so that the figures now available cover only the first half of the company's financial year. The aggregate receipts for the period amounted to £4,351,279, showing an increase of £606,225. For the first five months the increase in receipts was £511,750, and as the expenses expanded by £395,870, the increase in net earnings was £115,880. The labour question is, of course, an element of grave importance in the dividend prospect, but this satisfactory increase in profits has done much to minimise the effect on profits of the strike outbreak, and the feeling in the market has been quite hopeful.

Undeservedly scant success was accorded to the issue of Grand Trunk Pacific Guaranteed Bonds, a large proportion of which went to the underwriters. Two millions sterling of 3 per cent. First Mortgage Sterling Bonds, redeemable in 1962, were offered at 82½ per cent. through the Bank of Montreal, and can now be obtained at a small discount. As both principal and interest are guaranteed by the Dominion Government, the security is, of course, irreproachable, and the bonds form an excellent investment of the gilt-edged class.

CANADIAN GOVERNMENT SECURITIES.

Title.	Present Amount.	When Redeemable.	Price.	Yield.	Interest Payable.
4% Inter)) Guaranteed colonial)) by Great	1,341,400	1910	101	—	) 1 Apr.—1 Oct.
4% ,,) Britain.	1,700,000	1913	102	3⅝	)
3½% 1884 Regd. Stock	4,676,830	1909–34	99½	—	1 June—1 Dec.
3% Inscribed Stock (t)	8,594,877	1938	91	3¼	1 Jan.—1 July.
2½% ,, ,, (t)	1,592,105	1947	79	3 9⁄16	1 Apr.—1 Oct.
PROVINCIAL.					
BRITISH COLUMBIA.					
3% Inscribed Stock .	2,045,760	1941	85½	3 13⁄16	1 Jan.—1 July.
MANITOBA.					
5% Sterling Bonds .	308,000	1923	108	4 3⁄16	1 Jan.—1 July.
4% ,, Debs. .	205,000	1928	102	3⅞	1 May—1 Nov.
NOVA SCOTIA.					
3% Stock	164,000	1949	81	3 15⁄16	1 Jan.—1 July.
QUEBEC.					
3% Inscribed . . .	1,897,820	1937	85½	3⅞	1 Apr.—1 Oct.
MUNICIPAL.					
Hamilton (City of) 4%	482,800	1934	101	4	1 Apr.—1 Oct.
Montreal 3% Deb.) Stock . . . .)	1,440,000	permanent	81	3 11⁄16	) 1 May—1 Nov.
Do. 4% Cons. ,,	1,821,917	1932	103	3 13⁄16	)
Quebec 4% Debs. . .	385,000	1923	101	3⅞	) 1 Jan.—1 July.
Do. 3½% Con. Stock .	504,196	drawings	92	3⅞	)
Toronto 5% Con. Debs.	136,700	1919–20*	106	4 3⁄16	)
Do. 4% Stg. Bonds .	300,910	1922–28*	101	3⅞	) 1 Jan.—1 July.
Do. 3½% Bonds . .	1,169,844	1929	93	4	)
Vancouver 4% Bonds .	121,200	1931	101	4	1 Apr.—1 Oct.
Do. 4% 40-year Bonds	117,200	1932	102	3⅞	7 Feb.—7 Aug.
Winnipeg 5% Debs. .	138,000	1914	103	4¼	30 Apr.—31 Oct.

(t) Eligible for Trustee investments.
* Yield calculated on earlier date of redemption.

CANADIAN RAILWAYS, BANKS AND COMPANIES.

Title.	Number of Shares or Amount.	Dividend for last Year.	Paid up per Share.	Price.	Yield
RAILWAYS.		%			
Canadian Pacific Shares . .	1,500,000	7	$100	194$\frac{1}{4}$	3$\frac{9}{16}$
Do. 4% Preference	£11,328,082	4	Stock	107	3$\frac{11}{16}$
Do. 5% Stg. 1st Mtg. Bd. 1915	£7,191,500	5	,,	105	3$\frac{7}{8}$
Do. 4% Cons. Deb. Stock . .	£25,315,001	4	,,	109	3$\frac{5}{8}$
Grand Trunk Ordinary . .	£22,475,985	nil.	,,	26$\frac{7}{8}$	nil.
Do. 5% 1st Preference . . .	£3,420,000	5	,,	109	4$\frac{9}{16}$
Do. 5% 2nd ,, . . .	£2,530,000	5	,,	98	5$\frac{1}{16}$
Do. 4% 3rd ,, . . .	£7,168,055	nil.	,,	57$\frac{3}{4}$	nil.
Do. 4% Guaranteed . . .	£9,840,011	4	,,	93$\frac{1}{2}$	4$\frac{1}{4}$
Do. 5% Perp. Deb. Stock . .	£4,270,375	5	,,	126	3$\frac{15}{16}$
Do. 4% Cons. Deb. Stock . .	£15,821,571	4	,,	102$\frac{1}{2}$	3$\frac{7}{8}$
BANKS AND COMPANIES.					
Bank of Montreal	140,000	10	$100	252	3$\frac{15}{16}$
Bank of British North America	20,000	7	50	75$\frac{1}{2}$	4$\frac{5}{8}$
Canadian Bank of Commerce .	200,000	9	$50	£21	4$\frac{7}{16}$
Canada Company	8,319	29s. per sh.	1	30	4$\frac{13}{16}$
Hudson's Bay	100,000	50s. per sh.	10*	103$\frac{1}{2}x$	2$\frac{3}{8}$
Trust and Loan of Canada .	60,000	8	5	6$\frac{1}{4}$	6$\frac{3}{8}$
Do. new	25,000	8	3	3$\frac{1}{4}$	7$\frac{3}{8}$
British Columbia Electric Railway . . . Def.	£600,000	8	Stock	143$\frac{1}{2}$	5$\frac{9}{16}$
British Columbia Electric Railway . . . Prefd.	£600,000	6	Stock	126	4$\frac{3}{4}$

* £1 capital repaid 1904.
(x) Ex dividend.

NEWFOUNDLAND GOVERNMENT SECURITIES.

Title.	Present Amount.	When Redeemable.	Price.	Yield.	Interest Payable.
3$\frac{1}{2}$% Sterling Bonds .	2,178,800	1941-7-8†	93	3$\frac{13}{16}$	1 Jan.—1 July.
3% Sterling ,, .	325,000	1947	80	4$\frac{1}{16}$	1 Jan.—1 July.
4% Inscribed Stock .	320,000	1913–38*	101	3$\frac{5}{8}$	1 Jan.—1 July.
4% ,, ,, .	455,647	1935	109	3$\frac{7}{16}$	1 Jan.—1 July.
4% Cons. Ins. ,, .	200,000	1936	104	3$\frac{3}{4}$	1 Jan.—1 July.

* Yield calculated on earlier date of redemption.
† Yield calculated on latest date.

Revenue returns from the Australian States are still encouraging. The net revenue of New South Wales for June amounted to £1,770,918, an increase of £525,876 over that for the corresponding month of last year. Among the principal heads of increase were stamps, which produced £290,230 more, and railways, which showed an increase of £78,015. For the whole of the financial year, the net revenue amounted to £14,540,055 against £13,625,071. Stamps contributed £366,220 of the increase and railways £375,117. Victoria enjoyed an increase of

AUSTRALIAN GOVERNMENT SECURITIES.

Title.	Present Amount.	When Redeemable.	Price.	Yield.	Interest Payable.
NEW SOUTH WALES.					
4% Inscribed Stock (*t*)	9,686,300	1933	105	$3\frac{5}{8}$	1 Jan.—1 July.
$3\frac{1}{2}$% ,, ,, (*t*)	16,464,545	1924	$99\frac{1}{2}$	$3\frac{9}{16}$	1 Apr.—1 Oct.
3% ,, ,, (*t*)	12,480,000	1935	$88\frac{1}{2}$	$3\frac{3}{4}$	1 Apr.—1 Oct.
VICTORIA.					
4% Inscribed, 1885 .	5,970,000	1920	102	$3\frac{3}{4}$	1 Jan.—1 July.
$3\frac{1}{2}$% ,, 1889 (*t*)	5,000,000	1921–6*	98	$3\frac{11}{16}$	1 Jan.—1 July.
4% , . .	2,107,000	1911–26*	$100\frac{1}{2}$	$3\frac{11}{16}$	1 Jan.—1 July.
3% ,, (*t*) . .	5,211,331	1929–49†	$85\frac{1}{2}$	$3\frac{11}{16}$	1 Jan.—1 July.
QUEENSLAND.					
4% Bonds	10,267,400	1913–15*	$101\frac{1}{2}$	$3\frac{7}{16}$	1 Jan.—1 July.
4% Inscribed Stock (*t*)	7,939,000	1924	102	$3\frac{3}{4}$	1 Jan.—1 July.
$3\frac{1}{2}$% ,, ,, (*t*)	8,616,034	1921–30†	98	$3\frac{5}{8}$	1 Jan.—1 July.
3% ,, ,, (*t*)	4,274,213	1922–47†	$85\frac{1}{2}$	$3\frac{11}{16}$	1 Jan.—1 July.
SOUTH AUSTRALIA.					
4% Bonds	1,359,300	1916	102	$3\frac{13}{16}$	1 Apr.—1 Oct.
4% Inscribed Stock .	6,269,000	1916–7–36*	$102\frac{1}{2}$	$3\frac{11}{16}$	1 Apr.—1 Oct.
$3\frac{1}{2}$% ,, ,, (*t*)	2,517,800	1939	$98\frac{1}{2}$	$3\frac{9}{16}$	1 Jan.—1 July.
3% ,, ,, (*t*)	839,500	1916–26‡	$89\frac{1}{2}$	$3\frac{5}{16}$	1 Jan.—1 July.
3% ,, ,, (*t*)	2,760,100	1916 ‡ or after.	84	$3\frac{9}{16}$	1 Jan.—1 July.
WESTERN AUSTRALIA.					
4% Inscribed . . .	1,876,000	1911–31*	$101\frac{1}{2}$	$3\frac{11}{16}$	15 Apr.—15 Oct.
$3\frac{1}{2}$% ,, (*t*) . .	3,780,000	1920–35†	$97\frac{1}{2}$	$3\frac{11}{16}$	1 May—1 Nov.
3% ,, (*t*) . .	3,750,000	1915–35‡	88	$3\frac{3}{8}$	1 May—1 Nov.
3% ,, (*t*) . .	2,500,000	1927‡	89	$3\frac{5}{16}$	15 Jan.—15 July.
TASMANIA.					
$3\frac{1}{2}$% Inscbd. Stock (*t*)	4,156,500	1920–40*	$98\frac{1}{2}$	$3\frac{5}{8}$	1 Jan.—1 July.
4% ,, ,,	1,000,000	1920–40*	$102\frac{1}{2}$	$3\frac{11}{16}$	1 Jan.—1 July.
3% . . . . . (*t*)	450,000	1920–40†	86	$3\frac{3}{4}$	1 Jan.—1 July.

* Yield calculated on earlier date of redemption.
† Yield calculated on later date of redemption, though a portion of the loan may be redeemed earlier.
‡ No allowance for redemption.
(*t*) Eligible for Trustee Investment.

AUSTRALIAN MUNICIPAL AND OTHER BONDS.

Title.	Present Amount.	When Redeemable.	Price.	Yield.	Interest Payable.
Melbourne & Met. Bd. of Works 4% Debs.	1,000,000	1921	101	4	1 Apl.—1 Oct.
Do. City 4% Deb. .	850,000	1915–22*	100	4	1 Jan.—1 July.
Melbourne Trams Trust $4\frac{1}{2}$% Debs. .	1,650,000	1914–16*	101	$4\frac{3}{16}$	1 Jan.—1 July.
S. Melbourne $4\frac{1}{2}$% Debs.	128,700	1919	101	$4\frac{5}{16}$	1 Jan.—1 July.
Sydney 4% Debs. . .	640,000	1912–13	100	4	1 Jan.—1 July.
Do. 4% Debs. . . .	300,000	1919	100	4	1 Jan.—1 July.

* Yield calculated on earlier date of redemption.

£300,000 in the year's revenue, the total being £8,500,000. Here again, railways are the principal contributor, that source of revenue showing an increase of £249,000.

AUSTRALIAN RAILWAYS, BANKS AND COMPANIES.

Title.	Number of Shares or Amount.	Dividend for last Year.	Paid up.	Price.	Yield.
RAILWAYS.		%			
Emu Bay and Mount Bischoff . . .	12,000	6	5	4½	6⅝
Do. 4½% Irred. Deb. Stock	£130,900	4½	100	97	4⅝
Mid. of W. Aust. 4% Debs., Guartd. .	300,000	4	100	100	4
BANKS AND COMPANIES.					
Bank of Australasia	40,000	14	40	109½	5 1/16
Bank of New South Wales	125,000	10	20	44	4½
Union Bank of Australia £75 . . .	60,000	14	25	62½	5 9/16
Do. 4% Inscribed Stock Deposits . .	£600,000	4	100	98	4 1/16
Australian Mort. Land & Finance £25	80,000	12½	5	7¼	8 9/16
Do. 4% Perp. Deb. Stock	£1,900,000	4	100	101½	3 15/16
Dalgety & Co. £20	154,000	7	5	5¾	6 1/16
Do. 4½% Irred. Deb. Stock	£620,000	4½	100	108	4⅛
Goldsbrough Mort & Co. 4% A Deb. Stock Reduced	£1,067,137	4	100	85½	4⅝
Do. B Income Reduced	£711,340	5½	100	94	5 13/16
Australian Agricultural £25 . . .	20,000	£4½	21½	75	6
South Australian Company . . .	14,200	15	20	68½	4⅜
Trust & Agency of Australasia . . .	42,479	7½	1	¾	10
Do. 5% Cum. Pref.	87,500	5	10	9¾	5⅛

NEW ZEALAND MUNICIPAL AND OTHER SECURITIES.

Title.	Present Amount.	When Redeemable.	Price.	Yield.	Interest Payable.
Auckland 5% Deb. .	200,000	1934–8*	109	4⅜	1 Jan.—1 July.
Do. Hbr. Bd. 5% Debs.	150,000	1917	104	4 1/16	10 April—10 Oct.
Bank of N. Z. shares†	150,000	div. 12½%	10¼	4 1/16	—
Do. 4% Gua. Stock‡ .	£1,000,000	1914	101	3 13/16	April—Oct.
Christchurch 6% Drainage Loan. .	200,000	1926	120	4 3/16	30 June—31 Dec.
Lyttleton Hbr. Bd. 6%	200,000	1929	120	4⅜	1 Jan.—1 July.
Napier Hbr. Bd. 5% Debs.	300,000	1920	103	4 9/16	1 Jan.—1 July.
Do. 5% Debs. . . .	200,000	1928	104	4⅝	1 Jan.—1 July.
National Bank of N.Z. £7½ Shares £2½ paid	150,000	div. 13%	5½x	5⅞	Jan.—July.
Oamaru 5% Bds. . .	173,800	1920	94	5¾	1 Jan.—1 July.
Otago Hbr. Cons. Bds. 5%	443,100	1934	105	4⅝	1 Jan.—1 July.
Wellington 6% Impts. Loan	100,000	1914–29	110	—	1 Mar.—1 Sept.
Do. 6% Waterworks .	130,000	1929	121	4 7/16	1 Mar.—1 Sept.
Do. 4½% Debs. . .	165,000	1933	104	4¼	1 May—1 Nov.
Westport Hbr. 4% Debs.	150,000	1925	102	3⅞	1 Mar.—1 Sept.

* Yield calculated on earlier date of redemption.
† £6 13*s*. 4*d*. Shares with £3 6*s*. 8*d*. paid up.
‡ Guaranteed by New Zealand Government.
(*x*) **Ex dividend.**

NEW ZEALAND GOVERNMENT SECURITIES.

Title.	Present Amount.	When Redeemable.	Price.	Yield.	Interest Payable.
5% Bonds	266,300	1914	104x	3$\frac{7}{8}$	15 Jan.—15 July.
4% Inscribed Stock (t)	29,150,302	1929	104$\frac{1}{4}$	3$\frac{11}{16}$	1 May—1 Nov.
3½% Stock (t) . . .	13,754,532	1940	98	3$\frac{9}{16}$	1 Jan.—1 July.
3% Inscribed Stock (t)	9,659,980	1945	87$\frac{1}{2}$	3$\frac{3}{8}$	1 Apr.—1 Oct.

(t) Eligible for Trustee investments.
(x) Ex dividend.

There was an increase of nearly 400 ounces in the daily average gold production from the Transvaal during June, the total output being 625,181 ounces valued at £2,655,602. This table gives the returns month by month for several years past:

—	1910.	1909.	1908.	1907.	1906.	1905.
	£	£	£	£	£	£
January . .	2,554,451	2,612,836	2,380,124	2,283,741	1,820,739	1,568,508
February . .	2,445,088	2,400,892	2,301,971	2,096,434	1,731,664	1,545,371
March . .	2,578,877	2,580,498	2,442,022	2,287,391	1,884,815	1,698,340
April . .	2,629,535	2,578,804	2,403,500	2,281,110	1,865,785	1,695,550
May . .	2,693,785	2,652,699	2,472,143	2,227,838	1,959,062	1,768,734
June . .	2,655,602	2,621,818	2,442,329	2,155,976	2,021,813	1,751,412
July . . .	—	2,636,965	2,482,608	2,262,813	2,089,004	1,781,944
August . .	—	2,597,646	2,496,869	2,357,602	2,162,583	1,820,496
September .	—	2,575,760	2,496,112	2,285,424	2,145,575	1,769,124
October . .	—	2,558,902	2,624,012	2,351,344	2,296,361	1,765,047
November .	—	2,539,146	2,609,685	2,335,406	2,265,625	1,804,253
December .	—	2,569,822	2,806,235	2,478,659	2,336,961	1,833,295
Total * .	15,557,333	30,925,788	29,957,610	27,403,738	24,579,987	20,802,074

* Including undeclared amounts omitted from the monthly returns.

The report of the General Mining and Finance Corporation, Limited, for the year ended December 31, 1909, submitted at the meeting in Johannesburg on May 21, states that the working profit, after deducting administration expenses and depreciation of office furniture, amounted to £500,339. This amount added to the balance of unappropriated profit brought forward from 1908 of £59,551, makes a total available profit of £559,890. Out of this has been paid dividend No. 5 of 15 per cent., declared in March, 1910, on the ordinary shares absorbing £281,100, and a dividend of £31 6s. 8d. per share on the Founders' shares, absorbing £31,333 6s. 8d., or a total of £312,433 6s. 8d., leaving a balance of unappropriated profit (subject to sundry commissions payable to certain officials under agreements for services and bonus to staff) to be carried forward to 1910 of £313,802. The usual practice has been followed of taking the share and stock holdings into the balance-sheet either at cost or at the Stock

Exchange making-up prices current at the date the accounts were made up, whichever is the lower. The book cost of the share investments is considerably less than the market prices at the date of the accounts, but of this unrealised profit no account has been taken and in no case has an asset been written up. There is also a considerable appreciation in the value of mining claims above the cost at which they stand in the books.

The major portion of the share investments are in the nine mines under the management and control of the Corporation. These are:—Meyer and Charlton Gold Mining Company, Limited; Roodepoort United Main Reef Gold Mining Company, Limited; New Goch Gold Mines, Limited; Van Ryn Gold Mines Estate, Limited; Aurora West United Gold Mining Company, Limited; West Rand Consolidated Mines, Limited; Cinderella Deep, Limited; New Steyn Estate Gold Mines, Limited; and Rand Collieries, Limited. The total issued share capital at December 31, 1909, of these nine companies amounted to £5,358,354. They own properties on the Main Reef Series comprising 6,253 claims and also freehold land 19,005 acres in extent, and coal rights over about 5,910 acres. The operations of the seven producing mines under the control of the Corporation show continued expansion and improved results. Collectively, the Meyer and Charlton, New Goch, Roodepoort United, Van Ryn, Aurora West, Cinderella Deep and West Rand Consolidated crushed 1,550,780 tons of ore, yielding gold and other revenue to the amount of £2,148,498, for a gross profit of £773,000. At the end of the past year, 745 stamps were running, as compared with 655 in December, 1908. The total working expenditure of these seven mines for the year under report was £1,375,490, equal to 17s. 9d. per ton crushed: as compared with 18s. 2d. for the previous year, 21s. 5d. for 1907, and 23s. 1d. per ton for 1906. The payable ore reserves at December 31 last amounted in the aggregate to 3,869,745 tons of an average assay value of 6·4 dwts. per ton. The Meyer and Charlton declared dividends for the year amounting to £65,000, or 45 per cent. on the issued capital; the Van Ryn distributed £225,000 representing 45 per cent. for the year; the Roodepoort United declared dividends amounting to £80,500, equal to 17½ per cent. on the increased capital of the company; the New Goch declared its first dividend of 10 per cent., absorbing £55,000; and the West Rand Consolidated also declared its first dividend of 3¾ per cent., amounting to £74,228.

The net profits earned during the year by the two remaining producing mines—the Cinderella Deep and the Aurora West—were expended on additions to their respective surface equipments. In giving detailed figures relating to the Witwatersrand Gold Mining Industry, the directors point out that the considerable progress would have been still more marked but for the prejudicial effects of the abnormal rainfall in the early part of the year, and the temporary shortage of native labour during the past few months. They also draw particular attention, in congratulating shareholders on the highly satisfactory results obtained by the Corporation during the past year, to the important changes which have been effected during the period under review, or which are on the eve of being made, in regard to the greatly improved prospects of the subsidiary companies. Every one of the companies under the management of the Corporation is in a stronger position at the present time than at the beginning of the year under report—either by reason of large accretions to its mining area and equipment, or by the provision of a considerable amount of additional working capital for the expansion of its operations, or the liquidation of its previously existing liabilities. The directors add that the Corporation and the mines which it controls are to-day in a sounder position than ever hitherto attained, and express the opinion that the prejudicial factors, such as a temporary shortage of native labour, which to some extent during the past year affected the economical working of the mines, are of only a passing nature.

Very satisfactory figures were shown by the Rand native labour return for June, the decrease on the month in the number of Kaffirs employed in the gold mines being 533. Thus, during May and June there has been a net decrease of only 383, whereas during the corresponding period of last year, the decrease was

SOUTH AFRICAN GOVERNMENT SECURITIES.

Title.	Present Amount.	When Redeemable.	Price.	Yield.	Interest Payable.
CAPE COLONY.	£				
4½% Bonds	485,000	dwgs.	102	$4\frac{7}{16}$	15 Apr.—15 Oct.
4% 1883 Inscribed .	8,733,195	1923	103	$3\frac{3}{4}$	1 June—1 Dec.
4% 1886 ,, .	9,997,566	1916-36*	102½	$3\frac{11}{16}$	15 Apr.—15 Oct.
3½% 1886 ,, (t).	15,443,014	1929-49†	99½	$3\frac{7}{8}$	1 Jan.—1 July.
3% 1886 ,, (t).	7,553,590	1933-43†	86½	$3\frac{3}{4}$	1 Feb.—1 Aug.
NATAL.					
4½% Bonds, 1876 . .	758,700	1919	105	4	15 Mar.—15 Sep.
4% Inscribed (t) . .	3,026,444	1937	106	$3\frac{5}{8}$	Apr.—Oct.
3½% ,, (t) . .	3,714,917	1914-39†	99	$3\frac{1}{2}$	1 June—1 Dec.
3% ,, (t) . .	6,000,000	1929-49†	85½	$3\frac{11}{16}$	1 Jan.—1 July.
TRANSVAAL.					
3% Guartd. Stock (t) .	35,000,000	1923-53†	94¼	$3\frac{1}{4}$	1 May—1 Nov.

* Yield calculated on earlier date of redemption.
† Yield calculated on later date of redemption.
(t) Eligible for Trustee investments.

4,641. The following table shows the course of the fluctuations in the labour supply during the past two years:

Month.	Natives Joined.	Natives Left.	Net Gain on Month.	Natives Employed end of Month.	Chinese Employed end of Month.
June 1908	9,360	8,985	375	129,871	21,636
July ,,	11,725	9,257	2,468	132,339	18,413
August ,,	11,988	10,799	1,209	133,548	17,006
September ,,	14,129	11,497	2,632	136,180	14,655
October ,,	14,754	11,769	2,985	139,165	12,317
November ,,	12,324	10,163	2,161	141,326	12,298
December ,,	17,404	10,008	7,396	148,722	12,283
January 1909	13,551	11,609	1,942	150,664	10,045
February ,,	18,018	10,844	7,174	157,838	10,034
March ,,	16,184	11,979	4,205	162,043	9,997
April ,,	12,102	11,244	858	162,901	7,734
May ,,	7,717	12,339	4,622*	158,279	7,717
June ,,	8,335	12,354	4,019*	154,260	5,378
July ,,	7,826	12,612	4,786*	149,474	5,370
August ,,	10,089	12,642	2,553*	146,291	5,361
September ,,	11,747	13,811	2,064*	144,857	3,204
October ,,	14,656	13,762	894	152,563‡	3,199
November ,,	13,942	13,742	200	152,763	1,799
December ,,	17,293	13,348	3,945	156,708	nil.
January 1910	—	—	3,954	160,662	nil.
February ,,	—	—	9,109	169,771	nil.
March ,,	—	—	8,574	178,345	nil.
April ,,	—	—	5,469	183,814	nil.
May ,,	—	—	150	183,964	nil.
June ,,	—	—	533*	183,431	nil.

* Net loss. ‡ Including new members of Native Labour Association.

Rhodesia's gold output showed a further reduction during June amounting to £214,709 against £224,888 for the preceding

SOUTH AFRICAN RAILWAYS, BANKS, AND COMPANIES.

Title.	Number of Shares or Amount.	Dividend for last Year.	Paid up.	Price.	Yield.
Railways.					
Mashonaland 5% Debs.	£2,500,000	5	100	99	5
Rhodesia Rlys. 5% 1st Mort. Debs. guar. by B.S.A. Co. till 1915. . .	£2,000,000	5	100	102	$4\frac{7}{8}$
Royal Trans-African 5% Debs. Rep. .	£1,855,000	5	100	87	$5\frac{11}{16}$
Banks and Companies.					
African Banking Corporation £10 shares	80,000	$5\frac{1}{2}$	5	$4\frac{7}{8}$	$5\frac{5}{8}$
Bank of Africa £18¾	160,000	5	$6\frac{1}{4}$	7	$4\frac{7}{16}$
Natal Bank £10	148,232	8	$2\frac{1}{2}$	$3\frac{3}{8}x$	$5\frac{7}{8}$
National Bank of S. Africa £10 . .	110,000	3	10	$11\frac{3}{4}$	$2\frac{1}{2}$
Standard Bank of S. Africa £100 . .	61,941	10	25	$59\frac{1}{2}$	$4\frac{3}{16}$
Ohlsson's Cape Breweries	60,000	nil	5	$4\frac{1}{4}$	—
South African Breweries	965,279	10	1	$1\frac{15}{32}x$	$6\frac{3}{4}$
British South Africa (Chartered) . .	8,046,020	nil	1	$1\frac{17}{32}$	nil
Do. 5% Debs. Red.	£1,250,000	5	100	107	$4\frac{5}{8}$
Natal Land and Colonization . . .	68,066	4	5	$4\frac{1}{4}$	$4\frac{11}{16}$
Cape Town & District Gas Light & Coke	10,000	nil	10	$3\frac{1}{2}$	—
Kimberley Waterworks £10 . . .	45,000	5	7	$5\frac{1}{4}$	$6\frac{5}{8}$

(x) Ex dividend.

SOUTH AFRICAN MUNICIPAL SECURITIES.

Title.	Present Amount.	When Redeemable.	Price.	Yield.	Interest Payable.
	£				
Bloemfontein 4% . .	663,000	1954	99	4	1 Jan.—1 July.
Cape Town 4% . .	1,861,750	1953	102	$3\frac{7}{8}$	1 Jan.—1 July.
Durban 4% . . .	850,000	1951-3	101	$3\frac{15}{16}$	30 June—31 Dec.
Johannesburg 4% .	5,500,000	1933-4	$100\frac{1}{2}$	4	1 April—1 Oct.
Krugersdorp 4% . .	100,000	1930	96	$4\frac{5}{16}$	1 June—1 Dec.
Pietermaritzburg 4%	825,000	1949-53	99	4	30 June—31 Dec.
Port Elizabeth 4% .	376,946	1964	99	4	30 June—31 Dec.
Pretoria 4% . . .	1,000,000	1939	100	4	1 Jan.—1 July.
Rand Water Board 4%	3,400,000	1935	100	4	1 Jan.—1 July.

month, and £217,520 for June last year. This table enables comparison with the returns for several years past:

Month.	1910.	1909.	1908.	1907.	1906.
	£	£	£	£	£
January . .	227,511	204,666	199,380	168,240	155,337
February . .	203,888	192,497	191,635	145,397	137,561
March . . .	228,385	202,157	200,615	167,424	160,722
April . . .	228,213	222,700	212,935	175,210	157,108
May . . .	224,888	225,032	223,867	189,216	169,218
June . . .	214,709	217,600	224,920	192,506	170,083
July . . .	—	225,234	228,151	191,681	173,313
August . . .	—	228,296	220,792	192,106	179,000
September. .	—	213,249	204,262	192,186	173,973
October . .	—	222,653	205,466	191,478	161,360
November . .	—	236,307	196,668	183,058	175,656
December . .	—	233,397	217,316	190,383	171,770
Total .	1,327,594	2,623,788	2,526,007	2,178,885	1,985,101

Other minerals produced from Southern Rhodesia during June comprised 19,318 ounces of silver, 67 tons of lead, 3 tons of copper, 15,191 tons of coal, 5,901 tons of chrome ore and 70 tons of asbestos.

CROWN COLONY SECURITIES.

Title.	Present Amount.	When Redeemable.	Price.	Yield.	Interest Payable.
Barbadoes $3\frac{1}{2}$% ins. (*t*)	375,000	1925-42*	98	$3\frac{3}{4}$	1 Mar.—1 Sep.
Brit. Guiana 3% ins. (*t*)	250,000	1923-45†	84	$3\frac{7}{8}$	1 Feb.—1 Aug.
Ceylon 4% ins. (*t*). .	1,076,100	1934	109	$3\frac{7}{16}$	15 Feb.—15 Aug.
Do. 3% ins. (*t*). . .	2,850,000	1940	88	$3\frac{11}{16}$	1 May—1 Nov.
Hong-Kong $3\frac{1}{2}$% ins (*t*)	1,485,733	1918-43†	98	$3\frac{5}{8}$	15 Apr.—15 Oct.
Jamaica 4% ins. (*t*) .	1,099,048	1934	107	$3\frac{9}{16}$	15 Feb.—15 Aug.
Do. $3\frac{1}{2}$% ins. (*t*) . .	1,455,500	1919-49†	97	$3\frac{11}{16}$	24 Jan.—24 July.
Mauritius 3% guar. Great Britain (*t*) .	600,000	1940	92	$3\frac{3}{8}$	1 Jan.—1 July.
Do. 4% ins. (*t*). . .	482,390	1937	105	$3\frac{3}{4}$	1 Feb.—1 Aug.
Sierra Leone $3\frac{1}{2}$% ins. (*t*)	720,051	1929-54†	$98\frac{1}{2}$	$3\frac{9}{16}$	1 June—1 Dec.
Trinidad 4% ins. . .	422,593	1917-42*	104	$3\frac{1}{2}$	15 Mar.—15 Sep.
Do. 3% ins. (*t*). . .	600,000	1922-44†	85	$3\frac{3}{4}$	15 Jan.—15 July.
Hong-Kong & Shanghai Bank Shares .	120,000	Div. £4	$£89\frac{1}{2}$	$4\frac{7}{16}$	Feb.—Aug.

* Yield calculated on shorter period. † Yield calculated on longer period.
(*t*) Eligible for Trustee investments.

Rubber shares have still been suffering from the aftermath of the boom in new issues, the special settlements in which have been involving a good deal of liquidation. In these circumstances

RUBBER SHARES.

Company.	Issued Capital.	Area planted.	Nominal Value of Share.	Amount paid-up.	Price.
	£	Acres.			
Anglo-Malay	150,000	3,391	2*s.*	2*s.*	28*s.* 6*d.*
Batu Tiga	60,000	1,545	£1	£1	6
Bukit Rajah	66,700	2,772	£1	£1	20
Consolidated Malay	62,007	1,710	£1	2*s.*	31*s.* 6*d.*
Highlands and Lowlands	317,353	4,707	£1	£1	$6\frac{3}{4}$
Kepitigalla	225,000	3,127	£1	£1	$1\frac{1}{8}$
Kuala Lumpur	180,000	2,611	£1	£1	$10\frac{1}{8}$
Lanadron	269,780	4,570	£1	£1	$7\frac{5}{8}$
Linggi	100,000	4,192	2*s.*	2*s.*	62*s.* 6*d.*
Pataling	22,500	1,454	2*s.*	2*s.*	$3\frac{5}{8}$
Straits (Bertam)	200,000	2,270	2*s.*	2*s.*	8*s.* 6*d.*
Vallambrosa	50,600	1,807	2*s.*	2*s.*	55*s.*

new business has been meagre, but a distinctly healthier tone has been adopted by the market, and the prices of the good shares are now generally higher than they were a month ago.

In Egyptian financial circles anticipations of the results of the next cotton crop are beginning to play an important part. With the labour dispute settled in the Lancashire trade, and with a shortage in American cotton, a good cotton crop with high prices would confer on Egyptian commerce a benefit of which it

EGYPTIAN SECURITIES.

Title.	Amount or Number of Shares.	Dividend for last Year.	Paid up.	Price.	Yield.
Egyptian Govt. Guaranteed Loan (*t*)	£7,414,700	3	99	98	$3\frac{1}{16}$
,, Unified Debt	£55,971,960	4	100	$100\frac{3}{4}$	$3\frac{15}{16}$
National Bank of Egypt	300,000	9	10	$20\frac{1}{4}$	$4\frac{7}{16}$
Bank of Egypt	50,000	15	$12\frac{1}{2}$	$30\frac{1}{2}$	$6\frac{1}{8}$
Agricultural Bank of Egypt, Ordinary	496,000	$5\frac{1}{4}$	5	$7\frac{1}{8}$	$3\frac{5}{8}$
,, ,, ,, Preferred	125,000	4	10	$9\frac{1}{8}$	$4\frac{3}{8}$
,, ,, ,, Bonds	£2,350,000	$3\frac{1}{2}$	100	86	$4\frac{1}{16}$

(*t*) Eligible for Trustee investments.

is sadly in need after last year's crop disappointment. Already hopes of a good crop have been stimulating a little speculative buying of Egyptian land shares, but it is, of course, too early yet to form any reliable estimates as to the ultimate quantity of cotton that will be harvested.

TRUSTEE.

July 21, 1910.

THE EMPIRE REVIEW

"Far as the breeze can bear, the billows foam,
Survey our empire, and behold our home."—*Byron.*

VOL. XX.　　SEPTEMBER, 1910.　　No. 116

THE APPROACHING CENSUS

SOME OBSERVATIONS ON THE NUMBERING OF THE PEOPLE

By GEORGE T. BISSET-SMITH

H.M. Registration Examiner

THAT acknowledged measure in many ways of the evolution of the Empire, basis for legislation and administration, the Census of our population not only pictures the present, but indicates both the direction in which we are travelling and the rate of progress we are making. In short the Census is the stocktaking of our national life; greatest of all statistical operations.

Births and deaths—additions and subtractions—are recorded daily: while the British Census is still only decennial. In France it is quinquennial; and it is probable that in 1916 we shall follow France, for it is generally agreed among statisticians that strong necessity arises for an intermediate numbering of the people. Such intermediate Census might fulfil its object by counting only the numbers, its main purpose being the ratification of intercensal estimates. Owing to the inconstancy of industrial conditions, the fluctuations of population are more frequent to-day than in former decades. Estimates of the population in particular localities made upon the basis of the increase shown at the last Census are, accordingly, apt to be erroneous, and the amount of error tends to increase in the decennium. Glasgow, for example, is following London in showing a centrifugal displacement of population; the growth of its central area is now almost arrested, while its marginal zone is developing. Its population on the basis of the increase revealed at the Census of 1901 was, in 1905, 24,512 greater than the number arrived at by the Medical Officer of Health, whose figure is now more than 70,000 less than the Census estimate. Aberdeen is another illustration of the inability of those concerned to frame, upon the basis of the results of preceding Censuses, sufficiently accurate estimates of population existing at any given date between one census and another. Industrial depression and displacement (including increased emigration to Canada and Australia) have stopped even the genetic increase of Aberdeen, and its population is less by 10,000 than the estimate published by the Registrar-General. Similar instances are furnished by several of the seventy-six towns of England, as to which birth and death-rates are put forth also upon the basis of an intercensal estimate, requiring rectification. The necessity for a quinquennial ascertainment of the numbers (with age and sex) of the population has, indeed, been admitted. The only objection is that of cost. Obviously, the present system involves a waste of public money, in, for instance, the preparation and publication of death-rates which are wrong and misleading. And I would emphasise the important consideration that the intermediate counting need not be so comprehensive—nor so expensive—as the usual decennial Census.

In ancient Rome the Census was quinquennial. The main object of the Roman Census, however, was to ascertain what a man was worth, for purposes of assessment.* The quinquennial registering and rating of the *assidui* in ancient Rome had also a connection with recruiting for the army and the exercise of political rights. The *proletarii* being excluded, it was not a complete enumeration of the people; but it was taken every quinquennium: and the greater masses and mobility of men to-day make ten years far too long an interval to elapse between the national numberings of the people of Great Britain and Ireland. The State of Queensland and the Dominion of New Zealand take an elaborate Census every five years.

The Census Schedule is the blue paper half yard measure of our people. It is called the Occupier's Schedule in England and Wales, the Householder's Schedule in Scotland, and the Family Return Form in Ireland. It was introduced for the first time at the fifth British Census (1841) in much the same shape as for the coming Census. But it has been altered here and there since 1851, especially in the compartment headed *Profession or Occupation*. One-third, indeed, of the space in the Schedule to be filled up by the occupier or householder is now devoted to details regarding occupation; and one-fourth of the whole Schedule is filled with precise instructions as to the stating of employment. The particular branch of the trade, or industry,

---

* Cicero, De Leg., III. C. 3.

and the material worked or dealt in, have to be specified ; also, whether the man is an employer (other than that of domestic servants), a worker for an employer, working on his own account, or carrying on a trade or industry at home. To a non-statistical mind, this precision may appear over-elaborate ; but it should be borne in mind that the key to the•condition of a country lies in reliable details of its occupations.

The careful and intelligent classification of occupations, with the numbers and ages of those engaged in them, affords results of the greatest value. Statistics generally show only quantity, but such final figures reveal something of a country's quality. They picture the condition of our country so clearly that, on comparing the figures of previous decades, we can see at a glance our industrial changes and development. Electricity, for example, was shown at the last Census * to employ many thousands, whereas thirty years ago it gave occupation only to a few hundreds. The classification of occupations is the most delicate and difficult part of the final work of tabulating the information in the Schedules ; and its importance is thus emphasised in the Census of England Report for 1871 :—" The number of a nation is limited by its organisation—in professions, trades, and industries. Without government, without defence, without the sciences, without literature and the arts, without tools, without dwellings, without agriculture, without commerce, without roads, without ships, without mines—without all the complicated mechanism of industry, society would cease to exist, and men would lose their highest prerogatives." The Census is therefore the stock-taking not only of our number, but also of our civilisation, as set forth in our occupations. It ascertains what all live by, distinguishing those who obtain their support from the land from those engaged in trade ; and, in detail, the Census Reports give the number supported by any particular profession, trade or industry.

In our three earliest Censuses—1801, 1811, and 1821—there was a rough division of the people under the three headings of Agriculture, Trade, and Others. A more detailed tabulation was attempted in 1831, and in 1841 all the principal occupations were recorded. In 1851 the exhaustive method of tabulation now in use was originated : and the same year saw the introduction of the Census Schedule filled up by the occupier. The system of tabulation used at the central Census office groups all occupations into twenty-two great classes or orders ; with numerous sub-classes ; in all, about four hundred occupations ; and the persons employed are subdivided by sex and quinquennial age-periods. Imperial and Local Government, Defence of the Country, Religion,

* 1901.

Law and Medicine, Art and Literature, Science and Education, Agriculture and Minerals, form the main leading divisions into which are classed the particulars as to profession and occupation.

The following statement gives the essence of the Summary of Occupations at the phase and period of civilisation reached at the Census of 1901, in a form easily understood.

PERCENTAGE, IN SIX GENERAL DIVISIONS, OF OCCUPATIONS IN THE UNITED KINGDOM.

Class.	Percentage.
Professional persons	3·3
Commercial	4·4
Domestic	6·2
Agricultural and fishing	6·7
Industrial	23·9
Children, and adults with no specified occupation	55·5
	100·0

Birthplaces.—There is a double value in the column in the Census Schedule headed "Where Born"; for it shows not only the birthplaces, but also something of the migrations of the people. As men mature, they leave birthplaces for "work places." Such migration is greater in Scotland than in England—where notwithstanding the constant migration from country to town the native population still shows, upon the whole, a habit of stationariness. Of the natives of England and Wales, no less than 75·19 were enumerated in their native countries at the Census of 1881; and the disturbance in the distribution of the people caused by industrial development and increased facilities of locomotion led to only a comparatively small decrease in twenty years of the percentage of stationary natives to 70·76 in 1901

Ages.—Changes in the proportions of age and sex are of fundamental importance in regulating the strength, development and character of a nation. The difference in value to society between a mature man and a child recently entered upon existence being so obviously great and incalculable, it is very necessary to have ages stated. Age (last birthday) and sex are accordingly required to be given; the ages of infants under one year being inserted in months. Statistics as to age were first attempted formally in 1821; but the answering of the question was then optional, and the attempt was so unsuccessful that, except for the ancient and biblical division into those under and those over twenty years, no notice was taken of age in the following Census of 1831. The Census of 1841 was much more stringent; it provided that the numbering should be simultaneous, in one day, and required the occupation, birthplace, and the exact age.

It is in the matter of age that a slight element of fiction appears now and then in the Schedules; for careful study reveals that there are more of the fair sex aged about twenty-five than can be accounted for. Women of twenty-five in 1901 must have been fifteen in 1891; but the women entered in the returns as twenty-five exceed the young girls of fifteen, of whom they should be only the naturally diminished survivors! It may be offered as a partial explanation that twenty-five is looked upon as the golden age for matrimony, to be older than which means the facing at once the possibility of remaining an old maid; and in spite of the opening of many occupations and professions to women, marriage seems to be still looked upon as the most desirable career for woman. Any person who refuses to give information, or who wilfully gives false information as to any of the particulars in the Census-Schedule, is liable to a fine not exceeding five pounds. After all the Schedules for Scotland had been centralised in 1891, a lady, deeply veiled, handed in the sum of five pounds, with half-a-crown for acknowledgment in *The Scotsman*, mentioning that she had entered her age wrongly. This instance is unique. Payments for income-tax arrears and understatements are not uncommonly made in such anonymous fashion, but I have never heard of a single other case of voluntary payment of conscience-money for erroneous information in the Census. And I know of only one conviction (of a woman in Glasgow) for a false return at last Census.

APPROXIMATE AGE TABLE FOR THE UNITED KINGDOM, CALCULATED FOR CENSUS REPORTS.

Age.	Percentage.
Under 4 years inclusive	12·0
From 5–14 ,, ,,	22·8
,, 15–24 ,, ,,	19·6
,, 25–34 ,, ,,	14·7
,, 35–44 ,, ,,	11·3
,, 45–54 ,, ,,	8·7
,, 55–64 ,, ,,	5·9
,, 65–74 ,, ,,	3·5
,, 75–84 ,, ,,	1·3
,, 85–100 and upwards	0·2
	100·0

As a result partly of increased longevity but chiefly of the falling birth-rate, our population is becoming an older one, with a decreasing basis for the coming generation. The percentage of boys and girls under 10 has diminished at each Census. In 1881 it was 25·7 of the total population in England and Wales; in 1891, 24; in 1901 it had become as low as 22·1; and it is safe to say that the percentage of 1911 will be even less, for the percentage of the births has deceased significantly in the last decade.

Infirmities, etc.—More delicate even than the question of age is the last query in the Schedule, relating to infirmities, which inquires whether the person enumerated is blind, deaf, dumb, imbecile or lunatic. The term " afflicted " or " infirm " are not admissible, the prescribed descriptions being; Deaf and dumb; Blind; Lunatic, and Imbecile. The Schedule of 1901 had: " Imbecile, Feebleminded." * The final word was objected to and the objection was admitted to be valid. Information as to the bodily infirmities of blindness and the like are readily given ; but, possibly, parents or guardians are reluctant, in some instances, to record mental weakness, especially where that weakness is .not fully apparent as an incapacitating infirmity. And one is somewhat doubtful as to the value of the Census record of the mentally unsound. The information, however, although it may not be complete, is in a way valuable, the use of the information collected being to afford some indication of the deductions to be made in calculating the strength of a nation, just as allowance has to be made for the very young and the very old.

The Census Schedule collects also particulars of Sex and Conjugal Condition.

Sex.—The number of males born is greater than that of females, but the mortality of males is heavier ; with the result that the proportion of females to males shown at the Census of 1881 was 51·3 to 50, and the proportion has since increased by ·2 in each decade, being 51·7 in 1901.

Marriage.—The mean age of men and women at marriage has risen from 28 and 25·7 in 1867–70, to 28·4 and 26·2 in 1896–1900. The number of wives in England on the Census night of 1901 was 5,717,537, the number of husbands 5,611,381, a difference of 106,156, which is explained mainly by the large body of married men absent then owing to the South African War. There was no column for divorced person in 1901.

On the outside of the Census Schedule it is stated that— " The Return is required for carrying out the provisions of the Census Act. The contents of the Schedules will be treated as confidential ; they will be published in General Abstracts only, and strict care will be taken that the Returns are not used for the gratification of curiosity, or for other purposes than those of the Census." Census reports make public no individual particulars, and mention no names of persons. There is, therefore, no direct use made of the first column in the Schedule, headed " Name and Surname." The instruction is to write first the name of the head of the family, followed by the names of his wife, children, and other relatives ; then the names of any visitors, boarders and servants. Double Schedules are supplied for large houses and

* In col. 10.

hotels. For public institutions and barracks or camps, special enumeration books are issued to be filled up by the head of the institution or the chief resident officer, and in the barracks the paid enumerator is generally the barrack-master or quartermaster.

Five different Schedules are printed for the enumeration of similar places in Ireland, with headings, barrack, workhouse, hospital, prison, or college and boarding-school return. The Green Isle also devotes four forms to recording the number of students or pupils " on the books of each College or Boarding-school on any day or days of the fortnight ending about the middle of May 1911," and other similar information which the heads of educational establishments in Ireland are required to give during the progress of the Census. Education is not included in the English and Scottish Census, but the Irish Family Schedule asks the enumerator to ascertain whether each person can read and write, read only, or cannot read. The Royal Irish Constabulary chiefly act as enumerators for the Emerald Isle, directed as to their duties and the multiplicity of forms by twenty pages of " Instructions to Enumerators." The Dublin Metropolitan Police also act as enumerators. In England and Scotland the enumerator is required to be a person of some address and intelligence who can write well, and is not less than eighteen nor more than sixty-five years of age. Enumerators are the modern representatives of the high officials mentioned in Numbers as appointed to help Moses to take " the sum of all the congregation of the children of Israel, after their families, by the house of their fathers."

Date of Census.—In terms of the Act passed on 3rd August, the next Census is to be taken as on Sunday, the second day of April, in the year 1911. Various opinions have been expressed from time to time as to the date upon which the Census should be taken, and the dates have ranged from the 10th of March in 1801 to the 6th of June in 1841. The most suitable season is the spring. In winter the enumerators, especially in country districts, would have difficulty in getting over the ground; and, in order to find the population in their usual home, it is necessary to fix the date for a time before the summer movements of the people are in progress. By long usage, therefore, the day fixed is the Sunday nearest to the 1st of April. The fixing of the 2nd of April, 1911, for the national numbering is thus in accordance with reason and precedent.

Religion.—At every British Census there is an agitation for the collection of statistics regarding religion. The Irish Census Act, indeed, includes a provision for taking account of religions, with a proviso, however, that " no person shall be subject to any such penalty for refusing to state his religious profession."

Only a very small number of persons refuse; and it is concluded therefore that the people in Ireland (a gradually decreasing population) do not object to the question as unduly inquisitorial. The inquiry in Ireland, however, which has been made successfully at five previous Censuses, is intended mainly to ascertain the proportion of Protestants to Catholics; and the former are requested to name their "particular Church, Denomination, or Body." Basing their proposal upon the success of the religious Census in Ireland, and ignoring the different conditions of the countries, enthusiastic statisticians have again and again urged upon the Government the adoption of a similar question in the Schedule for Great Britain. In 1880 the subject was debated very warmly and thoroughly in Parliament, and the religious question was rejected. It has been so ever since—the usual question in Parliament as to its introduction having recently received the stereotyped reply in the negative; and the amendment by the Lords rejected in the Commons.

It may be mentioned that in 1851 an attempt was made towards a Census of Religions in England and Scotland. In that year, the church accommodation was enumerated, and returns were made of those attending the different churches on Census Sunday, March 30, 1851. Admittedly imperfect, these figures were not worth much. In other countries, however, and in our Colonies the information is obtained, and is of value from a statistical standpoint. In Great Britain the question is complicated by the fact that there are over two hundred different religious sects, and all might demand tabulation! "If it were proposed to take a Religious Census, do you think it would be worth while tabulating every different sect, or dividing between what is your Established Church in Scotland, and what is your Nonconformist Church in Scotland merely?" was a question put by the Census Committee of 1890, to which the Registrar-General replied:—"I think, if the Census were taken at all, that probably those who wish to have it taken would desire that it should be made as minute as possible." In their Report the Census Committee conclude their observations on this subject, by stating that "Reasons of weight, mainly of a political character, have been urged against the requirement of returns under this head." If exacted by a penalty, the Religious Census might be objectionable; and if optional, it might prove incomplete, unsatisfactory and untrustworthy; requiring, in any case, too many discounts to be of statistical value.

Religious beliefs are almost automatically inviolate; they cannot be expressed readily in the brief terms of a schedule. At best a Religious Census would be rather a Census of Churchmen. And what of the children? Census-taking has its limits. The great analytical process can be extended only with the utmost care and caution. To widen it too much would be to weaken it. And judging from the personal experience of three Censuses I may add that an initial objection to a census of religious professions is that the enumerator might be apt to insert in the Schedule his own denomination in those cases where he completed the Census Schedule, or corrected it as erroneous, both of which he is authorised to do by his instructions. A large number of persons, in city districts especially, attend and are attached to no church regularly; and if a Census enumerator belonged to a body called so, he might be tempted to return, in many urban localities, a large number of the people as belonging to the indefinite denomination of " Go-as-You-please Christians."

Housing.—But although some families can live, apparently, without any professed religion, they nearly all require a house or shelter of some kind. The question of housing is of the first importance, and it is tackled very thoroughly in the Scottish Census.* In the application of the Act to Scotland, a complete return of the windowed rooms occupied by each family has long been required to be made by the enumerator. At previous Censuses, the English Schedule asked a statement of the number of rooms only where the rooms occupied by the persons named were fewer than five rooms. Henceforth there is to be uniformity in this respect, and the occupier in England of a large house will be required to state the number of rooms in his mansion equally with the dweller in a small or slum house, for whose benefit only the question was put in Censuses prior to that of 1911. The desirability of uniformity in the statistics of house accommodation has been advocated again and again by statisticians and sociologists; and it is satisfactory to learn that comparable figures as to "the number of rooms inhabited" are to be collected at the coming Census. The number of storeys to a house might be entered with advantage—especially in Scotland, where the houses are so much divided horizontally; and perhaps other information as to the style and character of the various streets might be recorded. Much regarding the standard of comfort and living in a city may be learned from an intelligent study of the statistics of housing; and the figures for Scotland show a steady continuance of improvement in the housing of the people. Aberdeen has the highest percentage of persons living in houses of seven rooms, and Edinburgh of houses of ten or more rooms.

* Full figures as to houses, persons, and windowed rooms have been obtained in Scotland since 1861; and these statistics have formed the basis of improvement in the housing of the people—especially in Edinburgh, Glasgow, Dundee and Aberdeen, where during the last three decades many overcrowded and insanitary dwellings have been reformed.

Shipping.—The Navy is enumerated by the Admiralty. To take a Census of all who go down to the sea in ships seems impossible; but the subtlety of the Census mind is equal to the emergency, and by means of the officers of the Customs and the coastguard it is easily accomplished. Persons on board vessels in ports are enumerated by the Customs officials, aided, on occasion, by the respective foreign Consuls. Coasting and foreign vessels arriving early in April are to be enumerated. British vessels reaching port up to June 30 are included, in order to take in the long-sea ships from China, India and Australasia. A special Schedule is prepared on which are provided spaces for showing the place at which the Schedule is delivered to the master, the position of the vessel on Census Sunday (April 2); and the number of persons—crew or passengers—on shore on the Census night. The Customs officers at the various ports fill in the compartments stating the port to which the ship belongs; her tonnage; whether steam or sailing; and how employed. The occupation columns here are easily filled for the most part, and show the rating of each of the crew. From the various ports, the Schedules are sent to the Registrar-General of Shipping and Seamen in London, who forwards them (in accordance with the localities indicated in the Schedules) to the Registrars-General of England, Ireland, and Scotland. Maritime greatness has moulded our destiny; and hitherto each survey, each decennial and Imperial Census has shown the unrivalled spread of our race. True as the words were when Daniel Webster spoke them nearly eighty years ago, how much more true are they now, that her "morning drumbeat, following the sun and keeping company with the hours, circles the earth with one continuous and unbroken strain of the martial airs of England."

An innovation is to be attempted in 1911 by asking the duration of marriage and the number of children born of the marriage, the facts being required as *data* for the proper discussion of the birthrate and the fertility of marriage. From the information given in the Schedules it should be possible to prepare valuable tables of average ages of parents at the time of the births of their children, and of the average number of children born during fixed periods of married life. Such details were required in the death and birth registers of Scotland in 1855, when compulsory civil registration commenced, but the obtaining and recording of such family-histories-in-brief was relinquished as too inquisitorial and elaborate for ordinary daily Registration. To ascertain how long people have been married, and how many children they have had, will not always be an easy task. The question will, necessarily, be somewhat complicated in Scotland by peculiarities of illegitimacy and legitimation by subsequent marriage. A woman who has had illegitimate children before marriage is an instance of the difficulty; and it may thus not be easy to differentiate the families of a woman who has been two or three times married, in cases complicated by illegitimacy.

Of the coming Census much more might be said. The purpose of this paper, however, is to give a general account of the analytical and statistical process of the Population Census, the main objects of which are :—The total number of the population, their conjugal condition, and the proportion of the sexes; their fertility; their varying occupations; their birthplaces, and their migration. I have avoided the use of tables of figures which might repel the non-statistical reader; and I will conclude by pointing out that—given good units—population is strength, and by emphasising the historical fact, full of a practical moral for Great Britain, as well as for the Dominions overseas, that the only disease of which a nation can die is lack of efficient men.

Each survey of the progress of the Empire proves our vast development. In 1871 a universal numbering of the inhabitants of the British Empire showed a population all over the world of 235 millions, occupying about 77,700,000 square miles; 435 millions occupying over 12 million square miles is a moderate estimate to-day of the population of that great Empire of which (in the words of Lord Rosebery) "We are the tenants in fee, and of which we inherit the responsibility and the glory."

The crowning study of mankind is Man. Highest of all science is that dealing with the human race, and revealing the causes which lead to progressive and relative dominance—to progressive physical and mental development. Viewed as a measurement of the whole social organism, the Population Census is of the deepest interest to the legislator and the sociologist, and studied in all their aspects, the statistics of our numbers, occupations, and effective fertility, should indicate the economic condition of the Empire. No country can continue powerful without a progressive population.

GEORGE T. BISSET-SMITH.

FOREIGN AFFAIRS

By EDWARD DICEY, C.B.

THE ANNEXATION OF KOREA

THE impending annexation of Korea by Japan takes us back in memory some fifteen years—to the days of the China-Japan war. At the time hostilities broke out Korea was nominally under the suzerainty of China. I say nominally, because Japan had twice conquered the Hermit Kingdom, and insisted on regarding it as a Japanese dependency, although she had never occupied the country, while the Chinese Government had successfully exacted tribute from the Peninsula. The Korean ruler, however, had frequently objected to pay this tribute, but did not hesitate to appeal to China whenever he expected any interference from Japan. The situation, therefore, was somewhat peculiar, and matters were not improved when it was discovered by China and by Japan that the Emperor of Korea was endeavouring to enter into independent relations with foreign Powers. Except to the immediate neighbourhood surrounding the newly-opened Treaty Ports, foreigners were excluded from the country. No roads or railways existed, and even in the towns the streets were of a most primitive character. Sanitation was unknown, and things generally were in a most unsatisfactory state. That reforms were necessary no one can deny; but it is a little difficult to see on what ground Japan based her right to insist on Korea carrying out a programme of reform drawn up at Tokio. Still, so it was, and failing to succeed by peaceful methods, Japan invaded the Peninsula for the third time. China protested, and hence the war.

Probably even in those days Japan saw the commercial importance of Korea, and as China appeared to disregard her suzerain powers Japan thought she might as well step in and secure possession. But Japan had reckoned without Russia. She defeated China, and China surrendered her claims in Korea; but Russia stepped in and refused to allow annexation. Japan appealed to this country for assistance, but Lord Rosebery, then

Foreign Minister, did not see his way to interfere. Japan was helpless, and had to rest content with the disappearance of China and the recognition of Japanese influence, while leaving Korea practically independent. Russia, in fact, was the chief Power which benefited by the Treaty of Shimonoseki. With China's wings clipped, she lost no time in establishing herself in Southern Manchuria, and not long afterwards occupied and fortified Port Arthur after solemnly promising she would do nothing of the kind. From her position in Manchuria Russia kept a sharp eye on Korea, and any scheme promoted by Japan for civilising the country or promoting trade between Japan and Korea was soon checkmated by the influence of Russia. In fact for some years Russia watched over the Korean Emperor, and whenever anything was mooted it had first to be submitted to the Russian Legation, which virtually held sway in the Korean capital. In these circumstances no wonder the relations between Japan and Russia became strained, and as Russia refused to give way, but on the other hand tightened her hold on what in reality were Japan's possessions, the only way out of the difficulty was an appeal to force. Hence the Russo-Japan War, the results of which are too recent to need reciting.

There was no occasion for Japan to appeal for aid to a third Power this time. The utter discomfiture of Russia by an Eastern race led to Japan jumping at once into the position of a First-Class Power, and Japan took very good care that this time she retained the spoils of war. Russia retired from Southern Manchuria, and her influence in Korea became a thing of the past. Early in 1904 an agreement was signed at Seoul on behalf of Japan and Korea, the Japanese Government undertaking to ensure the safety of the Korean Imperial House, and guaranteeing the independence and territorial integrity of the country, while the Korean Government, placing full confidence in the Japanese Government, agreed to adopt Japanese advice with respect to administrative improvements. Under the Russo-Japanese treaty of peace signed in the following year, Russia acknowledged Japan's paramount interests in Korea and engaged not to obstruct nor interfere with any measures of guidance, protection or control which Japan might take. The Anglo-Japanese agreement contains similar recognition on the part of Great Britain. Next year saw a further advance on the part of Japan, and an arrangement was come to giving the Japanese Government the control and direction of the foreign relations of Korea, and allowing a Japanese Resident-General to be stationed at Seoul. By a later agreement still the terms of all administrative measures, and all high official appointments were made subject to the approval of the Resident-General, and Japanese subjects became eligible for official positions in Korea.

As a result the entire administration of the Peninsula was transferred to the nominees of Japan. The way for annexation was thus cleared of all obstacles, and nothing remained but for Japan to enter into possession whenever she felt inclined to make the move.

Whether the Koreans altogether appreciated the change from the influence of Russia to that of Japan is another story. Personally I do not think they did, and the fault lay with Japan. Instead of taking care that the occupation was everything it should be, they allowed anyone to follow the troops; thus Korea became the happy hunting-ground for the lower orders of Japan, and the army itself was more or less demoralised: many Koreans were robbed of their land, and in place of the civilising influences that were expected, the position was worse than before. The late Prince Ito was appointed to restore order and to put things right in the Peninsula, and during three years he worked hard to accomplish his mission; but matters had gone too far, and it is doubtful whether military methods were the best in all the circumstances. The subsequent murder of the Prince by a Korean deprived Japan of a really great man, and the whole world sympathised with the stricken nation. Perhaps the sacrifice of Japan's brightest statesman was too great a price to pay for the mistakes that had been made, but one thing is certain, since that terrible event the voice of complaint in Korea if not silenced has been but seldom heard. Japan awakened to a sense of her responsibilities, and as a natural consequence Korea is gradually becoming a country where order and justice prevails. Indeed everything points to a new era for Korea when its annexation by Japan is completed.

It is significant that the St. Petersburg correspondent of the *Times*, after announcing that the Russian Government has been apprised of the impending annexation of Korea as well as of the fact that the Korean Government have concluded a treaty with Japan providing for that event, observes: "It had been hoped here that Japan would refrain from what was apparently a superfluous measure, but Russia will certainly not raise serious objections to it, and the event is not likely to prejudice Russo-Japanese relations." It would seem from this statement that Japan had gone out of her way to impress upon Russia she was a defeated nation; but when one remembers the part Russia has played in keeping Japan out of her just rights in Korea, and that but for Russia's policy in the Far East Japan would never have had to go to war a second time about Korea, it seems expecting too much that Japan should abandon the ordinary methods of diplomacy merely to avoid hurting Russia's susceptibilities.

From Reuter's correspondent at Seoul we have some interesting details regarding the negotiations that led to the annexation. " It is," we are told, "stated that the Emperor Yi-Syek and ex-Emperor Yi Heni willingly gave their assent, and the only hesitation shown was when the titles of the former Emperor were discussed. The Japanese proposed the title of Grand Duke, but the Emperor insisted upon being styled 'whang' or king. To this the Japanese finally consented. It was also agreed that the Princes of the Imperial House should be treated as Japanese Princes, should receive an annuity of 750,000 dollars, and should be allowed to reside where they pleased. Some high Korean dignitaries are to be created Japanese Peers, and Koreans will also be appointed Privy Councillors and officials of the Provincial Administration when competent. According to the new Resident-General, the Koreans, under the annexation, will enjoy exactly the same rights in Korea as the Japanese. It is the wish and command of the Japanese Emperor that every effort shall be made to make the Koreans feel that there is no humiliation, but rather a relief, in annexation."

Everything, therefore, seems to have been done to make the annexation as easy as possible for the Korean Imperial House, and the outlook for the future of Korea appears much brighter than before. There is, however, one matter which greatly concerns the other Powers interested in Korea, and these include Great Britain, Germany and the United States of America. It is well known that the new Japanese commercial treaties impose heavy duties on all foreign manufactures that enter the Empire of Japan; should those same duties be imposed on all foreign manufactures entering Korea, there is little doubt that the ready acquiescence of foreign powers to the annexation would undergo an immediate change. The *Tageblatt* correctly diagnoses the position when it says " Japan has gained the object she has followed throughout decades of stiff-necked diplomacy and two victorious wars. It was worth much to Japan to consummate the annexation before the treaty with England expired. Other States, among them Germany, would only protest if Japan intended to close the open door in Korea." Whatever may be contemplated in the future, and I for one am not over sanguine about Japan's tariff assurances, it is understood that although the treaties with foreign Powers lapse with the annexation, the present Customs Tariff of Korea will be continued "for an indefinite period" under Japanese rule. I take it this understanding was communicated to the foreign Powers interested before their assent to the annexation was formally given, and I assume that in future all foreigners will enjoy the same rights in Korea as they do now in Japan. One matter, however, I have not seen noticed, that is the jurisdiction of the Consular Courts. Presumably these courts disappear with annexation, but something will have to be done to make their past decisions operative in the future.

On the whole I welcome the annexation, and it is certainly a feather in the cap of Japanese diplomacy that after so many rebuffs the Japanese government should have finally defeated all opposition and come out triumphant. Korea is absolutely necessary for Japan. She must have an outlet for her surplus population, and one may perhaps be permitted to hope, now that outlet has been secured, we may hear less of Japanese migration to the British Colonies.

THE EMPEROR FRANCIS JOSEPH

The occasion of the Emperor Francis Joseph's eightieth birth-day has been marked in Austria-Hungary with great rejoicing, and deservedly so. No monarch has served his country better than the Austrian Emperor has done, and no monarch has been called upon to decide more momentous issues within his own kingdom. Both in heart and mind this "Grand Old Man" of Europe has shown himself equal to all demands made on him, while his tact and sympathy have gained for him a place in the Concert of Europe such as no other sovereign has ever filled. The friendship between the aged Emperor and King Edward was an enduring friendship, and had our late Sovereign's life been spared he would undoubtedly have joined the family gathering at Ischl, which assembled the other day to do honour to the illustrious head of the Austro-Hungarian nation. But "the King is dead—long live the King!" and it is highly satis-factory to know that the friendship between the two Royal Houses will suffer no diminution.

"Some years ago," said Count Mensdorff, when proposing the toast of the "King and the Royal Family" at the dinner given by the Austro-Hungarian colony in London, "King George and Queen Mary visited the Emperor of Austria, and they were assured that the friendship which had lasted for so long a period between the monarchs of the two countries would be continued during the present reign." That such would be the case one felt certain, but the timely assurance of the Austrian Ambassador is none the less welcome. Very truly spoke Count Mensdorff when he said that the people of this country venerated the Emperor Francis Joseph because of their appreciation of what his Majesty had done to advance Austro-Hungarian interests during the last sixty-two years, and particularly because they perceived how powerful his influence had been in the interests of peace. We do not forget his kindliness during the South

African War, and we are pleased to remember the many occasions on which he has found himself in agreement with British foreign policy. That the two nations differed over the annexation of Bosnia and Herzegovina is well known, but it was more on account of the moment selected and the methods adopted than because of the actual annexation, which, in common with other great Powers, we knew to be inevitable. No other course was open to us than to raise the objections we did, even if those objections had not the ring of reality about them, and I, for one, am bound to say that the protest made by this country against the annexation of Bosnia and Herzegovina never seemed to me to be a genuine protest, and I do not think his Majesty's Government were altogether sorry when Germany happily came to the rescue and pulled the chestnuts out of the fire for all parties. Indeed, if it had not been for the timely intervention of Germany, things would certainly not have fallen out so smoothly as they did, and this country might have found herself involved in the hostilities that for some months threatened to open in the Near East. At the time I drew attention in these pages to the true inwardness of Germany's overtures to Russia, and pointed out that the Kaiser was rendering valuable service to the cause of peace by explaining to Russia the consequences that must follow any attempt on her part to disturb the *status quo*. It was a delicate matter and one that Germany alone could undertake, and in undertaking it she laid herself open to be misunderstood in many of the Chancelleries of Europe. That she was so misunderstood is an open secret, but the fact that the German Emperor, thinking only of preserving the peace of Europe, disregarded all other issues, is deserving of all praise.

A good story is told of the Emperor Francis Joseph by the *Times* correspondent at Vienna. It runs thus : " Of Galgotzy, a taciturn old soldier whose very name brings a glow of pleasure to the cheek of every Austro-Hungarian officer, a characteristic story is told. After the occupation of Bosnia-Herzegovina, Galgotzy was set to build a military road. Funds were short and the sum available for the purpose seemed hopelessly insufficient. By dint of hard work and ingenuity, Galgotzy succeeded, nevertheless, in performing his task, and thereupon reported: ' Road built ; 25,000 florins received, 25,000 florins spent ; remains nothing.—Galgotzy.' Dissatisfied with so summary an account, the audit officials applied for a detailed statement of expenditure. Galgotzy ignored the application, which was presently renewed in peremptory form. Impatient of red-tape he replied :—' Road built ; 25,000 florins received, 25,000 florins spent ; remains nothing. Whoever doubts it is an ass.' Shocked by such impropriety, a red-tapist-in-chief submitted Galgotzy's 'account' to the Emperor, who blandly inquired 'Do you then doubt it?'"

Indeed few men have more accurately gauged the character of Austria-Hungary's ruler than the *Times* correspondent at Vienna, and I take leave to reproduce from this writer's interesting appreciation of the Emperor the reference made to his humanity. "It is the human side of Francis Joseph's character—his humour, his goodness of heart, his simplicity—that call forth such rejoicings as those celebrated in Austria-Hungary. A monarch who, when told that his shooting trophies had taken first prize at the Sports Exhibition, slily asked the committee: 'Was there no "protection" about the award?'; who associated his Diamond Jubilee in 1908 with care for needy children; who lives without luxury, sleeps on a hard camp bed, rises early, and has ever an ear for a tale of misfortune or injustice, could scarcely fail so to impress his outward personality upon the minds of generation after generation of his subjects as to become in a sense a household god and joint possession of all. Of the lonely Imperial statesman in the study at the Hofburg, at Schönbrunn, or in the Villa at Ischl, where Ministers and generals come and go and sheaves of documents are daily examined, annotated and signed, the public at large knows little, and is unable to guess the Emperor's real policy or to discern how often his name is taken in vain to cloak bureaucratic indolence or intrigue. So noiseless is his life and so unobtrusively methodical his work that even important personages sometimes forget that his hand still firmly grasps the helm of State; but when storms arise and collisions threaten, they too awaken to the fact that of all Francis Joseph's cares and occupations the guardianship of international peace most constantly claims his thought. And it is his endeavour and achievement in this regard which non-Austrians especially requite with feelings of thankfulness." *

No wonder the Emperor is universally beloved by his own people and universally respected by all nationalities. He is a great man in the best and truest sense of the term; and the part he has played in assisting to preserve the peace of Europe cannot be too highly estimated. May his life be spared for many years to come.

ANGLO-GERMAN RELATIONS

The question of Anglo-German relations is always with us. Yet there was a time when no one troubled to discuss them. It was sufficient to know that the two Powers sprang from a common stock, believed in the same religion, and had similar

* See *Times*, August 8.

characteristics. As a matter of course they were the best of friends. To-day the relations between this country and Germany is a frequent and sometimes an acrimonious topic, and yet the facts recited above are the same as then. What has happened to bring about the change? The solution of the problem is not so difficult as at first sight it appears. In the days I refer to Germany was a comparatively poor country; she came to us for her manufactures as well as for her raw material, and often we acted as middlemen, selling to Germany the produce of more distant lands. All that is altered to-day. Germany is a rich country, manufactures for herself, deals direct and is getting fast hold of the markets of the world. And all honour to Germany for what she has done.

While we slept Germany was awake. While we played Germany worked. Compulsory service made not only soldiers but increased the physique of the nation. Technical education brought out ideas. Scientific tariffs did the rest. When we were talking of sending commercial agents to foreign countries and to our own colonies Germany had them there. While our merchants insisted on their old methods of packing and selling, Germany consulted the requirements of buyers. She packed her goods to suit the country of import. She manufactured to suit her clients and her agents looked after the rest. No one can find fault with Germany for doing what we ourselves should have done. It may be said, "But of late years we have done the same." I am not so sure of that; but in any case it is little use shutting the door after the horse is stolen. Germany is now our greatest commercial rival, if we set aside the United States, and, like all rivals, she does not always get accepted on her merits. Then came the naval question. Germany had acquired large interests in all lands; she became a colonising Power, and her possessions were scattered over all seas. Not unnaturally she began to build a strong navy. Germany must protect her commercial interests and her subjects, just as other nations; but this building of a strong navy raised awkward questions in a country whose policy was that its navy should be equal to that of any two other Powers, wherever they are or whatever they may be. It became necessary for Great Britain to build more battleships, and to build them faster. But all this cost money, and that meant further taxation. Here, then, we have in a nutshell the reasons why we hear so much to-day about Anglo-German relations.

The absurdity of discord between the two nations should be patent to all; but with certain cliques the German scare is used to serve any purpose that is uppermost. No thought is given to the evil effects of such base insinuations. Just as in party politics the most unscrupulous cries often obtain the widest hearing, so it is with the suggestion that Germany is trying to supplant us politically. But, like all counterfeit coin, the suggestion has no true ring, and I am glad to say that the scaremongers in both countries are being found out. Common-sense is once more prevailing, and it is now being generally recognised that, instead of railing at Germany for going one better than ourselves in the commercial world and striving all she can to build for herself a strong navy, our duty is to put our own house in order. What we have to do is to push Britain's commerce in all the neutral markets, to enter into a preferential arrangement with our colonies, so as to secure a larger portion of their markets, to institute a scientific tariff, in order to give our own workmen a chance of employing their labour and our manufacturers a chance of selling their goods in foreign markets, and, above and beyond all, to make our own navy so strong and so efficient that by no remote possibility could we suffer defeat on the seas by any combination that may be brought against us.

Quite recently the Prime Minister has told us that our relations with Germany are of the most friendly kind. The Foreign Secretary gives us the same assurance. In these circumstances I do not think we need pay much attention to the voices of the would-be alarmists. All that is necessary is for the two nations to try and understand each other better. Our German friends should endeavour to see more of this country and we should see more of their country. The more we know of one another the more we are likely to appreciate and sympathise with each other's ambitions. That is one reason why I rejoice to see the visits of British working-men to Germany. I do not care whether they go over at the expense of the Tariff Reform League or the Free Trade Union. Once bring the working men of the two countries together and war scares will soon become a dead letter. If the black bread scandal has done harm in some quarters it has materially assisted towards a better understanding between the working classes of the two nations. Nothing a working man dislikes more than being deceived, and every labour party that has visited Germany has returned, if not converted to Tariff Reform, at any rate with his eyes opened to the fact that the black bread cry so recklessly used by the Chancellor of the Exchequer and Radicals generally at the last general election for their own party purposes, is as false as was the cry of the yellow slaves in chains. Indirectly this may be a good thing for the party to which I belong; but, glad as I am that my party should profit, I am far more concerned that the result of the evil doing has led to a truer knowledge of working class conditions in

Germany, and a truer knowledge of the feelings entertained by the people of Germany for the people of this country.

Similarly with the visit of the burgomasters to England and that of our municipal authorities to Germany and many more visits of a like character. Just now a number of German students, accompanied by several professors, are, I hear, sojourning in our midst to take note of our educational system. This is as it should be. All this forgathering is of incalculable benefit to the peoples of both countries. It opens the eyes of the German people as well as the eyes of the British people. An ounce of fact is worth a ton of argument. Our visitors go back to Germany and tell their German friends what they see and hear, and the British visitors to Germany do the same. In this way the real feeling of the two countries becomes known, and, as every true Briton and every true German is aware, the feeling of the two peoples for one another is one of the greatest kindliness and the highest esteem.

As we go to press, an announcement is made of a gift by Sir Ernest Cassel designed to benefit Germans in this country and Britons in Germany who find themselves in distressed circumstances. Regarding the particulars we are somewhat in the dark, but that a German by birth, resident in England, should have conceived a scheme of this character as a memorial to King Edward, who, of all people, was ever anxious to see not only friendly but cordial relations between this country and Germany, indicates that the matter uppermost in the minds of thoughtful men is to do all in their power to restore the old feeling of amity and goodwill that of late has suffered from a mistaken idea of the aims and objects of both countries.

EDWARD DICEY.

OVER-GOVERNMENT IN AUSTRALIA

POLITICIANS AND PAYMENT OF MEMBERS

By F. A. W. GISBORNE

(Our Special Correspondent in Australia)

APPEARANCES point to an early aggressive movement on the part of the promoters of unification in the Commonwealth of Australia. So far, efforts in that direction have been persistent, but indirect and insidious. The direct assault is soon likely to supersede the flank movement. The present Labour Government is undoubtedly unificationist as a whole, though the ranks of the party include a considerable number of dissentients. The iron discipline of the Caucus, however, bestows absolute authority on a bare majority, and it may safely be affirmed that the majority of the present Parliamentary Labour Party favours the practical nullifying of existing State Rights.

The Federal Parliament is endowed with formidable powers. It can tax the people as it pleases, and the graduated Land Tax shortly to be imposed is a proof that the present Ministry is inclined to consider little moral restraints when it can hope to derive benefit by the exercise of its legal rights. The measure referred to must tend to bring on the States financial embarrassment, and the approaching issue of a Commonwealth paper currency, apart from its general effects on business transactions, will appreciably accentuate that embarrassment. Moreover, a fresh referendum is soon to be taken, with a view to the establishment of a Federal industrial autocracy. All these encroachments, and more likely to follow, tend to create a general feeling of uneasiness among those who uphold the constitutional rights of the State Governments, and among property-owners in general, who lean to a great extent on the various State Councils for protection against attacks on their interests. Before the crisis of the struggle is reached a brief analysis of the questions involved, and of the respective arguments of the contending parties, unificationists and anti-unificationists, may be attempted.

The case for unification may first be stated. No candid person can deny that it is a strong one. It would, in fact, be absolutely convincing, were it not for some unfortunate circumstances that will be explained later. That the machinery of government in Australia to-day is excessive, cumbrous and inordinately costly practically every one admits. So great is the friction that the power actually exercised is but a minute fraction of that generated ; so vast the multitude of counsellors that wisdom is drowned amid the clamour of tongues. Half a dozen skilled English or Anglo-Indian administrators, if invested with full powers, could manage the public affairs of Australia infinitely better, and at infinitely less cost, than they are now managed by the politicians that come and go on the political stage. But there is an unfortunate element of truth in a saying, expressive of the very quintessence of opportunism, ascribed to the late Sir Henry Campbell-Bannerman. The average Australian at least believes that good government is no substitute for government by the people. True, the attractive phrase " government by the people ' is always misleading. It simply implies that a dominant party, or faction, governs in the people's name, and frequently at the people's expense. But the very charm of the expression quite overpowers the fallacy it embodies. A wiser man than the late Prime Minister of the Motherland, in his defence before the Athenian dicastery, had the courage to utter a truth which, in a modified form, is as applicable to modern as well as to ancient popular governments. " Let not the truth offend you . . . but wherever the people is sovereign, no man who shall dare honestly to oppose injustice, frequent and extravagant injustice, can avoid destruction." A modern Socrates would, indeed, escape the hemlock, but he would scarcely become a popular idol ; and any hopes he might entertain of winning political distinction would certainly be disappointed.

The unwieldiness and cost of Parliamentary government in Australia to-day may be illustrated by the quotation of a few facts and figures borrowed from the last Commonwealth Year Book. These do not include the ordinary administrative charges, which together with pensions and various allowance, amount to a considerable additional sum each year. Including the Federal Parliament, the various legislatures embrace a body of no less than 670 members, a number exactly equal to that of the members of the House of Commons. Of these, 241 belong to the Senate and the State Councils ; the remainder to the various Lower Chambers. There are seven independent, or semi-independent legislatures in the continent, with fifty-four executive Ministers, all drawing high salaries. In addition, as symbols of the Imperial connection, there are six Governors and a Governor-General with their respective staffs. To accommodate all these legislators and dignitaries, and the multitudinous functionaries connected with the various departments, numerous superb public buildings have to be maintained.

In regard to cost, the total annual expenditure involved in the maintenance of the establishments of the Governor-General and the State Governors, including salaries, amounts approximately to £50,000. No patriotic Briton would grudge this tribute to the sentiment of Imperial citizenship, setting aside the very substantial benefits derived from the influence and counsels of statesmen of wide experience, mature judgment and absolute impartiality. The colonial Governor, like the Sovereign at home, is the umpire or referee in the rather squalid strife of parties; his office is honoured, and his services valued, by all that is respectable in Australian public opinion. But, so far as Parliaments are concerned, there is practical unanimity in considering these both unnecessarily large and unnecessarily expensive. For the privilege of maintaining a larger proportionate number of legislators than any other civilised country in the world—nearly one to each 6,700 of the population—Australia, with the important exception of New South Wales, after deducting the sum of £52,964 furnished towards the support of the Governor-General and the six Governors with their respective staffs, pays the handsome yearly amount of £387,305. The figures for New South Wales, whose Parliament contains no fewer than 146 members, 90 of whom receive £300 a year a-piece, are not yet obtainable; and if these were included the total cost of maintaining the Australian Parliaments alone would come to about £450,000. Including all expenses connected with the establishments of the Governor-General and the Governors the total cost of Parliamentary government in the Commonwealth must certainly now exceed £500,000 each year. A heavy bill for a population still under four and a half millions to meet.

The Federal Parliament is naturally the most expensive luxury. Its 111 members, each enjoying the substantial yearly stipend of £600, and already hungering for more, claim no less than £154,936 of the sum above mentioned, various costly extras included. In the States the dignity, or avarice, of politicians is more easily satisfied. Members of the Lower Chambers in New South Wales, Victoria and Queensland receive £300 apiece, those of South Australia and West Australia £200, and of Tasmania £100. The very capable members of the Councils in New South Wales, Victoria and Queensland serve gratuitously; and the examples of these and other similar bodies seem to justify the reflection that Australia, like other countries, is irrational enough to pay highly for a rather indifferent political article when she could get the best for nothing. Her responsible ministers, too, might remember that the President of the Swiss Confederation with its twenty-two Sovereign States receives a yearly salary of but £540; while his six colleagues in the Federal Council receive but £480 apiece, each of these high officials, moreover, being required to renounce all private business and to devote his whole time and abilities to the service of the public. There seems no good reason why the members of the Commonwealth Government in Australia should receive nearly four times as large an annual amount as the responsible rulers of the Swiss Republic.

But, large as is the sum the Australian taxpayer is called on to find to reward the multitude of law-makers (who, certainly, to do them justice, strive their utmost to give him, in quantity, full value for his money), there are besides considerable additions. Royal Commissions, for instance, are numerous and costly. By rather a sad irony the men who have helped to pass very bad laws are afterwards remunerated for seeking remedies for the evils they have themselves caused. The system would be a very convenient one, say, to tailors. The customer whose coat was outrageously tight might enjoy the privilege of paying for the necessary alterations, in addition to the initial cost of the garment, with a certain amount of temporary inconvenience thrown in. The Parliamentary picnic, too, has become quite an established institution, and the indulgent taxpayer is beginning to regard it as scarcely worthy even of a jest. Excursion parties of legislators are continually wandering about the continent in search of information. Not very long ago a contingent of Federal legislators visited Port Darwin; the sugar-growing districts of N. Queensland were inspected on another occasion; and quite a number of luxurious exploring expeditions have been made by hardy Parliamentary pioneers in search of a site for the future federal capital. These jaunts, of course, are paid for by the country. Whenever a protest is raised they are indignantly defended as " educative." The taxpayer might retort that, since he pays liberally men who are supposed at least to have qualified themselves beforehand for the work they voluntarily undertook, it is scarcely fair that he should have to pay for their education as well. The defence put foward, if allowed, would justify an apprentice to an engineer in claiming, not only wages at the full rate paid to a skilled workman, but additional allowances to enable him to make extensive foreign tours, and to attend classes at a technical school.

The fact that the practice of bestowing substantial emoluments, both direct and indirect, on legislators has tended, in Australia at least, to the inordinate increase of their number, as well as to a plethora of ill-considered legislation, is beyond dispute. The present system is a naked appeal to cupidity rather than

patriotism.   It substitutes sordid for honourable motives, and in
a large degree excludes from public life men of independent means
and minds, actuated solely by the sentiment of honourable ambition.   On the other hand, it invites needy adventurers of all
kinds to enter the political arena, and substitutes quantity of
both laws and law-makers for quality.   The generalisation,
indeed, is justified, after a survey of the proceedings of the
principal popularly-elected legislative bodies in the world to-day,
that the ability and dignity displayed by them are usually in
inverse ratio to the pecuniary rewards bestowed on their
respective members.   Thus, in the United States, members of
Congress receive £1000 annually, and those of the French
Chamber of Deputies £600, with, in the latter case, prospective
pensions to boot.   Neither body at the present time excels either
in wisdom, independence, or freedom from corrupt influences.
Neither, moreover, offers to the world a model of decorum or of
manners.   At the other extreme, the unpaid members of the
British Parliament have hitherto—excepting the political em-
ployées of Mr. Patrick Ford and the militant trade-unionist—
been distinguished, with but few exceptions, by the essential
qualities befitting both the legislator and the gentleman.   The
very efficient members of the German Reichstag receive but
£150 annually, subject to fines for non-attendance, and their
legislative brethren in Switzerland, Norway and Denmark, are
paid only a meagre 16s. 8d., 14s. 7d., and 13s. per sitting,
respectively.

Of course, in Australia as elsewhere, much is said in denunciation of the iniquity of depriving the people of the services of able
men who cannot afford to serve their country gratuitously.   The
argument, by the way, is much more commonly heard among
professional politicians than among electors.   It may be replied
that indigent ability is more hurtful even than honest mediocrity
when applied to the conduct of State affairs, for it is usually
accompanied by moral weakness and a lack of a sense of
responsibility.   The man of natural talents who fails within a
reasonable period to win for himself a modest competence,
in the great majority of cases will be found to be lacking
in application, vicious or extravagant.   Neither indolence nor
wastefulness fits a man for undertaking high and important
duties, no matter what his natural talents may be.   As a general
rule, he only can be safely entrusted with a share in managing
the affairs of others who has proved his ability to manage his
own with success.   Poverty, too, subjects men to temptations
against which those whose positions are assured are comparatively
immune.   And, most important of all, the sense of independence
and of responsibility is far stronger in the legislator whose living

does not depend on the successful capture of votes, than in him to whom politics are a livelihood.

The hireling legislator fails to win popular respect. He is regarded as a servant paid to obey the capricious orders of his master, the mob, under peril of ignominious discharge. Consequently, to do what is temporarily popular, rather than what is wise, becomes the golden rule of the successful politician. Whenever Demos, in a paroxysm of fury, throws himself on his back and kicks and bellows, his political nurses rush to him and fill his mouth with sugar plums stolen from his elder brother's pocket. He may be ill afterwards, that matters little, his rage is appeased for the time. An absolute lack of political independence is the curse of Australia to-day, and it is to be attributed mainly to the two-fold evil of universal suffrage and payment of members. By their operation the most important and vital interests of the country, those connected with the soil, enjoy no effective representation, either in the Federal Parliament or the Lower Chambers of the State Legislatures; and the class of legislators that was the glory and salvation of Great Britain in the perilous years immediately following the dawn of the last century, has been almost entirely expelled from the deliberative assemblies of the Australian continent.

That the causes briefly traced have induced political deterioration, as well as enhanced prodigiously the ordinary expenses of government in the Commonwealth, is undeniable. Fortunately, so far, the atmosphere, though dusty, has been pure. But when, as in the United States to-day, the squalid evils that beset all absolute democracies shall display themselves—when the struggle between the demagogue and the plutocrat, the man who bribes with promises of other people's money, and the man who bribes with his own, shall begin—Australia may have reason to lament the absence from her councils of men who, under existing conditions, have to submit to political ostracism.

The subject of payment of members of Parliament has been treated at some length, because it bears strongly on the question of Australian unification. By paying legislators, as before said, encouragement is directly offered to the increase of their number, and the multiplication of law-makers is followed by a corresponding multiplication of laws. The administration of the latter necessarily entails the appointment of large numbers of salaried officials. France with her 800,000 "fonctionnaires" should serve as a warning to the Australian public of the dangers of legislative excess. The establishment of a parasitic bureaucracy in any country is fatal both to freedom and economy, and already the number of quite unnecessary offices created, and restrictions imposed on the commercial and industrial classes in the continent, is arousing much discontent. "Commerce is like a timid maiden," said Peter the Great more than two centuries ago, "who is scared by rough usage, and must be won by gentle means." The results of well-meaning but ignorant legislative interference with trade operations in the Commonwealth of late years testify to the truth of the remark. Reference has been made in a previous article in this Review (April 1910) to the multitude of industrial measures now operative in Australia, and still the number tends to increase in deference to the demands of the insatiable trade union leaders.

Pas trop gouverner is a wholesome maxim to be observed by legislators. Too few laws are always better than too many. Of course the many experimental measures now in force in Australia, or projected, are well meant. They represent the aspirations of zealous, but frequently rather youthful and inexperienced legislators who reach the haven of Parliament after the storm of each successive general election. The energetic Parliamentary novice is a source of terror to the sober citizen—indeed, general elections, alike in State and Commonwealth, with the violent changes of policy that frequently follow, attended by a virulent epidemic of legislation, are becoming most serious public inflictions. What is sport to the politician is death to the tranquillity of the country. A healthy man has reason to complain if he be forcibly dosed with nauseous medicines at brief intervals to cure him of entirely imaginary maladies.

The ambiguity and confusion that distinguish the land legislation of New South Wales, for instance, was pointedly commented on by the then Acting Chief Justice, Sir George Simpson, not long ago. "Somebody really should be appointed," the learned judge remarked in the course of proceedings before the State Full Court in connection with a land dispute, "to look thoroughly into these Acts of Parliament, to examine a Bill before it is introduced and watch it during its course in both Houses, so that in the end this perpetual conflict as to what the Legislature means might be avoided. It is becoming a most fearful tax upon the public." He proceeded to recommend the appointment of a revising body similar to the Parliamentary Revision Committee in England to examine and check all legislation with a view to the removal of obscurities. The ambiguous and sometimes contradictory provisions contained in the various industrial enactments particularly have provided judges and counsel with an unending succession of legal conundrums of the most intricate kind, while the aggregate bill of costs unfortunate suitors have had to pay for these intellectual exercises promises soon to equal the value of a Dreadnought.

All this confusion points to two conclusions. Australian

legislators are both too numerous and too inexperienced for the satisfactory discharge of their duties. In democracies at ordinary times the rule is that force of character rather than real intellectual and moral superiority gains the supremacy; the energy of well-meaning ignorance carries all before it. This is peculiarly the case with Australia at the present time. Judgment has to yield to prejudice, and the claims of common fairness are too often overlooked in the desire to attain some impossible end. Sincerity, after all, is but a poor substitute for experience and wisdom—in politics it is often a dangerous virtue. The man who rides a political hobby requires delicate handling. He is quite incorrigible when his hobby rides him.

The friction, confusion and exorbitant cost of government in Australia to-day would make the case for unification within reasonable limits irresistible were it possible for the educated and property-owning classes in the Commonwealth to hold perfect confidence in the Federal Legislature. But unfortunately the rather sorry record of the latter body since its first establishment has not inspired the necessary confidence. Over-government, the anti-unificationist contends, is at least better than misgovernment. Too many cooks, even of very moderate talents, are better than one who persists in spilling the fat into the fire, and continually threatens a disastrous conflagration. By common consent the public departments transferred by the States to the Commonwealth have been consistently mismanaged since Federation took place, and expenses have been enormously augmented. Political union was advocated and achieved principally in order that a homogeneous and effective Defence Force should be created. After ten years no such force yet exists. The postal service is hopelessly disorganised, and grave complaints are constantly brought against the Customs department. Worse still, not a penny has yet been paid, either in the way of purchase-money or rent, by the Federal Government for the numerous and costly public buildings taken over from the State Governments; and the clear provisions of the Constitution have in this as other respects been cynically disregarded. Seeing that many of these buildings were originally built with borrowed money on which the State taxpayers have to pay interest the injustice as well as impolicy of this neglect cannot be excused. While exceedingly generous to themselves the members of the Commonwealth Parliament have hitherto forgotten to be just to the States, or faithful to their Constitutional obligations. Here lies the real and—at present—insuperable obstacle to unification. Legislative bodies that do not exercise wisely and justly what powers they have cannot expect to be endowed with yet wider powers.

To remedy existing evils, and to establish the confidence that

is essential to the enlargement of the Federal authority certain
reforms are eminently desirable. If a rational limitation of the
franchise on which both Chambers of the Commonwealth Parliament are now elected by virtue of the Constitution must be
regarded, for the present at all events, as outside the pale of
practical politics, a considerable improvement both in the quality
and the representative character of their members might be
effected by the introduction of the system of proportional voting.
The pernicious "ticket" evil would then be destroyed, and the
body of representatives returned at each election would at least
be a faithful reflex of the mass of public opinion.* If the property
qualification, whose essential virtues lie in its insistence on a
sense of responsibility both in the voter and in the candidate,
be regarded as obsolete, it were surely consistent with the
orthodox canons of democracy that certain restrictions as to age
should be imposed on all classes alike. Youth, as a rule, is too
hasty ; age too cautious. Might not the privilege of the franchise
only be conferred on such citizens as were not less than, say,
twenty-five, nor more than sixty-five years of age? Moderation
and judgment would then have at least a better chance than
recklessness and prejudice to sway the national policy. Youth,
after all, is more at home in the football field than in the council
chamber.

Most certainly the present ridiculous latitude allowed to
candidates for the Commonwealth Senate should be restricted.
It is not too much to say that at present any man qualified by
residence may stand either for that body or its companion
Chamber who is old enough to defy his parents, educated
enough to write his own name, and moral enough to keep
out of gaol. The age of eligibility for the Senate should
at least be raised to thirty—better, with an unlimited franchise,
to thirty-five. And, if the suggestion be not too audacious,
seeing that doctors, lawyers, chemists, engineers, and other professional men have to pass severe educational tests before they
are allowed to practise, while skilled handicraftsmen serve also
varying periods of apprenticeship, may it not be hinted that even
aspirants for positions that convey power, not merely over the
interests of individuals, but over the interests and very lives of
nations, should afford some evidences of their competency for
such exalted functions before being endowed with them? To
be able to talk fluent nonsense from a public platform, to win

---

* Mr. Deakin recently pointed out in a speech delivered shortly after the first
meeting of the new Parliament that at the late General Election 18 Labour
senators were elected by 671,000 votes, while 662,000 Liberal votes didn't return
a single senator. Similar anomalies occurred in the elections for the House of
Representatives.

the votes of many idle Pauls by promising to rob industrious Peter for their benefit, to hold out fallacious hopes, and to appeal to the human weakness denounced by the tenth commandment, these may be the accomplishments of the successful politician, but they lie wholly outside the art of the statesman.

It is statesmen that Australia is in sore need of to-day. She has multitudes of able men, but she has not yet produced a really great man. His time will yet come. When a credulous and long-suffering patient finds himself reduced to death's door under the ministrations of costly quacks, he usually seeks in the end the services of the skilled physician. When the adversity which neither man nor nation on this troubled orb can hope entirely to escape shall overtake Australia, and her safety depend, perhaps, on her ready brain and on her strong right arm, history justifies the hope that the true leader, whether Pitt or Washington, Napoleon or Bismarck, will appear. The storm will awake the captain, under whom the riotous crew will be brought to due obedience and to well-directed, resolute action, for the common weal. To such a man Australia may yet owe deliverance, lasting union, and the blessings of good government. Possibly, to him also, the Empire may be indebted for the completion of the crowning work of Imperial unification.

F. A. W. GISBORNE.

TASMANIA, *July* 12.

THE TYRANNY OF HERTZOGISM

By A SOUTH AFRICAN

In his reiterated appeals for co-operation, General Botha has expressed the opinion that "if there was one question which should be kept outside the domain of party politics, it was education," and he has also deplored the Separatist School movement. Mr. Burton, a member of General Botha's Cabinet, told a Venterstad audience that he was as tired of the word Hertzogism as he had been of the word Krugerism. The *Cape Times* replied that "it is not the word, but the thing, which is nauseous and nauseating, and Mr. Burton may depend upon it that South Africa will not agree to drop the word until the thing is as definitely abandoned as the various objectionable things once indicated by the term Krugerism. The Minister for Native Affairs may doubt, if he chooses, 'whether the man in the street knows what Hertzogism really means,' but the men in the streets of Harrismith, Ficksburg, and Bloemfontein, who are pushing on with the establishment of separate schools, largely from money contributed from their own pockets, show that such a doubt is extremely foolish." The tyrannical educational policy of the party in power in the Free State amply justified the institution of separate schools. General Hertzog's policy has aroused racial animosity, retarded education, and robbed the Free State of valued and efficient public servants. Referring to the dismissed inspectors, Mr. Gunn very truly remarks: "For its flagrant injustice, for the irregularity of the procedure, for the flimsiness of the accusations and of the so-called evidence, and for some other astounding circumstances connected with it, the action of the Government of the Orange River Colony must stand without a parallel in the history of British administration."

General Botha's conciliatory speeches have been cancelled by his deeds in the constitution of his Cabinet, and the South African electors who desire to carry out the Act of Union in the spirit of the Convention, can no longer feel the confidence with which they welcomed the Premier's appointment, because fine words butter no parsnips to parents who are anxious for their children's welfare, and who deplore the increasing racial estrangement consequent on the Hertzog Act. As the Johannesburg *Leader* justly pointed out: "The minority in the Free State is being oppressed through the efforts of a gentleman whom General Botha has taken into his Cabinet, and for whom he is responsible. Self-respecting South Africans will not tolerate this, and until the wrong is righted there can be no peace in the country. We do not doubt General Botha's words are good. Let us have the action without which they are so much rigmarole." Mr. Frazer, one of the inspectors dismissed by the late Government, has been engaged by the Free State Council of Education to organise the new system of separatist schools. He condemns the Hertzog School Act as "a system which has put an end to true educational progress, and produces at its best confusion of thought and speech," and declares the Hertzog Acts to be anti-British in conception and practice.

The fair and liberal spirit of the Council governing the separatist movement is shown in the following statement of policy, for parents in every way are given a wide option.

1. The schools established and controlled by the Free State Council of Education shall be called the Council Schools of the Orange Free State, and all pupils attending such schools shall be instructed in accordance with the principles set forth in the language clause of the Act of Union.

2. *Curriculum.*—The subjects and the course of instruction in the Council schools shall be those generally indicated in the Transvaal Code of 1909.

3. *English and Dutch as languages in every Council school.*—Both English and Dutch shall be taught as languages to all pupils in attendance, unless their parents request exemption from the instruction in either language.

4. *English and Dutch as medium of instruction.*—(1) The medium of instruction in the sub-standards of the Council schools shall be the home language of the child, and if the parents so desire the other language shall be gradually introduced as a medium; (2) above the sub-standards the medium shall be English or Dutch, as the parents may decide, but every pupil shall throughout his school course be instructed in all subjects, save the second language, through the medium of one language.

5. *The general qualifications of teachers.*—All efficient teachers, unilingual and bilingual, shall be eligible irrespective of race or nationality for all suitable appointments in the Council schools.

Commenting on the captain and crew of the Nationalist Ministry, with special reference to educational policy, the *Cape Times* fairly sums up the situation, daily evidenced in the election campaign, as follows :—" General Botha implores the originators of the movement for separate schools in the Free State to stay their hand in the interests of what he calls 'co-operation'; but these people are convinced that at the end of five years, with Hertzogism unvetoed and even unchecked (as the Prime Minister says is inevitable) by the Union Parliament, there will scarcely be an English teacher left in the Free State. How can the

Prime Minister expect parents who will suffer from this sort of thing to be consoled by the reflection that they are 'co-operating'? Then, again, General Botha forgets that others remember what General Hertzog has publicly said. The suggestion now is to let things alone in the Free State. That the policy is bad, the Prime Minister admits: but in five years' time all will be well. Unfortunately we have General Hertzog's deliberate statement that he and his fellow-apostles of State-compulsion in bilingualism are determined that their policy shall not only triumph in the Free State, but be extended to every province in South Africa. It is quite natural that the Prime Minister should be anxious, with the general elections at hand, to let such an utterance pass into oblivion: but it is absurd to suggest that the Unionists are attempting to use education for merely electioneering purposes simply because they refuse to help General Botha to electioneer. The Ministerialists have themselves to blame if they are damaged by publicity and quotations from their own utterances. General Hertzog and the fanatics have not publicly recanted, neither have they shown the smallest sign that their intentions have changed. All we have is a statement that the Prime Minister's policy is not that of the Free State: that he speaks for the Cabinet: but that the Cabinet are quite helpless in the matter. Surely the position is clearly one where the safest course for all who disapprove of Hertzogism, is to return to the Union Parliament an opposition which will not be so easily satisfied that the resources of Constitutionalism are exhausted."

All persons interested in the progress of education in South Africa, especially in Cape Colony, and its general prospect under Union, will find food for reflection in the admirable Presidential address delivered by Mr. Anders, a leading head-master, before the South African Teachers' Association at Mossel Bay.* He remarked that it was open to serious doubt whether the Orange River Colony (Free State) interpretation of Section 137 of the Act of Union was in harmony with what the Convention intended it to be, adding that he would probably have ignored the Orange River Colony trouble were it not for the fact that the "Unie" "applauds the Hertzog Acts and plaintively asks when Cape Colony is to share in such unmitigated blessings."

Mr. Anders referred to Mr. Hugh Gunn's comment in his last report: "For the effective working of the dual medium it is, of course, essential that the schools should be provided with capable bilingual teachers, and at the present time the supply of such teachers is inadequate." A similar warning was quoted from the annual report of the Director of Education of the Transvaal, in

* June 21.

which the Inspector of the West Circuit writes: "In English I see no improvement, but many evidences of deterioration. Less time is now given to English . . . surprisingly few farm school teachers really are able to write correct questions upon the reading matter of the first, second, and third standard readers." After giving specimens of everyday errors, the inspector proceeds: "How can one expect great progress from the scholar? My constant experience is that ability to read English is no guarantee of ability to use it. And I am every day more firmly of opinion that the truly bilingual teacher is exceedingly rare. In my circuit I count them on the fingers of one hand. And the number of teachers who read for either pleasure and instruction is lamentably small."

The President of the Teachers' Association added: "It is safe to assert that what holds good in this respect in the Transvaal will hold good in many districts of Cape Colony. And what of the parent? My experience has taught me that our Dutch farmers are exceedingly anxious their children should be proficient in English; they know that their children must compete with those not of their own race, and very naturally they lay claim to every means by which they may be so equipped as to fight the battle for existence successfully. If, therefore, sound Dutch teaching is provided, and it must be provided, and the teacher is judicious as he should be, the difficulties will vanish of themselves."

Mr. Anders eulogised the late Professor Hofmeyr, and I can endorse every word of his tribute to the memory of that true educationist, a man of saintly character and the broadest sympathies. No English teacher was handicapped who worked in schools in any way directed by the beloved professor at Stellenbosch, who expressed his views thus : "I say, let those who believe there is a future before our Dutch language have a fair chance of helping it on, only let them do it in such a way as not to injure or irritate others." One more reference to the Presidential address: Mr. Anders pointed to the fact that thousands of pupils of non-Dutch parentage take up the study of Dutch voluntarily, and that would-be compulsion was impolitic. The other side of the story is not so pleasing when he continued : "The treatment English is receiving in certain educational centres gives rise to grave misgivings. Some advocates of a thorough knowledge of both languages strangely enough deprecate English being practised in conversation; English is looked upon as a sort of foreign language. What is the net result? Graduates whose command of the English language, and often of the Dutch language as well, fall short of what might reasonably be expected. It is not infrequent to find just the man weak at English proclaim the doctrine of equal rights the loudest. The cry is becoming louder day by day that English is deteriorating, and one need not go far for proofs. It is pitiable to see teachers, even graduates, stand before a class, struggling to get through a decent English sentence."

It was significant that, at the second session* of the South African Teachers' Association, the following message of greeting was received from Mr. F. S. Malan, Minister of Education : "I take a very keen and deep interest 'in the deliberations of your association. Although the administration of education, other than Higher Education, at present falls under the Provincial Council, I hope your association will promote the interests of the Union by fostering a healthy national spirit in connection with educational institutions of the Union.   I believe many educational difficulties of the Union can only be solved by teachers who are bilingual, national, and in sympathy with the character of the people." A member of the late Cape House of Assembly expressed the opinion that in South Africa " the future race was not going to be Dutch or English, but something differing from both, and the language would not be English, as spoken at present, but English modified by the introduction of Dutch, where the idiom was more expressive."   A cheerful prospect for those of us to whom the " Voices of our Fathers " speak eloquently in the priceless heritage of English literature, and who regard that heritage as one of the many good gifts to be handed on to children trained to receive it with understanding sympathy, and to cherish it with other privileges of Imperial citizenship.

The *Herald*, at Port Elizabeth, after pointing out that the British Free Staters had been compelled to make heavy sacrifices to provide new schools, since an impossible law had been imposed on them, concluded as follows : " The Prime Minister cannot allow himself to be treated as a cipher by the obstinate and misguided men who accepted office under him.   The Union Parliament has the power of the purse, and, were General Botha to intimate to the Free State authorities that, unless some common-sense was evidenced in the control of education, grants would be withheld, he would have very little further trouble in that quarter ; in fact, he has the power, if he has also the courage to use it, that will end a situation which is growing dangerous. "

According to the Hertzog Act the children in the Free State have to be taught in every subject through both the English and Dutch mediums by teachers who are at any rate supposed to be conversant with both languages.   Mr. Hugh Gunn, late Director of Education in the Orange River Colony, has pointed out that this practically prevents the appointment of British-born or uni-lingual teachers, " even at the request of the parents or the School

* June 22.

Committee, as the State, through its legislation, restricts their judgment and discretion as far as the linguistic qualifications of the staff are concerned." Mr. Gunn has further shown that the British-born teachers were thus discouraged and made to feel that " at best they were only tolerated by the Government." In his opinion " the only result of the policy could be to oust them gradually from the service, and to prevent their places being filled —even at the request of the communities—by candidates from Great Britain."

A specimen of South African bilingualism was given recently in the *Bloemfontein Post*. More than a nodding acquaintance with Cape Dutch is needed to recognise its shortcomings as an educational medium, but the pitiful absurdity of the "dual" lesson is sufficient to show readers that the protest against the reactionary and regrettable forces represented by the Hertzog extremists, is no mere party cry, but a struggle for justice and for the true welfare of all South African children.

SOUTH AFRICAN.

CANADA'S EXPERIMENTAL FARMS

THEIR WORK AND THEIR METHODS

By ELIZABETH WALMSLEY

FEW chapters in the history of Western Canada's development are of greater interest and of greater significance than those dealing with the Experimental Farms, established by the Dominion Government in the mutual interest of the land and her settlers, and with the men who have made these farms a recognised power in agriculture, in science, and in education.

The Dominion Department of Agriculture succeeded a provincial department of a similar nature, presided over by the Minister of Agriculture at Quebec. In the first session of the first Dominion Parliament, an Act was passed for the re-organisation of the Quebec department on a new and more efficient basis, and in 1886, a number of Experimental Farms were established throughout the country. To the five original farms at Ottawa (467 acres), Nappan (Nova Scotia, 300 acres), Brandon (Manitoba, 625 acres), Indian Head (Saskatchewan, 680 acres), and Agassiz, B.C. (300 acres), have been added those at Lethbridge, South Alberta (400 acres), and Lacombe, North Alberta (150 acres.) Each of the local farms is managed by a Superintendent, but the general control is exercised from the central farm at Ottawa, where are carried out the principal scientific investigations.

Canada also possesses many admirable Agricultural Colleges similar to those in this country. These colleges are situated at Truro (Nova Scotia), Guelph* (Ontario), at Ste. Anne de Bellevue, a little west of Montreal, and near Winnipeg (Manitoba), while it is expected that the Saskatchewan College will open its classes this autumn. But although these colleges play an important rôle in the educative system of Canada, they can hardly be regarded as an immediate part of that admirable machinery the Dominion has devised in its Experimental Farms for the vast business of turning its hundreds and thousands of

* These colleges are enterprises of the provincial governments.

immigrants, year by year, into successful farmers. The colleges provide the farms with superintendents, horticulturists, chemists, cerealists, botanists, entomologists, and the various departments of the Government with geographers, hydrographers, mineralogists, inspectors of fisheries, and similar officials, but it is the farms which metamorphose cobblers, soldiers, sailors, clerks, engineers, waiters, masons—all the rank and file of every trade and profession besides that of the land—into expert grain growers and scientific ranchers. The colleges supply the officers, and the farms the mass of that great army of men who have beaten their swords into ploughshares, and set about the conquest of the great North-west.

In Canada, farming in all its branches is looked upon not only as the first national concern, but as the great social force *par excellence* " for the humanising of the people, and the cultivating of a proper spirit of pride of race." It is to be hoped that England will arrest in time her gradual metamorphosis from an agricultural to a manufacturing country, lest the cry of " back to the land," which many people trust will point out the remedy for the innumerable social and economic evils that have grown up in the process, like a pestilential by-product, should become for her an anachronism. England had better forfeit her farm labourers to Canada if she cannot prevent their drifting into the cities, for the wage-earner over here has a fine chance, there, of dealing not with another man's land and crops all his life, but with his own. " Back to the land " should really be " emigrate." Millions of glorious acres are to be had practically for the asking in Canada, and Canada in providing for her own expansion has also provided for the wholesale regeneration of England's—of Europe's—pale-faced, city-worn, devitalised men and women and children. This indeed is the view taken by men in the Dominion who are not only agriculturists but humanitarians.

" Agriculture," said Dr. Robertson, Principal of the Macdonald College, Montreal, " is the greatest educational experience England's people have ever had for teaching citizenship, self-reliance, and every kind of adventurous courage." And what has been done in the Motherland can be done in Canada. England must, however, see to it that she sends over the right sort of raw material to manufacture into farmers, for success or failure in homesteading results less from any element of chance than from a man's own character. " It's the land *and* the man," as a Saskatchewan farmer observed when discussing an instance of failure, " and the first two years out here depend more upon the man than on the land . . . the land is no good to men who can't or won't work." Canada has made it sufficiently clear that while she will do all in her power to aid and teach and encourage good and likely settlers she will undertake no philanthropic

experiments.   Settlers throughout the country have the right
of access to the Government farms for assistance and counsel,
free of charge, and the large and constantly increasing demand
for literature, the rapidly extending correspondence, and the
readiness shown by the settlers everywhere to co-operate with
the work of the Experimental Farms furnish strong evidence of
a growing desire for expert information.

There is moreover another side to Dr. Robertson's view of the
value of agriculture as a means of citizen-making.   Canada is
confronted with the vast problem of how best to assimilate all
the heterogeneous elements of the tide of immigration flowing
in upon her.   What can a national flag mean to all those strange
Sclavic peoples who have no knowledge of its traditions, and
little conception of its meaning ?   What does the British flag
with the Canadian wreath in the corner signify to Galician and
Dukhoboor ?   What does Canada's national anthem, brand new
as it is, signify to the alien Chinaman, the subjugated Indian, the
homesick Italian and the triumphant Yankee ?   Empire Day and
Dominion Day stand for a good deal, but unity of interest, of
effort, of experience, stand for much more, and in agriculture is
to be found the solution of the riddle how to weld Canada's
population into one great people.   Here again all the thanks
will be due to the work of the Experimental Farms.

Canada's system of weed inspection often astonishes the
English farmer.   Perhaps it hardly matters, over here, if a
pocket handkerchief of a field, neatly hedged in by fences or the
white high road of the English countryside, gets infested with
mustard, but mustard spreading for hundreds of acres over the
great wheat floors of the prairie would be quite another matter.
Hence each Province in the West draws up a list of the weeds
which deserve to come under the heading of " noxious " for her
particular purposes, organises a small corps of " weed-inspectors,"
and keeps them driving about the country all the summer at $5
or $4 a day expatiating remedially on the subject to the various
farmers.   In the winter these inspectors, or field-agents, as they
are sometimes called, lecture in the various local centres to the
little groups of settlers belonging to this, that, or the other
agricultural association.   In this they follow up the lecturing
activities of the superintendents of the local Experimental Farms,
who are always more or less on the move in the interests of such
societies and meetings, organising seed fairs, cattle shows and
what not.   Judged by the principle that prevention is better than
cure, the work of these inspectors is invaluable.   They are in
close touch with the heads of their department, and the farms
behind them are busy devising all sorts of weed-destroyers in aid
of such farmers whose crops must be condemned.

"While the Noxious Weeds Act gives the inspector power to order the destruction of all or any part of a crop," so runs the field-agent's *vade mecum*, "you are to avoid if possible taking any arbitrary action which would be likely to create ill-feeling. You should rather make it clear to offenders against the Act that the object of enforcing it is to afford protection to them as well as to their neighbours, and that it is distinctly in the interest of every farmer to assist the inspector in his efforts to have the weeds kept under control. In all your dealings with the farmers it will be well to remember that although you are invested with certain powers, your duty is not so much judicial as educative." Together with these clear-sighted instructions Alberta—for one—supplies her weed inspectors with sheaves of bulletins for distribution, with a specimen case of the seeds of all the weeds upon which he is to wage relentless war, and with a splendid technical volume, well illustrated, called 'The Farm Weeds of Canada' calculated to rouse life-long interest in the young botany of the virgin prairies.

From the weeds alone one might write the history of the invasion of the West! The stinkweed, for instance, was introduced from Europe to Manitoba in the days of the fur trade; the Russian thistle first made its appearance in South Dakota in 1873, the seeds having been brought from Russia with flax seed. Through the agencies of the wind and the railroad and by importation of foul seed grain from infested areas it has now spread over a wide range and is found to a greater or lesser extent in the prairie provinces. Mr. Henderson, late Chief Inspector of Weeds in Alberta, told me last summer that this weed first made its appearance in Southern Alberta in 1894 along the line of the C.P.R., and that since then it has lost no time in combating the farmers' crops over wide acres for light and air and nourishment. Every weed has its own history and has scored it far and wide on the face of the land.

No less than twenty-one Annual Reports were written for the Minister of Agriculture by the late Dr. Fletcher, entomologist and botanist to the Dominion Experimental Farms, and these, says Dr. Saunders, "have been of great value to the farmers of Canada by instructing them how to recognise their (weed and) insect enemies, as well as their insect friends, and have at the same time instructed them as to the most practical measures to adopt for the destruction of the more injurious species." The Hessian fly, the Wheat-joint worm, the Cinch bug, the Grain aphis, the Clover seed midge, the Hop-flea beetle, the Apple leaf hopper, root maggots, moths, cankerworms, the Pear leaf blister Mite, and countless other insect pests have received much unwelcome attention at the hands of Dr. Fletcher and his successors, while such grain blights as "smut" and "rust" have also been diligently studied. Dr. Fletcher's bulletins on all these subjects form indeed an agricultural literature by themselves at once highly scientific and eminently practical.

Again the lengthy and carefully conducted experiments of the farms in horticulture, arboriculture, fruit-growing, bee-keeping, poultry-keeping, dairying, stock-raising, and dry-farming, are all undertaken with a view to advising settlers as to the best and most expeditious ways of utilising their sections and quarter sections. Free samples of high quality grain are distributed, either for the purposes of co-operative experiment, or to set the farmer on his legs again after some severe loss caused by frost or fire. The number of farmers who united with the farms in making observations on the cultivation of these samples in 1908 was no less than 38,748. "It is remarkable," says the Report, "how rapidly a supply of grain may be built up from a single four or five pound sample. Take for instance a sample of oats. The four pounds received will, if well cared for, usually produce from three to four bushels. This sown on two acres of land will at a very moderate estimate give one hundred bushels, and sometimes much more, but taking the lower figure as the basis for this calculation, the crop at the end of the second year would be sufficient to sow fifty acres, which at the same moderate computation would furnish 2,500 bushels available for seed or sale at the end of the third year." Granted, of course, that the seasons were good and propitious.

In arranging such a matter as a rotation of crops best suited to any given locality or requirements the farmer has only to send to the experimental farm nearest at hand, state particulars as to site and soil, and he will receive in return such-and-such a schedule exactly calculated to meet the case, a schedule which is the direct result of practical experiment. In arranging a rotation it is very necessary to have some knowledge of the food requirements of different crops, and to know something of the values of the residues from the different crops included. Certain forage crops need an abundance of nitrates, other crops need more phosphates, hence do well after some forage crop has taken up the super-abundance of free nitrates found after sod. It is evident therefore that a good rotation will include (1) meadow or pasture, (2) roots or corn, (3) some cereal crop. Farmers of course know this all the world over, but the Canadian immigrant is not necessarily a farmer, so the experimental farms, or experience and possibly years of failure have to tell him.

In view again of the vast importance of making the best possible use of barnyard manure it is difficult to estimate the value of just one item of information which an experimental farm might arrive at whereas the ordinary farmer has no facilities for discovering it. That fresh manure is equal ton for ton in crop-producing power to rotted manure (which experiments have shown to lose during the process of rotting about 60 per cent. of its weight) is a fact for which even farmers by profession may thank the experts for demonstrating.

Yet there are not lacking persons who will scoff at the yields on experimental farms. "Anyone," they say, "could do that with the Government behind them; the farm doesn't have to pay its way." Such critics forget, as *The Edmonton Daily Bulletin* has pointed out, that men don't get the care of such farms until they have made good on other farms, and if they did they could not hold the job two years, for no amount of money without brains and skill to direct it can make two bushels of wheat grow where most men grow but one, or make Scotch firs succeed where wolf willow is the natural growth.

These men who have graduated in the school of hard work and self-help for this larger sphere of usefulness in the development of the West, are men Canada may well be proud of. Take for instance, Mr. Angus Mackay, Superintendent of the Experimental Farm at Indian Head, Saskatchewan, who is a Canadian of Scotch descent. He farmed in Saskatchewan for some years before he was asked to occupy his present responsible post, and was practically the discoverer of the secret of successful wheat-growing on the illimitable plains of that province. To the initiate the word "dry-farming" will explain the secret. Then there is Mr. Bedford, until recently Superintendent of the Farm at Brandon, Manitoba, who has been called "the uncrowned king of agriculture."

"He farms as to the manner born, and one readily believes that any wilderness would blossom as the rose under the spell of his almost uncanny knowledge of plant life. Ignorance of agriculture will never be laid at Mr. Bedford's door, for he comes of generations of Kent and Sussex farmers, emigrated to Ontario when twelve years of age, and later homesteaded in the Darlingford district, Southern Manitoba, in 1877, when the railroad was yet 350 miles from Winnipeg. The character of the man, his passion for good farming, and his knowledge of the essentials of success in his business, are well illustrated in the manner of his securing the first seed for his homestead.

"One day he informed his neighbours that he was going away to locate some good seed grain. 'When will you be back?' they asked. 'I don't know; it depends on how soon I find seed to suit me,' was the reply. One could readily excuse a young homesteader a hundred miles from a large town if his standards in this matter were not very high and he took almost any seed he could get, assuring himself that he would clean it well and hand-pick the growing crop. Such a man was not young Bedford. He walked eighty miles from farm to farm and stopping-place to stopping-place before he returned from his historic seed hunt, but he had located pure seed of high quality and bought 130 bushels of it. As a result of his tramp and subsequent skill in handling the product, while other men were laboriously hauling their crop to Emerson, sixty-five miles distant, the nearest market, Mr. Bedford was able to sell his entire crop year after year for seed purposes, and have men pay higher prices for his grain right in his own yard than he could have obtained had he teamed it to Emerson! His first crop of oats yielded eighty-four bushels to the acre and fetched—literally fetched—for farmers came and hauled then away—seventy-five cents a bushel! The only load of grain he ever hauled to Emerson was wheat, and the price obtained after drawing it sixty-five miles was sixty-five cents!

"This was the man to whom the superintendency of the new experimental farm at Brandon, comprising some 700 acres, was offered in 1887 without any seeking on his part, and certainly the men at Ottawa responsible for the manning of the farms were well advised and very fortunate when they secured two such men as Angus Mackay and Spencer A. Bedford to inaugurate this new and important work in the West. During the last year of Mr. Bedford's superintendency he estimated that no fewer than eighteen thousand farmers and others visited the farm, and three thousand letters were dispatched, besides many hundreds of circulars. From these figures and the fact that the farm superintendents address from twelve to twenty gatherings each year, some idea of the amount of information disseminated annually from such stations may be obtained."

Mr. James Murray, who has now succeeded Mr. Bedford at Brandon, is a "Canadian born" from Ontario. He was trained at the Guelph Agricultural College, and "has been a government official since the day he left it, being first with the Dominion Government in the east engaged in seed testing work, and later in charge of the work of the seed branch in the entire west, which work involved the introduction of such new and now successful methods of spreading the gospel of good seed as grain field competitions, seed fairs, and the work of the Canadian Seed Growers' Association. While in this work Mr. Murray attracted the notice of the new Saskatchewan Government, and in the spring of 1906 entered its service as superintendent of the newly-formed Department of Fairs and Institutes. In the following spring he returned to his old love and re-entered the service of the Dominion Government as superintendent of the Brandon farm. Thus Mr. Murray has started a series of experiments in fattening steers in the open air during the winter months, whereby it is hoped to prove conclusively that elaborate and expensive buildings are not at all essential or even necessary to profitable steer-feeding even with such winters as the West enjoys.   The growing of fodder corn for ensilage and of alfalfa for stock-feeding and the rebuilding of worn out soils are other lines which, as in the past, are also receiving much attention."*

Again, Mr. Fairfield at Lethbridge, and Mr. Hutton, B.S.A., at Lacombe, both College men, are doing magnificent work at their posts at the head of Alberta's farmers.

It would be unfair, of course, in any general estimate of the agriculturally educative forces at work in Canada to omit the influence of the agricultural journals, but numberless as they seem to be, there is nothing to distinguish them from similar journals in other countries.   They are eminently practical and useful, but they do not mean for Canadian immigrants what the Experimental Farms mean, nor can it be said that the work they do has a tithe of the national and ethical value of that so ably carried on under the direction of Dr. William Saunders.

ELIZABETH WALMSLEY.

* These extracts are from *The Edmonton Daily Bulletin* of Oct. 4, 1909.

THE HEALTH OF THE BRITISH AND GERMAN ARMIES: A CONTRAST

By Lieut.-Colonel WILLIAM HILL-CLIMO, M.D.,
Army Medical Staff (Retired)

THE public consider that the health of the Regular Army is good when the hospital admissions and the death and invaliding ratios are lower than in previous years. While at the present time these statistics indicate the good effects which modern sanitary methods and a more rational system of training the soldier have in reducing mortality in the Home Army from preventible diseases, they afford little information as to the general health of the Army, its powers of endurance and ability to resist disease in war, or as to the nation's health capacity for military service. Necessarily this is the case in a short service army, which is raised by voluntary enlistment, and composed of young men, who come from and return to civil life in quick succession, whereby their health statistics become merged in those of the civil population.

The problem is rendered more difficult by the fact that the out-patient system of medical treatment, a recent innovation, lowers the admission rates into hospital during the first two years of the soldier's service, and candidates for enlistment, who in former years would have been rejected for medical reasons, are now passed fit for service. It is obvious that these statistics are not sufficiently informing to determine the physical efficiency of the troops on the outbreak of war, much less the nation's capacity for military service. Of the health of the Territorial Army, which should be typical of the health of the nation, there are no records, but with the greater latitude allowed in its recruitment, its physical inferiority to the Regular Army is notorious.

On all these points continental nations, even in a time of profound peace, are in possession of full information. That is one of the advantages accruing to a nation from compulsory service, for all males, at a certain fixed age, are medically examined and the results recorded ; in addition the organisation of their medical service is on a regimental basis, so that the medical officers of corps units are intimately acquainted with the health of the men. The British medical service was organised on the same lines until some time after short service was adopted, which gave the Government the opportunity of abolishing the regimental system and substituting for it the posting of medical officers to districts and stations.

No comparison of the health of armies can be effective without considering the organisation of their respective medical services, for personal supervision of health is essential, which is the more complete when the relations of the medical service to the army it serves are close and intimate. In the German Army that has always been the case, for, besides the necessity for immediate preparedness for war, the German people, with that genius for thoroughness which is so characteristic of them, recognise what folly it would be to have the organisation of the medical service during peace different from what it must be in war. This necessity, for preparedness for war is not apparent to the British nation; it is often said that after war breaks out a period of six months' grace is assured to the nation, so that the time is ample to make every preparation. This may or may not be, but the belief in that policy cost the nation dearly, for the weakening of the supervision of the health of the Army which preceded and continued up to the South African War was in no small measure the immediate cause of our unpreparedness, and of the great loss of treasure and of life that war caused.

Let me recall the facts, for nations and governments have short memories. Advantage was taken of the adoption of short service to abolish the regimental system as being no longer required owing to the short time that the rank and file would have to serve with the colours. The War Office approached the question sympathetically from its financial side, while the medical department hoped to free itself from an irksome duty. There was constant friction between officers commanding corps and medical officers in regard to sanitary duties. So obsessed was the late Sir Thomas Crawford with the idea that short service gave the medical service the opportunity to be relieved from this invidious position, without detriment to the soldier's health, that, when he was appointed Director-General, he said he would endeavour to fix the responsibility for sanitary duties upon regimental quartermasters. His position was the more uncomfortable, because senior medical officers had not kept in touch with the progress of modern sanitary science, and they consequently had little liking for the new ideas which their juniors, fresh from the schools, had brought with them; it was in truth a case of putting new wine into old bottles.

It was not surprising, therefore, that on the outbreak of the South African War the physical efficiency of the Army for field service was not known until the troops were mobilised, when it was found that 33·76 per cent., non-commissioned officers and men, were medically unfit. Had this information been available earlier the military authorities would have made adequate provision to meet the requirements of the war and the medical department for the care and treatment of the sick, for they could hardly fail to have recognised that an army so constituted would suffer severely from epidemic diseases in the field, more especially as before the war enteric fever was more prevalent among the troops quartered in South Africa than in India. This lesson of the war led to the reorganisation of the medical service on progressive lines, whereby the personal supervision of the health of the recruit during training and of the soldier in barracks has become an every-day duty. The work too now covers a wider range, for the department is represented in the Intelligence Branch of the Imperial General Staff, and the A.M.D. Reports, since 1906, give statistics from which a comparison can be made between the health of the Home Army and of the male civil population of similar ages, and of certain foreign armies. These statistics should correct the erroneous opinions which are frequently expressed of the effects of military service upon health. For instance, it is a common belief in large centres of industry that the life of the soldier cannot be other than unhealthy, though for the legend of "the soldier's heart," which has been a deterrent to enlistment, and from which the Army Medical Department has not yet emancipated itself, a distinguished medical officer was mainly responsible, but that is an old story, for which, at the time, there was some justification. On the other hand, the advocates of universal military service find in the improvement which they allege would take place in the health of the nation one of their strongest arguments.

These opinions, widely different as they are, are susceptible of a simple explanation, for the pessimist is wedded to the traditions of the past, and thinks of the health of the Army as it was fifty years ago, when its insanitary conditions were a reproach and a byword. My experience dates from 1861; it recalls crowded and badly-ventilated barracks, with floors polluted by constant expectoration, the men huddled together on plank bedsteads and straw palliasses, which were often damp and soiled; their food badly cooked and insufficient, with long intervals between meals; and the means of ablution scanty, making personal cleanliness an ever-present difficulty. It was no wonder that, with these conditions, the admissions into hospital and the mortality were always high, but besides there was a constant stream of invalids, who returned to the civil population, carrying with them the marks of disease to every town and village ; the memory of evil dies hard.

Contrast that picture of the soldier's life with what it is to-day ; the change is phenomenal. His barracks provide him with dining halls ; with separate rooms in which his clothes are dried and aired ; with sleeping apartments furnished with iron cots and coir mattresses ; and with bath-rooms with hot and cold water supply. Besides, there are regimental institutions—recreation and reading-rooms with supper bars ; in brief, everything is done to promote health and to make for comfort. His food is varied and well cooked, which, with regular exercise and early hours, conduce to physical efficiency. The discipline to which he is subjected no longer destroys his self-respect, for it appeals to his intelligence and develops self-control, without which there cannot be a healthy mind in a healthy body. Compared with his civilian brother, who may be a clerk in some city office, the amenities of life which he enjoys are in many respects superior, but in comparison with the classes from which the majority of the recruits for the Regular Army come, it would be mere waste of time to discuss the question further, for the advantage is altogether on the side of the soldier.

It is not surprising, therefore, that these differences in the hygienic conditions of the Home Army and of the civil population find their counterpart in their respective rates of mortality. The table below, compiled from the A.M.D. Reports for the years 1906, 1907 and 1908, gives the average death-rates from all causes, per million, for the three years' period, of soldiers serving in the United Kingdom, and of males in the civil population, of similar ages, in England and Wales, for the three years period—1905, 1906 and 1907 ; the death-rates for diseases of the heart are also given with the view of correcting the erroneous opinions which are held on that subject.

Average Death Rates per million, of the Regular Army serving in the United Kingdom for the three years' period— 1906, 1907 and 1908.	Average Death Rates in England and Wales, per million, of males aged 15–35 years for the three years' period— 1905, 1906 and 1907.
From all causes 2,860	4,889
Diseases of the Heart 246	314

These figures show that for every five deaths from all causes in the Regular Army serving in the United Kingdom, there are eight deaths in the male civil population, of similar ages, and that the deaths from diseases of the heart are 20 per cent. higher in the civil population than in the Army. The scoffer at universal military service as a means of improving national health will find in these statistics no support for his views, which are as unsound as they are unpatriotic. But the lesson for the nation is a serious one ; it should consider how is it that there is so marked an inferiority in the health of the civil population, an inferiority which in the case of a great national emergency would cripple its military efficiency. All the more is this necessary, because the organisation and training of the Territorial Army lend themselves to hiding the truth from the nation. Even the health of the Regular Army, good as it is in comparison with that of the civil population, is inferior to that of the armies of the great European Powers. Germany looms large in popular estimation for the great strength of its army and for its capacity to build battleships and to manufacture the *matériel* of war, but the public would not be less profitably employed in turning the searchlight on itself and considering the physical condition of our own people side by side with that of other nations.

With this intent it will be helpful to compare the health of the British and German armies, the respective protagonists of the voluntary and compulsory systems of army organisation, which is based upon the selection of the recruit. In this inquiry two questions present themselves, they are interdependent, but they must be separately considered, namely, the health capacity for military service of the respective populations from which these armies are raised, and the effect which military service has upon national health and character.

AVERAGE DEATH RATES PER 1,000 OF STRENGTH.*

	Of the Regular Army serving in the United Kingdom for the years 1906, 1907 and 1908.	Of the German Army for the years 1903–4, 1904–5 and 1905–6.
Deaths from all causes	2·86	1·66
„ „ Diseases of the Heart	0·34	0·03
„ „ Enteric Fever . .	0·10	0·09
„ „ Tubercle of the Lung	0·24	0·12

It has been said "that the moral of an armed force is good, when that force, collectively considered, is in a healthy physiological condition." That being so, in what relation, in the light of the above statistics, do the British and German armies stand to each other? The British Army is on a lower plane, for the mortality from all causes is seven-tenths greater than in the German Army; for diseases of the heart there are eleven deaths in the British Army to one in the German Army; for enteric fever these proportions are ten to nine; and for tubercle of lung there are two deaths in the British Army to one in the German Army. The most optimistic Secretary of State would do well to consider what these differences mean; they have not hitherto received official appreciation.

The conclusion to be drawn from these figures is that the •

* This table is compiled from the A.M.D. Reports for the years 1906, 1907 and 1908. I am also indebted to Major Ostertag, Military Attaché, German Embassy, for the Medical Report, etc., of the German Army for the year 1905–6.

British nation from a health point of view is less capable of military service, at the present time, than the German. How otherwise can the relatively greater mortality in the British Army be accounted for ? It is said, with great truth, that armies which are raised by voluntary enlistment are not so healthy as armies whose recruitment is compulsory ; but in the present case that explanation will not suffice, for the British Army is recruited from the classes which form five-sixths of the population, and according to the medical reports of recruiting the selected candidates are physically superior to youths of the same age in civil life. Apart from the obligation which each soldier owes to himself and to his country to keep sound and fit, the health of armies depends upon the health of the people from which they are recruited ; upon the sanitary conditions common to both ; upon climate ; and upon military service.

There is no European army more happily circumstanced than the British in regard to sanitary environment and to climate ; the lower death-rate in the Home Army, as compared with that of the male civil population of similar ages, is conclusive that the cause does not lie with military service ; besides, the improvement which takes place in the physique of the recruit during training is a matter of common knowledge. All nations which have adopted universal military service, at first unwillingly but of necessity, now recognise its value in the improvement which takes place in the health and character of the people, and for that reason they make the sacrifice, if sacrifice it be, gladly. Reluctantly, therefore, the conclusion is come to that the causes of the greater mortality in the British Army will be found in the people themselves ; for this reason the vital statistics of Great Britain and the German Empire will be compared, and a brief reference will be made to their political and economic conditions, upon which the health of nations so largely depends.

In estimating racial quality the marriage and birth rates must be considered equally with the death rates ; they are no less informing. A high marriage rate indicates, in white races, good wages and comfortable circumstances ; in brief, a healthy environment, though it is not necessarily the result of a higher civilisation. Associated with a high birth rate it leads to the healthy evolution of a race. On the other hand the lowering of the birth rate in European countries is not due to a loss of fertility but to artificial restrictions, a degradation which must be reflected in the health of succeeding generations. But a high birth rate increases the general death rate owing to the large number of deaths of infants under one year after birth, also because of the greater liability of young people to zymotic diseases, to which the Anglo-Saxon and the Teutonic races are specially susceptible. Hence the death rates of different nations should have the causes specified, for besides the effect which a high infantile mortality rate has in increasing the total death rate, it may be increased by extraneous and accidental conditions, quite apart from racial quality.

These observations must be kept in mind when investigating international vital statistics, because in official reports only deaths from preventible diseases are given under their respective headings, while the deaths which are due to all other causes, and which are chiefly constitutional, are bulked together. Notwithstanding, the figures in the two following tables, which have been compiled from the Registrar-General's Report for the year 1906, are approximately correct.

YEAR 1905.*

	Proportion per 1,000 of Population.		Deaths of Children under 1 year to 1,000 Births.
	Persons Married.	Births.	
United Kingdom (Great Britain and Ireland)	14·6	26·9	124
German Empire	16·1	33·0	205

PROPORTION OF DEATHS PER 1,000 OF POPULATION IN 1905.

	United Kingdom (Great Britain and Ireland).	German Empire.
(1) Mortality from all causes.	15·5	19·8
(2) ,, ,, zymotic diseases	3·6	6·0
(3) ,, of children under 1 year after birth .	3·3	6·7
Balance of deaths (excluding 2 and 3)	8·6	7·1

If high marriage and birth rates indicate superior racial quality, the advantage is with Germany. But the total death rate is markedly against it; and when from the total death rate there are deducted the deaths of infants under one year after birth and deaths from zymotic diseases, the balance remains in favour of Germany, for the deaths which took place from all other causes in 1905 were one-sixth greater in the United Kingdom. Hence in Germany in 1890 the proportion per 1,000 persons between 40 to 60 years was 182. And at 60 years and over, 80. Whereas in England and Wales these proportions in 1891 were respectively 174 and 74.

On the face of it these are perplexing facts, but they are reconcilable when the political and economic conditions of the two countries are considered, for from them have sprung up forces which powerfully influence the growth and character of their respective populations. These forces operate in the German Empire to make a virile people, and they are primarily due to its geographical position; its frontiers being conterminous with other powerful States, it has been compelled to train its manhood to arms, ready at all times for its defence. For similar reasons and to keep its people at home it protects home industries,

* The year 1905 is chosen, as it was the year of the last German census.

and it raises to the fullest possible extent its own food supplies. With a rapidly-increasing population its economic conditions will become more acute; but even so, the dominating factor will remain political, though with a wider field of action. The United Kingdom from its insular position and with an all-powerful navy has been saved from this necessity; but that time has passed, for the power of production of other countries, in the last twenty years, has been so phenomenal, while behind them there are such strong political forces that, if we are to hold our own without curtailment, we must take the lesson to heart and give ungrudgingly personal service to the State.

It is universal military service which has improved the health of the adult population in Germany, and which at the same time has given them a keener sense of public duty and of the personal obligations which it imposes; it is this recognition which has made German methods so thorough, beginning with the education of the young. The greater knowledge which it gives of wide world politics permits legislation on social and economic questions, which have failed to command support in a British House of Commons, and which one of its leaders characterised as being foreign to the genius of the British people. For instance, though the German Government contributes to infirmity and old age pensions, both employers and employed have equally to bear their share. By doing so there becomes developed thrift and a sense of personal responsibility which are no mean factors in the mainten-ance of health. By the protection of Home industries Germany supports nine-tenths of her population with the produce of the soil, and has thereby been able to arrest the great flow of emigration which took place up to 1892.

How different are the conditions which prevail in Great Britain, and how little is done by responsible officials to bring home to the democracy a sense of public duty. Successive Secretaries of State try to raise an army for home defence, with apologies for the necessity; our poor laws penalise the really deserving poor; and the free gift of old age pensions, without contributory insurance by employers and employed, demoralises the recipients. So is it with our free trade policy, which has destroyed rural life, the healthiest of all, and which permits foreign food supplies, of which the latest is Chinese pork, to take the place of home grown produce to the detriment of the health of the people. The infelicitous comparison of the Chancellor of the Exchequer of the food of the British and German workman is welcomed in that it has attracted attention to so important a subject. A visit to the market-place of any large continental town should correct many erroneous opinions, for there will be seen the consumer purchasing direct from the producer; the food supplies are fresh, not kept in greengrocers' shops to reach the poor when they become stale or faked.

If the United Kingdom wishes to emulate the German Empire in the growth of a virile people two conditions are essential; the adoption of universal military service and the return in large numbers of the people to the land. But universal service should be continuous for a period of two years, in the interests of national health; with its military necessities this paper does not deal. No nation can preserve a healthy stock, unless a large proportion of the population is engaged in rural employment.

With a fuller knowledge of international affairs and of the value of physical exercises and discipline public opinion is moving strongly in favour of both these measures. A study of German methods shows that the great obstacle to their early adoption is the attitude of the Government to the people. When it should lead, it follows; it is this want of leadership which makes our methods so poor in comparison with German practice. Hence there has grown up among our people a disinclination for personal service, which the German people do not understand, much less would they tolerate it. Happily a new spirit is being infused into the nation. The Boys' Brigade, the Boys' Scouts Brigade, the National Service League and other kindred institutions are all working towards this end. If Germany competes with us in building Dreadnoughts, she has a perfect right to do so ; to cavil at her action or to attempt to limit it by compromise, are the hysterical efforts of a people enfeebled and worn out by success. If competition there must be between two kindred nations, let it be in the building up of a healthy people : the spirit of the rising generation only wants *the man* to guide and show the way.

W. HILL-CLIMO.

THE LOST TRINITY OF THE COUNTRYSIDE

By wILLIAM S. WALKER (*Coo-ee*).

AFTER long residence in England and Scotland, an Australian has awakened to the fact that the things he has always held in reverence concerning the Mother Country are fallacies. Worse even, the very materials upon which he has built his faith, almost his religion, are non-existent. He has read continuously of the beauty, the vast utility, the wealth of the countryside. English hamlets embowered in festoons of English roses, cornfields verdant in spring, yellow in harvest, for the bread that strengthens the heart of man. The great oxen that make the Englishman the man he is, the malt that brews the barley-bree, the output and input of granaries, the orchards, the healthy country life, the whole box and dice of lavish literary ideas shakes out its legends in "sixes" upon a large and joyous countryside.

Such things used to be, they are supposed by persons who do not know or do not think, to exist now; but beyond the dim remembrance of them in the country itself, the plain truth is that they have utterly vanished. The trinity of the countryside used to be the squire, the farmer, the farm labourer, and the healthy fox-hunting parson used to give all three his benediction from the pulpit on the Sunday. To-day the country squire is gone, his estate more or less sequestrated or mortgaged, the farmer runs a little dairy herd, the country is thrown open to grass field after grass field and the ploughshare is far between them. On an average one cultivated field is found to eight or ten used for cattle and sheep pasture. Well and highly ordured these fields are from the droppings of countless seasons, unkempt, moundy, and ragged, they offend the eye and injure the health. Bare, unpeopled, unworked is the countryside to-day. Yet people still believe in English beef and corn. Fallacies both. England did and could furnish these life-giving, money-making, health-giving necessities, even to a margin for export, but she doesn't now, and doesn't know why she doesn't. She sits down and imagines she is all right, eating chilled foreign beef and foreign corn made bread. She won't supply her own needs because she can't. She has forgotten the way and fancies she doesn't need anything else. It is all right. She accepts the pap-spoon and feeding-bottle of foreign supply with unpardonable ignorance and apathy.

Sixty-three years of Free Trade have dumped the squire out of existence. The big farmers' sons of the glorious days of old have gone to protected countries oversea, and the labourers still required for the small amount of hedging, ditching and gathering into barns, are old men and lads, here and there in batches, as they can with difficulty be mustered together. Free Trade has slogged the country and every trade and profession within it almost out of existence, and made us unable to pay our own way by our own home produce and industries, the first sign of a nation drifting to decay. In Scotland the farm labourers are going to other lands as hard as ever they can. The Scotch landlords and the Scotch farmers are in the same fix as those in England. Scotch thistles are stocking the fields. Where the landlords own the estates they are glad to let to strangers or sell to the middleman or titled dumper.

We give everything away. Fruit won't sell because of foreign fruit. Every trade is hampered, every industry is on the down-grade. A steamer comes into a trading port dunnaged with Cardiff coal for a foreign country. She completes her loading with valuable china clay and returns with an import selection of French slates to put on our houses, and repeats the performance year in year out, while we have heaps of slates of our own. Money, free money, free goods almost for the foreigner, who gets all the profit of the bargain as well, and England looks on supinely and takes no steps to make her many industries pay. Canada, Australia and New Zealand jumped at a bound to prosperity when they adopted protective tariffs. Why should the mother-country refuse to save herself?

Our baby beef, one and a half to two years, goes to London, the country people have to eat a barren cow, or perhaps a tuberculous calf. Baby bullocks cost £23 a-piece, and it doesn't pay a butcher to sell this meat at chilled beef prices. The prime ox beef that Mr. Lloyd George cajoled a certain section of his constituents with is as extinct as the dodo. The prime ox should be four or five years old and weigh as a prime ox should. There is no beef in England of this sort, and we multiply inventions of excuse and palliation for the lack of it every day. There is no corn except the pretence of it. The squire, the farmer, the farm labourer, exist only as the vanishing impoverished ghosts of old well exchequered days, when the farmer ran his greyhounds, brewed his own beer, and rode to hounds as the Squire's right-hand man. Ask the old men in any village and they will tell the same tale.

The country industries most noticeable are the elevating and elevated advertisements—it may be great Free Trade advertisements of protected cocoa—the bathos with the sublime of the external, whether displayed or kept in the heart, and no man is to be seen over the great spaces of a day's journey, which lie untilled and unsought save by wandering birds. One might come across a human being snaring rabbits or trapping pheasants under the Chancellor's poaching hints, but silence reigns supreme through the far spreading areas of the Lost Trinity of the Country Side. Why are not the old gates of country prosperity, respectability and progress thrown open? Because they are banged, barred, and bolted by Free Trade. Let us away with this policy of suicide and protect ourselves under Tariff Reform.

WILLIAM S. WALKER (Coo-ee).

COTTON-GROWING IN RHODESIA

Lancashire's need will be Rhodesia's opportunity. "Empire grown cotton" is a matter of vital importance to the looms of Lancashire, and the news that the British South Africa Company and the British Cotton-Growing Association mutually agreed, some little time ago, to provide the necessary means to develop the cultivation of cotton in Northern Rhodesia, is proof that both Lancashire and Rhodesia realise the fact. The expert recently despatched to Rhodesia by the British Cotton-Growing Association has now returned, and his report is at present being considered by the Board of the Chartered Company and the Council of the Association. Large areas of land in Northern Rhodesia are known to be suitable for the cultivation of cotton, and a heavy yield of lint per acre has been obtained in the Loangwa Valley District. The average price of recent consignments of Rhodesian cotton sold in Liverpool is about 10d. per lb., whilst the average total cost landed in Liverpool has not exceeded 5d. per lb. With regard to transport, North-Western Rhodesia is served by the Congo extension of the Rhodesia Railways which (about 250 miles north of the Victoria Falls) crosses the Kafue River, a valuable feeder for the railway. Several plantations have already been started near the line and in close proximity to the river. The point where the railway crosses the Kafue is regarded as the most favourable site for the establishment of a Central Hydraulic Baling Press and Power Ginnery, the erection of which is now under consideration.

WANTED—AN IMPERIAL COUNCIL

By CHARLES STUART-LINTON

It is now an established fact that the Dominions have decided to build local navies of their own, instead of participating in one Imperial navy. This departure renders an improvement in our political relations not only desirable, but essential, if the unity of the Empire is to be continued. Some Imperial machinery must be created whereby the external relations of the several units of the Empire may be determined by some representative body; otherwise our foreign policy will become not only disjointed but chaotic.

The problem awaiting solution is, how can this machinery be provided. Are we to admit the colonies to the present so-called Imperial Parliament, which is also the local Parliament of the United Kingdom? This would, I fear, only complicate the situation. Are we, on the other hand, to create a new Imperial parliament—a federal parliament for the Empire, separate from the Parliament of the United Kingdom? Such a change would, I anticipate, be considered revolutionary, yet in the best interests of the Empire it is to be hoped that such a change may eventually be encompassed. Meanwhile something must be arranged. The Imperial Conference which meets every four years will not alone suffice.

For present day conditions, therefore, it seems that the creation of some sort of Imperial Council is the only hope of meeting the difficulty. This method has been steadily advocated for years, and it would appear that it is in a fair way to being realised. Among the many people who have written in favour of this plan may be mentioned the Duke of Argyll, Earl Grey, and the late Mr. W. E. Forster, founder of the Imperial Federation League. Their views, in this regard, are similar to the paper read by Mr. Greswell before the London Chamber of Commerce in 1888, when he said:

The Imperial assembly which we want must be an independent body, constitutional in its origin, representative in its character, and supreme in its decisions. Such a body we have already in existence in the Privy Council. Its members are chosen, irrespective of party considerations, from among the most eminent of those who have done service to the State. To this body Colonists of distinguished public service could be elected. In constituting the Imperial committee of the Privy Council, representation might be given to every part of the Empire, in proportion to the several contributions to expenditure for Imperial defence.

Since the first discussion of the question by Earl Grey in the early eighties, four different schemes have been evolved. One is the establishment of a permanent Imperial Committee of the Privy Council; a purely advisory body, having with it a permanent Bureau of Imperial Intelligence to collect and codify all information regarding Imperial subjects. A second is to have an enlarged Cabinet, another Cabinet for purely Imperial questions. To this enlarged Cabinet statesmen from the States over-sea would be called. This body would be both advisory and executive in authority. It would have the virtue of indefinite expansion, and, in the process of evolution the two Cabinets might become separated. A third, in a way similar to the second, came from Mr. R. B. Wise, who advocated that the High-Commissioners of Canada, Australia and South Africa should form a sub-committee of the Cabinet and be consulted on Imperial affairs. But these bodies would not be representative in character, and there would be little hope of their becoming so. The fourth scheme, that of a periodical Imperial Conference, which is in effect in being, meets this defect to some extent, but the trouble is that the Imperial Conference has neither permanent organisation nor executive powers, and is unrecognised by our Constitution.

All four proposals are far from perfect. Perhaps the most satisfactory is the quatrennial Imperial Conference. This, at least, represents the colonies in person, though most inadequately and indirectly. Something perhaps might be evolved by moulding the four proposals together. The Imperial Conference might be woven into the Cabinet, making it of an Imperial character. At the beginning, the Imperial Cabinet would be only the Cabinet of the United Kingdom, with the addition of a few colonial statesmen; but in a process of evolution the Imperial and local characters of the Cabinet might become separated. Its Imperial character would then take upon itself the administration of the Empire, and its local character would resume business for the government of the United Kingdom. The Imperial Cabinet would then account both to the Parliament of the United Kingdom and the parliaments of the daughter-States.

Meanwhile something more is needed, a permanent Imperial Committee of the Privy Council to assist the Imperial Cabinet.

This would be a purely consultative body, debating between the sessions of the Imperial Cabinet the same questions as would be dealt with by that Cabinet, and assisting the Cabinet of the United Kingdom on matters of a pressing Imperial nature. The Imperial Conference of 1907 made a step forward, when it initiated the idea of a permanent Imperial Commission—an Intelligence Department for the Imperial Conference, under the control of the Colonial Office.

Working on these suggestions we should have in our Government, first, an Imperial Cabinet, composed, at the commencement, of the Cabinet of the United Kingdom, with Colonial statesmen, and sitting periodically in an Imperial Conference; secondly, an advisory permanent Imperial Committee of the Privy Council, assisted by an Imperial Intelligence Department with a permanent secretariat.

Such a council, with nominated representatives debating on important Imperial questions, is the principle of Norman government, a parliament being that of the Anglo-Saxon. It is true that the present Imperial Parliament is in a measure derived from the Privy Council of our Norman Sovereigns, and therefore, it might be said to develop eventually into a proper federal parliament. But that derivation is confined to the Upper House, the House of Lords, and not to the popular body, the House of Commons. Yet a House of Commons was finally developed, and in time, the Imperial Council might expand into a bicameral Imperial Parliament.

Before that period, however, the Imperial Council might have developed into a useful makeshift for transacting the business of the Empire. It might, under a confederation and pending a more satisfactory federation, assume functions similar to those of the Council of Delegations of the Austro-Hungarian Empire. That Empire, however, can hardly be called a confederation. It is little more than a permanent association of two independent States. The Empire has no common Constitution and no common executive. All questions of customs and of the naval and military forces have to be governed by specified treaties for the same, drawn up jointly in the separate parliaments of Austria and Hungary. The defects of this system, however, are realised by none more keenly than the subjects of that Empire themselves. Were the British Empire to adopt this as a permanent scheme for Imperial unity it would before long likely find itself in as unsatisfactory a state as did the United States under their Articles of Confederation, prior to the founding of their wonderful Constitution. Such a condition would not mean federation, but at most a brittle confederation, incapable of withstanding great shocks. As a temporary scheme of Imperial unity, however, there is something to be said for it, so long as it is realised that it would be only temporary—a mere stage in our political evolution as an Empire.

Possibly the process of evolution may have begun with the Colonial Conferences which, beginning in 1887, afterwards became regular quatrennial occurrences, ultimately changing the name Colonial to Imperial and adding a permanent secretariat. The Imperial Conference might develop into an Imperial Council, still meeting every four years, with, of course, the permanent secretariat. The Imperial Council might then become an annual affair, and subsequently form part of the Imperial machinery of government. Finally, it might expand into a true federal Imperial parliament, with an upper and a lower house, establishing an Imperial Constitution graduating from confederation to federation, making the Empire from a Statenbund into a Bundesstaat. This after all is probably the way federation will come. We are a conservative people and are slow to change. We incline rather toward evolution than revolution. Let us trust that the process has really begun.

CHARLES E. T. STUART-LINTON.

INDIAN AND COLONIAL INVESTMENTS*

IT has been another dreary holiday month in the Stock Exchange. Day after day has passed with scarcely a ripple of activity in the markets, and in these circumstances the general tendency of prices has been to sink, but considering the scanty support they have received, investment securities have held up fairly well, and of most markets it can be said that it would require but a slight accession of new business to send prices more or less rapidly upward.

In company with Consols, Indian Government securities have been distinctly out of favour, and there has been very little demand for the railway stocks, although the results of the working of the companies for the first half of the year make on the whole a very satisfactory display. In only two cases was there any important decline in gross receipts, and in one of these the falling off was more than counteracted by a decrease in working expenses. In fact, economies in the cost of working are quite a gratifying feature of the results.

During the month there have been published also the results of the two great Canadian railway systems. As had already been indicated here, the Canadian Pacific's results were such that the

INDIAN GOVERNMENT SECURITIES.

Title.	Present Amount.	When Redeemable.	Price.	Yield.	Interest Payable.
INDIA.	£				
3½% Stock (t . . .	85,304,848	1931	95	3½⅟₆	Quarterly.
3% " (t) . . .	66,724,530	1948	82	3⅝	"
2½% " Inscribed (t)	11,892,207	1926	68	3⅝	"
3½% Rupee Paper 1854–5	..	(a)	96	3⅝	30 June—31 Dec.
3% " " 1896–7	..	1916	79½	3¾	30 June—30 Dec.

(t) Eligible for Trustee investments.
(a) Redeemable at a Quarter's notice.

* The tabular matter in this article will appear month by month, the figures being corrected to date. Stocks eligible for Trustee investments are so designated.— ED.

INDIAN RAILWAYS AND BANKS.

Title.	Subscribed.	Last year's dividend.	Share or Stock.	Price.	Yield.
RAILWAYS.	£				
Assam—Bengal, L., guaranteed 3%	1,500,000	3	100	79	3¾
Bengal and North-Western (Limited)	3,000,000	7½	100	141¾	5¼
Bengal Dooars, L.	400,000	4	100	86½	4⅝
Bengal Nagpur (L), gtd. 4%+¼th profits	3,000,000	5	100	102	4⅞
Burma Guar. 2½% and propn. of profits	3,000,000	5¼	100	109	$4\frac{13}{16}$
Delhi Umballa Kalka, L., guar. 3½% + net earnings	800,000	7	100	144½	$4\frac{13}{16}$
East Indian Def. ann. cap. g. 4% + ⅛ sur. profits (t)	1,912,804	5½	100	98	$5\frac{9}{16}$
Do. do, class "D," repayable 1953 (t)	4,637,196	4⅞	100	114¼	4¼
Do. 4½% perpet. deb. stock (t)	1,435,650	4½	100	118	$3\frac{13}{16}$
Do. new 3% deb. red. (t)	8,000,000	3	100	79½	3¾
Great Indian Peninsula 4% deb. Stock (t)	2,701,450	4	100	106	3¾
Do. 3% Gua. and $\frac{1}{20}$ surp. profits 1925 (t)	2,575,000	3	100	96	3⅛
Indian Mid. L. gua. 4% & ¼ surp. profits (t)	2,250,000	4	100	98½	$4\frac{1}{16}$
Madras and South Mahratta	5,000,000	4	100	101¾	3⅞
Nizam's State Rail. Gtd. 5% Stock	2,000,000	5	100	110¼	4½
Do. 3½% red. mort. debs.	1,074,700	3½	100	85	$4\frac{1}{16}$
Rohilkund and Kumaon, Limited	400,000	7	100	130	5⅜
South Behar, Limited	379,580	5	100	103	$4\frac{13}{16}$
South Indian 4½% per. deb. stock, gtd.	425,000	4½	100	118	$3\frac{13}{16}$
Do. capital stock	1,000,000	7½	100	102½	$7\frac{5}{16}$
Southern Punjab, Limited	1,000,000	7½	100	135	5½
Do. 3½% deb. stock red.	500,000	3½	100	88	$3\frac{15}{16}$
West of India Portuguese Guar. L.	800,000	5	100	95¼	5¼
Do. 5% debenture stock	550,000	5	100	101½	4⅞
BANKS.	Number of Shares.				
Chartered Bank of India, Australia, and China	60,000	14	20	58½	4¾
National Bank of India	64,000	12	12½	42½	3½

(t) Eligible for Trustee investments.

directors could easily have paid a very much larger dividend than the usual 7 per cent. Nevertheless, when the decision to increase the rate to 8 per cent. was announced, it seemed to take the market completely by surprise. The figures of the profit statement for the financial year, which ended on June 30, show wonderful progress.

The gross receipts amounted to $94,989,500 against $76,313,300 for the preceding year, an increase of nearly 25 per cent. The working expenses, on the other hand, showed a much smaller rate of increase, so that the net revenue grew from $22,955,600 to $33,840,000, an increase of nearly 50 per cent. After adding extra receipts, and deducting fixed charges and $900,000 for an appropriation to the steamboat replacement fund, against $800,000 a year ago, there remained a distributable balance of $26,278,700 against $14,955,100 a year ago. After payment of dividends there was a surplus of $13,896,600 against $3,847,200. Since these results were announced the shares have gone above the double-century, but sympathy with the American market has brought them down again to the extent of a few points.

In its more modest way the Grand Trunk system also has shown considerable improvement. The company's financial year ends on December 31 so that the results covered only six months. During this period the gross receipts were £3,321,600, an increase of £455,200, of which £376,800 was absorbed in additional working expenses, the net revenue being £865,600 against £787,200 for the corresponding period of last year. Included in the working expenses was a sum of £120,000 written off engine and car renewal suspense account. After making the usual adjustments and allowing for dividends ranking before that on the Guaranteed stock there is a surplus of £347,200 against £279,900, and the directors declare the full dividends for the

CANADIAN GOVERNMENT SECURITIES.

Title.	Present Amount.	When Redeemable.	Price.	Yield.	Interest Payable.
4% Inter)) Guaranteed colonial} } by Great	1,341,400	1910	101	—	}1 Apr.—1 Oct.
4% „ } Britain.	1,700,000	1913	102	$3\frac{5}{8}$	}
3½% 1884 Regd. Stock	4,676,830	1909–34	100	—	1 June—1 Dec.
3% Inscribed Stock (t)	8,594,877	1938	91	$3\frac{1}{2}$	1 Jan.—1 July.
2½% „ „ (t)	1,592,105	1947	77	$3\frac{11}{16}$	1 Apr.—1 Oct.

PROVINCIAL.

BRITISH COLUMBIA.

3% Inscribed Stock .	2,045,760	1941	85½	$3\frac{13}{16}$	1 Jan.—1 July.

MANITOBA.

5% Sterling Bonds .	308,000	1923	108	$4\frac{3}{16}$	1 Jan.—1 July.
4% „ Debs. .	205,000	1928	102	$3\frac{7}{8}$	1 May—1 Nov.

NOVA SCOTIA.

3% Stock	164,000	1949	81	$3\frac{15}{16}$	1 Jan.—1 July.

QUEBEC.

3% Inscribed . . .	1,897,820	1937	85½	$3\frac{15}{16}$	1 Apr.—1 Oct.

MUNICIPAL.

Hamilton (City of) 4%	482,800	1934	102	$3\frac{7}{8}$	1 Apr.—1 Oct.
Montreal 3% Deb.) Stock . . . .}	1,440,000	permanent	81	$3\frac{11}{16}$	}1 May—1 Nov.
Do. 4% Cons. „ .	1,821,917	1932	104	$3\frac{3}{4}$	}
Quebec 4% Debs. . .	385,000	1923	101	$3\frac{15}{16}$	}1 Jan.—1 July.
Do. 3½% Con. Stock .	504,196	drawings	92	$3\frac{3}{4}$	}
Toronto 5% Con. Debs.	136,700	1919–20*	106	$4\frac{1}{2}$	}
Do. 4% Stg. Bonds .	300,910	1922–28*	101	$3\frac{15}{16}$	}1 Jan.—1 July.
Do. 3½% Bonds . .	1,169,844	1929	93	4	}
Vancouver 4% Bonds	121,200	1931	101	4	1 Apr.—1 Oct.
Do. 4% 40-year Bonds	117,200	1932	100	4	7 Feb.—7 Aug.
Winnipeg 5% Debs. .	188,000	1914	103	$4\frac{7}{16}$	30 Apr.—31 Oct.

(t) Eligible for Trustee investments.
* Yield calculated on earlier date of redemption.

CANADIAN RAILWAYS, BANKS AND COMPANIES.

Title.	Number of Shares or Amount.	Dividend for last Year.	Paid up per Share.	Price.	Yield
RAILWAYS.		%			
Canadian Pacific Shares . .	1,500,000	7	$100	199	$3\frac{1}{2}$
Do. 4% Preference	£11,328,082	4	Stock	107	$3\frac{11}{16}$
Do. 5% Stg. 1st Mtg. Bd. 1915	£7,191,500	5	"	$105\frac{1}{2}$	$3\frac{3}{4}$
Do. 4% Cons. Deb. Stock . .	£25,315,001	4	"	109	$3\frac{5}{8}$
Grand Trunk Ordinary . .	£22,475,985	nil.	"	$27\frac{5}{8}$	nil.
Do. 5% 1st Preference . . .	£3,420,000	5	"	$110\frac{1}{2}$	$4\frac{1}{2}$
Do. 5% 2nd " . . .	£2,530,000	5	"	100	5
Do. 4% 3rd " . . .	£7,168,055	nil.	"	$58\frac{3}{4}$	nil.
Do. 4% Guaranteed . . .	£9,840,011	4	"	$93\frac{1}{2}$	$4\frac{1}{4}$
Do. 5% Perp. Deb. Stock . .	£4,270,375	5	"	126	$3\frac{15}{16}$
Do. 4% Cons. Deb. Stock . .	£15,821,571	4	"	$102\frac{1}{2}$	$3\frac{7}{8}$
BANKS AND COMPANIES.					
Bank of Montreal	140,000	10	$100	247	$4\frac{1}{16}$
Bank of British North America	20,000	7	50	$75\frac{1}{2}$	$4\frac{5}{8}$
Canadian Bank of Commerce .	200,000	9	$50	£21	$4\frac{7}{16}$
Canada Company	8,319	29s. per sh.	1	30	$4\frac{13}{16}$
Hudson's Bay	100,000	50s. per sh.	10*	$99\frac{1}{2}$	$2\frac{1}{2}$
Trust and Loan of Canada .	60,000	8	5	$6\frac{3}{8}$	$6\frac{1}{4}$
Do. new	25,000	8	3	$3\frac{1}{4}$	$7\frac{3}{8}$
British Columbia Electric Railway . . . Def.	£600,000	8	Stock	145	$5\frac{1}{2}$
British Columbia Electric Railway . . . Prefd.	£600,000	6	Stock	126	$4\frac{3}{4}$

* £1 capital repaid 1904.

NEWFOUNDLAND GOVERNMENT SECURITIES.

Title.	Present Amount.	When Redeemable.	Price.	Yield.	Interest Payable.
$3\frac{1}{2}$% Sterling Bonds .	2,178,800	1941-7-8†	93	$3\frac{13}{16}$	1 Jan.—1 July.
3% Sterling " .	325,000	1947	80	$4\frac{1}{16}$	
4% Inscribed Stock .	320,000	1913-38*	101	$3\frac{13}{16}$	
4% " " .	455,647	1935	105	$3\frac{11}{16}$	
4% Cons. Ins. " .	200,000	1936	104	$3\frac{3}{4}$	

* Yield calculated on earlier date of redemption.
† Yield calculated on latest date.

half-year on the First and Second Preference as well as the Guaranteed stocks, whereas a year ago the Second Preference received nothing. There still remains £12,600 to be brought forward to the current half-year against £9,900 last time.

New issues of all kinds have been comparatively rare during the past few holiday weeks, but there have been placed through the Bank of Montreal £94,600 of $4\frac{1}{2}$ per cent. debentures of the City of Regina, the capital of Saskatchewan, which is destined to become one of the Dominion's greatest cities at no distant date. The debentures are redeemable between 1930 and 1950, and were issued at 101 per cent.

AUSTRALIAN GOVERNMENT SECURITIES.

Title.	Present Amount.	When Redeemable.	Price.	Yield.	Interest Payable.
NEW SOUTH WALES.					
4% Inscribed Stock (*t*)	9,686,300	1933	105	$3\frac{11}{16}$	1 Jan.—1 July.
3½% ,, ,, (*t*)	16,464,545	1924	99½	$3\frac{5}{8}$	} 1 Apr.—1 Oct.
3% ,, ,, (*t*)	12,480,000	1935	88	$3\frac{13}{16}$	
VICTORIA.					
4% Inscribed, 1885 .	5,970,000	1920	102	$3\frac{13}{16}$	
3½% ,, 1889 (*t*)	5,000,000	1921–6*	98	$3\frac{11}{16}$	
4% ,,	2,107,000	1911–26*	100½	4	} 1 Jan.—1 July.
3% ,, (*t*) . .	5,211,331	1929–49†	85½	$3\frac{11}{16}$	
QUEENSLAND.					
4% Bonds	10,267,400	1913–15*	101½	$3\frac{5}{8}$	
4% Inscribed Stock (*t*)	7,939,000	1924	102	$3\frac{13}{16}$	
3½% ,, /,, (*t*)	8,616,034	1921–30†	98	$3\frac{5}{8}$	} 1 Jan.—1 July.
3% ,, ,, (*t*)	4,274,213	1922–47†	85½	$3\frac{11}{16}$	
SOUTH AUSTRALIA.					
4% Bonds	1,359,300	1916	102	$3\frac{13}{16}$	} 1 Apr.—1 Oct.
4% Inscribed Stock .	6,269,000	1916-7–36*	103	$3\frac{5}{8}$	
3½% ,, ,, (*t*)	2,517,800	1939	98½	$3\frac{9}{16}$	
3% ,, ,, (*t*)	839,500	1916–26‡	89½	$3\frac{9}{16}$	} 1 Jan.—1 July.
3% ,, ,, (*t*)	2,760,100	1916 ‡ or after.	84	$3\frac{9}{16}$	
WESTERN AUSTRALIA.					
4% Inscribed . . .	1,876,000	1911–31*	101½	$3\frac{11}{16}$	15 Apr.—15 Oct.
3½% ,, (*t*) . .	3,780,000	1920–35†	97½	$3\frac{11}{16}$	} 1 May—1 Nov.
3% ,, (*t*) . . .	3,750,000	1915–35‡	88	$3\frac{5}{8}$	
3% ,, (*t*) . .	2,500,000	1927‡	89½	$3\frac{5}{16}$	15 Jan.—15 July.
TASMANIA.					
3½% Inscbd. Stock (*t*)	4,156,500	1920–40*	99	$3\frac{9}{16}$	
4% ,, ,,	1,000,000	1920–40*	102½	$3\frac{3}{4}$	} 1 Jan.—1 July.
3% . . . . . (*t*)	450,000	1920–40†	86	$3\frac{3}{4}$	

* Yield calculated on earlier date of redemption.
† Yield calculated on later date of redemption, though a portion of the loan may be redeemed earlier.
‡ No allowance for redemption.
(*t*) Eligible for Trustee Investment.

AUSTRALIAN MUNICIPAL AND OTHER BONDS.

Title.	Present Amount.	When Redeemable.	Price.	Yield.	Interest Payable.
Melbourne & Met. Bd. of Works 4% Debs.	1,000,000	1921	101	4	1 Apl.—1 Oct.
Do. City 4% Deb. .	850,000	1915–22*	101	$3\frac{7}{8}$	
Melbourne Trams Trust 4½% Debs. .	1,650,000	1914–16*	102	$4\frac{1}{16}$	} 1 Jan.—1 July.
S. Melbourne 4½% Debs.	128,700	1919	101	$4\frac{3}{8}$	
Sydney 4% Debs. . .	640,000	1912–13	101	$3\frac{11}{16}$	} 1 Jan.—1 July.
Do. 4% Debs. . . .	300,000	1919	101	$3\frac{7}{8}$	

* Yield calculated on earlier date of redemption.

In Australian financial circles there has naturally been a good deal of discussion over the proposed Commonwealth note

AUSTRALIAN RAILWAYS, BANKS AND COMPANIES.

Title.	Number of Shares or Amount.	Dividend for last Year.	Paid up.	Price.	Yield.
RAILWAYS.		%			
Emu Bay and Mount Bischoff . . .	12,000	6	5	$4\frac{1}{2}$	$6\frac{5}{8}$
Do. $4\frac{1}{2}$% Irred. Deb. Stock	£130,900	$4\frac{1}{2}$	100	97	$4\frac{5}{8}$
Mid. of W. Aust. 4% Debs., Guartd. .	300,000	4	100	100	4
BANKS AND COMPANIES.					
Bank of Australasia	40,000	14	40	114	4
Bank of New South Wales	125,000	10	20	$44\frac{1}{2}$	$4\frac{7}{16}$
Union Bank of Australia £75 . . .	60,000	14	25	$61\frac{1}{2}$	$5\frac{11}{16}$
Do. 4% Inscribed Stock Deposits . .	£600,000	4	100	99	4
Australian Mort. Land & Finance £25	80,000	$12\frac{1}{2}$	5	$7\frac{1}{4}$	$8\frac{9}{16}$
Do. 4% Perp. Deb. Stock	£1,900,000	4	100	$100\frac{1}{2}$	$3\frac{15}{16}$
Dalgety & Co. £20	154,000	7	5	$5\frac{3}{4}$	$6\frac{1}{16}$
Do. $4\frac{1}{2}$% Irred. Deb. Stock	£620,000	$4\frac{1}{2}$	100	108	$4\frac{1}{8}$
Goldsbrough Mort & Co. 4% A Deb. Stock Reduced	£1,067,137	4	100	$85\frac{1}{2}$	$4\frac{5}{8}$
Do. B Income Reduced	£711,340	$5\frac{1}{2}$	100	94	$5\frac{13}{16}$
Australian Agricultural £25 . . .	20,000	£$4\frac{1}{2}$	$21\frac{1}{2}$	74	$6\frac{1}{16}$
South Australian Company . . .	14,200	15	20	$68\frac{1}{2}$	$4\frac{3}{8}$
Trust & Agency of Australasia . . .	42,479	$7\frac{1}{2}$	1	$\frac{3}{4}$	10
Do. 5% Cum. Pref.	87,500	5	10	$9\frac{3}{4}$	$5\frac{1}{8}$

NEW ZEALAND MUNICIPAL AND OTHER SECURITIES.

Title.	Present Amount.	When Redeemable.	Price.	Yield.	Interest Payable.
Auckland 5% Deb. .	200,000	1934–8*	109	$4\frac{3}{8}$	1 Jan.—1 July.
Do. Hbr. Bd. 5% Debs.	150,000	1917	104	$4\frac{9}{16}$	10 April—10 Oct.
Bank of N. Z. shares†	150,000	div. $12\frac{1}{2}$%	$10\frac{1}{2}$	$3\frac{15}{16}$	—
Do. 4% Gua. Stock‡ .	£1,000,000	1914	101	4	April—Oct.
Christchurch 6% Drainage Loan. .	200,000	1926	121	$4\frac{3}{16}$	30 June—31 Dec.
Lyttleton Hbr. Bd. 6%	200,000	1929	121	$4\frac{3}{8}$	
Napier Hbr. Bd. 5% Debs.	300,000	1920	104	$4\frac{1}{2}$	1 Jan.—1 July.
Do. 5% Debs.	200,000	1928	104	$4\frac{11}{16}$	
National Bank of N.Z. £$7\frac{1}{2}$ Shares £$2\frac{1}{2}$ paid	150,000	div. 13%	$5\frac{1}{2}$	$5\frac{7}{8}$	Jan.—July.
Oamaru 5% Bds. . . .	173,800	1920	94	$5\frac{7}{8}$	1 Jan.—1 July.
Otago Hbr. Cons. Bds. 5%	443,100	1934	105	$4\frac{5}{8}$	1 Jan.—1 July.
Wellington 6% Impts. Loan	100,000	1914–29	110	—	1 Mar.—1 Sept.
Do. 6% Waterworks .	130,000	1929	121	$4\frac{7}{16}$	1 Mar.—1 Sept.
Do. $4\frac{1}{2}$% Debs. . .	165,000	1933	104	$4\frac{1}{4}$	1 May—1 Nov.
Westport Hbr. 4% Debs.	150,000	1925	102	$3\frac{7}{8}$	1 Mar.—1 Sept.

* Yield calculated on earlier date of redemption.
† £6 13*s.* 4*d.* Shares with £3 6*s.* 8*d.* paid up.
‡ Guaranteed by New Zealand Government.

NEW ZEALAND GOVERNMENT SECURITIES.

Title.	Present Amount.	When Redeemable.	Price.	Yield.	Interest Payable.
5% Bonds	266,300	1914	104	3⅞	15 Jan.—15 July.
4% Inscribed Stock (t)	29,150,302	1929	104½	3¹¹⁄₁₆	1 May—1 Nov.
3½% Stock (t) . . .	13,754,532	1940	98	3⁹⁄₁₆	1 Jan.—1 July.
3% Inscribed Stock (t)	9,659,980	1945	88	3⅝	1 Apr.—1 Oct.

(t) Eligible for Trustee Investments.

issue, and in London monetary quarters the definite official formulation of the Ministry's scheme will be closely scanned. There is an inclination to believe that the amount of the authorised note issue will very soon swell to proportions considerably greater than the four millions sterling that inspired organs have suggested. For a definite statement on this and other important items of financial policy the new Government's first Budget is awaited with exceptionally keen interest.

July's output of gold from the Transvaal amounted to 638,714 ounces valued at £2,713,083. This total has been only once exceeded, but the daily average production was less than that for the preceding month. This table gives the returns month by month for several years past:

Month.	1910.	1909.	1908.	1907.	1906.	1905.
	£	£	£	£	£	£
January . .	2,554,451	2,612,836	2,380,124	2,283,741	1,820,739	1,568,508
February .	2,445,088	2,400,892	2,301,971	2,096,434	1,731,664	1,545,371
March . .	2,578,877	2,580,498	2,442,022	2,287,391	1,884,815	1,698,340
April . . .	2,629,535	2,578,804	2,403,500	2,281,110	1,865,785	1,695,550
May . . .	2,693,785	2,652,699	2,472,143	2,227,838	1,959,062	1,768,734
June . . .	2,655,602	2,621,818	2,442,329	2,155,976	2,021,813	1,751,412
July . . .	2,713,083	2,636,965	2,482,608	2,262,813	2,089,004	1,781,944
August . .	—	2,597,646	2,496,869	2,357,602	2,162,583	1,820,496
September .	—	2,575,760	2,496,112	2,285,424	2,145,575	1,769,124
October . .	—	2,558,902	2,624,012	2,351,344	2,296,361	1,765,047
November .	—	2,539,146	2,609,685	2,335,406	2,265,625	1,804,253
December .	—	2,569,822	2,806,235	2,478,659	2,336,961	1,833,295
Total * .	18,270,421	30,925,788	29,957,610	27,403,738	24,579,987	20,802,074

* Including undeclared amounts omitted from the monthly returns.

The diminution during July of the native labour supply at the gold mines was again considerably less than a year ago, the supply at the end of the month exceeding by nearly 30,000 hands the total employed, both Kaffirs and Chinese, a year ago.

The following table shows the course of the labour supply during the past two years :

Month.	Natives Joined.	Natives Left.	Net Gain on Month.	Natives Employed end of Month.	Chinese Employed end of Month.
July 1908	11,725	9,257	2,468	132,339	18,413
August ,,	11,988	10,799	1,209	133,548	17,006
September ,,	14,129	11,497	2,632	136,180	14,655
October ,,	14,754	11,769	2,985	139,165	12,317
November ,,	12,324	10,163	2,161	141,326	12,298
December ,,	17,404	10,008	7,396	148,722	12,283
January 1909	13,551	11,609	1,942	150,664	10,045
February ,,	18,018	10,844	7,174	157,838	10,084
March ,,	16,184	11,979	4,205	162,043	9,997
April ,,	12,102	11,244	858	162,901	7,734
May ,,	7,717	12,339	4,622*	158,279	7,717
June ,,	8,335	12,354	4,019*	154,260	5,378
July ,,	7,826	12,612	4,786*	149,474	5,370
August ,,	10,089	12,642	2,553*	146,291	5,361
September ,,	11,747	13,811	2,064*	144,857	3,204
October ,,	14,656	13,762	894	152,563‡	3,199
November ,,	13,942	13,742	200	152,763	1,799
December ,,	17,293	13,348	3,945	156,708	nil.
January 1910	—	—	3,954	160,662	nil.
February ,,	—	—	9,109	169,771	nil.
March ,,	—	—	8,574	178,345	nil.
April ,,	—	—	5,469	183,814	nil.
May ,,	—	—	150	183,964	nil.
June ,,	—	—	533*	183,431	nil.
July ,,	—	—	1,917*	181,514	nil.

* Net loss.   ‡ Including new members of Native Labour Association.

SOUTH AFRICAN GOVERNMENT SECURITIES:

Title.	Present Amount.	When Redeemable.	Price.	Yield.	Interest Payable.
CAPE COLONY.	£				
4½% Bonds	485,000	dwgs.	102	4$\frac{7}{8}$	15 Apr.—15 Oct.
4% Inscribed .	3,733,195	1923	103	3$\frac{3}{4}$	1 June—1 Dec.
4% 1888 ,, .	9,997,566	1916–36*	102½	3$\frac{11}{16}$	15 Apr.—15 Oct.
3½% 1886 ,, (t).	15,443,014	1929–49†	100	3$\frac{1}{2}$	1 Jan.—1 July.
3% 1886 ,, (t).	7,553,590	1933–43†	87	3$\frac{11}{16}$	1 Feb.—1 Aug.
NATAL.					
4½% Bonds, 1876 . .	758,700	1919	105	4	15 Mar.—15 Sep.
4% Inscribed (t) . .	3,026,444	1937	108	3$\frac{9}{16}$	Apr.—Oct.
3½% ,, (t) . .	3,714,917	1914–39†	99	3$\frac{9}{16}$	1 June—1 Dec.
3% ,, (t) . .	6,000,000	1929–49†	86	3$\frac{11}{16}$	1 Jan.—1 July.
TRANSVAAL.					
3% Guartd. Stock (t) .	35,000,000	1923–53†	93$\frac{3}{4}$	3$\frac{1}{4}$	1 May—1 Nov.

* Yield calculated on earlier date of redemption.
✦ Yield calculated on later date of redemption.
(t) Eligible for Trustee investments.

Rhodesia's gold output last month was somewhat disappointing, amounting to £195,233 against £214,709 for the preceding month, and £225,234 for the corresponding month of last year, as will be seen from the following table showing the monthly returns for some years past:

Month.	1910.	1909.	1908.	1907.	1906.
	£	£	£	£	£
January	227,511	204,666	199,380	168,240	155,337
February	203,888	192,497	191,635	145,397	137,561
March	228,385	202,157	200,615	167,424	160,722
April	228,213	222,700	212,935	175,210	157,108
May	224,888	225,032	223,867	189,216	169,218
June	214,709	217,600	224,920	192,506	170,083
July	195,233	225,234	228,151	191,681	173,313
August	—	228,296	220,792	192,106	179,000
September	—	213,249	204,262	192,186	173,973
October	—	222,653	205,466	191,478	161,360
November	—	236,307	196,668	183,058	175,656
December	—	233,397	217,316	190,383	171,770
Total	1,522,827	2,623,788	2,526,007	2,178,885	1,985,101

SOUTH AFRICAN RAILWAYS, BANKS, AND COMPANIES.

Title.	Number of Shares or Amount.	Dividend for last Year.	Paid up.	Price.	Yield.
Railways.					
Mashonaland 5% Debs.	£2,500,000	5	100	99	5
Rhodesia Rlys. 5% 1st Mort. Debs. guar. by B.S.A. Co. till 1915	£2,000,000	5	100	102	$4\frac{7}{8}$
Royal Trans-African 5% Debs. Rep.	£1,853,700	5	100	87	$5\frac{11}{16}$
Banks and Companies.					
African Banking Corporation £10 shares	80,000	$5\frac{1}{2}$	5	$4\frac{7}{8}$	$5\frac{5}{8}$
Bank of Africa £$18\frac{3}{4}$	160,000	5	$6\frac{1}{4}$	$6\frac{3}{4}$	$4\frac{5}{8}$
Natal Bank £10	148,232	8	$2\frac{1}{2}$	$3\frac{3}{8}$	$5\frac{7}{8}$
National Bank of S. Africa £10	110,000	3	10	$11\frac{3}{4}$	$2\frac{1}{2}$
Standard Bank of S. Africa £100	61,941	10	25	60	$4\frac{1}{8}$
Ohlsson's Cape Breweries	60,000	nil	5	4	—
South African Breweries	965,279	10	1	$1\frac{17}{32}$	$6\frac{1}{2}$
British South Africa (Chartered)	8,053,061	nil	1	$1\frac{1}{16}$	nil
Do. 5% Debs. Red.	£1,250,000	5	100	$105\frac{1}{2}$	$4\frac{11}{16}$
Natal Land and Colonization	68,066	4	5	$4\frac{1}{4}$	$4\frac{11}{16}$
Cape Town & District Gas Light & Coke	10,000	nil	10	$3\frac{1}{2}$	—
Kimberley Waterworks £10	45,000	5	7	$5\frac{1}{4}$	$6\frac{5}{8}$

SOUTH AFRICAN MUNICIPAL SECURITIES.

Title.	Present Amount.	When Redeemable.	Price.	Yield.	Interest Payable.
	£				
Bloemfontein 4%	663,000	1954	99	$4\frac{1}{16}$	1 Jan.—1 July.
Cape Town 4%	1,861,750	1953	103	$3\frac{7}{8}$	1 Jan.—1 July.
Durban 4%	850,000	1951-3	101	$3\frac{15}{16}$	30 June—31 Dec.
Johannesburg 4%	5,500,000	1933-4	$100\frac{1}{2}$	4	1 April—1 Oct.
Krugersdorp 4%	100,000	1930	96	$4\frac{5}{16}$	1 June—1 Dec.
Pietermaritzburg 4%	825,000	1949-53	99	$4\frac{1}{16}$	30 June—31 Dec.
Port Elizabeth 4%	374,060	1964	100	4	30 June—31 Dec.
Pretoria 4%	1,000,000	1939	101	$3\frac{15}{16}$	1 Jan.—1 July.
Rand Water Board 4%	3,400,000	1935	$100\frac{1}{2}$	4	1 Jan.—1 July.

CROWN COLONY SECURITIES.

Title.	Present Amount.	When Redeemable.	Price.	Yield.	Interest Payable.
Barbadoes 3½% ins. (*t*)	375,000	1925-42*	98	3¾	1 Mar.—1 Sep.
Brit. Guiana 3% ins. (*t*)	250,000	1923-45†	84	3 13/16	1 Feb.—1 Aug.
Ceylon 4% ins. (*t*) . .	1,076,100	1934	107	3½	15 Feb.—15 Aug.
Do. 3% ins. (*t*) . . .	2,850,000	1940	87½	3 11/16	1 May—1 Nov.
Hong-Kong 3½% ins (*t*)	1,485,733	1918-43†	98½	3⅝	15 Apr.—15 Oct.
Jamaica 4% ins. (*t*) .	1,099,048	1934	106	3 9/16	15 Feb.—15 Aug.
Do. 3½% ins. (*t*) . .	1,455,500	1919-49†	97	3⅝	24 Jan.—24 July.
Mauritius 3% guar. Great Britain (*t*) .	600,000	1940	92	3⅜	1 Jan.—1 July.
Do. 4% ins. (*t*) . . .	482,390	1937	106	3⅝	1 Feb.—1 Aug.
Sierra Leone 3½% ins. (*t*)	720,051	1929-54†	98½	3 9/16	1 June—1 Dec.
Trinidad 4% ins. . . .	422,593	1917-42*	104	3½	15 Mar.—15 Sep.
Do. 3% ins. (*t*) . . .	600,000	1922-44†	86	3 11/16	15 Jan.—15 July.
Hong-Kong & Shanghai Bank Shares .	120,000	Div. £4	£90	4 7/16	Feb.—Aug.

* Yield calculated on shorter period. † Yield calculated on longer period.
(*t*) Eligible for Trustee investments.

EGYPTIAN SECURITIES.

Title.	Amount or Number of Shares.	Dividend for last Year.	Paid up.	Price.	Yield.
Egyptian Govt. Guaranteed Loan (*t*) .	£7,414,700	3	99	98	3 1/16
" Unified Debt	£55,971,960	4	100	101½	3 15/16
National Bank of Egypt	300,000	9	10	21¼	4 3/16
Bank of Egypt	50,000	15	12½	29½	6 5/16
Agricultural Bank of Egypt, Ordinary	496,000	5¼	5	7⅝	3 7/16
" " " Preferred	125,000	4	10	9⅛	4⅜
" " " Bonds .	£2,350,000	3½	100	86	4 1/16

(*t*) Eligible for Trustee investments.

RUBBER SHARES.

Company.	Issued Capital.	Area planted.	Nominal Value of Share.	Amount paid-up.	Price.
	£	Acres.			
Anglo-Malay	150,000	3,391	2*s.*	2*s.*	25*s.*
Batu Tiga	60,000	1,545	£1	£1	5
Bukit Rajah	66,700	2,772	£1	£1	18
Consolidated Malay . . .	62,007	1,710	£1	2*s.*	27*s.* 9*d.*
Highlands and Lowlands .	317,353	4,707	£1	£1	6
Kepitigalla	225,000	3,127	£1	£1	⅞
Kuala Lumpur	180,000	2,611	£1	£1	9
Lanadron	269,780	4,570	£1	£1	6½
Linggi	100,000	4,192	2*s.*	2*s.*	55*s.*
Pataling.	22,500	1,454	2*s.*	2*s.*	3¼
Straits (Bertam)	200,000	2,541	2*s.*	2*s.*	8*s.*
Vallambrosa	50,600	1,807	2*s.*	2*s.*	43*s.* 9*d.*

There has been a slight revival of interest in Egyptian securities, but after last year's disappointment the public cannot be expected to take much of a hand in the market until the cotton crop reaches a more advanced stage.

Rubber shares have suffered another fall in company with the price of the raw product, but as far as can be seen at present there is every likelihood of a sufficient demand on the part of investors to keep the best class of shares from remaining long in the depths. Indeed, I should not be surprised to see a considerable rise shortly in all first-class rubber stock.

TRUSTEE.

August 22, 1910.

NOTICE TO CONTRIBUTORS.—The Editor of THE EMPIRE REVIEW cannot hold himself responsible in any case for the return of MS. He will, however, always be glad to consider any contributions which may be submitted to him; and when postage-stamps are enclosed every effort will be made to return rejected contributions promptly. Contributors are specially requested to put their names and addresses on their manuscripts, and to have them typewritten.

THE EMPIRE REVIEW

"Far as the breeze can bear, the billows foam,
Survey our empire, and behold our home."—*Byron.*

Vol. XX.   OCTOBER, 1910.   No. 117

THE APPROACHING CENSUS

II.—SOME ASPECTS OF POPULATION

By GEORGE T. BISSET-SMITH

H.M. Registration Examiner

MARRIAGE, the apex of life, is not reached by all; but we must all enter and depart from the world, must be born and must die. " I have three ' lines '; everybody must have two of them," was my reply to a partner in a commercial firm whom I met in a hotel at St. Andrews. He was at the Mecca of golf on business bent, but found little doing; and had observed me busy working. I had not golfed; everyone is assumed to golf at St. Andrews; otherwise you are regarded as a cumberer of the ground. My commercial friend, doubtless envious of my "getting all the business," wondered what was my line. He understood the mystery at once when I explained that I dealt with records of birth, death and marriage: the elemental factors of life and national numbers.

In a former article* I gave "some observations on the numbering of the people," in the present paper I propose to set forth briefly some aspects of population considered mainly in connection with the approaching Census.

Population is the basis of all public service and administration; and the importance of the population Census as a measure of our progress and a picture of our whole national work, is too little understood and appreciated. Never even seen by the majority of the public, the Census volumes are studied only by statisticians and sociologists, and only referred to occasionally by statesmen,

* See September issue.

administrators, and political economists. Rightly regarded, the Census figures reveal the garnered harvests of the human race, and it should always be remembered that the species is its own highest, its sole essential product. Generation after generation takes to itself the form of a body, emerges (as Carlyle puts it) from the inane, and hastens stormfully across the astonished earth. And in healthy conditions by far the larger number of these lives flitting across the stage of life go to swell the figures of our national stock-taking. To quote Adam Smith, "The most decisive mark of the prosperity of any country is the increase of the number of its inhabitants."

The population question is perennial. It is also chameleon-like, differing in colour according to time and place. During the last hundred and twenty years diametrically different opinions have been accepted, at least for a period. In one decade the cry was that we had not sufficient men for our Navy, a plausible enough cry while the struggle against Napoleon was in progress. The Census of 1801 showed that England and Wales had a population of 9,000,000. Cobbett denied the possibility of there being so many people, pointing out that, if it were true, in a hundred years our population would number 29,000,000. As a matter of fact, in 1901 the population of England and Wales exceeded 32,500,000.

Fear of over-population had its long day, begun by Malthus, and continued by well-meaning men like John Stuart Mill. Malthus invented the phrase "struggle for existence;" but he did not see far ahead, for when the Northern Kingdom had a population of less than a couple of millions he wrote: "Scotland is certainly over-peopled." Malthus, indeed, owing to the absence of reliable figures, worked at first a good deal in the dark; and, therefore, rather exaggerated the magnitude and the urgency of the danger which he discovered, and the possibilities of which he emphasised so effectively.

To-day it is generally agreed that population is strength and that its healthful increase adds to a nation's progress. Mere density or number, however, is not enough; there must be individual quality as well as numbers for real strength. As shown in India and China, over-population has obvious evils. But no country can continue powerful without a progressive population. The later Romans went down before the incursions of the barbarians—free tribes of purer habits, who had multiplied strongly in their native North, then fittingly named *officina nationum*, the storehouse of nations. Aristotle and Plato recommended the preservation of a fit proportion between territory and population; an insufficient population being dangerous to the independence, and an excess to the good order, of the State. Among the means of restriction mentioned by Aristotle were late marriages—men not to marry before thirty-seven, and the destruction of weak offspring.

The subject of population seems never to have been considered scientifically in this country until about the end of the eighteenth century; and the thorough treatment of the various aspects of the question arose synchronously with the large increase in the numbers of the people, and the troubles relative to a sufficient food-supply, consequent upon the changes in national life, resulting from the rapid and general development of industry.

Great Britain had passed through the barbaric, the pastoral, and the agricultural periods, and had reached an industrial epoch, when the essay of Malthus on population appeared. That work is more mentioned than read to-day—later on I shall comment on its main doctrines. Previous to the publication of the 'Principles of Population,' the world was content, for the most part, to multiply without worrying about the philosophy of population. Opinions which to a statistician appear very curious prevailed in pre-Malthus and pre-Census periods: and before giving some modern figures, it may be interesting to glance at a few of the remarkable conclusions put forward. To count is a very modern plan; the older writers preferred to guess as to numbers, and generally their guesses overshot the mark; guesses almost invariably tend towards extravagance.

Statistics of actual numbers not being available, many eighteenth-century writers arrived at conclusions not supported by facts, assigning, for example, an enormous population to several nations of antiquity. The opinion that the world supported a much larger number of people in ancient than in modern times was accepted by Robert Wallace (1697–1771) in his book on 'Various Prospects of Mankind, Nature, and Providence,' an Edinburgh work which stimulated Malthus. Hume is more sceptical in his elaborate and learned essay entitled, "The Populousness of Ancient Nations" (1741). He points out significantly that Diodorus Siculus, a contemporary of Cæsar, and who lived at that period of antiquity represented generally as most populous, complains of the desolation which then prevailed, gives the preference to former times, and has recourse to ancient fables as a foundation for his opinion. But Montesquieu believed that the ancient world *regorgéainent d'habitants;* even the accurate Gibbon made far too large an estimate of the Roman Empire. The entire population of the Empire under Augustus is reckoned at 85 millions, 40 millions being in the European, and 45 millions in the Asiatic provinces. Gibbon's calculation is "one hundred and twenty millions of persons: a degree of population which possibly exceeded that of modern Europe, and forms the most numerous society that has ever been united under one form of Government." * To-day, 130 years after the time at which Gibbon penned this sentence, the British Empire has a population of nearly 440 millions.

Population appears to have been a current question in the eighteenth century. "Whether by the encouragement of proper laws the number of births in Great Britain might not be nearly doubled, or, at least, greatly increased," was a subject brought in 1763 by Professor Reid before the Aberdeen Philosophical Society. And Malthus was anticipated by a discussion, in 1766, in the same Society, upon the other view of the subject, "Whether good policy may not sometimes justify the laying a restraint upon population in a State?"

The opinion that population was stationary was expressed by Botero, and, later, by Buffon. That unsupported view appears also in the article by Damilaville in Diderot's Encyclopédie (1765). The sum of men, asserts the encyclopædist, taken together is to-day equal to that of an epoch of antiquity, and to that which it will be in future ages. If (he adds) there have been periods when a greater or lesser scarcity of men appeared to exist, it was not because the total number was less, but that the population was migratory, and thus there occurred local diminutions of population. Voltaire estimated, in 1753, that the globe contained sixteen hundred millions ; an estimate somewhat larger than that even of its present population, for such guesses almost always exceed actuality. In our own age of inquiry and statistics, the number of formally enumerated countries is fairly satisfactory ; the principal exceptions being Africa, China, Turkey, Persia, the wild tracts of Central and South America, and the large islands of the South-Eastern Seas.

At every Census population figures are coming more out of the region of conjecture into that of definite enumeration. The percentage of the population of Europe now enumerated regularly is nearly 99 ; of America, 93 ; of Oceania, 85 ; of Asia, 37 ; of Africa, over 12 ; and the total population of the world at the beginning of 1901 was approximately, 1,583,621,000.

TABLE SHOWING THE POPULATION OF THE GLOBE AT THE 1901 CENSUS.

Continent.	Total Population Partly Estimated.	Percentage Enumerated.	Inhabitants per Sq. Mile.
Europe . . .	393,622,000	98·4	104
Asia	874,282,000	37·0	55
Africa	164,319,000	12·1	14
America . . .	145,661,000	92·8	9
Oceania . . .	5,652,000	84·5	1·6
Polar Regions . .	85,000	...	...
The World . . .	1,583,621,000	...	...

* 'History of the Decline and Fall of the Roman Empire,' Chapter II.

The population which can be supported by a country depends largely upon the resources and the requirements of the people. Pastoral communities need a large area. Agricultural populations also must generally be sparse; but where a people with few wants have a fertile soil, as in portions of India, Egypt and China, an enormous population can be supported. In most countries, however, mineral resources and manufacturing industries are necessary for the maintenance of a dense population. The United Kingdom has a population of 300 to the square mile. In some areas of England, however, it is 500. Japan has 290 to the square mile; Canada, 1·5 and Siberia, 1. If the present rate of increase continues for 200 years, the world will have (it has been asserted) the maximum population which the earth has been estimated to be able to support under existing conditions, namely, 6,000 millions.

The marriage-rate of England is affected apparently as a whole by the value of exports, the marriages going up and down synchronously with the exports. Thus, a curve of value of exports is followed fairly closely by the fluctuations in the yearly number of marriages. Sex-distribution also affects the nuptiality of a country. In most populations there are more women than men. But more boys are born than girls, the ratio being about 207 to 200. The male death-rate is, however, higher than that of the female, partly because men lead harder lives. Age-distribution is also a factor. In young countries, profiting by immigration, there is always a larger proportion of both men and women at the marriageable and child-producing period.

The numbers of births and deaths in any civilised country can readily be obtained. It would thus, at first glance, seem easy to calculate the rate; but, in reality, it is almost impossible, for the basis of calculation — the exact population — cannot generally be procured. For the purposes of reports, it has to be assumed that the increase of the population continues at the same rate as revealed by the last Census. And this assumption (that the increase of population continues), while occasionally unreliable in the case of a smaller area, gives for a large community, and especially for a whole country, generally a fairly accurate estimate of the number of its inhabitants. But birth- and death-rates are sometimes only reasonable approximations for certain limited areas.

In 1876 the birth-rate per thousand of the population in Scotland was 35, and in France 26·2. In 1893 it was 31 and 22·1 respectively: while in 1902 it had fallen further to 29·2 in Scotland, the lowest on record, and to 22 in France, where the decrease in natality constitutes a national danger.

TABLE SHOWING EMIGRANTS FROM UNITED KINGDOM TO NON-EUROPEAN
COUNTRIES, 1876-1900.

Quinquennial Period.	English.		Scots.		Irish.		Total.
	Number.	Per Cent.	Number.	Per Cent.	Number.	Per Cent.	Number.
1876–1880	425,550	60	70,596	10	213,236	30	709,382
1881–1885	760,124	59	133,527	10	398,658	31	1,292,309
1886–1890	788,841	62	141,568	11	335,817	27	1,266,226
1891–1895	617,869	63	100,878	10	259,827	27	978,574
1896–1900	478,022	63	85,104	11	201,090	26	764,216
1876–1900	3,070,406	61	531,673	10	1,408,628	28	5,010,707

As nuptiality and natality are the forces at work increasing
population, so death and emigration diminish it. From the
United Kingdom there is a steady outflow of emigrants, so that
never can the alteration of the population be determined by the
simple process of merely deducting the deaths from the births.
Not a little of the increase in population is due not to increase in
births, but to the diminution of deaths. The birth-rate has
declined. There has, however, been an even greater proportionate
decline in the death-rate, and the diminution of the annual death-
rate to 15, 14, 13 or thereby, per thousand, affects very favourably
the increase of population.

That the decrease of births in the mother-country is bad for
Greater Britain appears to be a fair deduction from the figures in
the above tabular statement, which reveals a falling-off in emigration from 1890 onwards. And the table below shows that, next
to the United States, the greatest annual rate of increase is now
accredited to our formidable commercial rival, Germany.

TABLE SHOWING THE ANNUAL RATE PER CENT. OF INCREASE, IN A CENTURY,
OF THE UNITED STATES AND EUROPE.

Country.	1800–1850.	1850–1900.	By Last Census.
United States	3·00	2·39	1·90
England and Wales	1·41	1·21	1·15
France	0·52	0·20	0·13
Belgium	0·76	0·88	1·06
Spain	0·48	0·51	0·54
Italy	0·56	0·58	0·69
Holland	0·73	1·01	1·24
Austria	0·58	0·79	0·89
Hungary	0·57	0·75	0·95
Norway	0·94	0·92	1·10
Sweden	0·79	0·78	0·71
Denmark	0·84	1·11	1·09
Finland	0·91	0·92	1·01
Germany	0·96	0·99	1·50

The treatise of Malthus was entitled originally "An Essay on the Principle of Population as it affects the Future Improvement of Society, with Remarks on the Speculations of Mr. Godwin, Monsieur Condorcet, and other Writers." The work startled the world, which hitherto had been content mostly to multiply without much scientific speculation as to the Philosophy of Population.

A mind of original caste, trained out of the ordinary mental ruts of the time, was required for an inquiry so remarkable. The British schoolboy at that period was reared upon routine, rather dulling to the edge of inquiring intellect. Such education tended to produce men suitable to administer things exactly as they are established, but not to encourage originators, and one is not surprised to learn that Malthus was never at a public school, but was taught by private tutors. At home the boy breathed an atmosphere of social philosophy. His father was a cultured gentleman of independent fortune; a friend, and one of the executors of Rousseau. Malthus was ninth wrangler, a Fellow of Jesus College, Cambridge, and entered the Church. The beginnings of the essay are noteworthy. The father of Malthus, a comfortable optimist, was inclined to the cheerful views of Godwin and Condorcet on the Perfectibility of Human Society. But, in their prolonged discussions, Malthus maintained that the perfecting of human prosperity and happiness would always be hindered by the tendency of population to increase faster than the means of subsistence. The father asked the son to put his views and arguments into writing, thereafter recommending publication: and, thus composed, the famous essay first saw the light in 1798.

To a clear understanding of the essay, it is advisable to glance, not only at its genesis, but also at the condition of this country at that period: and in the early years of Malthus, when the impressions received were strongest, that condition was one of want, trouble, and transition. Industry was rising with astounding rapidity. Population was increasing at a rate regarded as alarming; whilst a succession of bad seasons had produced scarcity of food and impoverished the agricultural classes. Heavy customs and import duties impeded exchange. Black and ominous appeared the outlook for an overcrowded community—fit time for the acceptance of the views of Malthus.

Belief that space and subsistence were abundant and unfailing explains much of the neglect of the subject of population until the appearance of the epoch-making essay. Much of Asia and nearly all Africa was yet unknown or unexplored. Australia was only very partially colonised; and the great American continent seemed likely to be able to receive our superfluous sons and daughters for many centuries. With the widening of geographical knowledge, however, it was seen that the uninhabited spaces of the globe were not so immeasurably vast as had been imagined.

Demographic conceptions also altered very much with the fall of feudalism, under which the chief care of every superior, as of every sovereign, was to have a large number of men fit to bear arms ; an economic organisation which became obsolete with the rise of industry and capitalism, revolutionising the general idea of the value of men. The conditions of the time were thus most favourable to the full acceptance of Malthusianism, of which the following are the three main propositions :—

(a) Population is necessarily limited by the means of subsistence.

(b) Population invariably increases where the means of subsistence increase, unless prevented by some very powerful and obvious checks.

(c) These checks, and the checks which repress the superior power of population, and keep its effects on a level with the means of subsistence, are all resolvable into moral restraint, vice, and misery.

As already pointed out, Malthus had to work without reliable figures ; and had the national numbering of the people commenced a century earlier, Malthus would have been saved from several statistical errors. After the first Census (1801), Malthus brought out a revised edition of his essay, and four following editions in 1806, 1807, 1817, and 1826. The so-called "law" relating to the geometrical increase of population formulated by Malthus has been gradually repealed. It is to the effect that :—Population, when unchecked, doubles in twenty-five years, increasing in geometrical ratio. The means of subsistence increase only in arithmetical ratio.

If the doubling dictum worked out in practice, the population of this island, 11 millions in 1800, would have been 176 millions in 1900, and would reach 352 millions in 1925! There is much virtue, therefore, in the italicised qualifying words "when unchecked." For at all times the checks upon mankind multiplying operate through disease, want, war, vice, circumstances, and will.

In regard to the means of subsistence, the general introduction of machinery has increased the industrial capacity of mankind more than tenfold. It is, accordingly, no longer allowable to call, even by courtesy, the hypothesis of Malthus a law. Statistics prove that his theory is in disagreement with the reliable and concrete data as to population and subsistence; indeed, the more complete the statistical material, the severer is the falsification and refutation of the Malthusian statement regarding geometrical increase. Malthusianism, accordingly, is not only dead, but buried without hope of resurrection. It was the most remarkable paralogism ever accepted by unstatistical and short-sighted philosophy.

Malthus, to do him justice, has been a good deal misrepresented in recent times, much that is said of his views being from second-hand acquaintance. He did not deny that an increase of population is both a great positive good in itself and absolutely necessary to a further increase in the annual produce of the land and labour of any country. His opinions are thus diametrically opposed to the doctrines now popularly associated with the name of Malthus.

The birth-rate of Great Britain was at its greatest about 1876; in 1877 came into notice the doctrine promulgated by Mrs. Besant and Mr. Charles Bradlaugh as a means of ameliorating the condition of the wage-earner. Malthus had advocated moral restraint; he disapproved distinctly of any immoral restraint, and this earnest and upright English clergyman would have heard with horror the views inculcated by the so-called Malthusian League. It is, indeed, a curious irony of fate that the name of Malthus has come to be associated with practices he so expressly disowned and against which the medical profession, as a body, has generally given strong condemnatory opinion, Neo-Malthusian practices being denounced by most doctors as degrading mentally and morally, and frequently injurious to both sexes in physical effects. In the words of honest Malthus : "I should always particularly reprobate any artificial and unnatural modes of checking population, both on account of their immorality and their tendency to remove a necessary stimulus to industry." Indeed, the overflow of the River of Life, the excess of Fertility, has been a cause of man's further advance.

Pressure of population is an important factor in human endeavour. Were it not for this pressure, as Herbert Spencer observes, so much thought and energy would not be spent daily on the business of life, and growth of mental power would not take place. Nothing but necessity could make men submit to this discipline, and nothing but this discipline could produce a continued progression. The long-continued application of adults is accentuated in the case of those who have children by a desire to give their offspring a good start, and is thus an incentive to higher education, to the life-long mental development of man.

The subject of man's fertility is of great interest at this epoch. The scientist and philosopher are agreed that the degree of fertility is proportionate inversely to the grade of development, and that, therefore, higher degrees of evolution must be accompanied by lower rates of multiplication. "Individuation" and "Genesis" vary inversely.

Pressure of population has increased the ability to maintain existence, but has decreased the ability and the will to multiply. That is partly why the death-rate and the birth-rate are both decreasing on an average. The effect is not a uniform effect, but a general one. All may not advance under the discipline of life in these days, but, in the nature of things, only those who do advance are successful and survive. Those who fail and succumb are those, in the average, whose energy and strength of self-preservation are least, while those who advance and successfully continue the race are matured by the struggle, and constitute the select of their generation.

"Life is not for work and learning," said Spencer, "but work and learning are for life." Man's progress in the future must lie in the development of mind. The body has developed to a stand-still. Culture of mind tends to diminish fertility. Pressure of population disappears as its end is attained. Man's advance is complete physically. It must now be psychical. And, again in Spencer's words, "This greater emotional and intellectual development does not mean a mentally laborious life, for, as it gradually becomes organic, it will become spontaneous and pleasurable."

Action should not be repressive, but progressive. Advancing evolution must be accompanied by declining fertility, moving towards a time when the amount of life shall be the greatest possible—that is, in its highest form; and the rate of reproduction that suited to the requirements of communities. Tendency is shown towards self-adjustment—the movement of things towards equilibrium; a reduction of births accompanying a diminution of deaths; the balancing of mortality and natality.

The twin goals to which the biologist and the philosopher point are :—

    (a) The Improvement of the People—"Racial Eugenics"— Good-breeding, in every sense of the phrase.

    (b) The conscious and rational adjustment of the "struggle for" into the "culture of" existence.

Gradually the "struggle for life" is reaching the higher standard of "the struggle for the life of others."

During the last century our Empire showed a steady advance in population. Inclusive of the Indian Feudatory States, the British Empire had a population of about 259 millions in 1861. Twenty years later it had reached nearly 310 millions. Largely owing to acquisitions, the total had grown to more than 381 millions at the Census of 1891.

The largest aggregate of population ever united under one political control, the British Empire, is also the most varied in condition, physical and sociological. The Empire contains more than a fourth of the population of the globe, and more than a fifth of its inhabitable area. ⸱ Its growth during the last thirty years has been from a population of 235 millions and an area of about 7,770,000 square miles, to 420 millions and an area of about 12,000,000 square miles ; while its trade is about one-third of that of the whole world, thus accounting for its immense wealth and predominance.

TABLE SHOWING THE POPULATION OF THE BRITISH EMPIRE, 1903.

Division of the Empire.	White Inhabitants (including French and Dutch).	Native Inhabitants : Brown, Black and Yellow.
United Kingdom . .	42,000,000	..
Australia and Islands . .	5,000,000	700,000
Canada . . .	5,500,000	100,000
India and Ceylon . .	100,000	300,000,000
West Indies and Bermuda .	100,000	1,700,000
Africa	1,100,000	60,000,000
Total of White . .	53,800,000	362,500,000
Do. Native . .	362,500,000	
Grand Total . . .	416,300,000	

Are we worthy of this prodigious inheritance—the British Empire? Is the race which holds it capable of maintaining and developing it? This nation might do worse than inquire— " Suppose that when it decennially takes stock of its population. that it took stock of a little more. Suppose when it numbered the people, that it tested their plight—that it inquired if their condition were better or worse than it was ten years before ; and so as to the position of our industries, of our education, of our naval and military systems."

That was the suggestion of Lord Rosebery in his Rectorial Address upon Questions of Empire, delivered in 1900 at Glasgow. It is characteristically thorough. And⸱ the quotation may be continued: "The general result would probably be satisfactory ; but it may be predicted with much more certainty that weaknesses and abuses and stagnation would be discovered, an ill condition which is apt, when neglected, to be contagious and dangerous. . . The shadow of the future is as vain as all other shadows. Prosperity, while it endures, is the drug, the haschish, which blinds men to all but golden visions."

With its careful analysis of Occupations, the Census of 1911 will be a test of the people's plight, of their progress and condition; and a Report is to appear on the population of the whole Empire.

In view of the debate in Parliament this year regarding the question of taking a Census of religion in England, Wales, and Scotland, it is noteworthy that for the Census in 1901 of the Empire statistics are available for 319 millions, being about four-fifths of the total population. No returns were made regarding the religion of the remaining 79 millions.

Of the 319 millions, more than 20 millions, exclusive of the population of Great Britain, were returned as professing one or other form of Christianity. Over 295 millions were classified under non-Christian religions, while the remainder, amounting to fewer than 4 millions, were classed as having no religion or as "indefinitely expressed." If to these numbers the population of Great Britain at the Census of 1901, 37 millions, and—representing the Christians in the Colonies where no religious Census was taken—a further half million is added, there is reached a total of over $57\frac{1}{2}$ millions. According to the Registrar-General, that number, approaching 60 millions, may be taken as the total number of persons classified as Christians in the British Empire at last Census.

With regard to a religious Census, as some statements in my September article have been quoted as being against the inclusion of a question in the British Schedule, I may be allowed to emphasise the fact that my objections are evolved from experience and are not in any way the result of personal predilection. Indeed, personally, I see no objection to the obtaining of data regarding religious beliefs. It is the difficulty of securing reliable replies that gives one pause. Had a question been inserted in the British Schedule—to adapt Gibbon's famous phrase—"sighed as a lover, but obeyed as a son"—the Census official would have obeyed zealously as a civil servant, but, possibly, sighed as a statistician. In the Upper House, Lord Newton asserted in the discussion that "Any man would rather state his religion than his income." A Scotsman surely is not ashamed to own his Church, and not only is a church a spiritual entity, but it has also an organised social side which does good work; such an organisation forming an aspect of national life not to be ignored even by the least spiritual. The only point is the procuring of quite reliable information; and I may quote the late Dr. Ogle's reply to the Census Committee with respect to the question of a return of religious belief: "I have no special view about it myself. I am afraid you would not get very accurate returns. Of course there would be no difficulty whatsoever in tabulating the information given except cost. There are, I believe, not far from 200 religious sects, and the smaller a sect is the more will it insist upon being recognised; consequently, you would have to tabulate these returns, trustworthy or not, under a very large number of headings. But of course that is only a matter of cost; there would be no difficulty about tabulation if the data were given."

Some years ago I discussed vital registration and the Census with an Austrian, when I learned that "State your religion" was a question in the Austrian Schedule, a document which is as large as an open sheet of, say, *The Daily Telegraph*. Along with it is distributed six pages of instructions. The head of the family is required to state, among other things, on the Schedule: The precise place and date of birth; number of years of residence in present place; the principal and secondary languages used in the family; the principal and collateral occupations, and the number of workmen, artisans and apprentices he employs. Whether unemployed? Number of domestic animals? Description of each room? Have you a bath-room? Gas or electricity? How much rent do you pay? And proof is required wherever documentary evidence can be procured; birth and marriage certificates, for instance, being demanded; and mis-statement is punished severely. Austria puts up with this exhaustive inquisition, but I do not think the average Briton would readily answer such a series of inquiries; and I mention the foregoing questions to indicate how far a census is carried on the Continent. I understand that the German Census Schedule also contains an inquiry as to religion, which I am assured is answered without a thought of refusal.

The British Census is less comprehensive. The success of our Census is, indeed, a result of its comparative simplicity and of continuity of system. The British Schedule has grown, however, with time; but its development has been reasonable. Innovations have been introduced with great care and only after prolonged deliberation. In another article I shall hope to explain, with some completeness, the fresh features, still under discussion, of the approaching enumeration; and I may conclude this paper with a brief preliminary sketch of the rise of the Census.

The Census was probably the most important function discharged by the Censor in ancient Rome; and he kept a register of property and imposed taxes upon the basis of the information obtained at the Census. Although necessarily statistical in character, the Roman enumeration was thus fiscal mainly in purpose. The Censor watched over the morals of the Romans, and possibly the information procured at the Census had some influence upon legislation. Its main object, however, was the apportionment, according to their property, of the duties and rights of citizens. The Romans were divided into six classes, which were sub-divided into centuries. The subdivision was made according to a ratio calculated upon wealth and numbers. The Roman Census showed the number and respective class of all free persons, their domestic position as husbands and wives, fathers and mothers, sons and daughters. Slaves and freedmen were enumerated with the possessions of the head of the house. Land was classified according to its character and produce. The Census was conducted every five years. It was followed by a sacrifice of purification (lustration), and the period of five years came hence to be called lustrum. The grading by property qualification gave such phrases as Census senatorius, and Census equester. In later times we have *Census dominicatus*, a feudal tax to the lord or superior, and *Census duplicatus*, a feudal casualty, a double tax. Old English writers use cense, which became abbreviated into the modern cess.

No numbering of the people took place in the Middle Ages, however, and the word Census at that period was applied only to taxation, which did not require an enumeration of the inhabitants. Economic ends and the adjustment of social rank did not call during a period of 1,700 years at least for a Census in England ; nor was it until the eighteenth century that the subject was discussed practically in Great Britain.

The purpose and scheme of the Census Schedule of this country are familiar ; its chief purpose is demographical, and its scheme necessarily simple. Simplicity indeed is the first requisite of a successful Census ; for the questions have to be answered not only by the educated and methodical, but by the ignorant and careless. Unlike the Roman Census—a Register by the Censor of the citizens and their property—the modern Census is universal, and the replies are recorded by the informants themselves in the Schedules. Accordingly, the questions put at the Census must be quite clear, definite, and not difficult to answer nor inquisitorial.

The primary purpose of the Census is to ascertain the population of a given place at a given time. This is *la population de fait* of France, as distinguished from *la population de droit*. The latter comprises all usually resident in the district including those temporarily absent ; it excludes those only temporary present. *La population municipale* is *la population de droit* minus prisoners in gaols, patients in hospitals, scholars resident in schools, the army, and members of convents, and the like. The Census of the United States being prescribed by its constitution, has a total population, a general population, and a constitutional population ; the last excludes residents in Indian Reservations, the Territories, and the District of Columbia. *La population de fait* is the aim of the British Census, which includes the Channel Islands and the Isle of Man.

Two hundred years ago, our forefathers resented much

Government interference and bureaucracy. Upon the Continent, where men were less free and rule was more despotic and much more centralised, statistical inquiries into the numbers of the inhabitants were carried out whenever occasion arose in particular areas. In the words of the well-known statistician Dr. W. Farr:—" It was in Britain, with its abstinent Government and unrestrained people that the want of population statistics became most flagrantly conspicuous. It is difficult at present to realise the idea that, long after Adam Smith's time, the number of the inhabitants of the British Empire could only be guessed at as the populousness of China is at the present day; and, as in all matters of statistics, which have their own simple solution through specific inquiry, the guesses about the population of the Empire were not only vague but extravagantly contradictory."

The Roman Census, as we have seen, was not that of persons only, but also of property ; but the British Census has never yet attempted, although it has frequently been suggested, anything in the direction of a record of possessions or their value. A proposal for a Census of Great Britain first appeared in 1753, and was contained in a Bill for taking an annual account of the total number of the people, and of marriages, births and deaths ; also of the poor receiving alms. But this Bill was thrown out in the Lords, who took the popular side on this question. The Bill was received with a virulence of animadversion that to-day seems astounding. The member for the City of York said :—" I did not believe that there was any set of men, or indeed, any individual of the human species, so presumptuous and so abandoned, as to make the proposal we have just heard. . . . I hold this project to be totally subversive of the last remains of English liberty. . . . The new Bill will direct the imposition of new taxes, and, indeed, the addition of a very few words will make it the most effectual engine of rapacity and oppression that was ever used against an injured people. . . . Moreover, an annual register of our people will acquaint our enemies abroad with our weakness." The scheme was denounced, further, as being borrowed from " our natural enemies," the French, and as " costly and impracticable," and likely to be followed by an " epidemical distemper ! " These Biblical and other objections to the Census gradually disappeared. A great change in the public mind had come about before 1800, when a new Bill was introduced. Instead of the fear that the population was falling off, and that an enumeration would betray the insufficiency of our supply of soldiers, an alarm had arisen that the people were increasing too rapidly for the means of subsistence—a scare partly due to a dearth at this time, but more to the publication in 1798 of the essay by Malthus on the ' Principles of Population.' It was now seen that a Census was for several reasons absolutely necessary, and the British Population Bill was passed without opposition in November 1800. The periodical enumeration of the people of Great Britain, which was thus originated in March 1801, has been repeated ever since in the first year of each decennium.

The Census (Ireland) Act, 1910 (10 Edw. 7 & 1 Geo. 5) was passed on July 26th, 1910, and the Census (Great Britain) Act, 1910 (10 Edw. 7 & 1 Geo. 5) received the royal assent on August 3rd. Both these Acts authorise an inquiry into the Fertility of Marriage. Very suggestive and sinister has been the decline in the rate of increase shown in our population in recent decennia. This steady falling-off in the birth-rate has affected the whole Empire, and accordingly a consideration of Fertility of Marriage has been deemed desirable as a special feature of the approaching Census.

The method and details of collecting and tabulating such information and other new features I propose to treat in a further contribution dealing specially with the fresh features of the coming Census. Incidentally, I may describe the machinery of the Census; the growth of London and Glasgow, of the population of India and America; touching upon the decline of Ireland's numbers; and explain that massing together into stupendous aggregations which is the outstanding result revealed at all recent Censuses. It is a movement of concentration accompanied by expansion, seen in the most striking way in Birmingham, Manchester, Greater Glasgow, and Greater London. Men are forsaking birth-places for work-places, and thus, perforce, the country for the city.

GEORGE T. BISSET-SMITH.

THE SOUTH AFRICAN ELECTIONS

SIDELIGHTS FROM SPEECHES

By A SOUTH AFRICAN

AT Smithfield on August 19th, General Hertzog concluded a most virulent speech by asserting that "the Unionist method of fighting is that of the slanderer and the racialist. They have sown the wind, let them be careful lest they reap the whirlwind." The South African electorate has answered this warning in a manner hardly encouraging to the Hertzog extremists, and by returning Dr. Jameson unopposed for Albany and by a large majority for the Harbour Division of Capetown has evidently accepted General Botha's judgment regarding the distinguished leader of the Unionist party: "I have always found Dr. Jameson as anxious as I am that racialism should be avoided."

Addressing an audience at Graham's Town,* Dr. Jameson, with equal courtesy, expressed his personal conviction of General Botha's sincerity: "I hoped (he said) to present you with a Government composed of the best men that could be got, irrespective of race or party divisions. That was my desire; instead of that, I am here as leader of the Opposition Party, determined to make the most strenuous efforts I can against the first Union Government of South Africa. You will say, Why? Why this going back? My answer is, the constitution of the present Government. I will premise at once by saying that throughout these negotiations, and the previous negotiations during the convention and subsequent to the convention, up to the last time I saw the Prime Minister, about ten days ago, I have never had to complain of anything but candid truth from him. I believe he is in absolute accord with not only the broad principles of the Unionist party programme, but every detail that I am in favour of. But he is in the hopeless position of a minority in his own cabinet, and we know that the majority rules the minority. I know he is perfectly at one with me in the

* August 18th.

spirit. You will say : ' Why not give the Prime Minister a chance ? ' Certainly I will, and the only chance he can get is through a large Unionist minority if not a majority." To prove the truth of this summary of the situation Dr. Jameson referred to past acts and past speeches of the majority of the Botha Cabinet, adding : " And remember that their past speeches and past acts have not been contradicted by present speeches or acts."

That the record of the past was being emphasised and reiterated became painfully evident as the election campaign proceeded. The *Cape Times* truly expressed the regret and misgiving felt by all moderate South Africans when it uttered an emphatic protest against the bitter racialism so violently expressed by General Hertzog. A few specimens of this gentleman's oratory will suffice : " I do believe it would not be saying too much if it were alleged that the largest portion of their time (the Opposition) is being spent in inventing fiction and preparing it for the daily press." The Opposition " gang " are accused of distortion and misrepresentation, of endeavouring to flood South Africa with racialism " under the hypocritical pretext of protecting the rights of those who were English-speaking " ; furthermore, " they have at their service almost the whole daily press of South Africa, fed by men crammed with hatred towards Dutch-speaking South Africans, men whose only virtue lies in the readiness and faithfulness with which they prostitute their talents and journalistic skill for the sake of their pay." Dr. Jameson's dignity and forbearance under this storm of groundless abuse enhanced his great personal influence. The *Cape Times*, however, justly condemned these outbursts by pointing out that " A politician who uses such language regarding the great majority of English-speaking South Africans—for the great majority belong to Dr. Jameson's party, and recognise him as their leader—is an offence anywhere ; but in a South African Cabinet at the present juncture he is a public danger." Since the above comment appeared, the result of the elections shows that Hertzogism is not to continue its harmful influence unchecked. The fact that General Botha's appointment as Prime Minister was so widely welcomed by English-speaking South Africans is sufficient answer to General Hertzog's outrageous calumnies. In previous numbers of *The Empire Review* I have already tried to indicate some of the reasons why confidence in General Botha's judgment was shaken in South Africa, but, as the *Bloemfontein Post* has pointed out, the Union Prime Minister may find his defeat at Pretoria a blessing, " if he reads the lesson aright."

Some curious " Liberal " chickens are coming home to roost in South Africa. In a speech eulogising the Liberal Colonial policy,

General Hertzog said : " If the great and noble British statesmen who followed Mr. Chamberlain and the other participators in the criminal war have not had the power to restore their independence to the Republics, they have at least given us that which comes nearest to that independence—full and free self-government, with the recognition of a status of equals within the Imperial State building." Referring to this criticism of Mr. Chamberlain and his colleagues, the *Cape Times* remarks : " Now no one expects General Hertzog to agree with the policy of the war ; but every citizen of the British Empire has a right to expect a politician who is at present a Minister of the British Crown to refrain from denouncing a war waged by the Crown as ' criminal.' No South African of British extraction has the smallest desire to reopen questions which we had all imagined were to be regarded as closed ; but if, in his capacity as Minister, General Hertzog insists on doing so, then he must understand that thousands who are quite as patriotic South Africans as he is, refuse to be dragooned into accepting his views on the war." In face of General Hertzog's statement I confess that I find it difficult to understand General Botha's utterance at Pretoria a few days later : " Everyone would have noticed that the leaders of his party had studiously refrained from any reference to their pre-war differences. What possibly could be gained by raking up the dreadful past ? What good would be done by opening old wounds, which to all intents and purposes were healed ? Every true patriot had almost insensibly avoided any unpleasant reference to those sad events."

It would seem that the Prime Minister might well have addressed this warning and rebuke to his own Minister of Justice, for as Mr. Alexander (now elected as Unionist member for the Castle Division, Cape Town) justly remarked : " They had in the Ministry a man who had done more to cause the racial flames, which had practically died out, to spring up again than any other man in the history of South Africa. He referred to General Hertzog. His policy in the Free State, which consisted in forcing all the children in the country to learn every subject in both languages, if it were not so tragical in its influence and effect upon the education of children, would be farcical. He considered that the parents should decide the matter for themselves. General Hertzog was the apostle of compulsion, and it was absurd for the Ministry to say that it was not responsible for what he did." Speaking at Cape Town on August 30, Dr. Jameson referred to General Hertzog's education policy, and English teachers leaving the Free State in consequence. Bearing in mind the part the Chinese agitation played in the last English elections, one wonders if the Liberal leaders approve of the Free State door being practically slammed in the face of British teachers? As Dr. Jameson shrewdly pointed out: "There are more ways of killing a cat without shooting it, and what the Director of Education had charged General Hertzog with was what he knew to be a fact, which was that at the present moment at least two-thirds of the English teachers in the Orange Free State had gone from the country; and if things were not changed, the other third would have gone too."

The reasons for this deplorable state of affairs have been fully explained by Mr. Hugh Gunn, and, on August 24, he again cited some of the more important points: "General Hertzog's own law lays it down that teachers must learn Dutch in three years or else be removed—whatever that may mean. Besides, the second circular issued by the Department showed clearly that unilingual teachers could look for no promotion. 'Whenever vacancies hereafter occur,' the circular stated, 'it will be necessary, in order to meet the requirements of the law, to appoint teachers who have a competent knowledge of both languages.' If setting a three-year limit in which to learn Dutch or take the consequences, and blocking the road to promotion isn't threatening the English teacher, what is?" Questioned regarding General Hertzog's statement as to the larger salaries in the Transvaal and elsewhere having tempted many of the imported teachers to leave the Free State service, Mr. Gunn emphatically replied: "I could cite General Hertzog cases of teachers who took largely reduced salaries elsewhere, simply in order to get out of the atmosphere created by the Hertzog policy. Many begged to be given posts at a bare living wage in Rhodesia, anywhere away from the Free State locality which had become so intolerable for them. No, there are two reasons why the bulk of the imported teachers have left, and the rest wish to leave. In the first place, the Hertzog Act excited racial animosities all over the Free State, stirring Dutch-speaking people up against English-speaking people. After three years of perfect peace before General Hertzog came into power, local feeling was being roused to a deplorably high pitch. And in the second place, English teachers know only too well that if the bitter faction appealed to General Hertzog against them, the Minister would always lend a ready ear and take the anti-British side." This treatment of English teachers seems a unique way of requiting the unparalleled generosity shown to the Free State by the Liberal Government.

One wonders also if the Liberal leaders endorse the immigration policy of their Free State admirer. It would appear that "the great and noble British statesmen" are being smitten in more ways than one in the Nationalist house of their supposed friends in South Africa, for Mr. Merriman, when referring to the Union Premiership in his speech at Victoria West on August 19, stated that : " The Progressive party and the magnates were entirely in favour of starting on the Transvaal lines, and, of course the opinion of these worthies was bound to have great weight with the Liberal Government in England." The immigration question is of such wide Imperial interest that the divergence between extreme Nationalist and moderate Unionist opinions is noteworthy. The encouragement of European immigration was one of the planks of the Nationalist programme issued by General Botha, but General Hertzog's views hardly coincide with those of his chief. In his Smithfield speech the Minister of Justice declared that : " There is nothing more detestable than the cry for immigration from outside, when it is taken into consideration the bad results which will be the fruits thereof, if under existing circumstances this is persisted in. The capitalists, from whom that cry now goes forth, will, it is true, be benefited thereby, but what of the labourer who must earn his bread by the sweat of his brow ? What about the South African who is now in the towns, languishing for help to be given the opportunity for removing to the land to find relief for himself and his children ? " After a tirade against the capitalists, to whom he imputed the worst motives, General Hertzog continued : " I repeat, there must be immigration from the towns to the land, but under present circumstances Government-aided immigration from outside to South Africa would be a crime—a crime against the labourer, who will not go on to the land, but just as much a crime against the poor man in South Africa, be he a labourer or not, who does not wish to go on the land. Of the moral mischief and personal ruin, which will be the result of the failure of an immigration undertaking, I will not even speak. Anyone of us can easily imagine it. To be a powerful people it is necessary that our hearts and manly vigour should be protected."

Replying to General Hertzog on the immigration question, Dr. Jameson voiced his opinions at Capetown on August 30 :— " I will pass by the expression ' criminal war,' and likewise the abuse of myself and my friends, and I will go at once to the portion where General Hertzog deals with one of the headings— one of the most important headings—of the Pretoria programme. We know that one of the headings is the advocacy of immigration and land settlement. What do we find General Hertzog saying on this subject? ' There is nothing more detestable than the cry for immigration from outside when it is taken into con- sideration with the bad results which will be the fruits thereof.' And further he says ' that immigration at the present moment would be a crime.' Well," continued Dr. Jameson, he asked them to remember these words ; and he asked them, " how did that stand up against General Botha's speeches—not once, but many times repeated—in the earlier days before, and, yes, after the formation of the Union Government, when he had said that what they wanted in this country was capital and people ; when he had further said that there were millions of acres in this country uncultivated and unoccupied, and there was room for millions to come in from oversea, to cultivate and occupy the land ? Now, they had General Hertzog's statement that it would be a crime to encourage immigration at the present moment; and why did General Hertzog at the present moment call a halt to immigration? He (General Hertzog) was a student of history, and the history of the country, from the days of Van Riebeck, from the days of the ancestors of General Hertzog to the present moment. How had the country been peopled and built up but by means of immigration ? Why did General Hertzog say that at that moment they must stop, and that it would be a crime to bring any-body in ?

" He (Dr. Jameson) quite agreed with General Botha that if there were any people in the country desirous of going on the land, let them be helped to do so, but was there any reason why they should stop immigration, and why the Government should not assist immigration from abroad ? Mr. Merriman had said the other day that they had a million and a quarter white people in the country and five million natives. If they should preach the domination of the white races in the country, was that domination going to be preserved if they were going to limit the white people, when they knew that the black people could produce ten to every one the white people could ? How did this balance with redress by immigration ? How were they to main-tain their position as the dominant races ? But he asked General Hertzog to give them a reason for all this ? He (Dr. Jameson) knew he could give a reason, but would not. He would provide it for the General. It was because, before Union took place, General Hertzog and his faction were in power. Union took place with their help on certain conditions, and these conditions they saw being whittled away day by day. General Hertzog wanted that power confirmed and not interfered with by an influx of enlightened citizens into this country. That was the reason why General Hertzog wanted the flow of immigration stopped, and cried ' Hold, enough ! ' Well, as he had said all they had in the Pretoria programme was the advocacy of immigration and land settlement. But to that statement on the Unionist pro-gramme they had added the method by which land settlement could be brought about, by giving the Government the power of the acquisition of land for the purposes of settlement.

"General Hertzog told them that all the land was in the hands of the capitalists. But not all. Let him be perfectly accurate. He said that the majority of the land was in the hands of the capitalists. Well, all he could say, was that it was an absolute untruth. They knew that the vast majority of the land that was suitable for the purposes of closer settlement was contained in those big farms of hundreds of morgen of which only a portion was used. They were the friends of General Hertzog who would refuse the power to the Government to acquire land for the purpose. They knew that the capitalists did not get the land for the land, but for its mineral-bearing possibilities. General Botha and General Hertzog knew this very well. But that was why they were not in favour of giving the Government the power of acquiring the land by going into the market and getting land at a fair price, so that the settler would not be burdened to such a tremendous extent as if the land had to be purchased at enormous costs by bids being rushed up. If the Government got that power and the settler were placed on the land, then a settler would be enabled to get a good honest living."

With telling effect Dr. Jameson cited Ruskin's ' Harbours of England,' showing the inner meaning of the allegory of the harbours being the medium through which the fellowship of mankind had been brought about, and that it applied to the harbours of South Africa as well as of England, so that really intercommunication between man and man was the ideal to keep in view, as "it was only through that that they were able to build up those new nationalities as part of the British Empire," and only by taking a wide view of the destinies of South Africa could the country advance on right and broad lines.

To follow many of the ins and outs of South African election questions and present results would require more space than is available. Much sympathy has been felt for General Botha in his unenviable position, the Unionists demanding a detailed enunciation of his policy, and asking why he did not repudiate contradictions of his stated principles and rebuke racial speeches by his own ministers, while the reactionaries in his own party were wanting their own way and insisting often on taking it. General Botha would declare a promising policy in the towns which would be quite differently interpreted by Mr. Fischer and other Nationalist leaders to suit country constituencies, while so-called "friendly warnings" would be addressed to General Botha, through a section of the Nationalist press, not to be too British or so immoderate in his expressions of loyalty.

On various important matters, immigration, land settlement, education, the native and drink questions, it was noticed that members of the Cabinet were evidently not in agreement, and General Smuts (Minister of the Interior), who is considered a dominating power in the Union Cabinet, made a remarkable statement in reply to heckling, when he admitted : " Provisionally, General Botha has published a programme, but as soon as the party is formed, all over South Africa it will be one common programme which will be settled by a Congress that will be held, a Congress that will be the foundation of the new party." Many South African electors were thus placed in the position of bewildered little Alice in Wonderland, for·the political situation grew " curiouser and curiouser." General Botha had formed a Ministry on strict party lines, excluding political leaders who had generously co-operated to make Union possible, and followed this up by challenging Sir Percy Fitzpatrick in Pretoria East. After constituting a party Cabinet, the Union Prime Minister declared his programme at Pretoria, appealed for co-operation and the obliteration of old party lines, and invited South Africans to join his new party, the " Nationalist," which was to govern the country on non-party principles. General Smuts, Minister of the Interior (in more ways than one) at a later date ̇declared the Pretoria programme to be purely provisional—presumably for election purposes—and there was no party, it was yet to be formed. Meanwhile the old familiar Bond programme was daily seen emerging as each Minister went about the country expounding his own political creed. One was constantly reminded of a familiar ditty on South African co-operation in which it was amusingly set forth that the typical Dutch-speaking South African " never will co-operate with no one but himself," and as this form of co-operation is favoured by the Bond and therefore suits his views, he generally sticks to that organisation, though rifts within even that lute have lately appeared.

Doubtless some or all of these difficulties were contributory causes leading to the defeat of General Botha and two other members of his Cabinet, Mr. Hull, Minister of Finance, whom Sir George Farrar defeated by an overwhelming majority, and Mr. Moor, Minister of Commerce and Industries, and late Premier of Natal. General Botha's prestige and personal influence are so great that it was hardly thought possible that Sir Percy Fitzpatrick could win the day in the historic Pretorian conflict. The Union Prime Minister was evidently confident of the safety of his own position, as, speaking to a great audience at the Town Hall, Pretoria, on August 30, he made some uncomplimentary references to his opponent's tactics which he said were not likely to appeal to " the intelligent and independent voter of Pretoria East." General Botha added that he himself made no such appeal as Sir Percy's (the latter having said that if not elected for Pretoria East he would not accept a seat elsewhere, though he had been offered a safe seat), " because in the first place he was going to beat him, and, in the second place, because he was going to be a sportsman, and he considered such an appeal unsportsmanlike and undignified ; and, lastly, because of all possible appeals this was the one most likely to be treated with contempt."

The intelligent and independent and sportsmanlike electorate of Pretoria East has already answered a notable challenge by returning Sir Percy Fitzpatrick, a genuine and patriotic South African ; and that the author of ' Jock of the Bushveld ' knows how to win South African votes and hearts has been amply demonstrated at Pretoria and Johannesburg. For the rest, " So long," as we say in South Africa.

A SOUTH AFRICAN.

SOUTH AFRICA AND BRITISH CAPITAL

Last year, the *Cape Times* observes, we called attention to the notable increase in the inflow of British capital to South Africa in 1909, as compared with 1908. The statistics for the first half of 1910 indicate an unexpected swing back in the pendulum. London's new capital creations in the half-year ending June 30 were far above any previous record, amounting to no less than 188 millions sterling ; but of this gigantic amount something less than 2½ millions were destined for South Africa, whereas in the first half of 1909 we took 9½ millions. Of the decrease (7 millions) a little over one million is due to a curtailment in the demands of the mining companies, leaving 6 millions sterling to be accounted for by restricted applications on account of Government, public corporations, or the requirements of industry other than mining enterprise. The Bankers' Institute might find an interesting subject for inquiry in tracing the shrinkage in detail through the various channels of inflow. No doubt South Africa would have taken more capital had the rubber and oil " booms " not been so powerfully attractive. In the first half of 1909, according to the *Economist's* figures, rubber companies took only a million sterling, whereas in the first six months of the current year they absorbed the colossal sum of 16½ millions : oil issues following with 8½ millions.

FOREIGN AFFAIRS

By EDWARD DICEY, C.B.

THE NEW TURKISH LOAN

WITH the annexation of Korea by Japan things in the Far East may be regarded as having settled down for a time, and until China awakens to a fuller knowledge of her latent strength it may be said, without fear of contradiction, that Japan will continue to exert a controlling influence in that part of the world. Accordingly Great Britain, as Japan's ally and Russia's friend, may consider her position in the Far East, if not exactly what is termed safe, at any rate free from any hostile attack as long as the present understandings and the present *ententes* remain in force. But as we get nearer home the diplomatic barometer falls a little, and in Persia a difference of opinion has unfortunately arisen between the various Powers taking part in the progress and development of the Shah's dominions as to what constitutes political and what economic interests. Happily these differences have been smoothed over for a time, but there is no reason to suppose that a final settlement has been reached, and it cannot be denied that in Persia there are still international difficulties requiring the most careful adjustment in order to prevent offence being given or taken.

In the Near East the outlook is anything but satisfactory. Here British influence has to contend with the constant activities of other European Powers, as well as with opposing interests of factions within the Ottoman Empire. Every European interest appears to centre in Turkey, and the interest of one Power seems invariably to conflict with that of another Power or group of Powers. Constantinople has ever been regarded as the powder magazine of Europe, and oft-times it has required the most careful handling on the part of the accredited representatives of foreign Courts to prevent a conflagration. Just now Turkey is again the source of anxiety. In some quarters fears are entertained that British influence in Turkish territory is on the wane, and that another Power, Germany, now occupies first place with the Turkish Government, if not with the Turkish people. Certainly, German influence in the Near East has gained ground very fast during the last decade, and it is therefore but natural that the status of Germany in Turkey should have become more important. But whatever may be the case with other Powers, it is Germany's commercial rather than her political influence in Turkey that brings her in conflict with us, and for this, I fear, we have only ourselves to blame. For very many years Germany has placed commerce in the forefront of her foreign policy. Markets she has aimed at and markets she has secured; while we rested on our oars Germany strained every nerve to sell her goods and obtain trading concessions, with the not very surprising result that she has now attained a position in which she meets us on equal terms.

But it will be said that the present difficulty with Turkey has its political side, in fact that politics have a large if not a predominant share in the tension that has arisen with France over the Turkish loan.

Let us examine the situation. That Turkey wants money, and wants it badly, is an open secret; moreover she wants a considerable sum if she is to develop' her resources, as well as put her affairs in order. As might be expected she turned to France for help, but France, too, has looked with jealous eyes on the growing trade between Turkey and Germany, and if a new Turkish loan is to be quoted on the Paris Bourse, the French Government require that the Ottoman Government must hold out some prospect of orders being placed in France. Attached to this condition is a further one regarding the character of the financial guarantees, and a third involving the observance of certain political restrictions. Perhaps the nature of the conditions was best described by the *Journal des Débats*, when the report was current in Constantinople that the Turkish Minister of Finance had succeeded in inducing the French Government to pledge itself in principle to making the advance. The French journal at once contradicted that report by stating that neither the Minister for Foreign Affairs, nor the Minister of Finance, nor the Prime Minister, had pledged themselves to anything. On the contrary, in view of the existing financial situation of the Ottoman Empire, they had reserved to themselves the right of examining with special attention, on the one hand, the conditions upon which it would be possible to sanction the admission of a new Turkish loan to quotation, and, on the other hand, the character of the genuine guarantees which would have to be required for the protection of the bondholders. "It goes without saying," continued the writer, "that the French Government would likewise be obliged to take into consideration the question of general political expediency." On the same occasion the *Liberté* observed that neither the French Government nor public opinion could forget that if in addition to Turkey's debt of £100,000,000 a fresh draft upon French savings was to be made, unimpeachable guarantees, which could be called upon at a moment's notice, must be required. " Similarly, neither the Government nor public opinion can tolerate the pretension that money obtained upon credit from France should be devoted to paying for German goods, or to promoting the diminution and oppression of French interests in Turkey."

Clearly these pronouncements by no means indicated that the loan was *un fait accompli*, and they certainly give colour to the rumour that questions of "general political expediency" were under consideration; in fact, no attempt was made to hide the suspicions entertained in Paris that a portion of the money was required to meet engagements or, more correctly, to allow of Turkey entering into engagements of a political nature that were regarded by the French Government to be inimical to French interests in the Near East. As soon as these suspicions were bruited abroad, the Turkish Grand Vizier, Hakki Pasha, paid a visit to M. Pichon in the Jura, and endeavoured to explain them away, and he was so far successful that the negotiations proceeded; but the improvement in the negotiations turned out to be only temporary, and a further hitch soon occurred.

For some time it has been common knowledge that the relations between the Ottoman Bank and the Constitutional Ottoman Government have been somewhat strained, and the fact that the proposed new loan to Turkey is being promoted by the Crédit Mobilier has not tended to conciliate matters. It is commonly asserted, with what amount of accuracy I know not, that the opposition of the Ottoman Bank to the loan has had a good deal to do with the failure of the negotiations. And the assertion gains support from some of the more influential of the Turkish journals which vent their spleen not so much on the action of the French Government, as on that of the Ottoman Bank and its allies. That the intervention of the Ottoman Bank in the transaction is no sinecure is evident from the following telegram sent from the *Times* correspondent at Constantinople on September 22nd : "A Ministerial Council was held here this morning. It is stated on good authority that the Council discussed a telegram received last night from Hakki Pasha stating that the French Government still insisted on the control of State expenditure by the Ottoman Bank, and that it was resolved to reply stating the readiness of Turkey to lodge State revenues in the bank, but rejecting all control."

Whether or not an agreement is come to between the French

and Ottoman Governments in the matter of the loan, it may be taken for granted that France will not give way altogether on the question of political and economic guarantees, but how far her conditions in these respects may be modified remains a doubtful quantity, especially if it be correct that the Young Turks have approached Sir Ernest Cassel and a group of private financiers. Indeed it is said that in the event of the negotiations with France failing, Sir Ernest has undertaken to find the whole of the money required by the Turkish Government, presumably without insisting on the political and economic guarantees that appear so necessary to France. Another report attributes to Sir Ernest the *rôle* of mediator, while a third report is that he is to bring out his loan in London, and that this country is prepared to do what France has refused. For myself, I do not pay much attention to any of these reports, and the attempt in certain quarters to make a possible refusal by France or a possible acceptance by a private syndicate a question of high international policy is in my opinion both unfortunate and reprehensible. Of course, this country would not purposely do anything opposed directly to French interests, nor is Sir Ernest Cassel likely to do what the British Government would not do. That Sir Ernest was consulted I have no doubt whatever, but he is far too wise a man of business to give the consultation away and lay all his cards on the table, to be turned over at will by political partisans. In the end, I should not be surprised to see both sides arriving at a compromise which will remove the objections of the Ottoman Bank and reconcile with the public interest the rights which the Mobilier group have acquired by their contract with Djarid Bey; in fact, a general shake-hands all round. What concerns this country far more than the loan itself is to see that British industry is to the fore in the developments that it may be assumed the Turkish Government intend to embark upon at an early date.

REPORTED NEW ALLIANCES

The Franco-Turkish difficulties over the loan are further intensified by the report of an alliance between Turkey on the one hand and Germany and Austria-Hungary on the other. Nothing is said about Italy, so it is a little difficult to make out whether the suggestion is an addition to the Triple Alliance or the formation of a new triple *entente*. In any event, it may be assumed that if either were under consideration Italy would certainly be in the know. As, therefore, silence reigns in Rome, I think we may conclude that the report had its origin in one of the many conversations which emanate from interested parties

in Constantinople and Vienna.   Personally, I can see nothing
but further complications in Turkey allying herself either with
Germany or Austria-Hungary, and, while I do not doubt that
the Young Turks see in such an alliance possible advantages for
a more vigorous policy, I very much doubt whether the Old
Turks desire the combination, and I feel certain that the
German Emperor, who, of all men, is desirous to preserve the
peace of Europe, would himself set his face against any proposal
of the kind.   I quite appreciate the anxiety of Turkey to see
herself strengthened, and one sympathises with the Porte in her
difficulties with Greece, but appreciation and sympathy are one
thing, and an alliance with the two strongest military Powers
in Central Europe another.   I dismiss, therefore, at once, any
addition to the Triple Alliance, and the suggestion of a new triple
entente I regard as being unworthy of serious consideration.

Then we have another and more persistent rumour thrust
upon us, namely, that a military convention has been signed
between Turkey and Roumania.   Here, again, I think we should
tread with caution, more especially as the report coincides with
the apparent rupture between Turkey and France over the loan
question.   Indeed, the rush of rumours seems more than a
coincidence, and lends support to the view expressed by the
Cologne Gazette that " an attack has been made all along the
line in order to show the world that the real cause of all
discord has only to be looked for in the intrigues of Germany,
by whose side, as thanks for German support in the Bosnian
question, stands faithfully Austria-Hungary."   That Germany
rendered a real service to the peace of Europe when she brought
Russia to a full-stop I have frequently pointed out; in fact, had
it not been for German intervention, I very much fear that
nothing could have prevented war in the Balkans.   Accordingly,
not only Austria-Hungary but all the Powers have reason to thank
Germany for her timely assistance.   It is childish to suppose
that Germany would have done what she did to secure peace
in Europe after the annexation of Bosnia and Herzegovina by
Austria-Hungary, if she was really the instigator of a military
alliance between Turkey and Roumania.   Naturally the two
Governments have a perfect right to approach one another if
they choose to do so, but the abstract right in no way gives
colour to the suggestion that the matter is an accomplished fact.
It is well known that a change of this kind might invite serious
consequences in other directions, and it is certainly neither to
the interest of Germany nor of Austria-Hungary to do anything
that would tend to cause a breach of the peace.   There are
many reasons why Roumania should refrain from entering into
a convention with Turkey, and I am inclined to throw in my

lot with the writer in the *Tageblatt*, who reminds us that "the identity of Turkish and Roumanian interests in the Balkans renders superfluous any positive or written engagements especially on the part of Roumania, as the latter State derives the greatest advantage from keeping a free hand in Balkan affairs." Moreover, a convention of this kind would have the appearance of a direct attack on Russia, and Roumania can hardly afford to take such a course.

KING AND KAISER

The visit of Prince Henry of Prussia to this country has given an opportunity for many personal courtesies, and the happy time spent with his royal relatives in the Highlands is not likely soon to pass from his memory. In Scotland he felt himself at home, and it greatly pleased both the King and the Queen that the Kaiser's brother should come and pay them a visit so soon after the accession. Nothing could possibly show greater family affection, and it would be well, I think, if that section of the public which is under the impression that friendship between this country and Germany is impossible were to remember that the very opposite view is held in the highest quarters, and that between the two Royal families the closest intimacy has always existed.

It was a happy suggestion that when the German Crown Prince goes to India he should be the guest not only of India but of Great Britain. As the *Times* very properly says, it would be a gracious act, and a special compliment to the Crown Prince, if Great Britain participated in the pleasure of entertaining him. Let us hope that the suggestion will fructify, and that some announcement will soon be made to the effect that the *Times* has but anticipated the view of the British Government. The Crown Prince is deservedly popular in England, and he may rest assured that in India he will be received with acclamation, not alone as the near relative of our own illustrious sovereign but for his own good and great qualities. In himself the Crown Prince is a charming personality, and a practical education has tended to bring out his special qualifications. When to his intimate knowledge of internal affairs he has added a knowledge of external affairs such as a tour of the world must give him, he cannot fail to be when the time comes, and may it be far distant, the worthy successor of a worthy father.

And here I should like to refer to the very able article contributed by Lord Esher to the *Deutsche Rundschau* on the subject of the late King and Germany. The object Lord Esher had in view in writing his paper was twofold—to refute the theory so

widely believed on the Continent of Europe that King Edward
initiated a policy of hostility to Germany, and to show that his
late Majesty did all in his power to promote a more friendly
understanding between the peoples of the two countries. Dealing
with the question of armaments, Lord Esher tells us that while
King Edward was at one with the majority of his people in the
wish to maintain the sea power of Great Britain on the highest
step which it must occupy if it is to fulfil the purposes of national
defence and afford a guarantee for the inviolability of British
territory, he had no ulterior thoughts, and never had a hostile
intention. "Least of all would it have occurred to the King to
look with feelings of jealousy, of irritation, or of uneasiness, at
the growing power of the German Empire. In this respect he
shared, not the nervous anxiety of a few fanatics, but the sound
conviction of by far the greater part of the British nation, that
within the four quarters of the world there is room enough for
Great Britain and Germany." Continuing, Lord Esher says, "The
press feuds which were fought out in Great Britain and Germany
by people who meant the best, and were guided by patriotic
motives, but did not understand the matter, annoyed and saddened
him. He abominated the stirring up of hatred and disunion."

On the much-vexed question of Germany's navy, Lord Esher,
who of all persons may be said to have had the ear of King
Edward, points out that "the late King was far too reasonable,
his knowledge of the world was too thorough, and his understanding of the conditions of commercial rivalry among the
European States too clear for him not absolutely to appreciate
the real meaning of the efforts of the German Emperor and the
German people to increase German sea-power, and to peg out a
broader area for German colonial undertakings. . . . When his
attention was drawn to the remarkable little book, 'Europe's
Optical Delusion,' which created a good deal of sensation in
England, and was brought to the notice of the German Emperor
and the Crown Prince by English friends, its main idea, that war
between Great Britain and Germany would, from the point of
view of both nations, be Dog Day madness, seemed to be quite
a familiar one to the King. To whichever victory might fall, it
would be a disaster for both nations. That was the idea which
one could hear from him almost every day. At the same time,
he could not regard disarmament or limitation of armaments
under existing circumstances as anything else than a fantastical
dream, and he could never understand how any intelligent human
being could believe that he had ever proposed either the one or
the other to the German Emperor." *

On the personal relations between the Kaiser and the late

* *Daily Telegraph*, September 1, 1910.

King much has been said at different times. Often it was rumoured that they were strained. That the Kaiser was jealous of King Edward, and that King Edward resented certain actions of the Kaiser. For years I have endeavoured in a humble way to show these assertions had no foundation in fact, that the closest and most affectionate relations existed between the two Monarchs, and it is therefore with great satisfaction that I find my views fully borne out by Lord Esher, who states :—

> Nobody could be long in the entourage of King Edward without perceiving that he loved Germany and the German people. No one could have seen the King and the Emperor in one another's society without noticing that both men, in spite of their so different temperaments, and in spite of the divergency of their ideals, had a noteworthy resemblance to one another, that blood is thicker than water, and that not only mutual esteem, but a real liking, was the basis of their intercourse. There are many people who remember how, last January, the King, deeply moved, mentioned that he had addressed a cordial letter to the Emperor for the latter's birthday, and expressed to him a keen desire that Germany and England might always co-operate in the interests of peace, a co-operation which they could always render possible. Perhaps the Emperor, when a few weeks later he stood by King George in the hall of William Rufus, where the great dead was lying in state, thought of this friendly letter and its noble-minded contents.*

There is no doubt that Lord Esher's article is correct in every particular, and the only pity is that it could not have appeared in the lifetime of King Edward. Had such a course been possible a great deal of misunderstanding would have been avoided, for the exposure of the myth regarding a breach between King Edward and the Emperor William would have opened the eyes of the public, both in this country and Germany, to the unreality of the jealousies which a certain section of the Press in both countries made it their business to foment. King George is following in his father's footsteps, and whenever an occasion offers he does not fail to emphasise the true feelings which bind the Royal family of this country to the Royal family of Germany. As to what passed between the King and the Kaiser's brother at Balmoral I have no means of knowing, but one thing may be regarded as certain, that the King was hardly likely to allow the opportunity to pass without doing everything in his power to bring about more friendly relations between the two nations.

At Vienna the German Emperor is having a triumphal progress, and there is little doubt that the meeting between the two Emperors will further strengthen and consolidate the alliance

* *Daily Telegraph*, September 1, 1910.

between the two Powers. The visit to the Rathaus was most popular, and the Kaiser's reference to the close understanding that exists between Germany and Austria-Hungary met with an enthusiastic reception. The words, "Methinks I read in your resolve the agreement of the City of Vienna with the action of an ally in taking his stand in shining armour at a grave moment by the side of your most gracious Sovereign," were cheered to the echo, and the applause broke out afresh with the explanation, "this was at once an injunction of duty and of friendship, for the alliance has, to the weal of the world, passed into and pervades as an imponderable element the convictions and the life of both peoples." With the strength of the Triple Alliance and in the continuance of the ententes between Great Britain and France and Great Britain and Russia the peace of Europe is built up. There remains only one further understanding to make that peace for ever secure, and that is an entente between this country and Germany. Let us hope it may not be far distant.

EDWARD DICEY.

OPENINGS FOR CAPITAL IN SEYCHELLES

From time to time inquiries are received as to whether Seychelles provides a suitable opening for Europeans who desire to take up tropical planting. In reply, it may be clearly laid down that the Colony is most unsuitable for white labourers of the working class without capital: wages are low, and the European working man would find it impossible to do more than eke out a bare living. But for a white man with capital, Seychelles provides as good an opening as most other tropical countries. Coconuts and rubber thrive, and vanilla is favoured by conditions perhaps unequalled in any other part of the world. Land, however, or rather good land, is not always easy to get, and it is advisable that any intending purchaser should come out and look round for himself. The price of land may be put down at Rs. 100 an acre, and for a man to succeed he should have a capital of at least £2,000. An estate properly worked would yield a steady minimum of say 12 per cent., and in good vanilla years the percentage would be much higher. No planter, however, if he hopes for success, should put all his capital into vanilla, seeing that both yield and price are extremely capricious. The influx of Indians, mainly from the Malabar coast, still continues, and most of the retail trade has passed into the hands of Indians and Chinese. Both races make excellent shopkeepers, and, so far, the Colony has benefited from their introduction.

LAND SETTLEMENT IN AUSTRALIA

By the Hon. HUGH McKENZIE, M.L.A.

(Minister for Lands, Victoria, Australia)

An Australian visiting Great Britain cannot help feeling a glow of satisfaction at the manifest interest which the people of the United Kingdom, and especially the commercial community, show in the development of the Commonwealth. And it was with no slight degree of gratification that I availed myself of the privilege of placing before the London Chamber of Commerce some indication of the immense industrial developments upon which the Australian continent is now entering. I readily accept the invitation to repeat some of my observations in the pages of *The Empire Review*.

Perhaps the most conspicuous feature is the effort being made to people the vacant land. To this end many of the States are offering land to settlers on most generous terms, and under conditions that will enable any man who has industry and thrift to secure a home. This organised movement to obtain farmers marks a transition period in our political and industrial life. The early settlement of Australia was devoted to the use of its natural opportunities. It began with the discovery of gold, and was followed by the use of the native grass, which grows during the winter rains and cures under the summer sun. The genial climate of Australia enables live stock to grow to maturity without either hand feeding or shelter. But while the gold mines and the great pastoral estates have been important factors in creating the wealth and trade which have enriched the country, they did not develop its full possibilities. Australia is now, however, entering upon this era.

The field of development occupies an entire continent equal in size to the United States. In this immense area there are at present only a little over four million people, or about one and four-tenths to the square mile, and nearly half these people live in the large cities. The land which is to support the population of the future, and on which the future commerce must depend, is practically unused. In many respects the conditions for development are unrivalled. The whole continent is under one Federal Government. There are no conflicting nations or local jealousies to interfere. The long coast line gives ready access to the markets of the world. The six States are wisely and economically governed, under laws which, in their justice and progressive spirit, have attracted enlightened study and favourable comment in all parts of the universe. In this work Victoria occupies a conspicuous position, seeing that it is the pioneer State in the matter of irrigated agriculture, which is destined, more than any other influence, to make agriculture in Australia safe and profitable, and the continent itself a country of dense population.

Victoria and New South Wales are the foremost States in population and in agricultural and manufacturing development. The number and importance of manufactures is extending, and is helped by an abundance of cheap coal in New South Wales, and the rapidly developing coal deposits of Victoria. But the future expansion of trade and commerce must depend chiefly upon the agricultural development of the country. In discussing this I propose to deal specifically with Victoria, and explain something of the conditions of life there, and the policy of the State Government in endeavouring to improve both the conditions at home, and the extension of our commercial relationship abroad.

For this purpose let me take as a starting-point a quarter of a century ago, when wool, cereals and gold were our chief exports. The fruit, the dairy and the meat trade, have all been established since then. The butter exports 25 years ago were only worth £69,000, and no meat was shipped at all. In 1900 the value of butter exports had risen to £1,490,000. Six years later to over £2,000,000. And advices by cable inform us that for 1910 they will amount to 20,000 tons, the largest total on record. In 1900 the frozen meat trade was £441,000. In 1906 it had reached to £658,000. The fruit trade, which is destined to become an important industry in the near future, is just beginning. Both the fruit and the frozen meat trades have been retarded by lack of proper distributing facilities in Great Britain, and this is one of the questions I am now investigating with a view to its improvement. I have not the complete figures for last year, but the total exports for the six months ending June amounted to £14,360,000, which is £842,000 more than the same period of 1909, and exceeds the imports by £1,738,000.

No State is better organised than Victoria to do its business economically. State ownership of railways is not only proving a source of revenue, capable of large expansion, but it is also an effective agency in promoting the development and possibilities of the rural districts. By the establishment of Government cool stores, the organisation of dairying, the support of technical schools and the giving of expert advice in all branches of agriculture, the Government has contributed greatly to the prosperity of the community.

Victoria has been a pioneer in many co-operative enterprises, which have proven so successful in countries like Denmark and Holland. This policy has materially increased the revenues of the State. No country can show a sounder financial condition. Taxes are very light. Many permanent improvements are being paid for out of revenue, and the income from railways and irrigation works are certain to increase largely in the near future, as a result of the rapid settlement now taking place. Notwithstanding the great industrial development which the State has undertaken, the Victorian public debt at the end of the financial year for June 30th, 1909, was only £55,100,000. Of this, £40,980,000 is on account of moneys raised by the State for railway construction. A further £8,537,000 was raised for State water supply works, and other water supply works financed by the State. £1,707,000 of the public debt has been used for land purchases for closer settlement. And the balance of the public debt, £3,876,000, was raised for docks, harbour works, and other public requirements. The interest on the public debt for 1908 was £1,874,000; the income from State works, £4,474,000; the working expenses on the railways, water supply works, etc., £2,545,000; so that we have available to pay interest on the public debt a sum of £1,929,000. In other words, the net returns from the State works were sufficient to pay the interest on the whole of the public debt of the State and to show a surplus of £55,000.

The *per capita* production of Australia averages £36, the highest in the world.

The country that makes money can spend money, and the extent of the purchases of Australia in the United Kingdom is one of the surest evidences of the prosperity of its people. Trade statistics show that among all the customers of the United Kingdom, Australia stands third, being surpassed by only two countries in the world, India and Germany. And this is the situation while agriculture is in its infancy. Individually the Australian is by far the largest buyer of British goods. Man for man he buys 50 per cent. more than any other customer.

TABLE SHOWING PURCHASES FROM THE UNITED KINGDOM IN 1908.

Country.	Value of Goods Bought.
India	£49,429,000
Germany	33,400,000
Australia	22,942,000
France	22,320,000
U.S.A.	21,303,000
Canada	12,243,960

The trade development between Australia and the United Kingdom is being fostered by the Commonwealth, which gives the Motherland a preference, and while we are endeavouring to build up our own manufactures at the same time we are strengthening those of the United Kingdom by the low tariff given them compared with the manufactures of other competing countries. Before many years the Island Continent will be not only the best customer of what the United Kingdom has to sell, but the best place for the United Kingdom to buy her food supplies. The thousands of people settling on the land each year mean more wheat, meat, butter and fruit to fill British ships and supply British households, and also mean that money now sent to foreign lands may be kept within the Empire.

In this connection irrigation is a factor of fundamental importance. Irrigation is as necessary to the full agricultural development of Australia as it is in India or Western America. This, I trust, warrants an explanation of the extensive irrigation schemes on which the State of Victoria is engaged. The even temperature, the dry air, and the sunshiny days of Australia give it a healthy and enjoyable climate for men and animals. These advantages carry with them one inevitable drawback, a low rainfall. About three-fourths of the continent has an average rainfall of twenty inches or less. This is ample for the growing of cereal crops or the pasturing of live stock if it falls at the right time; but such farming is of low acreage value, and only capable of supporting a limited population. The climate of Australia, however, renders it possible, with irrigation, to grow an extraordinary variety of high-priced crops, and to give increased returns which will support a dense population. Especially is this true of Victoria, which occupies the most southerly and coolest part of the continent. The records of Melbourne for the last fifty-two years show an average summer temperature of sixty-six degrees, and an average winter temperature of fifty degrees, or only sixteen degrees difference. This enables the Victorian farmer who can irrigate to grow all the products of the temperate zone, and many products of the semi-tropics.

On existing forty and fifty-acre farms there can be found the leading farm crops of England and the fruits of Southern France and Spain. Oranges and pineapples grow in the same orchard. Quinces, tokay and raisin grapes alike reach perfection in the open air. Such a wide variety of products adds immensely to the comfort of living, and also lessens its cost. The thrifty farmer can load his table with what are usually regarded as luxuries, yet all are home grown. With irrigation the home can be surrounded with flowers, fruit and foliage, the lawns can be kept green, and rural life invested with rare attractions and charm. The irrigation districts of Victoria are already becoming districts of lovely homes and a stimulating social and intellectual life. It is difficult to overstate the value of such environment in conferring happiness on the wives and children who live in the midst of its influence, as well as on the characters of the future citizens of the State.

The Victorian irrigation farm is, however, more than a comfortable place to live. It is a place to make money. For dairying or stock fattening no country has greater advantages. The mild sunny winters enable stock to live in the open the year through. Stabling or hand feeding are not required. That cuts off the chief expense of dairying in countries having severe winters. With irrigation there is always green feed, and a uniformity of production can be maintained. We have many butter factories, and the business of marketing dairy produce is well organised. The freight rate on butter from Melbourne to London is one halfpenny per pound, or less than many English farmers pay.

In the irrigation districts lucerne is the most valuable crop. The sunshine of the irrigation districts is what is needed for its growth and curing. The long seasons, combined with ability to apply water when needed, enable five and six crops to be cut in a year. On good land these cuttings will yield a ton to the cutting. Lucerne hay always commands a good price, frequently selling for £5 a ton, and in the dry seasons even higher. Large areas of irrigated land devoted to the production of fodder crops are destined to be a safeguard against losses to the pastoral areas, and a valuable aid to the regular and prosperous development of the whole country. The pastoral areas will give to the grower of fodder crops a home market in ordinary years, and an emergency market, with high prices, in dry years.

The fruit-grower in Victoria has great advantages. Being in the southern hemisphere enables him to land fresh fruits on the markets of the northern hemisphere in the winter and spring months. Cases of Australian grapes of 24 lbs., landed in London this season, were sold as high as 33s. a case. The profits from fruit-growing in the irrigated areas are reflected by the high prices obtained for land in the fruit districts. At Mildura orchards in full bearing fetch as much as £120 an acre, and rent in some instances is £5 to £10 an acre a year.

Realising the benefits which would follow irrigated agriculture on a large scale, the State of Victoria is building a system of irrigation works, that when completed will provide irrigation water for more than a million acres of land, and water for domestic and stock purposes for more than ten million acres. On these works about $3\frac{1}{2}$ millions sterling have already been expended. About 250,000 acres are being irrigated, and there is a surplus water supply for another quarter of a million acres. The completion of this scheme will create homes for half a million people, and expand both the local and oversea trade of the State. Without requiring any extension of mileage, it will multiply many times the business of existing railway lines, and greatly increase their profits. The State, however, requires more people to utilise the surplus water supply now available, and we are anxious to secure the farmers and farm workers needed to develop these lands.

In order to provide homes for the new settlers, the State has re-purchased from private owners large areas of land, which have been under cultivation without irrigation for many years, and this land it is now sub-dividing into small holdings, and offering what are practically ready-made farms, which include a water supply delivered on each farm ready for use; and if desired, the State will erect houses, so that those who select irrigation lands can at once begin their reproductive work. The terms for payment are exceedingly liberal, being $31\frac{1}{2}$ years for the land, and 15 years for the house. The settlement of these areas will give a stimulus to our exports of meats, dairy produce and fruits not possible otherwise. It will almost double our rural population, and result in a large expansion of our commerce with Europe and with the densely-peopled countries of the East.

A glance at the map shows the advantage which Australia enjoys by its proximity to the most thickly peopled portion of the globe now supplied with canned vegetables, meats and fruits from other countries. The Australian trade with the East is increasing steadily, and is being aided by State subsidies to two steamship lines, and the location of trade commissioners in the East to further our commercial interests. What is needed to improve the trade relations between the Commonwealth and the Mother Country is cheap and comfortable transportation. There have been great advances in this respect during the last few years. The passenger vessels are now better equipped, larger and faster than they were a few years ago, and every advance of this character brings the two countries closer together; but the difficulties now being experienced in securing accommodation on the vessels show that more ships and larger ships are necessary in the near future.

I would say in conclusion that the experience I have gained during my tour throughout Great Britain will be of very great value to me in my public capacity, and I wish to express my warm appreciation of the courtesies which have been extended to me during my visit.

HUGH McKENZIE.

EDUCATION IN EAST CENTRAL AFRICA

THE GERMAN SYSTEM OUTLINED

By R. HARRISON HARRIS

In the matter of educating the native races of Africa it must be admitted that Germany, in her East African colony, has tackled this difficult question far more vigorously than ourselves. Indeed, the subject has been shelved by successive British administrations. We have long realised that something must eventually be done to improve the condition of the native, but the results likely to accrue from the introduction of any systematic education have appeared so uncertain, and any mere tinkering with the condition of the native population so inimical to the welfare of the people as a whole, that it has been deemed wiser to leave the problem alone.

The German Government, on the other hand, having once determined on educating the African, lost no time in starting an experimental school at Tanga, a port on the east coast, under the control of Herr R. Blank, since promoted to the important post of Director of Education in German East Africa. The results of the Tanga experiment proved so satisfactory that in the course of the last ten years schools have been established in all the large towns in German territory from the coast to the lakes. The difficulty which the diversity of the languages and dialects of the tribes of the interior would otherwise have caused has been avoided by the adoption of the commercial language, Swahili, the *lingua franca* of the coast, for all educational purposes. This language is used officially, and, with perhaps the exception of the more remote tribes, is understood by the whole male population of Central Africa. No one will deny that the gradual extinction of the native dialects is, from some points of view, to be deplored, but at the same time the value of a widespread and general knowledge of Swahili for commercial purposes cannot be over-estimated. A second difficulty, that of enforcing regular attendance, was experienced for a time, but the simple process of imprisoning the parents of delinquents eventually proved effectual.

For educational purposes the Colony is divided into districts, each containing a central school in the chief town, with out-schools in the more thickly populated villages. These central schools provide for the education of native and Hindu boys, who work together; they also accommodate the more intelligent boys from the out-schools, who are provided with sleeping accommodation and granted a food allowance of about 3d. a day. The school course is a simple one in which the three Rs occupy a prominent place. It includes a knowledge of local geography and history and a working knowledge of the German language; while elementary instruction is also given as to the cause, effect and treatment of the prevalent native diseases. Religious knowledge is not included in the curriculum, but care is taken to emphasise the evils of the grosser native customs and the unreality of the claims and doctrines of the New Islam movement.

The ordinary school training ceases when a boy is thirteen or fourteen, and he should then have reached the equivalent of the English 3rd or 4th standard. If a pupil has shown special ability he is passed into the upper school, otherwise he is allowed to leave school, and given a " chit " to show that he has finished his training. The boys in the upper school continue their work, and are either trained as school-teachers or clerks or drafted into the school workshops and instructed in such practical handicrafts as carpentering, printing and bookbinding. Boys who have been taught a craft are afterwards apprenticed for long periods to skilled government workmen; those trained for school work serve first as pupil teachers, then as teachers in the central school, and eventually have charge of a village school. As many as possible of the out-school boys are encouraged to take up this work, so that they may go back to their own tribes as teachers and so bridge over the slight language difficulty. Some of the clerks are employed in business houses, but the greater number find work in government departments, and become sorters and postmen in the towns, letter collectors on the trains, ticket-clerks, station-masters and telegraphists on the railways, magistrates' clerks, interpreters and customs clerks.

The greater part of the actual teaching work is placed in the hands of natives, and this plan has been found to work well, though the native teacher cannot be left without European supervision. As a whole the teachers are both trustworthy and painstaking, but have little idea of progression. Efforts are made to show the boys that education is not opposed to manual work, and for this purpose a certain number of hours in each week are allotted to plantation or porterage work. It was an interesting sight to see the boys of Tanga school toiling up from the shore each morning carrying on their heads loads of stone, lime, and other materials for rebuilding their school.

The out-schools are necessarily more primitive than the central schools. Each is in charge of one or more native teachers sent from the central school, who live in the village and enjoy a position second only to that of the chief. The work done in the out-schools is similar to that of the central schools, but far more elementary in character; the number of scholars in each out-school ranges from fifty to a hundred and fifty.

The German system of native education raises the native to a higher level of utility, teaches him the dignity of labour, instructs him in the knowledge of the German Empire and of the honour due to the Kaiser and his representatives, and places before him the advantages of civilisation. There is no doubt that the training received in the schools has had a most beneficial effect on the native youth. It will, however, take many years before the whole country can be appreciably affected, but the effect of what has been done is already noticeable in the general demeanour of the younger generations to any one landing at a German coast town after visiting Mombasa or Zanzibar.

Here it is interesting to recall that it was mainly to combat the teaching of the apostles of the New Islam movement, now so sedulously spreading their doctrines all over East Central Africa, that the German system of native schools was instituted. Ostensibly the New Islam movement is a religious one, but it is strongly leavened with the idea of Africa for the African, and emanating as it does from fanatical Zanzibar, it might well prove a grave danger, not only to the colony, but to European power in Central Africa. As already indicated, the aim of these native schools is not only to be seats of learning, but also centres of German influence, and that this aim has been realised to some extent was seen in the Maji-maji rebellion of 1905-6. The rising, it will be remembered, was due to the promulgation of the New Islam teaching, and was an effort to throw off all foreign power. Europeans, Hindus and even Arabs were either killed or driven off to the coast, and there was danger of the rising spreading all over the colony. It was then the Germans saw that their policy had been framed on the right lines; for the rising was checked by the action of the Yao tribes which had benefited from the teaching and influence of the government and missionary schools.* These natives not

* The majority of schools in the Yao country were those of the Universities' Mission, which, working on similar lines to the government schools, had been established for some twenty years in the country.

only refused to join the rebels, but assisted the government troops to disperse them.

Such, in outline, is the scheme on which the authorities in German East Central Africa have based their hopes. With true insight they have advanced no active propaganda against Islam, but have taken active steps to capture the youth of the country, believing that the child is the father of the man.

But while the Germans in the neighbouring colony are fully alive to the advantages of native education and have evolved a sound workable system, the British have avoided dealing with the question. It is true that in Zanzibar during the last two or three years some attempt has been made to institute Government schools for native instruction, but a system which makes a point of teaching Arabic and the Quran to a Swahili population is hardly likely to be successful.

Education in Africa has many opponents, particularly among the settlers, who think that the native should be left in his pristine state, and believe that attempts to civilise him are ill-advised. My purpose here, however, is not to discuss these views, but rather to advocate the adoption of a reliable system of education, both as a part of the white man's duty to the black whom he has brought within the influence of civilisation, and as a safeguard and a remedial measure.

We see from time to time in consular and missionary reports accounts of the progress of Mohammedanism in Central Africa ; but few persons realise that the pernicious crusade of what may be called the New Islam Movement is in any way different from the Islam of the last century.* Those of us, however, who possess any knowledge of the undercurrents of African life have noted with some anxiety the rapid growth of the movement on the mainland, coupled with the signs of unrest at Zanzibar. As things now are the apostles of Islam are given a free field, and under the guise of religion induce the ignorant natives to give their allegiance to the movement. Certainly its followers are called Mohammedans, but they know absolutely nothing about the tenets of the Islamic faith, their only creed being "Africa for the Africans." The poor African, mazed and bewildered by the sudden influx of civilisation, which has resulted in the slackening of the ties that bound him so closely to his chief and tribe, falls a ready victim to these designing fanatics who, under a smiling exterior, veil a fierce hatred of the white man and all that comes in his train.

---

* That the German authorities recognise the danger of the situation is shown by the action of the Governor of the Lindi (Bezirksamt) district (which includes the districts affected by the Maji-maji outbreak), who has lately issued an order forbidding any but officially recognised Mullahs to engage in teaching.

Knowing as I do the characteristic loyalty of the East African native to his chief, his parents and the heads of his village, it appears to me that the British authorities are somewhat lacking in not turning this trait to good account. That is, by means of education to lead them to centre their loyalty on the King-Emperor, and so frustrate the aims of the Pan-Africans. I readily acknowledge that much good educational work has been done by private agencies, but no widespread and lasting good can be effected until the Government take up the case in earnest. The system of education found so successful in German East Africa might well serve as a model for the British Colony, rather than one found successful under the different conditions of India or South Africa. And all I should purpose is to modify the German system to suit the conditions of a British Colony. There must be no half measures, nor can such an attitude as meets the eye in certain " up country " districts, where boys are taught the "equality of man" and allowed to walk and talk with European girls as if they were their equals, be sanctioned. It is needless to say that whatever system is adopted discipline must necessarily be of the strictest character, indeed the native would regard any other treatment as a sign of weakness and despise it accordingly.

Mombasa would be the natural starting place for an educational scheme based on the Swahili language. The initial difficulty would be to get a staff of teachers, though no doubt some educated natives could be obtained from the town and from Zanzibar, who after tuition in school method and work would be found service-able. The school work would be similar to that carried on in the German schools, and it would be advisable to give instruction in the Christian beliefs as opposed to Islam, and to enforce the duty of loyalty to the Crown and its representatives. I am strongly of opinion that the teaching of a European language, except in special cases, is quite unnecessary, if not distinctly harmful. The boys on leaving school could with advantage be entered on the register in connection with the recently projected labour scheme. The work done in the Upper School could be extended so as to include masonry work, tailoring, and some instruction in cookery would be useful.

In order to extend the system over the mainland as rapidly as possible, it would be well to open up out-schools first in two or three of the largest villages of the far interior, and leave the real Mombasa district to be developed afterwards. If, for instance, village schools were established in the Kikuyu and Kavaronda countries, they would serve as a basis for central schools at Nairobi and Kisumu. The boys coming from these out-schools, after going through a training at Mombasa, would be able to go back to their own country, and so bridge over the language difficulty which would be experienced at first. With these central schools firmly established it would be only a case of time before the surrounding districts were fully developed. As the schools produced capable teachers, the country might be gradually divided into districts, and in course of time the whole youth of the country would come under government training. Many questions of detail would have to be considered, and possibly actual practice would show the need for modifying in some respects the arrangements which have proved successful under German administration.

The Islamic movement has advanced so rapidly that it will be no easy matter to check it, and the British Government may yet be forced to adopt more strenuous measures than those here suggested. Education however will go far towards removing the danger, and the longer the inception of a sound system is delayed, the heavier will be the task of the pioneers and the greater the risk. The New Islam Movement must be either countered or crushed if the white race is to continue to rule in tropical Africa. The true policy is to prevent the necessity of crushing from arising.

R. HARRISON HARRIS.

AGRICULTURAL RETURNS OF CANADA

Official final estimates show the value of all crops in the Dominion of Canada during 1909 to be $532,992,100, an increase over that of 1908 of $100,458,100 ; the area of land cultivated last year was 30,065,556 acres. The largest output took place in relation to wheat and hay, the amounts being, respectively, 166,744,000 bushels, valued at $141,320,000, and (estimated) 11,877,100 tons, valued at $132,287,700. The value of the other crops produced in any quantity is given as follows : oats $122,390,000 ; potatoes $36,399,000 ; barley $25,434,000 ; turnips and other root crops $18,197,500 ; fodder corn $15,115,000 ; husking corn $12,760,000 ; mixed grains $10,916,000 ; peas $7,222,000 ; buckwheat $4,554,000 ; flax $2,761,000 ; beans $1,881,000 ; rye $1,254,000 ; sugar beets $500,000. The values of the crops produced by the different provinces were in the following order, beginning with the highest and excluding British Columbia: Ontario, Saskatchewan, Quebec, Manitoba, Nova Scotia, Alberta,,New Brunswick and Prince Edward Island.

THE ADVANCE OF QUEENSLAND

By W. EDWARD GRAHAM (*of Brisbane*)

QUEENSLAND, with a total population of rather less than 600,000 persons, now possesses some 4,000 miles of railways, a proportion of mileage to population which compares favourably with that of any other country in the world. Of this mileage, well over 3,500 have been built and are worked by the State itself. At the present time developments in this direction are proceeding more rapidly than in any other Australian State, some hundreds of miles being in course of construction, and more projected, for the most part comparatively short lines designed to give access to rich agricultural or forest areas now unused for lack of proper communication.

During the session the Government intend to seek legislative sanction for the initiation of a scheme which has long been a cherished dream with men who have realised something of the vast area and vaster possibilities of this State : the construction of a great trunk railway to open up the practically limitless pastoral districts of the Far West, and bring them into touch with the markets of the world. There are in Queensland at present three main lines running westward from the coast, the South Western, from Brisbane to Charleville, a distance of 483 miles; the Central, Rockhampton to Longreach, 428 miles; and the Great Northern, Townsville to Cloncurry, 480 miles. Brisbane and Rockhampton are connected by the North Coast Railway (396 miles in length), but the Great Northern system is completely isolated. The proposed new trunk line is intended not only to serve the far western country, but also to link the three systems together. No definite route has so far been decided upon, only a flying inspection (by motor-car) having been made of the country to be traversed. But the idea which apparently finds most favour is that the line should start from a point somewhere about 200 miles to the south-west of Charleville, and run in a north-westerly direction to Camooweal, on the South Australian border, a distance of about 600 miles, the three existing lines being extended westwards to meet it.

The benefits which the construction of such a railway would confer upon the State are well-nigh incalculable. There are in Western Queensland millions upon millions of acres of splendid grazing country, in every way suitable for pasturing sheep, but which for lack of communication with the rest of the world are now, to all intents and purposes, useless. It has been estimated that if these areas were made available—as the proposed line would make the greater part of them—from fourteen to twenty millions of sheep might in a very few years be added to the flocks of the State without any danger of over-stocking. And not only so, but the new railway, in the opinion of experts, would to a very large extent serve as a safeguard against losses through drought such as have been suffered from in the past. Almost the whole of Western Queensland, it should be remembered, lies within the great artesian basin, and underground supplies of water can almost always be obtained. Add to this advantage that of facilities for easy and rapid transport of sheep and cattle from one district to another—and it is rarely that dry conditions prevail in all parts alike at the same time—north and south as well as eastward to the coast, and to the pastoralist the word "drought" will lose most of its old-time terrors.

Meanwhile the seasons are good, prices of most primary products remain high, and the State of Queensland continues to enjoy a period of prosperity and progress perhaps unexampled in the whole of its history. A steady stream of immigration, small, but growing, has set in from Europe, and the new-comers, most of them of the agricultural class, are of a good type, and apparently well suited to the conditions of life and work in this State. Land settlement is proceeding at a rate unprecedented hitherto; during the month of June 751,464 acres were taken up, as against 271,695 acres of the corresponding period of last year; and at times the officials of the Lands Department have all they can do to keep pace with the constantly increasing demand. These figures refer to Crown lands only; but large areas of privately owned properties are also being divided up into smaller holdings, which are being eagerly sought after. Many of the old pastoral estates, especially in certain districts, are being dealt with in this way. Railways are being rapidly pushed forward to open up new agricultural areas—of which the supply seems to be practically unlimited—and everywhere forests and scrubs are giving place to homesteads and farms.

Though the whole of the State is thus on the crest, so to speak, of a wave of prosperity, it is in the larger towns, perhaps, that the effects are most apparent to the ordinary observer. In Brisbane, the capital, evidences of progress are showing themselves on every side. New buildings—residences, shops, offices, some of them of large size and imposing design—are going up in all directions, and others are projected ; and new wharves are being constructed to meet the increasing demand for accommodation for the over-sea and inter-state shipping trade. A prominent feature in the recent progress of the city has been the rapid increase of its importance as a wool-selling centre. It is only a few years ago that, in face of considerable opposition, especially from Sydney, regular sales were established here. The catalogues at first were insignificant, but each year showed a substantial advance, until at the present time the complete success of the movement is recognised as beyond question. The total amount of wool sold during 1909 exceeded that of 1908 by 56,000 bales, and the sales of the present year bid fair to outstrip those of the last by at least as much. The significance of this state of affairs is illustrated by the fact that within the last few months no less than five of the great Southern wool-broking firms have decided to establish themselves permanently in Brisbane.

The cost of the new wharves, warehouses and offices required for carrying on these operations, and which will be taken in hand as soon as possible, is set down as at least £250,000. Another southern firm has just begun the erection of new freezing and meat preserving works near the mouth of the river, at a cost of about £200,000. The City Council proposes to expend several hundred thousand pounds upon various municipal works, including a new Town Hall, for which plans are now in course of preparation. This building, for which a fine central site has been chosen, is estimated to cost about £200,000. Other important schemes, both public and private, are projected ; and altogether an unmistakable air of hope and confidence seems to pervade the entire community.

W. EDWARD GRAHAM.

NOTES ON SOUTHERN RHODESIA

HINTS TO PROSPECTIVE SETTLERS

SOUTHERN RHODESIA offers many advantages to the farmer. But the new settler should understand that, in order to become a successful farmer, there must be no lack of energy and good management, more especially if his available capital is limited. It is impossible to say what is the least amount of capital a man can start with, so much depends upon himself. It is generally considered that by the time he is able to take up his farm he should have at least £500 at his disposal, and naturally the more capital he has the better are his chances of success.

The whole of Southern Rhodesia is suitable for ranching, and in almost every district agriculture in some form may be profitably undertaken. Maize is the staple crop, and other valuable crops are tobacco, fruits, potatoes, oats and barley. It should not be overlooked that the labour of the country is native, and that some knowledge of the native language is therefore necessary; but this is quickly acquired, and the intelligence of the native enables him in a remarkably short time to grasp the drift of instructions on a very limited vocabulary. A knowledge of carpentry, with the ability to erect rough buildings of brick, which are usually made on the farm and are either burnt in kilns or sun-dried, will be found most useful; also some acquaintance with agricultural implements, more especially how to take to pieces and put together again such implements as ploughs and mowing-machines, comes in very handy. Some experiments in veterinary work, a knowledge of dairying and the management of cattle, sheep and pigs, are also invaluable. Anyone not possessing practical knowledge of this nature should acquire it before going out, and after arrival in Rhodesia should spend a few months with a local farmer, or on one of the British South Africa Company's

Home Farms,* in order to study local conditions of farming before taking up land of his own. The British South Africa Company do not recommend a new settler, unless provided with ample funds, to take a wife and young children to the Colony until he has selected a farm and provided a suitable home for them.

Farm labour being almost entirely done by the natives, it is very difficult to obtain employment of this nature, but skilled farm hands will become more in demand as the country develops. Generally speaking, farmers can obtain native labourers for an average wage, in addition to food, of 10s. to 12s. 6d. per month in Mashonaland and 15s. to 20s. in Matabeleland. The average food allowance is 2½ to 3 lbs. of meal per day, but where sweet potatoes, pumpkins, etc., are given that allowance is reduced. Native drivers from southern colonies get from about £3 per month upwards and rations. Local natives are often trained for ordinary farm driving. At certain seasons of the year the supply of native labour is inadequate, but arrangements have now been concluded under which labourers are being recruited in Nyasaland for Rhodesian farmers. It is hoped, therefore, that the labour supply will in future be more constant and abundant. Household work, is almost entirely performed by male natives, who are remarkably quick at learning and make excellent cooks. They receive from 15s. to £2 per month, with food. Good European domestic servants and nurses are occasionally in demand, at wages varying from £3 to £5 a month, with board and lodging, but they are warned against going out without a definite promise of employment.

Although the country is looking its best during the summer, it is preferable to arrive in the dry season, viz., May to September, and the earlier the better. The climate is delightful at this time of the year, and the newcomer cannot fail to appreciate the invigorating sunshine. When one knows that it will not rain, and that the day is bound to be reasonably warm, there is nothing more delightful than camping out in the open. This is the time to start building a house, although the most primitive shelter for the next few months is all that is

---

* The British South Africa Company has established home farms where, for a year or so, a limited number of approved settlers will be given lodging free [this does not include blankets and linen, which must be provided by the men themselves. It is estimated that a settler's board will cost him £5 per month. Settlers on these farms usually run their own mess] in return for their services, and where some knowledge of local farming conditions may be acquired before taking up farms of their own. These farms are in the centre of areas which are rapidly being settled. At present, farms have been established at Marandellas, about fifty miles south-east of Salisbury; the Premier Estate, near Umtali; Sinoia, in the Lomagundi District; and at Rhodesdale, in the Charter District.

required. Ploughing can be started immediately, and the land left exposed to the air until the planting season.

While the land is being broken up, the farmer erects temporary accommodation; at least he supervises whilst a few natives quickly put up two or three huts—a bedroom, a sitting-room, and a kitchen. If the farmer would like his dining-room to be rectangular, he must mark it out himself, because, though a native can build in a perfect circle, he cannot draw a straight line. Huts of this kind, made of poles and mud with a thatched roof, cost practically no more than the labour of erecting them. It is of the utmost importance, however, from a health point of view, that the huts should be regarded only as temporary accommodation during dry weather, and more durable buildings should be erected before the first rains.

Another form of hut is known as the "Kaytor" hut. These are circular and of corrugated iron, with iron roof-trees to carry thatch. They are quickly erected, and have door and windows. They are frequently brick-lined and generally have wooden floors. The advantage of these huts is that they can be easily moved from one site to another. Their approximate cost at Salisbury is as follows :—

Large huts, 16 feet diameter, 8 feet to eaves, with wooden door and two windows	£25 0 0
Small huts, 12 feet diameter, 7 feet to eaves	14 10 0
Small huts, 12 feet diameter, 6 feet to eaves, with wooden door and one window (two windows can be put in if required, at extra cost)	13 0 0

As soon as possible, after selecting the best site, the farmer should build more substantial premises. The best building material is brick, with iron roofing, wooden floors, and high foundations of local stone. Houses built of iron, lined with wood or green bricks, are also suitable. Materials for the manufacture of bricks of good quality are to be found on a large proportion of the farms available for settlement. Farmers estimate the cost of making bricks at from 15s. to 20s. per thousand, according to the price of labour and the distance wood and water have to be carried.

The following are the approximate prices of building material in Salisbury :—

Deals, 3″ by 9″	1s. 1d. per foot.
„ 4½″ by 3″	7¼d. „
„ 4½″ by 1½″	3¾d. „
„ 9″ by 1½″	7½d. „
Floorings, 6″ by ⅝″	2¾d. „
Ceilings, 6″ by ½″	1¾d. „
Doors, 4 panel, 2′ 6″ by 6′ 6″ by 1¼″	18s. 6d.
French Casements, 3′ 6″ by 6′ 8″ by 1½″	55s.

Cottage Casements, 8 by 10, 6-light	10s. 6d.
,, ,, 10 by 12, 4-light.	10s. 6d.
Windows, complete, 8 by 10	35s.
,, ,, 10 by 12	42s. 6d.
Corrugated Galvanised Iron :	
24-gauge, 6' to 9'	8½d. per foot.
,, 10'	8¾d. ,,
,, 11'	9d. ,,
,, 12'	9¼d. ,,

The clothing that is worn in England will be found quite suitable, except that fewer thick and a larger proportion of light clothes should be taken. Flannel and khaki are most frequently worn, and in the summer months (November to March) white duck or drill suits are common. Woollen or flannel clothing should be worn next to the skin, and at certain seasons of the year the cold at these altitudes renders a change of thick warm clothing indispensable. Ladies will be wise to take out a good supply of washing skirts. The hats chiefly worn (often by ladies as well) are the felt terai and the panama. Boots and shoes should be ordered a shade larger than those worn at home. A good waterproof, a warm overcoat, and khaki or cord riding breeches and leggings should be taken, and also a good supply of flannel shirts. On the whole, the less baggage taken the better ; it is wiser to take a moderate supply of clothing and replenish it as required, and it must be remembered that there are excellent shops in the towns, and that many of the clothes, such as khaki "slacks," most suitable for the veld, can be more easily and quite cheaply purchased locally.

The same remark as to clothing being purchased locally applies to equipment. Many of the fancy articles advertised, though doubtless excellent of their kind, are unnecessary and cumbersome. The farmer should be able to do things for himself, and a few useful carpentering tools will come in handy. General farm implements had better be procured locally. A sleeping sack and waterproof sheet make the most convenient bed for the veld. A few blankets should also be taken. The fire-arms found most useful are a double-barrel 12-bore shot-gun, one barrel choke, and a ·303 sporting rifle, though, if it is a case of one or the other, the former is recommended as being on the whole the more useful. Guns and ammunition can be bought locally. The duty on importing a gun is £1 for a single and 30s. for a double-barrel, plus 10 per cent. *ad valorem*. A permit is required to take firearms or ammunition (on which duty is also payable) into the country. This can be procured from the Company in London. The ordinary game licence (there is no gun licence) in Southern Rhodesia is £1 per annum.

As it is possible that settlers may be situated at some distance from the nearest town and doctor, they should provide themselves with a medicine chest containing a few simple remedies, including quinine in two and five grain doses. Care should be taken to see that the purpose and dose of the drugs are clearly marked on the bottle in English. A small supply of surgical dressings, bandages, lint and sticking-plaster, and a simple antiseptic, such as permanganate of potash, are also advisable. Except in outlying districts, medical aid can be quickly obtained. District surgeons reside in all the towns and larger centres, and there are many public hospitals scattered throughout the country. Drinking water and milk should be boiled. The new settler should also provide himself with a mosquito net. The net should be roomy and come down to the floor all round the bed, or tucked in all round under the mattress. The mesh should not be less than sixteen to the inch.

NEW SOUTH WALES AND IMMIGRATION

In an interesting and critical article on the speech made by the Premier of New South Wales, defining the Government's policy on the eve of the elections, the Australian correspondent of the *Times* says: " So far as it goes, then, the new Ministerial programme is in substance highly satisfactory. Criticism—and without criticism you will not get a fair understanding of State politics or of the Ministry's prospects—must deal in the main either with the one great omission or with the possibility of realising the programme. The omission, as I said at first, may be repaired. But circumstantial evidence points regrettably the other way. Ministers' present mood is almost anti-immigrationist, as far as operations on any effective scale are concerned. They pin their faith to the importation of expert adult agricultural labourers; they decry every attempt to bring out boys to be trained locally, and have transmuted the Dreadnought Farm scheme into one for giving a few youths of eighteen and upwards a year's agricultural education. Their methods, that is, might be admirable if there was no hurry for the next hundred years. Their friends, I find, excuse them partly on the ground that there is no great hurry, partly because they think a Labour Ministry would be even less progressive and would abolish assisted immigration altogether. If this is so, it is all the more important to encourage immigrants while we can, not to express fears that a thousand or so young immigrants per year will lower the standard of wages and disorganise the labour market."

DOMINIONS DEPARTMENT REPORT

LEADING FEATURES

SIR CHARLES LUCAS is to be warmly congratulated on his excellent report of the Dominions Department of the Colonial Office for the year 1909–10, and the fact that the year only closed on the 31st March and the Report was circulated in the following May shows that the question of being up-to-date has not been overlooked. Pressure on our space has prevented an earlier reference to this excellent work. To the text is added a selection of Acts of special interest passed in the Dominions during the same period, and the whole may be described as a most interesting record of colonial affairs covering a particularly active year. It is not possible to reproduce the entire Report in these columns; but doubtless many readers have already made themselves acquainted with its more salient points. Perhaps the divisions likely to attract more general attention are, the personal chapter, the section dealing with the work of the Imperial Defence Conference, and that devoted to the Commercial treaties entered into between Canada and Germany, and between Canada and the United States. A similar treaty has also been made between Canada and France, but as the ratifications were only exchanged during the year 1909–10, Sir Charles Lucas has very properly excluded that Convention from his survey.

Changes in the Colonial Personnel.

Hitherto no attempt has been made to catalogue the changes that occur in the Colonial *personnel* during the year. From the standpoint of reference such a catalogue has a very special interest, and particularly so to readers of *The Empire Review.* Sir Charles's Report tells us that Canada kept the same Governor-General, the same Prime Minister, and the same High Commissioner during the year. In Newfoundland Sir Ralph Williams followed Sir William MacGregor as Governor, and Sir E. Morris, who became Premier upon Sir Robert Bond's resignation, obtained a substantial majority at the subsequent general election. In

Australia Lord Dudley continued to hold the post of Governor-General of the Commonwealth. There was a change of Prime Ministers of the Commonwealth, Mr. Deakin again becoming Prime Minister in place of Mr. Fisher, the leader of the Labour party.* In March, 1910, the first High Commissioner for the Commonwealth, Sir George Reid, arrived in London and took up his duties. During the year Sir Frederick Bedford retired from the Government of Western Australia, and was succeeded by Sir Gerald Strickland, who in turn was followed as Governor of Tasmania by Major-General Sir Harry Barron. Lord Chelmsford succeeded Sir Harry Rawson as Governor of New South Wales, and his place as Governor of Queensland was taken by Sir William MacGregor, previously Governor of Newfoundland. In South Australia Mr. Peake succeeded Mr. Price, who died in office, and in Tasmania, following on a general election, Sir Elliot Lewis became Premier in succession to Captain Evans.

Movements in London.

In England Sir Cornthwaite Rason has retired from the Agent-Generalship of Western Australia; Mr. Kirkpatrick succeeded Mr. Jenkins as Agent-General of South Australia; Dr. McCall has taken the place of the late Mr. Dobson as Agent-General of Tasmania; and in the post of Agent-General for Queensland Major T. B. Robinson † has succeeded Sir Horace Tozer, who had held that post since 1898. In New Zealand Lord Plunket's term of office is now drawing to a close, and his successor has been appointed; Sir Joseph Ward has continued to be Prime Minister. New Zealand has also been represented in England by the same High Commissioner. Sir Walter Hely-Hutchinson has returned from the government of the Cape after a term of office prolonged to nine years, Sir H. Goold-Adams has returned from the Orange River Colony, and Sir Matthew Nathan has ceased to be Governor of Natal. Of that Colony Sir William Arbuckle is no longer Agent-General, and Mr. Russell is acting in his place. The appointment of Lord Gladstone to be the first Governor-General of united South Africa falls within the period under review.

Visitors and Obituary.

The all-important question of union brought Lord Selborne, the Premiers of the South African Colonies, and other leading South African representatives to England during the summer of 1909. The Imperial Defence Conference brought the Prime

---

* Since then Mr. Deakin's party has been defeated at the polls, and Mr. Fisher is again Prime Minister.

† Now Sir T. B. Robinson.

Minister of New Zealand and other statesmen from Canada and
Australasia, while the Premier of Western Australia * is at
present in this country on business connected with his State.
Among leading men in or connected with the Dominions who
have died during the year may be mentioned Sir Henry Strong,
formerly Chief Justice of Canada and a member of the Judicial
Committee of the Privy Council; Sir Henri Taschereau, Chief
Justice of the Province of Quebec; Sir Frederick Darley, Chief
Justice and Lieutenant-Governor of New South Wales; Sir
Frederick Houlder, Speaker of the House of Representatives in
the Commonwealth Parliament; Mr. Thomas Price, the Premier
of South Australia, who, himself a Labour member, led a combined following of Liberals and Labour men; Sir Thomas Bent,
late Premier of Victoria; Sir Charles Todd, who, as Postmaster-
General of South Australia, carried out the great enterprise of a
telegraph line from Adelaide to Port Darwin; and Mr. Hofmeyr,
who, outside office, played for many years a leading part in South
African politics.

The Canadian Navy.

The Imperial Defence Conference was convened under the
terms of the first Resolution of the Imperial Conference of 1907,
which provided that subsidiary conferences should be held " upon
matters of importance requiring consultation between two or more
Governments, which cannot conveniently be postponed until the
next Conference." The Canadian representatives considered that
the provision of a fleet unit in the Pacific, as suggested by the
Admiralty, was not opportune, and at their request the Admiralty
prepared alternative plans for the establishment of a Canadian
navy involving an annual expenditure of £600,000 and £400,000
respectively. Under the first of these two alternatives, which was
the one preferred by the Dominion Government, it was suggested
that that Government should provide a force of cruisers and
destroyers comprising four cruisers of the improved " Bristol "
class and one of the " Boadicea " class, and six destroyers of the
improved " River " class. The number of officers and men
required for this force of eleven ships was estimated to be 2,194.
Pending the completion of the new cruisers, it was proposed
that the Admiralty should lend to Canada two cruisers of the
" Apollo " class, so that the training of the new naval personnel
might be proceeded with at once. These vessels were to be
fitted and maintained at the cost of the Canadian Government,
the officers and men being volunteers from the Royal Navy
paid by Canada, until they could be replaced by Canadian
officers and men. A Bill for the organisation of the Canadian

* The Premier has since returned to Western Australia.

Naval Service, embodying the above scheme has, since the year closed, become law; and negotiations are in progress between the Canadian Government and the Admiralty for the purchase by the Canadian Government of the cruisers "Rainbow" (of the "Apollo" class) and "Niobe" (of the "Diadem" class). It is intended that the latter vessel shall take the place of the cruiser of the "Boadicea" class under the Admiralty scheme.

The Australian Fleet.

It was provisionally adopted—that Australia should provide a fleet unit to form part of the Eastern Fleet of the Empire, which, it was suggested, should, in future, be called the Pacific Fleet, and that this unit should comprise :—One armoured cruiser (new "Indomitable" class). Three unarmoured cruisers ("Bristol" class). Six destroyers ("River" class). Three submarines (C class). "These vessels should be manned as far as possible by Australian officers and seamen, and the numbers required to make up the full complement for immediate purposes should be lent by the Royal Navy. In peace time, and while on the Australian station, this fleet unit would be under the exclusive control of the Commonwealth Government as regards their movements and general administration; but officers and men should be governed by regulations similar to the King's regulations, and be under naval discipline, and when with vessels of the Royal Navy the senior officer should take command of the whole. Further, when placed by the Commonwealth Government at the disposal of the Admiralty in war time, the vessels should be under the control of the naval Commander-in-Chief." The annual expenditure in connection with the maintenance of this fleet unit was estimated at £750,000 to be disbursed by the Commonwealth, but until the Commonwealth could take over the whole cost, the Imperial Government should contribute £250,000 annually "towards the maintenance of the complete fleet unit"; and until the existing Australian Squadron should be relieved by the new Australian fleet unit, the Commonwealth Government should continue to pay to the Imperial Government the annual subsidy of £200,000 payable under the existing agreement. A Naval Loan Act, providing for an expenditure of £3,500,000 for the establishment of the Australian fleet unit, has since been passed by the Commonwealth Parliament, and an order for an armoured cruiser, which will be the flagship of that fleet unit, has now been placed.

New Zealand's Naval Arrangements.

In addition to the gift of an armoured cruiser of the "Indomitable" type to the British Navy, which ship it was arranged should become the flagship of the fleet unit to be maintained on the China Station, the New Zealand Government undertook to continue to make unconditionally its annual contribution of £100,000 per annum to the navy; and it was agreed that, in order to maintain direct connection between New Zealand and the Royal Navy in a concrete form when the Australian fleet unit should have replaced the existing Australian Squadron, two of the "Bristol" cruisers, together with three destroyers and two submarines, should be detached from the fleet unit maintained on the China Station, and be stationed in New Zealand waters in time of peace, the ships in New Zealand waters being manned as far as possible by New Zealand officers and men. These ships should remain under the flag of the Admiral on the China Station, and there should be an interchange in the service of cruisers between New Zealand and Chinese waters. On the completion of the China unit the present agreement with New Zealand should be terminated, and the contribution of £100,000 per annum, should be applied to making good the difference in the local rates of pay to New Zealanders over and above what would be paid under the ordinary British rate. A Naval Loan Act providing for the necessary expenditure has been passed by the New Zealand Parliament, and an order for an armoured cruiser, to be paid for by New Zealand, has now been placed. It is hoped that all the naval arrangements sketched out above will be in operation by the end of 1912. South Africa and Newfoundland have taken no new departure; and pending the formation of the government and parliament of the Union of South Africa, the South African representatives were not in a position to give an authoritative expression of views.

Military Matters.

The representatives of the self-governing Dominions at the Conference having signified their general concurrence in the proposition "That each part of the Empire is willing to make its preparations on such lines as will enable it, should it so desire, to take its share in the general defence of the Empire," a sub-conference on military defence was assembled under the Chairmanship of the Chief of the General Staff to consider in detail "Proposals for so organising the military forces of the Empire as to ensure their effective co-operation in the event of war," which were prepared and laid before the Conference by the Chief of the General Staff. The sub-conference submitted valuable recommendations for assimilating the organisation, administration, and training of the military forces of the self-governing Dominions to the practice of the regular army in these matters. The arrangements for the establishment of local sections of the Imperial General Staff, in accordance with Mr. Haldane's resolution which was accepted by the Colonial Conference of 1907, were discussed, and details of the procedure to be followed in cases of the loan and interchange of officers were provisionally agreed to. A Defence Act has since been passed by the Parliament of the Commonwealth of Australia, under which provision is made for the introduction of universal military training, and a similar Act has been passed by the New Zealand Parliament. In the case of New Zealand the General Staff, at the request of the Prime Minister of the Dominion, drew up a scheme for the re-organisation of the military forces of that Dominion at once for local defence and for expeditionary action over-seas. Since the Defence Conference took place, Australia and New Zealand have had the great advantage of a visit from Lord Kitchener for the purpose of advice on military matters. After calling at Port Darwin, he went on to Queensland, and after visiting and inspecting camps in all the mainland Australian States in turn he went over to Tasmania, and thence to New Zealand.

Canada, France and Germany.

The year has been a fruitful one to Canada in the matter of international agreements. The final stage has been reached in connection with the Franco-Canadian Commercial Conventions. A Convention and a Supplementary Convention regulating the commercial relations between Canada and France were signed at Paris on the 19th of September, 1907, and the 23rd of January, 1909, respectively, and the ratifications of both were exchanged on the 1st of February, 1910. At the beginning of 1910 informal negotiations were undertaken between Mr. Fielding, the Canadian Minister of Finance, on behalf of the Dominion Government, and Dr. Karl Lang, the German Consul-General at Montreal, for the removal of the surtax of $33\frac{1}{3}$ per cent. imposed on German imports into Canada; and on the 15th of February last a provisional commercial agreement was arranged. Under its terms Germany has abandoned the contention that her imports into Canada should receive the same treatment as is accorded by the Dominion Government to imports from Great Britain, and has agreed to give to Canada the conventional rates of the German tariff upon nearly all the important articles which are sent from Canada to Germany. The Dominion Government in return has removed the surtax upon German imports into Canada. The agreement is avowedly provisional only, contemplating, at a future date, a general and formal convention for the regulation of commercial relations between Canada and Germany.

Canada and the United States.

At the end of March a satisfactory arrangement was arrived at between the Dominion of Canada and the United States Government regarding trade relations. Under the new tariff legislation of the United States the President was empowered to grant the minimum tariff to countries which did not discriminate unduly against the United States, and the question was raised whether the Canadian Treaty with France, the scope of which was extended automatically under the most-favoured-nation clauses in treaties with foreign Powers to various foreign nations, was not, in effect, such a discrimination against the United States. Some concern was also felt in the States with regard to the prospect of prohibition by the provincial Government of Quebec of the export of pulp produced on Crown lands within the Province. The Government of the United States appear to have considered that the Canadian Government should, in order to be admitted to the benefits of the minimum tariff, concede to the States the same treatment as is conceded to France under the Conventions of 1907 and 1909. On the other hand, the Canadian Government contended that they did not discriminate as against the United States; that the concessions made to France were made in return for counter-concessions, and that the United States Government itself had consistently adopted the view that most-favoured-nation clauses in treaties did not entitle a country to claim the benefit of special concessions made in return for other special concessions. Eventually a compromise was reached under which the United States Government have accepted the principle that they are not entitled to the full privileges of the French treaties, and they have agreed to give Canada the benefit of the minimum tariff in return for specific concessions on thirteen articles on which concessions were made to France in the Franco-Canadian Conventions.

INDIAN AND COLONIAL INVESTMENTS*

THERE has been no relief during the past month from the general dulness of the investment markets. Dealers are still waiting wearily for the public demand to increase, but, for one reason or another, the public shows no signs of relinquishing its attitude of aloofness. The troubles and rumours of troubles connected with labour have been one powerful deterrent to investment and speculation, such a factor producing a feeling of nervousness that is not confined to the securities immediately concerned. Meantime, the monetary position cannot be blamed. Money is quite as easy as is usual at this season of the year, and much easier than was expected a little while ago.

Following a further dip in Consols, Indian Government securities have fallen further, and the prices of the railway stocks have still failed to respond to the results of the past half-year. Native unrest continues to act as a deterrent to investment in this market.

A summary of the results of the Canadian Pacific Railway for its past financial year was published last month. These figures are now supplemented by the fuller details of the directors' report and accounts. Perhaps the most interesting part of the accounts

INDIAN GOVERNMENT SECURITIES.

Title.	Present Amount.	When Redeemable.	Price.	Yield.	Interest Payable.
INDIA.	£				
3½% Stock (*t*) . . .	85,304,848	1931	93¾	3¾	Quarterly.
3% ,, (*t*) . . .	66,724,530	1948	80¾	3¹¹⁄₁₆	,,
2½% ,, Inscribed (*t*)	11,892,207	1926	67	3¹¹⁄₁₆	,,
3½% Rupee Paper 1854–5	..	(*a*)	94½	3¹¹⁄₁₆	30 June—31 Dec.
3% ,, ,, 1896–7	..	1916	79½	3¾	30 June—30 Dec.

(*t*) Eligible for Trustee investments.
(*a*) Redeemable at a Quarter's notice.

* The tabular matter in this article will appear month by month, the figures being corrected to date. Stocks eligible for Trustee investments are so designated.—ED.

INDIAN RAILWAYS AND BANKS.

Title.	Subscribed.	Last year's dividend.	Share or Stock.	Price.	Yield.
RAILWAYS.	£				
Assam—Bengal, L., guaranteed 3%	1,500,000	3	100	$79\frac{1}{4}$	$3\frac{3}{4}$
Bengal and North-Western (Limited)	3,000,000	$7\frac{1}{2}$	100	$141\frac{1}{2}$	$5\frac{1}{4}$
Bengal Dooars, L.	400,000	$4\frac{1}{2}$	100	87	$5\frac{3}{16}$
Bengal Nagpur (L), gtd. 4% + $\frac{1}{4}$th profits	3,000,000	5	100	102	$4\frac{7}{8}$
Burma Guar. $2\frac{1}{2}$% and propn. of profits	3,000,000	$5\frac{1}{4}$	100	$109\frac{1}{2}$	$4\frac{3}{4}$
Delhi Umballa Kalka, L., guar. $3\frac{1}{4}$% + net earnings	800,000	7	100	$144\frac{1}{2}$	$4\frac{13}{16}$
East Indian Def. ann. cap. g. 4% + $\frac{1}{5}$ sur. profits (*t*)	1,912,804	$5\frac{7}{20}$	100	97	$5\frac{9}{16}$
Do. do, class "D," repayable 1953 (*t*)	4,637,196	$4\frac{3}{4}$	100	113	$4\frac{1}{4}$
Do. $4\frac{1}{2}$% perpet. deb. stock (*t*)	1,435,650	$4\frac{1}{2}$	100	116	$3\frac{7}{8}$
Do. new 3% deb. red. (*t*)	8,000,000	3	100	$79\frac{1}{2}$	$3\frac{3}{4}$
Great Indian Peninsula 4% deb. Stock (*t*)	2,701,450	4	100	106	$3\frac{3}{4}$
Do. 3% Gua. and $\frac{1}{20}$ surp. profits 1925 (*t*)	2,575,000	3	100	$95\frac{1}{4}$	$3\frac{1}{8}$
Indian Mid. L. gua. 4% & $\frac{1}{4}$ surp. profits (*t*)	2,250,000	4	100	99	4
Madras and South Mahratta	5,000,000	4	100	$102\frac{1}{4}$	$3\frac{7}{8}$
Nizam's State Rail. Gtd. 5% Stock	2,000,000	5	100	$110\frac{1}{4}$	$4\frac{1}{2}$
Do. $3\frac{1}{2}$% red. mort. debs.	1,074,700	$3\frac{1}{2}$	100	85	$4\frac{1}{16}$
Rohilkund and Kumaon, Limited	400,000	7	100	130	$5\frac{3}{8}$
South Behar, Limited	379,580	5	100	103	$4\frac{13}{16}$
South Indian $4\frac{1}{2}$% per. deb. stock, gtd.	425,000	$4\frac{1}{2}$	100	118	$3\frac{13}{16}$
Do. capital stock	1,000,000	$7\frac{1}{2}$	100	$104\frac{1}{2}$	$7\frac{1}{8}$
Southern Punjab, Limited	1,000,000	$7\frac{1}{2}$	100	$136\frac{1}{4}$	$5\frac{1}{2}$
Do. $3\frac{1}{2}$% deb. stock red.	500,000	$3\frac{1}{2}$	100	88	$3\frac{15}{16}$
West of India Portuguese Guar. L.	800,000	5	100	$95\frac{1}{4}$	$5\frac{1}{4}$
Do. 5% debenture stock	550,000	5	100	$101\frac{1}{2}$	$4\frac{7}{8}$
BANKS.	Number of Shares.				
Chartered Bank of India, Australia, and China	60,000	14	20	$58\frac{1}{2}$	$4\frac{3}{4}$
National Bank of India	64,000	12	$12\frac{1}{2}$	$43\frac{1}{2}x$	$3\frac{7}{16}$

(*t*) Eligible for Trustee investments.
(*x*) Ex dividend.

is that relating to the company's enormous land holdings. In the balance-sheet there appears the item "Land Grant: Sales of Land and Town Sites, $43,762,195." The balance-sheet takes no account of the unsold land consisting of 7,539,722 acres of agricultural land, and, in addition, 4,474,094 acres in British Columbia. The balance-sheet item is obtained by deducting from the net proceeds, amounting to $79,955,716, the sum of $36,195,521 expended in railway construction and equipment and deducted from the balance-sheet valuation of the cost of the property. The unsold land, valued conservatively at ten dollars an acre, amounts to $120,138,000, which added to the balance-sheet item gives a total valuation of $163,900,000 in respect of the company's land assets alone—or $13,900,000 more than the entire share capital. Thus in the present quotation of 194 the railway undertaking is valued at only 94. In the light of these considerations, the stock can scarcely be said to be over-valued.

That the directors intend to develop the land assets to the best advantage is indicated by their decision to irrigate a further 1,100,000 acres at an estimated expenditure of $8,500,000 to be spread over a period of about three years.

In the case of the Grand Trunk the full details of the report are still awaited. Meantime, the periodical returns relating to the new half-year show that the loss involved in the strike was much less than had been generally anticipated. The July revenue statement shows a decrease of £63,800 in gross receipts, but expenses were cut down by £46,050, so that the decline in net receipts was only £17,750. The weekly returns since issued show that the decrease in gross receipts since the beginning of the half-year has been reduced to £45,381, of which £32,268 was

CANADIAN GOVERNMENT SECURITIES.

Title.	Present Amount.	When Redeemable.	Price.	Yield.	Interest Payable.
4% Intercolonial } Guaranteed by Great Britain.	1,341,400	1910	101	—	1 Apr.—1 Oct.
4% „ } Guaranteed by Great Britain.	1,700,000	1913	103	3¼	1 Apr.—1 Oct.
3½% 1884 Regd. Stock	4,676,830	1909–34	100	—	1 June—1 Dec.
3% Inscribed Stock (t)	8,594,877	1938	91	3½	1 Jan.—1 July.
2½% „ „ (t)	1,592,105	1947	76x	3 11/16	1 Apr.—1 Oct.
PROVINCIAL.					
British Columbia.					
3% Inscribed Stock .	2,045,760	1941	85½	3 13/16	1 Jan.—1 July.
Manitoba.					
5% Sterling Bonds .	308,000	1923	108	4 3/16	1 Jan.—1 July.
4% „ Debs. .	205,000	1928	102	3⅞	1 May—1 Nov.
Nova Scotia.					
3% Stock	164,000	1949	81	4	1 Jan.—1 July.
Quebec.					
3% Inscribed . . .	1,897,820	1937	84x	3 15/16	1 Apr.—1 Oct.
MUNICIPAL.					
Hamilton (City of) 4%	482,800	1934	102	3⅞	1 Apr.—1 Oct.
Montreal 3% Deb. Stock	1,440,000	permanent	81	3¾	1 May—1 Nov.
Do. 4% Cons. „ .	1,821,917	1932	104	3¾	1 May—1 Nov.
Quebec 4% Debs. . .	385,000	1923	101	3 15/16	1 Jan.—1 July.
Do. 3½% Con. Stock .	504,196	drawings	92	3 13/16	1 Jan.—1 July.
Toronto 5% Con. Debs.	136,700	1919–20*	106	4¼	1 Jan.—1 July.
Do. 4% Stg. Bonds .	300,910	1922–28*	101	3 15/16	1 Jan.—1 July.
Do. 3½% Bonds . .	1,169,844	1929	93	4 1/16	1 Jan.—1 July.
Vancouver 4% Bonds	121,200	1931	101	4	1 Apr.—1 Oct.
Do. 4% 40-year Bonds	117,200	1932	100	4	7 Feb.—7 Aug.
Winnipeg 5% Debs. .	138,000	1914	103	4 7/16	30 Apr.—31 Oct.

(t) Eligible for Trustee investments.
* Yield calculated on earlier date of redemption.
(x) Ex dividend.

CANADIAN RAILWAYS, BANKS AND COMPANIES.

Title.	Number of Shares or Amount.	Dividend for last Year.	Paid up per Share.	Price.	Yield
RAILWAYS.		%			
Canadian Pacific Shares . .	1,500,000	7	$100	194	3$\frac{9}{16}$
Do. 4% Preference	£11,328,082	4	Stock	105x	3$\frac{3}{4}$
Do. 5% Stg. 1st Mtg. Bd. 1915	£7,191,500	5	,,	105$\frac{1}{2}$	3$\frac{3}{4}$
Do. 4% Cons. Deb. Stock .	£25,315,001	4	,,	109	3$\frac{5}{8}$
Grand Trunk Ordinary . .	£22,475,985	nil.	,,	26$\frac{7}{8}$	nil.
Do. 5% 1st Preference . . .	£3,420,000	5	,,	111	4$\frac{1}{2}$
Do. 5% 2nd ,, . . .	£2,530,000	5	,,	99$\frac{1}{2}$	5
Do. 4% 3rd ,, . . .	£7,168,055	nil.	,,	57$\frac{3}{4}$	nil.
Do. 4% Guaranteed . . .	£9,840,011	4	,,	93$\frac{1}{2}$	4$\frac{1}{4}$
Do. 5% Perp. Deb. Stock . .	£4,270,375	5	,,	126	3$\frac{15}{16}$
Do. 4% Cons. Deb. Stock . .	£15,821,571	4	,,	102$\frac{1}{2}$	3$\frac{7}{8}$
BANKS AND COMPANIES.					
Bank of Montreal	140,000	10	$100	247	4$\frac{1}{16}$
Bank of British North America	20,000	7	50	76	4$\frac{9}{16}$
Canadian Bank of Commerce .	200,000	9	$50	£20$\frac{3}{4}$	4$\frac{1}{2}$
Canada Company	8,319	30s. per sh.	1	29	5$\frac{1}{4}$
Hudson's Bay	100,000	80s. per sh.	10*	103$\frac{1}{2}$	3$\frac{3}{4}$
Trust and Loan of Canada .	75,000	8	5	6$\frac{5}{8}$	6$\frac{1}{4}$
Do. new	25,000	8	3	3$\frac{1}{4}$	7$\frac{3}{4}$
British Columbia Elec-\ Def.	£600,000	8	Stock	145	5$\frac{1}{4}$
tric Railway . . . / Prefd.	£600,000	6	Stock	126	4$\frac{3}{4}$

* £1 capital repaid 1904.
(x) Ex dividend.

NEWFOUNDLAND GOVERNMENT SECURITIES.

Title.	Present Amount.	When Redeemable.	Price.	Yield.	Interest Payable.
3$\frac{1}{2}$% Sterling Bonds .	2,178,800	1941–7–8†	93	3$\frac{7}{8}$	
3% Sterling ,, .	325,000	1947	80	4$\frac{1}{16}$	
4% Inscribed Stock .	320,000	1913–38*	101	3$\frac{13}{16}$	1 Jan.—1 July.
4% ,, ,, .	455,647	1935	105	3$\frac{11}{16}$	
4% Cons. Ins. ,, .	200,000	1936	104	3$\frac{3}{4}$	

* Yield calculated on earlier date of redemption.
† Yield calculated on latest date.

on the Grand Trunk Western, the main line actually showing an increase of £5,516.

In its report for the half-year ended June 30, the Bank of British North America shows a profit of £64,119 including £20,545 brought forward. The usual interim dividend at the rate of 6 per cent. per annum is announced, and after making various provisions for the benefit of the staff, the increased amount of £30,605 is carried forward. Since the date of the

AUSTRALIAN GOVERNMENT SECURITIES.

Title.	Present Amount.	When Redeemable.	Price.	Yield.	Interest Payable.
NEW SOUTH WALES.					
4% Inscribed Stock (*t*)	9,686,300	1933	105	$3\frac{11}{16}$	1 Jan.—1 July.
3½% ,, ,, (*t*)	16,464,545	1924	98	$3\frac{3}{4}$	⎫
3% ,, ,, (*t*)	12,480,000	1935	86½	$3\frac{5}{8}$	⎭1 Apr.—1 Oct.
VICTORIA.					
4% Inscribed, 1885 .	5,970,000	1920	102	$3\frac{13}{16}$	
3½% ,, 1889 (*t*)	5,000,000	1921–6*	98	$3\frac{3}{4}$	⎫
4% , . . .	2,107,000	1911–26*	101	$3\frac{11}{16}$	⎬1 Jan.—1 July.
3% ,, (*t*) . .	5,211,331	1929–49†	85½	$3\frac{13}{16}$	⎭
QUEENSLAND.					
4% Bonds	10,267,400	1913–15*	101¼	$3\frac{5}{8}$	
4% Inscribed Stock (*t*)	7,939,000	1924	102	$3\frac{13}{16}$	⎫
3½% ,, ,, (*t*)	8,616,034	1921–30†	98	$3\frac{5}{8}$	⎬1 Jan.—1 July.
3% ,, ,, (*t*)	4,274,213	1922–47†	85	$3\frac{3}{4}$	⎭
SOUTH AUSTRALIA.					
4% Bonds	1,359,300	1916	102	$3\frac{13}{16}$	⎫1 Apl.—1 Oct.
4% Inscribed Stock .	6,269,000	1916–7–36*	101	4	⎭
3½% ,, ,, (*t*)	2,517,800	1939	98½	$3\frac{9}{16}$	
3% ,, ,, (*t*)	839,500	1916–26‡	89½	$3\frac{5}{16}$	⎬1 Jan.—1 July.
3% ,, ,, (*t*)	2,760,100	1916 ‡ or after.	83½	$3\frac{9}{16}$	⎭
WESTERN AUSTRALIA.					
4% Inscribed . .	1,876,000	1911–31*	102	$3\frac{7}{16}$	15 Apr.—15 Oct.
3½% ,, (*t*) . .	3,780,000	1920–35†	97¼	$3\frac{11}{16}$	⎫1 May—1 Nov.
3% ,, (*t*) . .	3,750,000	1915–35‡	88	$3\frac{7}{8}$	⎭
3% ,, (*t*) . .	2,500,000	1927‡	89½	$3\frac{5}{16}$	15 Jan.—15 July.
TASMANIA.					
3½% Inscbd. Stock (*t*)	4,156,500	1920–40*	99	$3\frac{5}{8}$	⎫
4% ,, ,,	1,000,000	1920–40*	102¼	$3\frac{3}{4}$	⎬1 Jan.—1 July.
3% . . . . . (*t*)	450,000	1920–40†	86	$3\frac{13}{16}$	⎭

* Yield calculated on earlier date of redemption.

† Yield calculated on later date of redemption, though a portion of the loan may be redeemed earlier.

‡ No allowance for redemption.

(*t*) Eligible for Trustee Investment.

AUSTRALIAN MUNICIPAL AND OTHER BONDS.

Title.	Present Amount.	When Redeemable.	Price.	Yield.	Interest Payable.
Melbourne & Met. Bd. of Works 4% Debs.	1,000,000	1921	101	4	1 Apl.—1 Oct.
Do. City 4% Deb. .	850,000	1915–22*	101	$3\frac{7}{8}$	⎫
Melbourne Trams Trust 4½% Debs. .	1,650,000	1914–16*	102	$4\frac{1}{16}$	⎬1 Jan.—1 July.
S. Melbourne 4½% Debs.	128,700	1919	102	$4\frac{1}{4}$	⎭
Sydney 4% Debs. . .	640,000	1912–13	101	$3\frac{11}{16}$	⎫1 Jan.—1 July.
Do. 4% Debs. . . .	300,000	1919	101	$3\frac{7}{8}$	⎭

* Yield calculated on earlier date of redemption.

last report, the bank has opened new branches at Prince Rupert and two other towns in British Columbia, five towns in Saskatchewan and one in Alberta.

Splendid progress is shown by the half-yearly report of the Commercial Banking Company of Sydney. The deposit and current accounts at June 30 amounted to £18,321,000 against £15,971,800 at the corresponding date last year, thus showing the satisfactory increase of £2,349,200 on the year. The net profits for the half-year amounted to £123,900 against £111,100, and after paying the usual dividend at the rate of 10 per cent. per annum, giving a bonus to the staff, and transferring £40,000 to reserve, the directors are able to increase the carry-forward to £34,600. The total reserve is now brought up to £1,380,000 against a paid-up capital of £1,500,000.

AUSTRALIAN RAILWAYS, BANKS AND COMPANIES.

Title.	Number of Shares or Amount.	Dividend for last Year.	Paid up.	Price.	Yield.
RAILWAYS.		%			
Emu Bay and Mount Bischoff . . .	12,000	6	5	4½	6⅝
Do. 4½% Irred. Deb. Stock	£130,900	4½	100	97	4⅝
Mid. of W. Aust. 4% Debs., Guartd. .	300,000	4	100	100	4
BANKS AND COMPANIES.					
Bank of Australasia	40,000	14	40	117	4¾
Bank of New South Wales	125,000	10	20	45	4 7/16
Union Bank of Australia £75 . . .	60,000	14	25	62½	5 9/16
Do. 4% Inscribed Stock Deposits . .	£600,000	4	100	99	4
Australian Mort. Land & Finance £25	80,000	12½	5	7¼	8 9/16
Do. 4% Perp. Deb. Stock	£1,900,000	4	100	100½	3 15/16
Dalgety & Co. £20	154,000	7	5	5¾	6 1/16
Do. 4½% Irred. Deb. Stock	£620,000	4½	100	108	4⅛
Goldsbrough Mort & Co. 4% A Deb. Stock Reduced	£1,067,137	4	100	86½	4⅝
Do. B Income Reduced	£711,340	5½	100	95	5¾
Australian Agricultural £25 . . .	20,000	£4	21½	74	5 3/16
South Australian Company . . .	14,200	16½	20	66½	4⅞
Trust & Agency of Australasia . . .	42,479	7½	1	¾	10
Do. 5% Cum. Pref.	87,500	5	10	9¾	5⅛

NEW ZEALAND GOVERNMENT SECURITIES.

Title.	Present Amount.	When Redeemable.	Price.	Yield.	Interest Payable.
5% Bonds	266,300	1914	104	4	15 Jan.—15 July.
4% Inscribed Stock (*t*)	29,150,302	1929	105	3 11/16	1 May—1 Nov.
3½% Stock (*t*) . . .	13,754,532	1940	98	3⅝	1 Jan.—1 July.
3% Inscribed Stock (*t*)	9,659,980	1945	86½	3¾	1 Apr.—1 Oct.

(*t*) Eligible for Trustee investments.

NEW ZEALAND MUNICIPAL AND OTHER SECURITIES.

Title.	Present Amount.	When Redeemable.	Price.	Yield.	Interest Payable.
Auckland 5% Deb. .	200,000	1934–8*	109	$4\frac{3}{8}$	1 Jan.—1 July.
Do. Hbr. Bd. 5% Debs.	150,000	1917	105	$4\frac{3}{8}$	10 April—10 Oct.
Bank of N. Z. shares†	150,000	div. $12\frac{1}{2}$%	$10\frac{1}{2}$	$3\frac{15}{16}$	—
Do. 4% Gua. Stock‡ .	£1,000,000	1914	102	$3\frac{11}{16}$	April—Oct.
Christchurch 6% Drainage Loan. .	200,000	1926	121	$4\frac{3}{16}$	30 June—31 Dec.
Lyttleton Hbr. Bd. 6%	200,000	1929	121	$4\frac{3}{8}$	1 Jan.—1 July.
Napier Hbr. Bd. 5% Debs.	300,000	1920	104	$4\frac{1}{2}$	1 Jan.—1 July.
Do. 5% Debs.	200,000	1928	104	$4\frac{11}{16}$	1 Jan.—1 July.
National Bank of N.Z. £$7\frac{1}{2}$ Shares £$2\frac{1}{2}$ paid	150,000	div. 12%	$5\frac{7}{16}$	$5\frac{1}{2}$	Jan.—July.
Oamaru 5% Bds. . .	173,800	1920	94	$5\frac{7}{8}$	1 Jan.—1 July.
Otago Hbr. Cons. Bds. 5%	443,100	1934	105	$4\frac{5}{8}$	1 Jan.—1 July.
Wellington 6% Impts. Loan	100,000	1914–29	108	—	1 Mar.—1 Sept.
Do. 6% Waterworks .	130,000	1929	118	$4\frac{1}{2}$	1 Mar.—1 Sept.
Do. $4\frac{1}{2}$% Debs. . .	165,000	1933	104	$4\frac{5}{16}$	1 May—1 Nov.
Westport Hbr. 4% Debs.	150,000	1925	100	4	1 Mar.—1 Sept.

* Yield calculated on earlier date of redemption.
† £6 13*s.* 4*d.* Shares with £3 6*s.* 8*d.* paid up.
‡ Guaranteed by New Zealand Government.

If the revised scheme of capital reduction and reorganisation put forward by the directors of the Midland Railway of Western Australia is carried through, the company will enter upon a new and, it is hoped, more prosperous era. The scheme is necessarily of a very complicated character, and the difficulties of reconciling the various interests have been great, but the directors seem to have performed their task on very fair lines, and it is to be hoped that the scheme will pass. The directors seem already to have inaugurated a more vigorous policy with regard to colonisation. They have decided to put in operation a scheme for sub-dividing certain lands into 300-acre farms. Each farm will be fenced; 100 acres cleared and ploughed ready for sowing; provision made for water supply; and a house (three, four or five rooms, as may be required), sheds, stables and out-buildings will be erected. These "ready-made" farms will be offered, in the first instance, to farmers in Great Britain, on terms extending over twenty years. The results of this interesting scheme will be watched with interest.

August's production of gold in the Transvaal exceeded all previous returns except that for December 1908, in which was included a quantity of gold previously held in reserve. For all practical purposes, therefore, last month's return was a "record"

one. This table gives the returns month by month for several
years past :—

Month.	1910.	1909.	1908.	1907.	1906.	1905.
	£	£	£	£	£	£
January . .	2,554,451	2,612,836	2,380,124	2,283,741	1,820,739	1,568,508
February .	2,445,088	2,400,892	2,301,971	2,096,434	1,731,664	1,545,371
March . .	2,578,877	2,580,498	2,442,022	2,287,391	1,884,815	1,698,340
April. . .	2,629,535	2,578,804	2,403,500	2,281,110	1,865,785	1,695,550
May . . .	2,693,785	2,652,699	2,472,143	2,227,838	1,959,062	1,768,734
June . . .	2,655,602	2,621,818	2,442,329	2,155,976	2,021,813	1,751,412
July . . .	2,713,083	2,636,965	2,482,608	2,262,813	2,089,004	1,781,944
August . .	2,757,919	2,597,646	2,496,869	2,357,602	2,162,583	1,820,496
September .	—	2,575,760	2,496,112	2,285,424	2,145,575	1,769,124
October . .	—	2,558,902	2,624,012	2,351,344	2,296,361	1,765,047
November .	—	2,539,146	2,609,685	2,335,406	2,265,625	1,804,253
December .	—	2,569,822	2,806,235	2,478,659	2,336,961	1,833,295
Total * .	21,028,340	30,925,788	29,957,610	27,403,738	24,579,987	20,802,074

* Including undeclared amounts omitted from the monthly returns.

Satisfactory returns were also issued in respect of native
labour. During August the supply of Kaffirs at the gold mines
showed a diminution of only 683, whereas the reduction due to
seasonal causes is usually much greater than this. During the
corresponding month of last year it was 2,553. This statement
gives details of the returns for the past two years :—

Month.	Natives Joined.	Natives Left.	Net Gain on Month.	Natives Employed end of Month.	Chinese Employed end of Month.
August 1908	11,988	10,799	1,209	133,548	17,006
September ,,	14,129	11,497	2,632	136,180	14,655
October ,,	14,754	11,769	2,985	139,165	12,317
November ,,	12,324	10,163	2,161	141,326	12,298
December ,,	17,404	10,008	7,396	148,722	12,283
January 1909	13,551	11,609	1,942	150,664	10,045
February ,,	18,018	10,844	7,174	157,838	10,034
March ,,	16,184	11,979	4,205	162,043	9,997
April ,,	12,102	11,244	858	162,901	7,734
May ,,	7,717	12,339	4,622*	158,279	7,717
June ,,	8,335	12,354	4,019*	154,260	5,378
July ,,	7,826	12,612	4,786*	149,474	5,370
August ,,	10,089	12,642	2,553*	146,291	5,361
September ,,	11,747	13,811	2,064*	144,857	3,204
October ,,	14,656	13,762	894	152,563‡	3,199
November ,,	13,942	13,742	200	152,763	1,799
December ,,	17,293	13,348	3,945	156,708	nil.
January 1910	—	—	3,954	160,662	nil.
February ,,	—	—	9,109	169,771	nil.
March ,,	—	—	8,574	178,345	nil.
April ,,	—	—	5,469	183,814	nil.
May ,,	—	—	150	183,964	nil.
June ,,	—	—	533*	183,431	nil.
July ,,	—	—	1,917*	181,514	nil.
August ,,	—	—	683*	180,831	nil.

* Net loss.   ‡ Including new members of Native Labour Association.

SOUTH AFRICAN GOVERNMENT SECURITIES.

Title.	Present Amount.	When Redeemable.	Price.	Yield.	Interest Payable.
CAPE COLONY.	£				
$4\frac{1}{2}$% Bonds	485,000	dwgs.	102	$4\frac{7}{16}$	15 Apr.—15 Oct.
4% 1883 Inscribed .	3,733,195	1923	$103\frac{1}{2}$	$3\frac{3}{4}$	1 June—1 Dec.
4% 1886 " .	9,997,566	1916-36*	$102\frac{1}{2}$	$3\frac{11}{16}$	15 Apr.—15 Oct.
$3\frac{1}{2}$% 1886 " (t).	15,443,014	1929-49†	100	$3\frac{1}{2}$	1 Jan.—1 July.
3% 1886 " (t).	7,553,590	1933-43†	87	$3\frac{11}{16}$	1 Feb.—1 Aug.
NATAL.					
$4\frac{1}{2}$% Bonds, 1876 . .	758,700	1919	103x	$4\frac{1}{16}$	15 Mar.—15 Sep.
4% Inscribed (t) . .	3,026,444	1937	106	$3\frac{11}{16}$	Apr.—Oct.
$3\frac{1}{2}$% " (t) . .	3,714,917	1914-39†	$98\frac{1}{2}$	$3\frac{9}{16}$	1 June—1 Dec.
3% " (t) . .	6,000,000	1929-49†	86	$3\frac{11}{16}$	1 Jan.—1 July.
TRANSVAAL.					
3% Guartd. Stock (t) .	35,000,000	1923-53†	$93\frac{1}{4}$	$3\frac{5}{16}$	1 May—1 Nov.

* Yield calculated on earlier date of redemption.
† Yield calculated on later date of redemption.
(t) Eligible for Trustee investments.
(x) Ex dividend.

SOUTH AFRICAN RAILWAYS, BANKS, AND COMPANIES.

Title.	Number of Shares or Amount.	Dividend for last Year.	Paid up.	Price.	Yield.
RAILWAYS.					
Mashonaland 5% Debs.	£2,500,000	5	100	$99\frac{1}{2}$	5
Rhodesia Rlys. 5% 1st Mort. Debs. guar. by B.S.A. Co. till 1915 . . .	£2,000,000	5	100	$100\frac{1}{2}$	$4\frac{15}{16}$
Royal Trans-African 5% Debs. Rep. .	£1,853,700	5	100	90	$5\frac{1}{2}$
BANKS AND COMPANIES.					
African Banking Corporation £10 shares	80,000	$5\frac{1}{2}$	5	$4\frac{7}{8}$	$5\frac{5}{8}$
Bank of Africa £$18\frac{3}{4}$	160,000	5	$6\frac{1}{4}$	$7\frac{1}{4}$	$4\frac{1}{4}$
Natal Bank £10	148,232	8	$2\frac{1}{2}$	$3\frac{3}{8}$	$5\frac{7}{8}$
National Bank of S. Africa £10 . .	110,000	3	10	12	$2\frac{1}{2}$
Standard Bank of S. Africa £100 . .	61,941	10	25	$63\frac{1}{2}$	$3\frac{15}{16}$
Ohlsson's Cape Breweries	60,000	nil	5	$3\frac{3}{4}$	—
South African Breweries	965,279	10	1	$1\frac{17}{32}$	$6\frac{1}{2}$
British South Africa (Chartered) . .	8,053,425	nil	1	$1\frac{29}{32}$	nil
Do. 5% Debs. Red.	£1,250,000	5	100	$105\frac{1}{2}$	$4\frac{11}{16}$
Natal Land and Colonization . . .	68,066	4	5	$4\frac{1}{4}$	$4\frac{11}{16}$
Cape Town & District Gas Light & Coke	10,000	nil	10	$3\frac{1}{2}$	—
Kimberley Waterworks £10 . . .	45,000	5	7	$5\frac{1}{4}$	$6\frac{5}{8}$

Rhodesia's gold output for August showed a further somewhat disappointing diminution. The total production for the month amounted to 45,458 ounces, valued at £191,423, which is £3,810 less than the value for the preceding month, and £36,873 less than

that for August last year. This statement enables comparison
with the monthly returns for several years past :—

MONTH.	1910.	1909.	1908.	1907.	1906.
	£	£	£	£	£
January . .	227,511	204,666	199,380	168,240	155,337
February . .	203,888	192,497	191,635	145,397	137,561
March . . .	228,385	202,157	200,615	167,424	160,722
April . . .	228,213	222,700	212,935	175,210	157,108
May . . .	224,888	225,032	223,867	189,216	169,218
June . . .	214,709	217,600	224,920	192,506	170,083
July . . .	195,233	225,234	228,151	191,681	173,313
August . . .	191,423	228,296	220,792	192,106	179,000
September . .	—	213,249	204,262	192,186	173,973
October . .	—	222,653	205,466	191,478	161,360
November . .	—	236,307	196,668	183,058	175,656
December . .	—	233,397	217,316	190,383	171,770
Total .	1,714,250	2,623,788	2,526,007	2,178,885	1,985,101

SOUTH AFRICAN MUNICIPAL SECURITIES.

Title.	Present Amount.	When Redeemable.	Price.	Yield.	Interest Payable.
	£				
Bloemfontein 4% . .	763,000	1954	99	$4\frac{7}{16}$	1 Jan.—1 July.
Cape Town 4% . .	1,861,750	1953	103	$3\frac{3}{4}$	1 Jan.—1 July.
Durban 4% . . .	850,000	1951–3	101	$3\frac{15}{16}$	30 June—31 Dec.
Johannesburg 4% .	5,500,000	1933–4	99	$4\frac{1}{2}$	1 April—1 Oct.
Krugersdorp 4% . .	100,000	1930	96	$4\frac{3}{4}$	1 June—1 Dec.
Pietermaritzburg 4%	825,000	1949–53	99	$4\frac{1}{16}$	30 June—31 Dec.
Port Elizabeth 4% .	374,060	1964	100	4	30 June—31 Dec.
Pretoria 4% . . .	1,000,000	1939	101	$3\frac{15}{16}$	1 Jan.—1 July.
Rand Water Board 4%	3,400,000	1935	101	$3\frac{15}{16}$	1 Jan.—1 July.

CROWN COLONY SECURITIES.

Title.	Present Amount.	When Redeemable.	Price.	Yield.	Interest Payable.
Barbadoes 3½% ins. (t)	375,000	1925–42*	96	$3\frac{13}{16}$	1 Mar.—1 Sep.
Brit. Guiana 3% ins. (t)	250,000	1923–45†	85	$3\frac{3}{4}$	1 Feb.—1 Aug.
Ceylon 4% ins. (t). .	1,076,100	1934	107	$3\frac{1}{4}$	15 Feb.—15 Aug.
Do. 3% ins. (t). .	2,850,000	1940	87	$3\frac{3}{4}$	1 May—1 Nov.
Hong-Kong 3½% ins (t)	1,485,733	1918–43†	$98\frac{1}{2}$	$3\frac{5}{8}$	15 Apr.—15 Oct.
Jamaica 4% ins. (t) .	1,099,048	1934	106	$3\frac{9}{16}$	15 Feb.—15 Aug.
Do. 3½% ins. (t) . .	1,455,500	1919–49†	97	$3\frac{5}{8}$	24 Jan.—24 July.
Mauritius 3% guar.⎫ Great Britain (t) .⎬	600,000	1940	92	$3\frac{7}{16}$	1 Jan.—1 July.
Do. 4% ins. (t). . .	482,390	1937	106	$3\frac{5}{8}$	1 Feb.—1 Aug.
Sierra Leone 3½% ins. (t)	720,051	1929–54†	$98\frac{1}{2}$	$3\frac{9}{16}$	1 June—1 Dec.
Trinidad 4% ins. . .	422,593	1917–42*	102	$3\frac{5}{8}$	15 Mar.—15 Sep.
Do. 3% ins. (t). . .	600,000	1922–44†	86	$3\frac{3}{4}$	15 Jan.—15 July.
Hong-Kong & Shang-⎫ hai Bank Shares .⎬	120,000	Div. £4½	£87½	$4\frac{7}{8}$	Feb.—Aug.

* Yield calculated on shorter period.   † Yield calculated on longer period.
(t) Eligible for Trustee investments.

Further relapses in the price of rubber have induced fresh selling of rubber shares by nervous holders, and weak bulls and bear operations also seem to have been carried on extensively. Big interim dividend announcements by the leading companies have failed to stay the decline, although they have attracted some quiet purchases by astute investors.

RUBBER SHARES.

Company.	Issued Capital.	Area planted.	Nominal Value of Share.	Amount paid-up.	Price.
	£	Acres.			
Anglo-Malay	150,000	3,391	2*s.*	2*s.*	23*s.*
Batu Tiga	60,000	1,545	£1	£1	$4\frac{1}{2}$
Bukit Rajah	66,700	2,772	£1	£1	$15\frac{1}{2}$
Consolidated Malay	62,007	1,710	£1	2*s.*	24*s.*
Highlands and Lowlands	317,353	4,707	£1	£1	$5\frac{1}{8}$
Kepitigalla	225,000	3,127	£1	£1	$\frac{7}{8}$
Kuala Lumpur	180,000	2,611	£1	£1	$7\frac{3}{4}$
Lanadron	269,780	4,570	£1	£1	$5\frac{3}{8}$
Linggi	100,000	4,192	2*s.*	2*s.*	50*s.* 6*d.*
Pataling	22,500	1,454	2*s.*	2*s.*	$2\frac{13}{16}$
Straits (Bertam)	200,000	2,541	2*s.*	2*s.*	7*s.*
Vallambrosa	50,600	1,807	2*s.*	2*s.*	40*s.* 9*d.*

EGYPTIAN SECURITIES.

Title.	Amount or Number of Shares.	Dividend for last Year.	Paid up.	Price.	Yield.
Egyptian Govt. Guaranteed Loan (*t*)	£7,414,700	3	99	95	$3\frac{1}{8}$
" Unified Debt	£55,971,960	4	100	$101\frac{3}{4}$	$3\frac{7}{8}$
National Bank of Egypt	300,000	9	10	21	$4\frac{1}{4}$
Bank of Egypt	50,000	15	$12\frac{1}{2}$	$29\frac{1}{2}$	$6\frac{5}{16}$
Agricultural Bank of Egypt, Ordinary	496,000	$5\frac{1}{4}$	5	$7\frac{1}{2}$	$3\frac{1}{2}$
" " " Preferred	125,000	4	10	$9\frac{1}{8}$	$4\frac{3}{8}$
" " " Bonds	£2,350,000	$3\frac{1}{2}$	100	$86\frac{1}{2}$	4

(*t*) Eligible for Trustee investments.

TRUSTEE.

September 23, 1910.

NOTICE TO CONTRIBUTORS.—The Editor of THE EMPIRE REVIEW cannot hold himself responsible in any case for the return of MS. He will, however, always be glad to consider any contributions which may be submitted to him; and when postage-stamps are enclosed every effort will be made to return rejected contributions promptly. Contributors are specially requested to put their names and addresses on their manuscripts, and to have them typewritten.

THE EMPIRE REVIEW

"Far as the breeze can bear, the billows foam,
Survey our empire, and behold our home."—*Byron.*

| VOL. XX. | NOVEMBER, 1910. | No. 118 |

THE LATE PRINCE FRANCIS OF TECK

A MEMOIR AND AN APPRECIATION

By the EDITOR

THE death of Prince Francis of Teck, after a comparatively short illness, in the flower of manhood, leaves a void in many a heart, for he was greatly liked and much respected by a wide and varied circle of friends and acquaintances. Terribly sad indeed is the crushing blow that has fallen so unexpectedly on his family, and the heart of the nation will go out in undivided sympathy to England's Queen, who, stricken with grief but with all a sister's devotion, watched by the bedside of her brother until death came to end the vigil, and he whom she so dearly loved passed calmly and peacefully away.

It takes one back a good many years in memory to the early days of happy married life which followed the union of Princess Mary Adelaide and Prince Teck. The bride was the younger daughter of the Duke and Duchess of Cambridge and first cousin to Queen Victoria. She was a great favourite both at Court and in Society, and possessed a most charming personality, which grew even more marked as years passed on, and gained for her the title of the "People's Princess." The bridegroom was a soldier, very popular with his brother officers, a special friend of the Emperor of Austria, and much liked in Vienna, where his good looks gained for him the sobriquet of "der schöner Uhlan." His father, Duke Alexander of Würtemberg, married Claudine Comtesse de Rhédey, on whom the Emperor of Austria conferred the title of Comtesse de Hohenstein, subsequently raising their son, Count Hohenstein, to the rank of prince, giving him the surname of Teck, one of the titles of the King of Würtemberg, and making him a Serene Highness. A few years after his marriage with Princess Mary the King of Würtemberg bestowed a dukedom upon Prince Teck, and Queen Victoria raised him to the rank of his Highness.

Her late Majesty gave the newly-married couple the apartments which she and the Duchess of Kent occupied for so many years at Kensington Palace, and it was there Prince Francis was born on January 9, 1870. Although his father's name was Francis, the name was, I believe, selected mainly as a compliment to the Emperor of Austria, who continued to retain the warmest regard for his young friend now Duke of Teck. Writing to a lady in 1872, the Duchess says, "Dolly (the present Duke of Teck) and Frank (the name Prince Francis was always known by in the family) are splendid specimens of boyhood, the one golden-haired the other chestnut-brown, and fully answer their sister's (Queen Mary) appellation of 'Beauty Boys.'" Prince Francis passed his boyhood at White Lodge, the country home of his parents, who made it a rule to spend as much time as possible with their children. When eight years old he went with his elder brother and their tutor to spend the holidays at Hopetoun. This was the first time either of them had stayed away without their mother, but the Duchess had promised to pay some visits abroad, and so she readily accepted Lady Hopetoun's offer to take care of the two elder boys until her return. Still, her thoughts were always with them, and in a letter to Lady Hopetoun the fond mother says : "I know full well that you will take every care of Dolly and Frank, and my only fear is that I am entrusting them to too kind and tender hands, and that the naughty good-for-nothings stand a very fair chance of being tremendously spoilt, though I think I may rely upon you keeping them in tolerable order and for my sake not allowing them to get unruly and above themselves. We, of course, give them over entirely into your charge. The only suggestion I would make is that some work be done of a morning before the expeditions, and that the boys do not, as a rule, sit up too late." Princess Mary was very proud of her three boys, and her thoughts constantly turned to their careers and how they would acquit themselves in after-life. In due time each was sent to a public school, Prince Francis going first to Wellington and afterwards to Cheltenham, where he won the Hornby Prize for German, open to the whole College.

"The Duchess of Teck often talked to me about her boys," said the Bishop of Peterborough. "Sometimes with tears in her eyes—her devotion to them was very great." On another occasion she remarked to her old friend Mrs. Dalrymple, "I pray they may each of them in turn grow up a credit to us all and be thorough English boys ; they are so as yet, thank God." It had always been Princess Mary's wish that her sons should be soldiers, and as one after the other entered the Army her motherly heart rejoiced to see that wish fulfilled. After passing through Sandhurst Prince Francis received a commission in the 9th Lancers, but in a very short time was transferred to the 60th Rifles, later on joining the 17th Dragoon Guards. He was attached for a year to the staff of the general officer commanding at Quetta, acting as aide-de-camp, when he was seconded for service in the Egyptian Army. He served under Lord Kitchener on the Nile, taking part in the battles of Atbara and Omdurman. Returning home he became aide-de-camp to Sir Leslie Rundle, then commanding the South-Eastern District, vacating that appointment to take up the post of Staff Captain of the Remount Establishment in Dublin. When the South African War broke out he was selected for similar work during the campaign. He was frequently mentioned in despatches, was awarded the Queen's Medal with three clasps, given Brevet rank and the Distinguished Service Order.

Soon after the war ended he retired from the Army and manifested a taste for business. The City had a special attraction for him, and he longed to take a leading part in the world of finance. Opportunities were not wanting, but difficulties stood in the way. These proved insurmountable, and he was compelled to relinquish a career which in many ways he was eminently fitted to follow. If not a deep thinker, his thoughts came very rapidly, and he was quick to see and seize upon a point. He was a man of commanding presence, and one could not be in his company without being impressed with his great earnestness and capacity for driving home an argument. Courteous to a degree, as became his Royal birth, he invariably won over an opponent, and was always on the best of terms with everyone who had the privilege of his acquaintance.

Although Prince Francis retired from the Army he continued to take the keenest interest in military affairs ; he had his own views on the problems which divide the experts, and did not fail to express them when opportunity offered. A strong advocate of military training, he desired to see an improvement in the physique of London lads. In the welfare of young men he took the greatest interest and was always ready to help on a promising youth. He was particularly attracted to the Claud Eliot Lads' Club, of which he was president. Often he would go down to Hoxton of an evening and join the members of the club in their drill and gymnastics, and on these occasions he never forgot to drive home in a kindly manner a few words of helpful advice.

No better host existed than Prince Francis of Teck; he always gave you of the best, and he took infinite trouble to see you enjoyed yourself. He had seen a good deal of people and of the world in general, and possessed an easy flow of conversation, which delighted his friends and greatly entertained his guests. Although his manner was most unassuming he never forgot his position, and always bore himself with becoming dignity. In his own private circle he was at all times the life and soul of the party, and his merry laugh and cheery ways made him a great favourite. He dearly loved society, and society will miss him much, for he was eagerly sought after, not because he was a member of the Royal Family, but for himself. Like the late King Edward, Prince Francis was essentially human; he understood mankind, and mankind understood him. By nature he was genial and full of sympathy; he enjoyed life and liked to see others enjoying life. Unselfish to a degree, he was never happier than when making others happy. If he could do a good turn to anyone he would go out of his way to do it, and if his means were small his generosity was large.

Being a bachelor he used his clubs freely. His service club was the Naval and Military, and at one time he frequented White's and the Bachelors' a good deal. Later on he was more often seen at the Marlborough, but perhaps the club that appealed to him most was the Beefsteak. Not only did he serve on the committee of the Club, where his advice was obviously of great value, but he joined the House Committee and took much interest in the domestic arrangements. A few years ago he became president of the Excelsior, and seldom missed taking the chair at the dinners which are the feature of this Club. But it was in connection with the Royal Automobile Club that he was perhaps best known. It is not too much to say that Prince Francis made the club what it has become. When accepting the invitation to become its chairman he said : "I will do my best to promote the welfare of the Club in every possible way. I will leave no stone unturned to see that the interests of the automobile world of Great Britain and Ireland receive careful attention." That he kept his word goes without saying; he was always thinking out new plans to make the club more successful, always doing or suggesting something. In the new house he was greatly interested; he worked hard for its success, and it is most pathetic to think that he should have been called away just as his labours were nearing completion.

In the world of sport he will be equally regretted. A good shot, he was much in request for shooting parties. A fine rider, he held his own in the hunting-field and was especially at home in Ireland, where his unaffected manner and goodness of heart gained him a host of friends and admirers, especially amongst the poor folk, many of whom treasure up some kind word spoken or some kind' deed done in the course of "the daily round, the common task." He was a good judge of a horse, and it was in no small measure due to his efforts that the Richmond Show owed its success year after year. A keen automobilist himself, he did everything in his power to help on the motor industry, and it will be a very difficult task to fill his place in this connection. Like his father and mother, Prince Francis was devoted to music ; as a boy he used to take part in the musical evenings at White Lodge. As he grew older his passion for music increased, and he was seldom absent from a performance at the Opera. The theatre also found in him a warm supporter. In fact he had the greatest admiration for art in every form, and numbered amongst his personal friends many of the prominent artists of the day. He was most constant in his friendships ; once a friend of Prince Francis always a friend. If he had not met you for some time he would place his hand on your shoulder and say, "Well, my old friend, come and tell me what you have been doing all this long time." His memory was very good, both for faces and names, and he would often recall incidents in conversation that his friends had forgotten. He was thorough in all things. In discussing matters he liked to talk them out, and never hurried away from one person to speak to another. He would always listen to men who were authorities on subjects, and in this way kept himself in touch with the chief movements of the day.

His last work will long be remembered ; it may almost be called his life work. No one felt more for the suffering poor than did Prince Francis. For many years he had assisted the Middlesex Hospital, first as Governor, then as Vice-President and Deputy-Chairman. Six months ago he was elected to the important post of Chairman of the Weekly Board of Management. At that time the debt on the hospital had reached £20,000. In a few months Prince Francis had cleared off this heavy liability. Not content with having performed so gigantic a task and in so short a time, he conceived the idea of adding to the income of the hospital a sufficient sum to ensure that the incomings met the outgoings, and in a letter to the Press on the eve of leaving for Balmoral to recruit his strength after his first illness he said : "But my task is not yet finished. The debt of £20,000 has been removed, but that liability represented the accumulated deficits between income and expenditure for three years ; and from this it it obvious that until a steady and permanent addition of £7,000 per annum is made to the hospital's income its financial position is not secure, and every third year the Governors will find them-

selves face to face with a crisis similar to that which has now
happily been averted. It is my ambition to substitute for such a
hand-to-mouth administration as this one which will provide the
Governors with an income sufficient to meet the normal expenses
of the year, so that they may apply themselves solely to seeing
that it is expended to the best advantage in the interest of those
whom the hospital serves, and, directly I am able to do so, it is
my intention to devote my time and energy to building up an
adequate annual subscription and donation list."

Alas! the subsequent illness which proved fatal prevented
Prince Francis from carrying out his noble resolve. Referring to
the Prince's work for the Middlesex Hospital the Secretary-
Superintendent said, "He has worked here for seven or eight
hours a day, week in week out for months. He was beloved by
everyone on the staff, from the highest to the lowest, and his
interest in their welfare was second only to that of his interest in
the hospital." It was entirely due to the efforts of Prince Francis
that the students of the medical school possessed their own sports
ground. In scientific directions he was equally interested, and
cancer patients will ever have cause to remember him for being
the means of arranging with the trustees of the late Mr. Barnato
that the money left by that gentleman for the maintenance of
some hospital should be allocated to the Cancer Charity.
Preaching in the Middlesex Hospital chapel on the day of the
funeral the chaplain said, "the Prince cared not only for the
hospital but for the individual patients. It would be impossible
to exaggerate the loss sustained by the hospital through his
untimely death." And he could have added with equal truth, it
will be well-nigh impossible to fill his place.

With the late King Edward he was a special favourite: he
would talk to his Majesty about the things he observed and the
persons he met in various walks of life. Perhaps more than
any other member of the Royal Family, Prince Francis may be
said to have mixed with the people: he had a broad mind, and
a mind of his own ; he did not accept an opinion immediately or
because a certain individual had expressed it, but thought things
out for himself and passed his own judgment. He was also a
favourite with the German Emperor, as well as with the
Emperor of Austria. In the home circle he was greatly beloved,
and his death will be an irreparable loss to his royal sister
and brothers. His affectionate disposition and boyish spirits
particularly endeared him to children, and the grief of the
younger members of his family must be well-nigh inconsolable.
King George was very much attached to his brother-in-law.
The two cousins saw a good deal of one another, and the grief
of the King is no less than that of the Queen. Men like Prince

Francis can ill be spared; the nation is the poorer for his death; he will be mourned by persons of all classes, for his heart was big and his humanity cosmopolitan.

Simple as the funeral ceremony was, the scene was most impressive. The coffin, borne to its last resting-place on a gun-carriage, was carried into St. George's Chapel, Windsor, on the shoulders of the soldier bearers and remained on the catafalque in the choir with the King, the Duke of Teck and Prince Alexander of Teck standing at the head until, as the Dean pronounced the solemn committal sentences, the mortal remains of Prince Francis were slowly lowered into the vault below. Within the Chapel were assembled the Prince's friends, bidden to attend as the guests of His Majesty. Men and women, representative of the several interests with which the Prince had been connected. All were there together with the envoys of foreign sovereigns and the high officers of the Army. Never has more genuine feeling been shown at the obsequies of any member of the royal family.

Near by in the cloisters were laid out the floral tributes sent from far and near in memory of the dead Prince, each bearing some personal inscription telling of affection and respect; their number was very large, and many were of surpassing beauty. And so, amid these historic surroundings, was laid to rest a gallant soldier, a true gentleman and a faithful friend.

CLEMENT KINLOCH-COOKE.

THE APPROACHING CENSUS

III.—NEW FEATURES OF THE COMING ENUMERATION

By GEORGE T. BISSET-SMITH

H.M. Registration Examiner

IN my two previous articles I have dealt generally with the Census and population. In this paper, after a brief sketch of methods and machinery, I purpose dealing more particularly with the fresh features of the coming Census. More than at any previous Census, public attention is likely to be attracted by the new questions to the value and importance of the national numbering; accordingly some understanding of the procedure is necessary in order that the householder may realise that, in the Census, the individual himself is nothing—only a unit in a great group. A knowledge of the spirit in which the Census is carried through by the Registration Departments cannot fail to increase public confidence, and tend to prevent the possibility of any reluctance arising to answer questions. Further, it should be borne in mind that all the Schedules are strictly confidential, and that the facts are published only in general abstracts.

The general manner of Census-taking is much the same all over the world. In England, from 1801-1831, the Census was taken by overseers of the poor. The Census Act of 1841 directed that the work should be under the control of the Registrar-General, whose department had been created to enforce, from July 1, 1837, the registration of births, deaths and marriages. From 1841 the responsibility for the accuracy of the information given in the Schedule was shifted from the Census Enumerator to the householder, who filled in the facts as to his own household. In Scotland, parochial schoolmasters were employed chiefly as the Census Enumerators in country districts, and the Scottish Census of 1841 and that of 1851 were taken upon commission from London, through the agency of the Sheriffs in counties and of the Chief Magistrates in the royal and parliamentary burghs.

When a system of compulsory registration was established in

Scotland * similar machinery was used for carrying out the national numbering of the people in North Britain. The Registrar-General· for Scotland is the engineer-in-chief of the Census machinery under the Census Act for Great Britain, as the Registrar-General of England is in England and Wales ; the supreme head of the English Census being the President of the Local Government Board, and of the Scottish, the Secretary for Scotland. By reason of their skill in statistical work, the departments of the Registrars-General for the three countries—England, Scotland and Ireland—are considered to be specially fitted for carrying out the Census. Each department has much experience in statistics, and their Medical Superintendents of Statistics have eminent qualifications for dealing with the greatest of all statistical undertakings.

In Ireland, the Lord-Lieutenant is vested with the authority of taking the Census, and the Enumerator there acts under instructions issued by the Chief or Under-Secretary to the Lord-Lieutenant, in terms of the Census (Ireland) Act, 1910. The Irish Census is taken by the Royal Irish Constabulary and Dublin Metropolitan Police, and these officers and men—being disciplined, well-educated, and acquainted minutely with the localities—perform the work in a manner more intelligent and reliable than do the majority of other Enumerators. Under the black and white banner of the statistical army, Census Enumerators are enrolled in thousands. These temporary recruits are drilled in their duties and, armed with millions of Census Schedules, they singly take their separate marches to invade every household, and thus secure the simultaneous enumeration of every person in these Isles alive at midnight on Sunday, April 2, 1911.

As regards public institutions in which upwards of one hundred persons usually reside, the Governor, or other Chief Resident Officer, is appointed Enumerator. Prisons, poorhouses, hospital and lunatic asylums are in this category ; also barracks containing one hundred soldiers, the Barracks Master or Quartermaster being entrusted with the enumeration. The Enumerator is required to be a person of some address, intelligence and tact, who can write well, and is not less than eighteen nor more than sixty-five years of age. Enumerators, it should be borne in mind, are not, as it were, mere account collectors, to be treated with scant courtesy, but temporary Government officials doing national work. They are, indeed, the modern representatives of the early Enumerators mentioned in the Book of Numbers appointed to help Moses to take " the sum of all the congregation of the children of Israel, after their families, by the house of their fathers." And it should tend to give dignity to the bearing and courage to the heart of the Census man of the twentieth century

* From January 1, 1855.

to remember, when not well received, that he has the honour of being in considerable measure the successor of these " renowned of the congregation, princes of the tribes of their fathers, heads of thousands in Israel."

Each registration district constitutes a principal Census Division, for which a plan is drawn up dividing it into suitable portions, capable of being overtaken by one Enumerator. Obviously, it is very desirable that an Enumerator should be acquainted with the ways of the people, and he must obtain an accurate knowledge of the boundaries of his district. Maps aid much in enabling an Enumerator to follow intelligently the local boundaries. Any clergyman or any professional man who takes an interest in the people of the place may be invited to act as Enumerator.* With the exception, however, of a few clergymen in the country, professional men do not generally act in this capacity. The remuneration is moderate, and a professional man could only be induced to take up the work by reason of his interest in the social condition of the people. My own experience of a mixed district in Edinburgh twenty years ago was varied, giving a painful insight into the poverty and discomfort in which so large a proportion of our population live, especially in the poorer parts of great cities.

The revision of the plan of division of the previous Census is a work requiring much care, especially where considerable inter-censal changes had taken place. The registrar requires to survey his district; form a general mental picture of the altered conditions; and then proceed to the necessary readjustment in detail. Administrative areas and divisions render the task complex in England and Scotland. In England there are some eighteen of these divisions; in Scotland the divisions are also numerous, embracing the civil parish, the ecclesiastical or the *quoad sacra* parish, School Board district; water or drainage district; parliamentary constituency; and the village, town, or burgh—royal, municipal and police ; public health areas.

The leading principles of enumeration are the same in England, Scotland and Ireland. Differences in detail are necessitated by national divergences in division and administration. In all three, the skilled and suitable machinery of registration is utilised in taking this stupendous inventory of the human commonwealth. The Registrar-General is practically the chief in command of the Census, controlling the whole operation from the central office. In England, the registrars are guided locally by the super-intendent registrars; while in Scotland (where there are no superintendent registrars) the registrars have their plans of division and enumerators approved by the sheriffs and sheriff-

* ' The Instructions to Local Officers.'

clerks in the counties and in Edinburgh, Glasgow, Dundee, Aberdeen, Greenock, Paisley, Leith, and Perth, by the Chief Magistrate and the Town Clerk. Summarily, the duties of the Registrar consist in arranging for the simultaneous enumeration of every soul in his district at the date of the Census. Familiar with the localities, the Registrars are able to supervise the enumeration. But except when a Registrar is unable to obtain a person to fill a vacancy at the last hour, he is not to act himself as Enumerator; for upon the Census collection day he is instructed to watch vigilantly the progress of his Enumerators. In Scotland, the Enumerator enters in a compartment upon the back of the Schedule the number of windowed rooms in each house. England is now to follow the example of Scotland in securing full details as to housing; the Act for 1911 requiring for both countries an enumeration of " the number of rooms inhabited." *

To prepare a plan of division and to select suitable Enumerators is the preliminary duty of the Registrar. The work of the Enumerator, acting under the Registrar, is to leave during the week previous a Census Schedule with every occupier of a house in his enumeration district, taking a note of every schedule so left. On the morning following Census Sunday, he begins to collect the Schedules. Where necessary, he helps the householder with advice in filling in details; sometimes, indeed, the Enumerator himself requires to complete the Schedule. In his notebook he records the number of persons temporarily absent or temporarily present, distinguishing males and females, and giving reasons for absence or presence: also the uninhabited and the unoccupied houses and the houses being built. Enumerators also ascertain the number of persons living in the open air, or sleeping in tents, caravans, sheds, barns, and of those living upon inland waters in canal boats and barges. Persons sleeping on board vessels of the Royal Navy or of the Mercantile Marine in the various harbours, docks, and roadsteads, or sailing in home waters upon the Census night, the returns of which are not obtained by the Registrars, are collected and forwarded through the Board of Admiralty in the case of the Royal Navy, and in the case of the Mercantile Marine by the Registrar General of Shipping and Seamen; the Schedules in the latter case being collected by the officers of H.M. Customs at the various ports of the United Kingdom.

The Schedules having been all collected, the English and Scottish Enumerator copies the particulars clearly into a large enumeration book. In Ireland (and it is understood in 1911, also in England) such transcribing is not necessary, the original Schedules being used in the Central Office. In the enumeration

* Section 4 (1) d.

book there is made, finally, a summary of its contents, showing precisely the population, rooms, and houses in each enumeration district. This summary is checked by the Registrar, who is sometimes in cities assisted specially by an expert at accounting. In 1881 I checked a number of enumeration books, finding that some excellent Enumerators failed in meticulous accuracy in this final summary of their arduous task. When the enumeration books have all been revised, the Registrar prepares a statement of the total population and other particulars pertaining to the whole of his registration district. Then, conscious of an important duty well done, the Registrar receives his fees, and waits patiently for the payment of the *bonus*, which was remitted to him when the tabulation at the Census office had advanced sufficiently to show that the general character of the work warranted the awarding of that additional remuneration which was given at last Census as a stimulus to accuracy.

Writing with some experience of three Censuses, I may remark that scarcely a Schedule comes into an Enumerator's hands but requires some amendment. Most often males and females are entered inadvertently in the same age columns. Rarely is the occupation stated with sufficient precision for purposes of tabulation and classification. Very frequently the county of the birthplace is wrong. And surprising it is to find how few occupiers are certain as to the exact number of windowed rooms in their house !

A complete and complex system of checks is necessary to secure accuracy in any Census : the Enumerator checks the householder ; the Registrar checks the Enumerator ; the Registrar is checked by his immediate official superior ; and the Census Office revises, checks, collates, tabulates and summarises the whole, evolving definite results from the mass of detail by well-planned and careful statistical methods.

The Dominions overseas have mostly followed the method of the Mother-country in Census matters. The Australian States, however, attempt to ascertain an astounding number of facts regarding land and house property, sheep and cattle : and Canada follows the United States in having an extremely exhaustive series of questions regarding its population (in 1901) of some four millions British and one and a half French. In magnitude and complexity the Imperial Census of India is the very Mount Everest of national numbering ; and always thoroughly well prepared, it succeeds wonderfully. What possibilities there are in India's prodigious population ! Population statistics are history in repose, just as human history is statistics in motion. As in the United States and Canada, the census of India has to be rehearsed, the Enumerators being allowed a prolonged period for completing their task. The population is divided, on the basis of language, into 118 groups and twelve leading divisions. Of its 300 millions about 295 are brown, and only a little over 100,000 white persons.

The area of England is 58,310 square miles; Ireland, 32,353; and Scotland, 30,406; their respective percentages of the whole area being 48, 27, and 25. The population of the United Kingdom on the night of the 31st of March, 1901, amounted to 41,454,724 persons, showing an increase of 3,721,802 upon the population enumerated at the previous Census in 1891. This increase exceeded by nearly a million the increase recorded in the preceding decennium 1881-91. The natural increase of population in the United Kingdom during the intercensal period 1891-1901, by excess of births over deaths, was 4,311,543; it appears, therefore, that the loss of population in the United Kingdom during the period through excess of emigration over immigration amounted to about 590,000.

TABLE SHOWING POPULATION OF THE UNITED KINGDOM AT NINE SUCCESSIVE CENSUSES.

	1821.	1831.	1841.	1851.	1861.
United Kingdom .	20,893,584	24,028,584	26,730,929	27,390,629,	28,927,485
England . .	11,281,883	13,090,523	15,002,443	16,921,888	18,945,444
Wales . . .	718,353	806,274	911,705	1,085,721	1,111,780
Scotland . .	2,091,521	2,364,386	2,620,184	2,888,742	3,062,294
Ireland . . .	6,801,827	7,767,401	8,196,597	6,574,278	5,798,967

	1871.	1881.	1891.	1901.
United Kingdom .	31,484,661	34,884,848	37,732,922	41,454,724
England . .	21,495,131	24,613,926	27,483,490	30,805,466
Wales . . .	1,217,135	1,360,513	1,519,035	1,720,609
Scotland . .	3,360,018	3,735,573	4,025,647	4,472,103
Ireland . . .	5,412,377	5,174,836	4,704,750	4,456,546

Constantly receiving a stream of emigrants from these Isles, the United States of America has long since outgrown the old country. Since 1870 the population of the United States has increased at the rate of 12,000,000 in each decennial period. The population in 1870 was 38,558,371; in 1880, 50,155,783; in 1890, 62,622,250; in 1900, 76,295,220; in 1910, over 90,000,000. The population of the United States in 1830 was only 12,866,020; in 1800, 5,308,483; and in 1790, 3,929,214. Greater New York had a population of 3,437,202 in 1900, against 2,500,000 in 1880. In 1910, the population numbers 4,766,883. America has got ahead of the old country in the size of her census schedule. Property, industries, and churches are included in the United

States census returns, which occupy fully five years, and are issued in twenty-five large volumes. In spite of the United States being largely agricultural, the increase in the urban population between 1870 and 1900 was about 17 millions. In earlier times Great Britain's non-agricultural population was in all the world the largest; now, however, the industrial inhabitants are increasing portentously not only in the States, but also in France and Germany. These three great rivals have now a large mass of industrial population. The United States and Germany are travelling upwards more rapidly than ourselves, and have larger additions to their population to draw upon.

The first fact shown by the Census is the alteration in total number. Much more than numerical information, however, is given by the Census, which indicates not only the vitality but also the movement of the population. Spots have been darkened with population while others have thinned. Purely agricultural counties are being deserted for manufacturing, coal-field and industrial districts. If the recruiting grounds—the healthy nurseries for towns—are being too much depleted, it is a fact to be deplored; and certainly there is a general tendency shown to swarm into towns. Much of the energy and health of our largest cities is due to arrivals from the country. Edinburgh is being steadily recruited from the Counties of Fife and Perth; Glasgow from Argyll and adjoining counties, as Dundee from Forfarshire, and the City of Aberdeen from its large county area.

The rural depopulation problem is partly one of housing. Cottar houses have decayed. They have not been replaced by houses meeting modern requirements. Quiet country hamlets are taking on the aspect of Sleepy Hollows. Rural tradesmen are declining. Blacksmiths are losing importance—both as tradesmen and gossips: they still mend carts; but complex reapers and binders are repaired chiefly by fresh fittings. And the trades of rural tailors and shoemakers are being ruined by machine-made boots and clothes manufactured in cities. The Deserted Village has created the crowded City.

Massing of persons together into stupendous aggregations is the chief feature of all recent censuses. It is a movement of concentration accompanied by expansion. The movement has its climax in the metropolis. Greater London, with its 6,600,000 inhabitants (estimate for 1910 is over 7½ millions) is, however, really a federation of 29 self-governing boroughs. Its population equals that of all Belgium, is greater than that of Portugal or Sweden, half again as much as Scotland or Ireland, and quite twice that of Switzerland.

The total number of the population, their conjugal condition, and the proportion of the sexes, their ages, their dwellings, their occupations, their birthplaces, and their migration,—these are the main objects of the great analytical process of the Population Census, to which has now been added the question of fertility.

TABLE SHOWING GROWTH OF CITIES, HAVING 100,000 INHABITANTS OR MORE, IN THE UNITED KINGDOM, GERMANY, AND FRANCE, FROM THE FIRST BRITISH CENSUS TO THE LAST.

Census.	UNITED KINGDOM.		GERMAN EMPIRE.		FRANCE.	
	No. of Cities.	Population at Census.	No. of Cities.	Population at Census.	No. of Cities.	Population at Census.
1801 . .	2	1,100,000	2	272,000	3	766,000
1851 . .	11	4,620,000	6	998,000	5	1,716,040
1871 . .	18	7,120,000	10	2,200,000	9	3,280,000
1901 . .	39	13,522,000	33	9,129,000	15	5,466,000

Every schoolboy remembers the trouncing administered to Sadler's * "Law of Population" by Macaulay. Sadler promulgated a crude theory that population was fertile in inverse ratio to number. Macaulay, applying the rule to an isolated couple in Canada, brought out a ridiculously large result. Sadler wrote a "Refutation," and Macaulay refuted Sadler's "Refutation" with increased directness of speech and scathing severity. But the fact actually appears to be that something could be said for Sadler's theory. Especially when it is expressed as a tendency for fertility to diminish with density of population. But the causes are by no means all natural. Macaulay's little problem in proportion, stated when London had a population of only 1½ millions and the average fertility of a London marriage was 2·35, was to allow a couple in Canada the same area as occupied by all Londoners and to state as two people to 1½ millions; so should 2·35 be to the absurd answer (2 : 1,500,000 :: 2·35); the answer being the progeny of the couple, so used to reduce the "Law" promulgated by Sadler to a ridiculous assertion. Macaulay is not at his best on this non-literary topic; and very probably most Fellows of the Royal Statistical Society regard his two Essays on Sadler's work with only modified admiration. Sadler is an avowed opponent of artificial limitation and of Malthus.

Volitional limitation of families is now general in Great Britain. The chief reason for the restriction is poverty. Recognising that the middle-class taxpayer should be encouraged to raise a family of fair size, the Government has been good enough to allow an annual abatement of £10 for income-tax in respect of each child under sixteen. That is a very moderate measure. But it is valuable as an indication of a national conviction that the families of the great middle-class should be

* M. T. Sadler, M.P.

larger. Possibly the burden may be lightened more and more until the income-tax is taken off altogether from the household contributing children to the common wealth of the kingdom. For as Ruskin wrote a generation ago the true veins of wealth are purple—and not in Rock but in Flesh. The final purpose of all wealth indeed should be the producing as many as possible full-breathed, bright-eyed, and happy-hearted human creatures. Among national manufactures, that of souls of a good quality, wrote Ruskin, may at last be regarded as a quite leadingly lucrative one. And we all remember the Roman matron who led forth her sons, saying, " These are my jewels."

Sadler's work on the Law of Population is an elaborate statistical disquisition in two octavo volumes published at London in 1830. Its full title is sufficiently explanatory : " A Treatise in Six Books in Disproof of the Superfecundity of Human Beings ; and Developing the Real Principle of their Increase." Its style is forceful and florid. This, for instance, is Mr. Sadler's manner of explaining that population causes progress :—

Population really does press against the level of the means of subsistence, and, still elevating that level, it continues to urge society through advancing stages till at length the strong and resistless hand of necessity presses the secret spring of human prosperity, and the portals of Providence fly open and disclose to the enraptured gaze the promised land of contented and rewarded labour.

The opinion of Sadler is diametrically opposed to that of Malthus ; for in the principle of population as enounced by Malthus it is asserted that there is an inherent evil productive of miseries. Sadler's law is that the prolificness of human beings otherwise similarly circumstanced varies inversely as their number. This attempt to connect density and decrease of fertility is not based upon facts such as connect density of population and increase of death rate. But it does appear that there is a tendency for the fecundity of the human race to diminish as population becomes more condensed and concentrated. Certainly, child-bearing is lessened It seems to be, indeed, a question in certain classes of limitation of families rather than of real decrease in potential fertility. The Registrar-General for England is the authority for the statement that seventy-nine per cent. of the recent diminution in the birth-rate is due to deliberate restriction of child-bearing.

The problem is many-sided. The factor of limitation is admitted. But Spencer pointed out half a century ago (1852) that the degrees of fertility of organisms from the highest to the lowest are naturally determined, that is, are physically caused. Degree of fertility is inversely proportionate to the grade of development ; as measured here by size (as in the elephant), there by structure, and commonly by all of these. Individuation, in

short, is antagonistic to Genesis. For instance, in its natural
state the rose has only five petals, and multiplies rapidly. When
perfected by cultivation (the stamina changed into petals), the
development is at the expense of fertility: and it can be re-
produced only by planting (or grafting) shoots. Individuality
implies an increase of the higher functions. Superior races have
a low birth-rate. Inferior races are very prolific. Always, however, we should remember that the successful survival and the
importance of a species depend not so much on quantity as on
quality. Lower rates of multiplication accompany higher degrees
of evolution.

Excess of fertility, to a certain extent, has been the cause of
man's further evolution. Is man now voluntarily limiting too
much the progress resulting from pressure of population? The
voice of Sadler says: Let man take heed how he rashly violates
his trust. And he bursts into rhyme, which I quote not for its
poetic beauty but for its pungent appropriateness:

> What myriads wait in Destiny's dark womb
> Doubtful of life or an eternal tomb!
> 'Tis his to blot them from the book of fate,
> Or, like a second Deity, create;
> To dry the stream of being in its source,
> Or bid it, widening, win its restless course;
> While, earth and heaven replenishing, the flood
> Rolls to its Ocean fount, and rests in God.

Excellent, perhaps, but should the unfit increase? The
parasitical classes have much guano in their composition.
Degenerates multiply. Weeds spread quickly. The thriftless
vagrant is often prolific. Not now is the struggle for existence
allowed to work out among mankind, as in animals, to a fatal
finish. Mental, moral, and physical inferiors do not suffer
irremediably; and efficient superiors have to relinquish much of
their reward to maintain those who have failed in life's fight.
Efficiency has to support the parasite inefficiency.

Defective and diseased persons are maintained by charity and the
State. But for the best parentage there is no substantial assistance. Mr. H. G. Wells advocates the endowment of motherhood.

The modern State [he says] has got to pay for its children if it really wants
them—and more particularly it has to pay for the children of good homes. The
alternative to that is racial replacement and social decay. Mr. Wells suggests
that payment should be made to the mother as the administrator of the family
budget, and that the amount should be made dependent upon the quality of
the home in which the children are being reared. The amount is thus to vary
with the standing of the home, and the health and physical development of
the children. "Be it remembered" (he says emphatically), "we do not want
any children; we want good quality children."

Which of the classes are failing to reproduce? That question
is to be tackled for the first time in the coming Census. House-

holders will be required to state the duration of their marriage and the number of children born of the union, and the number dead. We must breed wisely. Healthy children are wanted. Rapidly and recklessly are multiplying the relatively unfit and improvident, while the artizan and middle-classes moodily restrict their families and strive to keep pace with their monthly bills. For all human life is largely a matter of £ s. d. Social conditions render children a heavy burden on the more desirable parents of the population. Good stocks are checking their growth. Weak and careless oafs continue to have abundant offspring. Selective deterioration is thus operating both ways: the good tree is not growing, while the bad is branching out in all directions. The parasite may kill that upon which it feeds and flourishes. We are now in these Isles face to face with the hydra-headed problem of the fatal fertility of the unfit.

Obviously the remedy is to encourage parents capable of producing healthy children. Young-age pensions for parents? As I have already pointed out the Government, recognizing the national danger, has made a beginning with the £10 abatement on income-tax; possibly the next move to encourage middle-class parenthood may be the exemption from tax of all income spent in the maintenance and education of children of the fit and deserving. The better strains will then probably increase. Those who take thought for to-morrow will not then continue comparatively childless, and the average quality of the race will cease its deadly downward deterioration.

The only disease of which nations have died is lack of efficient men. In recent decades the decline in our national fertility has been the subject of grave consideration. For thirty years the birth-rate has fallen steadily, but there has been no accompanying and corresponding diminution in the marriage-rate. Information regarding the duration of marriages and the number of children born of the marriage should provide fairly reliable data for the study of the childbearing in different classes.* These statistics have been collected in other countries, especially in the last two Censuses of the United States. The figures obtained have been useful in arriving at conclusions regarding natality and infantile mortality. The method of tabulating the new information was discussed very fully at a recent meeting of the Royal Statistical Society.

Scotland showed the way here more than half a century ago. The numbers of "Issue living and deceased" of parents were recorded in the Scottish Registers of 1855. In the case of widows and widowers there was entered in the marriage Schedule the number of "children by each former marriage," and one of the double columns of the Death Register of 1855 is headed "If

* Section 4 (1) c., Census Act of 1910 for Great Britain. 10 Edw. 7 & 1 Geo. V.

deceased was married, to whom," and issue in order of birth—their names and ages. In succeeding years, unfortunately, the collection of such complete sociological data was relinquished. It was deemed too elaborate for prompt daily registration. The success of the experiment in Scotland, however, leads to the conclusion that, at the decennial Census, questions as to marriage and "Children born thereof" can be well answered generally in very intelligent North Britain. Possibly more tact and trouble may be necessary in England.

In this connection I may quote from a communication of Mr. Noël A. Humphreys, a well-known authority on vital statistics, whose great experience has made him possibly very chary of approving innovations in so large and important an undertaking as the Census. (He has been engaged on all the five Censuses from 1861 to 1901 in preparing statistics.)   Mr. Humphreys maintains that the decline in the birth-rate is not simply a question of fertility, and that the Marriage and Birth Registers afford ample facilities for the further investigation of this important subject.   He writes :

Fully recognising, as all must do, the importance of the subject, I found myself unable to support in Committee this addition to the Schedule, doubting as I do the trustworthiness of the information that will therein be furnished. Many half-educated occupiers will find it most difficult to state correctly the date of their marriage and the number of children born; and many may object to admit the true number of children who have died young. I regret the additions to the Schedule, as I hold that if the Schedule is filled up by the occupier, as is the case in Great Britain, the trustworthiness of the information depends upon the simplicity of the questions, and on the absence of all temptation to give false answers. I think that the birth register is the safer source of information bearing on the fertility of marriage, and I always much regretted the abandonment of the valuable experiment in the Scottish birth register.

Mr. Birrell, by the way, when the new questions were proposed for the Irish Bill, observed that he could not tell the date of his marriage "without considerable research," although he could speak with considerable confidence as to the number of his children.

Further improvements may be expected in counting and tabulations, and the British Census of 1911, by reason of its wider scope and many new features, cannot fail to rank high above its eleven predecessors. Of the new features the chief are, as already explained, the questions to be answered concerning child-bearing, with duration of marriage. In the Census Schedule for England and Wales, the new questions appear in columns 6, 7, 8 and 9, under the general heading of " Particulars as to Marriage," their precise wording being : " State for each Married Woman entered on this Schedule the number of completed years the *present* Marriage has lasted (column 6). (If less than one year, write ' under one.') Children *born alive* to *present* Marriage. (If no children born alive write ' none ' in column 7.) The three columns (Nos. 7, 8 and 9) relating to the numbers of children are headed respectively : ' Total children *born alive*.' ' Children still living '; and ' Children who have died.' "

This inquiry into fertility of marriage was proposed originally by the Census Committee of the Royal Statistical Society. It is, however, well known that the recent marked decline of the birth-rate is not simply a question of fertility, as pointed out by Mr. Humphreys ; who also expressed (in a relative discussion) the hope that " without waiting a few years for the final results of the Census, the General Register Office would find it possible to publish statistics dealing with the relative birth-rates in different social grades in order to throw light on one of the most disturbing assertions of the students of eugenics."

The information collected as to child-bearing will be tabulated probably only in those cases where both parents· are enumerated in the same Schedule; but these are over 90 per cent. ; the husbands and wives appearing together in 1901 being 92·5 per cent. of the married couples in England. A table will be prepared showing the average fertility (as evidenced by the number of children *born alive*) of every class of couple, where the wife's Census age is under 45. Such a statement will record the past and the present condition of our country in the matter of child-bearing ; and the sections of such a table will be constructed on the basis of the parents' ages.

The position in life of the parents is also of primary importance, and similar sections will show the population arranged so as to represent social *strata*, arranged on the criteria chiefly of rooms and domestic servants; in an attempt to ascertain whether (as is so frequently asserted to-day) child-bearing decreases with the ascent of the social scale, and in continuance of Dr. Matthews Duncan's inquiry into the physical laws affecting the natural history of mankind.

The Population Census has now become more definitely a Census of Occupations ; and means are provided in the coming enumeration for making the table of occupations reveal our industrial condition. An additional query is added in the columns headed Profession or Occupation, with the purpose of obtaining precisely the number of persons employed in connection with each industry and service.

Thus, the new features of the 1911 Census are of the greatest national importance. One deals with the births of children ; the other with the means of their maintenance. Child-bearing is indicative of vitality ; occupation of national progress ; for, fully considered, Census Tables of Occupations picture our period and its phase of civilisation.

GEORGE T. BISSET-SMITH.

FOREIGN AFFAIRS

By EDWARD DICEY, C.B.

NEW SITUATION IN PORTUGAL

THE revolution in Portugal has come and gone and King Manoel is a fugitive in England. It is not easy to recall a more rapid change than that which has taken place in the government of Portugal. Within a week a country ruled over by a monarch apparently liked by his people, and certainly desiring to do all in his power for his country's good, has not only been deposed, but compelled to seek refuge in a foreign land, and in his place a Republic has been proclaimed, not after desperate fighting, for in effecting the transformation there was but little excess and comparatively little bloodshed, but by acclamation. In fact the Provisional Government entered into possession with scant opposition, amidst the plaudits of the people, and with the backing of the army and the navy.

There was but little more excitement politically than we see in this country after a change in parties at Westminster. The colonial possessions of Portugal fell into line with the new administration without demur, and if in some cases indifference was shown at Lorenzo Marques enthusiasm appears to have prevailed. No time was lost on the part of the Provisional Government in giving assurances to Great Britain that it was their desire and intention to preserve the ancient alliance between the two nations, and equally cordial messages were conveyed to the other Powers. So far, however, nothing has been done in the way of public recognition of the new *régime*, and this seems to vex the self-constituted legislators. It is said that the Powers are waiting for Great Britain to take the lead, seeing that we have so close an interest in Portugal, and it may be that we shall do so, provided it is thoroughly established that the new Government is the Government the people desire, and that it has the capacity as well as the force necessary to carry out its resolves.

Certainly it cannot be said that Portugal has been very fortunate of late years in her domestic policy, but no one can blame King Manoel. He did everything possible to reconcile the opposing influences, but it was all in vain. That he should make a stand for the Church of Rome was only in keeping with what has always been expected in a Roman Catholic country, and it is difficult to understand the anti-clerical intolerance which seems to be the prevailing note of the Provisional Government. But it is not for us to find fault with another country if it chooses to replace a monarchy by a Republic, but it is not easy to see what Portugal has to gain by the change. In King Manoel the Portuguese had a most excellent King, a man young in years and ready to do everything that was required of him, possessing a charming individuality and a true friend of the people. Indeed, if King Manoel did not satisfy his subjects, it is difficult to imagine any king who will. This argument would seem to tell in favour of the Republic lasting, but with a people so difficult to satisfy as the Portuguese it would be idle to attempt to prophecy.

It was thought at first that what had happened in Portugal might spread to the adjoining country—Spain ; but happily there are no signs to warrant any such course of events. The Spanish King and his English Queen are both extremely popular, and while a certain number of revolutionary spirits made holiday when the revolution in Portugal was proceeding, nothing has happened in Spain that would in any way lead the authorities to suppose that the Spanish people desire any other government than the one they now enjoy. The royal visit to Valentia has proved a triumphal progress, and when the King and Queen took their seats in the royal box at the bullfight which brought their visit to a close, the enthusiasm of the public was immense. Without doubt the tour has been a signal success, and if this is the kind of reception meted out to the Spanish monarch and his queen in the heart of Republicanism, it is only fair to draw the conclusion that elsewhere in their domains their recognition would be equally cordial. I have not the least doubt that King Alphonso inspires his subjects with admiration and respect, but I must be allowed to say that the presence of the Queen was often the occasion for a special ovation.

THE TURKISH LOAN AND AFTER

When writing last month, although things did not look very bright respecting an immediate settlement between Turkey and France in the matter of the loan, I had great hopes that the outstanding difficulties would be bridged over and the loan floated on the Paris Bourse.

That I was not alone in my conclusion will be patent to anyone who has followed the progress of events. In all influential circles the same view was expressed. The Vienna correspondent of the *Times* tells us that the failure of the Franco-Turkish Loan came even as a surprise to political and financial circles in that country, where it might be presumed the latest information would be available. Only a day or so ago, a leading financier in Vienna, referred to by the sender of the telegram as having exceptional opportunities of studying the financial situation in Turkey, expressed to him the decided opinion that the negotiations with France would be successfully concluded. For myself, I went so far as to anticipate that the intervention of Sir Ernest Cassel was of good omen, and that matters would work out in the end very much as the Turkish Government desired. To-day, as I sit down to write, the position has undergone a change, a decided change. Negotiations between the French and the Turkish Governments have been broken off, the reason being, it is stated, the refusal of the Turkish Government to agree to the proposal that two French officers should be appointed to the control of the Public Accounts Department and the *Cour des Compte*. This condition, it appears, was at first accepted by the Turkish Ambassador, but when submitted by him in final form to the Porte, it was at once rejected.

Nothing however appears to have transpired regarding the political considerations, which at one time were mentioned as being a necessary part of the bargain. These seem to have entirely disappeared. In their place we are now informed that exclusive of the proposal above referred to and the demand that French industries should benefit out of the loan, the only other request put forward was one dealing with the status of Algerian and Tunisian subjects, the French Government contending that these persons being French subjects must be treated by Turkey as such, a theory the Paris correspondent of the *Morning Post* explains as particularly objectionable to Young Turks with Pan-Islamite tendencies. As to what answer has been given to this request nothing is said. All we know is that the matter has been postponed, not however indefinitely, for it is assumed that the question will come up for settlement in the near future quite apart from the financial negotiations. Thus the fate of the Turkish loan has followed that of the Hungarian loan, with the inevitable result that the matter will pass into the hands of the German syndicate. The amount urgently needed is £6,000,000, but it is hardly expected that sum will prove sufficient to meet Turkish requirements. In any event I do not doubt that the German and Austrian banks will have little difficulty in financing Turkey if they are definitely approached by the Turkish Government, and setting aside the views expressed at the meeting of Mohammedans at Constantinople, there is every reason to suppose an approach will be made if not to Vienna at any rate to Berlin.

The action of France opens up an entirely new vista in the matter of loan negotiations between the different Powers. Admittedly it has been the custom of allies to accommodate one another with financial advances, but the fact that no alliance existed has not hitherto stood in the way of financial arrangements between·two friendly States. Presumably if the members of the Triple Alliance wanted money they would try and raise it amongst themselves, but on the other hand they might wish to go outside, and, indeed, have often done so, and the Power lending the money has never, so far as I am aware, made political conditions an essential part of the bargain. The refusal of France to assist Turkey, coming as it does so quickly on the refusal to assist Hungary with a loan on business conditions alone, is a novel matter in the world of international finance, and if this policy is a settled policy it means that France will only lend to Russia or Great Britain. In these circumstances it would not be surprising if we find Germany and Austria-Hungary and Italy following suit. Moreover, the refusal of France to accommodate Turkey may tend to force Turkey into the Triple Alliance, or at any rate furnish Turkey with an excuse for making common cause with the members of that alliance.

Now that Turkey knows she cannot look to France for aid, she will no longer regard France quite in the same way she has done in the past, and with France naturally goes Russia. This in itself would not be a matter of great concern to us, but unfortunately, owing to our *ententes*, Great Britain is drawn in, and we stand to jeopardise if not to lose that hold which for many years we have always had on the Porte. I confess I do not like this reshuffling of the cards. I do not like to see Turkey slipping away, as it were, from her old friends and forming new friendships, especially just now, when we appear to have incurred the displeasure of the Young Turks by our altogether legitimate action in Persia. It may not yet be too late to come to some understanding, and it would certainly be in the interests of this country if the *status quo* between France and Turkey could be resumed. Not that I credit the report that Turkey is about to join hands politically with Germany and Austria-Hungary; but, after the rebuff Turkey has received from France, and the apparent readiness of the German syndicate to supply her with the money she needs, although it may be on more onerous financial terms, it will not be surprising to find that the contracts which it had been hoped the Turkish Government might have placed with British contractors will now go to German contractors. What we in this country want is commerce, and what Germany wants is commerce; the failure of the loan negotiations with France will certainly not be to our advantage, but if I interpret the result correctly it will be very much to the advantage of Germany, for that nation may now look forward, and legitimately look forward, to obtaining a commercial ascendency in a quarter where it was always expected British enterprise might count, if not on preferential terms, at any rate on friendly recognition.

For some time it has been an open secret that British influence in Turkey is on the decline, and the action of France, backed up as it has been by Russia, is not likely to stop its further decline. Germany, it is said, has been moving diplomatically in Turkey. And why not? This country had better opportunities than Germany ever had; and if British interests in Turkey suffer, the blame must rest on France and Russia, and not on Germany. It may be urged, and with apparent reason, that the loan fell through because Turkey refused to accept what may be regarded as ordinary business precautions; but while I cannot blame France for insisting on proper control of Turkish finance, I think it will be found that this control involved an undertaking on the part of Turkey to adopt a certain outside policy closely connected with the political considerations of which so much was said last month. And if this is the case, one can scarcely feel surprised at the course taken by the Turkish Government. No country cares to have her foreign or domestic policy dictated to her by any other country, and in my opinion it would have been more in accordance with precedent had France remained content with conditions which did not raise issues calculated to offend so very inflammable a Government as that at present responsible for the administration of the Turkish Empire.

Things might have turned out differently if some outside negotiator had been called in to advise. At one time it was said that Sir Ernest Cassel was willing to undertake that very difficult and delicate position, but France, we are told, declined his assistance. How far this is so I have no means of telling, but if Sir Ernest Cassel were indeed willing, no better course could have been adopted. As things now are, the ship of State in Turkey is drifting towards the shores of Germany and Austria; whether she will effect a landing is the crucial question. Certainly France does not show any sign of opposing the passage; on the other hand, she would seem to have gone out of her way to accept the post of pilot.

THE BRITISH NOTE TO PERSIA

In passing from the question of the Turkish loan to that of the British Note to Persia one does not get rid of Turkey. For some unexplained reason the Young Turks see in our suggestions a movement directed against their interests, and are ready to fan their opposition into a flame at any moment. All this is much to be regretted, and it is to be hoped that the calm official statement of the Foreign Office will allay their suspicions and bring about a truer understanding of the issues.

Nor is Turkey the only nation that views with alarm Great Britain's endeavours to assist the Persian Government in restoring order within her own dominions. A small but active section of the German Press read into the Note an intention on the part of this country and Russia to partition Persia and destroy Persian independence. Another section imagines that the Note is directed not so much to Teheran as to St. Petersburg, with the object of preventing Russian intrigue in Northern Persia. Fortunately the more staid press of Germany has not been thus misled, and it is satisfactory to find that the German Government appreciates the position, and is in no way disposed to take umbrage at our contemplated action. No encroachment whatever is intended on the integrity of Persia, and the British Government are not sending Indian troops to police the Southern part of the Shah's estate. The police force it is proposed to raise if necessary will be raised in Persia itself, and the only Indian troops it is suggested should be employed are a few Indian officers. Everyone agrees that it is time the Southern caravan routes were properly safe-guarded, and no fault can possibly be' found with this country for taking steps to bring about so very desirable a change.

But before any steps are taken the Persian Government are to be given ample time to put their own house in order, and with the new loan an accomplished fact, British intervention may not be required. The imaginative suggestion that the Note is really addressed to St. Petersburg and not to Teheran hardly seems to call for a reply, seeing that the draft was submitted to Russia before it was sent to the Persian Government. I have on a former occasion referred at length to the position of Great Britain and Russia in Persia, and I do not propose to travel over that ground again. As regards our understanding with Russia generally in the East, this was very fully set out by Lord Hardinge at the recent banquet given to him as Viceroy-designate of India. His remarks, it is true, were mainly directed to India, and he prefaced his speech by outlining the situation in India and the East before the Russian *entente*. No one is better able to give this explanation, since he was the moving figure in the negotiations that led up to the Anglo-Russian understanding.

As I said at the time, I have my doubts whether the bargain will be maintained in the same spirit on both sides, but so far I am bound to say the arrangement has been kept. But because

Russia and Great Britain have preponderating influences in Persia, and these influences are political as well as commercial, it does not follow that Germany's economic interests in that country are not to receive equal consideration, and I should not wonder if much of the misunderstanding that has arisen over the British Note is traceable to the somewhat arrogant manner in which Russia endeavoured to treat Germany when difficulties of an international character arose in Persia a few months ago. But for the Russian *entente* we should not on that occasion have fallen foul of Germany, and while we gain in many ways by the closer relations between the two countries, we undoubtedly suffer in others, particularly in our relations with Germany.

Not that Germany opposed the *entente*; on the other hand she assisted at the ceremony, but Russia is so closely involved with all burning questions in the Near East that she is a dangerous partner to have, when anything happens in that part of the world likely to disturb the peace of Europe. So far we have managed to steer clear of shoals, but it cannot be denied that the Russian *entente* is not altogether a bed of roses.

As we go to press an inconvenient telegram has been sent to the German Emperor by the members of the Persian Saadet Committee and their Turkish allies. I say inconvenient, for its tenour must be equally inconvenient to the German Emperor as it is to the British Government. I append the translation taken from the message of the *Times* correspondent at Constantinople, dated October 25.

Sire,—The Persians, who belong to the great Moslem family, which in all its difficulties has found noble and generous protection and aid in the person of your Imperial Majesty, and who for the past five years have struggled with such self-sacrifice to free their country, have been deeply affected by the threats of invasion contained in the recent ultimatum of the British Government.

Remembering at this supreme moment the glorious words which your Gracious Majesty deigned to utter over the tomb of Saladin, where it pleased you, Sire, to gladden the hearts of 350 million Moslems by the generous promise of the exalted support which your Glorious Majesty would accord them in their efforts to safeguard their rights; remembering, too, the noble deeds whereby your Glorious Majesty won the gratitude of the Moslem world in connection with the Moorish and Macedonian questions, Persians are full of hope that your Gracious Majesty will on this occasion, too, not refuse to intervene to remove the danger by which their country is threatened.

It is thus that at a grand meeting held yesterday in Constantinople, attended by thousands of Moslems, both of the Ottoman Empire and of Persia, we have been charged with the extreme honour of respectfully bringing to your Glorious Majesty's knowledge the hopes and sentiments of devotion and gratitude which animated all present.

The Moslem world, which after God and the glorious Khalifate builds all hopes on the generosity of your Gracious Majesty, firmly believes that your Majesty will deign to grant it your high support to bring about a favourable settle ent of the crisis through which it is now passing.

The world of Islam offers its most sincere and ardent prayers for the perpetual happiness of your Gracious Majesty, of her Majesty the Empress, and of the great German nation.

It will, I think, be well to await the reply before commenting on the telegram. The German Emperor is hardly likely to send an answer without the most careful consideration. But that the telegram should have been despatched at all is a matter of regret. That it was sent under a misapprehension of the real state of affairs there can be no doubt, for there are no "threats of invasion" in the British Note, and it may be assumed that in the reply this and other inaccuracies will escape attention.

But all said and done, so deliberate an action on the part of the Moslems cannot be treated lightly. Fortunately the relations between this country and the German Government are of a most friendly character, and it may be taken for granted that a potentate who has done so much to secure and maintain the peace of the world as the German Emperor has done, is not likely to do anything that might place that peace in jeopardy. We must not take too seriously the comments of that section of the German press which seems to see evil in everything this country does, any more than we place any confidence in that section of the British press which seems to see evil in everything Germany does. Rather let us look to the sound common sense of the two peoples to back up the two Governments in their endeavours to steer a peaceful course.

This is no time for pin-pricks. No sane person desires to see anything untoward happen, anything that might cause a conflagration, and if this is to be prevented, and it must be prevented at all costs, let us try to place the present friendly relations between this country and Germany on a still firmer footing. If that could be accomplished, and I see no reason why it should not be, I feel certain that many of the difficult questions that are now pending would melt away, and in place of the storms that are constantly arising we should have a perpetual calm.

EDWARD DICEY.

NOTES BY A PAPUAN JUDGE

By J. H. P. MURRAY,

Lieut.-Governor and Chief Judicial Officer of Papua

JUSTICE is administered in Papua under the provisions of the Queensland Criminal Code, slightly modified by local enactments; trials are held before the Chief Judicial Officer sitting alone, except that a white man charged with a capital offence must be tried by a jury of four.

Trials of white men are, however, exceedingly rare, and there has been only one instance of trial by jury; that was about two years ago at Port Moresby, and resulted in an acquittal. Crime is also rare among the natives who have been brought under Government influence; what crime there is among them is of the petty larceny type, with a good many cases of sorcery and adultery, which have been made criminal offences by local legislation. Among the native tribes beyond the limits of Government control the principal, in fact, almost the only crime is murder. This, in their eyes, is, as a rule, not a crime at all; sometimes it is a duty, sometimes a necessary part of social etiquette, sometimes a relaxation. There are some occasions on which, though the murder is not regarded with any disapproval, it is considered " good form " to pay a price for the murdered man, and an accused person always regards " payment " as a good defence to the charge. Indeed it is generally very difficult to convince him that such a plea is not allowed in law; sometimes I have had to give it up in despair, and have seen a prisoner led off to gaol loudly explaining, with vigorous gesticulations, that he has paid a pig, a tomahawk, and a necklace of dog's teeth for the murdered man, and that it was a great deal more than he was worth. The price of a man varies in different parts of the Territory, and, strange as it may seem in a land where the women do most of the work, the price of a woman is always less than that of a man.

There is a great sameness about the murder cases which come before the Court. It is true that cases frequently occur of apparently unprovoked attack upon unoffending villages, where the only motive one can find is simple lust for blood, but most murders are committed either to "pay back" for some previous murder, real or supposed, or else to comply with native etiquette, or to assure the social position of the assassin. A curious thing is that you generally find a pig mixed up in the case at some stage or other—in fact "cherchez le porc" would not be a bad maxim for a Papuan detective.

When the process of "paying back" once commences it can never come to an end, because there is always a life to be "paid for." It is encouraged by the rooted conviction entertained by all but the most civilised Papuans that, except in the case of the old and decrepit, there is no such thing as a natural death, so that when a young man or woman dies suddenly, or even after an illness, the death is ascribed to the machinations of some sorcerer, and a life must be taken in payment. This sometimes applies even when a native is taken by a crocodile or dies from snake bite; it is true that in the latter case the man's death is regarded in some places as due to the fact that his wife did not give him enough breakfast (a theory which used to be attended with disastrous results to the wife), but it is also attributed to the malevolence of an enemy—for snakes as well as crocodiles are regarded as being under the control of sorcerers. A belief is however gaining ground in a part of the Papuan Gulf that the crocodiles are in league with the Government, based upon the fact that a prisoner escaping from gaol was severely lacerated by one of these creatures while crossing a river. Crawling to the nearest village constable, the disgusted criminal gave himself up to justice, bitterly disappointed at the "unsportsmanlike" conduct of the Government in making such alliance. "No good we fight along Government now, alligator he help Government," was the way in which his complaint was eventually presented.

The Government itself is pictured by the less civilised native as a kind of benevolent but capricious monster of very uncertain temper, so that the alliance with crocodiles, though ungentlemanly, is not altogether unnatural. "Government he wild" is the usual way of stating official disapproval, and the alliance of a "wild" Government with "wild" crocodiles produces a combination with which it is as well to be on good terms. Still the crocodiles are by no means all under Government control; the great mass of them remain faithful to the sorcerers and will not attack a man unless bidden by a sorcerer to do so. I had to cross a river once which was reputed to be full of crocodiles, and I asked an old man who was with me if he was not afraid. He said that he was not. "A crocodile won't touch you," he explained, "unless some one has made puri puri (sorcery) against you—and if some one has made puri puri against you, you are a lost man in any case—he will get you somehow—if not with a crocodile then in some other way. So the crocodiles really do not matter." Fortunately they did not matter on this occasion, as we all got across safely.

To return to the blood-feud. If every death must be avenged, incessant warfare is the necessary result, for when once the system of "paying back" begins it can hardly cease until one side is exterminated. Sometimes, by accident, the guilty man is killed, but of course in many instances, as for example in the case of death from sickness, there is no guilty man. I remember a case of three men who were tried by me for a murder committed at the back of the Rigo district; the wife of one of them had died and it was therefore necessary to get payment—the only question was from whom the payment was to be taken. Fortunately (so he thought) the bereaved husband had some leaves which he had picked from a tree in the neighbourhood, and which had the power to call up the spirits of the living and the dead, so he put these under his head and went to sleep, and saw in his dreams his dead wife and the faces of some natives of a neighbouring village. These faces looked angry, so it was clear that they were those of the murderers of his wife, and vengeance was consequently taken, not upon them, but upon some other natives of their village, for, as a rule, in Papua it does not matter much about the individual so long as you hit what you take to be the right family or community. In this case, if the Government had not stepped in and spoiled sport, there was a very pretty vendetta which would have lasted till one or other of the villages concerned became extinct or sought refuge elsewhere. As it was, the murderers served three years in Port Moresby gaol, and went back to their village with minds at least partly disabused of the idea of divination by leaf, and thoroughly convinced that murder, though attractive as a pastime, was hardly worth the candle.

Similar cases of murders to avenge the death of persons killed by puri puri are very numerous throughout Papua; the death is generally attributed to some well-known sorcerer, and steps are taken accordingly (that is if the relatives are not too terrified to act) without further evidence, but sometimes the wizard or witch is actually seen, as recently in the East of Papua, where a man saw an old woman fly "all the same pigeon" into a house where she tore open his brother's breast as he lay ill and helpless, and gnawed his liver. The man killed the old dame on her return, and the brother got well. So too, also in the East end, a native saw two sorcerers place leaves in the path where his father, a vigorous middle-aged man, was walking; when his father came to the leaves his legs failed him and he fell. His son carried him to the village, where he died, clearly from puri puri. So the son collected his friends and killed the sorcerers; and indeed one could hardly blame him.

Of a similar nature was the case of a village constable in the North of the Territory. He had arrested a sorcerer and was taking him up the river in a canoe to the magistrate. While they were in the canoe the sorcerer took a long string and a number of small pieces of stick, and said to the village constable, "You remember your eldest brother? I killed him. And your sister? I killed her too. And I killed your other brothers, and your father and mother, and your friends so and so," tying a piece of stick on to the string each time that he mentioned a murder. The village constable stood it until the twenty-second piece of stick, and then he and his crew seized the sorcerer and held him head downwards in the water till he was drowned.

In this last case I was strongly tempted to bring in a verdict of " Served him right," and indeed sorcerers terrorise and black-mail their fellow-villagers in some districts to such an extent that one is almost glad sometimes to see their victims get even with them. The sorcerer, however, occasionally finds himself between the devil and the deep sea, and one of them, I remember, complained, not without reason, of the difficulties of his position. " The village people come," he said, " and ask me to make puri puri for them. If I do the Government gets ' wild ' and puts me in gaol " (sorcery is punished with imprisonment), "if I say I won't they think that I am making puri puri against them and may try to kill me—so what am I to do ? "

The belief in sorcery is no doubt genuine even in the most civilised natives, and is not likely to die out for many generations; when it does, the task of administration will be much easier. As it is I have known cases where intelligent and civilised natives have killed a sorcerer and then given themselves up to the police, saying that they did not consider the Government penalty for sorcery severe enough, and that they were determined to punish the sorcerer even at the price of a long term of imprisonment.

Another class of murders are those which are committed from motives of vanity, for the sake of social distinction, or to comply with the demands of local etiquette. In some districts there are certain feathers which none but homicides are allowed to wear, and these insignia are of course objects of ambition to the gilded youth of the village. It does not seem to matter much who is killed or how—to sneak round a tree and kill a baby would apparently entitle the assassin to the same consideration as to kill a man in hand-to-hand fight—but the girls are apt to discourage the advances of men who have not earned the badge of the homicide, and this fact is sometimes put forward by the accused in mitigation of sentence. I remember one case which I tried not long ago in the Cape Nelson district on the East Coast, where the prisoner had killed an old woman who was drawing water from a river, and where this excuse was offered—only in that case the object of the prisoner's affections was a married woman. She had objected to his suit on the grounds that he had killed no one, so he sallied forth and took the easiest chance he could find. On my remonstrating with him on the impropriety of paying attentions to a married woman he informed me that there were no girls in the village, as they had all been killed and eaten in a recent raid. The position of a young man who found himself in a village where all the women were either married or eaten was no doubt a difficult one, and I hope that I took it into consideration in passing sentence.

Among one of the tribes near Port Moresby it is, or was, the custom for a man who built a new house to paint the posts with a mixture called paila, made of cocoanut oil and red clay, but by native custom it was not permitted to use the paila unless a man had been killed to celebrate the building of the house. This custom was the cause of one of the few murders of white men in recent years in Papua. A leading man among the Koetapu called Hariki wished to build a house at a village which he had founded, and his ambition led him to plan the death of a white resident who lived on the Laloki River, about ten miles out of Port Moresby.

The case is described as follows in my report for the year 1906-7. " The crime was committed in April 1906, but the criminals were not brought to justice till the following October, as almost the whole population of Port Moresby, official and non-official, readily accepted the theory that the deceased had been taken by an alligator, his boots, pipe and hat having been placed by the murderers near the river in order to favour that delusion. The instigator of the crime was Hariki. His accomplices joined him either from fear, or because they were anxious to take part in a murder, in order that they might have the privilege of wearing certain feathers which are regarded as the insignia of the assassin.

" That they bore the unfortunate man no malice is obvious from the circumstance that, after they had killed him, they proceeded, under the guidance of one of the party who was skilled in charms, to bring him back to life. They succeeded, so they said, as far as the middle of his body, the lower part of which as well as his legs came to life, but, though they continued their incantations until nightfall, they could not get past a ghastly wound where a blow from a club had crushed his chest, and all above that remained dead. They therefore abandoned the attempt and buried the body, took what they could find in the house, and went away, leaving the boots in a position favourable to the alligator theory, which they intended to suggest so soon as their victim was missed. They were afterwards arrested and tried, with the result that Hariki was hanged, and his accomplices sentenced to terms of imprisonment varying from fourteen years to life."

It will be noticed that the death penalty was carried out in the case of Hariki; this is usual where a white man is murdered and is necessary for the protection of the small white community. An interesting incident appeared in the evidence in this case. Before the murder Hariki had sent a messenger to a village of the Koiari tribe inviting two natives, one a middle-aged man and the other a youth, to come to the village of Baruni to " roast some sago." The two men responded to the invitation, but after they had gone some distance the younger man was sent back to get his club. " Did you go back for your club?" I asked the elder man. " No," he replied, " I had mine—I knew what the message meant." "To roast sago" was evidently in former days a recognised euphemism for murder, but since the spread of the Government influence murder had gone out of fashion, and the younger man had not learnt the formula, though his comrade knew it well.

There are of course numerous cases of murder and manslaughter which arise from ordinary quarrels, from jealousy, and from other causes in much the same way as among white men, but there is a rather peculiar form of homicide which occasionally comes before the Court and which is sometimes rather difficult to understand. For instance, I have known cases where a man, grieving over the loss of a relative or over some slight that has been put upon him, has set fire to his house, quite regardless of whether anyone was inside, with the result, occasionally, that a child is burnt to death, and I recently tried a case of murder which was the direct outcome of grief over the death of a pig. The prisoners were brothers, and their pig bore the pretty name of Mehboma; but Mehboma died, and the brothers in their unquenchable grief went forth and killed the first man they saw. The victim had nothing to do with Mehboma's death, but the mourning brothers did not care for that—somebody had got to be killed over it. The prisoners told me that it was the custom of their village to show their grief in this way, so that their neighbours must occasionally have suffered rather severely.

Cases somewhat similar to this, where men are carried away by a sudden fury, are not uncommon in the west of the territory. " For instance," to quote from my report of 1908-9, " one man, irritated because a baby would not stop crying, killed, not the baby, but his own mother; and I remember a case in which a man split open the head of another because he could not find his knife—the other man had never seen the knife, but that was immaterial. So cases happen of accidental wounding caused by the habit these people have of discharging arrows at random when they have a headache or feel otherwise out of sorts."

The procedure on the trial of native cases is of necessity painfully irregular. The prisoner has of course not the faintest conception of pleading, and is generally eager to tell the Court all about the affair from start to finish, and the best way, I have found, is to let him go on, and, if there seems to be the slightest doubt of his guilt, to enter a plea of not guilty. As a rule, however, he does not give much assistance in one's attempt to suggest a defence, but insists upon inculpating himself beyond all hope of acquittal. He is arraigned perhaps with the formula, "True, you been kill that boy?" To which he almost invariably replies, "True, me been kill him." Then, perhaps, it is suggested to him by the judge that the killing was in self-defence. "I think that boy he want to kill you first time?" which generally elicits the reply, "He no want to kill me; he no catch him spear." Then a further suggestion—"I think you no want to kill that boy?" with the disheartening response, "My word, me want to kill him too much," with, as likely as not, the additition, "Behind me kai-kai that boy" ("afterwards I eat him"). Then comes the real crux of the case—"What for you kill that boy?" and the real defence, with its labyrinthine details of pigs, sorcery, and "paying back." In one case I had heard that the deceased had, immediately before his death, killed the prisoner's sister, but it took a long cross-examination to elicit the fact from the prisoner, who seemed to attach far more importance to the loss of a nose-stick which had been broken apparently by the same blow, and it was not until after a long discourse upon the value and beauty of the nose-stick that it occurred to him to mention the murder of his sister.

A Northern native who had killed his father excused himself on the ground that "the old man was not much good," and a favourite defence to a charge of killing women and children is that "plenty more he stop" (that is, there are plenty more women and children left).

A defence which showed that all the world is akin was raised recently at Samarai, where the prisoner urged that the murdered man was a bore. "All the time he talk, he talk, he talk too much." Needless to say that his sentence was not a very heavy one.

Witnesses of course are often called, and my experience has been that the natives who have not been in contact with white civilisation are on the whole truthful, though there are some districts to which this does not apply. Deceit is the natural defence of inferior races, but the uncivilised Papuan has not yet realised this—possibly because he does not admit his inferiority. There is of course always the possibility that the witness is mistaken, and I remember two cases in which a miscarriage of justice very nearly took place through a mistake by witnesses as to the identity of the culprits.

Strangely enough a man called Imiri was mixed up in both affairs. He is a native of one of the Uberi villages in the mountains behind Port Moresby, and he had, at the time I first came into contact with him, already served a sentence for some kind of homicide. This man was accused about six years ago of having taken part in a raid upon a mountain village not far from his home, in which most of the inhabitants were killed. The raid took place in the daytime, and the villagers fought for some time successfully at their stockade, until one of the attacking party, who had a rifle, fired a shot, upon which they retreated panic-stricken to the centre of the village, and the attacking party broke through the stockade and slaughtered them like sheep. There were, however, two eye-witnesses left alive—one who had hidden himself under a house, and another who was on his way back from his garden when the attack was made, and who had seen the whole thing from behind a tree. Both these witnesses identified Imiri as the man who had fired the shot, and stated further that, after firing, he had waved his rifle in the air and shouted, "It is I, Imiri, who have done this." Imiri flatly denied having been there at all, and called as a witness an old man who informed me that, when he was young, he had spent most of his spare time in raiding other villages, but that he had given up the practice now that the Government had come and spoiled all the fun in the country; he still, however, took an interest in whatever fighting went on, and he assured me that Imiri had nothing to do with this affair. The old man seemed to me to be telling the truth, so I let Imiri go, and it was fortunate that I did so, for the real offender, an ex-village constable, was afterwards apprehended, and admitted his guilt. It was said that he had really called out Imiri's name, though I confess that I am sceptical on this point.

The other case, in which Imiri also figured, was that of a raid upon an Ekiri village, in the ranges not far from Port Moresby. There were two Ekiri villages a couple of miles apart and one night, about five years ago, one of them was attacked and burnt, and nearly all the inhabitants murdered. There were two witnesses who had escaped from the massacre— one a youth who had heard the footsteps of the attacking party as he lay awake and had wisely taken to the bush, and the other a woman. The latter was sleeping in her house with her husband and her baby by her side when she was awakened by a blaze of light, and found the village in flames and her house full of armed men. Her husband was killed where he lay, the baby was driven through the floor by a blow from a club, and she dashed through the wall of the house receiving a wound in the back from a tomahawk as she went. Outside, the scene was as bright as day, and she saw the war party murdering all they could find. Of course she took to the bush as fast as her legs could carry her, but she positively identified the attacking party as belonging to Uberi, and Imiri as one of them.

Further investigation showed that Imiri and a party of men were absent from their village at the time of the massacre, and the case looked pretty black against Imiri, who, with some others, was arrested and committed for trial. At the trial he was quite unmoved. "You thought at first that I was in the other raid," he said, "and afterwards you found out that I had nothing to do with it. You will find that we had nothing to do with this one either; we were away on a fishing expedition. Send us back to gaol and make further inquiries, and you will find that I am telling the truth." Further inquiries were made, and sure enough it turned out to be as Imiri had said; the raid was not the work of Uberi at all, but of the Hagari tribe, who had come from high up in the Main Range in response to a challenge which had been sent to them. It appeared that a youth of one Ekiri village loved a maiden of the other, but the old men would not let them marry. On this the youth became desperate—" Suppose he no catch that girl no good that boy live, more better he die," was the way in which it was explained to me—and he challenged one of the chiefs of a powerful tribe in the Main Range to come down and fight. This he did by giving the chief an ornament called a Gebori as he passed through Ekiri on his way home from Port Moresby, where he had been to attend a dance; the Gebori is worn in the mouth when fighting, and to give it to another is equivalent to a challenge. Ekiri was a small village, and could have had no chance of repelling the attack even if the inhabitants had been prepared, which they were not, as the youth kept his own counsel. He himself was killed in the attack; the other Ekiri village where the girl lived was not molested.

In neither of these cases were the witnesses deliberately telling an untruth. The terrified woman flying from the murder of her husband and child could not be expected to take very careful note of the raiders; there was an old feud between Ekeri and Uberi, and, being satisfied that the attacking party must be from Uberi, she had no difficulty in identifying Imiri and the others.

The sentences passed in native murder cases vary from seven

years to twelve months, or even less, according to the degree of civilisation which has been reached by the prisoner—that is to say, he gets a heavier sentence in proportion as he ought to have known better. The gaol discipline is far from severe and the food is better and more plentiful than in the villages, but the deprivation of liberty and the separation from their friends is keenly felt by most natives, and attempts to escape are not infrequent. The escapee when recaptured (as he invariably is) often says, "I do not know why I ran away, but I thought of my village and I could not stop."

It would appear that the gaol treatment, though criticised sometimes as too lenient, has been successful, as subsequent convictions for serious offences are extremely rare, and returned prisoners almost invariably exercise a civilising influence in their village. It must be remembered that the Papuan murderer is by no means necessarily a bad man—he is generally a man who has merely followed the ordinary customs of his village and has had the bad luck to be caught—and the influence he exercises is entirely different from that which one would expect from an ordinary European convict.

Interpretation is often a matter of great difficulty. Papua is a regular Tower of Babel, and it is not uncommon to have two or even three interpreters. I remember one case at Cape Nelson where a man was charged with having killed and eaten a baby. The interpreters whose services had been utilised on the committal were not present when I arrived to try the case, so there was no means of communicating with the accused. Accordingly I took him with me on the Government steamer and, after some time, discovered a cook in Port Moresby gaol who apparently could speak to him; but then no one could speak to the cook. Eventually I was able, by the aid of three interpreters, to talk to the cook, so that the trial was eventually conducted with the aid of four.

In one case we had to travel for about a week into the mountains trying to find an interpreter. At last we reached the prisoner's village and tried him there; on that occasion I think only two interpreters were necessary. He was a man who had killed and eaten a women, and the people of his village, fearing that the Government would be "wild," for they had heard of the Government though they had never been visited, refused to allow him to remain, and so he was passed from village to village (each apprehensive of the "wildness" of the Government) until at last he came to a place where there was a constable who arrested him and brought him down to the Government station. When I reached his village he had been in custody nine months, and, as it appeared that the woman had been robbing his garden and it might have been argued that he was only getting his own back again, I let him go. I have seen him several times since, though I never went to his village again; he has, so far as I am aware, eaten no more women.

In all these cases where several interpreters are employed, extreme care must be taken to ensure that the version which eventually reaches the prisoner is at least reasonably like the evidence that has been given, but, so far as I have been able to test the matter, it would appear that the translation is far more accurate than one would be inclined to think. Occasionally, however, mistakes are made ; for instance, last year at Kokoda, I was trying a case in which two natives had cut the throat of another with a tomahawk, and then gouged out his eyes with a knife. "Why," I asked the first interpreter—of course in English, for by law all trials must be conducted in English—" why did they put out his eyes ; to cut his throat was surely enough?" and this was translated, rather to my horror, as follows : " The Governor says they were quite right to cut his throat, but they ought not to have put out his eyes." Fortunately I knew the language well enough to understand what was said and to correct the translation, but after the evidence has got beyond the first language one has to rely entirely on native interpreters, and the best one can do is to ensure, by careful examination and re-examination, that the danger of mistake and mistranslation is minimised.

The headquarters of the Central Court are at Port Moresby, but the judge wanders about the territory, bringing what, it is to be hoped, is justice to every man's door, though all attempts to fix anything like a regular circuit have hitherto been in vain. Various means of locomotion are employed in the coastal districts—steamer, sailing boat, whale boat, canoe, and occasionally horse-back—in fact, almost all methods except railway and motor car, neither of which exists in Papua. Inland the travelling is done on foot along native tracks, the distance being always reckoned by days. Stores, tents and other baggage are carried by natives, and the day's walk is limited by what a loaded " boy " can do in that time, so that, for instance, a distance of four days means as a rule the distance that loaded " boys " can travel in four days. In flat country a day may be taken to mean anything from fifteen to twenty miles, or perhaps a little more, but in the mountains it might easily be less than a third of this, for a native track in the mountains of Papua is a sight to shudder at ; there is a record of a Government party who, after going hard for three days of nine hours each, had travelled only eight miles, but I cannot vouch for the accuracy of this statement, as I was not one of them.

The weight of the load is of course an important item in reckoning the distance that a " boy " will carry, but in the case of a Government party the load is usually a light one, and a good deal less than that allowed in the case of regular carriers to the gold fields, who are allowed a much longer time to do the journey.

To a white man the travelling is often fatiguing almost to the limits of endurance, but, though full of minor discomforts, rarely presents anything that is worthy of the name of hardship or danger. Still one is occasionally placed in trying positions. It is difficult, for instance, for a middle-aged gentleman to maintain the dignity of the Court while balancing himself on a slippery log with a drop of ten feet beneath him, or while struggling across a so-called bridge with one line of twisted vine to walk on, and another to hold on to, and a mountain torrent 30 feet below; but it all sounds and looks much more difficult than it really is, and, with the assistance of that truly wonderful body of men, the native constabulary, one must indeed be a duffer if he cannot surmount any difficulty that even Papua is likely to offer. Incidents, humorous and interesting, are to be found at every turn, and the recollection of the loyalty of one's brother officers, and of the warm-hearted hospitality of the white population in general, and of many good friends among the natives, makes the prospect of returning to duty far from unpleasing even among the marvels of London.

J. H. P. MURRAY.

IMPERIAL DEFENCE

By F. A. W. GISBORNE

THE memorial recently signed by nearly 250 eminent naval and military officers in Great Britain appealing to the Government to sanction the issue of a loan of £100,000,000 in order to strengthen the national defences should be most carefully considered by those who are now mainly responsible for the safety of the Empire. Even at this late hour His Majesty's Ministers might, by a resolute and patriotic effort, redeem a rather sorry record of unwise legislation and unworthy intrigues. Without any loss of dignity whatever the Prime Minister and his colleagues have the opportunity of atoning for past omissions and transgressions by a prompt acceptance of the advice offered by men, compared with whom in knowledge of all the essential conditions affecting the national safety the majority of the parliamentary supporters of the present British Ministry are but children. The call of patriotism is clear. In the presence of danger the idle wrangles and bickerings of party should cease. Throughout the whole of the self-governing British world the great question of Imperial defence overshadows all others and claims immediate attention.

Popular institutions, unhappily, have been conclusively proved by history to be inimical to permanent military and naval efficiency. The mob mind has always lacked prescience, patience, and self-sacrifice. It snatches at passing gratifications and neglects what is essential to permanent security. The rebuke administered by Demosthenes over two thousand years ago to the pleasure-loving Athenians for having assented to the fatuous decree by which certain funds that had been previously devoted to the maintenance of the fleet were transferred to the support of the public games may soon, unless present tendencies be checked, be applied to the modern recipients of unearned pensions and the devotees of football. All competent naval and military experts agree in holding that the exclusive parliamentary control of national armaments is a dangerous absurdity. It suggests the direction of the movements and mechanism of a modern battleship by a scratch crew of landsmen suffering from chronic sea-sickness. A foreign critic might smile to perceive in England to-day one eminent barrister supreme over the Army, and another over the Navy; and might wonder whether the people who consented to these extraordinary appointments would not soon insist upon the elevation of Lord Roberts or Lord Kitchener to the office of Lord Chancellor. But the position is far too serious for the British citizen, either at home or abroad, whose dearest interests are imperilled by a system that is the negation of elementary common sense, to share such mirth; and he would fain hope that the small vanities and ambitions of politicians, in the self-governing Dominions as well as in Great Britain herself, might soon be subordinated to the dictates of prudence and wise policy.

England should not disdain to learn from her Eastern ally a few wholesome lessons in the art both of preparing for and of conducting war. "The strength of Japan," wrote Kuropatkin, referring to the Japanese achievements in the late contest, " was in the complete union of her people, army, and Government, and it was this union that gave her the victory." Such a union emphatically does not now exist in the British Empire. Precious time is being wasted over interminable and useless discussions, empty compliments, and diplomatic trivialities. Volubility is usurping the place of ability. Wisdom is being stifled with words, some of a peculiarly mischievous kind. Not very long ago a British Minister of War actually disclaimed in a public speech all wish to arouse a "military spirit" in the nation. Such deference to the sentimental simpleton excites wonder. The true military spirit is exactly what the nation requires and what should be encouraged in every possible way. Without it an army is worth little more, either for defence or attack, than a mob of housemaids armed with brooms. A nation becomes decadent as it loses its militancy. The degenerate Greeks of the Lower Empire, Gibbon informs us, excommunicated for three years every citizen who was courageous enough to fight for his country. There are yet, apparently, Christians of an equally primitive type in the British Parliament to-day who seem disposed to follow that ancient and ignoble precedent. It is Christianity of the kind practised by the Crusader and the Ironside that bestows on nations both security and greatness.

Granting the first and indispensable condition of the existence of a spirit of true patriotism in all classes of the population, the essentials to a sound system of Imperial defence are two-fold. Compulsory military service must be adopted throughout the

Empire, and a supreme council of high military and naval officers, representative of the Mother Country and the various dependencies, must be created and endowed with full authority over the Imperial naval and military forces, wherever situated. The funds for the support of these forces should be provided, in just proportions, by the various Parliaments; but the powers of the latter in regard to naval and military affairs should be strictly confined to the domain of finance. The ineptitude of the parliamentary system of army management in the case of Great Britain has been painfully proved by the only two serious wars, neither of which, fortunately, endangered her actual safety, waged by her since the days of Napoleon. A similar system prevailing in the United States at the time of the Civil War led to no less than 200,000 cases of desertion from the ranks of the victorious army alone, and a frightful amount of avoidable mortality and expense. The total abolition of so pernicious a system is the first reform that a wise statesman would undertake. A nation in time of danger cannot safely confide the care of its defenders to the hands of men who, in all matters pertaining to the military art, are ignorant of everything save their own ignorance.

As before remarked, a real union of the naval and military forces of the Empire, and their subjection to undivided control, is the first and most essential condition necessary to security. Painful evidences have recently been afforded that this paramount need is still either ignored or underestimated both in the Commonwealth of Australia and the Dominion of Canada. The proposed creation of local fleets subject to the direct control of the local legislatures, with some vague proviso that they should be placed at the service of the Mother Country in time of war, cannot satisfy the requirements either of strategy or Imperial patriotism. So fatal a course should be strenuously resisted, and the hope might have been entertained that the British Government, accepting the unanimous opinion of its expert advisers, would ere this have stated in firm but courteous terms its objections to so disastrous a policy. But, on the contrary, one at least of His Majesty's present Ministers seems actually to have encouraged its adoption. Lord Crewe is reported to have made the following remarks in the course of a speech delivered at the dinner given to the Australian High Commissioner, Sir George Reid:—"We have to note that the representatives of the Commonwealth entered most heartily into the ideas of the War Office with regard to common action and an Imperial General Staff so far as those ideals could be brought into being, and I confess in the progress of that conference nothing gave me greater pleasure than the evidence, which was not confined to Australia, but extended also to the other great Dominions, that while carefully safeguarding their position as regards matters of Imperial defence —that is to say, carefully, and I think properly, emphasising the fact that no Dominion would consider itself bound to go to war at the beck and call of this Government and this country, but would keep an absolutely free hand in the matter; yet at the same time they were most anxious, both as regards the provision of an Imperial General Staff, and also as regards the assimilation, so far as possible, of armament and equipments, to make their forces part of the great Imperial whole, so that in time of need they could be worked and used together with our forces at home." The passage quoted is, indeed, in style, with its abundance of qualifying phrases and clauses, a masterpiece of Gladstonian prolixity; in substance it shows a profound ignorance of the very rudiments of the great problem of Imperial Defence.

In my opinion a more inept and mischievous utterance no Minister of the Crown in modern times ever made himself responsible for. If Lord Crewe's words mean anything they signify that, should Great Britain become involved in war, even were that war provoked by the act of one of her Colonies, she could claim no right to call on any of the latter for assistance, but would have to wait until it was offered. No necessary concentration of Imperial forces could be effected before the actual outbreak of hostilities, and ordinary precautions might be delayed until too late, and fatal revelations made by the interminable chatter of ignorant politicians. London, quite conceivably, under the conditions so suavely anticipated by Lord Crewe, might be forced to capitulate ere a Canadian or Australian vessel of war was within a thousand miles of the English Channel. In fact, his words imply an unqualified recognition of colonial independence, and might well have been used by Cobden himself. It is to be hoped that the Government will absolutely dissociate itself from a doctrine which, if carried into practice, must mean the final dissolution of the Empire at the first shock. If joint naval and military action on the part of all its forces in the event of war be not obligatory and pre-arranged, real union does not exist. Lord Crewe's words were perhaps intended to flatter the vanity of certain colonial politicians: every patriotic citizen in Greater Britain, however, will emphatically repudiate them as false to the Imperial ideal and unworthy of a responsible Minister of the Crown.

In truth too many idle compliments are now bestowed by prominent public men in England on their political brethren in the over-sea Dominions. It seems to be the fashion to refer in unvarying terms of obsequious and rather nauseous flattery alike to Canadians, South Africans, Australians, and to all the inhabitants of the United States without distinction from President to prize-fighter. A little candid and manly advice would be more appreciated. Courtly phrases may create a momentarily pleasing impression, but they inspire neither confidence nor respect. After all, colonials are not wholly ignorant of the problems of naval and military defence, and they do not like to be treated as though they were schoolboys subject to the benevolent discipline of the new educationist. Every educated Canadian and Australian knows that unity of command is essential to success in war. He recognises also the truth of Adam Smith's words : "The colonial assemblies cannot be supposed to be the proper judges of what is necessary for the defence and the support of the whole Empire." He desires to see Parliamentary control of the joint naval and military forces strictly limited to matters of finance, and to see also an Imperial Council of War created in which Canada, South Africa, Australia and India would enjoy representation as well as the Mother Country.

Fair representation would be a *sine quâ non* to the constitution of such a body. From it the poison of political influence would be excluded, and the Parliamentary busy-body or sentimentalist would not be permitted to endanger the most vital national interests by mischievous interference with the plans of men who thoroughly understood the science of warfare. Over its deliberations the Sovereign, as Chief of the Empire, would naturally preside ; and besides its ordinary functions of organisation and administration the Council would enjoy the sole right to appoint officers over the naval and military forces, both in peace and war, from the Commander-in-Chief downwards. "An army controlled by more than one mind is as many times useless as are numbered the minds that direct it." An indisputable military as well as naval axiom is thus tersely expressed by the author of a striking work, 'The Valour of Ignorance,' recently written by a distinguished American officer, General Homer Lea. No nation can with impunity neglect it. Several minds may devise a plan ; one only can safely execute it. A perusal of the book just referred to, from which an additional passage or two will later be borrowed, might earnestly be recommended to all those who are particularly interested in the great problem of national defence.

A highly-equipped and sufficient naval and military force, homogeneous in composition and directed by a single authority, is absolutely necessary to the safety of the Empire. The effusive assurances of orators, the fitful emotionalism of crowds, the soothing purr of the diplomatist—these have no influence whatever on the main currents of national destiny. If fine speeches could have saved nations, neither Greece nor Rome would have fallen. The sword is still the master both of tongue and pen. "Of all broken reeds sentimentality is the most broken reed on which righteousness can lean." Still less, Mr. Roosevelt might have added, can Empire safely lean on it. War must be regarded as a certainty in the future. The forces of expanding populations, the struggle among the nations, not only for dominion and trade, but for very life, cannot be restrained by oratorical platitudes and episcopal benedictions. Only by the artificial limitation of human increase, by the scientific selection of the fit among the species, and by the moral revolution accompanying such a change, can the ultimate appeal to tooth and talon be prevented. So long as the combative instincts survive, so long as boys fight in public schools and men in public-houses, so long as a hundred men are constrained to live on land that can only support fifty in comfort, there will be war.

Would any sane statesman, it might be asked, openly proclaim the hostility of his country towards a rival, so as to warn it of the meditated blow? Does not every responsible ruler of a rising and martial nation sincerely desire and work for peace until his country's preparations for war have been perfected? A man attacked while loading his weapon has but a poor chance of victory. It is, at root, the clash of national interests that produces war—not race animosities or the ambitions of rulers. With nations moving on converging lines collisions from time to time are unavoidable; and the business of the true statesman is to foresee and to provide against such collisions. Facts, to the candid mind, speak for themselves and convey their own warning. The British Empire, with the exception of that of Russia and the American territories which, by the Monroe Doctrine, are practically dependencies of the United States, is the only Empire existing to-day that contains almost limitless areas of unoccupied lands fit for European settlement. It possesses also the most desirable coaling and commercial stations in the world. The increasing populations of powerful foreign countries, Asiatic as well as European, require room; their industrial classes need markets for their products, and supplies of raw material guaranteed by the protection afforded by their own flags to feed their factories. A successful war against Great Britain would give any such nation all it needed for a century's expansion. While, under present conditions, it could in any event lose but little, it might gain world supremacy. For the British pacifist to propose disarmament to a martial nation suffering from land hunger were like a millionaire expressing to a starving pauper an amiable wish that both might live amicably together without change of relative material condition. Arbitration too, where vital issues are involved, is a mere chimera. "The idea of International Arbitration as a substitute for natural laws that govern the existence of political entities arises not only from a denial of their fiats and an ignorance of their application, but from a total misconception of war, its causes and its meaning." * Plain truth is here expressed. The continued possession of so goodly a heritage as the British Empire depends, not merely on the determination of its citizens to defend their rights, but on wise provision and preparation on the part of its rulers. "The man who opposes, in time of peace, suitable preparation for war, is as unpatriotic and detrimental to the nation as he who shirks his duty or deserts his post in time of battle." † Truer words were never written. May their truth be practically recognised by all British statesmen and peoples ere the hour of battle shall strike. .

It is somewhat disquieting, however, to observe the emphasis generally laid on the fact that Great Britain's military and naval preparations are solely defensive. A very slight acquaintance with history demonstrates the truth that at all times in the past nations have owed their safety as well as their greatness to offensive rather than defensive action. A country that stands solely on the defensive is doomed. Scipio, not Fabius, was the deliverer of Rome. The flank attack on Spain and the rear attack on Africa saved the Republic from Hannibal—not the resistance of the home legions. The initial spring of Frederick the Great on Saxony in 1756 saved Prussia from ruin in the Seven Years' War. Wellington's refusal to follow the timid counsels of pusillanimous British Ministers, who would have confined his operations to Portugal, resulted in the expulsion of the French army from Spain. Cæsar did not await the onslaught of Pompey in Italy ; Napoleon's power began to crumble from the day on which the forces of the Allies commenced a vigorous attack. The recent example given by Japan at the outset of the late war, and a hundred others afforded by history, teach the same lesson. The forces of the British Empire, therefore, when the supreme crisis shall arise, must be prepared to strike at the enemy at once, and strike hard. To enable them to do so mobile bodies of troops, adequate in number and equipment, must be maintained, in addition to sufficient forces for home defence.

It is with deep concern that the over-sea Briton observes a non-recognition in English political circles of what is a mere commonplace of the military art. Almost entire reliance seems to be placed on the Navy. Yet the latter alone, no matter how powerful and ably directed, could never strike a decisive blow against a formidable Continental Power. "As all wars have been, so in the future will they be, determined by land warfare." ‡ Persia

* 'The Valour of Ignorance,' page 76.
† *Ibid*, page 6.
‡ *Ibid*, page 223.

was overthrown at Platæa, not Salamis. Aegospotami did not necessitate the fall of Athens. She succumbed after that crushing naval defeat solely because of her inability to invade Spartan territories or to protect her peninsular allies. A country that possesses only a strong navy unsupported by an equally strong army, when contending with an enemy powerful both on land and sea, is like a man with one arm striving against an opponent with two. Being compelled to ward off his adversary's attacks he must limit his action to self-protection, and can never deliver a knock-down blow. The recent concentration of British naval forces in the North Sea, so sadly suggestive of the recall of the Roman legions to Italy in the reign of the Emperor Honorius, is a melancholy admission of military impotence. It is extraordinary that even so distinguished a disciple of the blue-water school as Mr. Archibald Hurd should entirely fail to perceive the vital need, both to Great Britain herself and the Empire, of a powerful and well-trained army based on compulsory service. "Only when the naval superiority of one nation over another is so positive as to prohibit the hazard of battle can it be said that that nation is in a position to neglect with impunity its military forces and land defences." * Great Britain, certainly, cannot now claim such an overwhelming superiority over her chief naval rivals. Her navy, as matters now stand, on the outbreak of war would be thrown entirely on the defensive in order to protect the vessels bearing over-sea food supplies, and to ensure immunity from invasion. The moral effects of such an attitude on officers and crews placed between an enterprising enemy animated by hopes of victory in front, and timorous, unarmed multitudes, fearful alike of conquest and starvation, behind would be most discouraging. The navy would be in the position of a chained' bear baited by dogs able to attack and retreat as they pleased. And, apart from these considerations, there is the important question of foreign alliances. What European or other nation would ally itself with a Power that could give it no appreciable assistance either to invade the enemy's territories or to defend its own? *Ententes* do not include the use of powder and shot. How could Great Britain hope, single-handed, not merely to repel, but to inflict a decisive blow on a nation that numbered its armed and trained defenders by millions? Any advantages she might gain would be purely negative, and won at tremendous cost; a single defeat might mean destruction.

An effective scheme of Imperial defence requires, therefore, as the second of its two essential conditions, that Great Britain, like Australia, should discard the voluntary in favour of the compulsory system of military service. To strengthen the limbs

* 'The Valour of Ignorance,' p. 260.

while the very heart of the Empire remained unguarded were wasted labour. Territorials who, according to their originator, Mr. Haldane, would require six months' grace after the declaration of war to fit themselves for active service, are a mere delusion. In six days the decisive battle might have been fought and lost. Expeditionary corps at home affiliated to similar bodies of mobile troops in the Colonies, all under one control, should be held ready to embark and invade the territories of the enemy, if possible, before the latter was prepared to take similar action. To leave the initiative to the foe were a most fatal blunder. Precautions such as have been briefly outlined would render the Empire invulnerable, and would do more than the idle declamations of a thousand Peace Societies to maintain international concord. The potentialities of Imperial power, both on land and sea, have but to be transformed into actualities —a task surely not beyond the capabilities of British statesmanship and patriotism—and all schemes of hostile aggression meditated abroad will be baffled, the prevailing anxieties will be appeased, and the dark cloud of war will lose its terrors.

To say that military weakness provokes attack is but to repeat an ancient and indisputable truism attested by every page of history. Weakness accompanied by wealth presents double temptations to martial ambition. Commercialism and sentimentalism—the former the source of opulence, the latter of feebleness—have proved the ruin of many great empires in the past. Aggravated by the evil spirit of domestic faction, and the lack of self-denial and forethought inseparable from popular institutions, they threaten the existence of the British Empire to-day. It is full time that all the better elements in that Empire should unite in a vigorous effort to combat evils which, if unchecked, must end in frightful disaster. In scientific organisation, in provident statesmanship, in martial spirit and in true patriotism, Japan has set an example which Great Britain and her daughter States might well follow.

Let the fact be calmly recognised that war is a certainty of the future, probably of the near future. It is as much a part of the majestic scheme of Nature as the tornado and the thunderstorm. Attended for a time by havoc and destruction, its ultimate effects are good. Wordsworth's opinion concerning those effects was far more philosophic and true than that of the short-sighted, timorous humanitarian to-day. As Moltke said, war is the school of the noblest human virtues. It is the supreme test both of individual and of national fitness. It is the creator and the preserver, as well as the destroyer of nations. The British race as a whole, we may feel assured, still possesses all the qualities of virility, courage and patriotism necessary to enable it to emerge triumphantly, though not without wound and transient disaster, from the approaching ordeal. But the high and ennobling attributes just mentioned cannot avail in an age of scientific warfare without wise statesmanship, directive ability and scientific preparation. On the statesmen of the Empire is imposed the supreme task of supplying those requisites; their watchword should be—Unite and prepare.

F. A. W. GISBORNE.

EDUCATION IN BECHUANALAND

Education in the Bechuanaland Protectorate is mainly in the hands of the London Missionary Society, to whom a grant of £500 per annum is made in consideration of services rendered by them. The Dutch Reformed Church some years ago established a Mission in the Bakhatla Reserve and has schools in Mochudi, the chief native town, and at other places in that reserve. The annual grant in aid of education made to this denomination is £150. The Administration also contributes a sum of £150 per annum to the Tiger Kloof Institution, which was established a few years ago by the London Missionary Society, near Vryburg, with the object of imparting technical instruction to the Bechuanas both of the Cape Colony and Protectorate. The idea is to give, in addition to a moderate amount of book-learning, a sound practical knowledge of elementary carpentry and masonry to the boys. There is no intention of so equipping them as to make them rivals of European artisans, but to enable them to meet the requirements of their own people, among whom an inclination to substitute buildings of European appearance for the picturesque native huts has for long been noticeable, particularly in parts where they are brought most closely in touch with civilisation. In consideration of the grant the Society agreed to accept twelve pupils from the Protectorate free of charge. From the first the Protectorate natives have been alive to the advantages offered them at Tiger Kloof, and there has never been any lack of candidates for vacancies as they occur. There is an excellent little school for European children at Serowe, Khama's town, to which the Government makes a grant of £100; and to a Railway School at Artesia a contribution of £30 was made during the year. By arrangement with the Government of Basutoland the Inspector of Education of that Territory visits the Bechuanaland Protectorate once a year and inspects the various schools.

POLITICS AND STATISTICS IN INDIA

By A RESIDENT IN INDIA.

No civilised person to-day can regard statistics as anything else than the necessary basis of good government. An ignorant government must be a bad one however excellent its intentions, because it cannot tell where its assistance is needed, it cannot tell with what degree of weight its taxation presses upon the various classes of the people, nor can it form any opinion as to the way in which the classes are modifying their relations between themselves, whether one is fattening at the expense of another or not. But efficient administration presupposes that the Government has and acts on this knowledge, which in its most convenient form becomes what we know as official statistics.

But there are circumstances where statistics may be more or less replaced by other agencies. For example, a country in which the population possesses a considerable degree of education, and in which there exists a well-informed and reliable press, is evidently in less urgent need of official statistics than a country where education extends to only a small part of the population and where the press is, on the whole, ignorant and unreliable. There is thus a suspicion of irony about this matter, for the first is also the country where it is easiest to collect accurate statistics, and the second is that where accurate figures are practically out of the question.

Unhappily India comes most decidedly under the latter head. The Indian Government is an alien government, which cannot off-hand understand the ways of thought and mode of life of its subjects. Again, India is a vast and complicated country. There is an element of obscurity residing in the mere mass of the 300,000,000 people it contains. Then again, it is divided up among innumerable different castes and sub-castes, among different religions, among different races, so that in almost every question of importance the cross-pull of hostile interests defies analysis. Then, too, the people of India are still singularly ignorant. On the whole, it is not unfair to call them singularly improvident as well. They are quite incapable of grasping more than what they see around them. If their village is prosperous, with a good harvest, high prices, and low land-assessment, if the *sowcar* does not thrive among them and the lawyer does not extort the whole value of their land on pretext of defending them against some preposterous claim, then the whole of India must be prosperous and contented. But if the monsoon, however good on the average, should have missed their district in some one of its vagaries, then they fancy the whole land must be lying famine-stricken. Lastly, the popular press in India is in the last degree ignorant, mendacious, persistent in stirring up strife and in spreading false reports.

The Government of India is therefore in more urgent need of reliable figures than perhaps any other government in the world ; and it has done much to supply itself with figures of a sort. But it must be admitted that Indian statistics are not all that one desires. They are imperfect and inaccurate. They are inaccurate partly because of the apathetic ignorance of the people, partly because of " the sinister interests " of those who collect or give them, and partly also because the methods adopted to collect them are frequently imperfect. The attitude of the uneducated Indian towards statistical operations was one of suspicion but now is well on its way towards indifference. At first, with the ingrained habits bred by centuries of oppression, statistical inquiries meant new taxes to the average Indian. Now that he has discovered that an enumeration of his cattle does not lead to the confiscation of half of them, he is content to smile at it as a harmless fad of the Sirkar, like his worrying him about sanitation. But that any good should ever come of it, that Government might come to his assistance by reason of these inquiries, is an idea which the Indian peasant could never be made to grasp.

Then to support the invincible ignorance of the peasant we have " the sinister interests " of those who collect statistics——subordinate Government servants, mostly Brahmins. How these operate may easily be seen from an illustration or two. Every collector has to report on the crop out-turns in the district. He might, of course, go and sit in the sun all day long and watch the threshing and measuring of the crop on selected typical fields. But as a matter of fact he rarely does so. It is too hot and too tedious. Accordingly he deputes a subordinate, who in all probability never goes near the threshing floor. He looks to see what the out-turn was in the previous year, and adds a little or subtracts a little as he thinks the harvest was better or worse. There are stories told about district officers who took the crop out-turns seriously, who selected fields with care and verified the amount of grain that they really produced. But when their reports went in, they were told officially that the amounts were much greater than they possibly could be, that the normal out-turn was only two-thirds of what they had reported, and that the year was below normal, and so forth. Indeed, everybody who troubles to inquire into the matter knows quite well that the crop reports are underestimated by between 30 and 50 per cent., and this of course goes some way to explain how it was that Mr. Digby, Mr. Naoroji Dadhabhoy and Mr. Dutt were able to deduce such awful pictures of Indian poverty from the crop reports, when it is obvious to all observers that India has grown in wealth and prosperity. But there is good reason for the lowness of the crop reports. The land-revenue is assessed on calculations based on the average out-turn : and consequently a faithful report might lead to an enhancement of the rates at the next revision of the settlement. The Brahmins are large land-holders ; and therefore every Brahmin official conceives it to be his duty to keep the rates as low as possible by every means in his power.

The case is exactly reversed with the price reports, for when the prices of food-grains reach what is called " scarcity rates," all Government servants drawing up to Rs.20 a month receive an additional allowance. Now the prices are generally obtained by a *peon* going to the local bazaar and reporting to someone in the collector's office. But the *peon* is one of those persons who would benefit by the allowance ; the clerk in the office would probably benefit as well. So it comes to pass that there are active and obvious temptations towards exaggerating the prices of food-grains—at least towards maintaining them as nearly as possible at the scarcity level.

These cases, too, afford typical examples of what passes for statistics in India. Reports are accepted without check. The district officers are often enough too busy with other matters to supervise the figures that are sent out of their offices on the testimony of ignorant or interested persons. There is the most urgent need for a revision of the statistical methods at present in use. It is ridiculous that the out-turn reports should be made by one who has not really checked the out-turn of a single piece of land. It is ridiculous that the price reports, on which among other things depends the question whether the famine machinery shall be called into action or not, should be left to a *peon* on Rs.10 a month. What is really needed is a separate statistical establishment ; but, with its common parsimony, the Indian Government has preferred to assign statistical duties to officers already too busy to attend to them, with the result that statistics have gone to the wall and something neither reliable nor accurate has been put in their place.

On the whole one is led to feel that the Indian Government has shrunk from the expense which real statistics would probably involve in India, and a similar reflection is produced by certain defects in the substance of the statistics themselves. The least inaccurate statistics in India are the sea-borne trade returns. Next come the figures for the larger cities. But the statistics for the country districts, that is for nine-tenths of British India, are either imperfect, as has been described above, or altogether lacking. To give a single example, Madras is supposed to be held mainly by small proprietors who cultivate their own lands. It is therefore of the last importance to the efficient government of Madras that the position of the ryot should be accurately known. Before it can have any general policy worthy of the name the Madras Government should possess clear information of a statistical character regarding the indebtedness of the cultivator, the extent to which holdings are passing into non-agricultural hands, the accumulation of people upon the soil. A short time ago it was proposed that a Record of Rights should be prepared, such as would give this information. At present, the Revenue Settlement does not give the necessary details, but only records the person liable for the revenue assessed on each piece of land. Nor does the Registration Department. The latter merely registers documents. Thus A may mortgage a piece of land to B. The mortgage deed must be registered, but there is nothing to show whether the mortgage is *bonâ fide* or not. It would probably surprise Englishmen if they could know the percentage of fraudulent documents that are annually registered with a view to subsequent false claims and law-suits. But this sort of thing is encouraged by the intricacy of Indian land rights. A, B, C and D may be the co-heirs of a piece of land which they hold as undivided property. A may sell his share; B may mortgage his; C may die early leaving two young sons; and D may leave the village to seek his fortune in the Presidency town and only turn up again years after, or his heirs may appear suddenly to demand his rights. It is not difficult to imagine what endless lawsuits, genuine and fraudulent, might be based on this quite ordinary state of things. But it is equally clear that an exact Record of Rights, which could only be altered after notice given to all the parties interested, would in the first place render the administration of the law more regular and easy, and, in the second place, afford such information to Government as it certainly should have at its disposal.

The importance of the matter really lies in the fact that there is reason to believe that the ryots' rights in the soil have been seriously diminished in the last generation. Two classes at all events, Government servants and pleaders, have in recent times made very large savings. It is well known that their favourite form of investment is either the downright purchase or mortgage of landed property. But the extent to which the ryots have lost ground is, however, uncertain. Conflicting opinions are held by those best qualified to judge, and the matter could only be cleared up by a statistical survey which was strongly staffed enough to give accurate returns. But the Madras Government have resolved not to move in the matter.

As has been said above, this points to a carelessness of the value of statistics that is highly regrettable. The connection between economic and political movements has been too often demonstrated to need more than mention here. But its truth has recently been illustrated in India with singular poignancy. The unrest in its more violent and anarchic aspects coincided, as Sir Bampfylde Fuller recently pointed out, with an abnormal rise in Indian prices, which, by harassing the educated salaried classes, exposed them to become preachers and plotters of sedition. It would not of course be true to say that the rise in prices was the cause of sedition. It only gave sedition its opportunity. But that effect is obvious enough, and it does small credit to the Government that they should but recently, under the pressure of popular outcry, have set about inquiring into the causes of the rise in prices which dates from 1905. In the same way they seem disinclined to take any steps for ascertaining the actual condition of the present. But should that condition deteriorate, as there is reason to believe it is likely to do, under the pressure of continual purchases and foreclosures, then stringent legislation would become necessary, such as had to be passed in the Punjab where sales to a non-agriculturist have had to be prohibited.

And after all, the condition of the agriculturist must always be the prime object of interest to the Indian statesman. It must always be his chief consideration, the motive of nine-tenths of his executive actions. Is it not then reasonable to ask that steps be taken to improve the statistics relating to Indian land, so that one may know its real resources, the actual prices that the grower can obtain, the way in which he keeps his head above water or falls into the hands of the money-lender, and finally the tenure on which he holds his land, whether he is retaining full proprietorship or whether he is being ousted by those classes our rule has created and educated, which thrive by reason of the courts and system of appeals we have established, but which in their method of aggrandisement have never learnt the duty of mercy to those who chance to be under their power ?

MADRASSI.

SIDELIGHTS ON COLONIAL LIFE

The Editor will be glad to receive voluntary contributions to these pages
from oversea readers.

South African Fauna.

It is intended to present to the King a collection of animals
representative of the fauna of South Africa. In every case the
animals will be the gift of private individuals; it is not the
intention of the Union to buy animals. Sportsmen and lovers
of animals in the different provinces of the Union are being asked
to form committees to achieve the object in view. According
to a circular that has been issued of the large animals, young
ones are more desirable: of the full grown, those partially
tamed would be most appreciated. Indeed it may be said that
every animal is wanted except baboons and leopards (tiger).
Bats, field-mice, hedgehogs, meer-cats or muishonds, wild cats,
porcupines, or golden moles, wild dogs and hyænas; jackals,
other than the black-backed; bonte, bless, and springboks; kudu
or hartebeest, rooi rhebok (which has never been seen alive in
England, if in Europe), klipspringer or grey rhebok, grys, stein
or blaawbok. Buffaloes or elephants will be acceptable; the
mountain zebra is especially desired. Game birds would be
greatly appreciated, and lizards, tortoises, and snakes would also
be gladly received. All the donations are to be suitably acknowledged on printed forms, headed, "His Majesty the King's
South African Collection," which, we are told, the donors will
doubtless treasure as a memento of their generosity as well as
of the opening by Royalty of the first Parliament of the Union.

The Navy and South Africa.

Addressing a large audience at a political meeting on the eve
of the poll at Cape Town, Mr. Jagger is reported to have
made the following pertinent observations on the matter of
Imperial defence: "In the first place, I think we ought to
take every step for the local defence of our own harbours.
There can be no question about it that we should make a
greater contribution towards the cost of the Imperial Navy,
because what was the position to-day? Here in this country
we have something over twenty millions sterling in revenue,
and are only contributing £75,000 towards the cost of the
Navy, which does not amount to 1s. 3d. per head of population.

To put it in another way, and on the insurance basis, it does not amount to £2 per cent. on the total inward and outward trade of the country. Contrast that with Great Britain, which has to pay forty millions towards the Navy, almost £1 per head, for every man, woman, and child." He thought his audience would agree with him when he said that no self-respecting people could allow such a state of affairs to continue —that they should receive all the benefit here, and let others bear the burden. They were bound by their sense of self-respect and sense of justice to make a more adequate contribution towards the maintenance of the Imperial Navy.

International Copyright Convention.

As long ago as 1878 a Royal Commission reported that the British Copyright Law stood in urgent need of revision and amendment. Unfortunately it has not hitherto been found possible to give full effect to the recommendations of the Royal Commission, owing to the difficulty of the questions involved. A new importance, however, attaches to the matter by the revision of the International Copyright Convention, carried out by the International Conference held at Berlin in October and November 1908. The revised Convention, signed *ad referendum* by the British delegates on behalf of His Majesty's Government, embodied certain alterations which cannot be put into force in the British Empire without a change in the existing law. The revised Convention was examined, from the point of view of the interests of the United Kingdom, by a strong Departmental Committee, presided over by Lord Gorell, which reported in December 1909 substantially in favour of the ratification of the Convention. Before, however, any action could be taken to carry out the recommendations of the Committee it was necessary to ascertain the views of the other parts of the Empire. A Conference of representatives of all the self-governing Dominions, convened as a subsidiary Conference of the Imperial Conference, and comprising also a representative of the India Office, accordingly met to consider in what manner the existing uniformity of the law on copyright could best be maintained and in what respects the existing law should be modified, the basis for discussion being the revised Copyright Convention.

Imperial Copyright Law.

This Conference reported (1) That it recognises the urgent need of a new and uniform Law of Copyright throughout the Empire, and recommends that an Act dealing with all the essentials of Imperial Copyright Law should be passed by the Imperial Parliament, and that this Act, except such of its provisions as are expressly restricted to the United Kingdom, should be expressed to extend to all the British possessions : provided that the Act shall not extend to a self-governing Dominion unless declared by the Legislature of that Dominion to be in force therein, either without any modifications or additions, or with such modifications and additions relating exclusively to procedure and remedies as may be enacted by such Legislature. (2) That any self-governing Dominion which adopts the new Act should be at liberty subsequently to withdraw from the Act, and for that purpose to repeal it so far as it is operative in that Dominion, subject always to treaty obligations and respect for existing rights. (3) That where a self-governing Dominion has passed legislation substantially identical with the new Imperial Act, except for the omission of any provisions which are expressly restricted to the United Kingdom, or for such modifications as are verbal only, or are necessary to adapt the Act to the circumstances of the Dominion, or relate exclusively to procedure or remedies or to works first published within or the authors whereof are resident in the Dominion, the Dominion should, for the purposes of the rights conferred by the Act, be treated as if it were a Dominion to which the Act extends. (4) That a self-governing Dominion which neither adopts the Imperial Act nor passes substantially identical legislation, should not enjoy in other parts of the Empire any rights except such as may be conferred by Order in Council, or, within a self-governing Dominion, by Order of the Governor in Council. (5) That the Legislature of any British possession (whether a self-governing Dominion or not) to which the new Imperial Act extends, should have power to modify or add to any of its provisions in its application to the possession ; but, except so far as such modifications and additions relate to procedure and remedies, they should apply only to works the authors whereof are resident in the possession and to works first published therein.

Things in Pretoria.

In the course of an interview with a representative of the *Cape Times*, a prominent member of the Pretoria Town Council said : " The decision to make Pretoria the administrative capital means a great deal to the city, and the Council intend to take full advantage of it by carrying out an extensive programme of public works, and, more important still, by developing such industrial resources as we possess. Already conditions are much more satisfactory, and no one engaged in business at Pretoria can fail to realise how much more freely the public is spending money, and how much greater is the general prosperity than it was even six months ago. We have a white population of about 25,000, and clearly before new industries—and we have practically none of importance at present—can be established, we must have a much larger supply of labour. That is one of our principal objects—to improve the labour supply, and, above all, we want to attract and use white labour where possible. The Council is doing much in this direction, for, apart from the work created by schemes for public undertakings, we contemplate offering special inducements to manufacturers to take up sites within the municipality. We shall offer them cheap power and lighting, and other advantages, while the central position of Pretoria is all in its favour. We are also turning our attention to the exploitation of our extensive town lands, and have appointed a committee to go into the question of developing the mineral wealth available. Coal, iron, diamonds and cinnabar are known to exist, and we shall offer the town lands for prospecting as soon as our scheme has been passed in its entirety. Rents in Pretoria have gone up of late, but not higher than is warranted by the new prosperity, and in any case we do not intend this to hinder an influx of white working people, for we have a scheme under consideration for laying out erven at Pretoria West for sale at reasonable rates to this class of resident, so as to render them independent of speculators."

Agriculture in Bahamas.

From an excellent report of the Board of Agriculture (Bahamas) for the year 1909, recently published, one learns that "The total value of the shipments of sisal fibre, which is the most important product of the colony, was £42,627. In view of the extended production of this fibre in other parts of the world, ways are being sought of increasing the number of its uses. The export of pine-apples was worth £22,853; the market for this fruit, either green or canned, is entirely in the United States, on account of the inability to compete with the cheaply produced Singapore pineapple in England. Grape fruits were exported to the value of £1,264, and the shipments of oranges were worth £412, the numbers of the fruits being respectively, 276,576 and 465,050. The complaint is made that the citrus industry requires care in the handling and shipment of its products; and it is stated that more information is wanted as to possible markets. In the exports of cotton, an increase of £85 was shown, the total value being £319. The popularity of this crop in the Out Islands is increasing, and it is likely that the coming year will see an extension of the area planted. As regards tobacco, 23,800 cigars, valued at £122, were exported. Among minor products were exports to the following values: tomatoes £148, preserved guavas £97, bananas £67, pumpkins £66, and onions £48. The production of these is showing a fairly rapid growth, as increased amounts are being employed for local consumption."

Labour Hostility to British Immigrants.

Commenting on the refusal of the Labour Council to accept the invitation of the British Immigration League to elect two representatives on the committee of that organisation, *The Sun* of Sydney, New South Wales, observes :—" It will have the effect of confirming the view held by a number of people that the Labour party are uncompromisingly hostile to immigration. It seems that in this case, as happens in so many political and industrial matters, the voice of the extremists speaks for the whole body. Considered even from the standpoint of the most narrow-minded unionist, the Labour Council's decision was a blunder. These men take the view that until the land is opened up immigration to Australia should be stopped altogether. They declare the Immigration League to be engaging in a campaign that is inimical to the interest of the workers—that they are encouraging people to come here for whom work can be found only at the sacrifice of men at present in employment. The invitation by the league was prompted by a desire to make their committee as representative as possible of all sections of the community and to give accredited representatives of organised labour an opportunity of stating the facts as they know them, and of preventing any unconscious injustice being done to Australian workmen. In effect, the league said to the Labour Council : ' You complain that the men we are bringing out are affecting the local labour market. Will you appoint two delegates to supply us with information concerning the prospects of work which we might otherwise be unable to obtain, and see that the selection of immigrants introduced under our auspices is in the best interests of the country generally ? ' That considerate and well-meant invitation was turned down—certainly by a narrow majority, but still rejected."

Australian Criticism.

" The Immigration League," *The Sun* continues, " will not be deterred in their patriotic endeavours to populate this dangerously empty country, and they will, as hitherto, take every possible precaution to ensure that the people they bring here will prove neither a menace to our own workers nor a burden to the State. So far they have been exceedingly successful in avoiding errors in both respects, but should they in the future fail to completely realise the restrictions of the local labour market in certain directions, the Labour Council will be a party to any injustice which may be done to their fellows. Their attitude is not only petty and silly, but it is unpatriotic as well. The peril of allowing

Australia to remain empty and undefended cannot be too strongly emphasised. We cannot possibly hope to hold this country unless we people and develop it. That warning is being constantly sounded, and it is a pity that a certain section of the Labour party should so persistently ignore it. The idea that the restriction of population encourages prosperity is such an extraordinarily absurd one that it is remarkable that men who are far-seeing on other subjects should entertain it for a moment. The vigorous development of Australia means the opening up of new avenues of employment and the initiation of an era of national activity from which the workers will substantially benefit. We do not believe that the Labour party, as a party, are hostile to immigration, but it certainly looks as though the narrow-minded, unpatriotic section are swaying the larger number, who, while not antagonistic, are much less enthusiastic than they should be."

Canada and The West Indies.

In a booklet published by the Imperial Department of Agriculture for the West Indies much useful information has been collected with the primary object of placing manufacturers and merchants in Canada in possession of reliable facts and statistics relative to the development of the resources of the British West Indies and British Guiana, and the possibilities for trade between that part of the world and the Dominion. The tabulated statements show that the value of Canadian imports into the British West Indies and British Guiana amounted in the year ending March 31, 1909, to £391,940; while the value of the West Indian exports to Canada was £1,682,156, a total volume of trade between the two countries of £2,074,096. Further particulars tell us that in the year 1908–9, British Guiana exported to Canada produce, mostly sugar, to the value of $3,662,654, while the imports of Canadian goods were $605,413. From Barbados, sugar to the value of $499,076 and molasses to the value of $642,240 were sent to Canada, and imports of the value of $728,022 received. The value of the imports from Canada into Jamaica in 1908–9 was $824,837, or 7·1 per cent. of the total imports, and the value of the exports to Canada from Jamaica was 4·3 per cent. of the total exports. Trinidad in 1908–9 sent exports to the value of $1,344,566 to British North America, and received imports of the value of $468,346. These figures show that a very considerable trade is carried on between Canada and the West Indies and British Guiana. The Dominion Government offers a reduction of Customs duties for produce grown in the British Colonies, and on this and other grounds it is eminently desirable that closer commercial relations should be encouraged **between the West Indies and Canada.**

INDIAN AND COLONIAL INVESTMENTS*

INVESTMENT securities have made little progress during the past month, but the healthy condition of the markets has been indicated by the resistance they have offered to depressing factors. The revolution in Portugal and the sudden outbreak of the big strike in France were both events which, had markets been less sound, might have produced a much more disturbing effect than was actually the case. The appearance of one or two new issues of competitive securities has been another adverse influence, but even this has produced but little effect on prices. Consols, however, have been an exception, new record low prices having been touched. The Indian Government's policy of issuing its latest loan in short-term bonds instead of the usual inscribed stock has been fully justified by the results. The loan was put up for tender, and the average price obtained for the four millions sterling of 3½ per cent. Bonds was £99 11s. 7d. Thus the Government obtains its money at interest amounting to just a trifle over 3½ per cent. It would obviously have had to pay much more onerous terms if it had issued 3½ per cent. Stock, the market price of which is about 93½.

INDIAN GOVERNMENT SECURITIES.

Title.	Present Amount.	When Redeemable.	Price.	Yield.	Interest Payable.
INDIA.	£				
3½% Stock (t) . . .	85,304,848	1931	93¾	3⅟₁₆	Quarterly.
3% „ (t) . . .	66,724,530	1948	80½	3⅟₁₆	„
2½% „ Inscribed (t)	11,892,207	1926	67¾	3⅟₁₆	„
3½% Rupee Paper 1854–5	..	(a)	94½	3⅟₁₆	30 June—31 Dec.
3% „ „ 1896–7	..	1916	79½	3¾	30 June—30 Dec.

(t) Eligible for Trustee investments.
(a) Redeemable at a Quarter's notice.

* The tabular matter in this article will appear month by month, the figures being corrected to date. Stocks eligible for Trustee investments are so designated.— ED.

INDIAN RAILWAYS AND BANKS.

Title.	Subscribed.	Last year's dividend.	Share or Stock.	Price.	Yield.
RAILWAYS.	£				
Assam—Bengal, L., guaranteed 3%	1,500,000	3	100	79	3 3/4
Bengal and North-Western (Limited)	3,000,000	7 1/2	100	142 1/2	5 1/4
Bengal Dooars, L.	400,000	4 1/2	100	87	5 1/8
Bengal Nagpur (L), gtd. 4% + 1/4th profits	3,000,000	5	100	102	4 7/8
Burma Guar. 2 1/2% and propn. of profits	3,000,000	5 1/4	100	108	4 13/16
Delhi Umballa Kalka, L., guar. 3 1/2% + net earnings	800,000	7	100	144 3/4	4 13/16
East Indian Def. ann. cap. g. 4% + 1/5 sur. profits (t)	1,912,804	5 7/20	100	96	5 9/16
Do. do, class "D," repayable 1953 (t)	4,637,196	4 3/4	100	111	4 1/4
Do. 4 1/2% perpet. deb. stock (t)	1,435,650	4 1/2	100	116	3 7/8
Do. new 3% deb. red. (t)	8,000,000	3	100	79x	3 1/4
Great Indian Peninsula 4% deb. Stock (t)	2,701,450	4	100	106	3 3/4
Do. 3% Gua. and 1/20 surp. profits 1925 (t)	2,575,000	3	100	99	3
Indian Mid. L. gua. 4% & 1/4 surp. profits (t)	2,250,000	4	100	100	4
Madras and South Mahratta	5,000,000	4	100	102 1/2	3 7/8
Nizam's State Rail. Gtd. 5% Stock	2,000,000	5	100	110	4 1/2
Do. 3 1/2% red. mort. debs.	1,074,700	3 1/2	100	85	4 1/16
Rohilkund and Kumaon, Limited	400,000	7	100	130	5 3/8
South Behar, Limited	379,580	5	100	103	4 13/16
South Indian 4 1/2% per. deb. stock, gtd.	425,000	4 1/2	100	118	3 13/16
Do. capital stock	1,000,000	7 1/2	100	104 3/4	7 1/8
Southern Punjab, Limited	1,000,000	7 1/2	100	136 1/2	5 7/16
Do. 3 1/2% deb. stock red.	500,000	3 1/2	100	86	4 1/16
West of India Portuguese Guar. L.	800,000	5	100	95	5 1/4
Do. 5% debenture stock	550,000	5	100	100 1/2	4 15/16
BANKS.	Number of Shares.				
Chartered Bank of India, Australia, and China	60,000	14	20	57 1/2	4 13/16
National Bank of India	64,000	12	12 1/2	46	3 1/4

(t) Eligible for Trustee investments.
(x) Ex dividend.

Canada has been represented in the new issue market by an offer of a million sterling of City of Montreal 4 per cent. Stock at 101½, which brings the City's Consolidated Debt up to nearly nine millions sterling. Its rateable value, however, is over fifty-five millions sterling; the rate of taxation, apart from the school rate, is at present only 1 per cent., and the waterworks and other properties owned by the city amount to over three millions sterling.

Considerable interest attaches, of course, to the Canadian Pacific President's remarks, at the annual meeting in Montreal, on the vexed question of the disposal of the company's land assets and their proceeds. After dealing with the results of the railway undertaking Sir Thomas Shaughnessy said: "Apart from your surplus earnings you have extraneous assets in deferred payments or land mortgages, cash proceeds of land sales and other items of a like character in process of realisation that may be roughly estimated at fifty million dollars, without taking into account your unsold lands, and in the ordinary course this amount should be substantially augmented within the next few years. In the opinion of your directors the best interests of the company and its shareholders will be subserved by keeping intact a considerable portion of these assets instead of resorting to the policy ordinarily characterised as melon-cutting, which has not always proved a boon to the beneficiaries."

This seems an eminently sound course at the present juncture. But there still remains the question of the current income which these assets produce, and which is much in excess of the 1 per cent. per annum distributed to the shareholders in respect of the land branch of the company's undertaking. With regard to these

CANADIAN GOVERNMENT SECURITIES.

Title.	Present Amount.	When Redeemable.	Price.	Yield.	Interest Payable.
4% Intercolonial } Guaranteed by Great Britain.	1,341,400	1910	101	—	1 Apr.—1 Oct.
4% ,, } Guaranteed by Great Britain.	1,700,000	1913	101	3⅝	1 Apr.—1 Oct.
3½% 1884 Regd. Stock	4,676,830	1909–34	100	—	1 June—1 Dec.
3% Inscribed Stock (t)	8,594,877	1938	91	3½	1 Jan.—1 July.
2½% ,, ,, (t)	1,592,105	1947	76	3 11/16	1 Apr.—1 Oct.
PROVINCIAL.					
BRITISH COLUMBIA.					
3% Inscribed Stock .	2,045,760	1941	85½	3 13/16	1 Jan.—1 July.
MANITOBA.					
5% Sterling Bonds .	308,000	1923	109	4 3/16	1 Jan.—1 July.
4% ,, Debs. .	205,000	1928	102	3⅞	1 May—1 Nov.
NOVA SCOTIA.					
3% Stock	164,000	1949	81	4	1 Jan.—1 July.
QUEBEC.					
3% Inscribed . . .	1,897,820	1937	84	3 15/16	1 Apr.—1 Oct.
MUNICIPAL.					
Hamilton (City of) 4%	482,800	1934	100	4	1 Apr.—1 Oct.
Montreal 3% Deb. Stock	1,440,000	permanent	80x	3¾	1 May—1 Nov.
Do. 4% Cons. ,, .	1,821,917	1932	102x	3 13/16	1 May—1 Nov.
Quebec 4% Debs. . .	385,000	1923	101	4	1 Jan.—1 July.
Do. 3½% Con. Stock .	504,196	drawings	92	3 13/16	1 Jan.—1 July.
Toronto 5% Con. Debs.	136,700	1919–20*	106	4 5/16	1 Jan.—1 July.
Do. 4% Stg. Bonds .	300,910	1922–28*	101	4	1 Jan.—1 July.
Do. 3½% Bonds . .	1,169,844	1929	93	4 1/16	1 Jan.—1 July.
Vancouver 4% Bonds	121,200	1931	100	4	1 Apr.—1 Oct.
Do. 4% 40-year Bonds	117,200	1932	100	4	7 Feb.—7 Aug.
Winnipeg 5% Debs. .	138,000	1914	103	4 9/16	30 Apr.—31 Oct.

(t) Eligible for Trustee investments.
* Yield calculated on earlier date of redemption.
(x) Ex dividend.

CANADIAN RAILWAYS, BANKS AND COMPANIES.

Title.	Number of Shares or Amount.	Dividend for last Year.	Paid up per Share.	Price.	Yield
RAILWAYS.		%			
Canadian Pacific Shares . .	1,800,000	7	$100	202	3$\frac{7}{8}$
Do. 4% Preference	£11,328,082	4	Stock	105	3$\frac{3}{4}$
Do. 5% Stg. 1st Mtg. Bd. 1915	£7,191,500	5	,,	106$\frac{1}{2}$	3$\frac{1}{2}$
Do. 4% Cons. Deb. Stock . .	£25,315,001	4	,,	108	3$\frac{11}{16}$
Grand Trunk Ordinary . .	£22,475,985	nil.	,,	27$\frac{3}{8}$	nil.
Do. 5% 1st Preference . . .	£3,420,000	5	,,	111	4$\frac{1}{2}$
Do. 5% 2nd ,, . . .	£2,530,000	5	,,	99$\frac{1}{2}$	5
Do. 4% 3rd ,, . . .	£7,168,055	nil.	,,	57	nil.
Do. 4% Guaranteed . . .	£9,840,011	4	,,	93$\frac{1}{2}$	4$\frac{1}{4}$
Do. 5% Perp. Deb. Stock . .	£4,270,375	5	,,	126	3$\frac{15}{16}$
Do. 4% Cons. Deb. Stock . .	£15,821,571	4	,,	101$\frac{1}{2}$	3$\frac{15}{16}$
BANKS AND COMPANIES.					
Bank of Montreal	140,000	10	$100	251	4
Bank of British North America	20,000	7	50	76$\frac{1}{2}$	4$\frac{9}{16}$
Canadian Bank of Commerce .	200,000	9	$50	£21	4$\frac{7}{16}$
Canada Company	8,319	30s. per sh.	1	28	5$\frac{5}{16}$
Hudson's Bay	100,000	80s. per sh.	10*	102	3$\frac{7}{8}$
Trust and Loan of Canada .	75,000	8	5	6$\frac{3}{8}$	6$\frac{1}{4}$
Do. new	25,000	8	3	3$\frac{1}{4}$	7$\frac{3}{8}$
British Columbia Elec-) Def.	£600,000	8	Stock	139	5$\frac{3}{4}$
tric Railway . . . ∫ Prefd.	£600,000	6	Stock	119	5

* £1 capital repaid 1904.

NEWFOUNDLAND GOVERNMENT SECURITIES.

Title.	Present Amount.	When Redeemable.	Price.	Yield.	Interest Payable.
3$\frac{1}{2}$% Sterling Bonds .	2,178,800	1941-7-8†	93	3$\frac{7}{8}$	
3% Sterling ,, .	325,000	1947	80	4$\frac{1}{16}$	
4% Inscribed Stock .	320,000	1913-38*	101	4	1 Jan.—1 July.
4% ,, ,, .	455,647	1935	105	3$\frac{11}{16}$	
4% Cons. Ins. ,, .	200,000	1936	104	3$\frac{13}{16}$	

* Yield calculated on earlier date of redemption.
† Yield calculated on latest date.

the President agrees that " there is every reason why the share-holders of the present day should expect such advantage in the way of income from those assets as may be possible without unduly encroaching on the principal," and he adds that it is the intention of the directors to determine during the coming year how this can best be brought about. Thus by the time the next meeting comes round, the shareholders should be in possession of the directors' proposals. There is an idea that some announcement may be made at no distant date.

‚ In the Grand Trunk report, supplementing the preliminary profit statement previously published, it is shown that the engine and car renewal suspense account had been reduced by June 30 to £75,578, sums amounting to £122,117 having been charged against the half-year's revenue to diminish this account. Moreover, ten passenger engines and one dining and six first-class passenger cars were built, and thirty-five freight engines and ten baggage cars purchased, on revenue account, no additions to the rolling stock having been made at the expense of capital during the half-year. All this, of course, constitutes a further step towards putting the capital account on a sounder basis.

Western Australia, with its liberal offers of free grants of farm lands, and its Agricultural Bank making advances to farmers for improvements and stocking, is one of the foremost exponents of the policy of assisted colonisation, and some figures recently

AUSTRALIAN GOVERNMENT SECURITIES.

Title.	Present Amount.	When Redeemable.	Price.	Yield.	Interest Payable.
NEW SOUTH WALES.					
4% Inscribed Stock (*t*)	9,686,300	1933	105	$3\frac{11}{16}$	1 Jan.—1 July.
3½% „ „ (*t*)	16,464,545	1924	98	$3\frac{11}{16}$	}1 Apr.—1 Oct.
3% „ „ (*t*)	12,480,000	1935	86½	$3\frac{13}{16}$	
VICTORIA.					
4% Inscribed, 1885 .	5,970,000	1920	102	$3\frac{7}{8}$	
3½% „ 1889 (*t*)	5,000,000	1921–6*	98	$3\frac{3}{4}$	}1 Jan.—1 July.
4% ' . . .	2,107,000	1911–26*	101	4	
3% „ (*t*) . .	5,211,331	1929–49†	85½	$3\frac{11}{16}$	
QUEENSLAND.					
4% Bonds	10,267,400	1913–15*	101¼	$3\frac{13}{16}$	
4% Inscribed Stock (*t*)	7,939,000	1924	102¼	$3\frac{13}{16}$	}1 Jan.—1 July.
3½% „ „ (*t*)	8,616,034	1921–30†	98	$3\frac{6}{8}$	
3% „ „ (*t*)	4,274,213	1922–47†	84½	$3\frac{13}{16}$	
SOUTH AUSTRALIA.					
4% Bonds	1,359,300	1916	100	4	}1 Apr.—1 Oct.
4% Inscribed Stock .	6,269,000	1916–7–36*	101	$3\frac{13}{16}$	
3½% „ „ (*t*)	2,517,800	1939	98½	$3\frac{9}{16}$	
3% „ „ (*t*)	839,500	1916–26‡	89½	$3\frac{5}{16}$	}1 Jan.—1 July.
3% „ „ (*t*)	2,760,100	1916 ‡ or after.	83½	$3\frac{1}{16}$	
WESTERN AUSTRALIA.					
4% Inscribed . . .	1,876,000	1911–31*	100	4	15 Apr.—15 Oct.
3½% „ (*t*) . .	3,780,000	1920–35†	96	$3\frac{13}{16}$	}1 May—1 Nov.
3% „ (*t*) . .	3,750,000	1915–35‡	86½	$3\frac{1}{2}$	
3% „ (*t*) . .	2,500,000	1927‡	89½	$3\frac{5}{16}$	15 Jan.—15 July.
TASMANIA.					
3½% Inscbd. Stock (*t*)	4,156,500	1920–40*	99	$3\frac{5}{8}$	
4% „ „	1,000,000	1920–40*	102¼	$3\frac{13}{16}$	}1 Jan.—1 July.
3% . . . . . (*t*)	450,000	1920–40†	86	$3\frac{13}{16}$	

* Yield calculated on earlier date of redemption.
† Yield calculated on later date of redemption, though a portion of the loan may be redeemed earlier.
‡ No allowance for redemption.
(*t*) **Eligible for Trustee Investment.**

AUSTRALIAN MUNICIPAL AND OTHER BONDS.

Title.	Present Amount.	When Redeemable.	Price.	Yield.	Interest Payable.
Melbourne & Met. Bd. of Works 4% Debs.	1,000,000	1921	100	4	1 Apl.—1 Oct.
Do. City 4% Deb.	850,000	1915-22*	102	3¾	1 Jan.—1 July.
Melbourne Trams Trust 4½% Debs.	1,650,000	1914-16*	102	4 3/16	1 Jan.—1 July.
S. Melbourne 4½% Debs.	128,700	1919	102	4 5/16	1 Jan.—1 July.
Sydney 4% Debs. . .	640,000	1912-13	101	4	1 Jan.—1 July.
Do. 4% Debs. . . .	300,000	1919	101	4	1 Jan.—1 July.

* Yield calculated on earlier date of redemption.

AUSTRALIAN RAILWAYS, BANKS AND COMPANIES.

Title.	Number of Shares or Amount.	Dividend for last Year.	Paid up.	Price.	Yield.
Railways.		%			
Emu Bay and Mount Bischoff . . .	12,000	6	5	4½	6⅝
Do. 4½% Irred. Deb. Stock	£130,900	4½	100	97	4⅝
Mid. of W. Aust. 4% Debs., Guartd. .	300,000	4	100	100	4
Banks and Companies.					
Bank of Australasia	40,000	14	40	115	4 13/16
Bank of New South Wales	125,000	10	20	45	4 7/16
Union Bank of Australia £75 . . .	60,000	14	25	63½	5½
Do. 4% Inscribed Stock Deposits . .	£600,000	4	100	99	4
Australian Mort. Land & Finance £25	80,000	12½	5	7¼	8 9/16
Do. 4% Perp. Deb. Stock	£1,900,000	4	100	100½	3 15/16
Dalgety & Co. £20	154,000	7	5	5¾	6 1/16
Do. 4½% Irred. Deb. Stock	£620,000	4½	100	108	4⅛
Goldsbrough Mort & Co. 4% A Deb. Stock Reduced	£1,067,137	4	100	87½	4 9/16
Do. B Income Reduced	£711,340	5½	100	97	5⅝
Australian Agricultural £25 . . .	20,000	£4	21½	74	5⅜
South Australian Company . . .	14,200	16¼	20	66½	4⅞
Trust & Agency of Australasia . . .	42,479	7½	1	¾	10
Do. 5% Cum. Pref.	87,500	5	10	9¾	5⅛

NEW ZEALAND GOVERNMENT SECURITIES.

Title.	Present Amount.	When Redeemable.	Price.	Yield.	Interest Payable.
5% Bonds	266,300	1914	104	4⅛	15 Jan.—15 July.
4% Inscribed Stock (*t*)	29,150,302	1929	103½	3 13/16	1 May—1 Nov.
3½% Stock (*t*) . . .	13,754,532	1940	98½	3 9/16	1 Jan.—1 July.
3% Inscribed Stock (*t*)	9,659,980	1945	86½	3 11/16	1 Apr.—1 Oct.

(*t*) Eligible for Trustee investments.

quoted by the Minister of Lands indicate that its policy bears excellent fruit. Whereas the harvest of 1909 was a harvest of 585,339 acres, the 1910 crop was taken from 722,086 acres, an increase of 136,747 acres, while in the latter year there were 100,000 acres more lying fallow than in the preceding year. The next harvest, moreover, will be from 900,000 acres. The Minister further stated that if the labour is available, no less than half a million acres will be cleared during the coming season, against 223,000 acres prepared during the previous year.

NEW ZEALAND MUNICIPAL AND OTHER SECURITIES.

Title.	Present Amount.	When Redeemable.	Price.	Yield.	Interest Payable.
Auckland 5% Deb. .	200,000	1934–8*	109	$4\frac{7}{16}$	1 Jan.—1 July.
Do. Hbr. Bd. 5% Debs.	150,000	1917	104x	$4\frac{5}{16}$	10 April—10 Oct.
Bank of N. Z. shares†	150,000	div. 12½%	10½	$3\frac{13}{16}$	—
Do. 4% Gua. Stock‡ .	£1,000,000	1914	102	$3\frac{1}{16}$	April—Oct.
Christchurch 6% Drainage Loan. .	200,000	1926	121	$4\frac{1}{4}$	30 June—31 Dec.
Lyttleton Hbr. Bd. 6%	200,000	1929	121	$4\frac{7}{16}$	
Napier Hbr. Bd. 5% Debs. . . .	300,000	1920	104	$4\frac{9}{16}$	} 1 Jan.—1 July.
Do. 5% Debs. . . .	200,000	1923	104	$4\frac{11}{16}$	
National Bank of N.Z. £7½ Shares £2½ paid	150,000	div. 12%	5½	$5\frac{7}{16}$	Jan.—July.
Oamaru 5% Bds. . .	173,800	1920	94	$5\frac{15}{16}$	1 Jan.—1 July.
Otago Hbr. Cons. Bds. 5%	443,100	1934	105	$4\frac{11}{16}$	1 Jan.—1 July.
Wellington 6% Impts. Loan . . .	100,000	1914–29	108	—	1 Mar.—1 Sept.
Do. 6% Waterworks .	130,000	1929	118	$4\frac{9}{16}$	1 Mar.—1 Sept.
Do. 4½% Debs. . .	165,000	1933	104	$4\frac{5}{16}$	1 May—1 Nov.
Westport Hbr. 4% Debs.	150,000	1925	100	4	1 Mar.—1 Sept.

* Yield calculated on earlier date of redemption.
† £6 13s. 4d. Shares with £3 6s. 8d. paid up.
‡ Guaranteed by New Zealand Government.
(x) Ex dividend.

SOUTH AFRICAN GOVERNMENT SECURITIES.

Title.	Present Amount.	When Redeemable.	Price.	Yield.	Interest Payable.
CAPE COLONY.	£				
4½% Bonds . . .	485,000	dwgs.	101x	$4\frac{7}{16}$	15 Apr.—15 Oct.
4% 1883 Inscribed .	3,733,195	1923	103½	$3\frac{7}{8}$	1 June—1 Dec.
4% 1886 ,, .	9,997,566	1916–36*	100½	$3\frac{7}{8}$	15 Apr.—15 Oct.
3½% 1886 ,, (t).	15,443,014	1929–49†	100	$3\frac{1}{2}$	1 Jan.—1 July.
3% 1886 ,, (t).	7,553,590	1933–43†	87	$3\frac{11}{16}$	1 Feb.—1 Aug.
NATAL.					
4½% Bonds, 1876 . .	758,700	1919	103	$4\frac{1}{16}$	15 Mar.—15 Sep.
4% Inscribed (t) . .	3,026,444	1937	106	$3\frac{11}{16}$	Apr.—Oct.
3½% ,, (t) . .	3,714,917	1914–39†	98½	$3\frac{5}{8}$	1 June—1 Dec.
3% ,, (t) . .	6,000,000	1929–49†	86	$3\frac{11}{16}$	1 Jan.—1 July.
TRANSVAAL.					
3% Guartd. Stock (t) .	35,000,000	1923–53†	92	$3\frac{3}{8}$	1 May—1 Nov.

* Yield calculated on earlier date of redemption.
† Yield calculated on later date of redemption.
(t) Eligible for Trustee investments.
(x) Ex dividend.

Although the gold output from the Transvaal during September was a little less than that for August, the daily average showed an increase, and was, in fact, the highest on record, allowing for the inclusion of reserve gold in the record monthly return of December 1908.   This table gives the returns month by month for several years past :

Month.	1910.	1909.	1908.	1907.	1906.	1905.
	£	£	£	£	£	£
January . .	2,554,451	2,612,836	2,380,124	2,283,741	1,820,739	1,568,508
February . .	2,445,088	2,400,892	2,301,971	2,096,434	1,731,664	1,545,371
March . .	2,578,877	2,580,498	2,442,022	2,287,391	1,884,815	1,698,340
April . . .	2,629,535	2,578,804	2,403,500	2,281,110	1,865,785	1,695,550
May . . .	2,693,785	2,652,699	2,472,143	2,227,838	1,959,062	1,768,734
June . . .	2,655,602	2,621,818	2,442,329	2,155,976	2,021,813	1,751,412
July . . .	2,713,083	2,636,965	2,482,608	2,262,813	2,089,004	1,781,944
August . .	2,757,919	2,597,646	2,496,869	2,357,602	2,162,583	1,820,496
September .	2,747,853	2,575,760	2,496,112	2,285,424	2,145,575	1,769,124
October . .	—	2,558,902	2,624,012	2,351,344	2,296,361	1,765,047
November .	—	2,539,146	2,609,685	2,335,406	2,265,625	1,804,253
December .	—	2,569,822	2,806,235	2,478,659	2,336,961	1,833,295
Total * .	23,776,193	30,925,788	29,957,610	27,403,738	24,579,987	20,802,074

* Including undeclared amounts omitted from the monthly returns.

During September there was an encouraging increase in the native labour supply of the Transvaal gold mines, the month's gain being 1,369 hands, whereas during the corresponding month of last year there was a loss of 2,064.   This statement shows the variations in the supply during the past two years :

Month.	Natives Joined.	Natives Left.	Net Gain on Month.	Natives Employed end of Month.	Chinese Employed end of Month.
September 1908	14,129	11,497	2,632	136,180	14,655
October ,,	14,754	11,769	2,985	139,165	12,317
November ,,	12,324	10,163	2,161	141,326	12,298
December ,,	17,404	10,008	7,396	148,722	12,283
January 1909	13,551	11,609	1,942	150,664	10,045
February ,,	18,018	10,844	7,174	157,838	10,034
March ,,	16,184	11,979	4,205	162,043	9,997
April ,,	12,102	11,244	858	162,901	7,734
May ,,	7,717	12,339	4,622*	158,279	7,717
June ,,	8,335	12,354	4,019*	154,260	5,378
July ,,	7,826	12,612	4,786*	149,474	5,370
August ,,	10,089	12,642	2,553*	146,291	5,361
September ,,	11,747	13,811	2,064*	144,857	3,204
October ,,	14,656	13,762	894	152,563‡	3,199
November ,,	13,942	13,742	200	152,763	1,799
December ,,	17,293	13,348	3,945	156,708	nil.
January 1910	—	—	3,954	160,662	nil.
February ,,	—	—	9,109	169,771	nil.
March ,,	—	—	8,574	178,345	nil.
April ,,	—	—	5,469	183,814	nil.
May ,,	—	—	150	183,964	nil.
June ,,	—	—	533*	183,431	nil.
July ,,	—	—	1,917*	181,514	nil.
August ,,	—	—	688*	180,831	nil.
September ,,	—	—	1,369	182,200	nil.

* Net loss.   ‡ Including new members of Native Labour Association.

SOUTH AFRICAN RAILWAYS, BANKS, AND COMPANIES.

Title.	Number of Shares or Amount.	Dividend for last Year.	Paid up.	Price.	Yield.
RAILWAYS.					
Mashonaland 5% Debs.	£2,500,000	5	100	97	$5\frac{1}{8}$
Rhodesia Rlys. 5% 1st Mort. Debs. guar. by B.S.A. Co. till 1915. . .	£2,000,000	5	100	102	$4\frac{7}{8}$
Royal Trans-African 5% Debs. Rep. .	£1,853,700	5	100	$88\frac{1}{2}$	$5\frac{5}{8}$
BANKS AND COMPANIES.					
African Banking Corporation £10 shares	80,000	$5\frac{1}{2}$	5	$4\frac{7}{8}$	$5\frac{5}{8}$
Bank of Africa £$18\frac{3}{4}$	160,000	5	$6\frac{1}{4}$	7	$4\frac{7}{16}$
Natal Bank £10	148,232	8	$2\frac{1}{2}$	$3\frac{1}{2}$	$5\frac{11}{16}$
National Bank of S. Africa £10 . .	110,000	3	10	$12\frac{1}{4}$	$2\frac{7}{16}$
Standard Bank of S. Africa £100 . .	61,941	10	25	$63\frac{1}{2}$	$3\frac{15}{16}$
Ohlsson's Cape Breweries	60,000	nil	5	$4\frac{1}{4}$	—
South African Breweries	965,279	10	1	$1\frac{5}{8}$	$6\frac{1}{8}$
British South Africa (Chartered) . .	8,053,481	nil	1	$1\frac{19}{32}$	nil
Do. 5% Debs. Red.	£1,250,000	5	100	105	$4\frac{3}{4}$
Natal Land and Colonization . . .	68,066	4	5	$4\frac{1}{4}$	$4\frac{11}{16}$
Cape Town & District Gas Light & Coke	10,000	nil	10	$3\frac{1}{2}$	—
Kimberley Waterworks £10 . . .	45,000	5	7	$5x$	7

Rhodesia's gold output for September amounted to £178,950, a decrease of £12,473 as compared with August. The number of producing mines, it was pointed out, decreased by thirty-seven in consequence of the fact that several mines hitherto worked on a small scale by individuals have developed so satisfactorily that they have been taken over by large companies and are now closed down pending the erection of larger milling plants. This table gives the monthly returns for several years past:

MONTH.	1910.	1909.	1908.	1907.	1906.
	£	£	£	£	£
January . .	227,511	204,666	199,380	168,240	155,337
February . .	203,888	192,497	191,635	145,397	137,561
March . . .	228,385	202,157	200,615	167,424	160,722
April . . .	228,213	222,700	212,935	175,210	157,108
May . . .	224,888	225,032	223,867	189,216	169,218
June . . .	214,709	217,600	224,920	192,506	170,083
July . . .	195,233	225,234	228,151	191,681	173,313
August . . .	191,423	228,296	220,792	192,106	179,000
September. .	178,950	213,249	204,262	192,186	173,973
October . .	—	222,653	205,466	191,478	161,360
November . .	—	236,307	196,668	183,058	175,656
December . .	—	233,397	217,316	190,383	171,770
Total .	1,893,200	2,623,788	2,526,007	2,178,885	1,985,101

Two or three of the Crown Colonies, it is believed, are contemplating new issues. The Straits Settlements has already brought out its $2\frac{3}{4}$ millions sterling of $3\frac{1}{2}$ per cent. stock at $95\frac{1}{2}$.

SOUTH AFRICAN MUNICIPAL SECURITIES.

Title.	Present Amount.	When Redeemable.	Price.	Yield.	Interest Payable.
	£				
Bloemfontein 4% . .	763,000	1954	99	4$\frac{1}{16}$	1 Jan.—1 July.
Cape Town 4% . .	1,861,750	1953	103	3$\frac{7}{8}$	1 Jan.—1 July.
Durban 4% . . .	850,000	1951–3	101	4	30 June—31 Dec.
Johannesburg 4% .	5,500,000	1933–4	100	4	1 April—1 Oct.
Krugersdorp 4% . .	100,000	1930	96	4$\frac{3}{8}$	1 June—1 Dec.
Pietermaritzburg 4%	825,000	1949–53	100	4	30 June—31 Dec.
Port Elizabeth 4% .	374,060	1964	100	4	30 June—31 Dec.
Pretoria 4% . . .	1,000,000	1939	101	4	1 Jan.—1 July.
Rand Water Board 4%	3,400,000	1935	101	4	1 Jan.—1 July.

Although a trustee investment yielding £3 14s. per cent., the stock was not readily absorbed by the market. The proceeds are

CROWN COLONY SECURITIES.

Title.	Present Amount.	When Redeemable.	Price.	Yield.	Interest Payable.
Barbadoes 3$\frac{1}{2}$% ins. (t)	375,000	1925–42*	96	3$\frac{13}{12}$	1 Mar.—1 Sep.
Brit. Guiana 3% ins. (t)	250,000	1923–45†	85	3$\frac{13}{16}$	1 Feb.—1 Aug.
Ceylon 4% ins. (t). .	1,076,100	1934	107	3$\frac{9}{16}$	15 Feb.—15 Aug.
Do. 3% ins. (t). . .	2,850,000	1940	85	3$\frac{5}{8}$	1 May—1 Nov.
Hong-Kong 3$\frac{1}{2}$% ins (t)	1,485,733	1918–43†	97	3$\frac{5}{8}$	15 Apr.—15 Oct.
Jamaica 4% ins. (t) .	1,099,048	1934	106	3$\frac{5}{8}$	15 Feb.—15 Aug.
Do. 3$\frac{1}{2}$% ins. (t) .	1,455,500	1919–49†	97	3$\frac{5}{8}$	24 Jan.—24 July.
Mauritius 3% guar. \ Great Britain (t) ./	600,000	1940	93	3$\frac{3}{4}$	1 Jan.—1 July.
Do. 4% ins. (t). . .	482,390	1937	106	3$\frac{5}{8}$	1 Feb.—1 Aug.
Sierra Leone 3$\frac{1}{2}$% ins.(t)	720,051	1929–54†	98$\frac{1}{2}$	3$\frac{9}{16}$	1 June—1 Dec.
Trinidad 4% ins. . .	422,593	1917–42*	102	3$\frac{5}{8}$	15 Mar.—15 Sep.
Do. 3% ins. (t). . .	600,000	1922–44†	86	3$\frac{1}{4}$	15 Jan.—15 July.
Hong-Kong & Shang- \ hai Bank Shares ./	120,000	Div. £4$\frac{1}{4}$	£86$\frac{1}{2}$	4$\frac{7}{8}$	Feb.—Aug.

* Yield calculated on shorter period.   † Yield calculated on longer period.

(t) Eligible for Trustee investments.

RUBBER SHARES.

Company.	Issued Capital.	Area planted.	Nominal Value of Share.	Amount paid-up.	Price.
	£	Acres.			
Anglo-Malay	150,000	3,391	2s.	2s.	23s. 6d. x.d.
Batu Tiga	60,000	1,545	£1	£1	4$\frac{5}{8}$ x.d.
Bukit Rajah	66,700	2,772	£1	£1	15$\frac{1}{4}$ x.d.
Consolidated Malay . . .	62,007	1,710	£1	2s.	24s. 9d.
Highlands and Lowlands .	317,353	4,707	£1	£1	5$\frac{1}{16}$ x.d.
Kepitigalla	225,000	3,127	£1	£1	$\frac{15}{16}$
Kuala Lumpur	180,000	2,611	£1	£1	8$\frac{1}{8}$
Lanadron	269,780	4,570	£1	£1	5$\frac{5}{8}$
Linggi	100,000	4,192	2s.	2s.	43s. 6d.
Pataling.	22,500	1,454	2s.	2s.	2$\frac{11}{16}$
Straits (Bertam)	200,000	2,541	2s.	2s.	7s. 6d.
Vallambrosa	50,600	1,807	2s.	2s.	39s.

to be employed mainly on the extensions of the Tanjong Pagar Docks and the construction of the Singapore Harbour works. The trade of the colony is deriving considerable benefit from the greatly increased production of rubber.

EGYPTIAN SECURITIES.

Title.	Amount or Number of Shares.	Dividend for last Year.	Paid up.	Price.	Yield.
Egyptian Govt. Guaranteed Loan (t) .	£7,414,700	3	99	96	$3\frac{1}{16}$
„ Unified Debt	£55,971,960	4	100	$101\frac{1}{2}$	$3\frac{7}{8}$
National Bank of Egypt	300,000	9	10	$20\frac{3}{4}$	$4\frac{5}{16}$
Bank of Egypt	50,000	15	$12\frac{1}{2}$	$30\frac{1}{4}$	$6\frac{1}{8}$
Agricultural Bank of Egypt, Ordinary	496,000	$5\frac{1}{4}$	5	$7\frac{7}{8}$	$3\frac{7}{16}$
„ „ „ Preferred	125,000	4	10	$9\frac{1}{8}$	$4\frac{3}{8}$
„ „ „ Bonds .	£2,350,000	$3\frac{1}{2}$	100	85	$4\frac{1}{16}$

(t) Eligible for Trustee investments.

TRUSTEE.

October 21, 1910.

NOTICE TO CONTRIBUTORS.—The Editor of THE EMPIRE REVIEW cannot hold himself responsible in any case for the return of MS. He will, however, always be glad to consider any contributions which may be submitted to him; and when postage-stamps are enclosed every effort will be made to return rejected contributions promptly. Contributors are specially requested to put their names and addresses on their manuscripts, and to have them typewritten.

THE EMPIRE REVIEW

"Far as the breeze can bear, the billows foam,
Survey our empire, and behold our home."—*Byron.*

VOL. XX.   DECEMBER, 1910.   No. 119

THE FRONT DOOR OF AUSTRALIA

By F. A. W. GISBORNE

(Our Special Correspondent in Australia)

FACING the most populous regions on the earth's surface and separated from them only by the labyrinthine waters of the Malay Archipelago with narrow fringes of sea on either side, the north coast of Australia, in a geographical as well as political sense, is really the main façade of the continent. The splendid harbour of Port Darwin is its chief entrance. Northwards and westwards, within seven days' steaming distance of the most youthful, in regard to development, of the great habitable divisions of the globe, lie some of the most ancient civilisations that exist, and the most populous countries on the face of the earth.

The continent of the past stretches across the threshold of the continent of the future; excess of human life is to be found within 'a few days' travel of emptiness and solitude. The comparatively populous portions of Australia face far-sweeping oceans; a long and uninhabited coast in the north beckons to its shores the exuberant life of the East with its bustling and multitudinous activities. These and other considerations fasten themselves on the voyager's mind as his vessel ploughs through the green and turbid waters of the Arafura Sea on its way to Port Darwin. They suggest reflections of a more painful and sinister nature when attention is given to the portentous development of military and naval power that characterises the present age, and the continual lessening of distances by the increase of speed.

The vast regions known by the name of the Northern
Territory measures roughly 900 miles by 560 miles and possesses
a total length of coast-line of about 1,240 miles. Its area,
considerably exceeding half a million square miles, is about four
and a half times that of the United Kingdom. Its present
population amounts to barely a thousand white men and twice as
many Chinese. The only settlement it possesses worthy to be
called a town is Palmerston, usually styled Darwin by its residents,
or Port Darwin, a place containing in itself nearly one-third of
the total number of civilised inhabitants of the Territory. I
propose to offer the readers of this Review a brief description of
Port Darwin, and a sketch of the potentialities in regard to
production and trade of its hinterland, based on personal observation and on information derived from residents and official sources
in the course of a recent visit to the place.

The north coast of Australia differs essentially from the
eastern seaboard of the Continent in being uniformly low. No
coast range exists, and the country inland rises in a series of
gradual undulations or low terraces and not, as along the shores
of New South Wales and Queensland, with one bold spring to
heights varying from 2,000 to nearly 6,000 feet. This coastal
conformation, by the way, is of distinct advantage to the inland
regions of the north, allowing as it does the north-west monsoon to
distribute its pluvial favours fairly equally over enormous areas
in the interior, instead of confining them principally to the coast
belt. About Geraldton in North Queensland, for instance, some
150 inches of rain—occasionally nearly 200—fall annually. Fifty
miles due west of that locality the country languishes under a
meagre yearly dole of from ten to fifteen inches. Deluge and
drought thus exist side by side. On the other hand, it has been
computed that of the entire area of the Northern Territory only
6,300 square miles of country receive less than ten inches of rain
annually, 213,430 square miles receive from ten to twenty inches,
a fair allowance for pastoral purposes ; 96,790 from twenty to
thirty inches ; 120,600 from thirty to forty ; while the remaining
86,500 square miles, the distinctively tropical division of the
Territory, enjoy a yearly rainfall varying from fifty to rather over
eighty inches. Thus the extremes of humidity and aridity to
be found in other parts of Australia do not prevail in the
great northern province, a difference much to the latter's
advantage.

The entrance to Port Darwin is wide, about eight miles, and
there is no bar or obstruction of any kind except one small reef
so situated as to be of no danger whatever to navigation. Two
low mangrove-edged projections of the coast named respectively
East and West Point are to be seen on either side. After

steaming southwards up the harbour for about five miles Point Emery is passed, and then the course lies first south-east and then due east. A substantial iron jetty extends about a couple of hundred yards from the shore just below the town, and vessels lying at it, or anchored off shore, are completely sheltered, the harbour being landlocked, deep and spacious. A minimum depth at low tide of about four fathoms is to be found at the end of the present jetty, but a slight extension to it would accommodate the largest vessels in the world. Tidal influences at Port Darwin are strong, the difference between low water and high water level varying from about twenty-two to twenty-six feet. The rapidity of the current, therefore, at times makes the task of safely berthing a vessel at the jetty a little difficult.

Viewed from the sea, Palmerston presents a singularly picturesque appearance. The town is built on a level ironstone tableland elevated about seventy feet above the sea, and against the scarp, sloping abruptly to the beach, lean dense natural groves and shrubberies of a vivid green, with a house here and there nestling among them and a delicately tinted cliff occasionally breaking through the cascades of verdure. The site of the town occupies a small peninsula at the extremity of this low plateau, which terminates in a stretch of beach facing the jetty and flanked by two low detached eminences known as Fort Hill and Stokes' Hill, both of which are but fragments of the main tableland almost detached from it by the action of the sea. Beneath the latter of these hills the railway runs, and it is extended to the end of the jetty. Ascending the gentle rise that leads to the town, about one-third of a mile distant from the end of the jetty, the visitor first finds himself in the Chinese quarter—not a very attractive portion of the place, and one that offers outrage to the nose as well as eye. Palmerston, unfortunately, shows its back-yard rather than its front-garden to the new arrival on first landing, and if the place could be twisted round so that its slum quarter might be decently hidden, a stranger's first impression of it would be more favourable. Disreputable, malodorous blacks, also, slink about dressed in garments whose proper use would be as fertilisers of the soil rather than as clothing. One hundred and fifty or so sorry specimens of the ancient lords of the soil infest the streets and surroundings of Palmerston; and if they could be shipped off to some island, or transferred to some inland reserve, they and their present white neighbours would alike be better off. Very few European stores or places of business are to be seen, though evidences of the activities of the Mongolian trader are tolerably numerous. Three churches, however, exist, and the presence of two banks shows that Mammon, also, does not lack worshippers.

The general plan of the town is excellent, and its position chosen with admirable judgment. The porous reddish soil, sprinkled with ironstone gravel, allows the heaviest rain to soak away almost as rapidly as it falls. The place, by its comparative elevation, is naturally well drained, and there are no unwholesome swamps in its neighbourhood. Water of excellent quality is obtainable everywhere by sinking to depths varying from twenty to forty feet. The streets are wide and run at right angles in north-west and north-east directions. An odd and—to the eye at least—pleasing feature about them is that within a couple of hundred yards of the chief business quarter they plunge into the bush and form wide avenues bordered by the primeval forest, with a bungalow or two at intervals buried among the trees. As to buildings, the most important naturally are those in which Government business is transacted. These, as a rule, are low but substantially built of a very handsome kind of sandstone found in the neighbourhood. The residence of the supreme magistrate is a two-storied stone edifice beautifully situated on the edge of the high ground overlooking the harbour. About half-a-dozen other buildings in the place are built of stone, but galvanised iron is the material most commonly used, for walls as well as roofs. On account of the ravages committed by the white ant, wood is but sparingly employed, and the supports of the buildings are usually embedded in concrete to protect them against the pest. The floors likewise are made of concrete or cement. Broad verandahs surround all the residences, and most of these are completely closed in by means of interlaced strips of bamboo, for the sake of shade and coolness. Verandahs constitute the principal living and sleeping rooms in each house, a few curtains drawn across at intervals forming the necessary divisions. Gardens are not numerous, but each bungalow possesses a small shrubbery, and over its white-washed walls and roof masses of various creepers, the bignonia in particular, frequently riot luxuriantly. But while crowns of bloom and foliage greatly enhance the beauty of a dwelling and tend to coolness, these adornments are said to have the disagreeable effect of attracting innumerable insects, by no means to the comfort of the occupants. Ants and mosquitoes are the two great curses of the place, and the latter undoubtedly are largely responsible for the malaria that occasionally prevails.

As regards temperature, the first two columns of the table below give the highest and lowest readings, in the shade, during each period of twenty-four hours at Port Darwin during the year 1909. In the third column is shown the amount of rainfall in each month of the same year:

	Maximum.	Minimum.	Rainfall.
January	91·6	78·1	15·12 ins.
February	91·4	77·5	6·18 ,,
March	90·4	76·4	9·57 ,,
April	90·8	75·2	8·20 ,,
May	90·0	73·1	·11 ,,
June	89·0	71·9	0 ,,
July	88·6	68·9	0 ,,
August	90·2	72·2	1·09 ,,
September	91·0	73·6	·49 ,,
October	94·3	77·9	2·42 ,,
November	91·5	77·0	10·50 ,,
December	92·3	78·3	5·53 ,,

From the above table it will be seen that the average maximum of temperature at Port Darwin last year was 91° in the shade during the day, and the average minimum at night 75°, which figure represents the lowest mean temperature in the twenty-four hours. The mean temperature day and night throughout the year was 83°. The rainfall this year—rather under 60 inches—was below the normal. As many as 81 inches have been recorded, and the average is probably some 65 inches. The whole of the rain practically falls between the beginning of October and the end of April, December and the three following months being the wettest period of the year. From May to September the south-east, or dry, monsoon prevails, and four months out of these six are usually quite rainless. During the three weeks of my stay in August the thermometer registered over 90° in the shade every day, and once 98° was reached. The temperature at night could seldom have fallen below 80°. It can hardly be denied that these figures strongly support the contention that Port Darwin is not a place where Europeans can be expected to engage in hard and regular manual work. That the local climatic conditions are not favourable to the vitality and energy of the white inhabitants of the place even the most fervent apostle of the White Australia doctrine could hardly deny. Though the death-rate is not abnormal either among adults or children, pale complexions and weedy growths testify plainly to unsuitable climatic conditions. The tired expression is everywhere visible, and there is no energy of movement; practically no pedestrianism is cultivated, and very little manual work of any kind is done. Setting aside, however, the chief cause of the prevailing lethargy, the climate, Palmerston labours under several serious disadvantages in spite of its magnificent situation. On the land side it is completely isolated from the rest of Australia, and the mere stump of a railway it possesses confers very little benefit upon the town. The local trade is small. The total exports of the whole territory for last year were valued at only £278,270, and live stock driven overland to the southern States constituted the bulk of these.

Mail facilities are wretched. Frequently four weeks elapse without any delivery of letters from Europe or the rest of Australia. There is no regular subsidised service; two mails may be delivered within a week, and then a month or more may elapse before the next arrives. Comparatively few vessels call for passengers, and goods are alike scarce.

If we except pearl-shelling, there are no local industries, and the restrictions imposed, since federation, on the employment of coloured labour have considerably reduced the number of vessels engaged in this industry. At present only some twenty-five small luggers are employed, and the total output of shell last year was but sixty tons, with thirty-eight tons of trepang in addition. The commercial and industrial element in the local population is lamentably small; in fact, Government officials and those connected with the Eastern Extension Cable Company constitute a considerable majority of the local inhabitants, and this salaried class does not possess such substantial interests in the place as would encourage efforts to promote its prosperity. New blood of a vigorous enterprising type is needed, for an official *régime* means stagnation. Distance from the seat of government, Adelaide, and fatuous legislation imposed by politicians who are entirely ignorant of the conditions prevailing in a vast, tropical, undeveloped region accentuate the evils already mentioned. Apart from Commonwealth interference with the pearl-shelling industry, a more recent example of petty, unintelligent meddlesomeness may be mentioned. Fish of excellent quantity abound in the waters of the harbour, and hitherto the town has been fairly well supplied with this article of food by local Chinese fishermen. Now orders have been sent from Adelaide that within a short time no further fishing licences shall be issued to coloured men, whites alone, thenceforth, to be allowed to catch fish for sale. The result will certainly be a scarcity of Lenten fare in future. Possibly Chinese gardeners will next be fined for committing the sin of growing fruit and vegetables. Then a large addition to the present hospital accommodation will be required. White Australia as a policy may have its merits. As a fanaticism it threatens not only material loss and physical injury to the comparatively small number of white people living in the Australian tropics, but absolute danger to the future independence and integrity of the whole Commonwealth. It is not prudent under present conditions to adopt an attitude of consistent affront, of petty provocation, towards the representatives of people who outnumber the present population of Australia by more than a hundred to one.

Agriculture practically does not exist yet in the Northern Territory. About two miles out from Port Darwin there are, indeed, some very interesting Botanic Gardens to which the curator, Mr. Holtze, very kindly drove me, and pointed out a number of commercially valuable trees and plants there grown. Among these are to be seen the cocoanut, wine and African oil palm, sisal hemp, rice of several varieties, sugar-cane, cotton, tobacco, patchouli, cinnamon, citronella oil grass, coca, anatto and many different kinds of fruits. Important experiments have been made in particular in the cultivation of sisal hemp and upland or hill rice, products which Mr. Holtze regards as best suited to the climate, soil and labour conditions now prevailing in the Territory, and many thousands of plants of sisal hemp have been distributed among a few settlers with a view to establishing a new industry. It is too soon yet to express an opinion as to whether these experiments will prove successful. Farming in the Northern Territory is still an industry of the future.

The evils of land monopoly and absentee ownership are, unhappily, most pronounced in and about Palmerston. The residents bitterly complain that, owing to unwise profusion in the past, it is now almost imposible to obtain either a town allotment for building on, or a piece of land, within a reasonable distance outside, to cultivate. Both in the town and for many miles along the railway, as well as in other directions, the soil is in the grip of outside speculators, who have done absolutely nothing to improve their properties, and who refuse in most cases to sell an inch of them except on quite preposterous terms. When Palmerston was first founded, it is said, to encourage settlement a large number of half-acre building allotments were sold at a low price, and the purchaser of each allotment received also, by way of bonus, some 320 acres of country land as an absolute freehold, without any conditions as to residence or improvement. The result was that land fell wholesale into the hands of outside speculators, mostly wealthy men who could afford to wait. Among other absentee owners is a prominent British statesman, who owns, I have been informed, sixty town allotments and as many 320-acre blocks of country land besides. The prices asked for the few building sites in the town itself that can be obtained are unreasonably high. Would-be builders cannot obtain land on which to build ; would-be farmers cannot obtain land within easy reach of the town to farm. In the course of the railway journey to Pine Creek and back, a distance of 150 miles each way, I did not see a single animal larger than a goat, and goats were only to be seen near the houses of the railway officials. Not an acre of land was cleared, or fenced, or improved in any way, although the bulk of it was fair pastoral country and permanent waterholes were not infrequent.

The coming Federal land tax will, it is to be hoped, exercise sufficient pressure on the land monopolists to compel them to part with their properties on reasonable terms. At present the expansion of a place which is the natural port of thousands of square miles of territory, and a strategic point of the first importance is being artificially checked solely to subserve private interests. In regard to defensibility the erection of suitable forts armed with modern long-range guns on such points as Point Emery and East Point, supplemented by the use of submarine mines, would ensure to Port Darwin perfect safety from any direct attack by sea. But inasmuch as an enemy in command of the sea could easily land forces at high tide on the open beaches lying outside the harbour, and so take both town and forts in the rear (the abundance of natural cover obtainable would facilitate the operation), it follows that without a powerful garrison in reserve the erection of forts would be absolutely useless. For the effective defence of the place a fleet strong enough to render the task of landing a hostile force of great strength highly hazardous, and a local army strong enough to overpower such invading bodies as might escape the vigilance of the fleet would have to be provided. Both army and fleet would for a long time to come have to be recruited and supported by the southern States, and to enable the necessary men and stores to be expeditiously conveyed to the north, safe from attack by sea, the speedy completion of the trans-continental railway and its early duplication are of most vital importance. Until this task shall have been completed, in the event of Great Britain becoming involved in war with a naval Power of the first magnitude, Northern Australia will only be safe for so long a period as it would take a second-class Japanese cruiser to sail from Kobe to Port Darwin.

But, for the effective economic development of the Territory, a trans-continental railway in itself would not be sufficient. While such a work would undoubtedly stimulate in a large degree the mining and pastoral industries, labour conditions would still forbid the profitable exploitation of the agricultural resources of the coastal districts. At present, so far as I have been able to learn, only some two hundred acres of these have been, or are being, cultivated by white men, sisal hemp being grown chiefly, though the industry is still in the experimental stage. Sugar was once tried, but with unsatisfactory results. The site chosen for the plantation is said to have been dry ironstone country, and a shoemaker was appointed as manager. Naturally the enterprise failed. But undoubtedly sugar, cotton, rice, tobacco, rubber, and many other such products could be profitably grown near the coast and along the valleys of such rivers as the Victoria, Daly, Roper, Adelaide and Goyder, if cheap and efficient coloured labour were obtainable. The importation of such labour, in suitable quantities, under contract, into special tropical areas, outside which the employment of coolies should be prohibited, is, in my opinion, absolutely necessary to the full agricultural development of the hot and humid belt of country lying below an elevation of three hundred feet and extending all along the coast and great river valleys.

Approximately the region of tropical agriculture would embrace some 90,000 square miles, outside which the country might be reserved entirely for white men. That the establishment of a flourishing planting industry along the coast would greatly assist the progress of white settlement in the interior by providing profitable and easily accessible markets is obvious. Not only would the breeding of cattle, horses and sheep be encouraged, but in all probability, with the extension of railways, the cultivation of wheat would be undertaken on a large scale. The magnificent Barclay Tablelands, containing fully 20,000,000 acres of rich country, are said to be admirably adapted for wheat-growing. In fact the whole belt of country, computed to embrace about 80,000,000 acres, stretching across the full breadth of the Territory between Powell's Creek and the Catherine River, a region lying from 400 to 1,500 feet above sea level and enjoying a rainfall varying from fifteen to forty inches with a shade temperature fluctuating between 110° and 26°, will hereafter, in all probability, be to Australia what the western prairie States now are to Canada, a land of the farmer *par excellence*. Further south the Macdonnell Ranges, lying between the 23rd and 24th parallels of south latitude, culminating in Bald Hill, whose summit is nearly 4,000 feet above sea level, afford vast spaces of country eminently adapted for horse-breeding and a climate described as being absolutely perfect in salubrity and charm.

With a proper system of importation of coloured labour, under careful Government supervision, and limited to specified areas, in force, the harmonious development of the five main classes of industries suited to the Territory would proceed rapidly. The maritime industries of pearl-shelling, fishing and trepanging, would be carried on with licensed coloured crews working under the supervision of white men. Along the coast there would be a belt of plantations where coloured labour also would be employed, but where, at the same time, numerous opportunities of profitable employment under comfortable conditions would be afforded to white managers, engineers, superintendents, traders and others. Behind the planting areas would be the region of white agriculture, and further inland, though of course overlapping in places, vast territories would afford scope for the miner and the pastoralist.

Under such a condition of things the safety of the Northern Territory would be assured by the presence of a strong army of occupation, whose labours in times of peace would furnish abundant revenues for the maintenance of an effective defence force, both on land and sea. Port Darwin would become a naval and military base of the first magnitude, and the door now open would be securely locked. Coloured aliens would come to the Territory as servants and friends, not, possibly, as enemies and masters. Accompanying the intermittent and regulated inflow and outflow of Asiatics, a steady and increasing stream of European immigrants would pour into the vast empty spaces in the interior, where they and their descendants might live in health and prosperity. These are not mere dreams.

There are substantial, not shadowy, foundations for the confident optimism cherished by many who, like myself, have made a serious study of conditions prevailing in the northern portions of Australia on the spot, and who have taken some trouble to acquire reliable information concerning the potentialities of those vast empty regions, and to ascertain their chief needs, provided a rational policy in dealing with them be adopted in time. The solution of the problem of developing tropical territories is, after all, not far to seek. It lies, so far as Australia is concerned, in the subordination of racial prejudice, in the adoption of a policy of compromise, in emancipation from the tyranny of abstract principles, in the recognition of the fact that Nature is still the supreme arbitress of human destiny, in obedience to climatic laws. Extreme views are always false views. Wisdom always lies in the mean. White Australia, not only as a national ideal, but as a practicable policy, is admirable as applied to three-quarters of the Australian continent. If it be definitely and rigidly applied to the remaining quarter it will fail ; and its failure will be attended, not only by heavy loss, but by grave and abiding danger.

F. A. W. GISBORNE.

PORT DARWIN.

FOREIGN AFFAIRS

By EDWARD DICEY, C.B.

THE PRIME MINISTER ON THE SITUATION

It was extremely satisfactory to hear the Prime Minister say at the Guildhall Banquet that while there have been excitements and agitations in some quarters of the international horizon, "none have threatened any disturbance of the peace or of good relations between the Great Powers." Continuing, he laid it down that "The main objects of British policy are well known and are steadily and continuously pursued. Whenever apprehension exists we are always ready, and not only ready but glad, to join with others in using our influence on the side of appeasement and moderation. We have no desire nor have we any motive for embarking on adventurous schemes. Our Empire for its maintenance and our trade for its prosperity require, not adventure, but stability and peace." This is sound common sense, and will be received with acclamation throughout the Empire.

Regarding the matters that led up to the sending of the British Note to the Persian Government and the effect which it is hoped that Note may produce, Mr. Asquith, after pointing out that a certain amount of alarm had been caused by a report that his Majesty's Government were about to initiate a policy for active intervention in Persia, went on to say :—

For some time past the trade routes in the southern part of Persia have been in a condition of the greatest insecurity. British firms who have trading interests there have naturally requested us to do what was in our power to secure a remedy for this state of things. We have, therefore, pressed the Persian Government, urging them that, if they could not with their own resources police the roads, they should consent to a Persian force being levied, under the guidance of British officers, who would be lent from India for the purpose. If the obstacle in the way of the Persian Government re-establishing order is lack of funds, we will gladly facilitate the raising of money by any reasonable methods,

z 2

provided we can be sure that the proceeds will be efficiently and satisfactorily applied to the policing of the trade routes and the maintenance of security. It is impossible for a country which has drifted into the state of debility and chaos in which Persia was when the last Shah was deposed to rehabilitate itself without help from outside, and it is idle to suppose that Persia can gain strength and security by pursuing a policy of suspicion and hostility towards her two immediate neighbours, or towards either of them. Meanwhile, there is nothing in any proposal which we have urged the Persian Government to adopt in any way inconsistent with the independence or the integrity of that country. If the Persian Government will seek the good will of their neighbours their advances will meet with a ready response ; but if they will not do so, if their attitude is to be at once helpless and hostile, there must inevitably arise a state of confusion and chaos which would be a real danger to Persia herself and to every interest in Persia. In such an event we must reserve to ourselves the right to adopt any measures which may be found to be necessary for the protection of British interests.

This position is unassailable, and it is gratifying to know that, except in certain quarters in Russia and Turkey, the attitude of Great Britain meets with general approval.

Dealing with the vexed question of expenditure on armaments, the Prime Minister only voiced the opinion of all civilised nations when he said that the vast majority of the peoples in all the great countries of the world desire peace and are strongly opposed to war. Nor is anyone likely to quarrel with his subsequent words —:

What a paradox, then, it is—the greatest and in some ways, I think, the most tragic paradox of our time—that in almost every great country in turn one of the most prominent topics of Parliamentary debate is the increased expenditure upon armaments. One day it crops up in our own Parliament ; another day in that of Germany ; more recently still in the Austro-Hungarian Delegations. The larger the expenditure the more rapidly it seems to grow, so that each increase is not an attained *maximum*, but a starting-point for still further developments. We are sometimes told that the very size of these armaments is in itself a safeguard for peace ; but the mere collection of such a mass of explosive material, always accumulating, and always ready for use, is in itself a danger ; while the burden and pressure of taxation is in every country producing restlessness which, for the moment, may find its expression in internal disturbance, but which may well, under some new impulse, attempt to seek relief in external aggression. What then is to be said ? We all admit the evil ; we all deplore it. In what direction, in what quarter, are we to find a remedy ?

While no fault can be found with the Prime Minister for endeavouring to bring all nations to a common understanding, is he not beating the air ? Say what you will, do as you may, it is not the slightest use curtailing armaments when óther nations are arming. Depend on it, the best and safest policy is, if you want peace, to be prepared for war.

On the general position between this country and Germany there is little to add. It may, however, be safely said that relations are improving. The pin-pricks do not seem to go quite so deep and the ruffled waters more quickly assume a calm surface. The tact of the German Emperor in the matter of the telegram that caused a momentary sensation in the European chancelleries at the close of last month, cannot fail to have a salutary effect on the anti-German section in this country. Even the question of acceleration in the German navy no longer stirs up strife. People are beginning to see that after all it is sounder policy to set their own house in order than to be perpetually attacking another country for doing that which the British Government neglected to do from 1906--1908. Mr. Leyland, well known as an authority on naval affairs, has been through the German naval yards, and it is satisfactory to find that his opinion is against the acceleration theory. Seeing, I take it, is believing, and Mr. Leyland should know what he is talking about. But my point all along has been, acceleration or no acceleration, that is not our business ; Germany has a perfect right to do as she pleases, and we have no right to abuse her for so doing, while to challenge a statement made by the head of the German admiralty is hardly in accordance with the comity of nations. Let us see to it that our navy is strong enough to meet any combination that may be brought against us and leave other nations to manage their own affairs. That is the duty of the British Government, that is the duty of the British people.

One more word before I pass on : we have unfortunately another election forced upon us. Let my radical friends abstain from heaping every imaginary epithet on the German working classes because they prefer rye to wheaten bread; let us have no more vain stories about offal and horseflesh. I notice in a recent interesting and valuable contribution to the Anglo-German *entente* in the *Daily Chronicle* much to commend, but the paper would have been more complete had the writer offered some explanation of these regrettable attacks on the internal economy of a friendly nation. It is these attacks as much as anything else that annoy and vex the German people. I have no desire to revive old controversies, but I cannot but think that the tactics in this respect of the Government supporters at the last general election leave much room for improvement.

Before these lines appear the German Crown Prince will have arrived in India as the guest of the Indian Government. All who have the pleasure of personal acquaintance with His Royal Highness speak of him as a most charming personality; he is known to have a special leaning to England and all things English, and his stay in India cannot fail to forge another link in the chain of closer relations. He is sure to take note of what he sees and hears, and he may be relied on to use his information to the best purposes. I am glad we are to have a record of his tour in Asia; it is certain to be a most interesting record, not alone on account of the great literary ability of the gentleman who is to write the story, but by reason of the strong personality of the Crown Prince, which one may rest assured will be stamped on every page. I wish His Royal Highness the best of health to enjoy his travels, and I feel confident that he will leave India a great friend of the Indian people, and that the Indian people will ever remain a great friend of His Royal Highness.

THE CZAR'S VISIT TO POTSDAM

Not the least interesting event of the month is the visit of the Czar to the German Emperor. The close friendship that has always existed between the royal houses of Russia and Germany would in itself offer sufficient reason for a meeting between the two monarchs; but the fact that the Czar was attended by his new Minister of Foreign Affairs, M. Sazonoff, gives to the meeting a more public character than would otherwise have been the case. Not so very long ago one heard a good deal about a coolness in the relations between Germany and Russia; that was at the time of the annexation of Bosnia and Herzegovina by Germany's ally and neighbour, and the many outward and visible expressions of gratitude shown by the people of Austria-Hungary to the German Emperor during his recent stay at Vienna, again led to a report that the feeling between the two countries had not yet assumed its old cordiality. These reports were silenced when the Czar, who had been spending some weeks at Darmstadt with his Grand Ducal relatives, announced his intention of visiting the Kaiser at Potsdam. The German Emperor, if report tells truly, was delighted at the suggestion, and there can be no doubt that both countries are much gratified to see an end put to rumours which never really had any deep foundation.

That there were matters outstanding between the Foreign Offices of Berlin and St. Petersburg we can well understand, and that the Czar should desire to see them cleared up while he was in Germany was only in keeping with the usual order of things. Moreover, M. Sazonoff had not previously had an opportunity of meeting either Herr von Bethmann Hollweg or Herr von Kiderlen-Waechter. In these circumstances the presence of the new Russian Minister was eminently desirable, and as he is generally credited with possessing a more conciliatory manner than M. Isvolsky, it may be assumed that he did not leave Berlin before everything had been cleared up, and cleared up to the mutual satisfaction of both parties.

When it was first announced that M. Sazonoff was to join the Czar at Darmstadt and to accompany his sovereign to Potsdam, German opinion was busy with explanations. These, however, focussed themselves in a comparatively short time and found due expression in the following editorial of the *Cologne Gazette* :—

> We welcome the visit of the Czar to Potsdam as a very happy event, because it shows that the personal relations of the two Emperors at the present time are excellent, and that people in Russia value and desire to continue these relations. The presence of M. Sazonoff will in our opinion produce little change as a whole in the now firmly established policy of Russia. It may well be, on the other hand, that a man like Sazonoff, who is credited with pronounced political tendencies, will not so easily allow himself to be affected by influences of the moment and to be driven into a restless policy. It was rather the restlessness than the direction of the policy of M. Isvolsky which gave ground for complaint and sometimes failed to contribute to steady development of the general situation in Europe.

That the new Russian Minister took full advantage of his opportunities, and that the Emperors themselves did not hesitate to approach matters that were of burning interest to their respective countries are clear from the note in the *North German Gazette*, referring to the visit. After briefly reviewing the facts of the moment the writer goes on to say that " The Czar's visit has given occasion for repeated conversations between the sovereigns and the German and Russian statesmen, and for an exchange of views satisfactory to both parties upon political matters." If the wording in itself is not very informative, it supplies the keynote to the situation. Further light is thrown on the conversations by the St. Petersburg correspondent of the *Times*, who sends to his journal a most interesting statement, which he attributes to M. Sazonoff, regarding that minister's impression of his meeting with German statesmen. I do not think I can do better than reproduce it here.

> My conversations with Herr von Bethmann Hollweg and with Herr von Kiderlen-Waechter established the full consonance of the mutual interests of the two countries. No questions affecting the stability of the Triple *Entente* were

raised. All the conversations were based upon the assumption of its absolute maintenance. For that matter, no Russian Minister could dream of forswearing the alliance with France and the understanding with England. This is fully understood in Germany. There was not even an attempt to draw Russia into the rival group.

The concrete questions discussed dealt with the respective relations of Russia and Germany with Turkey and Persia. The German statesmen categorically repudiated any share whatsoever in bringing about the change noticeable in Turkish policy towards Russia. Regarding Persian matters, the discussion was confined to the Russian sphere of influence, as reference to the neutral zone would have necessitated the presence of British statesmen.

From this statement one may conclude that neither the triple alliance nor the triple *entente* are in any better or worse position from the meeting between the Czar and the German Emperor at Potsdam, while the relations between Russia and France stand exactly where they did. It may therefore be assumed that the main subjects of conversation were the positions in the Near East and Persia; and I do not doubt that the Russian Minister was not allowed to leave Germany without fully understanding that Germany had economic interests in Persia, and that she was determined to see that those interests were in no way set aside by the claims of other nations. But as regards active resistance in matters that do not directly concern her, the position taken up by Germany may well be gauged from the reply given by M. Sazonoff to the correspondent of the *Novoe Vremya*. "Turkey," says the correspondent, "is gradually occupying the frontier zone of Persia with troops. What attitude will Germany take if the neighbouring Powers offer resistance to Turkey in her aggressions?" To this invitation M. Sazonoff is credited with replying: "I am convinced that Germany will take no part in the matter." And, commenting on the Minister's words, the *Novoe Vremya* says :—

It would be premature to pass final judgment on the new political combination. For the present it may be noted that Germany refrains from opposing Russia's lawful interests in the Near and Middle East. Russia apparently pays for this negative commodity a positive price. She agrees, that is, to invigorate an unpromising German enterprise in Asia Minor. A saving clause in this transaction is afforded by the circumstance that the final arbiter will be Russia. If Germany fails to fulfil her promises Russia may retaliate by declining to link the future Persian railway with the German line. But the promise given by Russia, ever faithful to her obligations, even now raises the prospects of the German undertaking, which is dependent upon outside assistance.

But that is another story. Yet it goes far to support the contention that the more important part of the conversations at Potsdam had reference to the future, and not the past. It might perhaps serve a similarly useful purpose if King George and the German Emperor were to meet under like circumstances when the days of mourning are over. In this way many of the difficulties one sees ahead in Persia might be nipped in the bud, and an arrangement arrived at between Russia, Great Britain and Germany that would be materially beneficial to all three nations and satisfactory to all three peoples.

In concluding these few observations on the Czar's visit to Potsdam, one ought not to disregard the opinion of Austria-Hungary. The Austrian newspapers have not been very prolific in their comments; but what has been said has all been in favour of the meeting. The *Fremdenblatt* sees no cause for suspicion in any quarter, and in a well-reasoned article on the visit before it had taken place the writer observed: " In view of our intimate relations with Germany it can but be highly welcome to us if the meeting should offer the means of settling in friendly fashion differences possibly arising out of the manifold interpenetrations of the various political interests of Russia and Germany in the world. We regard the meeting besides, and in a more general sense, as an entirely satisfactory event from which the most beneficent effects will proceed." This hits off the situation exactly, and it is very satisfactory to see the Czar following in the footsteps of our own King Edward of blessed and glorious memory, and endeavouring to do all in his power to maintain the peace of Europe.

THE TURKISH LOAN AND AFTER

As I anticipated last month, the German and Austrian banks had no difficulty in finding the money that Turkey wanted to meet her immediate requirements: whether the syndicate will continue to finance Turkey on the same or any other terms is another question. But the main point to bear in mind is the fact that Turkey has secured the necessary funds without the assistance of France and without having to fulfil the political obligations France sought to impose on the Porte. Naturally in these circumstances Turkey is somewhat elated. That she will not forget her friends goes without saying, and while the *entente* with France has much to commend it, in the present instance it can scarcely be said to have worked out altogether to the advantage of the British contractor or the British merchant. It is a well-known axiom in international arrangements that finance and commerce go hand in hand. The mistake France made was in trying to make finance and policy go hand in hand, and unfortunately our Foreign Office fell an easy victim to French susceptibilities. I do not say that policy and finance have not an affinity, but if you define that affinity too closely, negotiations can hardly be expected to succeed. You are on far safer ground if you connect finance and commerce; that connection is understood both by nations and peoples, the other combination is sure to be misunderstood. Moreover, as in the case of France and Turkey, you turn away a customer and lose trade.

No greater mistake could be made than to suppose Germany wished to take the Turkish loan, and certainly Austria-Hungary did not want it. All that Germany did was to say to Turkey, " If you cannot get the money from France we will help you "; but every care was taken to impress upon Turkey to get the money from France if possible. Germany wants all the money she has got for herself, and Austria-Hungary has even less to spare; the very fact then that Germany has come to the assistance of Turkey under circumstances that carry heavy obligations on the part of Turkey must mean that Germany will in the end benefit commercially by the transaction; and rightly so. The nation that pays the piper calls the tune, and precious little tune will France or Great Britain be able to call; and all for what? Because France elected to insist on certain political conditions being fulfilled before she would consider another Turkish loan being quoted on the Paris Boùrse, and in order to carry out some implied understanding between this country and France the British Foreign Office refused to allow Sir Ernest Cassell to step into the breach and make things smooth all round. Had he done so British trade would doubtless have received a substantial benefit. As it is, both British trade and British enterprise have received a check. The sooner our Foreign Office understands that policy is one thing and *ententes* are one thing, but business is another quite separate from both, the better it will be for the commercial interests of this country.

I do not doubt that I shall be told my views are altogether too pessimistic, and I shall be confronted with the statement in the *Geni Gazeta*, which the *Times* correspondent quotes and which runs thus: " It would not beseem Ottoman courtesy, after this success, to adopt a spiteful attitude towards other nations. While we show gratitude to those who have supplied us with funds and enabled us to safeguard the national dignity, let us say to others on this occasion, We have been unable to come to an understanding on financial matters, This need not affect our friendship in other matters." But while fully admitting that the opinion expressed represents the general opinion of the Turkish press,

I see no reason to withdraw anything I have said. Of course, Turkey does not want to quarrel with France or with England, but Turkey knows that when she was in a tight place, Germany and Austria came to her aid. It seems to me we are driving the question of *ententes* to an absurdity. By all means let us have *ententes*, but do not let our *ententes* handicap our business with other countries.

The action of France in the first place, and of the British Foreign Office in the second place, forced Germany to lend the money to Turkey; if you doubt it read the following message emanating from Berlin and published in the *Neues Wiener Tageblatt*, while negotiations were proceeding :—

> The Turkish loan negotiations are in an awkward position. The claims of Turkey with regard to the ulterior consolidated loan are incredibly high and might eventually lead to complications on the German money market. On this account people here would not be at all displeased if France were to take over the loan. The Imperial Government would not regard it as a political defeat if the French were now to make the loan. Turkey would have Germany to thank if she were now to obtain a loan in France on better terms than was possible before. The German Imperial Government has hitherto always laid stress upon its readiness to help Turkey, but not to come into conflict with France. Therefore, should the question of concluding the loan in France again be raised, Germany would not only regard it without ill-will, but would rather welcome such a solution.

This message bears out all I have said as regards the policy pursued by Germany with regard to the loan. As to the matter of repayment we have only to sit still and await results. What France can do to make up for handicapping us in the scramble for Turkey's contracts I am at a loss to imagine. I confess myself in favour of the *entente cordiale*, but I see no reason why the country should be dragged into a dispute not of our making. France is jealous of Germany and refuses to lend money to Turkey because she supposes the money will be used to strengthen Germany's position in the Near East. An independent syndicate emanating from a British source offers to assist matters by taking over the loan and floating it in the London Stock Exchange, the *entente* steps in and the British Foreign Office stop the negotiations. Result, an Austro-German syndicate lends the money, and it naturally follows, as night the day, business in the future goes to Germany. That is the story in a nutshell. I wonder how the British trader likes it! Germany is our commercial rival, why then play into Germany's hands to assist the *amour propre* of France? Why?

NEW ROUTE TO INDIA

As we go to press comes the news that an influential group of Russian financiers and public men' are promoting an international company for the construction of a railway across Persia from the Caucasus to Baluchistan. The news reaches us through the *Times* correspondent at St.˙Petersburg, and there seems no reason to doubt the authenticity of the information. Presumably the suggested line will link up the Russian and Indian railway systems.

In a leading article the *Times* thus explains the route and the object in view :—

> The general outline of the scheme seems to be that from Baku, on the Caspian, a line should be carried southwards along the shores of that sea to the Persian frontier, and thence by way of Resht to Teheran, whence it would be continued *vid* Kerman to the Seistan frontier of Baluchistan and on to Nushki, where it would connect with the Indian railways. The Persian section of the line would be built and controlled by an international company, whilst Russia, on the one hand, and Great Britain, on the other, would naturally have complete control over the lines running through their own territories. It is estimated that the cost of the Persian section of the line, which would be 1,100 miles long, would not exceed fifteen millions sterling. The immediate object in view is the formation of a *société d'études*, which would undertake a preliminary survey of the country and apply for a concession from the Persian Government with a view to the ultimate creation of an international railway company.

The suggestion is not a new one. The *Novoe Vremya* points out that it was first considered at the time when the relations between Russia and England were very different to what they are to-day, but this organ of Russian opinion is careful to observe that, "No doubt the mere prospect of the realisation of the scheme will call forth the bitterest opposition on many sides. Old scores, unextinct prejudices, and political resentments will rise to the surface to impede this great work of peace simply because it has been initiated in Russia." But it adds, "reason will, we hope, finally overcome all obstacles." The new line will materially shorten the journey from this country to India. Instead of the twelve and a half days *vid* Brindisi, one will be able to travel from London to Bombay in seven days, or five days shorter than the Baghdad route *vid* the Persian Gulf and Karachi. The mention of Baghdad recalls the opposition of certain individuals and a certain section of the British press to Great Britain joining in that undertaking. I have not seen any opposition to the Russian proposal, but this is probably because it was made by Russian financiers and not by German bankers.

Some little while since I wrote at length on the matter of the Baghdad railway, and set out the commercial advantages that must accrue to the owners of that line as well as to Turkey and Persia, to say nothing of Germany. As the Foreign Office were quite willing to join in the Baghdad railway, it may be taken for granted that they will be even more ready to join in the new undertaking. I do not anticipate that Germany will offer any objection to the line provided she obtains adequate representation on the Board, and as the Persian portion is to be built by an international company it may be assumed that Germany will be invited to join and to find her portion of the £15,000,000, the amount it is said the trunk line will cost. With two railways connecting the East and the West the intervening territory should be well served with communications and new markets will be opened up for trade.

Before, however, any steps are taken it will be necessary to secure a concession from the Persian Government. I do not myself anticipate the least difficulty in this matter, but with so many nations having economic interests in the regions through which the line is to pass it may be assumed that the Persian Government will only grant the concession provided all these interests are properly safeguarded. I saw the other day that China had decided, when granting concessions to the Western Powers, to stipulate that whenever a concession was given to Great Britain, France, Russia or Germany, the Power securing the concession should allow a certain percentage to be taken up by the other three countries. This appears to me to be a good plan to follow in Persia. For example, if Russia secures a concession from Persia, then a proportion of the financial backing would go to each one of the other countries interested in Persia. If some plan of this kind were adopted all petty jealousies would disappear and much friction be avoided. An opportunity occurs now of reopening the Baghdad railway question and of making a general link-up all round. In fact the whole situation in Persia has undergone a change, and, with a recognition of each Power's sphere of influence, we should probably see an end to all those bickerings and quarrellings that do so much harm to commercial and industrial progress.

EDWARD DICEY.

THE VOLUNTARY SYSTEM OF ENGLISH NATIONAL DEFENCE

By Colonel ST. JOHN FANCOURT, C.B.

THE voluntary principle of national defence has been exploited in every conceivable manner for the last fifty years. We have never in that time had an army that could be relied on to defend England, and fight successfully in defence of our oversea dominions in case our fleets lost command of the sea. The Volunteer Force was an excellent patriotic movement which insured our country against isolated raids, but only so long as our Navy was all-powerful. The volunteers were called for at a time when Napoleon III. had built up a naval strength in the Channel almost equal to the ships of war we could spare from fleets engaged in patrolling our ocean-bordered Empire.

Statesmen of fifty years ago did not withdraw our oversea fleets to protect our shores as our present Government has done, when called on to meet the German naval strength in the North Sea. Palmerston turned to the people and told them to protect themselves, and they responded with the volunteer movement. The squire and his farm-hand learnt the manual exercise shoulder to shoulder in the ranks of the volunteers, much in the same way their fathers or grandfathers had done when the great Napoleon assembled his army at Boulogne for the invasion of England. It is problematical whether either of these volunteer armies could have defended England, had our Channel Fleet been out of the way or defeated, but it is quite certain the territorial force as at present organised cannot do so. The numerous devices by which the position of fleets can now be ascertained were not then available, nor was a fleet subject to any greater danger than storms or a fight in the open. In the ever-changing aspects of naval warfare due to new inventions, it is quite impossible to be assured that victory will lie with the strongest fleet, for some new kind of airship or submarine may prove so destructive as to oblige fleets to scatter. If the problem of throwing down bombs from aeroplanes or airships is to be soon solved, as appears likely, a few airships working by night might break up the battle formation of a whole fleet, as for its own preservation it must scatter. The argument that airship will meet airship is delusive in our case, for we are always laggards in military inventions. At the present time we have only three airships and few aeroplanes, while some other nations have many. It was particularly brought home to those who saw our own airship hovering over the troops engaged in the recent military manœuvres, and sending down messages and sketches, how very unpleasant it might be if it worked by night-time and dropped high explosives on a fleet.

The airship is a fly-by-night, and then only in still weather, and it would be difficult to carry sufficient explosives to do widespread damage. But it appears more than probable that the aeroplane is even now a most dangerous enemy, especially to coast defence. Even if we lit tar-smoke fires all along the coast, in order to shut out from the view of aeroplanes reconnoitring from the sea where our troops were massed, it is very doubtful if they would be wholly successful, for troops marching to the places they were ordered to defend would be seriously impeded by the smoke. An aeroplane that can rise from or come down on the sea is certain to be invented shortly. That would be invaluable to an invading army. The first nation to possess an aeroplane fleet and reliable airships which can work by night, will possess an enormous strategic advantage by sea and land. As matters stand at present we are far behind in the race. In many other ways the prospect is not pleasant.

The working-class Englishman who takes on in the army or navy, though a very brave man when he can see and fight his foe, is liable to serious demoralisation when death is dealt by an unseen hand. It is quite certain that the next naval war will be a very severe trial of that very kind. Floating mines, submarines, torpedoes, bombs from airships and five-mile range of fire all bring death from an unseen hand. In this connection it may be mentioned that for night fighting our troops have not proved as reliable as those of some other nations, and there have been some very lamentable disasters connected with it in quite recent years. The naval wars of the future must be fought under conditions which approximate closely to night operations on land, and it still remains to be proved whether our bluejackets will, under the new conditions, fight as well as their predecessors did in the old time. Our success in both land and sea warfare, and especially in the latter, has always depended on closing with the enemy, but under modern conditions of war that is now rarely possible. The necessary changes in battle tactics have proved most disadvantageous to us on land; we have yet to see how they will affect the efficiency of our sea service. We entered on the Boer War with the assured conviction of the leaders of our land forces that two or three divisions would finish the business in three months : the result we know.

There is no desire on anyone's part to exaggerate a national danger. The Navy will soon have guns which will have the power of firing straight up into the blue and burst shells with such noxious contents that an airship's crew would be as dead men for some time, and the airship would put them down anywhere. But these times are not yet, and while we wait for them we have to pass through the danger zone of the next three years. With trouble threatening in India which may absorb all our Regular Army at any time, with a Territorial Army quite unfit in its present condition to defend our shores, we have put all our eggs into one basket or, in other words, into the power of the Navy to defend England against invasion.

Under the recent conditions which govern naval warfare, officers and men are exposed in war time to a terribly severe strain on their nerves and endurance, and the strain is most severe on those who have to be ready for defence at any hour of the day or night. Our naval officers are probably the finest class of educated fighting men in the world. That they will do their duty nobly is a certainty, but at the same time it should be remembered that our Navy has not been engaged in a naval war for nearly a hundred years.

Lord Charles Beresford, whose ability as an Admiral and whose knowledge of his men cannot be disputed, has warned the public that our Navy, as it stands, is inadequate both in ships and seamen for the tasks it may be called on to perform in the event of war. That an officer of the highest rank in our naval service, who has recently commanded some of our great fleets, should have taken such extreme and unprecedented action, is proof positive that he considers the nation is in great danger if it depends on our present naval strength to preserve our prestige and trade in all parts of the Empire. The inference to be drawn from his patriotic protest is that our Navy must be largely increased or it must be relieved from coast defence duties. He appears to favour the view that if the Navy is made sufficiently strong, land defence is unnecessary. But with new conditions of warfare, this is a venturesome defensive policy to adopt. It is far easier and more economical to raise our land defensive power to such strength and efficiency as to make the invasion of England an impossible military operation, though our fleets were withdrawn from our shores to protect our Imperial interests. How this can be done is open to much argument, but I venture to think it is possible to propose measures of land defence which will protect the nation against invasion, and set the Navy free from coast defence duties.

In the earliest days of last century, when our country was in danger of invasion, we raised a great fighting force (partly by compulsion) equivalent to two million of men in the present day, allowing for the increase in the population. If a man was not a volunteer he was balloted for compulsory service in the militia. Every lad " at loose ends " was voted an " undesirable character " by the magistrates and swept into the Regular Army. The naval authorities despised the slow process of the ballot, and by means of their press-gangs seized every able-bodied seafaring man around our coasts, or from our merchant ships, where and when they required them. These men, when associated with the more worthy class who voluntarily fought for their country, became good soldiers and sailors and won the crowning victories of Trafalgar and Waterloo. In our day we have applied the compulsory principle to national " book-learning " education which, however desirable it may be, is a matter of detail when compared with the military education of our young men, for if they cannot defend England against invasion there will be no money available for education of any other kind. In the meantime, some classes of Englishmen ignore the necessity of national defence.

Had old age pensions been confined to men who had qualified themselves for the great work of national defence, and to the wives and widows of such men, the Territorial ranks and those of the Special Reserve would be full up to any strength considered necessary, and pressure could have been brought to bear on the men to make themselves efficient. The working-man who without payment undertakes to defend his country, and if necessary lay down his life for it must surely be considered a more meritorious person than one who refuses to bear such responsibilities. It is difficult to discover the merit in earning a weekly wage when the alternative is starvation or the work-house, but apparently the Government considered there was great merit, for they excluded from pensions the most necessitous class in the nation, those so poor that they had at some time to receive public assistance—a class largely composed of old soldiers, their widows and children.

The most recent demand made at the late Trade Union Congress was that the Territorial Army shall not be employed against their " brethren " engaged in trade riots. The delegates are rabid antimilitarists, so it is difficult to see how the Territorials are their " brethren." The delegates appeared to be ignorant of the fact that it is the duty of every citizen when called on to assist in keeping the law and securing rioters. This impudent demand on the Government is equivalent to asking permission to have licensed rioting and terrorism whenever the Regular Army is out of England. These people claim to represent a million and a half of English workmen. In the case of compulsory service, this is one of the classes we should have to draw on.

The assertion is frequently made that if the Territorial Army does not become efficient, we shall be driven to adopt conscription. But investigation will show that conscription is not the simple matter it appears to be. At present we raise an army of about 300,000 Regulars and Special Reserves by voluntary recruiting at the rate of 40,000 men per annum, on the standard of men of 5 feet 3 inches in height, 33 inches round the chest, sound in wind and limb, and a decent character. If there was no "qualification" standard, we could raise 600,000 by voluntary enlistment, but the majority of them would be practically useless for military purposes. Moreover, a conscript army is quite unsuitable for the military policing of our great Empire. For that alone we require an army of 200,000 men always abroad in time of peace, with a Reserve of 200,000 ready trained for a time of war. Hitherto, by fair means or foul, something approaching those numbers have been maintained in peace and war. A million of men raised by conscription without the standard of physical qualification and moral character, would not answer our purpose as well as this voluntary enlisted army.

It is a well-ascertained fact that not five per cent. of the factory hands of Great Britain are fit to do a soldier's duty. The scum of our great cities are a still more hopeless material from which to make soldiers who have to serve in all climates, and maintain the prestige of the British Army among the hundreds of millions of the other races we rule over. It should be remembered that we are now paying the price of England having been the workshop of the world for fifty years by an almost automatic decrease in the physique and health of those compelled to pursue indoor occupations under trying conditions. They form the bulk of those who would have to serve as soldiers under a system of conscription, even though it applied to all classes alike. So far as the Regular Army is concerned in peace time, any form of compulsory service appears to be unnecessary and inadvisable, but unless the Special Reserve (the old Militia Force) fill up more quickly than it does at present, some system of enforced enrolment must be adopted, otherwise the nation should be prepared to lose some of its oversea dominions, and, as a necessary consequence, their trade.

The Territorial Army is representative of the military spirit of the nation, but their class and numbers show that the military or patriotic spirit is confined to a very narrow area. Mr. Haldane has netted the sons of the aristocracy, the wealthy classes, the professional men, the tradesmen and their employés, but the impassioned appeals have not met with any response from the masses, and they are practically unrepresented in the ranks. The attendance at professional football matches and music-halls is a convincing proof of how hundreds of thousands of young men occupy the leisure which could be so profitably spent on the ranges or in the drill-halls of the Territorials.   We are told that these Saturday afternoon idlers would rush to arms if invasion threatened, but such a death-bed repentance would be quite useless, for it would be an act of military madness to draft thousands of untrained men into the ranks of the Territorial army at a critical time, as it could only result in the demoralisation of the whole force.

The Territorials cannot be reckoned at more than 250,000 able-bodied men, but though they are quite inadequate to the defence of the kingdom, they will, if given proper facilities of training, become a most valuable force.   At present they have reached the limit of the classes from which they draw recruits, and they have also reached the limit of their efficiency under present conditions.   We have, however, a ready means of increasing the recruiting field of the Territorials.   Let the Ballot Act for the Militia, which is still the law of the land, be applied to the Special Reserve, and ten to twenty thousand lads of from eighteen to twenty-five years of age be called up annually to serve in it under present conditions.   As the Territorials would not be liable to the ballot for the Special Reserve, there would be a rush to join their ranks in order to escape the more onerous conditions of the Special Reserve.   A four years' term of Territorial enlistment, full drills and a month's camp training could then be demanded from the Territorial Army and non-compliance with terms of enlistment would render the defaulter liable to discharge, when he would have to run his chance of being drifted into the Special Reserve by ballot.

This simple measure would also ensure the discipline of the Territorials, for without some penalty for disobedience it is most difficult to maintain.   As the Militia Ballot Act for the Special Reserve would, if fairly worked, apply to all classes alike, there could not be a cry of class favouritism raised by the democracy. Commanding officers of Territorial regiments would, of course, retain the power of only enlisting men whose character and physique were suitable to their ranks and those they rejected for any reason would remain liable to be called up for service in the Special Reserve.   As the latter is a paid service many youths and men not in regular work would prefer to serve in it rather than enter the Territorials.   On the other hand, all the sons of the well-to-do classes would eagerly undertake the light duties of Territorial soldiers, and thus the latter could be raised to an efficient force of half a million.

Every schoolboy knows that even in the best behaved school discipline cannot be preserved without penalties for disobedience. The penalty laid down for insubordination in the Territorials is imprisonment with hard labour, but it is practically impossible to enforce such a punishment without irretrievably destroying the recruiting market; men will not subject themselves to be pointed out as jail birds for offences which in civil life are not criminal. Dismissal from the Force is no doubt regarded as a disgrace by the vast majority of the Territorials, but it has been adequately proved in the last manœuvres that it is a gross injustice to hard-working officers of the Territorials to expect them to inculcate and maintain discipline without placing in their hands some power of imposing a penalty for disobedience. It should be in the power of a Territorial commanding officer to say to a man : "You are a slacker and no use to us; you can go, and I hope you will be balloted into the Special Reserve, where you will have to put in six months in barracks and under the Regulars' discipline." The Territorial thus dismissed would not appreciate his prospects in the Special Reserve, for if he could not stand the mild standard of the Territorial discipline, he would still less like discipline under the articles of war.

We should benefit greatly from three lines of defensive forces, thus :—1st, the Regulars, a voluntary and well paid offensive and defensive army for service abroad. 2nd, the Special Reserve (or Militia) in which all classes would be liable to serve, paid when serving, and under similar articles of war to the first, or Regular Army. 3rd, the Home Defence Army or Territorials, under similar conditions to the present Force, of voluntarily enlisted men, but the training on different and more efficient lines. By this plan the First Line Army would be fed in time of war by an effective Special Reserve. If it were considered advisable to keep up the Reserve of the Regular Army, they should only be placed under an obligation to serve in the ranks of the Territorials.

The present system of paying the reservist fourpence per day retaining fee to come forward in case of "national emergency" has been a complete failure. The fourpence per day has been the moral ruin of tens of thousands of men, while the Government has translated any and every kind of small campaign to mean "a national emergency." The reservists have been called away from their civil employments to their own detriment and that of their employers, and have been unable, in thousands of cases, to obtain regular work subsequently. Under the present Government plan

" national emergency " appears to mean whenever the services of the reservists are required ! ! It is most unsatisfactory to find that our " Expeditionary Force " can only be made effective for war by calling thousands of Reserve men away from their families and work. The Special Reserve or Militia is the natural supply for the 1st or Regular Line in case of war, but at present it is inadequate in numbers and disqualified by age and physique for service abroad. The Militia Ballot Act applied to the Special Reserve would remedy this state of affairs. It would not be conscription, for any man who wanted to escape the ballot would only have to enrol himself in the Territorial Army for Home Defence.

It is very doubtful if conscription would help us in any way if applied to either the Regular or Territorial Army, though National Service training might in a measure do so if there was any guarantee that the men so trained would join the Regulars or Territorials in time of war, for such vital matters cannot be left to chance.

There is dire need of immediate reform, as the present state of the Territorial Army is eminently unsatisfactory both in numbers and training. The essentials of a coast defence army are that its artillery should be able to stop landing parties, and for that straight shooting is positively necessary. The same may be said of the Infantry. Needless to say, the Territorial Force is far from complying with such conditions.

Under the present system an officer of Territorials must spend money, otherwise he is unpopular and recruiting falls off. There are numbers of excellent non-commissioned officers who would make admirable officers, but will not accept commissions because they cannot afford to spend what the men expect, consequently the Force is short of officers, or has to take men who do not make good officers. The money qualification is essential to a commanding officer and in most cases decides his appointment to command. With the driving power of the Militia Ballot Act, the recruiting for the Territorials would not depend on the spending power of the officers, for sixty thousand recruits per annum would be available to keep up a Territorial Establishment of half a million.

The Territorial officers, when recruited up to their Establishment, are quite good enough to carry out their duties in fixed defensive areas if they were constantly practised in the duties of its defence in peace time. In war time the commanding officers would doubtless have the assistance of one or two staff officers from the Regular Army, for the command of a thousand men in war requires technical knowledge and experience which a Territorial commanding officer has no opportunity of acquiring, however able and painstaking he may be.

Half a million of Territorials with improved opportunities of learning their work might safely be trusted with Home Defence against invasion. It is highly improbable they can ever become a mobile army able to fight in any extended theatre of war, and fall back or advance from position to position, but when crammed into a threatened defensive area where they would know the ranges, the cover and the interior lines well, they would be most formidable troops for any landing force to meet. The Territorials must learn in peace time the duties they would have to perform when England is in imminent danger of invasion. The effort made this year to teach them such duties was most instructive, though its full value was lost by the troops in position not being called on to resist a landing force, while they were called on to march and counter-march to resist an enemy who had taken them in the rear—a curious situation, which required a vivid imagination.

Our wide seaboard has so many vulnerable points of attack that practically the whole coast would have to be watched when war threatened, in order to prevent isolated raids. The Territorials would be mobilised at the most dangerous points so as to stop a landing in force ; not less than 100,000 men would be required at each of these points—say 400,000 in all—for it must be remembered that an enemy attacking by sea can get to a selected landing place quicker than the land troops ; the latter must therefore be in position on the first intimation of war, as it would take at least three days to get 100,000 even well-trained Territorials into a defensive area of the coast. Food and ammunition for 100,000 men are a most serious matter when required on the coast ; the railway connections are poor and the coast roads difficult. In the recent operations at Felixstowe, in which only a few thousand troops were engaged, some of the battalions were left without food all one day. That most important branch of the Territorial Army, the Army Service Corps, is quite unable to meet the demands which would be made on it in case of invasion. Even with the help of the Regular's Army Service Corps, the task of collecting and distributing three days' rations for 400,000 men at various points on the coast with only twenty-four hours' notice would be a most difficult and in some cases it would be an impossible task. A properly organised Territorial Defensive Army should have 400 motor-lorries available to carry the food-supply of 400,000 men when the troops are called to the coast. As matters stand at present the troops would be starved. People seem more concerned about providing nurses for the men than about feeding them, though the nurses will also starve unless they fall into the hands of the enemy.

The successful invasion of England would appear to be only possible if conducted on the following lines : 1st, A sudden declaration of war; 2nd, The separation of our naval strength south of the Thames from that to the north of it by the enemy sending down floating mines, fireships and various other devices which take a fleet time to get through; 3rd, That the enemy's northern flanking fleet should be strong enough to fight our North Sea Fleet on equal or superior terms, so as to enable their transports to pass on; 4th. That the enemy's southern flanking fleet should be strong enough to meet and beat off any ships of our Channel Fleet that managed to get through obstacles in the Channel and then be able to attack our North Sea Fleet when weakened by its previous action; 5th, The defeat or crippling of our Fleet.

The results of such naval action must be considered doubtful, but it is not in any way doubtful that while it was being fought, one hundred thousand men and more could land on our shores, unless the Territorials are better prepared in numbers and efficiency than they are at present. If the enemy's Fleet suffered defeat, the landed troops would be in an unpleasant situation, for they would have to sit down and entrench themselves while they drew supplies from the surrounding country. It would be a desperate task for the present Territorial troops to turn them out or make them prisoners, for in resisting the landing the Territorials would have suffered severely.

History has an unpleasant way of repeating itself. Some thousand years ago there reigned in England one Ethelred the Unready. In his time we read of the Danes establishing themselves in a defensive position in the Isle of Thanet and living on the surrounding country and refusing to come out and fight, "well knowing that the Englishmen who served at their own expense would disperse when tired of waiting"; and how the English army gradually melted away until Ethelred was glad to pay a great indemnity in order to get rid of the invaders. History also relates how the English then trusted to sea defence against the invaders and raised a powerful fleet, and how it was lost in a great and terrible storm, and our country was at the mercy of the invaders who landed where and when they chose. How Turkil in East Anglia and Kemsig in the Isle of Thanet pillaged and ravaged the country, exacting great ransoms from the cities, and how the untrained troops of England "who served at their own charges" were defeated again and again whenever they ventured a battle against the highly trained though comparatively few invaders.

The old chronicles mention the fact that the voluntary service armies melted away under the strenuous conditions of the campaigns. In our day such matters have not changed. East or west we learn the same lesson; the volunteer soldier soon grows weary of fighting for the lazy anti-militarist socialists who will not do a man's work and bear a hand in fighting for their homes and children. When he has done his share of bearing other men's burdens, he cries "enough," and takes himself off to look after his family and his personal interests. However noble self-sacrifice may be, he finds its limitations after three months of an experience in hardship, starvation, wounds and battles.

The United States Civil War supplies a curious example as to how far the voluntary system can be trusted, unless it has some backbone of compulsory service behind it. The Civil War was entered on with enthusiasm by the North. Tens of thousands of men engaged for a short time of service, but "melted away" by departing to their homes at the first opportunity, on the termination of their three months' engagements. Lincoln, the exponent of all democratic ideas, the anti-militarist, the apostle of freedom and "go as you please," then enforced conscription in order to carry his war through, and it was accepted by a race who boasted that they would never accept "compulsion" in any form. They were, without doubt, the last people in the world who would have been likely to accept compulsory service, but they did so, and after some severe examples in the cause of discipline, settled down to their work and won a victory over the Southern States Army mainly composed of volunteers.

In 1902, I put forward a scheme of Army Reform which was received with favour by some of the leading statesmen and generals. It was pointed out that we had 300,000 young men in England who attain soldiering age every year, and we might reckon on about 100,000 of them being willing to accept military duty (as officers or privates), provided we paid them their price in appreciation, money or Government employment: that they would give a sufficient supply of recruits to keep up a first line Regular highly paid Army of 150,000 stationed in India and Africa; a second Line (Militia) of 320,000 under periodical training in England and only abroad in time of great wars; a third Line (Territorials) of 430,000 always at home standing on the defensive; a fourth Line of Cadets 150,000 strong, trained and engaged to fill the vacancies in the first, second, and third Lines on reaching eighteen years of age.

The first Line of fighting soldiers always abroad was a highly paid force, assured of Government employment for life, subject to good behaviour; the second, third, and fourth Lines were to be paid for their military obligations by having a preferential claim on all government service paid for by taxation. In other words, no man or boy could be employed and paid by the Government or by local bodies, who was not a qualified fighting man or in process of becoming one. The same law was to be applied to the duke's son or the labourer's ; they had both alike to qualify as defensive national soldiers before they could receive the pay of a Prime Minister, or the wages of a humble municipal workman. The taxpayer has the command of well-paid Government employment, and can dictate his terms very much in the same way that the East 'Indian Railway authorities insist on every man they engage taking on himself the obligation to become an efficient volunteer soldier.   There is no compulsion about their conditions of railway employment, for if the men who want employment are not willing to qualify themselves for the defence of the railway, they can go elsewhere.

The scheme put forward in 1902 was modified by me and placed before the public in *The Empire Review* of February 1907 ; it was, in essentials of organisation and administration, that subsequently placed before the House of Commons by Mr. Haldane, but, unfortunately, the crucial point that the labourer was worthy of his hire, was missed out and " the patriotic spirit " of the nation was relied on to fill the ranks of the Territorial Army. The " patriotic spirit " made great demands.   Three hundred thousand officers and men were to be asked to give up all their holiday time, week in and week out, in order to train as soldiers under very arduous conditions.   In the event of war they were to be called out for six months and compelled to leave their professions and trades to serve under the articles of war on the pittance of a soldier's pay or be treated as deserters.   In return for such noble self-sacrifice (provided it became a reality by a threatened invasion) they were only offered the reward of " a patriotic spirit."   They were refused all preferential claim on the employment paid for by the public they made great sacrifices to protect.   They were not to have a single privilege which was not to be bestowed on that noble army of labour martyrs, who must earn their weekly wage or starve.   While our Cabinet Ministers rightly receive good pay for doing their duties and, in many cases, are pensioned, it is difficult to understand why they expect lesser men to perform their duty to the State without any kind of recompense or reward.   The Territorial Army might have been a great army amply sufficient for the defence of England, had it not been sacrificed to the exigencies of party government.

We have reached a state of affairs when even individuals or public companies can be challenged in Parliament as to the terms on which they engage those they employ, if their conditions are in any way concerned with national defence.   When an Insurance Company announced that they would only take on clerks who would engage for the defence of the country, they were not only within their business rights, but were carrying out a wise and patriotic policy, yet the Labour Members in the House of Commons raised a vehement protest against what they called indirect compulsion for national service.

The Boys' Brigade and Boy Scouts are rapidly in course of becoming a peace society movement. The latter was a Church and State movement, designed to train up boys for the Territorials, but when, a few months ago, the Central Committee pronounced the movement to be a purely educational one without any end in view of military training for National Defence, the Nonconformist "peace at any price" party set to work at once to capture the movement from which they before stood aloof. They have been very successful, and thousands of their boys have joined the scouts. Thus, wherever we turn, the sorry spectacle is witnessed of young Englishmen under the instruction of those who hold it to be wrong to educate youth in patriotic military principles of national defence, and wicked to teach them how to shoot and drill. The Boy Scouts are still flattered with the idea that they are receiving a military training, otherwise they would not join, and the familiar terms of " attack " here or " reconnaissance" there, getting through the lines of the enemy, or "hanging on to his flank," are still used, but if the boys are not being trained to take their place in the ranks of England's defensive force, and taught to be proud of their rôle, there is no military use for them. The Boys' and Church Lads' Brigades are religious and educational movements of immense national value from an educational and moral point of view, though of small military value. As matters now stand the Boy Scouts are outside the religious organisation of the Church Lads' Brigade and the Boys' Brigade and seriously interfere with their development, for as a purely secular movement, our boys naturally prefer to join the Scouts rather than incur religious obligations. In one word, the patriotic and military education of our youth can only be described as a sham.

The Cadet Corps of the Volunteers gave a most valuable military education to lads of all classes, but they are now dying out as the Church Lads' Brigade, the Boys' Brigade and the Boy Scouts are said to have taken their place. They have not done so and never can under a " peace " organisation, for the essence of the Volunteer Cadet system was to teach a lad that it was a great and glorious aspiration to qualify himself to be a soldier who could fight for his home in case of invasion.

Thus the Territorial Army's recruiting ground has been undermined in every direction. Their supply of recruits has fallen off so steadily that many county associations are losing their present men at the rate of fifty per month, notwithstanding they allow them to engage for one year only and excuse them camp training if they can give a good reason for exemption. Men enlisted on such terms are worse than useless in the Territorial ranks. A four years' term of enlistment, full musketry course and fifteen days' camp training was the irreducible minimum to which the House of Commons would agree when the Territorial Force was proposed. Now, three years after the Territorial Army has been formed, many corps have never done a musketry course but are accounted " efficients," and about half their men do not put in more than eight days in camp. The horse-supply is quite inadequate to the needs of the Force, yet no steps have been taken to provide motor-lorries for guns, food, ammunition, and ambulance trains, though it is quite certain the Territorials cannot mobilise on the coast without them. High angle guns on motors are necessary to prevent reconnoitring air-ships (which can reach our coast and return in a day) from obtaining information as to where our troops are concentrated, but we have none.

All these things cost money. If they cannot be provided the force is of little practical value as a factor in national defence. The Regular Army cannot leave England until such time as the Territorial Army is made efficient in numbers and training. The Imperial duties of both the Army and Navy can only be carried on in war time when the Territorials are qualified to defend our coast. As matters stand at present we require our Navy in home waters and our Regular Army for coast defence.

ST. JOHN FANCOURT.

THE BROAD STONE OF EMPIRE *

PROBLEMS OF CROWN COLONY ADMINISTRATION

[A Review]

By Sir HUBERT E. H. JERNINGHAM, K.C.M.G.

The only criticism one would venture on after careful perusal of these admirable volumes is that the title does not convey the meaning or object which the author had in view. Lever, the novelist, used to say that a good title to a book was more essential to that book than to the individual who wrote it, and it appears to me that Mr. Digby's ' Broad Stone of Honour,' cannot by any process of analogy be turned into a ' Broad Stone of Empire.'

But let that be, for one is the less disposed to quarrel about the title of the book that one is more than grateful to the friends who some time ago suggested to Sir Charles Bruce "that he should co-ordinate and expand his scattered contributions to a knowledge of the crown colonies and places within the Empire;" and to himself for the interesting method he has adopted of tracing the gradual development of these colonies, considered so useless only half a century ago, under a broader policy of colonial administration at home, a policy which was itself born out of the loyal attachment of those colonies to the Mother Country.

Sir Charles declares : " J'ai pris mon bien partout où je l'ai trouvé " and there is little doubt that in the same language the reader would reply "il a bien fait." The volumes are replete with interesting quotations bearing on the various problems of policy or government, selected with great judgment and peculiar aptness, whether to justify a postulate or bring into relief any given contrast.

The chapters on national policy, colonial policy and imperial policy, deserve special mention as chapters on British History as valuable as any we could have desired from the best acknowledged authorities, and monuments in themselves of the thoroughness with which the author has set himself to his task.

* 'The Broad Stone of Empire,' by Sir Charles Bruce, G.C.M.G. 2 vols. 30s. net. Macmillan & Co., Ltd.

There is something almost thrilling in the manner in which he describes how the conquests of territories beyond the seas during the Napoleonic wars constituted them ₐactual burdens on the nation during the years of want and poverty which succeeded the close of those wars and influenced the policy of Peace Retrenchment and Reform, which brought such men as John Stuart Mill, Cobden, Sir William Molesworth and even Gladstone to believe conscientiously "that England is sufficient to her own protection without the colonies and would be in a much stronger position if separated from them."—How the aspirations of the North American States towards a united North American Continent, which should include Canada, brought a change in British opinion causing Lord John Russell in 1838 to declare in the House of Commons that he "believed that the possession of our colonies tends materially to the prosperity of the Empire, and that on their preservation depends the continuance of our commercial marine, and on our commercial marine depends our naval power, and on our naval power mainly depends the strength and supremacy of our arms."—How a few years later the Imperial idea was born in England out of the ambitious policy of expansion publicly given out by President Johnson of the United States, who, regardless of "a mountainous debt, a depreciated currency, the reduction of the war taxes and the harassing problem of reconstruction involving the military control of eleven States," declared in a Presidential message that "comprehensive national policy would seem to sanction the acquisition and incorporation into one Federal Union of the several adjacent continential and insular communities.

British politicians began to be alarmed when such a declaration was followed by President Grant pleading for the annexation of San Domingo because "it commands the Caribbean Sea and the isthmus transits of commerce:" when Senator Sumner "advocated the Alaska treaty and urged that Canada ought to be ceded in adjustment of the Alabama affair:" when General Butler asked for the West Indies "as belonging to America by position and the laws of nature:" when Admiral Porter claimed St. Thomas "as a central point from which all or any of the West Indian Islands can be assailed."

As Sir Charles concludes: "All this had its bearing on the colonial policy of England." It was a main factor in concentrating English and Colonial opinion on that policy which found expression in the Colonial Institute, originally called the Colonial Society, founded in 1868, and incorporated by Royal Charter in 1882, and at whose preliminary meeting on June 26, 1868, the aim of the Society was declared to be "to arouse the country' from the indifference with which it treated colonial subjects, and by spreading a knowledge of the importance of the Colonial Empire to the interests of the United Kingdom."

It is difficult to say how influential the Colonial Institute has been in carrying out its aims, but it is a fact that through its lectures, its conferences, its publications, the peoples of the colonies have become better acquainted with the mother country and those of the latter more friendly disposed to their colonial brethren, a result which lies at the root of that imperialism which brought Canada and Australia to shed their blood in their Mother Country's cause, and to give the lie to Mr. Cobden's speech in 1865, wherein he sneeringly remarked, "We are told indeed of the loyalty of the Canadians : but this is an ironical term to apply to people who neither pay our taxes nor obey our laws, nor hold themselves liable to fight our battles."

"In the multitude of words there wanteth not sin," and Mr. Cobden used a great multitude of words even more than some politicians of the present day, but it is not the purpose of this article to enumerate sins of past politicians much less those of the present. The remark, however, leads us to recommend especially to the interested reader the careful perusal of Sir Charles Bruce's observations in the chapter on national policy on the gradual displacement of power in the political life of England from the time of the conquest to the present day. They are as full of interest as they are carefully, and in my opinion soundly thought out and expounded.

The chapter too, on the duties and responsibility of the Colonial Governor is too instructive not to deserve attention, though I think Sir Charles is over sanguine when he considers that ' there is no doubt that a governor will always be held to have the power necessary to meet any emergency that may arise and take immediate action for the safety of the colony." Unless orders in Council or further Imperial enactments have been issued within the last ten years to fill the breach, "there is no doubt" that he does not hold and never held the power necessary to meet all emergencies.

Sir Charles is better inspired when he pleads for the retired governors and urges what has been urged by other governors that there should be an advisory Council at the Colonial Office on the lines of a similar Council at the India Office.

The fate of retired governors has often been before the Colonial Secretary, and the Government of the day, and has not even yet been appreciated either fairly or equitably. Unless possessed of private means their lives on retirement are not the reward they should expect for all the expenditure of best energies, impaired health in bad climates, anxious hours in responsible position, and never-ending brain work in the cause of England and her colonies.

Lord Curzon of Kedleston quoted by Sir Charles after suggesting an advisory Council at the Colonial Office, "which would save the home authorities from many blunders and misunderstandings, inherent to home ignorance of distant localities, temper and requirements" pointed out that "there is within a three mile radius of Whitehall a reserve of knowledge, ability and experience in Imperial and administrative problems, unequalled in any other country," and he said no more than the truth.

Another appropriate quotation, unearthed by the author from an article on the constitution of Pennsylvania in 1759 by a Mr. Collier, depicts the actual situation—151 years later—of this useful but neglected class of Government servants who have shared Government responsibilities abroad and come home to be totally ignored. "There is no man long or much conversant with this overgrown city (London) who has not often found himself in company with the shades of departed governors doomed to wander out the residue of their lives full of the agonising remembrance of their past eminence and the severe sensation of present neglect."

Let us hope that the author at least will be spared the most harrowing of regrets as Dante styles it :

> Nessun maggior dolor ch'è ricordarsi
> Del tempo felice nella miseria.

and that when the Colonial Advisory Board is constituted, his knowledge, his experience, his broadness of view, and his tolerant spirit will entitle him to one of the first selections.

In the meantime I beg to offer him my best congratulations on a masterly and useful performance.

The space allowed to his present reviewer does not permit of touching on the many subjects such as health, labour law, education, religion, finance, transport and defence which as the result of colonial establishments peculiarly affect those establishments, but it may be justly said that all and each are treated with equal thoroughness and liberal-mindedness.

Indeed the whole work is worthy of much praise and should become the greatly needed "Vade mecum" for any one who is at all connected with or interested in this vast Empire of ours : for the work deals not only with the origin of Colonial and Empire problems but with their solutions whether attempted or realised and their effect for good or bad, the whole being written with a tolerant and charitable pen in a graphic, classical and admirable style.

HUBERT E. H. JERNINGHAM.

November 19.

A PLEA FOR A MORE SIMPLE CURRENCY

By W. W. HARDWICKE.

PUBLIC attention was first drawn to the advantages of the decimal system as applied to currency weights and measures in 1824 by Lord Wrottesley. It was again advocated in 1832 by Mr. Babbage, and in 1834 by General Pasley. But the first formal recommendation to the Government emanated from a royal commission, of which Sir George Airy was chairman, in 1841. Between this time and 1853 it was strongly and persistently advocated by Professor de Morgan, and in 1847 the florin of two shillings made its appearance.

Then, in 1852 appeared the petition of the Liverpool Chamber of Commerce to Parliament, and in 1853 a committee was appointed, whose report was unanimously in favour of a decimal currency weights and measures. In 1854 a paper was read upon the subject before the Royal Society of Arts, by Mr. Milles of the Bank of England, and exhaustively debated upon. In 1857 a second royal commission was appointed, in which Mr. Brown, M.P. for South Lancashire, brought in a motion which embraced the whole subject, and in which Mr. Gladstone took part, the result being in favour of a decimal currency to be followed by metric weights and measures. Subsequently a Decimal Association was formed, from which many publications on the subject have been issued. Then a petition to Parliament was presented, praying for the adoption of a decimal currency, taking the pound as the basis. This has been described as being one of the most influential petitions ever presented. It was signed by 1,200 merchants of the City of London alone, and was supported by the various chambers of commerce, banks, mercantile and commercial bodies, schoolmasters, engineers, physicians, etc.; and the Bank of England, besides adopting the decimal system in the buying and selling of bullion, contributed £100 to the funds of the Decimal Association. But, notwithstanding all these appeals to the Government of our country, and the fact that an Act of Parliament was passed in 1897, declaring the use of the metric system of weights and measures to be legal, nothing has been done with regard to the currency beyond the issue of a new florin of 2s., with the inscription upon it of "one-tenth of a pound," in lieu of the old one of 1s. 8d., and the issue in 1887 of a double florin or British dollar of 4s. The above inscription on the Victorian florin is, however, not seen on the Edwardian coins, for what reason it has not been explained.

Most of us are aware of the inconvenience of the present irregular system, the difficulties with which the business of international commerce is carried on, and the waste of valuable time involved in the conversion of money, weights, and measures, from one system to another, and in learning the complicated arithmetic rendered necessary by its use. We are also aware of the relief to these difficulties which would be obtained by the adoption of the decimal or all ten system, which has been adopted by every civilised nation in the world except Great Britain. That the decimal system of calculation is the most natural one is demonstrated by nature in the number of our fingers, which may be said to be nature's calculating machine ; and that it is the most rational one is shown by the many advantages it possesses. But, as occurs in all attempts at reformation, it has its opponents who prefer to stick to the old methods. These, in defending what is termed by them a "duodecimal system," assert exultantly that the number *twelve* has more divisions than *ten*. So it may have, but this advantage —the only one it possesses—is more apparent than real, and cannot be compared with the numerous advantages of the former, which is proved by the experience of decimal-using peoples. The advantages of greater subdivision may appear plausible at first, but it will be seen that in actually performing a division by 3, say of such a sum as 13s. 7¾d., no real advantage is gained, for after dividing the 13s., one shilling remains to be added to the 7¾d., leaving 19¾d. to be divided by 3, with the awkward result which is at once manifest. But in decimals the result is simple : fl. $6·81 \div 3 = $ fl. $2·27$. If our system were duodecimal throughout, it would still not possess the natural advantages of a decimal one. But neither the currency—except in so far as the shilling and penny are concerned—nor the old Imperial weights and measures, which are still used by a large majority, are duodecimal. They are irregular, the denominations having no affinity with each other, consisting of three different relation- ships in the former, and innumerable and variable relationships in the latter.

Few of us are probably aware of the simplicity with which our present currency might be converted into a decimal one, without interfering materially with the existing coins, and at the same time preserving intact our gold standard and penny—" the poor man's coin." In decimalising, it is not necessary that our unit should be exactly of the same value as that of some other decimal currency, for decimalisation itself is sufficient, it being as easy to convert amounts from one decimal notation to another, as it is difficult to convert from an irregular one to a decimal one, and *vice versâ*.

Our pound or sovereign consists of 10 florins, 20 shillings, 240 pence, and 960 farthings—the lowest denomination. Now it is obvious that by the addition of forty more farthings to the pound, *i.e.* four more to the florin, we should obtain a perfect decimal currency, and with the least amount of disturbance possible to the existing coins; the pound now consisting of 10 florins, and 1000 farthings or cents. The pound would be undisturbed, and the bronze coins practically so; the shilling remaining at the same value as before, but becoming a half-florin.

But the adoption of the pound as the unit would necessitate three decimal places for the fraction, thus: £53 5s. 1$\frac{1}{4}$d. would become £53·255; and as an article valued at 6d. in present money, would now be valued at £0·025, the arrangement would in daily practice become intolerable. With the florin, however, as the acting unit and chief coin of account—the pound being still the standard of value and essential unit, two decimal places only would be neccessary. The figures in any sum would be the same in both cases, but the point would be moved one place to the right in the latter case, thus: fl. 532·55, all the figures to the left of the first figure of the integer representing the higher denomination, so that the amount in pounds would be seen at once by simple inspection, *i.e.* at sight, without any arithmetical calculation; fl. 532·55 being synonymous with £53·255. The advantage of this is that, not only do we have only two decimal places for our fraction, but the pound could be used as a secondary unit for large amounts where fractions are absent or would not be considered, by simply changing the denominational sign and the position of the point. For instance, a house valued at fl. 4500·00 might be quoted still as of the value of £450. In the same manner the kilogram is used abroad as a secondary unit to the gramme for large amounts in weight; and the centimetre, as a secondary unit to the metre, for small measures of length.

The bronze coins would be slightly reduced in value—to be precise by $\frac{1}{25}$ or 4 per cent.—but the gold and silver coins would remain untouched as regards value. The very slight reduction in the value of the penny, halfpenny, and farthing would be so trifling as to be inappreciable. They would circulate as did the French 10 centime pieces, which got into circulation a short time ago, and remained till they were declared not to be legal tender, without a demur from the public.

STATE OF THE COINAGE.

		Value in Decimals.	Value in present Money.
			£ s. d.
Bronze	Cent	·01	$\frac{1}{25}$ {0 0 0¼
	Two cents or "half-penny" . .	·02	less {0 0 0½
	Four cents or "penny" . . .	·04	than {0 0 1
Aluminium (perforated)	Five cents or "half dime" . .	·05	0 0 1¼
	Ten cents or "dime" . . .	·10	0 0 2½
Silver	Twenty-five cents or "tester" .	·25	0 0 6
	Fifty cents or "shilling" . .	·50	0 1 0
	Florin	1·00	0 2 0
	One florin fifty . . .	1·50	0 3 0
	Double florin or "dollar" . .	2·00	0 4 0
Gold	Five florins or "half-sovereign" .	5·00	0 10 0
	Ten florins or "sovereign" . .	10·00	1 0 0
	Twenty florins or "royal" . .	20·00	2 0 0
	Fifty florins or "imperial" . .	50·00	5 0 0

Rule.—10 cents = 1 dime; 10 dimes = 1 florin.

The only coins to be withdrawn from circulation would be the threepenny piece, crown, and half-crown. The first of these is so minute a coin as to be easily lost, and its withdrawal would be regretted by no one. As it represents 12 cents, it would be antagonistic to the decimal series. It would be replaced by a tenth or "dime," of the value of 2½d., and be of aluminium or nickel, centrally perforated, and with smooth edges; the former metal for preference, as this is already in use at the mint for coins in Nigeria and East Africa and Uganda. Also a new coin would be issued of the same metal and distinguishing character-istics, of the value of 1¼d., as a half-dime or 5 cents. Their perforation and size would distinguish them from the silver and bronze coins, the 5 cent. piece being 2·2 cm., and the 10 cent. piece being 2·7 cm. in diameter, each being 2 mm. larger than the halfpenny and farthing, and 1 mm. less than the shilling and florin. The "dime" would be a useful coin, appreciated by those who object to carry about them a quantity of bronze coins; five representing a shilling. A silver "dime" might be issued as usual, in lieu of the threepenny piece for Maundy money. The crown and half-crown need not be withdrawn until later from circulation; the former being too large and unwieldy to carry about; and the latter, being fl. 1·25, would be represented by the more useful fl. 1·50 coin (= 3s.).

It must be borne in mind that the silver and bronze coins are not, as are the gold coins, of their intrinsic value, but are simply tokens, representing certain values in relation to the pound sterling, the sole standard of value in the present currency.

That some inconvenience must accompany any rearrangement

2 B 2

of our currency is obvious, but this would be confined to public officials, clerks, and those well able to cope with the change; and what little trouble existed would only be at first, *i.e.*, during the initiatory period. This ought, however, to obtain only that consideration it deserves, when it is realised what enormous benefits would be derived by a great commercial nation. The tariffs of the Post Office, Inland Revenue and Customs would, as will be obvious, require revising, but by the observance of the following rule, no difficulty would be felt. In computing prices, etc., sums of 6*d*. and 1*s*. would take their value relatively from the florin, but fractions of 6*d*., below and above this amount, would take their value relatively from the cent, thus: A 1*s*. 2*d*. licence would be computed as follows: the 1*s*. would be reckoned as 50 cents, and the 2*d*. as 8 cents = 58 cents. A 9*d*. bill of exchange would be reckoned as 25 and 12 cents = 37 cents; a 2½*d*. stamp would cost 6 cents; a 6*d*. telegram and stamp would cost each 25 cents; a 9*d*. stamp, 37 cents; and a 2*s*. 6*d*. one, fl. 1·25. To compensate for the slight advantage to the public on the sale of stamps, the duty on patent medicines up to and of the value of 30*s*., might be slightly raised when being retabulated as follows:—

		PRESENT DUTY.		NEW DUTY.	
	s.	*s.*	*d.*	*flor.*	*flor.*
Not exceeding 1	..	0	1½	0·50 ..	0·08
,,	2	.. 0	3	1·00 ..	0·15
,,	4	.. 0	6	2·00 ..	0·30
,,	10	.. 1	0	5·00 ..	0·60
,,	20	.. 2	0	10·00 ..	1·25
,,	30	.. 3	0	15·00 ..	1·50

The dozen would have to disappear with the disappearance of the duodecimal shilling-and-penny relationship. Articles which have been sold at per dozen would now be sold at per ten, for an equally easy and rapid method of reduction and multiplication can be obtained by the use of ten in the decimal or all-ten system. As a dozen articles sold at 30*s*. means one at 30*d*., so ten articles at fl. 3·00 would mean one at fl. 0·30, shown at once by simply moving the point one figure to the left; the relationship between the decimal florin and ten being the same as that between the duodecimal shilling and twelve. Not only this: the number ten is capable of wider and easier expansion than twelve, for it has the decimal advantage of unlimited increase and decrease by simply moving the point. As we moved it one figure to the left to reduce from ten to one, so, in finding the price of 100 or 1000, we move it to the right, and add the necessary noughts, thus : the articles sold at fl 3·00 per ten, would be equal to fl. 30·00 per 100, and fl. 300·00 per 1000. Such simplicity in reduction and multiplication could not be obtained under any system of irregular relationship such as our present one.

When new coins are issued, it is to be hoped that, besides the name of each coin, which occupies the lower portion of the reverse, the value, in cents if below a florin in value, and in florins if above, will be clearly shown in some convenient spot, which would not only be useful to the public generally, but to the foreigner who is generally so puzzled over the value of our coins. The retention of the title "*Fidei Defensor*" is both meaningless and obsolete, for it was one personal to Henry VIII.—not as king, but as author—upon whom it was conferred by the Pope of the day in acknowledgment of his having written a book in defence of Roman Catholicism, which Martin Luther was attacking. The incongruity is the more glaring as the occupants of the throne are not now defenders of that faith, but opponents to it.

The introduction of the new coinage could be effected on April 6th (the commencement of the statutory year of the Inland Revenue) of any year ; and such clauses as the following might be embodied in the Bill, that on and after April 6th, 19—: 1. Notwithstanding anything in the Currency Act of 1816, the florin of 2s., representing the tenth part of a pound sterling, shall be the acting unit of value and the chief coin of account. And all public and official accounts shall be kept in decimals, with the florin as integer and with two decimal places for the fraction, representing the tenth and hundredth of the said integer. 2. The farthing, half-penny, and penny shall represent the $\frac{1}{100}$, the $\frac{1}{50}$, and the $\frac{1}{25}$ of the florin, i.e., one cent, two cents, and four cents, respectively. 3. All charges or prices for any stamp, order, licence, duty, tax or other commodity, issued or sold by any Government department, and all sums of money mentioned or contained in any Act of Parliament, lease, agreement, or other stamped document, shall be computed as follows : sums of 6d. and 1s. shall take their value relatively from the florin as $\frac{1}{4}$ and $\frac{1}{2}$ florins, but fractions of 6d. below or above this amount, shall take their values relatively from the cent or hundredth part of the florin. 4. New coins of aluminium will be issued representing the following values respectively, viz. : Five cents, $\frac{1}{20}$ of a florin, and ten cents or "dime," $\frac{1}{10}$ of a florin. They shall be legal tender to, but for not more than sums of one florin. 5. The *colonial currency :* The special coins below the value of a cent (or decimal farthing) in use in some of our colonies, shall, in addition to the Imperial series, remain in circulation ; and their values, which have hitherto been taken from the farthing or $\frac{1}{96}$ of a florin, shall now be taken from the British cent. 6. The *Indian currency :* For all purposes whatsoever, the rupee shall represent the fixed value of 16 annas or British pence, and 64 British cents ; and the pice or pie shall represent the fixed value of one British cent.

W. W. HARDWICKE.

RURAL EDUCATION IN RHODESIA

By G. DUTHIE (*Director of Education*).

THE aim of this paper is to explain in a succinct form the present facilities for education in Rhodesia. The title is general, so that the paper may be of use to more than those interested in agriculture, but I propose to give special attention to education as it affects farmers and farmers' children.

It goes without saying that for farmers' children, as for other children, the first essential is a sound elementary education, and I think it may be fairly claimed that even in this territory, young as it is in the stage of development, this is within the reach of a very large proportion of its inhabitants. One need not delay over the children in towns or within the reach of schools. The main problem, and a difficult and costly one, is how can a State system best include the youth in outlying districts? Although the methods adopted have been explained on previous occasions it is likely that they are new to many, especially to new arrivals in the country, and I make no excuse for explaining them somewhat in detail.

The first method is by means of farm schools, and for the sake of those who are familiar with farm schools elsewhere I may explain that the "farm schools" implies something different from what it would signify in other States, as the conditions in Rhodesia for establishing these schools are much easier for the farmers. If ten children, can be collected together, of school age, the Government is prepared to consider the institution of a school on conditions which I shall explain. A schoolroom must be built by the farmers interested. This need not be more than a hut, a form of building which, if well constructed, is found to be very suitable on account of its cool shelter. It is naturally in the interest of the children, and therefore of the farmers, that the hut should be roomy and well lit. Benches and tables would also have to be provided by the farmers. The Government provides all other school requisites, and pays the teacher's salary. The school fees are per term (there are four terms in the year): 15s. for infants; 20s. for Standards I. and II.; 25s. for Standards III. and IV.; 30s. for standards over Standard IV. If there are three children the third pays half fees, and if more than three all others are free. The fees include all books and stationery, which are provided by Government. The farmers have to see that there is accommodation for the teacher, who would pay for board and lodging. Naturally it is in the interest of all that the teacher should be well housed. Farm schools have been established, one in South Melsetter, one in North Melsetter, one in the Imbeza valley near Penhalonga, one near Marandellas, and six in the Charter district. Several have been started along the railway line from Bulawayo to Plumtree, but owing to migration of the farmers these have had to be discontinued. Six others are under consideration in various parts of Rhodesia.

Now, for children on isolated farms, where ten children cannot be collected together. The Administration has established boarding schools at Melsetter, Umtali, Gwelo, and Enkeldoorn. The Beit Trustees have two boarding houses in Salisbury, and in connection with the new schools in Bulawayo, boarding houses will be arranged for. The boarding fees in these schools are not higher than £12 10s. a term, or £50 per annum. In addition to this a few incidental expenses have necessarily to be incurred. As many farmers require at present all their capital to work their farms, the Government has instituted a system of boarding grants of £20 per annum to assist in making it easy to send children to a boarding house. The number of these grants is one hundred, and to this the Beit Trustees have added one hundred more. The residence of the pupil must be more than three miles from a school, and the pupil must be eight years of age or over. As the grants are to aid parents who cannot afford to pay the full fee, a declaration is required to that effect. The total number of these grants has been taken up for the present, but the Administrator has stated that should the necessity for more be demonstrated, they may be forthcoming. It has to be remembered in this connection, that when a pupil reaches the sixth standard, Beit scholarships for boarders are available, £40 per annum for three years. These are to enable pupils to continue their studies to the matriculation standard of the Cape University. The total number of these scholarships is twenty every year, and they are awarded after competitive examination.

The next all-important question for parents in Rhodesia is the range and character of the education provided. In the minds of most, the education provided by Government is associated with what is commonly called elementary education, the main items of which are reading, writing, and arithmetic. In Rhodesia, the Administration provides much more than this, and undertakes education as far as the matriculation standard of the University of the Cape of Good Hope, so that the scope of State education here

includes secondary as well as primary education. There is, therefore, no necessity for a pupil to leave the territory before he is
ready to enter a university. As to the education of farmers'
children and agricultural education, which are not, of course,
necessarily the same, I would not indicate the possibilities. Sons
of farmers may wish to study for any of the professions. The
stepping-stone is matriculation, and it is at their feet. But
supposing they wish specially for an agricultural education, what
provisions are there? For those whose ambition it is to be
specialists in some particular branch of agricultural science, or to
study at an agricultural college, the best course is to proceed to
matriculation, so that they too are provided for. But, it may be
asked, is there any special preliminary training for those intending
to study at agricultural colleges? The answer is that it is possible
to matriculate by taking such subjects as chemistry, physical
science, botany, zoology, along with other subjects in the examination. It is impossible for us with so few pupils in the
schools to provide specialist teachers in all these subjects, but it
would be equally impossible for any schoolboy, even if he were
desirous and willing, to undertake all of these in addition to the
compulsory subjects. Therefore a wise selection had to be made.

The ordinary school curriculum includes English, mathematics, French, Latin, and science (physics and chemistry),
geography and history. These subjects are taught in the Salisbury
High Schools, and will be taught in the new schools in Bulawayo.
The advantages of choosing physics and chemistry as the science
to be taught are so overwhelming, and, if I may say so, so obvious
that there is simply the one choice. As a basis for agricultural
science none better could have been adopted. Among the other
subjects, there are only two to which a certain class of people may
object, but certainly not enlightened farmers; I mean Latin and
French. Supposing the argument is taken only on the lowest
possible utilitarian consideration—and by utilitarian I mean such
as have a cash value—elementary Latin is of great assistance in
the study of botany, zoology, pathology, and physiology, all of
which are necessary for the full scientific training of the modern
farmer. And as for French, I do not think any intelligent farmer
would object to his son learning the language of a people famed
for their cultivation, their intensive culture, their vine-growing,
and their study of all plants and animal diseases. But it is almost
an insult to suggest that the question should be viewed merely
from the low utilitarian point of view. A farmer, who is a farmer
and nothing more, may be of a certain value to the community,
but if he is to take an intelligent interest in the affairs of the State,
if he is to take a broad view of the advancement of the country, if
he is to be a useful settler, and if he is to take his part in the

government of the country, and perhaps in the framing of its legislation, it is essential that his education, specialised in his own particular work, should nevertheless be on the broadest possible base.

But while a curriculum for our schools has been chosen sufficiently broad to meet all cases consistently, with our available resources, it has to be added that subjects which more especially meet the needs of our future farmers have been included. For the cultivation of observation, for the efficient manipulation of tools, for the study of all living things, we have nature study, woodwork, and drawing. At the new Boys' High School, Bulawayo, a teacher has been appointed for his special knowledge of woodwork and science, as well as for his ability as a teacher. But the wide subject of nature has been still more specialised, and a farm "reader," which deals specially with farming in South Africa, has been introduced in our schools. In this connection I may say that Mr. Fletcher has offered prizes to the pupils in the new schools in Bulawayo for an examination in this book, just as Mr. Newton, the Treasurer, has done in Salisbury. We have also our maize-growing competitions for which the Government generously offers prizes. In our grass-collecting competition, a schoolboy on his first attempt succeeded in finding five new grasses in Matabeleland, some of which now go by his name.

In conclusion, allow me to indicate how a Rhodesian schoolboy with practically little assistance, from the age of 12 or 13 may reach the highest scientific agricultural education. At the age of 12 or 13 he ought to have finished his standard VI., and he is then eligible for a Beit scholarship of £40 per annum if he is a boarder, and £20 per annum if he is a day pupil. There are 20 such scholarships and they are available for three years, by the end of which period he ought to be able to pass a matriculation examination of the Cape University. At this stage he has another helping hand held out to him. There are three Beit bursaries of £100 each, available for three years, awaiting the three most successful candidates at the matriculation examination if they pass in the first or second grade. These are to enable Rhodesians to go into residence at one of the colleges in South Africa, and among these agricultural colleges are included. But suppose the budding agricultural scientist wishes to proceed further, it would be advisable for him to proceed to take the science degree at the Cape University, choosing such sciences as are best suited for his purpose. He would be able then to compete for one of the three Rhodes' scholarships of £300 a year, which are available for three years. He would be in a position then to apply himself to research work, which is specially provided for at Oxford University.

G. DUTHIE.

BULAWAYO.

FRENCH EXPLORATIONS AND PROJECTS IN AUSTRALIA

THE title of this paper is also the title of a book by Mr. Ernest Scott,* whose principal object is to clear up certain disputed points in connection with Napoleon's alleged association with Australia through the agency of Baudin's expedition between 1800 and 1804. The author's secondary aim is to discuss the truth of the assertion that this French explorer, or rather his subordinates, plagiarised Flinders' charts for the purpose of constructing their own. On the subsidiary point, however, all one need say is that on Mr. Scott's showing the assertion seems to have little foundation in fact. But the primary question— whether Napoleon's object in sending the expedition was to prepare the way for French colonisation—is of considerable interest, although perhaps in a negative sense.

If Napoleon actually desired to interfere with Australia, which Mr. Scott, in opposition to at least one distinguished scholar, considers he did not, and had he the opportunity to do so, which despite our strength at sea our politicians in the early years of the nineteenth century were quite capable of giving him, the consequent effects which his action would have had on present-day politics are too obvious to need explanation. Linked as it is with speculations on such a question, Baudin's expedition has always been of interest. It was but one of a long series of French expeditions. The Englishman Dampier and the Dutchman Tasman were, of course, by a long way the first in the field of Australian exploration, but the French by no means neglected research in those parts. Baudin's expedition was preceded by those of Bougainville in 1766, Marion Dufresne in 1771, and La Pérouse in 1785. It was followed by those of Freycinet in 1817 and Bougainville (son of the former explorer) in 1824. These were all purely scientific ventures, and no ulterior motives have ever been attributed to their patrons or commanders.

---

* Terre Napoléon. A History of French Explorations and Projects in Australia. By Ernest Scott. With eight illustrations and maps. 8vo. Methuen and Co, 1910.

Baudin's expenditure also had all the attributes of a scientific expedition, if the value of the scientific work done by its personnel would not lift it appreciably above the others. It was splendidly equipped by the Government, under the active patronage of Napoleon, and the ships carried a full complement of scientists of whom Péron is the best known. The collection of over one hundred thousand specimens, the discovery of more than two thousand five hundred new species, and, last but not least, the excellent classification and description of the collection by Péron earned the unstinted praise of the learned in France, and the resulting books, the first volume of 'Voyage de Découvertes' by Péron and a folio of drawings and charts by Freycinet, his subordinate, were published under the patronage of the Emperor. Péron unfortunately died in 1810. Freycinet completed the second volume of 'Voyage de Découvertes,' and also issued in 1812 an atlas of Australian maps and charts, including the first map of the whole Australian coast ever published. But to quote Mr. Scott:

the circumstances in which this result was effected were not such as secured any honour to the expedition, and must, when the facts became known, have been deeply deplored by instructed French people. Flinders was working at his own complete map of Australia in his miserable prison at Mauritius, while his splendidly won credit was being filched from him; and it was merely the misfortune which placed him in the power of General Decaen that debarred him from issuing what should have been the first finished outline of the vast island which he had been the earliest to circumnavigate. Historically the Carte Générale is interesting, but no honour attaches to it.

Thus though Baudin's and his companion's labours, praiseworthy as they were, deserve no extraordinary eulogies, we find Mr. Scott devotes a book to the expedition. It is their association with Napoleon that makes this voyage worthy of a lengthy discussion. As already stated, Mr. Scott's main aim was to ascertain whether Napoleon's intention was, using Baudin's expedition as agent and its scientific equipment as a screen, to acquire territory in Australia, and this necessitates a close examination of the voyage in all its aspects and the sifting of much evidence, direct and indirect. He had however, I believe, before writing, no ulterior motive for desiring his investigations to prove the existence of political aspirations or the reverse. The long standing discussion of the subject came to his notice while pursuing other inquiries, the nature of which he does not state. The points brought out by the close examination which he makes of the genesis, progress and results of the expedition are that it was promoted by scientists for scientific purposes only, though under the patronage of the First Consul, that it was not an isolated effort but one of a series, exactly similar in purpose, made by the French, that the nature of the equipment and personnel were in accord with its professed object, and that the work throughout never crossed the limits of genuine scientific research. The evidence which Mr. Scott brings forward is more of the circumstantial kind. He claims, and appearances certainly support him, that Bonaparte, during the Consulate, was quite capable of promoting research for its own sake, and he notes that practically no trace of any desire to colonise Australia is to be found in his correspondence or in his recorded sayings at St. Helena, where his whole life was passed under review. Any assertion therefore that Bonaparte had political motives when sending out Baudin is merely an assumption, perhaps a true one, but unsupported by even indirect evidence.

More attention still should be paid to another of Mr. Scott's arguments. He directs our notice to the fact that the Peace of Amiens was made and the treaty signed during Baudin's absence, so the period of his voyage covered that in which colonies were daily bartered and exchanged by the contracting powers: " We were then," as the author says, " in a concessionary mood." We actually ceded the Cape, Ceylon and other valuable possessions, and we were on the point of relinquishing Malta. Compared with them Australia was nothing to England. We sent our convicts there and that was about all, so it is reasonable to suppose that it was only because Napoleon did not mention the country during the negotiations that it was never ceded to him. It is, of course, quite true that as matters subsequently turned out, the cession would have affected us little, for the French, helpless at sea, could never have occupied Australia if we had chosen to hinder them. But one must not forget one important point, that Baudin's expedition had returned to France before Trafalgar was fought. Till that victory our supremacy at sea was by no means assured; we were relinquishing the Cape, the French held Mauritius, and there was no Suez Canal; so if Napoleon had asked for and been granted a free hand to take what he chose in Australia, there was at the time of Baudin's expedition no apparent reason why he should not be able to hold what he took. That he did not ask for any such concession is a conclusive proof that he did not consider it worth troubling about. There therefore appears as few reasons for considering that Baudin was sent as a political agent as there are outward evidences of his having acted in the manner of such.

The conclusion which I think any reader of Mr. Scott's book will come to is that the case against Napoleon has broken down completely and so to the author's credit stands the demolition of, to use his own words, " a little sporadic Napoleonic legend." A little legend he terms it, and so it may be, but no effort in the cause of true history is too little to be thankful for. Nobody has ever attempted to credit Napoleon with any intention, or even dreams, of Australian colonisation at times subsequent to Baudin's expedition. Such an idea can hardly have entered his mind, for the rapid development of our power at sea, culminating in absolute supremacy after Trafalgar, definitely separated France and Australia. It can hardly be doubted though that only the obvious impossibility of effective interference in oversea affairs can have prevented Napoleon, when Emperor, from striking at England through Australia. Napoleon III. is said to have cast his eyes towards Australia more than once, but he met with distinct discouragement from us, in the face of which, and of our unchallenged command of the sea, he of course could do nothing.

Mr. Scott concludes his book in emphasising the fact that "the people of no portion of the British Empire have greater reason to be grateful for the benefits conferred by the naval strength maintained by the mother country, during the past one hundred years, than have those who occupy Australia. Their country has indeed been in a special degree the nursling of sea power." It is perhaps an obvious conclusion, but, since many have forgotten that one portion of our Australian territory once bore the name of Terre Napoléon, and many choose to ignore that it was our power at sea which banished that name from the map, it is worthy of the prominence given it, and I cannot end my paper better than by endorsing Mr. Scott's statement.

UBIQUE.

SOUTH AFRICAN FISCAL PROBLEMS

OF the many questions that will come up for solution in the
Union Parliament, the most formidable relates to the framing
of the Customs tariff. In view of the importance of the matter
to South Africa, I was surprised to find so few references made
to it during the election. Probably this was due to the fact that
it has not yet become a burning question with party politicians.
The framing of a uniform tariff has proved exceedingly difficult
in the past, for the reason that, perhaps, in no other part of
the Empire do the clashing of sectional interests and prejudices
result in such bitterness of feeling. Long ago, when the
goods intended for consumption in the inland colonies passed
entirely through the ports of Cape Colony and Natal, the Governments of those colonies levied excessive charges on the goods. It
was this fact which moved the Transvaal to turn to its most
natural port Lourenco Marques, and the growing importance of
that port has ever since been a thorn in the flesh of the less
favourably situated ports of Natal and Cape Colony.

To allow each colony to frame a tariff in its own interests,
regardless of the conditions of its neighbours, could only result in
industrial strife and in the retarding of that commercial expansion
to which so many now look forward. Lord Milner saw the vital
necessity of securing harmony in tariff duties when he called a
conference of representatives of the various colonies at Bloemfontein in 1903. The conference resulted in the formation of
the existing Customs Union, which comprises the whole of
British South Africa, with the exception of North Eastern
Rhodesia and Nyasaland. From the date of the birth of the
Customs Union tariffs have been framed by a Customs convention. The results of the deliberations of the convention were
submitted to the various Governments for approval or rejection,
but with no power to amend. Rejection by any one Government meant a reconsideration of the entire tariff by the
Customs convention, or the secession of the colony in question
from the Customs Union—a step which could be effected on
giving twelve months' notice. Obviously the withdrawal of any
one colony from the Customs Union made the efforts of the

convention to frame a uniform tariff futile. In order to avoid complications the various Governments have often been induced to accept the tariff, by passing identical legislation for the purpose, even when their individual interests have not been served thereby. In view of this condition of affairs, it has been practically useless for the convention to try to frame a tariff that is suitable to the conditions of South Africa as a whole; efforts were rather made to satisfy the whims of various sections, with the result that the tariff was weakened by all sorts of compromises.

Although the Customs Union is far from satisfactory, its existence is justifiable in that it has maintained a measure of internal free trade, and has thus avoided the evils that would result from a divergent policy. Nevertheless it has had a precarious existence, being twice denounced by certain of the colonies since its inception.

Tariffs have hitherto been framed in secret, but future tariffs will be subjected to public debate in the Union Parliament. Wide differences of opinion exist respecting the classes of goods which should be subjected to a tax. In the inland towns, for instance, feeling tends to favour a more moderate system of protection in order to reduce the cost of living. On the other hand, agriculturists, and manufacturers in the coastal towns favour greater protective measures, as a means of encouraging the cultivation of domestic products, or the fostering of local industries. An Association of Manufacturers, in one of the leading ports, recognising that the question is likely to be an important one at future elections, has been busily preparing for this contingency, by issuing pamphlets intended to educate the public in the economic principles of protection.

Formerly, one fruitful source of divergence of opinion regarding the extent of Customs duties to be levied, lay in the fact that the financial positions of the different colonies were not the same. Some needed higher duties for revenue purposes, while others, already having a surplus in hand, naturally inclined to lower scales of duties. However, with the taking over of the assets and liabilities of the several colonies forming the Union, by the Central Government, the difficulty on this score is removed.

What will be the attitude of the Union Government towards this momentous question? Will it allow itself to become susceptible to sectional influences? Or will it disregard purely local pressure, and decide on a broad policy favourable to South Africa as a whole? Much will depend on the Minister in charge of the department which deals with the question. One thing, however, is certain. It is eminently necessary that he should possess both knowledge and experience.

"TRANSVAALER."

SIDELIGHTS ON COLONIAL LIFE

The Editor will be glad to receive voluntary contributions to these pages
from oversea readers.

Rhodesian Postage Stamps.

The British South Africa Company has just issued a new and attractive set of Rhodesian postage stamps. The stamps differ materially from previous issues in that they bear the portraits of the King and Queen, the consent of his Majesty being specially given in view of the Duke of Connaught's recent visit to Rhodesia as the representative of the Sovereign. The stamps, on which the word "Rhodesia" appears for the first time as an integral part of the stamp, are in two colours. They consist of eighteen values ranging from $\frac{1}{2}d$. to £1.

Irrigation in Cape Colony.

Some little time ago, *The Cape Times* tells us, in discussing the question of Closer Settlement in South Africa, it was pointed out by that journal that, according to the Census returns of 1904, the extent of land under cultivation in Cape Colony had increased by only half a million acres in thirty years. In stating the fact the writer remarked that in all probability the forthcoming Census would indicate a very much more rapid rate of development, and if one is to judge from the report of the Director of Irrigation, the past three or four years have been distinguished by a progress as remarkable as it is gratifying. Mr. Kanthack estimates that in the past three years approximately 100,000 acres of new land have been brought under irrigation at an expenditure of £550,000, or £5 10s. per acre. The net increase in the value of this land, according to a further estimate, amounts, after deducting the cost of the irrigation works, approximately to £1,850,000. This relates merely to irrigation works in which the irrigation Department has played a direct part—at a cost to the Government of only £36,000: and Mr. Kanthack believes that quite half as much again has been done wholly by private enterprise without the assistance of the Department. Moreover, it may be said that every irrigation work which is carried to a successful conclusion, is a direct incentive to neighbouring farmers to embark in similar enterprises. An interesting map, appended to Mr. Kanthack's report, shows the schemes which the Department has dealt with in the past three years. The chart of the Cape Province is plentifully dotted with little red spots indicating these "centres of infection," more especially in the midland districts, and with so many object-lessons before the eyes of the farmers they may look forward with some confidence to the rapid increase of the area of land under irrigation.

Cane Cultivation in Fiji.

With a view to the extension of cane cultivation in Fiji, the Government endeavoured in 1909 to 'obtain an option of large areas of land in the Sigatoka District, Viti Levu. The land was handed over by the native owners to the Government to be leased on their behalf and an option granted to the Colonial Sugar Refining Company over the areas in question estimated at approximately 5,000 acres. A difficulty in connection with an outlet for the produce from the district arose owing to the fact that the harbours along the coast were considered unfit for the anchorage of large vessels. The Colonial Sugar Refining Company have, however, entered upon the extension of their industry in these districts, and areas of land are now being planted in cane. As an outlet for their produce they are at present engaged in laying down some 40 or 50 miles of tramline to connect with the line from their Lautoka Mill to Nadi. It is anticipated that the work will be completed in 1912, at a cost estimated at £160,000, by which date a considerable crop of cane should be ready for crushing. This extension by the Colonial Sugar Refining Company will prove a large addition to the trade of the Colony.

Cyprus Laboratory.

The annual report of the Government Analyst at Cyprus affords testimony to the valuable work carried on there in the Government laboratory. During the year, 658 samples were analysed, and 203 preparations made. Of the analyses, 415 were of samples of food, drugs, and drinking waters, 160 were in connection with criminal cases, 38 were agricultural and industrial, and the rest were medical and miscellaneous. Out of 406 samples of food analysed, 71, or 17·4 per cent., were found to be adulterated, and of 9 samples of drinking water, 6 were declared to be of good quality, and 2 were found to contain an excess of saline matter. Since the passage of the Food and Drugs Law, 1905, the percentage of adulterated samples has fallen from 49·9 to 17.4, and the Government Analyst reports that there is a great improvement in the samples of milk, flour, butter, olive oil, curdled milk, sweets, and tinned foods, as compared with previous years. In consequence of complaints made to the Government by buyers of tithe grain, and assiduously circulated in the local press, that thousands of sacks of adulterated flour were imported into the island to the detriment of the local wheat market, 65 samples of flour imported at Larnaca were examined by the Government Analyst and found to be perfectly pure. In presence of this analysis the agitation against imported flour suddenly dropped. The eager search for minerals which is being prosecuted in many parts of the island has led to many samples being sent in for analysis; but no new mineral has been discovered. Among the samples of minerals was an interesting specimen of an ancient ingot of copper. Agriculturists have been assisted by the analysis of samples of soils to determine the presence of plant-food constituents, and by the examination of water for irrigation purposes. Many interesting and successful experiments were made in order to ascertain the best method of bleaching and cleaning sponges.

Canada and Reciprocity.

During the debate on the address Sir Richard Cartwright, Dominion Minister of Trade and Commerce, discussed the question of reciprocity negotiations with the United States at some length. After referring to many matters the Minister said :—

> There are more considerations in this matter than pounds, shillings, and pence. I have always been an advocate for Canada making herself more valuable to the Empire by promoting, as far as in her power lies, friendly relations between ourselves and the people of the United States.. In my opinion no one thing can be done by Canada or Canadian politicians which will be a hundredth part as great a service to the British Empire as promoting in every way equitable and friendly relations between the great Anglo-Saxon Powers. I will go further and say that if there is one thing more than another which would be calculated to bring about something like a condition of general disarmament, it would be a favourable alliance between those two great nations.

The New Hebrides.

The Sydney correspondent of the *Times* in a recent telegram observed : "The Bishop of Melanesia and the Presbyterian missionaries report gross violation of the Anglo-French Convention in several of the New Hebrides islands by French recruiters of labour. They say that liquor and cartridges are freely sold to the natives, their wives are kidnapped, and their children recruited for illegal purposes. Leprosy and other diseases have been introduced

among them.   The Bishop declares that matters have grown
worse since the condominium was established." This is exactly
what we expected and what we ventured to forcast in these pages
at the time the agreement was signed. No wonder the *Sydney
Morning Herald* says : We feel hot indignation against the
abominable atrocities.   The Federal Government cannot remain
silent and not insist on an inquiry.   Otherwise France and Great
Britain stand condemned before the bar of international opinion.

Ceylon Legislative Council.

A Blue-Book containing further correspondence relating to
the constitution of the Ceylon Legislative Council has just been
issued.   The Blue-Book covers the period from February 9 to
September 29 of the present year, and is in continuation of the
volume issued in March last.   In the first letter the Governor
states that he is taking steps for the appointment of a Commission
to consider and advise upon the details of the scheme laid down by
the Secretary of State for altering the constitution of the Legislative Council, and suggests modifications ; and the correspondence
closes with a telegram from the Governor to the Secretary of State
announcing that the Franchise Bill had passed with a few
unimportant amendments.   The correspondence contains evidences
of the opposition aroused in various sections of the community by
the new scheme.   Resolutions of the Planters' Association and
the Chamber of Commerce protesting against the abolition of the
principle of nomination were forwarded in March by the Governor,
who, in the same month, transmitted a report of a public meeting
of the general European community protesting against the
reduction of the European representation from three members to
two.   In his reply, dated April 14, the Secretary of State confirmed
his decision, stating that, in view of the size of the European
community and of the presence of European official members in
Council, he considered two members to be sufficient.   A representation by the Governor calling attention to the under-representation
of the Tamil community was favourably received by the Secretary
of State; who, in accordance with the Governor's suggestions,
agreed that this community should be represented by two
nominated members and that the Government Agent of the
Southern Province should be appointed a member of the Council
in order to preserve the official majority.*

* This analysis is taken from the *Times*, November 24.

MEMORIAL TO THE LATE PRINCE FRANCIS OF TECK.

I FEEL sure our readers, both at home and oversea, will be glad to have the opportunity of contributing to the Fund which is being raised as a token of appreciation of the splendid work done by the late Prince Francis of Teck in connection with the Middlesex Hospital.

The letter set out below from Prince Alexander of Teck, who, on the death of his brother, accepted the invitation of the Governors to become their Chairman, tells its own story. "I take up my brother's work," he says, "where he left off, and it is my earnest hope that I may ultimately achieve the object he sought to accomplish."

We, too, earnestly hope that he may be more than successful in the task he has so nobly undertaken, and as Editor of this Review I would venture to plead with our readers for help in so good a cause. Let us one and all rally round the grand old hospital that has done so much for the poor and needy of that great metropolis, so aptly and so correctly named the Heart of the Empire.

THE EDITOR.

To the Editor of THE EMPIRE REVIEW.

Sir,—The last letter written by my late brother in connection with his work at the Middlesex Hospital was one in which he expressed his grateful thanks to those who had responded to his appeal for £20,000 with the object of removing the debt upon that institution. He concluded his letter as follows:

"But my task is not yet finished. The debt of £20,000 has, it is true, been removed, but that liability represented the accumulated deficits between income and expenditure for three years, and from this it is obvious that, until a steady and permanent addition of £7,000 per annum is made to the hospital's income, its financial position is not secure, and every third year the Governors will find themselves face to face with a crisis similar to that which has now happily been averted.

"It is my ambition to substitute for such a hand-to-mouth administration as this one which will provide the Governors with an income sufficient to meet the normal expenses of the year, so that they may apply themselves solely to seeing that it is expended to the best advantage in the interests of those whom the hospital serves, and directly I am able to do so it is my intention to devote my time and energy to building up an adequate annual subscription and donation list. I feel sure that my confidence in the generosity of those to whom I apply will again be fully justified."

This was his ambition, the purpose to which he intended to devote his life, and, had he lived, I feel sure that his efforts would have been crowned with success.

There is a general feeling amongst his friends, and those who take a practical interest in the great work which the Middlesex Hospital performs, that no more appropriate tribute could be paid to his memory than by the establishment of an Endowment Fund which would produce £7,000 a year—the amount by which the normal annual expenditure exceeds the annual income.

I am conscious that the example which my brother set of devotion to the cause of succouring the afflicted poor, is one which it is difficult to follow, but I am determined, nevertheless, to do my utmost to imitate it, and to carry on the work which was so dear to him.

I have accordingly accepted the invitation of the Governors to become their Chairman; I take up my brother's work where he left off, and it is my earnest hope that I may ultimately achieve the object he sought to accomplish.

I will gratefully acknowledge all contributions to the Memorial Fund, which should be addressed to me at the Middlesex Hospital, Mortimer Street, London, W.—Yours, etc.,

ALEXANDER GEORGE OF TECK.

HENRY III. TOWER, WINDSOR CASTLE.

INDIAN AND COLONIAL INVESTMENTS *

ANOTHER political upheaval has come as a disturbing influence for the markets in investment securities, but so far it has produced little effect except to diminish business. Prices have not suffered much. At one time during the most acute stage of the political crisis India stocks, in fact, were quite strong, deriving considerable benefit from the announcement of the King's intention to hold the Coronation Durbar in person and from the enthusiasm with which the news was received in India. Indian railway stocks, too, have enjoyed a general rise, the improvement in trade indicated by the revenue returns creating a good impression.

Two rising Canadian cities have issued loans during the month on terms giving an excellent rate of interest to the subscriber. In both cases 4½ per cent. Debentures were offered through the Bank of Montreal at 101½ per cent., the City of Saskatoon placing £88,600 and the City of Moose Jaw £101,300. The loans are redeemable in 1940 and 1950 respectively, and the usual provision is made for the levy in every year of a rate sufficient to cover interest and the necessary sinking fund.

INDIAN GOVERNMENT SECURITIES.

Title.	Present Amount.	When Redeemable.	Price.	Yield.	Interest Payable.
INDIA.	£				
3½% Stock (*t*) . . .	85,304,848	1931	94	$3\frac{1}{16}$	Quarterly.
3% „ (*t*) . . .	66,724,530	1948	81¼	$3\frac{11}{16}$	„
2½% „ Inscribed (*t*)	11,892,207	1926	67	$3\frac{11}{16}$	„
3½% Rupee Paper 1854–5	..	(*a*)	93¾	$3\frac{3}{4}$	30 June—31 Dec.
3% „ „ 1896–7	..	1916	79¼	$3\frac{13}{16}$	30 June—30 Dec.

(*t*) Eligible for Trustee Investments.
(*a*) Redeemable at a Quarter's notice.

* The tabular matter in this article will appear month by month, the figures being corrected to date. Stocks eligible for Trustee investments are so designated.—ED.

INDIAN RAILWAYS AND BANKS.

Title.	Subscribed.	Last year's dividend.	Share or Stock.	Price.	Yield.
RAILWAYS.	£				
Assam—Bengal, L., guaranteed 3% .	1,500,000	3	100	79	3¾
Bengal and North-Western (Limited)	3,000,000	7½	100	144	5 3/16
Bengal Dooars, L.	400,000	4½	100	87	5⅛
Bengal Nagpur (L), gtd. 4%+¼th profits	3,000,000	5	100	102	4⅞
Burma Guar. 2½% and propn. of profits	3,000,000	5¼	100	107	4⅞
Delhi Umballa Kalka, L., guar. 3½% + net earnings	800,000	7	100	146	4¾
East Indian Def. ann. cap. g. 4% + ⅛ sur. profits (t)	1,912,804	5 7/20	100	96	5 9/16
Do. do, class "D," repayable 1953 (t) .	4,637,196	4¾	100	112½	4 3/16
Do. 4½% perpet. deb. stock (t) . . .	1,435,650	4½	100	116	3⅞
Do. new 3% deb. red. (t)	8,000,000	3	100	79	3¾
Great Indian Peninsula 4% deb. Stock (t)	2,701,450	4	100	106¼	3¾
Do. 3% Gua. and 1/20 surp. profits 1925 (t)	2,575,000	3	100	99	3
Indian Mid. L. gua. 4% & ¼ surp. profits (t)	2,250,000	4	100	100	4
Madras and South Mahratta . . .	5,000,000	4	100	103½	3 13/16
Nizam's State Rail. Gtd. 5% Stock .	2,000,000	5	100	107½x	4⅝
Do. 3½% red. mort. debs.	1,074,700	3½	100	85	4 1/16
Rohilkund and Kumaon, Limited . .	400,000	7	100	133	5¼
South Behar, Limited	379,580	5	100	103	4 13/16
South Indian 4½% per. deb. stock, gtd.	425,000	4½	100	118	3 13/16
Do. capital stock	1,000,000	7½	100	106½	7
Southern Punjab, Limited	1,000,000	7½	100	137	5 7/16
Do. 3½% deb. stock red.	500,000	3½	100	87	4
West of India Portuguese Guar. L. .	800,000	5	100	95	5¼
Do. 5% debenture stock	550,000	5	100	100½	4 15/16
BANKS.	Number of Shares.				
Chartered Bank of India, Australia, and China	60,000	14	20	57½	4 13/16
National Bank of India	64,000	12	12½	47	3 3/16

(t) Eligible for Trustee investments.
(x) Ex dividend.

Canadian railway traffic returns have begun to show the effects of the diminished grain harvest, but the big increase that the Canadian Pacific accumulated during the earlier part of the half year has not been appreciably reduced. The system shows an increase of $5,087,000 in receipts since July 1, and the net revenue statements up to September 30 show an aggregate increase of $2,212,000 in net earnings. The Grand Trunk's net revenue for the same period shows a decrease of £12,700 while the gross receipts, made up to November 21, show an aggregate increase of only £2,263.

Fresh attention has been drawn in the Stock Exchange to Australia's mineral resources by the wonderful discoveries at the Bullfinch Mine in the Yilgarn District. Of course, the area has still to be developed, but if it fulfils all the promises that have been made for it, even Kalgoorlie and the Golden Mile will, as the State Premier says, sink into insignificance. The

CANADIAN GOVERNMENT SECURITIES

Title.	Present Amount.	When Redeemable.	Price.	Yield.	Interest Payable.
3½% 1884 Regd. Stock	4,676,830	1909–34	98½x	—	1 June—1 Dec.
3% Inscribed Stock (t)	8,594,877	1938	91	3.9	1 Jan.—1 July.
2½% „ „ (t)	1,592,105	1947	76	3$\frac{11}{16}$	1 Apr.—1 Oct.
PROVINCIAL.					
BRITISH COLUMBIA.					
3% Inscribed Stock .	2,045,760	1941	85½	3$\frac{7}{8}$	1 Jan.—1 July.
MANITOBA.					
5% Sterling Bonds .	308,000	1923	109	4$\frac{3}{16}$	1 Jan.—1 July.
4% „ Debs. .	205,000	1928	101	3$\frac{7}{8}$	1 May—1 Nov.
NOVA SCOTIA.					
3% Stock	164,000	1949	81	4	1 Jan.—1 July.
QUEBEC.					
3% Inscribed . . .	1,897,820	1937	83½	4	1 Apr.—1 Oct.
MUNICIPAL.					
Hamilton (City of) 4%	482,800	1934	100	4	1 Apr.—1 Oct.
Montreal 3% Deb. Stock	1,440,000	permanent	80	3$\frac{3}{4}$	}1 May—1 Nov.
Do. 4% Cons. „ .	1,821,917	1932	102	3$\frac{13}{16}$	
Quebec 4% Debs. . .	385,000	1923	101	4	}1 Jan.—1 July.
Do. 3½% Con. Stock .	504,196	drawings	92	3$\frac{13}{16}$	
Toronto 5% Con. Debs.	136,700	1919–20*	106	4$\frac{5}{8}$	
Do. 4% Stg. Bonds .	300,910	1922–28*	101	4	}1 Jan.—1 July.
Do. 3½% Bonds . .	1,169,844	1929	93	4$\frac{1}{16}$	
Vancouver 4% Bonds	121,200	1931	101	3$\frac{13}{16}$	1 Apr.—1 Oct.
Do. 4% 40-year Bonds	117,200	1932	101	4	7 Feb.—7 Aug.
Winnipeg 5% Debs. .	138,000	1914	101	4$\frac{11}{16}$	30 Apr.—31 Oct.

(t) Eligible for Trustee Investments.
* Yield calculated on earlier date of redemption.
(x) Ex dividend.

Government has already taken active steps to facilitate the exploration of the field and a railway is projected.

New Zealand's big issue came at a rather unfortunate juncture. The political crisis and the turn of the screw in the money market were both adverse factors and quite a small proportion of the loan was taken by the public. The underwriters, however, are probably quite content, as the investment is a remunerative one, and it will not be long before the loan is absorbed by the general public. Five millions sterling of 3½ per cent. Four-year Convertible Debentures were offered at 98½ per cent. with a full six months' interest, payable on July 1, 1911, although the last call of 23 per cent. is not due until April 3. Of the proceeds of the issue a million and a quarter will be utilised to meet the payments in respect of the New Zealand Dreadnought cruiser now under con-

CANADIAN RAILWAYS, BANKS AND COMPANIES.

Title.	Number of Shares or Amount.	Dividend for last Year.	Paid up per Share.	Price.	Yield
RAILWAYS.		%			
Canadian Pacific Shares . .	1,800,000	7	$100	202 1/2	3 7/16
Do. 4% Preference	£11,328,082	4	Stock	104 1/2	3 13/16
Do. 5% Stg. 1st Mtg. Bd. 1915	£7,191,500	5	"	106 1/2	3 1/2
Do. 4% Cons. Deb. Stock . .	£25,315,001	4	"	107 1/2	3 11/16
Grand Trunk Ordinary . .	£22,475,985	nil.	"	24 5/8	nil.
Do. 5% 1st Preference . . .	£3,420,000	5	"	108	4 5/8
Do. 5% 2nd " . . .	£2,530,000	5	"	94 1/2	5 1/4
Do. 4% 3rd " . . .	£7,168,055	nil.	"	52 1/4	nil.
Do. 4% Guaranteed . . .	£9,840,011	4	"	92	4 5/16
Do. 5% Perp. Deb. Stock . .	£4,270,375	5	"	126	3 15/16
Do. 4% Cons. Deb. Stock . .	£15,821,571	4	"	101 1/2	3 15/16
BANKS AND COMPANIES.					
Bank of Montreal	140,000	10	$100	251	4
Bank of British North America	20,000	7	50	76 1/2	4 9/16
Canadian Bank of Commerce .	200,000	9	$50	£21 1/2	4 5/16
Canada Company	8,319	30s. per sh.	1	28	5 5/16
Hudson's Bay	100,000	80s. per sh.	10*	110	3 5/8
Trust and Loan of Canada .	75,000	8	5	6 3/8	6 1/4
Do. new	25,000	8	3	3 1/4	7 3/8
British Columbia Electric Railway . . . Def.	£600,000	8	Stock	148	5 3/8
British Columbia Electric Railway . . . Prefd.	£600,000	6	Stock	124	4 13/16

* £1 capital repaid 1904.

NEWFOUNDLAND GOVERNMENT SECURITIES.

Title.	Present Amount.	When Redeemable.	Price.	Yield.	Interest Payable.
3 1/2% Sterling Bonds .	2,178,800	1941-7-8†	93	3 7/8	1 Jan.—1 July.
3% Sterling " .	325,000	1947	80	4 1/8	1 Jan.—1 July.
4% Inscribed Stock .	320,000	1913-38*	101	4	1 Jan.—1 July.
4% " " .	455,647	1935	106	3 11/16	1 Jan.—1 July.
4% Cons. Ins. " .	200,000	1936	104	3 13/16	1 Jan.—1 July.

* Yield calculated on earlier date of redemption.
† Yield calculated on latest date.

struction. Each £100 debenture is convertible at the option of the holder into £102 of 3 1/2 per cent. Inscribed Stock redeemable in 1940. This stock is a trustee security and the option is an attractive one.

During the month there have been published the results of the great Consolidated Gold Fields Company of South Africa, and the report and the subsequent speech by Lord Harris, the chairman, at the annual meeting, have as usual afforded a useful indication of the position and progress of the South African gold mining industry. The company's realised net profits for the year

AUSTRALIAN GOVERNMENT SECURITIES.

Title.	Present Amount.	When Redeemable.	Price.	Yield.	Interest Payable.
NEW SOUTH WALES.					
4% Inscribed Stock (t)	9,686,300	1933	$105\frac{1}{2}$	$3\frac{11}{16}$	1 Jan.—1 July.
3½% " " (t)	16,464,545	1924	$97\frac{1}{4}$	$3\frac{3}{4}$	
3% " " (t)	12,480,000	· 1935	$85\frac{1}{2}$	$3\frac{7}{8}$	}1 Apr.—1 Oct.
VICTORIA.					
4% Inscribed, 1885 .	5,970,000	1920	$102\frac{1}{4}$	$3\frac{13}{16}$	
3½% , 1889 (t)	5,000,000	1921–6*	98	$3\frac{13}{16}$	
4% , . .	2,107,000	1911–26*	$101\frac{1}{4}$	$3\frac{11}{16}$	}1 Jan.—1 July.
3% ,, (t) . .	5,211,331	1929–49†	$85\frac{1}{4}$	$3\frac{3}{4}$	
QUEENSLAND.					
4% Bonds	10,267,400	1913–15*	$101\frac{1}{4}$	$3\frac{13}{16}$	
4% Inscribed Stock (t)	7,939,000	1924	103	$3\frac{3}{4}$	
3½% " " (t)	8,616,034	1921–30†	98	$3\frac{11}{16}$	}1 Jan.—1 July.
3% " " (t)	4,274,213	1922–47†	$84\frac{1}{2}$	$3\frac{13}{16}$	
SOUTH AUSTRALIA.					
4% Bonds . . .	1,359,300	1916	100	$4\frac{1}{16}$	}1 Apr.—1 Oct.
4% Inscribed Stock .	6,269,000	1916-7-36*	101	$3\frac{7}{8}$	
3½% " " (t)	2,517,800	1939	$98\frac{1}{2}$	$3\frac{5}{8}$	
3% " " (t)	839,500	1916–26‡	$89\frac{1}{4}$	$3\frac{3}{4}$	}1 Jan.—1 July.
3% " " (t)	2,760,100	1916 ‡ or after.	$88\frac{1}{2}$	$3\frac{5}{8}$	
WESTERN AUSTRALIA.					
4% Inscribed . .	1,876,000	1911–31*	$100\frac{1}{2}$	$3\frac{11}{16}$	15 Apr.—15 Oct.
3½% " (t) . .	3,780,000	1920–35†	96	$3\frac{3}{4}$	}1 May—1 Nov.
3% " (t) . .	3,750,000	1915–35‡	$86\frac{1}{2}$	$3\frac{7}{16}$	
3% " (t) . .	2,500,000	1927‡	$89\frac{1}{2}$	$3\frac{5}{8}$	15 Jan.—15 July.
TASMANIA.					
3½% Inscbd. Stock (t)	4,156,500	1920–40*	99	$3\frac{11}{16}$	
4% " "	1,000,000	1920–40*	103	$3\frac{3}{4}$	}1 Jan.—1 July.
3% . . . . . (t)	450,000	1920–40†	86	$3\frac{13}{16}$	

* Yield calculated on earlier date of redemption.
† Yield calculated on later date of redemption, though a portion of the loan may be redeemed earlier.
‡ No allowance for redemption.
(t) Eligible for Trustee Investment.

AUSTRALIAN MUNICIPAL AND OTHER BONDS.

Title.	Present Amount.	When Redeemable.	Price.	Yield.	Interest Payable.
Melbourne & Met. Bd. of Works 4% Debs.	1,000,000	1921	100	4	1 Apl.—1 Oct.
Do. City 4% Deb. .	850,000	1915–22*	100	$4\frac{3}{16}$	
Melbourne Trams Trust 4½% Debs. .	1,650,000	1914–16*	103	$4\frac{1}{16}$	}1 Jan.—1 July.
S. Melbourne 4½% Debs.	128,700	1919	102	$4\frac{3}{8}$	
Sydney 4% Debs. . .	640,000	1912–13	101	4	}1 Jan.—1 July.
Do. 4% Debs. . . .	300,000	1919	101	4	

* Yield calculated on earlier date of redemption.

AUSTRALIAN RAILWAYS, BANKS AND COMPANIES.

Title.	Number of Shares or Amount.	Dividend for last Year.	Paid up.	Price.	Yield.
RAILWAYS.		%			
Emu Bay and Mount Bischoff . . .	12,000	6	5	4½	6⅝
Do. 4½% Irred. Deb. Stock	£130,900	4½	100	97	4⅝
Mid. of W. Aust. 4% Debs., Guartd. .	300,000	4	100	100	4
BANKS AND COMPANIES.					
Bank of Australasia	40,000	14	40	114	4⅞
Bank of New South Wales	125,000	10	20	45	4 7/16
Union Bank of Australia £75 . . .	60,000	14	25	63½	5½
Do. 4% Inscribed Stock Deposits . .	£600,000	4	100	99	4
Australian Mort. Land & Finance £25	80,000	12½	5	7	8⅞
Do. 4% Perp. Deb. Stock	£1,900,000	4	100	100½	3 15/16
Dalgety & Co. £20	154,000	7	5	6	5 13/16
Do. 4½% Irred. Deb. Stock	£620,000	4½	100	108	4⅛
Goldsbrough Mort & Co. 4% A Deb. Stock Reduced	£1,067,137	4	100	88½	4½
Do. B Income Reduced	£711,340	5½	100	98	5 9/16
Australian Agricultural £25 . . .	20,000	£4	21½	74	5⅜
South Australian Company . . .	14,200	16¼	20	66½	4⅞
Trust & Agency of Australasia . . .	42,479	7½	1	⅝x	12
Do. 5% Cum. Pref.	87,500	5	10	9¾	5⅛

(x) Ex dividend.

NEW ZEALAND GOVERNMENT SECURITIES.

Title.	Present Amount.	When Redeemable.	Price.	Yield.	Interest Payable.
5% Bonds	266,300	1914	104	4¼	15 Jan.—15 July.
4% Inscribed Stock (t)	29,150,302	1929	103½	3 11/16	1 May—1 Nov.
3½% Stock (t) . . .	13,852,432	1940	97	3 11/16	1 Jan.—1 July.
3% Inscribed Stock (t)	9,659,980	1945	85½	3¾	1 Apr.—1 Oct.

(t) Eligible for Trustee investments.

ended June 30, 1910, largely derived from dividends on investments, amounted to close on a million sterling—to be exact, £993,381 13*s*. 8*d*. In addition to this, the share investments show, on current market prices, a large unrealised profit. A sum of £200,000 is appropriated out of profit as a further provision for writing down the prices at which investments in the shares of crushing mines stand in the books of the company, £9,981 goes in French Government duty and stamps, £75,000 is absorbed by the Preference dividend, and £900,000 is distributed to the ordinary shareholders, giving them a distribution of 7*s*. per share, or 35 per cent. for the year. The company's reserve stands at two millions sterling.

In its review of the year on the Rand the report gives first place to the native labour shortage. It is pointed out that the

NEW ZEALAND MUNICIPAL AND OTHER SECURITIES.

Title.	Present Amount.	When Redeemable.	Price.	Yield.	Interest Payable.
Auckland 5% Deb. .	200,000	1934–8*	109	$4\frac{7}{16}$	1 Jan.—1 July.
Do. Hbr. Bd. 5% Debs.	150,000	1917	104	$4\frac{7}{8}$	10 April—10 Oct.
Bank of N. Z. shares†	150,000	div. 12½%	10½	$3\frac{1}{16}$	—
Do. 4% Gua. Stock‡ .	£1,000,000	1914	100	4	April—Oct.
Christchurch 6% Drainage Loan. .	200,000	1926	121	$4\frac{5}{16}$	30 June—31 Dec.
Lyttleton Hbr. Bd. 6%	200,000	1929	121	$4\frac{7}{16}$	
Napier Hbr. Bd. 5% Debs.	300,000	1920	105	$4\frac{1}{2}$	1 Jan.—1 July.
Do. 5% Debs. . . .	200,000	1928	105	$4\frac{11}{16}$	
National Bank of N.Z. £7½ Shares £2½ paid	150,000	div. 12%	$5\frac{5}{8}$	$5\frac{5}{16}$	Jan.—July.
Oamaru 5% Bds. . .	173,800	1920	95	$5\frac{5}{8}$	1 Jan.—1 July.
Otago Hbr. Cons. Bds. 5%	443,100	1934	105	$4\frac{11}{16}$	1 Jan.—1 July.
Wellington 6% Impts. Loan	100,000	1914–29	108	—	1 Mar.—1 Sept.
Do. 6% Waterworks .	130,000	1929	119	$4\frac{1}{2}$	1 Mar.—1 Sept.
Do. 4½% Debs. . .	165,000	1933	102	$4\frac{5}{16}$	1 May—1 Nov.
Westport Hbr. 4% Debs.	150,000	1925	101	$3\frac{15}{16}$	1 Mar.—1 Sept.

* Yield calculated on earlier date of redemption.
† £6 13s. 4d. Shares with £3 6s. 8d. paid up.
‡ Guaranteed by New Zealand Government.

SOUTH AFRICAN GOVERNMENT SECURITIES.

Title.	Present Amount.	When Redeemable.	Price.	Yield.	Interest Payable.
Cape Colony.	£				
4½% Bonds . . .	485,000	dwgs.	101	$4\frac{7}{8}$	15 Apr.—15 Oct.
4% Inscribed .	3,733,195	1923	102	$3\frac{7}{8}$	1 June—1 Dec.
4% 1888 „ .	9,997,566	1916–36*	101½	$3\frac{11}{16}$	15 Apr.—15 Oct.
3½% 1886 „ (t).	15,443,014	1929–49†	100	$3\frac{1}{2}$	1 Jan.—1 July.
3% 1886 „ (t).	7,553,590	1933–43†	86½	$3\frac{3}{4}$	1 Feb.—1 Aug.
Natal.					
4½% Bonds, 1876 . .	758,700	1919	104	4	15 Mar.—15 Sep.
4% Inscribed (t) . .	3,026,444	1937	106	$3\frac{5}{8}$	Apr.—Oct.
3½% „ (t) . .	3,714,917	1914–39†	96½	$3\frac{3}{4}$	1 June—1 Dec.
3% „ (t) . .	6,000,000	1929–49†	85½	$3\frac{3}{4}$	1 Jan.—1 July.
Transvaal.					
3% Guartd. Stock (t) .	35,000,000	1923–53†	92¼	$3\frac{5}{16}$	1 May—1 Nov.

* Yield calculated on earlier date of redemption.
† Yield calculated on later date of redemption.
(t) Eligible for Trustee investments.

operations on the crushing mines in which the company is interested have been considerably hampered by the scarcity and to a certain extent by the inefficiency of the unskilled native labourer. While the actual number of natives at work has

SOUTH AFRICAN MUNICIPAL SECURITIES.

Title.	Present Amount.	When Re-deemable.	Price.	Yield.	Interest Payable.
	£				
Bloemfontein 4% . .	763,000	1954	99	4$\frac{1}{8}$	1 Jan.—1 July.
Cape Town 4% . .	1,861,750	1953	103	3$\frac{7}{8}$	1 Jan.—1 July.
Durban 4% . . .	850,000	1951–3	101	4	30 June—31 Dec.
Johannesburg 4% .	5,500,000	1933–4	100	4	1 April—1 Oct.
Krugersdorp 4% .	100,000	1930	94	4$\frac{9}{16}$	1 June—1 Dec.
Pietermaritzburg 4%	825,000	1949–53	100	4	30 June—31 Dec.
Port Elizabeth 4 % .	374,060	1964	100	4	30 June—31 Dec.
Pretoria 4% . . .	1,000,000	1939	100	4	1 Jan.—1 July.
Rand Water Board 4%	3,400,000	1935	101	4	1 Jan.—1 July.

SOUTH AFRICAN RAILWAYS, BANKS, AND COMPANIES.

Title.	Number of Shares or Amount.	Dividend for last Year.	Paid up.	Price.	Yield.
RAILWAYS.					
Mashonaland 5% Debs.	£2,500,000	5	100	97	5$\frac{1}{4}$
Rhodesia Rlys. 5% 1st Mort. Debs. guar. by B.S.A. Co. till 1915. . . }	£2,000,000	5	100	100$\frac{1}{2}$	4$\frac{15}{16}$
Royal Trans-African 5% Debs. Rep. .	£1,853,700	5	100	88$\frac{1}{2}$	5$\frac{5}{8}$
BANKS AND COMPANIES.					
African Banking Corporation £10 shares	80,000	5$\frac{1}{2}$	5	4$\frac{7}{8}$	5$\frac{5}{8}$
Bank of Africa £18$\frac{3}{4}$	160,000	5	6$\frac{1}{4}$	7	4$\frac{7}{16}$
Natal Bank £10	148,232	8	2$\frac{1}{2}$	3$\frac{1}{2}$	5$\frac{11}{16}$
National Bank of S. Africa £10	110,000	3	10	11$\frac{1}{2}$	2$\frac{9}{16}$
Standard Bank of S. Africa £100 . .	61,941	10	25	61$\frac{1}{2}$	4$\frac{1}{16}$
Ohlsson's Cape Breweries . . .	60,000	nil	5	4$\frac{3}{4}$	—
South African Breweries . . .	965,279	10	1	1$\frac{11}{16}$	5$\frac{7}{8}$
British South Africa (Chartered) . .	8,053,481	nil	1	1$\frac{17}{32}$	nil
Do. 5% Debs. Red.	£1,250,000	5	100	105$\frac{1}{4}$	4$\frac{11}{16}$
Natal Land and Colonization . . .	68,066	4	5	4$\frac{3}{8}$	4$\frac{9}{16}$
Cape Town & District Gas Light & Coke	10,000	nil	10	3$\frac{1}{2}$	—
Kimberley Waterworks £10 . . .	45,000	5	7	5	7

considerably increased during the year, it still fails to keep pace with the demand, which owing to the continued expansion of the mining industry is largely in excess of the numbers available. Every effort continues to be made to open up fresh sources of supply and to make the conditions of life on the mines as attractive as possible.

Moreover, the company's engineers have dealt with the position created by this labour shortage by methods which have varied according to the conditions prevailing at the respective mines; and it remains to be seen whether the adoption of mechanical appliances in place of manual labour in some cases, and the reduction of tonnage handled in others, will produce the same profitable results as in the past.   The directors think that this will eventually be the case, and that when the present transition stage has been passed, the results of the changes in methods will prove their justification.

Although October's output of gold from the Transvaal exceeded September's big returns, the daily average production showed a decrease. This statement gives the monthly returns for several years past :

Month.	1910.	1909.	1908.	1907.	1906.	1905.
	£	£	£	£	£	£
January . .	2,554,451	2,612,836	2,380,124	2,283,741	1,820,739	1,568,508
February .	2,445,088	2,400,892	2,301,971	2,096,434	1,731,664	1,545,371
March . .	2,578,877	2,580,498	2,442,022	2,287,391	1,884,815	1,698,340
April . . .	2,629,535	2,578,804	2,403,500	2,281,110	1,865,785	1,695,550
May . . .	2,693,785	2,652,699	2,472,143	2,227,838	1,959,062	1,768,734
June . . .	2,655,602	2,621,818	2,442,329	2,155,976	2,021,813	1,751,412
July . . .	2,713,083	2,636,965	2,482,608	2,262,813	2,089,004	1,781,944
August . .	2,757,919	2,597,646	2,496,869	2,357,602	2,162,583	1,820,496
September .	2,747,853	2,575,760	2,496,112	2,285,424	2,145,575	1,769,124
October . .	2,774,390	2,558,902	2,624,012	2,351,344	2,296,361	1,765,047
November .	—	2,539,146	2,609,685	2,335,406	2,265,625	1,804,253
December .	—	2,569,822	2,806,235	2,478,659	2,336,961	1,833,295
Total * .	26,550,583	30,925,788	29,957,610	27,403,738	24,579,987	20,802,074

* Including undeclared amounts omitted from the monthly returns.

October's return of native labour on the Rand was rather disappointing, the number of Kaffirs employed in the gold mines diminishing during the month by 2,097. This statement shows the course of the labour supply during the past two years :

Month.	Natives Joined.	Natives Left.	Net Gain on Month.	Natives Employed end of Month.	Chinese Employed end of Month.
October 1908	14,754	11,769	2,985	139,165	12,317
November ,,	12,324	10,163	2,161	141,326	12,298
December ,,	17,404	10,008	7,396	148,722	12,283
January 1909	13,551	11,609	1,942	150,664	10,045
February ,,	18,018	10,844	7,174	157,838	10,034
March ,,	16,184	11,979	4,205	162,043	9,997
April ,,	12,102	11,244	858	162,901	7,734
May ,,	7,717	12,339	4,622*	158,279	7,717
June ,,	8,335	12,354	4,019*	154,260	5,378
July ,,	7,826	12,612	4,786*	149,474	5,370
August ,,	10,089	12,642	2,553*	146,291	5,361
September ,,	11,747	13,811	2,064*	144,857	3,204
October ,,	14,656	13,762	894	152,563‡	3,199
November ,,	13,942	13,742	200	152,763	1,799
December ,,	17,293	13,348	3,945	156,708	nil.
January 1910	—	—	3,954	160,662	nil.
February ,,	—	—	9,109	169,771	nil.
March ,,	—	—	8,574	178,345	nil.
April ,,	—	—	5,469	183,814	nil.
May ,,	—	—	150	183,964	nil.
June ,,	—	—	533*	183,431	nil.
July ,,	—	—	1,917*	181,514	nil.
August ,,	—	—	688*	180,881	nil.
September ,,	—	—	1,369	182,200	nil.
October ,,	—	—	2,097*	180,103	nil.

* Net loss. ‡ Including new members of Native Labour Association.

Considerable recovery was shown by the Rhodesian gold output during October, the month's production being £234,928, which, with the exception of that for November last year, is the largest return ever published, as will be seen from this table giving the output month by month for several years past :

Month.	1910.	1909.	1908.	1907.	1906.
	£	£	£	£	£
January . .	227,511	204,666	199,380	168,240	155,337
February . .	203,888	192,497	191,635	145,397	137,561
March . . .	228,385	202,157	200,615	167,424	160,722
April . . .	228,213	222,700	212,935	175,210	157,108
May . . .	224,888	225,032	223,867	189,216	169,218
June . . .	214,709	217,600	224,920	192,506	170,083
July . . .	195,233	225,234	228,151	191,681	173,313
August . . .	191,423	228,296	220,792	192,106	179,000
September. .	178,950	213,249	204,262	192,186	173,973
October . .	234,928	222,653	205,466	191,478	161,360
November. .	—	236,307	196,668	183,058	175,656
December . .	—	233,397	217,316	190,383	171,770
Total .	2,128,128	2,623,788	2,526,007	2,178,885	1,985,101

The other mineral productions of Rhodesia during October were 16,717 ounces of silver, 59 tons of lead, 16,731 tons of coal, 2,856 tons of chrome ore, and 20 tons of asbestos.

CROWN COLONY SECURITIES.

Title.	Present Amount.	When Redeemable.	Price.	Yield.	Interest Payable.
Barbadoes 3½% ins. (*t*)	375,000	1925–42*	97	3¾	1 Mar.—1 Sep.
Brit. Guiana 3% ins. (*t*)	250,000	1923–45†	85	3 13/16	1 Feb.—1 Aug.
Ceylon 4% ins. (*t*). .	1,076,100	1934	107	3 9/16	15 Feb.—15 Aug.
Do. 3% ins. (*t*). . .	2,850,000	1940	85	3 13/16	1 May—1 Nov.
Hong-Kong 3½% ins (*t*)	1,485,733	1918–43†	97	3⅝	15 Apr.—15 Oct.
Jamaica 4% ins. (*t*) .	1,099,048	1934	106	3⅝	15 Feb.—15 Aug.
Do. 3½% ins. (*t*) . .	1,455,500	1919–49†	97	3⅝	24 Jan.—24 July.
Mauritius 3% guar. Great Britain (*t*) .	600,000	1940	93	3⅜	1 Jan.—1 July.
Do. 4% ins. (*t*). . .	482,390	1937	106	3 11/16	1 Feb.—1 Aug.
Sierra Leone 3½% ins. (*t*)	720,051	1929–54†	96½	3 11/16	1 June—1 Dec.
Trinidad 4% ins. . .	422,593	1917–42*	102	3¾	15 Mar.—15 Sep.
Do. 3% ins. (*t*). . .	600,000	1922–44†	86	3¾	15 Jan.—15 July.
Hong-Kong & Shanghai Bank Shares .	120,000	Div. £4¼	£86½	4 15/16	Feb.—Aug.

* Yield calculated on shorter period. Yield calculated on longer period.
(*t*) Eligible for Trustee investments.

Good prices and a good crop now seem assured for Egypt's staple agricultural industry, the cultivation of cotton; and commercial conditions in the country already begin to reflect the advent of more prosperous times.

RUBBER SHARES.

Company.	Issued Capital.	Area planted.	Nominal Value of Share.	Amount paid-up.	Price.
	£	Acres.			
Anglo-Malay	150,000	3,391	2*s*.	2*s*.	24*s*.
Batu Tiga	60,000	1,545	£1	£1	4½
Bukit Rajah	66,700	2,772	£1	£1	16
Consolidated Malay . . .	62,007	1,710	£1	2*s*.	24*s*.
Highlands and Lowlands .	317,353	4,707	£1	£1	5¼
Kepitigalla	225,000	3,127	£1	£1	15/16
Kuala Lumpur	180,000	2,611	£1	£1	8⅛
Lanadron	269,780	4,570	£1	£1	5¼
Linggi	100,000	4,192	2*s*.	2*s*.	45*s*. 9*d*.
Pataling.	22,500	1,454	2*s*.	2*s*.	2 15/16
Straits (Bertam)	200,000	2,541	2*s*.	2*s*.	7*s*. 3*d*.
Vallambrosa	50,600	1,807	2*s*.	2*s*.	39*s*. 9*d*.

EGYPTIAN SECURITIES.

Title.	Amount or Number of Shares.	Dividend for last Year.	Paid up.	Price.	Yield.
Egyptian Govt. Guaranteed Loan (*t*) .	£7,414,700	3	99	96	3 1/16
,, Unified Debt	£55,971,960	4	100	99¾	4
National Bank of Egypt	300,000	9	10	21½	4⅛
Bank of Egypt	50,000	15	12½	33½	5 9/16
Agricultural Bank of Egypt, Ordinary	496,000	5¼	5	7¾	3⅜
,, ,, ,, Preferred	125,000	4	10	9	4 7/16
,, ,, ,, Bonds .	£2,350,000	3½	100	85½	4 1/16

(*t*) Eligible for Trustee investments.

TRUSTEE.

November 24, 1910.

NOTICE TO CONTRIBUTORS.—The Editor of THE EMPIRE REVIEW cannot hold himself responsible in any case for the return of MS. He will, however, always be glad to consider any contributions which may be submitted to him; and when postage-stamps are enclosed every effort will be made to return rejected contributions promptly. Contributors are specially requested to put their names and addresses on their manuscripts, and to have them typewritten.

THE EMPIRE REVIEW

" Far as the breeze can bear, the billows foam,
Survey our empire, and behold our home."—Byron.

| VOL. XX. | JANUARY, 1911. | NO. 120 |

THE UNIFICATION OF HOME AND COLONIAL PATENT SYSTEMS

BY F. W. BENEY

PATENT systems are the outcome of a desire on the part of the State to encourage and foster the development of individual genius for the good of the community. To this end almost every country in the world has adopted some system of letters patent for invention; and in the main each system has been created and from time to time modified to suit the particular requirements and conditions of the State to which it applies. The oversea dominions have not failed to realise the value of a patent system, and in the great majority of cases some method exists for carrying into practical effect the idea of rewarding the labours of invention by the grant of a restricted monopoly.

In a general way each system may be said to have developed along its own particular line from one common basis, but although to a certain extent Imperial interests have been considered, wide divergences between the different systems have arisen which Imperial considerations have been powerless to check. And it is but natural that this should be so. Home needs and home considerations are ever the prime factors influencing legislative measures, but with the growth of the Imperial tie each member of the Imperial family begins to realise, more especially in matters of commerce, the great advantage which must accrue both to the Empire at large and to its own particular community from a clear and definite understanding, and an equitable give-and-take policy. The scope and validity of letters patent is a matter closely concerning the commercial relations between the units of the Empire, and the desire for a mutual understanding in this respect has found expression on all sides. For the most part this expression has been vague and intermittent, but at times it has crystallised into schemes within the sphere of practical utility.

In this article my purpose is to endeavour to show what has been accomplished in this direction and what it is possible to accomplish by working upon the lines suggested by leading statesmen and experts in the science of patents. At the last Imperial Conference, Mr. Deakin, on behalf of the Commonwealth of Australia, brought forward a resolution in these terms: "That it is desirable in the interests of inventors and the public that patents granted in Great Britain or in any colony possessing a Patent Office of a standard to be specified should be valid throughout the Empire." The use of the word "valid" is perhaps a little misleading; no State could reasonably be asked to guarantee the validity of a patent; the patent is granted, after inquiry as to novelty, but the question of validity is one that a Court of Law alone can determine. Mr. Deakin frankly stated that his resolution was intended merely to introduce the subject with a view to discussion so that some approach towards uniformity might be made. He admitted that at the moment absolute uniformity was not feasible, and suggested that reform should proceed on the basis of assimilation of methods, times and modes so as to render the various patent systems mutually comprehensible and available. Further, he recommended that as a first step towards this end the home Government should invite the Dominions to furnish schedules of particulars, setting forth their patent laws so as to enable a comparison being made and information being sent to each colony as to the steps to be taken to bring the local law into harmony with the legislation prevailing in other parts of the Empire.

The Board of Trade to a certain extent had anticipated Mr. Deakin's further proposal, and a memorandum on the mutual protection of patents, prepared by the Patent Office, was ready for submission to the conference. Mr. Lloyd George, at that time President of the Board of Trade, took part in the discussion and suggested that the resolution be amended so as to read thus:—"That greater uniformity of Patent laws throughout the Empire is desirable so far as local circumstances permit," adding that the principle of compulsory working of foreign patents, introduced for the first time by the Patent measure, then being debated in the House of Commons, should be extended as far as possible throughout the Empire. Eventually the resolution was agreed to in the following terms: "That it is desirable that His Majesty's Government, after full consideration with the colonies, should endeavour to provide such uniformity as may be practicable in the laws for the granting and protection of trade-marks and patents."

Soon after the Conference had concluded its sittings, the Patents and Designs (Amendment) Bill was passed, and the Consolidating Act is now in force, under the title of the Patents and Designs Act, 1907. A schedule of the statutes and ordinances governing the Patent Laws in the Dominions was also laid before Parliament last February, and in the near future a Blue-Book may be expected setting out at length those statutes and ordinances, with an explanation of the practice in the Patent Offices of the several Dominions.*

Sir Wiiliam (now Lord) Robson made it clear to the Conference that the task of unifying the Patent Laws presented several difficulties, and as an illustration he observed that unless the search for novelty made in the Patent Office of one colony on an application for the grant of a patent was as severe as that made in every other colony, Imperial scope for a patent would be obviously unfair to those colonies where the search was the most stringent. This is but one of many obstacles which would arise if the territorial scope of letters patent were extended to the whole Empire. For if a patent be given Imperial scope it follows that its validity might be questioned in any part of the Empire; and seeing that the task of an English Court in determining the validity of an English patent is often one of extreme responsibility, that task would be rendered much greater where a judgment adverse to the patent involved also complete loss of patent rights throughout the Dominions. For example, assuming that a patent granted anywhere in the Empire possessed Imperial scope, and that the patent law for the Empire in regard to validity was the same as the English law to-day, it would be a good defence to an action founded upon such a patent to prove prior publication or prior public user or prior common knowledge in any place coming within the territorial scope of the patent—in other words, in any part of the Empire. The heavy costs involved would give an unfair advantage to the wealthy defendant, and the delay necessitated by world-wide inquiries would be most embarrassing to all parties.

Again, in regard to practice in the Patent Office, complications would arise. In England an applicant for letters patent is given six months from the filing of his application and the general description of the invention in which to prepare the complete specification, describing the invention in detail and making the claims, and another six months may elapse before the specification is accepted. During that period the public cannot inspect the file, and it often happens that similar specifications from different

* An excellent little text-book giving a summary of the patent law and practice in each colony and foreign state has been written by Mr. W. C. Fairweather, 'Foreign and Colonial Patent Law, 1910.'

applicants overlap one another. This is unknown except to the Office, and consequently difficulties, perhaps oppositions, arise. These difficulties in the case of concurrent applications in various patent offices of the Empire, separated by thousands of miles, would be well-nigh insuperable, as they would render it necessary for every stage in the progress of a patent to be notified in detail, and at once, to every patent office in the Empire.

When a specification has been accepted by the Office the acceptance is advertised, and the file can be inspected. The right to oppose the grant of a patent within two months from the advertisement of acceptance would give rise to great inconvenience in the case of imperial patents ; and whether the grant were opposed in the office where the application was made or in any other office, the possibility of injustice would be increased. But perhaps the greatest objection to an imperial patent system is that indicated by Lord Robson, namely the varying efficiency of Patent Office searches in the different dominions. In Canada, for instance, a large staff of trained examiners is employed to search the records for prior patents, and an application for a patent may be refused on any of the following grounds,

> That the invention is not subject-matter for grant of letters-patent according to the law of Canada.*
> That the invention is already known to the public with consent of the inventor.
> That the invention is not new.
> That the invention has been described to the public in a book or by other means.
> That the invention has been already patented in Canada or elsewhere for more than one year.

Thus it will be seen that the Commissioner of Patents in Canada, in the granting of patents, has almost the power of an English judge, with regard to the field of his investigations, with the result that Canadian patents, although difficult to obtain, when obtained are seldom upset by the Courts. On an application in the United Kingdom the only test for novelty is a search, which is confined to previous British patents, while in New Zealand, both British and Colonial records are investigated, and in Rhodesia records of all countries. These variations are not merely haphazard, but in the main have been made to suit the requirements of each country. In an imperial system, unless all such variations are made to disappear, a task fraught with great expense, confusion, and often injustice to patentees must result ; for example, an applicant refused an imperial patent in Canada would outwit the

---

* Under this heading no patents for medicines are allowed as being not a matter of invention.

Canadian Office by obtaining one elsewhere, where the search was less stringent.

On a small scale we have an object-lesson regarding the confusion to be expected, in the case of Australia where, soon after Federation, an Act was passed by the Commonwealth unifying the patent system throughout Australia and providing for the grant of patents with federal scope (Act No. 21 of 1903). Under this Act, a person in possession of a State patent still running, can apply for a Commonwealth patent, and this is granted to him for the unexpired term with the proviso that if the invention has been published in another State of the Commonwealth before his Commonwealth application, that State is excepted from the scope of his Commonwealth patent. The proviso is necessary in order to be just to users in the other States where the invention has not been originally protected. After acceptance of a Commonwealth patent the original State patent may be surrendered, thereby saving the double payment of the periodic renewal fees.

Now if the State-patented invention had been a success, it would have been published in the other States, and a strict application of the Act would render its effect prohibitive. According to a letter sent by an Australian patent agent to the Chartered Institute of Patent Agents in London,* this part of the Act is not being strictly applied; no search by the Office is being made in the States for prior publication or user beyond the State patent records ; with the result that while many Commonwealth patents are being granted and their original State patents being surrendered, actions founded upon the former will result in the Commonwealth patent being upset by proof of publication in some State prior to the date of the grant of the federal patent and the patentee losing all his rights. This is a serious matter and there is no doubt with an Imperial system it would become infinitely more serious ; with the difficulties of a world-wide search by the Office, many mistakes would be made with disastrous consequences.

The insuperable difficulties in the way of an Imperial system such as that suggested by the original resolution at the last Imperial Conference preclude the possibility of unification in home and colonial law to the extent of granting Empire patents with Imperial scope ; much may, however, be done by way of action on the resolution as carried. A greater uniformity is possible both as regards colonial patent laws and simplification of practice under the International Convention, which is an agreement between many leading countries. Under the provisions of this Convention, inter alia, a patentee in one country, on applying for a patent

* Transactions of the Char. Inst. of Pat. Agents, Vol. 26, pp. 22–3.

for the same invention in another country within a certain time, can get his patent granted as of the date of his first home application. It is not possible in the space at my disposal to touch on more than a few of the chief points of disparity in which alteration is both needful and feasible.

According to English Law, a person who becomes acquainted with some invention in a foreign country, whether patented there or not, and applies for a patent for that invention in England is entitled to obtain one provided the invention has not been patented here already or is not about to be patented here by the foreign inventor under the International Convention. This person is known as the "true and first importer," and his rights have been recognised in English Common Law long previous to the Statute of Monopolies. In Australia the "importer" is not an "inventor" unless the invention be communicated to him by the foreign inventor. A similar rule is in force in New Zealand, and in the Transvaal "inventor" does not include "importer" nor does it in Canada.

By article four of the International Convention, of which amongst others the United Kingdom, Australia and New Zealand are members, an applicant in one country belonging to the Convention can, as stated above, obtain priority on a subsequent application within a limited period in another country. It would seem, therefore, that the Australian and New Zealand refusals to grant a patent to an unauthorised importer can be overcome, for the "importer" can first obtain his patent in England, and then apply as an "inventor" with the English patent as a basis under the Convention in either of those countries: but in the Transvaal and Canada, which remain outside the Convention, no such subtlety is possible.

In any event unification on this point would be beneficial. Although never yet legally decided the common view seems to be that Letters Patent are granted primarily as a reward for the disclosure to the public of something new and useful and only secondarily as a stimulant to inventive genius. There seems to be no good reason therefore why it should not be an imperial law that an "importer" should be considered as an "inventor" with regard to the country into which he imports, and this whether he imports from a foreign land or a colony.

The signing of the International Convention by all the Dominions is also a desirable step, and one which carries with it the necessity of several important modifications in the present laws. When a Convention application is made in England, a certified copy of the specification of the first foreign application must be filed, and a complete English specification with claims. Although the wording of the two specifications need not be identical yet the protection granted under such convention patent must not be substantially different from that granted in the foreign country according to the legal foreign interpretation of the foreign specification. This is a ruling of the Comptroller-General, dated, 1910 (B). It is a little difficult to approve. The Comptroller-General says the test is, " What has in fact been protected by the foreign patent ? " A fairer test seems to be, looking at the foreign document, what were the limits of the invention in the mind of the inventor when he filed his specification abroad ? In an action founded upon such English patent it is probable that disconformity between the foreign and English specifications would not *per se* avail as a defence, but that, if proved, evidence would be admitted to impeach the additional or surplus protection covered by the English patent on the usual grounds.

It will therefore be apparent that since the extent of protection granted under a convention, application in every Colony should be the same, for this is in accord with the Resolution, it would be necessary when applying the Convention to the Empire, to apply also the rules as to the interpretation of specifications filed with convention applications.

Before leaving this point mention should be made of a difficulty arising when an English application is made under the Convention to get the date of a foreign or colonial application, under which a *provisional* specification has been filed. In many countries, including England and most of the colonies, the usual practice as already noted is to file a provisional specification with the formal application, and file the complete specification six months or so later. A provisional specification is only an outline of the invention, which makes no claims, but must describe its nature, and, as far as possible, its limits. It is not until the complete specification has been filed abroad that it is possible to ascertain what is really protected there, and the English office will not accept an application till this has been done, and much delay is caused in getting through the English patent. It would conduce to fairer and earlier treatment of these cases both at home and in the colonies, if, when the foreign or Colonial patent, whose date is claimed under the Convention, has not passed beyond the provisional stage when the English application is made, the foreign provisional specification should be allowed to be filed, on the English application, and with that as a basis, the English patent should be completed in the usual way. It is submitted that the specification filed with the application, whether it is provisional or complete, is the only genuine test of what a man has really in his mind at the time of his application for patent rights. This would involve a modification of the Comptroller's ruling, and might be difficult to put into practice on some foreign convention applications, but could be worked with good effect as between the units of the Empire.

Some Imperial agreement might also be made as to allowing patent rights under the convention to the German "Gebrauchs-muster," which is in some countries treated as a patent, and in others as a design.

Now as to the question of compulsory manufacture. Under Section 27 of the Patents and Designs Act, 1907, the subject of an English patent must be manufactured, or at least an honest endeavour must be made to manufacture it in the United Kingdom within four years from its date : otherwise it is liable to be revoked on the ground that the article, the subject of the English patent, is mainly or exclusively manufactured abroad. The questions of compulsory working and of importation are quite distinct, though apt to be confused. In the United Kingdom provision was made for the revocation of patents and the granting of compulsory licences for non-working on certain conditions long before 1907; the 1907 Act introduced the rule as to importation. Mr. Justice Parker has held that it is immaterial for the purposes of this section whether the article manufactured abroad be patented there or not, as long as it is the subject of the English patent in question, and that if the article be manufactured in the United Kingdom to an extent which may reasonably be expected, having regard to what is done abroad, the case is taken out of the section.

The object of the section is to prevent anyone using his English patent to keep English manufacturers from competing with foreign manufacturers in the home market. And however much one may approve this principle it must be admitted that its application has fallen rather flat. During 1909 there were only seventeen successful petitions to revoke patents under the section, as against fifty-six unsuccessful.* On the other hand, it is true that a few large patent owning firms have put down works in this country and others have granted licences to English manufacturers, so that as a measure of bluff, it has met with some success.

On the second reading of the Bill in the House of Commons, Sir Alfred Mond stated that the effect of the compulsory working clauses in other countries was practically nil : it must, however, be said that any estimate of the effect of such clauses is largely speculative, and hence of little value.

A significant letter was sent in the early part of last year to the Chartered Institute of Patent Agents by Mr. Fitzpatrick in which it was stated that the working clauses were becoming very onerous to patentees, and the more so because they were being adopted

* Comptroller-General's Report for 1909.

by other countries.* On all sides these clauses were preventing inventors from taking out patents in Great Britain, and Mr. Fitzpatrick suggested that the severity of the Law might be mitigated by making manufacture in one part of the Empire equivalent to manufacture in any other part. This severity has been felt elsewhere, and it is pertinent to remark that Germany has made agreements with the United States, Austria and Italy that manufacture by citizens or subjects of one country in that country shall be equivalent to manufacture in the other. If the application of some such scheme to the colonies were feasible it would probably be welcome everywhere, except perhaps in Canada, where importation after one year is forbidden in view of the propinquity of the United States. All Colonial Patent Systems except those of Jamaica, Natal, Cape Colony and Nigeria, contain rules as to working, but at present Canada alone has dealt with importation.

Section 27 of the 1907 Act has however been adopted by Australia and will come into force in December 1911, with a modification making it possible for the patentee to get the revocation cancelled in certain circumstances.

The chief disadvantage of this equivalent manufacture scheme is that it would materially increase the cost of revocation petitions, since it might be necessary on a petition for revocation of an English patent to get evidence from all over the Empire, a thing that might deter many would-be petitioners on whom the State largely relies for making the working and importation clauses effective and meaning.

A reform to which there can be no objection is that of allowing the same times for the various stages in the passage of a patent through the Office in each colony; e.g., for leaving complete specification, for acceptance and for sealing. This would simplify the work under the convention considerably.

One of the most startling points of disparity between the systems is that of the defences available in an infringement action. It is impossible to tabulate these for the various countries here, but it may be said that while in England prior publication in the country of almost any kind, and invalidity of merely one of several claims in a specification are, *inter alia*, sufficient to upset the patent; in Natal practically the only defence is that the defendant was the real inventor or had himself previously published the invention; in Natal, too, invalidity of one claim will not affect the others. It would probably be impossible and certainly inadvisable to attempt to identify the laws on this point, but much could be done to equalise matters and encourage both inventor and manufacturer.

Then there seems no reason why, if an inventor has patents

* Mr. Radford pointed out the probability of this during the debate on the Bill.

in various countries for his invention, his colonial patent should expire *ipso facto* at the expiration of any of the foreign patents for his invention; yet this is the law all over South Africa except in Rhodesia and the Transvaal.

The avoidance of unfair conditions attached to the grant of licences and leases by owners of English and colonial patents, and especially by foreign owners, is a matter which has received attention here, and might with advantage be adopted throughout the Empire. One shudders to think what Lord Bramwell would have said as to this. But times have changed, and freedom of the individual, which with Lord Bramwell amounted almost to a mania, is now nearly forgotten when it clashes with national interests.

When these questions are seriously tackled and some attempt is made towards the unification of the various colonial systems, it is to be sincerely hoped that the colonies will endeavour to meet the Home Government in the spirit of co-operation.

This spirit was manifest during the last Conference when the matter was barely touched upon. Certain differences in the various systems are bound to remain, for they are necessitated by local conditions, but a tendency to uniformity is an excellent thing and a thing which should take a definite step forward in the near future. In other branches of the law this tendency has spread into the wider international field. A Conference attended by delegates from every important country was held in Brussels in September, 1909, to consider the policy and advisability of unifying maritime law. Concerning this Conference and future Conferences of the kind, Lord Justice Kennedy said.*

"I venture humbly and earnestly to express the hope that neither my country nor any other of the countries concerned will obstruct the path to attainment of a great common boon by clinging obstinately to theoretical symmetry, or look askance at a reasonable compromise where national rules have differed."

National laws are bound to differ widely, and colonial laws hardly less widely, for on such questions as religion, and marriage, public opinion varies enormously with geographical conditions. But in the main, economic questions are the same the world over. Mr. Bryce, in his 'Studies in History and Jurisprudence' †
says :—

"The more any department of law lies within the domain of economic interest, the more do the rules that belong to it tend to become the same in all countries, for in the domain of economic interest, reason and science have full play. But the more the element of human emotion enters any department

---

* Address on unification of law delivered before the Liverpool Board of legal studies.
† Vol. 1, p. 144.

of law, as, for instance, that which deals with the relations of husband and wife or of parent and child, or that which defines the freedom of the individual as against the State, the greater becomes the probability that existing divergences between the laws of different countries may in that department continue, or even that new divergences may appear."

Patent systems are so largely responsible for encouragement and stimulation of inventive genius, and inventive genius for higher civilisation, healthier living, and more widespread happiness, that anyone who believes that a nation's welfare depends upon the development of individual effort, and that his nation's future depends upon her imperial position, as an outcome of his belief must be desirous not only of strengthening and simplifying the various patent systems, but of enabling the whole Empire to advance along lines that in the opinion of her chief men lead through mutual fairness and sympathy to imperial progress.

F. W. BENEY.

APPOINTMENTS TO SURVEY DEPARTMENTS

The Secretary of State for the Colonies has approved of the selection of candidates for junior survey appointments in Crown Colonies and Protectorates. For the purpose of selecting surveyors, Ceylon, the Federated Malay States, and the East Africa and Uganda Protectorates will be grouped, and candidates will be required to pass the same tests and go through the same preliminary training. Candidates will, however, be allowed to indicate their preference for particular Colonies, and, if they wish, to await the occurrence of vacancies. Possibly other Colonies or Protectorates may be included in these arrangements, but for the present they will apply only to the countries named. Candidates must be between the ages of twenty-one and twenty-seven and should be unmarried, as the conditions of service for surveyors in the countries concerned are not suitable for a married man. Anyone wishing to become a candidate for these posts should apply in writing to the Private Secretary to the Secretary of State, Colonial Office, London, S.W. He will be required to fill in a form of application and to furnish testimonials and the name of two referees. If the information thus obtained is considered satisfactory, he will be asked to call at the Colonial Office for a personal interview, and, if accepted, will be nominated as a candidate. A candidate, not exempted, will be required to pass two tests: (a) A qualifying examination in mathematics, including algebra, geometry, and plane and spherical trigonometry; (b) A qualifying examination in the use and adjustment of surveying instruments.

FOREIGN AFFAIRS

By EDWARD DICEY, C.B.

THE GENERAL ELECTION AND FOREIGN OPINION

MR. ASQUITH has shot his arrow but failed to hit the mark. He comes back to office exactly as he left it, dependent for the political existence of his party on the Irish vote. It is a sorry spectacle and one that does not augur well for the country at large. The *Neue Freie Press* correctly gauged the situation when, writing after the results of the early polls had become known, the editor said, " the Liberal Party started for a mighty leap. It intended to humble the arrogant lords, who had unhinged the whole party system and had furiously opposed the plan of a Referendum to the historic rights of the House of Commons. But to do this a government needs a roaring success, the un-reserved support of the whole nation, the testimony of a brilliant election. Middling results are here of little use. Only a giant can hurl rocks." Referring to the future of the Liberal Party the same organ says: " A crisis is already beginning in the Asquith Cabinet, and a new chapter of English history—a con-centration from Right to Left under stress of iron necessity—is about to open."

Without lending myself to the editorial interpretation of the House of Lords question, the view of the Austrian-Hungarian organ fairly expresses the situation to-day. For actualities, how-ever, we must, to use the Prime Minister's phrase, " Wait and see." On the other hand, a new phase of energy may possibly open up for the Liberal Party. For instance, it will be interesting to see how far the weakness of the home position affects our status abroad. Possibly this very weakness will turn out to be a cause of strength, and Foreign Policy may prove a source of attraction to a Cabinet divided on domestic affairs.

ENGLAND AND GERMANY

Be this as it may, it is satisfactory to be able to record that the General Election through which we have just passed compares very favourably in one respect with that of last January; I refer to attacks on Germany and the German people. The chief offenders last January were the Chancellor of the Exchequer and the Home Secretary. Both these gentlemen are to be congratulated on mending their manners, and during the December campaign little or nothing was heard about black bread, offal, and other kindred subjects. There was also a decided tendency to avoid exaggeration concerning the German Navy; whenever that matter was referred to it was generally prefaced, at all events by speakers of any standing, with the statement that Germany had a perfect right to do as she liked as regards shipbuilding, and to adopt what naval policy she deemed best for the safety and security of the German Empire. In fact quite a different feeling prevailed on either side during the recent political contest to that of twelve months ago. So it was in Germany; the German press refrained from interference, and studiously avoided irritating comments. From first to last there seemed to be a tacit understanding in both countries that the least said the soonest mended, and it is gratifying to find that the fight has ended without Germany having received even a scratch much less a wound. I cannot but think all this a good omen, it seems to indicate that both nations have come to the conclusion that enough has been done in the direction of sowing seeds of discord, and that henceforward the policy of the two peoples should be to advance along the line of amity and friendship.

For some time past I have watched the slowing down process. Happily I see no signs of flames bursting out again. Things seem to be returning to the normal, to what they were before angry passions arose; a time of goodwill is approaching. The moment, then, should be opportune for burying the hatchet, and if, in place of trying to destroy the British constitution, Mr. Asquith and his colleagues were to direct their attention towards bringing about an *entente* between this country and Germany, appearances point to success. Of one thing I am very certain : any step in that direction would earn the gratitude of the people in both countries for, whatever may be said to the contrary, there never has existed any deep-rooted enmity between the two nations. All along it has been a constant pulling one against the other ; commercial rivalry led to political rivalry and naval programmes did the rest. Once get to close quarters and talk matters out at a round table and all should be well. Things have not gone anything like so far with Germany as they did with

France, and yet what close friends France and England are to-day. And how did it come about? France and this country made up their minds to end all causes of friction. No sooner was the decision arrived at than a way was found to carry it into effect, and what, at one time, was regarded as an impossibility, not only became possible, but resulted in the linking together of the two nations into a common bond of friendship. And if this could be done with France, what is to prevent it being done with Germany.

I do not doubt that Herr von Bethmann Hollweg touched the spot, at any rate on one side, when he told the Reichstag the other day that "the British Government had repeatedly expressed the view that to fix by agreement the naval strength of the individual Powers would tend appreciably to tranquillise international relations." This country, if I remember rightly, raised the same question at the Hague Conference, and ministers have referred to it more than once since that date, but the Imperial Chancellor told us quite frankly, that while admitting all this, we had never yet brought forward proposals that could be met with "a positive acceptance or a positive rejection." I certainly understood the Prime Minister to say in the House of Commons last session that Germany had definitely refused the British proposals for limitation of armaments. But if those proposals were not definite, the results could hardly be otherwise. At any rate it would now seem that all Germany awaits is some definite proposal from us. In that case what more easy than for Mr. Asquith to make it?

Herr von Bethmann Hollweg, holds out the olive branch, when he says:—

> We find ourselves at one with England in the desire to avoid rivalries in respect of armaments. But throughout the *pourparlers*—informal and conducted in a spirit of mutual friendliness—that have taken place from time to time we have always put in the foreground the idea that it is an open and frank discussion, followed by agreement concerning the economic and political interests on both sides, that is the surest means of removing mistrust of any kind in respect of the comparative strength of the two Powers by sea or by land. In itself the continuance of a frank and voluntary exchange of views on all those questions which are connected with these matters is a guarantee of friendly intent on either side, and should lead slowly but surely to the removal of the mistrust which has, unhappily, often made itself felt—not, indeed, on the part of the Governments, but in the public opinion of the two countries.

Surely nothing could be more outspoken, nothing more fair, nothing more opportune. Obviously, before two countries can talk about limitations of armaments with any sincerity, they must be on an outwardly friendly footing. With the feeling of mistrust that for several years, has animated the policy of both nations, when the interests abroad of either is concerned, unremoved, no progress is likely to be made towards a general reconciliation. Why not go to the root of the matter and remove all feeling of mistrust? Then having got rid of the source of annoyance, the rest should be all plain sailing. In Germany a strong desire is manifesting itself to be on better terms with England. I firmly believe that the same desire prevails here, and in reply to the German Imperial Chancellor I should be glad to see some equally concise and equally practical statement made by Sir Edward Grey. The time has passed for generalities, we have had enough and to spare ; let us get to business. Let us have an open and frank discussion and let that discussion be followed by an agreement concerning the economic and political interests on both sides. Then we can talk with some likelihood of success as to limitation of armaments. But I am convinced that without some arrangement of this kind, little practical good will be accomplished in that direction.·

From the interesting and important statement made by Herr Wermuth, the Secretary of State for the Imperial Treasury, when introducing the estimates to the Reichstag, we learn that while the German naval estimates have developed in accordance with the Navy Law, naval expenditure reached its highest point this year when the expenditure was £22,500,000. Henceforward the extraordinary estimates for construction will decline, but the ordinary estimates must necessarily continue to increase until 1917. With the decline in extraordinary expenditure on German naval construction comes also a decline in Germany's borrowings. Reviewing this part of German finance, since 1877 Herr Wermuth pointed out that between that year and 1880 the Government borrowed about £3,500,000 per annum: during the next decade the yearly average mounted up to £6,350,000. The following ten years showed a somewhat lower average, but between 1901 and 1909 the annual loans reached the high average of £14,350,000. For 1910 there was one of £7,400,000, but in the new estimates provision is made for a loan of £4,850,000 only. It would therefore seem that the financial policy of the new Chancellor is one of retrenchment ; that such a policy will be met with endorsement by the German nation needs no demonstration. Here it might not be altogether inopportune to mention that while the increased expenditure on the German navy from 1909-10 was £2,800,000, Great Britain's increase during the same period was £8,400,000, and that our total naval expenditure is not far short of being double that of Germany. It would, therefore, appear that Germany's chance of catching us up is

very remote; that being the case I can see no reason for the
scare generated by Mr. Asquith and Mr. McKenna the year
before last, and which even now makes its reappearance at
inopportune times.

Whether the lessening of Germany's extraordinary expenditure
on naval construction will have a counter-effect on this country's
naval estimates remains to be seen. Of one thing, however, I
feel certain, that Germany is not likely to do what the Radical
Government did and by implication upbraid a foreign and friendly
power for taking time by the forelock and setting its own house
in order. I confess the attitude of the German Navy League is
somewhat mysterious. It is true that the League is not pressing
for fresh legislation, but at the same time, it appears unnecessarily anxious to see that the Navy Law is carried out to
its full extent. As far as one can understand, it is the
intention of the Government to lay down only one battleship and
one large cruiser each year after 1912. But Grand Admiral von
Koester tells us that the League policy is "that from the year
1912 onwards Germany shall proceed with the regular annual
construction of three ships as substitutes for old ships, on the
ground that the legal total of, in round numbers, sixty ships
(thirty-eight battleships and twenty armoured cruisers with a life
of twenty years) justifies this decision and makes it possible to
provide substitutes at the proper time for the training ships
struck off the list." As no organic connection exists between the
Navy League and the German Admiralty probably the League's
programme is only the programme of an ultra-patriotic society.
All the same, it is a little disconcerting to read that the German
Government and the German Navy League are not agreed on the
legal interpretation of the Navy Law. Then again there is the
year 1917 to be met. What will happen then? Shall we repeat
what we have gone through these last few years, or will our
relations at that date be of an altogether different character?

This, I think, depends entirely how we meet the invitation
of the German Imperial Chancellor. If the Government is
so foolish as to let the opportunity pass we must drift further
apart, but if the Government accepts the olive branch the road
is clear of obstacles, all we have to do is to pass along it to
reconciliation. Then what matters it what the German Navy
League says or what happens in 1917? England and Germany
will be on the same footing as England and France and England
and Russia. The peace of Europe will be secured, and one might
almost say the peace of the world. Nothing would have given
more genuine pleasure to the late King Edward and nothing
would, I feel sure, give more genuine pleasure to King George
and the German Emperor than to see an Anglo-German *entente*.

With the Triple Alliance with Germany and Russia agreed on a political and economic understanding it only remains for Germany and England to follow suit, and then all the great Powers of Europe will be welded together into one common bond of unity and friendly feeling.

GERMANY AND RUSSIA

Herr von Bethmann Hollweg seems to have repeated very much what I said last month in these pages with regard to the significance of the meeting between the Czar and the Emperor William and the visit of M. Sazoroff to Berlin. As, however, his utterance is official and goes much further into particulars than my information warranted me in doing, I take leave to reproduce from the very full telegram of the *Times* correspondent the actual words of the Imperial Chancellor's statement:—

I would indicate [he said] as the result of the recent interview that it was once more established that neither Power commits itself to any combination which might have an aggressive point directed against the other. In harmony with this standpoint, we have had the opportunity of noting in particular that Germany and Russia have an equal interest in the maintenance of the *status quo* in the Balkans and throughout the Near East, and will accordingly, support no policy—from whatever quarter it might proceed—which is directed towards the disturbance of that *status quo*.

We have spoken in an open and friendly manner on the subject of our mutual interests in Persia. We have found ourselves at one in the view that our common interests in Persia demand the maintenance, or, as the case may be, the restoration of peace and order in that country. We are bound to desire that our trade with Persia shall not be disturbed and that it may further develop. Russia has the same desire with respect to her own trade, and in addition, as Persia's neighbour, she has a particular and well-grounded interest in the security of conditions in that district of Persia which marches with her frontier. We have gladly admitted that to this end Russia has need of an especial degree of influence in northern Persia, and we have accordingly been very ready to assent to her claim to all concessions for railways, roads, or telegraphs in that region, in order that she may be enabled to perform the tasks in which, as a neighbouring State, she is especially interested. Russia, on her part, will not only place no obstacles in the way of our trade, but will further facilitate the provision of a connection by which that portion of it which is conveyed by Baghdad to Khanikin may be imported into Persia.

We think that the discussion and agreement with Russia, in the course of which a number of points of detail were raised, will make it an easy matter for the two Governments to attain agreement on such new questions as may arise without change of attitude in respect of their policy in general. I may summarise my observations by saying that the conversations which took place during the Potsdam interview have removed more than one apparent misunderstanding, and have confirmed and strengthened the old relations of confidence between ourselves and Russia.

TURKISH POLICY AT HOME AND ABROAD

As to the Turkish Loan the German Imperial Chancellor's explanation goes far to confirm my own diagnosis of the situation. Without, however, mentioning the material benefits that must accrue to the German nation, we are officially informed that, the negotiations with France failed owing to difficulties which "in part were based on political grounds." As to what those grounds were no special enlightenment is afforded, but the reasons that prompted Germany and Austria to advance the loan may be gathered from the following observations:

The Imperial Government followed with its sympathy the financial operations which ensued. It did so, moved by the political consideration that Germany, in showing readiness to meet the pressing financial needs of Turkey, at the same time serves substantially her own well-approved policy, the policy of maintaining peace and the *status quo* in the East. A prime factor in the conduct of this policy is a strong Government in Turkey, strong enough to secure order at home and to command respect abroad. The Turkish Government has hitherto shown great devotion in carrying out this task, and has achieved gratifying success. It appeared, therefore, just and reasonable, on economic and political grounds, that we should stand by our friends the Turkish Government in overcoming the difficulties which had arisen out of their financial position, and provide them with the means to carry further the work of consolidation.

Here it may be convenient to call attention to the pronouncement of Hakki Pasha, the Grand Vizier, on Turkish policy made a few days earlier in the Chamber of Deputies. After referring to the disturbance in the provinces the Grand Vizier proceeded to deal with the loan negotiations, explaining that the French Government had proposed conditions incompatible with the national dignity. It does not appear, however, that much pressure was put upon Turkey by France to secure the loan, for the Grand Vizier was able to add that if the continuance of amicable relations between Turkey and France had depended on the result of the loan negotiations, he would have abstained from advising the policy ultimately followed. He was able also to assure his audience that Turkish relations with France remained and he trusted would remain of the friendliest character. Nor had Turkey's relations with England suffered, for Turkey had never approached the British Government with the object of raising a loan in London, nor had she any intention of entering the Triple Alliance.

A Special Report on the Ottoman Public Debt for 1909–10 has just been circulated amongst the British and Dutch bondholders. In the course of an able summary of political events, in which Sir Adam Block paid a warm tribute to the capacity of Djarid Bey, Minister of Finance, the President of the Council of Administration made the following allusions to the French loan negotiations :

The French Government finally put forward the following conditions :—

The Turkish Government shall designate, in agreement with the French Government, two officials, one of whom shall be the head of the Public Accounting Department at the Ministry of Finance. The other shall be entrusted with the duty of ensuring the proper working of the Audit Department, as laid down in the law now under consideration by the Chamber. The Turkish Government shall notify to the French Government the measures they propose to apply for the strict control of the Budget. Lastly, in the placing of Government orders for munitions of war, &c., to be defrayed out of the proceeds of the loan, France was to be accorded as good treatment as the most favoured nation.

The Minister of Finance considered that the new law, recently passed by the Chamber to regulate the Accounting Department of the Ministry of Finance, was in itself sufficient to centralize all payments at the Ministry of Finance and to control and check non-budgetary expenditure. So close is this control that the Minister of War has endeavoured recently to liberate himself from its effect. The law is perhaps too complicated, but its intention is excellent. Monsieur Laurent, the French adviser to the Ministry of Finance, states that it is a veritable code of budgetary legislation founded on the French law. Under its provisions no expenditure can be authorized without the visa of the Audit Department.

The view taken in official circles here was that these conditions were tantamount to the official intervention of a foreign Government in internal affairs, and it is hardly surprising that in the present temper of the " Young Turkey " party, at a moment when the spirit of national independence is awakening, the Government should find these conditions unacceptable. The opinion 'was widely circulated in the Turkish Press that seeing the security offered for the loan was first-rate, and that the general state of the Empire was certainly not worse than hitherto, political rather than merely financial considerations had influenced the action of the French Government to close the French market. The French market being closed and the London financiers having withdrawn, the Turkish Government had no other course but to turn to Germany and Austria.*

As regards Turkey's relations generally with foreign powers, the Grand Vizier's remarks are well summarized by the *Times* correspondent at Constantinople † in the following words :

As for their general foreign policy, the Government wished to be on the best terms with all the European Powers without leaning on one or other of the great alliances. Indeed, so far as questions of primary interest to Turkey were concerned—namely, the maintenance of the Constitution and integrity of Turkey and the *status quo* in the Near

* See *Times*, Dec. 15.

† See *Times*, Dec. 5.

East, the Powers were all favourably disposed. Relations with neighbouring States were friendly. Rumours of the conclusion of an alliance with Roumania were false. Both Governments were sufficiently interested in the maintenance of the *status quo* in the Balkans to be able to dispense with any formal agreement relative thereto. Relations with Greece had been somewhat disturbed on account of the conduct of the Hellenic Government, which aroused the suspicion that Greece wished to intervene in the affairs of Crete, which only concerned Turkey and the protecting Powers. It was hoped that the future conduct of Greece would dispel these suspicions.

The Cretan situation was unchanged. The Powers still considered that the time for a definite solution had not arrived. The Ottoman military movements in Persia were much exaggerated. Certain contested frontier districts had been in Turkish occupation since the days of the old *régime*, but the Ottoman troops would be withdrawn should the delimitation prove that the districts belonged to Persia. Persia was at present too much occupied with internal troubles to attend to the question. The British Note to Persia had been explained in a satisfactory manner. The Turkish Government was interested in the prosperity and integrity of its Moslem neighbour.

All this is most satisfactory and should tend to allay any misgivings that may have arisen as to events in the Near East. The satisfaction expressed as to the contents of the British Note to Persia should go far to appease the Moslems.

The purchase of two battleships from Germany was sharply criticised by Riza Pasha, late Minister of Marine, who urged among other matters that the ships were old and out of date. In replying the Grand Vizier explained that the addition to the navy was made in the interests of the defence of Turkey's extensive seaboard, justifying the purchase as being necessary to meet the exigencies of the political situation which made it advisable to guard against all eventualities. For my part I think the Grand Vizier did right, although I could have wished that the Turkish Government had purchased two of our old battleships instead of finding what they wanted in German yards. It is business we want, and our diplomats should not forget this when contracts are under consideration.

GERMANY'S POLICY TOWARDS SOCIALISM

On the question of German Internal affairs the most important remarks made by the Imperial Chancellor had reference to the fight against Socialism. What a pity we have not someone in a similar position in our Parliament who could speak with authority in the same way. Instead of that we have a Chancellor who sides with the Socialists, who does not hesitate to take the chair at a political meeting when an avowed Socialist is the candidate. Other members of the British Cabinet have similar leanings. Instead of allowing Mr. Keir Hardie's expressions to pass unnoticed why not deal with them from the Government Front Bench as Herr von Bethmann Hollweg did with the recent avowals of Republicanism by the Socialists in Germany. Brilliantly and forcibly did the Imperial Chancellor anathematize the Socialist doctrines. The German people, he said, must be shown plainly whither the Socialists were taking them, adding that persons who told the masses that they could not prosper unless the present order of things was thrown over and ruined, shared the blame if the masses applied this doctrine. Nor did he hesitate to attribute to the Social Democrats moral complicity in the rioting in Moobit.

Very correctly did the Imperial Chancellor voice the feelings of the German people when he said they were opposed, at heart, to the ultimate political aims and to the Utopian economic ambitions of Socialism. Concluding a speech that will long be remembered in the Reichstag he observed with emphasis that the policy of social help did not affect the position of the State towards Socialism, and its lawless and violent assaults would be beaten down by the employment of every resource which the State provided. That is the way to meet the canker worm which is eating itself into the minds of a section of our own working classes. Let them once know whither their demagogues and stump orators are leading them and they will soon turn upon their leaders and rend them in twain. Instead of that we in this country have to look on while highly placed members of the Cabinet lend the support of their position to secure the return to Parliament of advanced Socialists.

In replying to the Socialist criticism of the German tariff the Imperial Chancellor dotted the i's and crossed the t's of the arguments used by tariff reformers in this country. After showing what can be done with a weapon of defence by illustrating the negotiations between Germany and Sweden and Germany and Japan, in the matter of the recent commercial treaties, he turned to the Socialists and said :—

> Go and ask the business circle of the German people, go and ask agriculture, go and ask industry, go and ask trade whether there is anything in these quarters that we should abandon the foundations upon which our economic life has developed, and brilliantly developed, and that we should make experiments with some other system. In all circum-stances the people would refuse any such experiment, because it would take away the ground from under their feet.

One cannot but admire the outspoken language of the German Imperial Chancellor. Would that the British Cabinet could take a leaf out of his book. Failing the Cabinet, why not Mr. Balfour ? Let a leader who is trusted on one side come out and put his foot down on the harmful theories which are being spread broadcast over this country.

My warmest congratulations to Herr von Bethmann-Hollweg for what I must be allowed to say is one of the best speeches ever made by an Imperial Chancellor. Retrenchment at home in the matter of loans, denunciation of Socialist doctrines and a friendly attitude to all foreign nations may be said to be the three essential points of the speech. Sentiments like these cannot fail to advance the prosperity of Germany, and they should go far towards helping to secure the peace of the world.

What the German Emperor has said on many important occasions, what the German Ambassador has repeated time and again here, the Crown Prince has just said in India and the Imperial Chancellor has just said in the Reichstag. It is the desire of the people in Germany to be on friendly terms with the people of the United Kingdom. Towards this end King George and his illustrious father have done their part. It only remains for Mr. Asquith and Sir Edward Grey to take the necessary steps to accomplish a result that will redound to their own credit and to that of the British nation.

EDWARD DICEY.

OVER-SEA BRITISH ENTERPRISE AND INDUSTRY

SOME SUGGESTIONS FOR ENCOURAGEMENT

BY THE HON. SIR J. W. TAVERNER

(Agent-General for Victoria)

LET me give at the outset the latest official figures showing the splendid trade which is established between the mother-country and the Commonwealth of Australia—all being the outcome of British enterprise and industry : imports from Australia, £32,655,709; exports to Australia, £27,207,430, making a total trade of £59,863,139. When one finds that British enterprise within the Empire has built up this fine trade with the motherland, it will, I think, readily be conceded that the labours of our kinsmen are entitled to every encouragement.

I wish it to be clearly understood that my proposals could in no way clash with the fiscal policy now in force in the mother-country, and I have no desire in any way to dictate to the people of this country as to what fiscal policy they should adopt, that being a matter for them alone to decide. The Chancellor of the Exchequer at the late Imperial Conference said that he heartily concurred in the view presented by the colonial Ministers, that the Empire would be a great gainer if each of the products now purchased from foreign countries could be produced and purchased within the Empire, and any reasonable and workable plan that would tend to increase the proportions of the produce which is bought from us and from each other must necessarily enhance the resources of the Empire as a whole. A considerable part of the surplus population of the United Kingdom which now emigrate to foreign lands in search of a livelihood, might then find it profitable to remain under the flag, and the Empire would gain in riches of material and men. I agree with my colonial comrades that all this is worth concentrated effort, even if that effort cost us something. The federation of the free common-wealths is worth some sacrifice. One never knows when its strength may be essential to the great cause of human freedom, and that is priceless.

The position to-day is that our British pioneers who pitched their tents under the flag and those who followed are not receiving that recognition and support from the mother-country that they are entitled to as Britishers working hard and spending money in developing the resources of the Empire. I propose to point out, purely on business lines, some of the disabilities our over-sea enterprise labours under, and to suggest in what direction the mother-country might extend encouragement to those now working out the destinies of the Empire, and with the additional advantage of offering to those who are leaving the mother-country to pitch their tents under the flag, so that the Empire would gain in riches of material and men.

Let me first deal with the Port of London, which may be said to extend from London Bridge to Tilbury, a distance of about twenty-three miles. Just imagine, in this twentieth century—with a magnificent tidal river running through the City of London—our British mail weekly steamers are obliged to disembark their passengers and produce twenty-three miles from London while foreign passengers and produce are carried right up to London Bridge. What a convenience for foreign passengers, what an advantage for foreign produce over British—less handling, less exposure, less cost of insurance. It will be said that the British boats are too large; my reply to that is that British enterprise demanded larger boats for our trade—so much the better, and so much the more reason why the Port of London should keep pace with the development of British ship-building demanded by the increasing British trade, and place British people in a position to do trade in the Port of London under the best conditions, so that we may at least have fair competition with foreign traders.

As long ago as 1890, I reported to the Australian Governments upon the disadvantages under which Australian trade suffered owing to the obsolete methods of handling produce in the Port of London, and I recommended the erection of an Australian depot for the reception and distribution of Australian produce. The want of unanimity in the colonies resulted in no action being taken; vested interests in this country stood in the way of improving the Port; and we are practically in the same position now as we were ten years ago. What I said then I repeat to-day. It is absolutely necessary to reduce the number of handlings of perishable and other produce to a minimum, in order that the goods may be sold in the finest possible condition and at the least cost to the producer, enabling as high a price as possible to be returned to the consignor in Australia. Then there is the desirability of the Australian origin of the goods being kept before the British buyer, in order that the full benefit of improvement in quality may accrue to the Australian producer. I have made it my business to confer with some of the largest buyers and distributors of produce in Great Britain, and from one and all I have the most encouraging opinions as to the future of Australian produce on the market. The fact that our summer-grown goods arrive during the English winter, and that the quality of our products is beyond reproach, have convinced them that the Australian Colonies will obtain an increasingly strong hold. The universal opinion is that Australian produce has only to be known to be appreciated.

I am convinced that it is desirable that a large central receiving depot with ample cold storage accommodation be erected on the Thames, into which all Australian produce could be received direct from the ship's refrigerated hold. This would secure the arrival of the produce in the best condition and at the least possible cost. It would be inadvisable for the Australian Governments to interfere in any way with the actual distribution, but I am satisfied that the establishment of a central Australian receiving depot would in itself be invaluable in impressing upon buyers the Australian origin of goods. Ample cold storage accommodation would be provided, and the stores would be identified solely with the Australian trade both by name and reputation. Either space could be let out to producers' representatives, or they could be charged a rate for space occupied, or both these methods might be adopted.

I classify the advantages of a Central Depot under the following heads :—

> The increased importance and publicity this concentration of our trade would give to Australian produce generally.
> The chance it would offer of issuing reliable reports as to market prices and needs.
> The satisfaction it would give producers on account of the certainty of reliable and independent reports in cases where quality is complained of, as an examination would be made at the Central Depot before leaving.
> The certain improvement of quality through fewer handlings and no delay in discharging, and the advantages an essentially Australian wharf would have for dealing with Australian produce.

If the Central Depot were erected the process of handling would consist of discharging the butter in bulk into the depot, samples only being sent to Tooley Street. When the goods were sold the parcel would be delivered to the railway. That is two handlings—ship to depot; depot to rail. At present the system usually works thus :—The goods are discharged into a barge and towed up the river ten to twenty miles and there stored. When sold they are carted to the railway station. The handlings then are—ship to lighter; lighter to wharf for storage; wharf to cart; cart to railway. Or it might be increased by the goods being taken into their own store by the importing agents, when the process would be—ship to lighter; lighter to wharf; cart to store for storage; store to cart; cart to railway. A Central Depot in the first case would effect a saving of two handlings, and in the second a saving of three handlings.

The examination of canned goods is a matter which requires considerable experience, and some wharves in London practically command the trade on account of the reputation they have gained. An Australian wharf would be at least qualified to deal with Australian goods to the best advantage. The reputation of a country is founded on its reliability, and is formed, not by the standard of its best products, but of its worst. I have insisted very strongly on the absolute necessity for uniformity. I would insist just as strongly on the necessity for the Colonies never sending forward goods that are not perfectly sound. Every package exported should be calculated to improve our reputation rather than damage it.

As I have already said, I do not agree with Government interference with distribution, nor do I believe such interference would help the trade. If it is desirable to open shops in provincial centres, in the manner of the Argentine Meat Trade, I believe private enterprise, as in the case of the Argentine, will do so, and probably with far more satisfactory results than would be the case if a Government attempted to do it. The competition Australia has to meet is great, and in spite of the freight, which handicaps us, our natural advantages are such that with proper facilities we must take a front place in the race for trade. Present facilities, with the needless expense and risk of damage to our quality, are, however, not proper, and this is one direction in which Governments can interfere with advantage. It is to enable the producer to obtain the highest possible return for his produce, and at the same time to preserve and improve the reputation of the exporting Colonies of Australia on the British market that I submit these recommendations. They will, I feel sure, if acted upon, result most beneficially to interests that are national and entitled to Government sympathy and action.

Some two years ago the Imperial Government relieved the Port of London from certain vested interests which had previously hampered bringing the Port up to date. We have now to deal with the Port Authorities, and from what I can gather there is very little prospect of the very urgent Port improvements being carried out with the revenue at the disposal of the London

Port Authority. I would like to say here that the proposed Port rates are calculated to further hamper British trade. One has only to look at the map of the Port of London to be struck at once with the necessity of rooting up those prehistoric catacombs on the old East India Docks site, constructing a straight cut and providing the necessary warehouse accommodation so as to put us in a position equal to that of Hamburg or Bremen Ports for handling imported food supplies from our over-sea States. The Imperial Government might fairly be asked to look upon a work of this character as national, and come to the assistance of the Port Authority in helping them to complete a work of such vital importance to the enterprise and industry of our kinsmen over the seas as the bringing up to date of the Port of London.

From what I can gather, the Hamburg and Bremen Port Authorities received substantial financial assistance in carrying out their very excellent port accommodation. If the Home Government were to move in this matter they would render an Imperial service which would be much appreciated by the over-sea British producers who are loyally doing their part to make the Empire self-supporting. We are prepared to pay for the accommodation required·for the economic handling and distribution of the Empire's trade at the Port of London. The over-sea Governments have expended millions in harbour improvements, so surely it is time that London, with its great commercial reputation, its great Empire trade and immense potentialities, should wake up and face the position. Another direction in which I think British enterprise and industry could be encouraged by the Mother Country, is in assisting us in opening up direct trade with some of the leading British Ports, such as Manchester, Glasgow, Bristol and Hull, with a regular line of steamers at any rate during the period of the over-seas export trade.

It is gratifying to be able to say that during the last few years there has been a gradually increasing flow of people into our sunny land of Australia, the greater proportion of these new colonists seeking land. This, naturally, means an increase in production, resulting in an expansion of trade, and a greater need for improved Port accommodation· I speak more particularly with regard to food supplies and our perishable product trade. In this connection it is essential that there should be a direct and regular service during our export season. Geographically we are handicapped by distance; if we were within a week's journey from the Mother Country this special consideration would not be expected. Imperial Government subsidies would not, I venture to say, be inconsistent with Free Trade.

If the Imperial and Commonwealth Governments would a

the forthcoming Conference give consideration to matters of this kind with a view to co-operating, they would, in my judgment, accomplish good practical Imperial work.

I have touched upon two proposals which are important in the highest degree so far as encouraging British enterprise and industry by the Mother Parliament is concerned, and should be regarded as Empire work. I propose to suggest other methods of encouraging our over-sea enterprise and industry, which probably is more sensitive, inasmuch as it touches the Revenue duties of this country. Let me first of all deal with the British over-sea wine industry. Millions of British capital and much labour have gone into this natural industry; we are producing sound and pure wine, and notwithstanding the handicap of distance, we receive no encouragement from the Imperial Parliament in the direction of taxation as between British and foreign wines. Some encouragement could be extended without any surrender of the principles of the fiscal policy in force in this country.

France is our principal competitor. Mark how she treats British enterprise and industry. She imposes the maximum tariff upon our wine, also upon our fruit, butter, rabbits and meat. With regard to meat, she also inflicts vexatious regulations which practically make a trade in frozen meat impossible. Acts of this kind can hardly be reconciled with the spirit of the *entente cordiale* in which I venture to say it was intended by the late King that the British over-sea dominions should participate. About five years ago I paid a special visit to Paris and saw the Authorities, urging upon them the desirableness of removing the restrictions placed upon our meat trade, apart altogether from the question of duties. On two other occasions since, assisted by the British Chamber of Commerce in Paris, I have made representations, hoping that, in view of the excellent system of Government inspection of our meat for export which ensures only sound and healthy meat for human consumption, we should be recognised by the French Government, and our meat, accompanied by a Government certificate, accepted, but without avail. France is evidently only agreeable to granting concessions to her own Colonies and the Argentine.

I am strongly of opinion that the Imperial Government should follow the example of France and adopt a maximum and a minimum tariff. This would place the Government in a position to encourage British enterprise and industry within the Empire. Take the fruit industry—I refer principally to the dry fruits. British enterprise and labour in Australia are producing the finest of raisins, currants and apricots. Under the existing tariff, the Imperial Parliament imposes a tax of 7s. per cwt. on these products. With a maximum and minimum tariff in force, the Imperial Government would be in a position to offer encouragement to British enterprise by placing these products under a minimum tariff.

Then, again, note the action of the Austrian Government in regard to the importation of frozen meat. You will remember that recently an agitation was on foot in that country with a view to inducing the Government to allow frozen meat to be imported. The Australasians who attended the Congress on Refrigeration held in Vienna this year did all that was possible to bring under the notice of the Austrian Authorities the excellence of Australasian frozen meat, and offered, on behalf of their respective Governments, to co-operate with the Austrian Government in arranging for a trial shipment of Australasian meat to be sent to Vienna; but according to the *Standard's* Vienna correspondent, the feeling of the Government is expressed by an Austrian politician as follows: " We mean to get something for ourselves in return for the permission. Australia has nothing to give us, and Great Britain cannot give us anything that we have not got already because she has no tariff; so we turn to Argentina, where we can make a bargain."

With a maximum and minimum tariff in force in this country the Imperial Government would be in a position to inform the Austrian Government that Australia was a portion of the British Empire, and that two could play the game of tariff bargaining. If the Mother Country had this power, British enterprise and industry could be encouraged in many ways, and we would only be doing what other countries do for their own people. In my judgment it is a mistake to allow the shibboleths of sixty years ago to influence us in dealing with things as we find them to-day. We should approach this question without political bias, and with only one desire, that of promoting the prosperity and welfare of our own people.

With regard to the meat trade, four points which should not be lost sight of by the Mother Country are:—

That she only produces twenty per cent. of her meat requirements.

That British enterprise and industry pioneered and established the frozen meat trade.

That the Australasian meat export trade has placed within the reach of the people of this country good meat at reasonable prices.

That prior to the establishment of the Empire's meat export trade, fresh meat was a luxury.

Another aspect of the position that might be remembered is the fact that the over-sea States pay a living wage.

In Victoria and other parts of Australia irrigable lands are being brought under intense culture. We are providing our countrymen with freehold homes, and affording them opportunities of bringing up their families under the best possible conditions. This policy is going to build up a great fruit producing industry and an expanding export trade. If we are to be regarded as part and parcel of the Empire, surely we are entitled to seek the co-operation of the Mother Country in asking her to realise the great colonising work of British enterprise and industry that exists and is growing fast in the over-sea States of the Empire, and to appeal for the encouragement on the lines I have suggested in helping our own people to make the Empire self-supporting.

J. W. TAVERNER.

RUBBER IN THE MALAY STATES

The increase in the rubber acreage in the Federated Malay States, according to the annual report for 1909 of the Acting Resident-General just issued, is made up of 11,572 acres in Perak, 11,607 acres in Selangor, 4,640 acres in Negri Sembilan, and 1,086 acres in Pahang. The number of rubber estates in the Federated Malay States is returned as 377, their acreage being 500,431 acres, of which 196,953 acres has been planted up. The output of rubber is recorded as 6,083,493 lbs. (= 2,692 tons) as against 3,190,000 lbs. (= 1,425 tons) in 1908 : the percentage of increase works out as follows : Perak, 177 per cent. ; Selangor, 100 per cent. ; Negri Sembilan, 40 per cent. The lands under rubber in the several States were : Perak, 68,278 acres ; Selangor, 93,853 acres ; Negri Sembilan, 31,945 acres ; Pahang, 2,877 acres : Total, 196,953 acres. There was a steady upward movement in price from 5s. 0½d. per lb. in January to 9s. 8½d. in November : as it is estimated that it costs from 1s. to 1s. 3d. per lb. to place the rubber on the market, the prices quoted give a phenomenal profit. There was no serious amount of disease on estates, though root disease is still troublesome and costly. A fungal disease attacking the branch and stem of the tree appeared, but was quickly overcome ; white ants still give trouble, but are no longer a serious pest. It is to be regretted that these reports are not published earlier. There is no excuse for postponing the circulation of the 1909 report to October 1910 !

TRADE UNIONISM AND THE REFERENDUM

By F. A. W. GISBORNE

(Our Special Correspondent in Australia)

FOR expeditious legislation the present Federal Parliament in its first session will probably create a world's record. The new brooms, wielded with the greatest energy, have already swept about half a dozen measures of the highest importance into the Statute Book. Discussion has been a mere form; members have met to vote not to deliberate. Opposition speakers throughout have recognised the futility of argument when addressed to men determined to have their own way, and pledged to carry without material amendment every measure into use.[*]

Sir Anthony Absolute was a reasonable being compared to a member of a ministry controlled by the Labour Caucus. "You know I am compliance itself—when I am not thwarted; no one more easily led—when I have my own way." Such has been the consistent answer given by the Government to every appeal and remonstrance addressed to it. The Caucus exercises an absolute autocracy, controlling alike the Ministry and the majority in each chamber. Among the measures already passed, or now being hustled through their last stages, are included the Northern Territory Acceptance Bill, the Seat of Government Bill, the Postal Rates Bill, the Anti-Trust Bill, the Land Tax Bill, the Judiciary Bill, the Naval and Military Defence Bills, the Tariff Anomalies Bill, the Referendum Machinery Bill, and two measures intended to effect important changes in the Constitution, which are to be submitted to the popular judgment by referendum early next year. With the latter only it is proposed now to deal. The referendum has become so facile an instrument in the hands of party engineers to further party objects, and such levity is being shown by Australian politicians in using

---

[*] The leader of the Opposition in the Upper Chamber, Senator Millais, in declining on behalf of his party to discuss a measure just introduced by the Government, declared that "the Senate had ceased to be entitled to be regarded as a deliberative assembly." And the remark applies with equal truth to the House of Representatives.

the "extreme medicine" of the Constitution as "daily bread," that a brief inquiry is also justified as to whether that institution, now so popular, is not becoming an unsuitable and dangerous instrument of government.

The two proposed alterations of the Constitution are of a far-reaching, almost revolutionary character. One is designed to give full power to the Commonwealth to nationalise monopolies. Its principal clause runs thus: "When each House of Parliament in the same session has by resolution declared that the industry or business of producing or supplying any specified goods, or of supplying any specified services, is the subject of a monopoly, the Parliament shall have power to make laws for carrying on the industry or business by or under the control of the Commonwealth, and acquiring for that purpose any property used in connection with the industry or business." No word, it will be observed, is included defining the term "monopoly," nor is anything said about compensation. In certain political circles, too, the expression "acquire" is but a euphemism for confiscate. Its meaning in any case is vague; a pick-pocket, for instance, may be said to acquire purses. The inherent right of the free citizen to appeal for justice to the tribunals of his country is also ignored. A caucus-ridden legislature deliberating in secret might, should the people be foolish enough to grant the powers sought, at any moment, by a bare majority vote, summarily confiscate, without notice, the property of any individual or association in the Commonwealth, from a coal-mine to a pawnbroker's shop. Whenever any industrial conflict arose a demand would at once be raised that the industry affected should be nationalised, and the men employed in it engaged on their own terms by the State. A disastrous feeling of insecurity would prevail throughout all classes of producers, and among those connected with the great transport and distributing agencies; and the end might be that, instead of a few small monopolies in capable hands, there would exist one huge monopoly in incapable hands. Direct political management of industries is notoriously corrupt and inefficient. It is noticeable, also, that, while reviling visionary monopolists, the Labour-Socialistic party claims for its own partisans the sole enjoyment of the most pernicious form of monopoly of all, the monopoly of employment. Of the insistent demand for preference for unionists, and the motives that inspire it, something will be said later.

The second measure to be submitted for popular ratification is entitled the Constitution Amendment Legislative Powers Bill. This aims at giving the Commonwealth Parliament sole power to legislate concerning labour and employment, including "wages and conditions of labour and employment in any trade, industry or calling; and the prevention and settlement of industrial disputes, including disputes in relation to employment on or about railways the property of any State." These words, quoted from Clause 4, convey some idea of the comprehensive nature of the powers sought. If the desired alteration of the Constitution be effected an industrial dictatorship will be conferred on the Commonwealth Parliament, and no man can feel sure that he will be allowed to manage his own business in his own fashion. The Commonwealth Court will dictate wages, and he must pay them. A judge sitting in Melbourne, possibly, will be empowered to order the rate of remuneration to be paid on a sugar plantation in Northern Queensland, or on a pearl lugger off the coast of West Australia. Such a functionary, to carry out his duties properly, will require the gifts both of omnipresence and omniscience. When one considers how numerous and diverse are the industries carried on in different parts of Australia, how varying the climatic and other conditions, it is obvious that a single judge or body of judges cannot possibly wield the enormous powers conferred on them satisfactorily.

The rush of applications for increased wages or other concessions immediately after the Commonwealth assumed entire control over all industries would be so tremendous that, either many suitors would have to engage in the profitable study of the Book of Job, or their clamours for a hearing would compel the creation of a small army of supernumerary judges; and processions of litigants, witnesses and lawyers would enliven the most remote settlements in the continent. And, after all, the futility of the whole business is clear. If the wages ordered were too high to enable an employer to carry on his business at a profit, he would close his doors and his late employees would cease to receive any wages at all. If the scale were considered by the men to be too low there would be a strike, and the law, as has again and again already happened, would be openly defied. No uniformity would be possible, for evidently the carpenter in the back blocks, or at Port Darwin, would not be satisfied with the wages that his fellow craftsmen in Sydney or Melbourne would be glad to accept. But what judge or Court, with the best intentions in the world, could possibly fix rates in all trades to suit all local conditions? State interference in these matters has always failed, and always must fail.

But the attempt to bring the railway servants of the various Australian State Governments under the control of the Federal Parliament is worse than a folly. It is a clear breach of the understanding on which federation was effected. The management of its own railways is one of the exclusive rights of each individual State; but if an extraneous, irresponsible authority be allowed to fix the rate of wages and salaries to be paid by the

State Governments to the men they employ in working their lines, practically the States will be deprived of the right of managing their railways, the discipline and efficiency of the railway administration will be impaired, and the financial stability of the States imperilled. At present, thanks to good management, all the State railway services (except that of Tasmania, where political management still lingers) are yielding substantial profits; but if the mischievous proposal just referred to be adopted, losses are certain to be incurred through an early and substantial increase of expenses; unless, indeed, the public be penalised by a corresponding increase in fares and charges for freight. Considering, also, that the Australian railways have been built almost entirely by means of borrowed money, it is clear that any change that tends to render them unremunerative must weaken the credit of the States in the world's money markets. Railway servants in Australia are already paid probably higher wages all through than men engaged in similar work anywhere else in the world. The proposal to entrust the supervision of their interests solely to a Court created by, and responsible to, the Federal Parliament is not only morally unjustifiable, but an insult to the Governments under which they serve.

Of course the motive for this pernicious attempt to usurp the functions conferred by the Constitution solely on the States, and to excite discord between the States and their employees, lies wholly in political expediency. The 100,000 votes commanded by the railway men are of value to the Labour Party, and to gain them considerations of justice and public policy must be set aside. When Mr. W. H. Irvine declared that the Government was deliberately allowing Parliament to be used as an instrument for enabling the servants in the great services of the States to obtain control of those services he expressed an opinion universally held in all responsible circles of Australian society. The same speaker added that the proposal originated in "a deliberate political conspiracy between the Ministerial party and 100,000 railway men," and his words were fully justified. Recent experiences in France and elsewhere support the view held by an increasing number of thinkers that public servants drawing pay from the State should be required to accept such limitations of their franchise privileges as seem necessary to prevent the abuse of those privileges. The State servant in Australia and certain other countries is being taught to think that, in violation of a well-known Biblical precept, he is above his master. For his own sake, and to save him from painful disillusionment, he should not be allowed to become the prey of the demagogue.

The proposals just considered are the sequels to a measure previously passed by the Commonwealth Parliament known as the Conciliation and Arbitration Act Amendment Bill, whose leading provisions were afterwards declared unconstitutional. The original Act was an honest though not very successful attempt to deal with industrial disputes affecting two or more States, and was a comparatively moderate measure. By a wholesome reservation all trade unions whose funds were employed in any way for political purposes were excluded from its benefits ; and in consideration of the peculiar conditions attached to special kinds of employment " all persons engaged in domestic service, agricultural, viticultural, horticultural and dairying pursuits " were placed outside its purview. The amending measure, however, purported to sweep away all those restrictions, and to bring all classes of the State employees also under a single industrial jurisdiction. Clause 9 specifically granted powers to the Arbitration Court to fix a minimum wage, and also to bestow preference on unionists.

The evil effects of the minimum wage are sufficiently familiar to those who have observed the consequences that have followed its recent application to various industries. Necessarily it leads to the discharge of numerous elderly or partially infirm men, increases the prices of manufactured goods and living generally, and creates unemployment. Preference to unionists, however, is an outrage on the first principles of fairness. The obvious underlying motive is to coerce working men to renounce their independence and to join unions, where they may be subjected to the joint influences of intimidation and cajolery exercised by the managers of the unions in the interests of themselves and their Parliamentary delegates. The working man is virtually told that he will be forbidden to obtain employment unless he promise to obey the small group of unscrupulous schemers who control the unions. The political managers of the Labour Party know that voters, like sheep, are more easily driven in flocks than singly.

To illustrate the kind of pressure exercised, it may be mentioned that certain unions in Australia not only compel their members to contribute to the support of a Labour journal, but actually fine any man £3 if he be audacious enough to refuse to vote for the selected Labour candidate at an election. Abuses such as these must ultimately demand stern remedies. The trade unionists of Australia at present number from one-quarter to one-third of the whole body of manual workers. According to the figures published in the last " Commonwealth Year Book " there were in 1908 approximately 153,000 unionists belonging to 331 unions in the Commonwealth, not counting 15 unions in South Australia which furnished no returns. The total funds subscribed by the 331 associations amounted during the year to £166,738, and the expenditure was £159,950. There were also accumulated funds amounting in the agregate to £140,377 besides. As the managers of the unions have always opposed a State audit of their accounts the way in which the large revenues received were employed can only be conjectured. In New South Wales, indeed, a statement sanctioned by the authority of a State official, Mr. Trivett, and published a month or two ago in the *Sydney Morning Herald*, shows that in the year mentioned (1908) the members of the unions contributed £61,601 to the joint funds of those bodies, or about £2 per member. In return they received by way of benefits the sum of £12,165, and by way of out-of-employment pay £9,114, or £21,279 in all. Of the large sum remaining costs of management absorbed £28,256, and legal charges and "other expenses" absorbed the rest. If these figures may be regarded as typical of the expenditure of all the unions the eagerness of the officials belonging to such bodies to enrol fresh subscribers can easily be understood. Preference for unionists is a convenient lure whereby to attract them. Whether the people when appealed to next March will sanction the introduction of the industrial boycott as an instrument to strengthen political unionism at the expense of the independent worker and voter remains to be seen. The mob mind is not exactly discriminative, but it ought to be able to perceive the naked selfishness that animates the self-appointed champions of the rights of labour.

The cry "more pay" is sufficiently audible throughout Australia already. But should rural workers, domestic servants and State employees be invited to join the vociferous crowd demanding increased remuneration the response will be overwhelming. Farm labourers in certain districts, educated by professional agitators, are already organising, and an imposing scale of wages commencing at a minimum of 7s. a day for eight hours' work, and ascending to amounts which might well tempt half the curates in England to take off their coats and emigrate as ploughmen to Australia, has already been published as a hint to the farmer of what he may expect as soon as the proposed amendment of the Constitution has been made. The poor Australian farmer has cause to wring his hands. High duties imposed on imported agricultural implements, and high prices charged for those locally made by manufacturers compelled to pay high wages, already strike him severely. He has heavy taxes to meet also. By way of compensation, a sympathetic legislature affords him the derisory comfort of imposing high import duties on the products he is obliged, for lack of a home market, to sell abroad. And soon, to add to his trials, Wat Tyler may be busy among his hands inciting a general revolt against present labour conditions. Apart from the anxieties caused by an increased wages bill, an eight-hours' working day in uncertain weather during harvest or haymaking time will probably tend to the increase of lunacy in the country districts. If it be legally sanctioned the malady must have made considerable progress already among the general body of electors. By the original Act a proposed law for the alteration of the Constitution must be passed by an absolute majority of each House of Parliament; and not less than two or more than six months afterwards must be submitted in each State to the electors. If one House alone passes the amending measure twice by an absolute majority, an interval of three months being required to elapse between the two occasions, the resistance of the dissentient House is overruled. After the prescribed delay of not less than two months a referendum is taken, and if in a majority of the States a majority of the electors voting—not an absolute majority of the entire body—approve the proposed law, on receiving the assent of the Crown it becomes operative.

The checks on hasty innovation thus provided have proved in practice quite inadequate. The referendum provisions of the Constitution distinctly favour a zealous, highly-organised minority at the expense of the listless or disunited majority of citizens. Practically any constitutional change, unless it affect the proportionate representation in the Federal Legislature or the territorial limits of any individual State (in which case a majority of the voters in the State affected decide the matter), can be made by a bare majority, even of a minority of electors voting. Previous to federation it was forcibly urged by many of the foremost political thinkers in Australia that more powerful bulwarks should be raised against reckless alterations of the Constitution of the kind now meditated. At the Sydney Convention in 1891, Sir Samuel Griffiths (the present Chief Justice) and others proposed the election of Commonwealth and State Conventions, modelled on those provided for by the Constitution of the United States, to deal with proposed amendments, and at that time their views prevailed. At the subsequent session held at Adelaide, however, the majority of the members of the Convention changed their minds, and the present arrangement, based mainly on the Swiss practice, was accepted without, unfortunately, certain safeguards required in Switzerland. In Australia, for instance, a new election following on the acceptance by the people of the proposed amending measure is not required, and the electors, therefore, are not allowed to reconsider a possibly hasty decision.

In the German Empire a proposed alteration of the Constitution is rejected if fourteen votes out of the entire number of fifty-eight be cast against it in the Federal Council. No direct appeal to the people is provided for; statesmen are believed to be the best judges of what is best for the nation, and reason is considered a better guide than the mass of ignorance, passion and delusion which usually constitute the *vox populi*. In Japan a proposal to amend the Constitution can only be introduced to the Diet by Imperial Order, and at least two-thirds out of a minimum of two-thirds of the entire body of members must approve of it. In the United States, as is well known, the checks imposed on constitutional changes are extremely rigid. By Article V. of the Constitution it is declared that two-thirds of both Houses of Congress must first approve of any proposed amendment, or the legislatures of two-thirds of the several States, before a Convention can be summoned to discuss it. The decision of the Convention must then be ratified by the legislatures of three-fourths of the several States, or by Conventions of three-fourths of them, "as the one or the other mode of ratification may be proposed by the Congress." Certain safeguards, such as are embodied also in the Commonwealth Constitution, are provided to protect State rights. The chief object aimed at by the accomplished statesmen by whom the Constitution of the United States was framed was to prevent its becoming an instrument in the hands of reckless party leaders, and to preserve inviolate the foundations of order and freedom. To Hamilton, Washington, and the great Republicans of the golden age of American statesmanship, the demagogue was anathema.

The architects of the Australian Constitution possessed, it is to be feared, too confiding a trust in the infallibility of popular majorities. In adopting the Swiss in preference to the American system they were led away by a false analogy and overlooked essential differences of circumstance. With great military Powers facing her four frontiers Switzerland is subjected to restraints hitherto unknown to Australia. Historical traditions implant in the mind of each Swiss citizen a sense of responsibility, and deter him from the reckless misuse of his civic privileges. Self-interest is subordinated to the intense sentiment of patriotism sprung from memories of adversity suffered in the past, and successful struggles for emancipation. The average Australian working-man voter, on the other hand, is an entirely irresponsible being. Never having known danger he believes it does not exist. His political advisers teach him to love his country merely with the love of the dairyman for his cow. His patriotism consists largely of an eager anticipation of State favours.

The politicians who grovel before him for his vote never address him in the manly terms employed by Mr. John Burns to the working men of Manchester some years ago. They never speak of duty, of the need of industry, honesty and self-restraint; they simply flatter his weaknesses and appeal to his cupidity. He is taught to think that patriotism means getting as much as possible from one's country and giving as little as possible to it in return. His love of sport, too, influences most injuriously his political actions. He speculates in legislation as readily as he speculates in mining shares. He accepts the assurance of his political misleaders with the same airy confidence that he accepts a tip on the racecourse. His temperament, the product of a sunny and stimulating climate, is inimical to habits of deep reflection. He thinks that the walls, not merely of class privilege, but of natural disparities and economic law will fall at the blast of political oratory. Individually highly intelligent, collectively he is as credulous and simple as a child. When promised the moon he believes he will get the moon; and if he got it he would roar for the sun also. To expect wise decisions on questions whose solution demands the highest intellectual ability, the widest historical knowledge and the purest patriotism from large masses of such men subject to the influences of delusive oratory, mendacious invective, and calculated misrepresentation is to defy common sense. The referendum, or plebiscite, has always been the tyrant's most effective weapon. It threatens Australia to-day with the most oppressive, and at the same time most contemptible, form of tyranny—that of ignorance misled by roguery.

Reaction, however, must come soon. Troublous times are at hand which will compel men to look before they leap—to think before they vote. Political trade unionism in Australia is abusing the privileges conferred on it by law. Instead of confining itself to the legitimate and salutary functions of improving the condition of the worker and of bringing him into harmonious and mutually advantageous relations with his employer, it is seeking merely to use him as an instrument to enable a few schemers to grasp supreme power. Such an attempt must fail when the public conscience has fairly been aroused. There are already signs that the hour of awakening is at hand.

F. A. W. GISBORNE.

Nov. 13, 1910.

RACIALISM IN SOUTH AFRICA

By A TRANSVAAL CORRESPONDENT

In nearly every speech delivered to an English audience General Botha has deprecated and disclaimed racialism. Yet how, I ask, can he reconcile with these disclaimers the fact of his choice of a ministry almost entirely Dutch? Unless, indeed, the Boer idea of removing racialism is to leave nothing but Dutch.

In these circumstances, what chance is there for anti-racialism in the Union Parliament, and how far are the objections of the Uitlanders under the Kruger *régime* likely to be remedied by the Botha administration? The chief grievances of the Uitlanders were that they were debarred from the franchise and all share in the executive; that, while they contributed nearly the whole of the revenue, the proceeds were almost entirely spent on the Boer population, and that their children had no chance of growing up with British ideals. Now a great deal has been heard of Hertzogism in the Free State, but a far more insidious process of Afrikanderising the rising generation is going on in the Transvaal. Whereas after the war over seventy-five per cent. of the teachers were English the proportion now is scarcely twenty-five per cent. Promotion beyond the third grade is impossible, except in the case of teachers of a few technical subjects, unless the teacher can pass a searching examination, oral and written, in Dutch. Thus we have British children in schools, even in the suburbs of Johannesburg, taught by young Boers, the product of that hotbed of racialism, Stellenbosch Training College, whose lack of good-breeding and manners is only equalled by the superficiality of their attainments. In the country districts some of the teachers can barely speak broken English, much less write a fair composition in the language. Moreover, the teaching of English history has been eliminated from all but the two higher standards and only taught to these in a meagre epitome. The History of South Africa in use under the Milner *régime* has been replaced by a racial text-book which no English child can read without being ashamed of the Empire, and no Dutch child without thinking that the Dutch race has been systematically wronged.

By leaving to a certain extent the choice of teachers and the direction of the schools in the hands of local committees, Mr. Smuts was apparently confident that in all but large English centres his real wishes would be carried out without the odium of the proceedings falling on him. What a refined and highly qualified English teacher has to submit to in the matter of petty annoyance and espionage from an ignorant Dutch committee soon renders his or her position untenable. Even at Standerton, where English children constitute over forty per cent. of the pupils, an attempt was made by the Dutch committee to have some of the subjects taught wholly in Dutch. Luckily the English parents made such a stormy protest that the Education Office was compelled to modify the action of the local committee. Again, the Training College in the English centre, Johannesburg, is allowed to languish for want of proper Government support, while every help is given to the training establishments in Dutch districts, as, for example, Heidelberg.

The time occupied in instruction through the medium of Dutch in South Africa may be taken as time wasted. As regards practical use few English people realise that Dutch is not the language of the Afrikander Boer. The Africaanse Taal bears about the same relation to Dutch as "kitchen Kaffir" does to pure Zulu, and in fact has much the same origin, being the attempt on the part of the Hottentot and Malay slaves under the Dutch East India Company's rule to speak Dutch, and the rising generation of Dutch, on isolated farms, used the same patois among themselves. Even General Hertzog has admitted that Dutch was a foreign language to himself. True it is used to some extent in Government offices : but for some years to come anyone not fortunate enough to possess a Dutch name will have little chance of employment in a Government office. The language may possibly enable Dutch children to standardise their " Taal," but the " Taal " proper cannot be taught in school, though I believe an attempt has been made on the part of extreme racialists to make a sort of " school Taal."

Though it may be desirable for an English child to be conversant with the " Taal," there can be no question that in the case of Dutch children a knowledge of English is almost imperative ; that is, of course, if the parents wish them to advance beyond the bywoner stage. To say nothing of the disabilities in life and the dwarfing of the child's mind, which the exclusive use of a corrupt patois, totally devoid of terms to express modern thought entails, how can the child grow up with wide imperial views ? His horizon will be bounded by things South African or even by those of his own farm. The average Dutchman fully realises this, and I was recently in charge of a school where the committee (consisting entirely of Dutchmen) passed a regulation that nothing but English was to be spoken in school, and that the pupils were to be encouraged to speak English out of school. Even the Transvaal Education Office has admitted that Dutch children in country schools are growing up unable to express themselves adequately in English, and that the boys of the country cadet corps do not sometimes understand even the words of command in English.

Enough of educational matters. I pass on to the question of parliamentary representation. It might have been thought that in view of the elections for the Union Parliament, the Botha Government would have followed the example of Natal and had a complete revision of the voter's list. Those in authority, however, considered that they would better serve the interests of their own party by leaving things as they were. Six months' residence confers the franchise, but as the last voter's list was compiled two years ago many people entitled to vote were unable to do so as their names did not appear on the list. In this way over a thousand English voters in Johannesburg alone were disfranchised. Others found themselves on the roll of a district some hundreds of miles from the spot where they were then residing. It should also be noted that the Dutch population is less migratory than the British.

It is amusing to notice how the authorities responsible for the readjustment of the Union constituencies have attempted to nullify the English vote. The most ridiculous instance is that in which Parktown, the aristocratic suburb of Johannesburg, has been tacked on to a Dutch slum quarter. Barberton has been joined to the Dutch district of Carolina, from which it is separated by an impassable range of mountains; of course there was no difficulty in procuring Het Volk evidence to the effect that the adequate means of communication required by law between the parts of the new district existed. Similarly the Pilgrims Rest electors were coerced by scarcely veiled threats of quashing their railway scheme into being annexed to Lydenberg.

Obviously any adequate system of immigration would lessen the Dutch predominance. Hence the Nationalists say they are averse to immigration till they have settled all their own poor on the land. This means they are eager to establish a few more pauper Dutch settlements similar to the one at Delmas, preferably in a district where the English are at present in a majority. This they propose doing by bringing back to the land the incompetent bywoners who have drifted into the towns. Supported by Government doles they may be trusted to produce Het Volk voters, if nothing else. Nothing has been done to encourage or assist the Milner settlers, but every effort has been made ,by the Dutch press to belittle their work and besmirch their characters. As a matter of fact the Milner settlers have in most cases produced double what the average Boer does off the same acreage and have proved what can be done by real hard work.

Having shown what a small share Englishmen are likely to have in the legislature of South Africa, let us consider what share they are likely to possess in the executive. At present, except in the case of heads of departments, Englishmen are in the majority. But how long will this continue? The South African Constabulary have been done away with, the original members of the Transvaal Police, mostly discharged soldiers and as fine a body of men as any police force in the Empire, have been largely replaced by the slovenly, inept bywoner. One of the first steps of the Union Government was to retrench the head of the department and his second in command, both English officers. Already there is an agitation to make bilingualism the qualification for all public officials from railway ticket-collectors to magistrates. It is noteworthy that comparatively few Englishmen succeed in passing the legal test for magistracies. When one considers that the examiners are Dutch judges, and that though candidates' names are suppressed, it is very easy to detect a Dutch candidate by his idiom, the explanation is not hard to find. The Dutch party seem to think that, as the British Government has handed the country over to them, it is presumptuous on the part of any Englishmen even to criticize them. The boycotting of the *Witness* in the matter of withdrawing from its pages all Government notices, bears out this conclusion. That paper had been too outspoken in its strictures on the prospective Union Government. The Dutch predikants who seem to think that racialism is synonymous with Christianity have compared the Dutch in their " election sermons " to the Jews when restored to their country, and have urged the Dutch " to build up the walls of Jerusalem " without allowing the other inhabitants of the land to participate. The Boers as a class, by some inscrutable reasoning process, have persuaded themselves that they are God's chosen race.

General Botha's Government have been creating sinecure and unnecessary offices for their Dutch supporters. It will be sufficient to allude to the field cornets. The colony is saddled with an expense of nearly £40,000 a year for the upkeep of these. Their official duties were previously carried out by the police. The field cornet is generally a Dutchman who often cannot speak a word of English. The field cornets were chiefly employed during the elections as paid political agents for the Nationalists.

Many Englishmen in the Transvaal are so little influenced by racial sentiment that they would willingly support a Government entirely of Dutchmen, did it govern the country equally in the interest of both races. To the English working-man the Nationalists have appealed as representing the people's interests as against those of the capitalists ; but the English working-man is beginning to see that the big Dutch landowner, notably in the matter of closer settlement, is more opposed to his interests than any mining magnate. He also realises that the present Government has done nothing for the working-man except to pass a not altogether satisfactory compensation Act. No steps have been taken to enforce proper ventilation of the mines. And the action of the Government with regard to the strike and the subsequent strike legislation were certainly not likely to appeal to the working-classes.

What, however, has alienated English supporters more than anything else is the racial favouritism displayed in the disbursement of public funds. A sum of over £300,000 a year has been set aside to pension the officials of the late republic. Of the recipients of the £123,000 voted for the relief of those disabled during the war only four bore English names. The Government seem to have a stereotyped form in readiness to send to English applicants, " Your application is not borne out by the evidence." Most of these moves on the part of the Government seem to necessitate highly paid commissions composed of Dutch supporters. In the last instance £32,000 was thus spent. A sum of £750,000 was appropriated by Botha as Minister of Agriculture, without a vote, on the last day of the session of the late legislature as a loan to enable indigent burghers to procure cattle. That this loan will probably be of the nature of a dole is shown by the fact that sums of £300,000 have from time to time been written off the repatriation loan as bad debts. The poorer English settlers have the greatest difficulty in getting any help of this kind or by profiting by the land bank. This institution is principally taken advantage of by big Dutch landowners, who are thus able to borrow money at 4 per cent. to pay off mortgage bonds for which they were previously paying 10 per cent. A huge sum of nearly a quarter of a million has been spent on irrigation works to improve the value of Dutch back veldt farms. Meanwhile, in English centres the efficiency of institutions like the Johannesburg Public Library and Hospital is seriously impaired for want of Government support, and it must be recollected that the English section contribute about 80 per cent. of the revenue.

As a forecast of what is coming it may be mentioned that the Nationalist Union Government has already shown its want of loyalty by attempting to cancel Empire Day from the list of public holidays. It has proposed to stop recruiting for volunteer regiments. The volunteer movement, it may be explained, is almost entirely English. Finally, the Minister of Justice has directed that all summonses in magistrates' courts must be printed both in Dutch and English. This last racial absurdity, involving, as it does, a large extra expense to the taxpayer, is all the more ridiculous when one considers that in some parts of the Union, in fact in two-thirds of Natal, you may live for years without hearing a word of Dutch or even meeting a Dutch man. And as the English reader may have already gathered, Dutch proper is almost unintelligible to the average Boer. It is a standing joke that the Boer farmer on receipt of similar bilingual documents from the Transvaal Agricultural Department reads them in English and replies to them in the Taal.

After all, we have only ourselves to blame for the position of affairs, or rather, I should say, the fatuous action of the Home Government. By going straight for responsible government without any intermediate period we have given back to the Boers everything for which they fought unsuccessfully. And, no doubt, in the circumstances, General Botha, with others of his party, is like a more celebrated character in history, " astonished at his own moderation."

ONE WHO KNOWS.

IMPERIAL LITERATURE

THE CONFLICT OF COLOUR *

ONE must acknowledge having read this book with conflicting sensations of wonder whether its clever author intended it as a hoax or as a serious treatise on international politics. Everything about it is puzzling. It possesses a general introduction which does not deal with the subject-matter of the book itself and general matter which has no relation with the introduction.

We are informed that everything in the past is wrong, and we are not told what is best to do to remedy so sad a condition. Where one seeks for information one gets quotations which are irrelevant to the question in hand, and when the reader fancies he has stumbled at last upon the author's main idea he is calmly informed that before any change takes place "many years must pass." It follows that with the best will in the world one cannot see where the danger lies which we are to conjure by abjuring, all we have believed in hitherto, and logically conclude that if that danger is not immediate we may hope it will not threaten us for "many years yet." Seriously this new departure on the part of Mr. Putnam Weale, who hitherto has instructed us very fairly in matters oriental, creates in us an apprehension—and he will excuse me for saying so—that either his volume is premature or that his undertaking is still beyond his scope. If as I gather on the whole he fears for the white populations the development of the coloured races which people our globe, and wishes by timely warning to place " the English-speaking races especially " on their guard, it does not seem quite right to weaken their armour of defence by telling them in blunt language that the principles, which for two thousand years at least have been their strength, are wholly useless and antiquated, or that Asia and Africa are awakening because they have realised that their former weakness " lay in climatic disabilities " only.

"It is at last quite certain," writes Mr. Weale, " that the question of colour is the rock on which the Empire must split or on which may be builded the greatest edifice the world has ever

* 'The Conflict of Colour,' by B. L. Putnam Weale, 8vo., 10s. net. Macmillan and Co., Ltd., London.

seen." This is a Delphic pronouncement, for one is in the dark as to what is the Empire which is to split, or that which is to be "builded."

In another place we are told "Progress is in the air; superstition is no longer believed in; men are everywhere discontented; yet the old structures have been standing so long that the work of removing them can only be carried out slowly after the lapse of the very longest periods. Thus knowledge, though it has now admittedly spread far and wide, though it has accomplished much, has still an infinity of tasks to attend to; and many thousand suns must set before the work of political renovation is reasonably complete even in Europe. This fact, this stout survival of prejudice will have a most important general bearing on all political problems for many decades." To call knowledge " a stout survival of prejudice " is so bold a statement that the author is justified in declaring in a footnote to the above " that such remarks will sound offensive in the ears of many readers." He might more truly have said they are offensive because they are subversive of what is the main object of man's existence on this planet or in the great hereafter, and because it fringes on the border of impertinence as a message from the author to his readers.

That great changes are at hand and await time and opportunity: that climate influences character, and that Providence is oftenest on the side of the big battalions are mere platitudes which do not require an elaborate investigation into the merits of Creasy's 'Fifteen Battles of the World,' but number has not yet conquered knowledge, climate has not yet arrested purpose, and people who love liberty seek it in law and order and will continue to impose them.

HUBERT E. H. JERNINGHAM.

TWO BOOKS ABOUT NEW ZEALAND

' Memories of Maoriland ' * is a delightful story of travel in New Zealand by E. I. Massy, a name familiar to the readers of *The Empire Review*. The book is well illustrated and should make a very acceptable New Year's gift. It is brightly written and full of anecdote. The Maori legends are most fascinating. This little volume should interest a wide circle of readers. By the generosity of the author the proceeds of the sale will be handed over to the Maori girls' school, founded in memory of the late Queen Victoria.

* ' Memories of Maoriland ' (illustrated), by E. I. Massy. Messrs. Clowes and Sons, Ltd., Cockspur Street, London, S.W. Price 3s. 6d. net.

' The Heart of the Bush ' * is a pretty love story told by that well known and popular writer on New Zealand, Edith Searle Grossmann. From this book, as indeed from all the author's studies, one learns much about the Dominion and about colonial ways. The style is taking and the matter interesting, and if the narrative is somewhat out of the beaten track it suffers nothing on that account. Here too one gains an insight into some of the beautiful Maori legends and learns to appreciate the island scenery.

A BOOK OF REFERENCE

' Who's Who' for 1911 † fully sustains the great reputation obtained by this excellent book of reference. Each year the volume becomes more indispensable, and each year it seems more complete. Owing to the General Election taking place in December, the defeated candidates still see themselves recorded on the " old register " as M.P.'s. Similarly the successful candidates left out in the last Parliament by reason of an adverse verdict at the polls in January, find themselves without the magic words " M.P." after their names. But all this is excusable in the circumstances. Not the least merit of this annual volume is the fact that it is published in good time. So many reference books make their appearance in the spring that the example of ' Who's Who ' cannot be too highly commended. It is one of the most useful and most accurate compilations in the literary world, and no man of importance can afford to be without a copy.

* ' The Heart of the Bush,' by Edith Searle Grossmann. Sands and Co. : London, 15, King Street, W.C. ; Edinburgh, 37, George Street. Price, 6s.

† ' Who's Who,' 1911. A. and C. Black, Soho Square, London. Price, 10s. net.

THE COAL INDUSTRY IN INDIA

By A BENGAL RESIDENT

INDIA now stands ninth on the list of the great coal-producing countries of the world, just below Japan, the output for last year being a little over 11¼ million tons.* Of this total 94 per cent. was obtained in Bengal ; the balance, 238,000 tons coming from the Central Provinces, 305,000 tons from Eastern Bengal and Assam, 37,000 tons from the Punjaub, and 96 tons from the North-West Frontier Province. The quantity raised, however, was 854,000 tons less than in the preceding year, a fact I attribute to the depression in the industry which caused the closing down of several mines, and to the anxiety of managers to curtail expenditure and get rid of stocks that had been accumulating since the coal-boom in 1908.

About 93 per cent. of the total amount of coal produced in India is consumed within the country. During the last seven years the export trade has averaged only 7 per cent. of the production. The following statement taken from the statistics published by the Director of Commercial Intelligence in India shows the approximate amount of coal consumed in India during 1909 :—

	Tons
Railways (including railway workshops)	3,765,000
Port trusts	109,000
Bunker coal	989,000
Inland steamers	500,000
Jute mills	703,000
Cotton mills	862,000
Iron and brass foundries	528,000
Tea gardens	100,000
Consumption at collieries and wastage	1,181,000
Other forms of industrial and domestic consumption	3,110,000
Total	11,797,000

In Bengal the bulk of the mining is concentrated in the districts of Manbhum and Burdwan. During 1909, 278 mines in all were working in the Manbhum district, 216 in the Jharia coalfields and 62 in the Raniganj fields. In Burdwan 164 coal

* See " Annual Report of Chief Inspector of Coal Mines in India."

mines were open. The great Bokara-Ramgarh coalfield in Hayaribagh district, comprising an area of 140 square miles in extent, has not yet been worked. A railway is being constructed from a station on the East Indian Railway line right into the heart of the coal area; and, when this is finished, one may expect to see a revolution in the coal industry. Labour is plentiful and cheap in the neighbourhood, and as the coal lies close to the surface, if the quality should turn out to be good, there is every prospect of this area becoming the main coal-producing district in India.

The greater part of the capital used in the exploitation of the Bengal coalfields is European, and the agents and managers of the various coal companies are nearly all Europeans. A few smaller mines and one or two important companies, however, are in the hands of Indian agents and managers. The labour is entirely Indian. Though the coal industry of Bengal is one of the most important in India, it is only during the last ten years that any real progress has been made, due, no doubt, to the antiquated methods employed in raising the coal. The average number of tons raised per person employed is only 103 per annum as against 705 in the United States, 498 in Australia, 570 in Germany, 350 in Austria and 268 in the United Kingdom. It is true the Indian labourer is physically far less efficient than the European or the American; but, on the other hand, coal in Bengal lies comparatively near the surface, and is obtained without much effort.

Notwithstanding the industry is passing through a period of unusual depression, good Bengal coal sells at the pit's mouth at about Rs. 3 per ton, and the shares of first-class companies are among the most paying investments in the East. I append a list of some of the best known companies with their market quotations taken from the last issue of the Calcutta paper, *Capital* :—

Name of Company	Capital Paid up.	Paid up per Share.	Market Quota- tion.	Dividends per Cent.	
				1908.	1909.
	Rs.	Rs.	Rs.		
Aldïh	8,00,000	100	151	22½	19½
Bengal	39,00,000	100	760	70	55
Balgorah	8,00,000	10	16½	15	27½
Bhuskajuri	5,08,070	10	16⅛	10½	12½
New Beerbhum	7,20,000	10	44	60	55
Standard	8,00,000	10	19⅛	25	17½
Seebpore	2,80,480	7	28	41½	32½
Runeegunge	9,00,000	10	19⅝	60	30

Unfortunately the majority of coal companies are not paying

dividends. The causes are not far to seek. During the boom the enormous dividends declared produced a fever of speculation. Astute owners sold their properties at extravagant rates, and numerous over-capitalized companies were floated. Many of these concerns have already gone into liquidation, and the shares of others are selling far below their par value. Apart from the losses sustained by speculators in these over-capitalized companies, their existence has had a very unwholesome effect on the coal industry as a whole. The sale of hundreds of thousands of tons of poor coal at temptingly low rates tended to depreciate the value of first-class Bengal coal, and the export of inferior coal to Australia and various eastern ports discredited the industry of Bengal. I am glad to say, however, that signs of recovery are to be seen on all sides and the price of good Bengal coal is rising; but it will still take some time before the industry recovers completely from the effects of the boom, and the over-production which followed in its wake.

Coal mining in India has not hitherto been pursued as an exact science. The enormous deposits in the Jharia and Raniganj fields outcropping at the surface, have made it possible for mining to be carried on with little expert knowledge, and yet with considerable financial success. The result is that in all but the best managed companies the coal industry has been exploited with little regard for the future, and under a system, which, if continued, must be ruinous to the industry in the end. The last report of the Chief Inspector of Mines in India contains the following severe indictment of the system followed in Bengal :—

Huge galleries and small pillars—pillars quite inadequate for proper support of the surface—was the ordinary method adopted. The large area of the galleries, coupled with the fact that explosive gas was never seen, apparently did away with the need for ventilation; while the strong sandstone roof which overlies most of the coal seams in Bengal, obviated the necessity for safe-guarding the future of the roadways.

With a road that showed no signs of collapsing, it was manifest that the easiest coal to get was that which was weathered and fractured upon the sides of the pillars ; so pillars already small became steadily smaller. This could only last for a time, perhaps months, perhaps a year or two, until nature asserted herself, and the weight of the strata crushed out the weak pillars, and large areas, if not the whole mine, were irretrievably lost.

This is an oft-told story ; unfortunately it means a national loss, as such coal is lost for ever.

Another great defect is the absence of the panel system of working. The object of this system is to isolate areas of working in case of fire or inundation. The Chief Inspector of Mines has drawn the attention of managers to the necessity of adopting it in Bengal, but apparently his advice is disregarded. " One sees the spectacle," he writes, " of a large coal property, where the conditions are so pre-eminently suitable for panel working, being cut up in the old-fashioned and wholly unscientific way, into one continuous area of pillars with a range of six or seven inclines into the seam. In the case of fire or inundation in any part, the whole property is immediately in danger, and would in all probability be engulfed." The coal of Bengal is a national asset, and it is the bounden duty of agents and managers to develop the industry on sound economic lines. Of course, investors demand dividends, but it is a poor policy to sacrifice future prospects for a small immediate gain ; and, if the agents and managers continue to fail in their duty, it is the business of Government to step in and impose restrictions.

Bengal coal can never compete on equal terms with Welsh coal,* which possesses at least 20 per cent. more burning power. But for the best quality of Bengal coal there will always be a steady and increasing demand. The problem, however, is how to dispose of the second-class coal. Fortunately an enormous market is ready to hand, which only requires exploitation. It is well known that the forest areas of India are rapidly disappearing. As deforestation progresses, wood fuel is becoming daily more expensive, and in parts of the northern provinces it cannot now be obtained at all, with the result that the agricultural population have no other fuel except the dried cow-dung which they collect in their fields. The Indian agriculturist is habitually conservative ; but there can be no doubt that, if the coal companies would devote some of their energies to the preparation of a cheap, smokeless coke, and to its distribution among the agricultural and even the town population, the results could hardly fail to be successful. There are at least a hundred million agriculturists in India who cannot now procure sufficient wood or other fuel for ordinary domestic purposes at anything like a reasonable cost. The exploitation of this field promises most to the coal industry. It requires only enterprise and capital to attain success ; and when that is attained, the demand for Bengal coal will be, probably, ten times as great as it is at present.

If the greater part of Bengal coal is second class, there is plenty available for use as steam coal at fair rates, and the prospects for companies which raise a high percentage of Desharghur and first-class coal are sufficiently bright. The

---

* The relative values of Indian, Welsh, Japanese and Australian coal may be gauged from the following market quotations for the year 1909 :—

	Calcutta		Colombo		Singapore	
	Rs.	As.	Rs.	As.	Rs.	As.
Indian Coal	13	0	15	8	14	14
Japanese Coal	—		—		16	8
Welsh Coal	18	8	21	6	23	13
Australian Coal.	—		—		18	6

price of first-class coal has recently increased by 4 to 8 annas per ton. At the same time the output has decreased, exports have increased, and the accumulated stocks are being rapidly disposed of. For instance, according to *Capital*, the total decrease in raisings for the period May to July, 1910, was 17 per cent. as compared with the raisings for the same period in 1909. The total decrease in stocks at the end of July was 44 per cent. as compared with the stocks for the same period in 1909, and the increase in exports for the period January to July was 27 per cent. as compared with the exports for the same period in the previous year. The statistical position is, therefore, eminently sound.

The Indian railways are the best customers of the coal companies. They consume annually about 120 tons per open mile. In the year 1909, the total consumption of Indian coal by the railways was over $3\frac{1}{2}$ million tons. When the mileage at present under construction is completed, the consumption will exceed 4 million tons, or nearly as much as the total output of coal in India in the year 1899. Since that date, raisings have increased by about 250 per cent., and the number of persons employed in the industry has risen from 65,000 to 109,000.

X.

COCOA IN GRENADA

The Colonial Secretary in the course of an interesting report tells us that the cocoa crop in Grenada for the last financial year produced 67,329 bags, the largest recorded ; the nearest approach being the crop of 1904, when 67,225 bags were reaped. Unfortunately a further decline in prices took place. An examination of the world's statistics of the cocoa trade shows that consumption is not keeping pace with production. On the other hand, consumption itself is on the increase, especially in the United States of America, where cocoa as a beverage, compared with tea and coffee, is evidently becoming more popular. With the advance of competition, greater attention is being paid both to the cultivation and curing of cocoa in Grenada than in bygone years, with the pleasing result that there is a distinct improvement in the quantity and quality of the crops.

SIDELIGHTS ON COLONIAL LIFE

The Editor will be glad to receive voluntary contributions to these pages
from oversea readers.

Land Settlement in Rhodesia.

In the course of an interview with a representative of the
South African *Farmers' Advocate*, Major Apthorp, late Director
of Land Settlement in the Orange Free State, gives some
useful and up-to-date information respecting the prospects of
farmers in Rhodesia. Answering various questions put to him
by the interviewer, Major Apthorp said : "I went through the
district round Bulawayo, and also visited Rhodes' Farm in the
Matapos, now being farmed by Mr. Hull, who formerly had a
farm near Bloemfontein. It was interesting to observe what
energy combined with a practical knowledge of the best methods
of farming could produce. The farm is a magnificent property,
and the growing of lucerne will be a great feature in the management. Mr. Hull has levelled and terraced a considerable acreage.
The soil is excellent, and will grow practically anything. It is
irrigated most perfectly by means of a big dam. I was told that
there is a quantity of similar land available in Rhodesia, which
struck me as being a white man's country in every sense of the
word. It is a capital country for farming, and so far as I could
judge, offers great possibilities for irrigation, both on a large and
small scale. The terms offered to settlers by the Chartered
Company appear to be most liberal. Only 5 per cent. of the
purchase price has to be paid by way of annual rent, and no
payment is demanded until the second year of occupation. New
settlers are taking up land every day and there is still an
enormous quantity of land available for settlement. Every man
who wishes to settle in the country should go and see it for himself. I also travelled in the Salisbury district, and so far as I
could judge the settlers were doing well. It happened that I saw
the country at its worst, no spring rains having fallen. The
settlers I met everywhere seemed a superior class of men, full of
enthusiasm and enterprise.

Essentially a Stock Country.

" As regards capital a man should not have less than £1,000, as he would need money to stock his farm. The Chartered Company are not at present giving the same assistance to men who have taken up land as the Land Board in the Orange Free State does. There, for instance, a man can claim an advance from the Board to assist him in making improvements, provided funds are available ; whereas in Rhodesia, although the price of land is very favourable to the settler, he has, as it were, to work out his own salvation. He has to develop his land with his own resources, and make improvements at his own expense. The British South Africa Company, however, gives a rebate for certain improvements carried out to the satisfaction of the Company. Rhodesia seemed to me to be essentially a good stock country, but whether it is advisable to import thoroughbred herds or not under the present conditions I cannot tell. I saw a good herd of pure-bred Frieslands on a farm near Salisbury, and although the initial losses had been heavy the herd was certainly doing well. All the cattle I saw were in excellent condition considering the time of the year. Where men are breeding up from the Angoni and other local breeds with good bulls the improvement in the progeny is very marked. In my travels I saw some large herds of Angoni cattle. It should be an easy matter to obtain a market for good slaughter cattle. With the general establishment of creameries cattle-raising must make progress.

Farmers and their Crops.

" Several of the farmers foresee difficulties in regard to native labour. They cannot get the right kind. Most of the good boys go to the mines. Many of the natives available come from Nyasaland, and the farmers say three of them would not equal one Basuto boy. As to the mining regulations in some few cases these may be opposed to the interests of farmers, but the drawbacks are counterbalanced by the advantages. For example, if a farmer takes up land for bonâ fide farming purposes, and it proves to be a rich gold-bearing property, he receives a very useful share of the prize. Further, it is always an advantage to a farmer to be near a mine, and I know of a case where a farmer sold 3,000 or 4,000 bags of maize to a mine close to his door, at a good price and, of course, free of railway and other freights. Maize is the farmer's chief source of revenue, and near the mines they were getting 10s. a bag, and 9s. at Bulawayo when I was there. Mealies are certainly an important factor in the farming operations of the country, and I may mention that I should think dry farming in all its branches has a great future there as well as in the Orange Free State and other parts of South Africa."

Cotton in Nyasaland.

The native cotton industry in Nyasaland has made satisfactory progress, but if an important export trade is to be created, it is imperative that the interests of the natives should be aroused and their willing co-operation enlisted. The constitutional apathy of the local tribes towards all novel forms of industry seemed at one time to present an almost insuperable obstacle to the establishment of cotton as a general staple of native cultivation. It may even yet be premature to indulge in too sanguine predictions, or to assume that cotton will eventually take its place in every village garden and obtain a fair share of the attention now being given to cereals, such as maize and millet. This, however, is the object which the Protectorate Government has in view. Its accomplishment will necessarily be a gradual process, because, if the co-operation of natives is to be of any real and lasting value, it must be given freely and intelligently from a conviction of the benefits conferred on the cultivators themselves rather than from any unreasoning acquiescence in the wishes of those in authority. There can be no doubt that very encouraging progress has already been made towards this end. The native cotton crop last year amounted to 220 tons, an increase of 130 tons on that of the previous year.

The crop now approaching maturity promises well, and, as seed distribution has practically doubled in amount, there is reason to anticipate a further large increase in the output. The quality of native-grown Nyasaland Upland cotton has always been as good as, if not better than, European-grown Upland, but the native-grown Egyptian crop has in the past been very disappointing. A marked improvement, however, has resulted from teaching the natives how to grade their cotton, and a large proportion of the native crop from Port Herald, on the Lower Shire River, obtained 1s. 1d. per lb., one of the highest prices hitherto secured by Egyptian cotton in this Protectorate. Under the system at present in vogue natives grow and sell their cotton more or less under the auspices of the Resident of the district, who, while leaving the vendors a perfectly free choice as to the disposal of their produce, assists them in every possible way by seed distribution, by advice as to methods of cultivation, and in other ways. It is satisfactory to note that a few natives are now opening up independent plantations of their own, apart from the ordinary village gardens.

Education in Hong-Kong.

In Hong-Kong there are seventy-one Government and Grant Schools, the most important being Queen's College. Twenty-two are Upper Grade with a staff competent to give instruction on all subjects of the Seventh Standard, and upwards; they have an average attendance of 4,337, and the medium of instruction in all with the exception of five girls' schools, is English. The remaining schools are Lower Grade. They comprise one school for British Indians, where English and Urdu are taught; four Government and one Grant Anglo-Chinese Schools; and forty-three Grant Vernacular Schools. The average attendance at the Lower Grade schools is 2,223, making the total average attendance at both Grades, 6,560. The revenue from school fees is $68,204 ($40,792 from Queen's College) and is rapidly increasing owing to the numbers of Chinese desirous of an English education. Two schools are provided for children of British parentage. Both (one for boys, the other for girls) are under the Government. Last year the combined average attendance was eighty. As might be expected these schools have a strong patriotic bias, the boys' school providing a small but efficient cadet corps.

Higher education is represented by the Technical Institute, where instruction is given in Mathematics, Machine Drawing, Building Construction, Field Surveying and allied subjects; in Chemistry and Physics; in the English and French languages, and in Book-keeping and Shorthand. There is also a Teachers' Class which the junior Chinese masters of Government and Grant Schools are expected to attend. The Institute has a well equipped laboratory. The lecturers are chiefly Civil Servants recruited from the European staffs of Queen's College and the Public Works Department. A scheme for the foundation of a University is rapidly being matured, the building fund having been furnished by the generosity of Mr. H. N. Mody and the endowment fund by private subscription. It is hoped the University may be opened with chairs of Medicine, Engineering and Arts early in 1912.

INDIAN AND COLONIAL INVESTMENTS*

By TRUSTEE

"To many readers the careful article by an anonymous contributor, signing himself ' Trustee,' on ' Indian and Colonial Investments,' is as interesting as anything in the number, and if the tabular matter is kept up to date, as is promised, this article will no doubt be frequently consulted by investors."—*Times.*

" In *The Empire Review* there is an article on ' Indian and Colonial Investments.' One attraction of the article is a voluminous series of tables, in which particulars are given of what may be called Imperial investments. . . . This monthly article ought to become a recognised guide to those seeking sound investments."—*Westminster Gazette.*

ALTHOUGH business on the Stock Exchange has shown no improvement since the General Election came as a final damper on speculation, there are reasonable hopes of some revival of activity in the New Year, although after the great rubber excitement it is too much to expect that the public will support anything like another boom. Prices during the past month have been well maintained and in some cases, notably India Government securities, there has been a hopeful advance.

Somewhat divergent results are being shown by the Canadian railways. The Canadian Pacific's last monthly statement showed increases of $485,000 in receipts and $366,000 in expenses, leaving

INDIAN GOVERNMENT SECURITIES.

Title.	Present Amount.	When Redeemable.	Price.	Yield.	Interest Payable.
INDIA.	£				
3½% Stock (*t*) . . .	85,304,848	1931	94½	3¹¹₁₆	Quarterly.
3% ,, (*t*) . . .	66,724,530	1948	82¼	3⅝	,,
2½% ,, Inscribed (*t*)	11,892,207	1926	68	3¹¹₁₆	,,
3½% Rupee Paper 1854–5	..	(*a*)	95¼	3¹¹₁₆	30 June—31 Dec.
3% ,, ,, 1896–7	..	1916	79½	3¹³₁₆	30 June—30 Dec.

(*t*) Eligible for Trustee investments.
(*a*) Redeemable at a Quarter's notice.

* The tabular matter in this article will appear month by month, the figures being corrected to date. Stocks eligible for Trustee investments are so designated.—ED.

INDIAN RAILWAYS AND BANKS.

Title.	Subscribed.	Last year's dividend.	Share or Stock.	Price.	Yield.
RAILWAYS.	£				
Assam—Bengal, L., guaranteed 3%	1,500,000	3	100	$79\frac{1}{2}$	$3\frac{3}{4}$
Bengal and North-Western (Limited)	3,000,000	$7\frac{1}{2}$	100	$144\frac{1}{4}$	$5\frac{3}{16}$
Bengal Dooars, L.	400,000	$4\frac{1}{2}$	100	90	5
Bengal Nagpur (L), gtd. 4%+$\frac{1}{4}$th profits	3,000,000	5	100	$101x$	$4\frac{15}{16}$
Burma Guar. $2\frac{1}{2}$% and propn. of profits	3,000,000	$5\frac{1}{4}$	100	$108\frac{3}{4}$	$4\frac{13}{16}$
Delhi Umballa Kalka, L., guar. $3\frac{1}{2}$% + net earnings	800,000	7	100	$143\frac{1}{2}$	$4\frac{7}{8}$
East Indian Def. ann. cap. g. 4% + $\frac{1}{5}$ sur. profits (*t*)	1,912,804	$5\frac{7}{20}$	100	$95x$	$5\frac{5}{8}$
Do. do, class "D," repayable 1953 (*t*)	4,637,196	$4\frac{3}{4}$	100	$113\frac{1}{2}x$	$4\frac{1}{8}$
Do. $4\frac{1}{2}$% perpet. deb. stock (*t*)	1,435,650	$4\frac{1}{2}$	100	116	$3\frac{7}{8}$
Do. new 3% deb. red. (*t*)	8,000,000	3	100	$80\frac{3}{4}$	$3\frac{11}{16}$
Great Indian Peninsula 4% deb. Stock (*t*)	2,701,450	4	100	$105\frac{1}{2}$	$3\frac{3}{4}$
Do. 3% Gua. and $\frac{1}{10}$ surp. profits 1925 (*t*)	2,575,000	3	100	$99\frac{1}{2}x$	3
Madras and South Mahratta	5,000,000	4	100	$103x$	$3\frac{7}{8}$
Nizam's State Rail. Gtd. 5% Stock	2,000,000	5	100	$107\frac{1}{2}$	$4\frac{5}{8}$
Do. $3\frac{1}{2}$% red. mort. debs.	1,074,700	$3\frac{1}{2}$	100	$85\frac{1}{2}$	$4\frac{1}{16}$
Rohilkund and Kumaon, Limited	400,000	7	100	131	$5\frac{5}{16}$
South Behar, Limited	379,580	5	100	103	$4\frac{13}{16}$
South Indian $4\frac{1}{2}$% per. deb. stock, gtd.	425,000	$4\frac{1}{2}$	100	116	$3\frac{7}{8}$
Do. capital stock	1,000,000	$7\frac{1}{2}$	100	107	7
Southern Punjab, Limited	1,000,000	$7\frac{1}{2}$	100	$135\frac{1}{4}x$	$5\frac{1}{2}$
Do. $3\frac{1}{2}$% deb. stock red.	500,000	$3\frac{1}{2}$	100	89	$3\frac{7}{8}$
West of India Portuguese Guar. L.	800,000	5	100	95	$5\frac{1}{4}$
Do. 5% debenture stock	550,000	5	100	101	$4\frac{15}{16}$
BANKS.	Number of Shares.				
Chartered Bank of India, Australia, and China	60,000	14	20	57	$4\frac{7}{8}$
National Bank of India	64,000	12	$12\frac{1}{2}$	47	$3\frac{3}{16}$

(*t*) Eligible for Trustee investments.
(*x*) Ex dividend.

an increase of $119,000 in net earnings. For the first four months of the financial half-year this makes an increase of $2,331,000 in net earnings. In the latest profit statement of the Grand Trunk Railway it was shown that the increase in receipts was still being accompanied by a growth in working expenses. For October the gross receipts showed an increase of £32,400 but the working expenses advanced £43,700, so that there was a decrease of £11,300 in profit. The aggregate figures for the first four months of the half-year show that whereas the growth in receipts was only £2,700 the expenses increased by as much as £74,750, making a £72,050 diminution in profit. But £46,150 of this decrease was on the Grand Trunk Western, whose accounts are kept quite separately. Thus, the decrease directly concerning the Grand Trunk Company itself is £25,900.

At the meeting of the Bank of Montreal, in presenting the accounts for the year ended October 31, the directors were able to point with pardonable pride to the splendid position that the Bank

CANADIAN GOVERNMENT SECURITIES

Title.	Present Amount.	When Redeemable.	Price.	Yield.	Interest Payable.
3½% 1884 Regd. Stock	4,676,830	1909–34	100	—	1 June—1 Dec.
3% Inscribed Stock (*t*)	8,594,877	1938	89½	3⅝	1 Jan.—1 July.
2½% „ „ (*t*)	1,592,105	1947	76	3 11/16	1 Apr.—1 Oct.
PROVINCIAL.					
British Columbia.					
3% Inscribed Stock .	2,045,760	1941	84*x*	3⅞	1 Jan.—1 July.
Manitoba.					
5% Sterling Bonds .	308,000	1923	109	4 3/16	1 Jan.—1 July.
4% „ Debs. .	205,000	1928	101	3 15/16	1 May—1 Nov.
Nova Scotia.					
3% Stock	164,000	1949	80	4 1/16	1 Jan.—1 July.
Quebec.					
3% Inscribed . . .	1,897,820	1937	83½	4	1 Apr.—1 Oct.
MUNICIPAL.					
Hamilton (City of) 4%	482,800	1934	100	4	1 Apr.—1 Oct.
Montreal 3% Deb. Stock	1,440,000	permanent	80	3¾	1 May—1 Nov.
Do. 4% Cons. „ .	1,821,917	1932	102	3⅞	1 May—1 Nov.
Quebec 4% Debs. . .	385,000	1923	101	4	1 Jan.—1 July.
Do. 3½% Con. Stock .	504,196	drawings	91*x*	3 13/16	1 Jan.—1 July.
Toronto 5% Con. Debs.	136,700	1919–20*	106	4⅜	1 Jan.—1 July.
Do. 4% Stg. Bonds .	300,910	1922–28*	101	4	1 Jan.—1 July.
Do. 3½% Bonds . .	1,169,844	1929	93	4 1/16	1 Jan.—1 July.
Vancouver 4% Bonds	121,200	1931	101	3 15/16	1 Apr.—1 Oct.
Do. 4% 40-year Bonds	117,200	1932	101	4	7 Feb.—7 Aug.
Winnipeg 5% Debs. .	138,000	1914	103	4¼	30 Apr.—31 Oct.

(*t*) Eligible for Trustee investments.
* Yield calculated on earlier date of redemption.
(*x*) Ex dividend.

has attained. In the balance-sheet the deposits stand at £40,591,204 against £36,954,745 for the preceding year, while the current loans and discounts amount to £23,031,777 against £18,734,313. The dividend has been conservatively maintained at 10 per cent. per annum since 1882, but a bonus is now promised at no distant date. In the course of his speech, by the way, Mr. Angus, the president of the Bank, made some remarks that deserve the utmost possible dissemination. "Contributions through the Stock Exchanges and money markets of Europe to the financial enterprises of Canada have been," he said, "extremely generous of late, and it is eminently desirable that the confidence thus displayed should not be abused. Some offerings have been made, it is feared, by over-sanguine promoters, whose statements it would be hard to justify, and in relation to

CANADIAN RAILWAYS, BANKS AND COMPANIES.

Title.	Number of Shares or Amount.	Dividend for last Year.	Paid up per Share.	Price.	Yield.
RAILWAYS.		%			
Canadian Pacific Shares . .	1,800,000	7	$100	199	3½
Do. 4% Preference	£11,328,082	4	Stock	104½	3 13/16
Do. 5% Stg. 1st Mtg. Bd. 1915	£7,191,500	5	,,	106½	3½
Do. 4% Cons. Deb. Stock . .	£27,993,228	4	,,	105½x	3¾
Grand Trunk Ordinary . .	£22,475,985	nil.	,,	24¼	nil.
Do. 5% 1st Preference . . .	£3,420,000	5	,,	106	4 11/16
Do. 5% 2nd ,, . . .	£2,530,000	5	,,	95	5¼
Do. 4% 3rd ,, . . .	£7,168,055	nil.	,,	53¼	nil.
Do. 4% Guaranteed . . .	£9,840,011	4	,,	92	4 5/16
Do. 5% Perp. Deb. Stock . .	£4,270,375	5	,,	127	3⅞
Do. 4% Cons. Deb. Stock . .	£15,821,571	4	,,	101½	3 15/16
BANKS AND COMPANIES.					
Bank of Montreal	140,000	10	$100	255	4
Bank of British North America	20,000	7	50	76½	4 9/16
Canadian Bank of Commerce .	200,000	9	$50	£21¾	4¼
Canada Company	8,319	30s. per sh.	1	28	5 5/16
Hudson's Bay	100,000	80s. per sh.	10*	109½	3⅝
Trust and Loan of Canada .	75,000	8	5	6¼	6⅜
Do. new	25,000	8	3	3¼	7⅜
British Columbia Electric Railway Def.	£600,000	8	Stock	148	5⅜
British Columbia Electric Railway Prefd.	£600,000	6	Stock	125	4¾

* £1 capital repaid 1904.
(*x*) Ex dividend.

NEWFOUNDLAND GOVERNMENT SECURITIES.

Title.	Present Amount.	When Redeemable.	Price.	Yield.	Interest Payable.
3½% Sterling Bonds .	2,178,800	1941-7-8†	93	3⅞	1 Jan.—1 July.
3% Sterling ,, .	325,000	1947	80	4⅛	1 Jan.—1 July.
4% Inscribed Stock .	320,000	1913-38*	101	4	1 Jan.—1 July.
4% ,, ,, .	455,647	1935	104	3 11/16	1 Jan.—1 July.
4% Cons. Ins. ,, .	200,000	1936	102*x*	3 13/16	1 Jan.—1 July.

* Yield calculated on earlier date of redemption.
† Yield calculated on latest date.
(*x*) Ex dividend.

schemes where the advantages to buyers are not quite apparent. It might be well to consider that, while money-seeking investment is much more abundant in some countries than it is with us, there is seldom much lack of capital here for participation in enterprises that are unquestionably sound."

Considerably increased profits are indicated by the half-yearly dividend announcement of the Bank of New South Wales. The rate of dividend, 10 per cent. per annum, is the same as a year ago, but it has to be paid on an extra half-million sterling of

AUSTRALIAN GOVERNMENT SECURITIES.

Title.	Present Amount.	When Redeemable.	Price.	Yield.	Interest Payable.
New South Wales.					
4% Inscribed Stock (*t*)	9,686,300	1933	104	$3\frac{3}{4}$	1 Jan.—1 July.
$3\frac{1}{2}$% „ „ (*t*)	16,464,545	1924	$97\frac{1}{2}$	$3\frac{3}{4}$	1 Apr.—1 Oct.
3% „ „ (*t*)	12,480,000	1935	86	$3\frac{7}{8}$	
Victoria.					
4% Inscribed, 1885 .	5,970,000	1920	$101\frac{1}{2}$	$3\frac{15}{16}$	1 Jan.—1 July.
$3\frac{1}{2}$% „ 1889 (*t*)	5,000,000	1921–6*	$96\frac{1}{2}$	4	
4% „ . .	2,107,000	1911–26*	100	$4\frac{1}{2}$	
3% „ (*t*) . .	5,211,331	1929–49†	84	$3\frac{13}{16}$	
Queensland.					
4% Bonds	10,267,400	1913–15*	102	$3\frac{5}{8}$	1 Jan.—1 July.
4% Inscribed Stock (*t*)	7,939,000	1924	$101\frac{1}{2}$	$3\frac{15}{16}$	
$3\frac{1}{2}$% „ „ (*t*)	8,616,034	1921–30†	96	$3\frac{13}{16}$	
3% „ „ (*t*)	4,274,213	1922–47†	83	$3\frac{15}{16}$	
South Australia.					
4% Bonds	1,359,300	1916	101	$3\frac{7}{8}$	1 Apr.—1 Oct.
4% Inscribed Stock .	6,269,000	1916–7–36*	101	$3\frac{7}{8}$	
$3\frac{1}{2}$% „ „ (*t*)	2,517,800	1939	$96\frac{1}{2}x$	$3\frac{11}{16}$	1 Jan.—1 July.
3% „ „ (*t*)	839,500	1916–26‡	$88x$	$3\frac{3}{8}$	
3% „ „ (*t*)	2,760,100	1916 ‡ or after.	$81\frac{1}{2}x$	$3\frac{5}{8}$	
Western Australia.					
4% Inscribed . . .	1,876,000	1911–31*	101	$3\frac{11}{16}$	15 Apr.—15 Oct.
$3\frac{1}{2}$% „ (*t*) . .	3,780,000	1920–35†	$96\frac{1}{2}$	$3\frac{11}{16}$	1 May—1 Nov.
3% „ (*t*) . .	3,750,000	1915–35‡	$86\frac{1}{2}$	$3\frac{7}{16}$	
3% „ (*t*) . .	2,500,000	1927‡	$89\frac{1}{2}x$	$3\frac{5}{16}$	15 Jan.—15 July.
Tasmania.					
$3\frac{1}{2}$% Inscbd. Stock (*t*)	4,156,500	1920–40*	$97\frac{1}{2}$	$3\frac{7}{8}$	1 Jan.—1 July.
4% „ „	1,000,000	1920–40*	102	$3\frac{7}{8}$	
3% . . . . . (*t*)	450,000	1920–40†	85	$3\frac{7}{8}$	

* Yield calculated on earlier date of redemption.

† Yield calculated on later date of redemption, though a portion of the loan may be redeemed earlier.

‡ No allowance for redemption.

(*t*) Eligible for Trustee Investment.

(*x*) Ex dividend.

AUSTRALIAN MUNICIPAL AND OTHER BONDS.

Title.	Present Amount.	When Redeemable.	Price.	Yield.	Interest Payable.
Melbourne & Met. Bd. of Works 4% Debs.	1,000,000	1921	100	4	1 Apl.—1 Oct.
Do. City 4% Deb. .	850,000	1915–22*	100	$4\frac{3}{16}$	**1 Jan.—1 July.**
Melbourne Trams Trust $4\frac{1}{2}$% Debs. .	1,650,000	1914–16*	103	$4\frac{1}{16}$	
S. Melbourne $4\frac{1}{2}$% Debs.	128,700	1919	102	$4\frac{3}{8}$	1 Jan.—1 July.
Sydney 4% Debs. . .	640,000	1912–13	101	4	
Do. 4% Debs. . . .	300,000	1919	101	4	

* Yield calculated on earlier date of redemption.

capital. Moreover, although the appropriation of £43,200 to reserve is £6,800 less than last time, a sum of £10,000 is placed to fidelity guarantee and provident fund which received nothing a year ago, and the carry-forward of £57, 342 compares with £45,704.

South Australia will probably be making a substantial loan issue early in the New Year under the provisions of the Bill recently introduced. It gives powers for borrowing a total of £6,800,000, all of which is to be applied to reproductive works. Railways account for half the amount, while nearly two millions is for port improvements, and a large amount is to be provided for the purposes of the Government's closer settlement policy.

Ambitious railway projects have recently been put forward by the Queensland Government. They involve an expenditure of some six millions sterling to be spread over a period of about ten years.

AUSTRALIAN RAILWAYS, BANKS AND COMPANIES.

Title.	Number of Shares or Amount.	Dividend for last Year.	Paid up.	Price.	Yield.
RAILWAYS.		%			
Emu Bay and Mount Bischoff . . .	12,000	6	5	4½	6⅝
Do. 4½% Irred. Deb. Stock	£130,900	4½	100	97	4⅝
Mid. of W. Aust. 4% Debs., Guartd. .	300,000	4	100	102	3⅞
BANKS AND COMPANIES.					
Bank of Australasia	40,000	14	40	114½	4⅞
Bank of New South Wales	125,000	10	20	44	4½
Union Bank of Australia £75 . . .	60,000	14	25	62	5⅝
Do. 4% Inscribed Stock Deposits . .	£600,000	4	100	98*x*	4 1/16
Australian Mort. Land & Finance £25	80,000	12½	5	6⅞	9 1/16
Do. 4% Perp. Deb. Stock	£1,900,000	4	100	98½*x*	4 1/16
Dalgety & Co. £20	154,000	7	5	5⅞	5 15/16
Do. 4½% Irred. Deb. Stock	£620,000	4½	100	108	4⅛
Goldsbrough Mort & Co. 4% A Deb. Stock Reduced	£1,067,137	4	100	88½	4½
Do. B Income Reduced	£711,340	5½	100	99	5½
Australian Agricultural £25 . . .	20,000	£4	21½	68½	5 13/16
South Australian Company . . .	14,200	16¼	20	66½	4⅞
Trust & Agency of Australasia . . .	42,479	7½	1	⅝	12
Do. 5% Cum. Pref.	87,500	5	10	9¾	5⅛

(*x*) Ex dividend.

NEW ZEALAND GOVERNMENT SECURITIES.

Title.	Present Amount.	When Redeemable.	Price.	Yield.	Interest Payable.
5% Bonds	266,300	1914	105	4	15 Jan.—15 July.
4% Inscribed Stock (*t*)	29,150,302	1929	103½	3¾	1 May—1 Nov.
3½% Stock (*t*) . . .	**13,852,432**	**1940**	95½	3¾	1 Jan.—1 July.
3% Inscribed Stock (*t*)	**9,659,980**	**1945**	85	3 13/16	1 Apr.—1 Oct.

(*t*) Eligible for Trustee Investments.

NEW ZEALAND MUNICIPAL AND OTHER SECURITIES.

Title.	Present Amount.	When Redeemable.	Price.	Yield.	Interest Payable.
Auckland 5% Deb. .	200,000	1934–8*	109	$4\frac{7}{16}$	1 Jan.—1 July.
Do. Hbr. Bd. 5% Debs.	150,000	1917	104	$4\frac{3}{8}$	10 April—10 Oct.
Bank of N. Z. shares†	150,000	div. 12½%	$10\frac{1}{2}x$	$3\frac{1}{16}$	—
Do. 4% Gua. Stock‡ .	£1,000,000	1914	100	$4\frac{1}{8}$	April—Oct.
Christchurch 6% Drainage Loan. . }	200,000	1926	121	$4\frac{5}{16}$	30 June—31 Dec.
Lyttleton Hbr. Bd. 6%	200,000	1929	121	$4\frac{7}{16}$	
Napier Hbr. Bd. 5% Debs. . . . . }	300,000	1920	106	$4\frac{3}{8}$	}1 Jan.—1 July.
Do. 5% Debs.	200,000	1928	106	$4\frac{9}{16}$	
National Bank of N.Z. £7½ Shares £2¼ paid }	150,000	div. 12%	$5\frac{3}{4}$	$5\frac{3}{16}$	Jan.—July.
Oamaru 5% Bds. . . .	173,800	1920	98	$5\frac{7}{16}$	1 Jan.—1 July.
Otago Hbr. Cons. Bds. 5%. . . . . . }	443,100	1934	107	$4\frac{9}{16}$	1 Jan.—1 July.
Wellington 6% Impts. Loan . . . . }	100,000	1914–29	108	—	1 Mar.—1 Sept.
Do. 6% Waterworks .	130,000	1929	119	$4\frac{9}{16}$	1 Mar.—1 Sept.
Do. 4½% Debs. . .	165,000	1933	103	$4\frac{5}{16}$	1 May—1 Nov.
Westport Hbr. 4% Debs. . . . . }	150,000	1925	101	4	1 Mar.—1 Sept.

* Yield calculated on earlier date of redemption.
† £6 13s. 4d. Shares with £3 6s. 8d. paid up.
‡ Guaranteed by New Zealand Government.
(x) Ex dividend.

Presiding at the meeting of the Western Australian Bank at Perth, Mr. Loton was able to report a steadily expanding volume of business. The deposits in the balance-sheet showed an increase of over half a million sterling on the year, while the

SOUTH AFRICAN GOVERNMENT SECURITIES.

Title.	Present Amount.	When Redeemable.	Price.	Yield.	Interest Payable.
CAPE COLONY.	£				
4½% Bonds . . .	485,000	dwgs.	101	$4\frac{7}{8}$	15 Apr.—15 Oct.
4% 1883 Inscribed .	3,733,195	1923	102	$3\frac{3}{4}$	1 June—1 Dec.
4% 1886 „ .	9,997,566	1916–36*	$101\frac{1}{2}$	$3\frac{13}{16}$	15 Apr.—15 Oct.
3½% 1886 „ (t) .	15,443,014	1929–49†	98	$3\frac{5}{8}$	1 Jan.—1 July.
3% 1886 „ (t) .	7,553,590	1933–43†	86	$3\frac{13}{16}$	1 Feb.—1 Aug.
NATAL.					
4½% Bonds, 1876 . .	758,700	1919	104	$4\frac{1}{8}$	15 Mar.—15 Sep.
4% Inscribed (t) . .	3,026,444	1937	106	$3\frac{5}{8}$	Apr.—Oct.
3½% „ (t) . .	3,714,917	1914–39†	97	$3\frac{5}{8}$	1 June—1 Dec.
3% „ (t) . .	6,000,000	1929–49†	84	$3\frac{13}{16}$	1 Jan.—1 July.
TRANSVAAL.					
3% Guartd. Stock (t) .	35,000,000	1923–53†	93	$3\frac{1}{4}$	1 May—1 Nov.

* Yield calculated on earlier date of redemption.
† Yield calculated on later date of redemption.
(t) Eligible for Trustee investments.

SOUTH AFRICAN MUNICIPAL SECURITIES.

Title.	Present Amount.	When Redeemable.	Price.	Yield.	Interest Payable.
	£				
Bloemfontein 4% . .	763,000	1954	97	$4\frac{3}{16}$	1 Jan.—1 July.
Cape Town 4% . .	1,861,750	1953	101	4	1 Jan.—1 July.
Durban 4% . . .	850,000	1951–3	99	$4\frac{1}{16}$	30 June—31 Dec
Johannesburg 4% .	5,500,000	1933–4	$99\frac{1}{2}$	$4\frac{1}{16}$	1 April—1 Oct.
Krugersdorp 4% . .	100,000	1930	94	$4\frac{7}{16}$	1 June—1 Dec.
Pietermaritzburg 4%	825,000	1949–53	98x	$4\frac{1}{16}$	30 June—31 Dec.
Port Elizabeth 4 % .	874,060	1964	99	$4\frac{1}{16}$	30 June—31 Dec.
Pretoria 4% . . .	1,000,000	1939	98	$4\frac{1}{2}$	1 Jan.—1 July.
Rand Water Board 4%	3,400,000	1935	$99\frac{1}{2}$	$4\frac{1}{16}$	1 Jan.—1 July.

(*x*) Ex dividend.

SOUTH AFRICAN RAILWAYS, BANKS, AND COMPANIES.

Title.	Number of Shares or Amount.	Dividend for last Year.	Paid up.	Price.	Yield.
RAILWAYS.					
Mashonaland 5% Debs.	£2,500,000	5	100	$96\frac{1}{2}$	$5\frac{1}{8}$
Rhodesia Rlys. 5% 1st Mort. Debs. guar. by B.S.A. Co. till 1915. . .	£2,000,000	5	100	$99\frac{1}{2}$	5
Royal Trans-African 5% Debs. Rep. .	£1,853,700	5	100	$88\frac{1}{2}$	$5\frac{5}{8}$
BANKS AND COMPANIES.					
African Banking Corporation £10 shares	80,000	$5\frac{1}{2}$	5	$4\frac{3}{4}$	$5\frac{3}{4}$
Bank of Africa £18¾	160,000	5	$6\frac{1}{4}$	$6\frac{1}{4}$	$4\frac{3}{4}$
Natal Bank £10	148,232	8	$2\frac{1}{2}$	$3\frac{1}{2}$	$5\frac{11}{16}$
National Bank of S. Africa £10 . .	110,000	3	10	$11\frac{1}{2}$	$2\frac{5}{8}$
Standard Bank of S. Africa £100 . .	61,941	10	25	$60\frac{1}{2}$	$4\frac{1}{2}$
Ohlsson's Cape Breweries	60,000	nil	5	$4\frac{3}{8}$	—
South African Breweries	965,279	10	1	$1\frac{3}{4}x$	$5\frac{11}{16}$
British South Africa (Chartered) . .	8,053,499	nil	1	$1\frac{3}{4}$	nil
Do. 5% Debs. Red.	£1,250,000	5	100	106	$4\frac{11}{16}$
Natal Land and Colonization . . .	68,066	4	5	$4\frac{3}{8}$	$4\frac{9}{16}$
Cape Town & District Gas Light & Coke	10,000	nil	10	$3\frac{1}{4}$	—
Kimberley Waterworks £10 . . .	45,000	5	7	5	7

(*x*) Ex dividend.

amount of specie and bullion on hand stood at an unusually high figure. With regard to the general outlook in connection with the business, not only of the Bank but also of the public generally and also of the country, he said that he did not know that the prospects were ever brighter or sounder than they were now. The pastoral industry was doing well, thanks to fairly good seasons during the past few years, and to the recovery in prices to the producer for his stock during the last few months. There was a prospect of a first-rate clip from north to south and of good prices being obtained for the wool. Then, again, the pearling industry was doing well. The boom that was being experienced in connection with the new find at the Bullfinch Mine was just, to his mind, what the State wanted, and would be a great impetus to that particular industry. It was a very wonderful find, as far as was known, and he hoped that those people who were venturing money in mining would not be led away rashly to invest their means in wild speculative propositions, put before them before any development had taken place.

That dreaded additional taxation of the mining industry by the South African Parliament has proved to be of quite modest extent. Indeed, the 10 per cent. profit tax on the gold mines has been left quite unaltered, although the Finance Minister promises a graduation in favour of the poorer mines a year hence. The new taxes comprise a percentage on the profits from base minerals, and an extension of the 10 per cent. gold mine tax to the diamond mines in the Cape and the Orange Free State. This affects De Beers and Jagersfontein and takes the place of the Cape income-tax. The Premier Mine, being in the Transvaal, already pays a big proportion of its profits to the Exchequer in respect of the Government's holding of its shares.

November's output of gold from the Transvaal amounted to 642,591 ounces valued at £2,729,554. Although less than the return for the preceding month the daily average showed an increase, the discrepancy being due to the different lengths of the months. This table enables comparison with the monthly returns for several years past :

Month.	1910.	1909.	1908.	1907.	1906.	1905.
	£	£	£	£	£	£
January . .	2,554,451	2,612,836	2,380,124	2,283,741	1,820,739	1,568,508
February .	2,445,088	2,400,892	2,301,971	2,096,434	1,731,664	1,545,371
March . .	2,578,877	2,580,498	2,442,022	2,287,391	1,884,815	1,698,340
April . . .	2,629,535	2,578,804	2,403,500	2,281,110	1,865,785	1,695,550
May . . .	2,693,785	2,652,699	2,472,143	2,227,838	1,959,062	1,768,734
June . . .	2,655,602	2,621,818	2,442,329	2,155,976	2,021,813	1,751,412
July . . .	2,713,083	2,636,965	2,482,608	2,262,813	2,089,004	1,781,944
August . .	2,757,919	2,597,646	2,496,869	2,357,602	2,162,583	1,820,496
September .	2,747,853	2,575,760	2,496,112	2,285,424	2,145,575	1,769,124
October . .	2,774,390	2,558,902	2,624,012	2,351,344	2,296,361	1,765,047
November .	2,729,554	2,539,146	2,609,685	2,335,406	2,265,625	1,804,253
December .	—	2,569,822	2,806,235	2,478,659	2,336,961	1,833,295
Total * .	29,280,137	30,925,788	29,957,610	27,403,738	24,579,987	20,802,074

* Including undeclared amounts omitted from the monthly returns.

Somewhat disappointing native labour returns have been issued, a diminution of 2,076 Kaffirs occurring during November in the supply for the gold mines. This table shows the course of the supply during the past two years :

Month.	Natives Joined.	Natives Left.	Net Gain on Month.	Natives Employed end of Month.	Chinese Employed end of Month.
November 1908	12,324	10,163	2,161	141,326	12,298
December ,,	17,404	10,008	7,396	148,722	12,283
January 1909	13,551	11,609	1,942	150,664	10,045
February ,,	18,018	10,844	7,174	157,838	10,034
March ,,	16,184	11,979	4,205	162,043	9,997
April ,,	12,102	11,244	858	162,901	7,734
May ,,	7,717	12,339	4,622*	158,279	7,717
June ,,	8,335	12,354	4,019*	154,260	5,378
July ,,	7,826	12,612	4,786*	149,474	5,370
August ,,	10,089	12,642	2,553*	146,291	5,361
September ,,	11,747	13,811	2,064*	144,857	3,204
October ,,	14,656	13,762	894	152,563‡	3,199
November ,,	13,942	13,742	200	152,763	1,799
December ,,	17,293	13,348	3,945	156,708	nil.
January 1910	—	—	3,954	160,662	nil.
February ,,	—	—	9,109	169,771	nil.
March ,,	—	—	8,574	178,345	nil.
April ,,	—	—	5,469	183,814	nil.
May ,,	—	—	150	183,964	nil.
June ,,	—	—	533*	183,431	nil.
July ,,	—	—	1,917*	181,514	nil.
August ,,	—	—	683*	180,831	nil.
September ,,	—	—	1,369	182,200	nil.
October ,,	—	—	2,097*	180,103	nil.
November ,,	—	—	2,076*	178,027	nil.

* Net loss.   ‡ Including new members of Native Labour Association.

Rhodesia's output of gold for November exceeded all previous records, amounting as it did to 57,158 ounces valued at £240,573, the previous highest being £236,307 for the corresponding month of last year, as will be seen from the following table showing the returns month by month for five years past.

MONTH.	1910.	1909.	1908.	1907.	1906.
	£	£	£	£	£
January . .	227,511	204,666	199,380	168,240	155,337
February .	203,888	192,497	191,635	145,397	137,561
March . . .	228,385	202,157	200,615	167,424	160,722
April . . .	228,213	222,700	212,935	175,210	157,108
May . . .	224,888	225,032	223,867	189,216	169,218
June . . .	214,709	217,600	224,920	192,506	170,088
July . . .	195,233	225,234	228,151	191,681	173,313
August . .	191,423	228,296	220,792	192,106	179,000
September. .	178,950	213,249	204,262	192,186	173,973
October . .	234,928	222,653	205,466	191,478	161,360
November. .	240,573	236,307	196,668	183,058	175,656
December . .	—	233,397	217,316	190,383	171,770
Total .	2,368,701	2,623,788	2,526,007	2,178,885	1,985,101

Increased receipts and diminished expenses are estimated by the Egyptian Budget for 1911. The receipts are put at £E15,500,000, an increase of £E150,000, and the expenditure at £E15,000,000, a decrease of £E150,000. The estimated surplus is therefore £E500,000, against £E200,000 for 1910.

CROWN COLONY SECURITIES.

Title.	Present Amount.	When Redeemable	Price.	Yield.	Interest Payable.
Barbadoes 3½% ins. (*t*)	375,000	1925–42*	97	3¾	1 Mar.—1 Sep.
Brit. Guiana 3% ins. (*t*)	250,000	1923–45†	85	3 13/16	1 Feb.—1 Aug.
Ceylon 4% ins. (*t*). .	1,076,100	1934	107	3 9/16	15 Feb.—15 Aug.
Do. 3% ins. (*t*). . .	2,850,000	1940	85	3 13/16	1 May—1 Nov.
Hong-Kong 3½% ins (*t*)	1,485,733	1918–43†	97	3⅝	15 Apr.—15 Oct.
Jamaica 4% ins. (*t*) .	1,099,048	1934	106	3⅝	15 Feb.—15 Aug.
Do. 3½% ins. (*t*) . .	1,455,500	1919–49†	97	3 11/16	24 Jan.—24 July.
Mauritius 3% guar. Great Britain (*t*) .	600,000	1940	92	3 7/16	1 Jan.—1 July.
Do. 4% ins. (*t*). . .	482,390	1937	106	3 11/16	1 Feb.—1 Aug.
Sierra Leone 3½% ins. (*t*)	725,101	1929–54†	96½	3⅝	1 June—1 Dec.
Trinidad 4% ins. . .	422,593	1917–42*	102	3 13/16	15 Mar.—15 Sep.
Do. 3% ins. (*t*). . .	600,000	1922–44†	85*x*	3¾	15 Jan.—15 July.
Hong-Kong & Shanghai Bank Shares .	120,000	Div. £4½	£86	5	Feb.—Aug.

* Yield calculated on shorter period † Yield calculated on longer period.
(*t*) Eligible for Trustee investments. (*x*) Ex dividend.

RUBBER SHARES.

Company.	Issued Capital.	Area planted.	Nominal Value of Share.	Amount paid-up.	Price.
	£	Acres.			
Anglo-Malay	150,000	3,391	2*s.*	2*s.*	22*s.* 9*d.*
Batu Tiga	60,000	1,545	£1	£1	4⅜
Bukit Rajah	66,700	2,772	£1	£1	15½
Consolidated Malay . . .	62,007	1,710	£1	2*s.*	23*s.*
Highlands and Lowlands .	317,353	4,707	£1	£1	5⅛
Kepitigalla	225,000	3,127	£1	£1	⅞
Kuala Lumpur	180,000	2,611	£1	£1	8
Lanadron	269,780	4,570	£1	£1	5⅛*xd.*
Linggi	100,000	4,192	2*s.*	2*s.*	46*s.*
Pataling.	22,500	1,454	2*s.*	2*s.*	3
Straits (Bertam)	200,000	2,541	2*s.*	2*s.*	7*s.*
Vallambrosa	50,600	1,807	2*s.*	2*s.*	36*s.* *xd.*

(*x*) Ex dividend.

EGYPTIAN SECURITIES.

Title.	Amount or Number of Shares.	Dividend for last Year.	Paid up.	Price.	Yield.
Egyptian Govt. Guaranteed Loan (*t*) .	£7,414,700	3	99	96	3 1/16
,, Unified Debt	£55,971,960	4	100	100¼	3 15/16
National Bank of Egypt	300,000	9	10	21¼	4 3/16
Bank of Egypt	50,000	15	12½	33	5⅝
Agricultural Bank of Egypt, Ordinary	496,000	5½	5	7¼	3 9/16
,, ,, ,, Preferred	125,000	4	10	9	4 7/16
,, ,, ,, Bonds .	£2,350,000	3½	100	85½	4 1/16

(*t*) Eligible for Trustee investments.

TRUSTEE.

22 *December*, 1910.

Lightning Source UK Ltd.
Milton Keynes UK
UKHW021228051118
331794UK00011B/950/P